BEST PRACTICES
IN LITERACY INSTRUCTION

Also from
Linda B. Gambrell and Lesley Mandel Morrow

Best Practices in Literacy Instruction

FIFTH EDITION

EDITED BY

Linda B. Gambrell
Lesley Mandel Morrow

Foreword by Timothy Shanahan

THE GUILFORD PRESS
New York   London

© 2015 The Guilford Press
A Division of Guilford Publications, Inc.
370 Seventh Avenue, Suite 1200, New York, NY 10001
www.guilford.com

Printed in the United States of America

This book is printed on acid-free paper.

Last digit is print number: 9   8   7   6   5   4   3   2

Library of Congress Cataloging-in-Publication Data

Best practices in literacy instruction / edited by Linda B. Gambrell, Lesley
Mandel Morrow. — Fifth edition.
        pages cm
    Includes bibliographical references and index.
    ISBN 978-1-4625-1719-0 (paperback : acid-free paper) — ISBN 978-1-4625-
1720-6 (hardcover : acid-free paper)
    1. Language arts—United States.   2. Reading comprehension—United
States.   3. Literacy—United States.   I. Gambrell, Linda B.   II. Morrow,
Lesley Mandel.
    LB1576.B486 2014
    372.6—dc23

                                                          2014006720

About the Editors

 Linda B. Gambrell, PhD, is Distinguished Professor in the Eugene T. Moore School of Education at Clemson University. Her major research interests are in the areas of reading comprehension, literacy motivation, and the role of discussion in teaching and learning. Dr. Gambrell has published numerous books and articles on reading instruction, comprehension strategy instruction, and literacy motivation. She is a recipient of the Outstanding Teacher Educator in Reading Award from the International Reading Association (IRA), the Albert J. Kingston Award from the Literacy Research Association (LRA), the Laureate Award from the Association of Literacy Educators and Researchers (ALER), and, most recently, the Oscar S. Causey Award from the LRA. Dr. Gambrell is past president of the IRA, LRA, and ALER and a member of the Reading Hall of Fame.

 Lesley Mandel Morrow, PhD, is Distinguished Professor of Literacy and Director of the Center for Literacy Development at the Graduate School of Education at Rutgers, The State University of New Jersey. Her research, which she conducts with children and families from diverse backgrounds, deals with early literacy development and the organization and management of language arts programs and literacy-rich environments. Dr. Morrow has published more than 300 journal articles, chapters, and books. Her work has been recognized with awards including the Outstanding Teacher Educator in Reading Award and the William S. Gray Citation of Merit, both from the IRA, and the Oscar S. Causey Award from the LRA for outstanding contributions to reading research. Dr. Morrow is past president of the IRA and is a member and past president of the Reading Hall of Fame.

Contributors

 Peter Afflerbach, PhD, is Professor of Education at the University of Maryland. His research interests include reading assessment, reading comprehension, and the verbal reporting methodology. Dr. Afflerbach is a standing member of the Reading Committee of the National Assessment of Educational Progress and a member of the Literacy Research Panel of the International Reading Association (IRA). He has served as Chair of the Literacy Assessment Committee of the IRA and on the Common Core State Standards Review and Feedback Panels. Dr. Afflerbach is an author or editor of numerous books, including *Understanding and Using Reading Assessment, K–12, Second Edition*; *Handbook of Reading Research, Fourth Edition*; and the forthcoming *Handbook of Individual Differences in Reading: Reader, Text, and Context*. He has served as coeditor of the journal *Metacognition and Learning* and on the editorial advisory boards of *Reading Research Quarterly*, *The Reading Teacher*, *Journal of Educational Psychology*, and *Educational Researcher*. He is a former elementary school Title I reading teacher, middle school remedial reading and writing teacher, and high school English teacher.

 Janice F. Almasi, PhD, is the Carol Lee Robertson Endowed Professor of Literacy Education at the University of Kentucky. Her research focuses on comprehension; in particular, her work examines the strategic processing that occurs while children read, and as they discuss text with peers. Dr. Almasi is currently a Co-Principal Investigator on a federally funded grant in which she is helping design interventions to assist struggling readers' narrative comprehension. Her research has been acknowledged with several awards and has been published in the field of literacy's premier journals. She was recently elected to the Executive Board of the Literacy Research Association (LRA) and will serve as President of the LRA in 2015.

Camille L. Z. Blachowicz, PhD, is Co-Director of the Reading Leadership Institute at the National College of Education of National Louis University, where she is Distinguished Research Professor Emerita. She has researched, written, and presented extensively on the topic of vocabulary instruction, which is the subject of several of her books, including *Teaching Vocabulary in All Classrooms, No More "Look Up the List" Vocabulary Instruction,* and *Teaching Academic Vocabulary K–8: Effective Practices across the Curriculum.* Dr. Blachowicz has been both a Fulbright and a Spencer Fellow. She was named to the roster of Outstanding Teacher Educators in Reading by the IRA and is also a member of the Reading Hall of Fame.

 Karen Bromley, PhD, is a SUNY Distinguished Teaching Professor in the Graduate School of Education at Binghamton University, where she teaches courses in literacy assessment and instruction, language arts, and children's literature. Previously she taught third grade and was a reading specialist in New York and Maryland. Dr. Bromley is the recipient of the SUNY Chancellor's Award for Excellence in Teaching and the New York State Reading Educator Award. She was a board member of the IRA from 2009 until 2012. Dr. Bromley has worked extensively with classroom teachers and has written many articles and several books. Her newest book is *The Next Step in Vocabulary Instruction.* Other recent books include *50 Graphic Organizers for Reading, Writing and More* and *Writing for Educators: Personal Stories and Practical Advice.*

 Byeong-Young Cho, PhD, is Assistant Professor in the School of Education at Iowa State University. His major research interests are in the area of reading comprehension, new literacies, higher-order thinking, and reading assessment. Dr. Cho has published journal articles and book chapters on strategic reading and reading assessment. He is a recipient of the Outstanding Dissertation Award from the IRA.

 Sarah K. Clark, PhD, is Assistant Professor of Elementary Education at Utah State University. She teaches undergraduate courses in literacy assessment and instruction for struggling readers, as well as graduate courses in the supervision of school reading programs and effective practices of literacy specialists and literacy coaches. Dr. Clark's research interests are in the areas of literacy education, teacher preparation, and support for struggling readers. She has published in both national and international literacy and teacher education journals. In 2014, she was named Jerry Johns' Promising Researcher from the Association of Literacy Educators and Researchers (ALER).

 Maria Elliker Crassas, PhD, is a former elementary classroom teacher and a certified reading specialist. She recently earned her doctorate in Curriculum and Instruction from the University of Maryland, College Park. Dr. Crassas is interested in family literacy and is currently working with parents and families who are living in homeless shelters to create a reading community and develop their children's reading and language skills.

Patricia M. Cunningham, PhD, is Professor of Education at Wake Forest University. She formerly taught first and fourth grades and was a reading specialist and director of reading for a county school system. Dr. Cunningham's particular interest has always been in finding alternative ways to teach children for whom learning to read is difficult. She is the author of *Phonics They Use: Words for Reading and Writing*, which is currently available in its sixth edition, and, with Richard Allington, *Classrooms That Work* and *Schools That Work*. Dr. Cunningham's most recent publications include *What Really Matters in Spelling*, *What Really Matters in Writing*, and *What Really Matters in Vocabulary*.

 Michael Domínguez, MEd, is a PhD candidate in Literacy Studies at the University of Colorado at Boulder, where his interests include critical literacies, literacy and identity, teacher education, and Chicana/o studies and educational achievement for Chicana/o and Latina/o youth. He teaches courses in reading development for preservice teachers, and also serves as director for a summer academic program focused on community development and leadership for Latina/o youth from communities across Colorado. Before beginning his doctoral studies in Colorado, he was a middle school English and ESL teacher in North Las Vegas, Nevada.

 Nell K. Duke, EdD, is Professor of Literacy, Language, and Culture and Faculty Associate in the Combined Program in Education and Psychology at the University of Michigan. Her work focuses on early literacy development, particularly among children living in poverty. Her specific areas of expertise include the development of informational reading and writing in young children, comprehension development and instruction in early schooling, and issues of equity in literacy education. Dr. Duke currently serves as a member of the IRA Literacy Research Panel and Co-Principal Investigator on projects funded by the Institute of Education Sciences, the National Science Foundation, and the Spencer Foundation. She has received several awards, including the American Educational Research Association (AERA) Early Career Award. She is coauthor and coeditor of numerous books, including *Inside Information: Developing Powerful Readers and Writers of Informational Text through Project-Basd Instruction, K–5* and the *Handbook of Effective Literacy Instruction: Research-Based Practice K–8*.

 Patricia A. Edwards, PhD, is Distinguished Professor of Language and Literacy in the Department of Teacher Education and a Senior University Outreach Fellow at Michigan State University. A member of the Reading Hall of Fame, she is a nationally and internationally recognized expert in parent involvement; home, school, and community partnerships; multicultural literacy; early literacy; and family/intergenerational literacy, especially among poor and minority children. Dr. Edwards served on the Board of Directors of the IRA from 1998 to 2001 and as IRA president for 2010–2011. She was also the first African American president (2006–2007) of the LRA. Dr. Edwards is the coauthor of *A Path to Follow: Learning to Listen to Parents*, *Bridging Literacy and Equity: The Essential Guide to Social Equity Teaching,* and *Change Is Gonna Come:*

Transforming Literacy Education for African American Students, which won the LRA's Edward B. Fry Book Award for 2011. In 2012, she received the Albert J. Kingston Service Award from the LRA.

 Douglas Fisher, PhD, is Professor of Educational Leadership at San Diego State University and a teacher leader at Health Sciences High and Middle College. He is the recipient of an IRA Celebrate Literacy Award, the Farmer Award for Excellence in writing from the National Council of Teachers of English, as well as a Christa McAuliffe Award for Excellence in Teacher Education from the American Association of State Colleges and Universities. Dr. Fisher has published numerous articles on reading and literacy, differentiated instruction, and curriculum design, as well as books, such as *Text Complexity: Raising Rigor in Reading, Common Core English Language Arts in a PLC at Work, Rigorous Reading,* and *The Leader's Guide to Teaching English Learners.*

 Peter J. Fisher, PhD, is Professor of Education at the National College of Education of National Louis University, where he teaches graduate classes in literacy education. He has published numerous articles and chapters on vocabulary instruction and is a coauthor of the books *Teaching Vocabulary in All Classrooms, Teaching Academic Vocabulary K–8,* and *The Complete Guide to Tutoring Struggling Readers: Mapping Interventions to Purpose and the CCSS.*

 Michelle Flory, MEd, is a doctoral candidate and adjunct faculty member for multiple universities, including Utah State University, Ottawa University, and Utah Valley University. She teaches courses in literacy, curriculum, and elementary teaching methods. Her research interests include children's literature, intermediate students' reading comprehension, motivation, and effective teaching practices and teacher knowledge in literacy.

 Elena Forzani, MEd, is a Neag Fellow, doctoral student, and researcher with the New Literacies Research Lab at the University of Connecticut. Before joining the New Literacies Research Team, she taught first grade and high school English and reading. Her research interests focus on the way students read and comprehend disciplinary texts in digital literacies contexts. Ms. Forzani earned her master's of education in literacy from the University of Michigan.

 Nancy Frey, PhD, is Professor in the Department of Educational Leadership at San Diego State University. She is the recipient of the 2008 Early Career Achievement Award from the National Reading Conference (now LRA). Dr. Frey has published in *The Reading Teacher, Journal of Adolescent and Adult Literacy, English Journal, Voices in the Middle, Middle School Journal, Remedial and Special Education, TESOL Journal, Journal of Learning Disabilities, Early Childhood Education Journal,* and *Educational Leadership.* She has coauthored books on formative assessment (*Checking for Understanding* and *Formative Assessment Action Plan*), instructional design (*Better Learning for Structured Teaching*), data-driven instruction (*Using Data to Focus Instructional*

Improvement), and brain-based learning (*In a Reading State of Mind*). Dr. Frey is a credentialed special educator, reading specialist, and administrator in California, and has taught at the elementary, middle, and high school levels for two decades. She is a teacher-leader at Health Sciences High and Middle College.

Linda B. Gambrell (*see* About the Editors).

 Vicki B. Griffo, MA, is a doctoral candidate at the University of California, Berkeley. Her research interests are in reading development and disabilities, refining instructional methods, and developing teacher education. These interests first took root while she served as a first/second-grade teacher working with bilingual students in a rural, high-poverty district in central California. In 2002, she earned her MA as a reading specialist at the University of California, Berkeley. In the course of 10 years, she has conducted educational research on a variety of topics, such as improving reading comprehension and reading assessment and remediation of at-risk students.

 John T. Guthrie, PhD, is the Jean Mullan Professor Emeritus in the Department of Human Development at the University of Maryland. He is a member of the IRA Reading Hall of Fame and received the Oscar S. Causey Award for Outstanding Research from the National Reading Conference. Dr. Guthrie is a Fellow of the AERA and the American Psychological Association. He was given the University of Maryland Regent's Faculty Award for research/ scholarship/creative activity in 2004. In 2011, he was elected to the National Academy of Education, an honorary society of scholars that connects education research to policy. Dr. Guthrie was Principal Investigator for a federally funded grant to examine adolescents' motivation, engagement, and learning in a districtwide study of Concept-Oriented Reading Instruction. He has published several books and articles about motivation and engagement.

Kris D. Gutiérrez, PhD, is Professor of Learning Sciences and Literacy and holds the Inaugural Provost's Chair at the University of Colorado Boulder. She is also Professor Emerita of Social Research Methodology at the Graduate School of Education and Information Studies at the University of California, Los Angeles. Dr. Gutiérrez is a national leader in education, with an emphasis in literacy, learning, and interpretive approaches to inquiry. Her research examines learning in designed learning environments, with particular attention to students from nondominant communities and English learners. Her work on third spaces and syncretic approaches to literacy and new media literacies seeks to leverage students' everyday concepts and practices to ratchet up expansive forms of learning. Dr. Gutiérrez is a member of the National Academy of Education and is past president of the AERA and the National Conference on Research on Language and Literacy. She is a member of the National Board for the Institute of Education Sciences, where she currently serves as Vice-Chair. Her research has been published widely in premier academic journals, and she is a coauthor of *Learning and Expanding with Activity Theory*.

Susan J. Hart, EdD, is a reading specialist at Cassidy Elementary School in Lexington, Kentucky. She began her career as an elementary school teacher in the District of Columbia Public School System and also worked as a research assistant for Dr. Janice F. Almasi at the University of Kentucky, where she assisted with various research endeavors, including collecting and analyzing data related to the Kentucky Reading Project and implementation of response to intervention across the state of Kentucky. Her doctoral dissertation examined an online interactive community of practice that sought to better support teachers, specifically as it related to literacy and strategy instruction.

Jong-Yun Kim, PhD, received his doctoral degree from the Department of Teaching and Learning, Policy and Leadership, at the University of Maryland, College Park. His major research interests are reading comprehension of multiple texts; the relationship between reader beliefs, biases, and reading strategies; and classroom assessment of reading. He was a former high school teacher of Korean language and literature in South Korea.

Melanie R. Kuhn, PhD, is Associate Professor in Literacy Education at Boston University. Her instructional experience includes teaching in the Boston Public Schools and at Centre Academy in London. She was Co-Principal Investigator on an Interagency Education Research Initiative grant that explored the development of reading fluency with second graders. Dr. Kuhn has authored or coauthored three books—*Developing Fluent Readers: Teching Fluency as a Foundational Skill, Fluency in the Classroom,* and *The Hows and Whys of Fluency Instruction*—and numerous chapters and journal articles. In addition to reading fluency, her research interests include literacy instruction for struggling readers, comprehension development, and vocabulary instruction. She currently teaches courses on reading assessment and struggling readers.

Donald J. Leu, PhD, is Professor of Education and the Neag Endowed Chair in Literacy and Technology at the University of Connecticut. He directs the New Literacies Research Lab and is a member of the Reading Hall of Fame. He is a past president of the National Reading Conference (now LRA) and former member of the Board of Directors of the IRA. A graduate of Michigan State, Harvard, and the University of California, Berkeley, Dr. Leu's research focuses on the new skills and strategies required to read, write, and learn with Internet technologies and the best instructional practices that prepare students for these new literacies. He has received the A. B. Herr Award from the ALER, the Maryann Manning Medal from the University of Alabama, Birmingham, and the Friday Medal for Innovation and Leadership in Education from North Carolina State University.

Christina L. Madda, PhD, is Assistant Professor in the Department of Literacy Education at Northeastern Illinois University, where she teaches courses in literacy instruction for elementary grades, assessment and diagnosis, and technology integration. Her research interests include the use of iPads for intervention with struggling readers, developing the language of coaching within clinical settings, and writing instruction in bilingual classrooms. Dr. Madda is also involved with the Illinois Grow Your Own Teachers initiative that aims to improve urban education by creating a pipeline of highly qualified, community-based teachers of color. Her most recent publication in the *New Educator* journal addresses the potential of university–community partnerships like Grow Your Own Teachers to strengthen teacher preparation.

 Jacquelynn A. Malloy, PhD, is Assistant Professor of Elementary Education in the Eugene T. Moore School of Education at Clemson University, where she teaches the English language arts methods course and is developing a course on social justice and 21st-century learners. Her previous research focused on motivation, engagement, and teacher visioning, with publications in *The Reading Teacher, Literacy Research and Instruction,* and *The Yearbook of the Literacy Research Association.* Dr. Malloy's current research agenda builds on the theory of cognitive change offered through discussion, as outlined in a chapter in the *Handbook of Reading Disabilities Research.* She is currently conducting research on teaching practices involving discussion to support mathematical language and conceptual growth.

 Barbara A. Marinak, PhD, is Associate Professor in the School of Education and Human Services at Mount St. Mary's University. Her doctoral dissertation received the 2005 J. Estill Alexander Future Leaders in Literacy Dissertation Award from the ALER. Before joining the faculty at Mount St. Mary's, Dr. Marinak spent more than two decades in public education, where she held a variety of leadership positions. Her research interests include reading motivation, intervention practices, and the use of informational text. Dr. Marinak has published numerous journal articles and book chapters. Along with her colleagues Susan Anders Mazzoni and Linda B. Gambrell, she is the coauthor of *Maximizing Motivation for Literacy Learning: Grades K–6.*

 Nicole M. Martin, PhD, is Assistant Professor in the Department of Teacher Education and Higher Education at the University of North Carolina at Greensboro. Her research focuses on elementary students' reading comprehension, informational reading and writing, and literacy learning in urban schools. Dr. Martin has coauthored many journal articles, book chapters, and the book *Reading and Writing Genre with Purpose in K–8 Classrooms.* She has received several awards, including the Outstanding Dissertation Award Finalist Award and Teacher of the Year Award from the IRA.

 Chris L. Massey, PhD, is a doctoral candidate at Clemson University. He is a former middle school and high school teacher. His areas of interest include adolescent content-area literacy, disciplinary literacy, and reading motivation and comprehension of lesbian, gay, bisexual, transgender, and questioning adolescents. He has presented his research at the IRA, LRA, ALER, and the AERA conferences.

Susan Anders Mazzoni, MEd, is an independent literacy consultant who works with administrators and teachers to improve literacy practices in elementary school classrooms. Since the late 1990s, she has worked with teachers on implementing phonics, phonemic awareness, fluency, comprehension, and vocabulary instruction in ways that promote student engagement and literacy motivation. She has taught reading courses and served as a research assistant for the National Reading Research Center at the University of Maryland, College Park. Her research and publications address reading motivation, reading engagement, emergent literacy, and discussion. She is a coauthor of the book *Maximizing Motivation for Literacy Learning: Grades K–6.*

 Michael C. McKenna, PhD, is Thomas G. Jewell Professor of Reading at the University of Virginia. Before becoming a professor, he taught middle school math and English. He has authored, coauthored, or edited more than 20 books, including *Cracking the Common Core: Choosing and Using Texts in Grades 6–12* and *Assessment for Reading Instruction, Second Edition,* and over 100 articles, chapters, and technical reports on a range of literacy topics. Dr. McKenna's research has been sponsored by the National Reading Research Center and the Center for the Improvement of Early Reading Achievement. He is a corecipient of the Edward B. Fry Book Award from the LRA and the Award for Outstanding Academic Books from the American Library Association.

Lesley Mandel Morrow (*see* About the Editors).

 Lisa M. O'Brien, EdD, is an advanced doctoral student in Language and Literacy Education at Boston University. Her research focuses on understanding and implementing interventions that close early and later achievement gaps. She is particularly interested in the relationship between vocabulary and conceptual knowledge development and text comprehension.

 Jeanne R. Paratore, EdD, is Professor of Education and Director of the Reading Education and Literacy and Language Education Programs at Boston University. She directs the university-based reading and writing clinic and is research advisor to the Intergenerational Literacy Program, a family literacy program she founded in 1989 to support the English literacy learning of immigrant parents and their children. Dr. Paratore has conducted research and written widely on issues related to family literacy, classroom grouping practices, and interventions for struggling readers. She is a recipient of the New England Reading Association's Lifetime Achievement Award and a member of the Reading Hall of Fame.

 P. David Pearson, PhD, is Professor in the Language, Literacy, and Culture program in the Graduate School of Education at the University of California, Berkeley, where he served as Dean from 2001 to 2010. He has written scores of articles and chapters and written or edited several books about research and practice, most notably the *Handbook of Reading Research,* now in its fourth volume. Dr. Pearson has received numerous honors, including the William S. Gray Citation of Merit and the Albert J. Harris Award from the IRA, the Oscar S. Causey Award from the National Reading Conference (now LRA), the Alan Purves Award from the National Council of Teachers of English, and the Distinguished Contributions to Research in Education Award from the AERA. In 2012, the LRA established the P. David Pearson Scholarly Influence Award to honor research that exerts a long-term influence on literacy practices and/or policies.

Taffy E. Raphael, PhD, is Professor of Literacy Education at the University of Illinois at Chicago and President of SchoolRise LLC. Her research interests include comprehension and writing instruction, frameworks for literacy curriculum and instruction, and whole-school reform. Dr. Raphael designed and researched pedagogical frameworks such as Question Answer Relationships and Book Club. She has published several books and over 100 articles and chapters in leading journals and has been honored by awards such as the IRA's Outstanding Teacher Educator in Reading Award, the University of Illinois at Urbana–Champaign Distinguished Alumni Award, and the LRA's Oscar S. Causey Award for lifetime contributions to literacy research. Dr. Raphael is a fellow of the National Council of Research in Language and Literacy and a member of the Reading Hall of Fame. She served on the board of the LRA, where she also served as treasurer and president.

Timothy Rasinski, PhD, is Professor of Literacy Education at Kent State University. He began his career as an elementary and middle school teacher. Dr. Rasinski has written over 200 articles and has authored, coauthored, or edited over 50 books or curriculum programs on reading education, including *The Fluent Reader, Second Edition*, a best-selling book on reading fluency. His scholarly interests include reading fluency and word study, reading in the elementary and middle grades, and readers who struggle. Dr. Rasinski's research on reading has been cited by the National Reading Panel and has been published in journals such as *Reading Research Quarterly, The Reading Teacher, Reading Psychology*, and the *Journal of Educational Research*. He was the lead author for the fluency chapter in volume 4 of the *Handbook of Reading Research*. Dr. Rasinski has served on the Board of Directors of the IRA, as the president of the College Reading Association, and as coeditor of *The Reading Teacher* and the *Journal of Literacy Research*. In 2010 he was elected to the Reading Hall of Fame.

D. Ray Reutzel, PhD, is the Emma Eccles Jones Distinguished Professor and Endowed Chair of Early Childhood Education at Utah State University. He is the author of more than 200 published research reports, articles, books, book chapters, and monographs. Dr. Reutzel is a past editor of the journals *Literacy Research and Instruction* and *The Reading Teacher*. He received the 1999 A. B. Herr Award and the 2013 ALER Laureate Award from the ALER, and served as president of the organization from 2006 until 2007. He was presented the John C. Manning Public School Service Award from the IRA in May 2007 and served as a member of the Board of Directors from 2007 until 2010. Dr. Reutzel was recently elected to serve as a member of the LRA Board of Directors from 2012 until 2015. He is a member of the Reading Hall of Fame.

 Victoria J. Risko, EdD, is Professor Emerita at Vanderbilt University, having taught in the language, literacy, and culture area of the Department of Teaching and Learning. Her research focuses on teacher education and professional development, teacher reflection, reading comprehension and meaningful learning, and uses of cases and multimedia environments to enhance learning, especially the learning of English learners and readers who are experiencing difficulties. Dr. Risko was the 2011–2012 president of the IRA and is a former president of the ALER. Her most recent book, coauthored with Doris Walker-Dalhouse, is *Be That Teacher!: Breaking the Cycle for Struggling Readers.* She has published in numerous journals and research handbooks, and she is past coeditor of the "Research in the Classroom" column in *The Reading Teacher.* Dr. Risko has received the New York Chancellor's Award for Outstanding Teaching, a Distinguished Research in Education Award from the Association of Teacher Educators, the A. B. Herr Award and Laureate Award for distinguished contributions to reading education and research from the ALER, and the Literary Award for distinguished leadership and contributions to global literacy from the IRA. She is a member of the Reading Hall of Fame.

Nicole Timbrell, MEd, is a graduate student in the Department of Educational Psychology and a graduate assistant in the New Literacies Research Team at the University of Connecticut. She received her master of arts (English) from the University of Sydney. Her research interests are in the new literacies of online research and comprehension, and the use of technology in teaching reading and writing skills to adolescents. She is also a high school English teacher in Sydney, Australia.

Diane H. Tracey, EdD, is Professor of Education at Kean University, where she teaches graduate and undergraduate classes in literacy instruction. Her area of specialization is theoretical understanding of reading, resulting in the text *Lenses on Reading: An Introduction to Theories and Models,* coauthored with Lesley Mandel Morrow. She is presently engaged in two lines of research: teacher read-alouds in the classroom, and the applications of psychotherapeutic techniques to teaching and learning processes. Dr. Tracey currently serves as Secretary of the LRA and as coeditor of the *Journal of School Connections.* She has served on editorial review boards for the *Journal of Literacy Research, The Reading Teacher,* and the *National Reading Conference Yearbook,* and is a guest reviewer for *Reading Research Quarterly.* In 2010, Dr. Tracey received Kean University's Presidential Scholars Challenge Award. Prior to her work at the university level, she was an early childhood educator and a research assistant on a large, federally funded grant project studying children's reading disabilities.

Doris Walker-Dalhouse, PhD, is Professor of Literacy in the College of Education at Marquette University and Professor Emerita at Minnesota State University Moorhead. Her research, conducted in after-school reading programs with preservice teachers and struggling readers and their families, focuses on sociocultural factors in the literacy development of ethnically and culturally diverse learners. She has also published in numerous professional journals and research yearbooks. Dr. Walker-Dalhouse cochaired the IRA Response to Intervention Task Force and is presently cochair of Area 8, Literacy Learning and Practice in Multilingual and Multicultural Settings, of the LRA Annual Conference Committee. She is a past member of the Board of Directors of the IRA and the LRA; past coeditor of the Research in the Classroom column in *The Reading Teacher*; and recipient of the 2013 Albert J. Mazurkiewicz Special Services Award from the ALER.

Sharon Walpole, PhD, is Professor in the School of Education at the University of Delaware. She has experience as a high school teacher, an elementary school literacy coach, and a professional development designer. Dr. Walpole received the National Reading Conference (now LRA) Early Career Achievement Award in 2007. She has coauthored eight books about schoolwide initiatives, has served as a scientific reviewer for the Institute of Education Sciences Reading and Writing Panel, and is currently on the editorial boards of *Elementary School Journal* and *The Reading Teacher*. Dr. Walpole's research focuses on the design and implementation of schoolwide interventions and has been published in *Elementary School Journal, Educational Researcher, Reading Research Quarterly*, and *Reading and Writing Quarterly*.

Lisa Zawilinski, PhD, is Assistant Professor at the University of Hartford. Her research examines methods for helping young children develop literacy skills and strategies across various learning contexts. She focuses on the skills and strategies necessary for elementary grade students to communicate and gather information on the Internet. Dr. Zawilinski also examines how best to support preservice teachers as they explore and embed Internet technologies within their teaching. Her most recent study of elementary grade students explores the use of a blog for sharing information between first and fifth graders. Dr. Zawilinski has published in *The Reading Teacher, Reading Today*, and in a variety of other journals and books.

Foreword

How do you dice an onion?

There are lots of choices, of course. I know how I do it. First, I nip off the stem and shuck off all of the dried paper layers I can with my fingers. I slice the globe in two, and then halve those pieces again. Then, I take each quarter and slice it, trimming off slivers about a quarter of an inch at a time. At this point, it doesn't look much like an onion anymore, and I start rocking my knife back and forth across the shards until I decide it is diced enough.

My wife, Cyndie, is not impressed.

Of course, that's not how they do it on *Top Chef*, and no celebrity chef worth his or her salt would ever use such a brute force method to deconstruct an onion.

"Best practices" in onion dicing say that I take too much time and end up with too many uneven pieces of onion and too much juice—the more even the pieces, these culinary experts claim, the better they'll cook in your dish. My approach isn't completely crazy, however—these big-name cooks trim the stem, peel the skin, and even cut the onion in half much as I do. But then they get all fancy on us, slicing the wedges in two different directions so that the whole thing seems to fall apart magically on the cutting board into amazingly equal cubes of onion flesh.

Clearly, these "experts" slice onions better than me. But who cares? The only people who are going to eat my cooking are me, my family, and my friends—those who I care most about. . . . Perhaps it *would* be better to follow best practices of cooking rather than just soldiering on in my usual messy way.

The book you hold in your hands, now impressively in its fifth edition, obviously is not a cookbook, and you'll gain no unwanted calories following the advice of the experts who have written the chapters. And yet they all start with the same premise as my onion-slicing story: It matters how well you do things. In this case, it matters how you teach literacy: it matters to the students, it matters to their families, and, someday, it will matter to the society as they go out into the world of work and citizenship.

Every chapter here emphasizes some useful way teachers and other educators can help their students to reach higher levels of literacy attainment or to use literacy in ever-expanding ways within our society. As such, each chapter is much more than just a list of facts; each, instead, is an evidence-based argument aimed at persuading you, the reader, to adopt particular "best practices" in your schools and classrooms that can improve student achievement. In other words, slice the onions this way, and it won't be as messy and will result in tastier dishes.

What is a best practice in literacy education?

There was a time when that was a big bone of contention in literacy teaching. Disputes over how to teach reading, the so-called "reading wars," raged. Many educators embraced philosophies and beliefs about how best to teach reading that conflicted with the findings of actual research studies. Clearly, it matters how reading and writing are taught—some methods are more effective than others (i.e., the dishes will usually turn out better), and wise and dedicated professionals want things to come out as well as possible, whether we're talking about a pot of chili or a third grader.

As a result of those "reading wars"–era arguments, many educators have come to accept the value of research-based solutions to classroom problems, and the chapters throughout this book will provide lots of advice based on such studies.

But what does it mean to be a "best practice" or a "research-based" method? When someone tells me they have a "research-based approach for teaching reading," my first inclination is to grab my wallet and to run screaming from the room. Nevertheless, despite the disparate views on those concepts and their frequent misuse, the authors collected here have embraced a surprisingly consistent set of views about what constitutes a best practice.

A fundamental idea that may help teachers to make sense of arguments about best practice is that there are three different kinds of research. They all can be the basis of instructional practice, but they need to be weighed differently by practitioners.

First, there is "descriptive research." True to its name, such studies describe things. Descriptive studies include surveys, questionnaires, and observational studies, and they tell you things like 66% of elementary teachers place students in texts on the basis of reading levels rather than grade levels, or that 86% of elementary students with learning problems struggle with phonics, or that black students tend to lag behind their white counterparts in reading achievement. Such studies are great for identifying gaps and for tracking performance and practice, but they don't reveal much about what works. Thus, aiming some new program at the needs of African American students with the idea of trying to bridge the learning gap makes great sense, and yet such data don't reveal how to make such efforts work.

Second, there are "correlational studies." These investigations identify and measure the relationships among variables. When you are told that the best readers read more than the poorest ones or that the most fluent readers generally have the highest comprehension, you are hearing about correlations (National Institute of Child Health and Human Development, 2000). Often teachers are encouraged to use such evidence to guide their practices—if reading more is such a good idea, maybe teachers should assign more reading. Correlational data can be very useful, and yet, like descriptive studies, they usually don't divulge what works. For instance, correlational studies don't distinguish chickens from eggs (a worse error than misslicing the onions): The best readers certainly do read the most, but it is not clear from this whether more reading practice leads to higher achievement, or whether high achievement simply enables more students to engage in reading (if you can't read well, how much are you going to choose to read?).

Third, there are "experimental studies" that examine the effectiveness of particular instructional practices by actually trying them out with children and seeing if they confer any kind of advantage to the groups who experience them. That kind of research findings is obviously the "golden ticket." But it is important not to overstate such findings either. A positive research finding in education does not mean a practice necessarily works—it only means that it has been made to work by educators in the past. That's not a guarantee, but it's not nothing: "If they can make it work, then I can probably make it work, too."

Many people treat the results of such experimental studies as proof that a practice works. But there is more to it than that. For example, some studies are not especially well done, or some findings are replicated again and again ("If so many people have made this work successfully, then I'm even more sure that I could do it"). Finally, when we say something works, that simply means that the experimental group outdid the control group; but a question to ask is, how much better was it? Slicing onions properly may improve my cooking, and yet how much better would it be? Will my daughters notice the improvement? An outcome can be statistically significant, but not very important since the size of the impact is so tiny (it worked, but it conferred so little advantage no one cared).

The idea that best practices are research based is a good one, but there is clearly more to the idea than that (or this book would probably be called *Research-Based Practices in Literacy Instruction*). Has something been tried often enough that we should trust it? Is it practical? That is, could teachers really implement this result in America's classrooms without extraordinary levels of support? Does the approach make sense in terms of everything else that we know?

Thus, these chapters won't proffer technical summaries of research findings with instructional conclusions tacked on; they are better than that. Each author has viewed the research through his or her own expert lens of practicality and usefulness. The results of this process are well worth having (I've used earlier editions of this book in my own graduate classes to reinforce and extend the ideas I was hoping my students were gaining from me).

Probably the biggest difference between this version and the earlier editions is the emphasis on the Common Core State Standards. In the past, each state adopted its own educational standards. In 2009, 48 states decided to work together to revise their standards. The idea was that in core areas of the curriculum (such as reading and math), the states should have common or shared standards or goals. Children in Wichita, Kansas, are unlikely to need different reading skills than the kids in Seattle, Washington, or Dover, Delaware. As a result, 44 states now are aimed at the same educational outcomes in reading and writing.

Some critics of these standards have panned them because of their lack of research. I strongly support the new standards and want them realized for my own grandchildren. However, the critics are actually correct about this: We depend on research to tell us what works, not what we want. If someone says they want their kids to read complex texts, to summarize an author's message, or to critically examine how a text works, the right response isn't that we need a research study to determine whether we really want them—no more than we need a research investigation to tell us that we want tastier dishes, more money, happier spouses, and better weather. We just know that we want our students to become proficient readers and writers—and that's okay. This volume will help you to figure out how to accomplish that effectively.

TIMOTHY SHANAHAN, PhD
University of Illinois at Chicago

REFERENCE

National Institute of Child Health and Human Development. (2000). *Report of the National Reading Panel: Teaching children to read: An evidence based assessment of the scientific research literature on reading and its implications for reading instruction* (NIH Publication No. 00-4769). Washington, DC: U.S. Government Printing Office.

Introduction

In the first edition of *Best Practices in Literacy Instruction* (1999), Linda B. Gambrell, Lesley Mandel Morrow, Susan B. Neuman, and Michael Pressley invited leading literacy scholars and researchers to author chapters for a volume that would focus on evidence-based best practices for literacy instruction. In the introduction to the first edition, the editors argued that researchers and practitioners should consider a wide range of influences on literacy development. These influences included classroom context, motivation to read, teaching methods, social interaction, and teacher–student interaction. Gambrell and colleagues (1999) reminded us about the *what* and *how* of literacy research: "*What* research reveals about literacy instruction should inform *how* we go about the very important job of providing literacy experiences and instruction for our students" (pp. 1–2). Four editions and more than 15 years later, the fifth edition of *Best Practices in Literacy Instruction* continues to address evidence-based best practices in literacy instruction in light of emerging research and national policy. In addition, this edition continues to provide practical suggestions for enhancing the literacy development of all students. The fifth edition adds to the ongoing conversation about literacy instruction by addressing the influence of the Common Core State Standards (CCSS) on literacy instruction (National Governors Association [NGA] Center for Best Practices & Council of Chief State School Officers [CCSSO], 2010). Also, this edition addresses the centrality of motivation to read and its role within best practices in literacy instruction. Finally, it includes a stronger emphasis on topics such as the use of informational texts, close reading, and text complexity. Even though the volume is designed for both inservice and preservice teachers, the editors and authors hope teacher educators find it useful in professional development, as well as in courses for graduate students and reading specialists. The book should also benefit administrators who are interested in the success of their schools in both literacy development and CCSS implementation.

Most recently, literacy researchers have begun to address evidence-based practices and their relation to the CCSS (Neuman & Gambrell, 2013; Morrow, Wixson, & Shanahan, 2013; Morrow, Shanahan, & Wixson, 2013). The Standards are important to literacy researchers, literacy educators, and literacy instruction because the K–12 standards "help ensure that all students are college and career ready in literacy no later than the end of high school" (NGA & CCSSO, 2010, p. 3). That is, the CCSS provide a destination—a guide, if you will—for educators to assist with all students' preparation for life beyond high school. Whether students choose to go to college or to enter the workforce, the CCSS are in place to provide a general framework of *what* students should gain from their literacy experiences and instruction. *How* to get to literacy proficiency is left to the expertise of literacy educators. Across the literacy spectrum of reading, writing, speaking, listening, and language, the Standards address (1) reading: text complexity and comprehension growth in reading; (2) writing: text types, responding to reading, and research; (3) speaking and listening: flexible communication and collaboration; and (4) language: conventions, effective use, and vocabulary (NGA & CCSSO, 2010, p. 8). The Standards provide an endpoint, while the roadmap is left to teachers: "The Standards define what all students are expected to know and be able to do, not how teachers should teach" (NGA & CCSSO, 2010, p. 6). Simply put, the Standards define the *what*, while the *how* to get there is left to literacy educators who rely on evidence-based practices that will assist them in their classrooms as they provide effective literacy instruction to all students so they are better prepared to enter life experiences upon completion of their K–12 education.

The contributors to the fifth edition of *Best Practices in Literacy Instruction* actively tie classroom-based research, innovations, and instruction about literacy development to the CCSS. The editors and chapter authors believe that informed and empowered teachers are best able to integrate evidence-based strategies and traditional ideas about literacy instruction to best meet the needs of today's students while meeting the general tenets set forth in the Standards. Thus, the chapters in this edition provide not only evidence-based classroom strategies and techniques to assist in instructional decision making, but also informative discussions about the influences related to the CCSS and effective and comprehensive literacy instruction.

This edition has 18 chapters, which are organized into four parts: (I) Perspectives on Best Practices, (II) Best Practices for All Students,

(III) Evidence-Based Strategies for Literacy Learning and Teaching, and (IV) Perspectives on Special Issues. In Part I, the chapter authors discuss philosophies about literacy instruction that are linked to best practices. Specifically, the authors focus on how comprehensive literacy instruction integrates what we know about effective literacy instruction and effective teaching in order to provide balanced literacy instruction in keeping with the CCSS. Part II presents current, evidence-based information about classroom literacy practices that are effective for *all* students. Topics include early literacy, struggling readers, English language learners (ELLs), and adolescent literacy. Part III provides strategies for literacy instruction that are grounded in research and have been shown to be effective practices in classrooms. The topics discussed in this section include phonological awareness and phonics, vocabulary, narrative text comprehension, informational text comprehension, fluency, writing, and assessment. Part IV introduces new perspectives related to specific issues within the literacy field, including topics such as the new literacies of online research, differentiating instruction, family literacy, and professional development.

Part I: Perspectives on Best Practices

In Chapter 1, Linda B. Gambrell, Jacquelynn A. Malloy, Barbara A. Marinak, and Susan Anders Mazzoni contend that literacy achievement is unequal for children in U.S. schools and that any serious efforts to meet the CCSS and close the reading and writing achievement gap can be met only with instruction and assessments that are grounded in evidence-based practices and sound principles of learning. Then they discuss the importance of differentiated instruction using best practices to provide opportunities for literacy learning for all students along with meeting the demands of the CCSS. After presenting 10 evidence-based best practices for comprehensive literacy instruction, they discuss the vital role of teachers as decision makers. They propose that optimal literacy teaching and learning can be achieved only when teachers are given latitude to use their professional judgment about instructional decisions.

Vicki B. Griffo, Christina L. Madda, P. David Pearson, and Taffy E. Raphael revisit the construct of balance within the field of literacy in Chapter 2. In continuing the conversation about a balanced literacy curriculum, they outline issues that frame today's educational contexts and discuss evidence-based best practices and achieving balance in literacy teaching and learning. They assert that both scholarly evidence and the world in which students live and work demand literacy instruction that is multifaceted. After discussing the research base surrounding best practices in literacy instruction, the role of the teacher in a balanced literacy program, and the role of the CCSS, Griffo and her colleagues assert that a balanced and comprehensive literacy curriculum can be achieved only through artful orchestration by teachers.

In Chapter 3, John T. Guthrie discusses best practices for motivating students to read. Guthrie conveys the research evidence about the importance of motivation to read and relates the CCSS to motivation and engagement. He discusses three key motivations: interest, confidence, and dedication. Finally, he portrays classroom practices such as assuring relevance, providing choices, generating success, arranging collaborations, setting up thematic units, and emphasizing the importance of building value that foster motivation to read. Guthrie concludes that every teacher is a motivator, and when teachers empower students to become active readers by placing motivation first, they are rewarded with motivated readers.

Part II: Best Practices for All Students

In order to illustrate best practices in early literacy, Diane H. Tracey and Lesley Mandel Morrow, in Chapter 4, present a case study infused with connections to the CCSS for English language arts. The authors first present a brief overview of theories that inform best practices in early literacy. Then they present a summary of the initiatives that have impacted early literacy, including the CCSS. They follow this discussion with a research synthesis and research-based instructional strategies for early literacy, and they examine special issues such as digital literacies, ELLs, and response to intervention (RTI).

In Chapter 5, Victoria J. Risko and Doris Walker-Dalhouse argue that struggling readers need teachers who take a comprehensive and balanced view of their literacy processes. The authors identify current issues related to assessment and instruction of struggling readers, while situating the practices in research and authentic classrooms, including alignment with the CCSS. Risko and Walker-Dalhouse end their discussion of best practices for struggling readers with a call for an increase in documented accounts of teacher practices involving struggling readers in urban and rural settings, across multiple grade levels, and in national and international school settings.

Michael Domínguez and Kris D. Gutiérrez address the special considerations for ELLs in literacy instruction in Chapter 6. The authors argue for connected forms of learning that are both interesting to students and culturally and socially relevant. According to Domínguez and Gutiérrez, instructional practices should provide ELLs with a variety of opportunities to use communicative and written language within a variety of social contexts and from different identity positions. During their discussion of evidence-based best practices and the CCSS, the authors assert that the use of the term *dual language learners* (DLLs), rather than the term ELLs, provides an asset-based description of students who are immersed in a culture and society that are quite different from their own. In this chapter, the authors explore how discourse shapes and informs how we view our students' learning, as well as their potential.

In Chapter 7, Douglas Fisher and Nancy Frey focus on the unique needs of adolescents and their literacy development. After examining the growing knowledge base of disciplinary literacy, the authors provide four instructional practices that advance content learning and literacy knowledge, all of which are aligned with the CCSS: close reading, annotation, discussion, and writing with evidence. In a spirited and thought-provoking discussion surrounding the statement "Every teacher is a teacher of reading," the authors argue for instructional practices that transform knowledge, rather than those practices that rely on transmission. In their concluding remarks, Fisher and Frey assert that discipline-specific literacy, by drawing from literacy components, enables students to understand the world in which they live.

Part III: Evidence-Based Strategies for Literacy Learning and Teaching

After describing the role of phonemic awareness in learning to read, Patricia M. Cunningham, in Chapter 8, explores what research says about the best ways to teach phonics. She then summarizes "what we know" about multisyllabic word decoding, and, although research is scant, she concludes that what we do know leads us to believe that morphemes are the building blocks of big words, which is recognized by the CCSS. Descriptions of classroom practices consistent with what we know about phonemic awareness, phonics, and multisyllabic word decoding follows, and Cunningham ends the chapter by connecting activities to the CCSS.

Camille L. Z. Blachowicz and Peter J. Fisher discuss five research-based guidelines for vocabulary instruction in Chapter 9. Arguing that effective vocabulary instruction needs to be multifaceted and that vocabulary instruction should approach learning from many angles, the authors stress the need for comprehensive instruction as they share the research that underpins each of the guidelines as well as including examples and their Common Core connections. In a vivid and engaging description of a fourth-grade classroom where the teacher uses these best practices, the authors come full circle with their discussion of research-based guidelines for vocabulary instruction.

In Chapter 10, Janice F. Almasi and Susan J. Hart discuss best practices surrounding narrative text comprehension and explain how comprehension instruction links with the CCSS. The authors divide their chapter into three sections: what the current research has to say about comprehension, a description of the changes needed to recontextualize comprehension as a way to prepare strategic and reflective learners, and a description of adjustments within literacy classrooms that foster a transformational view of strategy instruction. These sections provide the authors with an opportunity to discuss the role of social context in comprehension instruction as well as the importance of both scaffolding during comprehension instruction and teaching readers to be strategic rather than just teaching strategies. Almasi and Hart assert that the shift from "the strategy" to "the student" is critical and requires teachers to move their focus from strategy instruction to a focus on the context in which they are taught.

In Chapter 11, Nell A. Duke and Nicole M. Martin explain the need to teach informational text comprehension across genres, tasks, and grade levels. The authors also identify research that supports strategies for scaffolding comprehension and develops strategic readers of informational text. With a powerful and pragmatic unit that uses research-supported practices, Duke and Martin describe how these practices support the development of the CCSS and informational text comprehension.

Melanie R. Kuhn and Timothy Rasinski, in Chapter 12, demonstrate how fluency is an important part in reading development and text comprehension. In this chapter, Kuhn and Rasinski discuss the role of fluency in both the reading process and reading achievement and its relation to the CCSS, outline effective fluency approaches, and close with future directions for research. Readers will glean the importance of fluency when the authors present effective fluency approaches. The Fluency Development Lesson, Fluency-Oriented Reading Instruction (FORI)/Wide FORI, and Fast Start are examples of approaches to fluency instruction that can positively impact students' reading abilities and assist them with understanding the challenging texts that are suggested by the CCSS.

In Chapter 13, Karen Bromley presents a research synthesis of evidence-based best practices for K–8 writing instruction, as well as a discussion about writing and the CCSS. Bromley discusses rubrics, student conferences, and student choice in the evidence-based practices for teachers of writing. Finally, in reflections and future directions, Bromley reminds us that teachers should be flexible, willing to collaborate, and creative in blending out-of-school literacies with in-school writing.

Peter Afflerbach, Byeong-Young Cho, Maria Elliker Crassas, and Jong-Yun Kim discuss attaining a balanced approach between instruction and reading assessment in Chapter 14. After discussing the current state of literacy assessment, Afflerbach et al. remind us when discussing best practices that teachers and teacher educators should reflect balance in assessment in order to produce information that is useful to multiple audiences. The authors then suggest that balance can be achieved in literacy assessment by using the CCSS. During this rich discussion, Afflerbach and his colleagues provide examples of balanced approaches and best practices in literacy assessment.

Part IV. Perspectives on Special Issues

In Chapter 15, Donald J. Leu, Lisa Zawilinski, Elena Forzani, and Nicole Timbrell explore best practices in new literacies and their relationship with online research and comprehension. They define a dual-level theory of new literacies and explain how we should interpret the CCSS in reading while integrating instruction in the new literacies of online research and comprehension with traditional reading comprehension. Next, they discuss 10 research-based principles for new literacies, such as using new literacies to help the last student become the first and teaching online search skills. In their conclusion, Leu and his colleagues predict that the new literacies will always be central for learning, and the future will include online literacy technologies that are currently not in existence.

In Chapter 16, D. Ray Reutzel, Sarah K. Clark, and Michelle Flory discuss how to organize effective literacy instruction while differentiating that instruction in order to meet the needs of all students. After providing an overview of global and national contexts that surround classroom literacy instruction, the authors discuss the CCSS and (1) evidence-based elements of literacy instruction and RTI; (2) the use of assessment data and RTI to inform the CCSS; (3) the use of multiple literacy instructional practices to use with RTI; (4) alternative grouping approaches and effective literacy instruction and RTI; and (5) scheduling a literacy instructional block and RTI. In their reflection, Reutzel, Clark, and Flory remind us that research has shown the advantages of small-group, differentiated literacy instruction.

Jeanne R. Paratore, Patricia A. Edwards, and Lisa M. O'Brien address issues related to family literacy and the CCSS in Chapter 17. The authors open the chapter with an explanation of the importance of parental involvement and then describe the families that attend U.S. schools in order to understand and plan appropriate forms of parental involvement. Finally, they give examples of evidence-based programs and list principles to guide teachers with their family planning.

In Chapter 18, Sharon Walpole and Michael C. McKenna argue that the key to effective professional development (PD) is specificity of training; that is, PD should be designed for immediate instructional application for particular students and instructional materials. Walpole and McKenna summarize what we know about the design and effects of PD and then provide a rationale for specific PD while recommending a cycle for PD. One of the highlights of this chapter is the authors' proposal of three promising PD practices: (1) school-based professional learning communities, (2) coaching, and (3) use of technology. As they close their chapter, Walpole and McKenna analyze current practices where the CCSS are the focus of the PD. Finally, the authors address concerns about PD, most of which revolve around the intensive nature of the suggested activities.

It is our hope is that the fifth edition of this volume will inspire teachers to use best practices in their literacy instruction so that *all* students become proficient readers and writers. Finally, we would like to thank our authors who contributed to this book; without them, a volume of best practices would not be possible.

LINDA B. GAMBRELL,
LESLEY MANDEL MORROW,
and CHRIS L. MASSEY

REFERENCES

Gambrell, L. B., Morrow, L. M., Neuman, S. B., & Pressley, M. (Eds.). (1999). *Best practices in literacy instruction*. New York: Guilford Press.

Morrow, L. M., Shanahan, T., & Wixson, K. K. (Eds.). (2013). *Teaching with the Common Core Standards for English language arts, PreK–2*. New York: Guilford Press.

Morrow, L. M., Wixson, K. K., & Shanahan, T. (Eds.). (2013). *Teaching with the Common Core Standards for English language arts, grades 3–5*. New York: Guilford Press.

National Governors Association Center for Best Practices & Council of Chief State School Officers. (2010). *Common Core State Standards for English language arts and literacy in history/social studies, science, and technical subjects*. Washington, DC: Authors. Retrieved from *www.corestandards.org/assets/ CCSSI_ELA%20Standards.pdf*.

Neuman, S. B., & Gambrell, L. B. (Eds.). (2013). *Reading instruction in the age of Common Core Standards*. Newark, DE: International Reading Association.

Contents

PART III. Evidence-Based Strategies for Literacy Learning and Teaching

PART IV. Perspectives on Special Issues

PART I

PERSPECTIVES ON BEST PRACTICES

CHAPTER 1

Evidence-Based Best Practices for Comprehensive Literacy Instruction in the Age of the Common Core Standards

Linda B. Gambrell
Jacquelynn A. Malloy
Barbara A. Marinak
Susan Anders Mazzoni

This chapter will:

- Present and discuss features of evidence-based best practices for comprehensive literacy instruction.

- Discuss the importance of differentiated instruction using best practices to provide *all* students with opportunities for literacy learning.

- Discuss the influence of the Common Core State Standards and other current initiatives on comprehensive literacy instruction.

- Present 10 evidence-based best practices for comprehensive literacy instruction.

- Discuss the important role of teachers as visionary decision makers who thoughtfully incorporate best practices for comprehensive literacy instruction.

It is a time of great challenge and opportunity for literacy teachers. The Common Core State Standards (CCSS; National Governors Association Center for Best Practices & Council of Chief State School Officers [NGA & CCSSO], 2010) challenge us to help our students develop high-level reading, writing, speaking, listening, viewing, and representing skills. It is also a time of great opportunity to ensure that our students are proficient, persistent, passionate, and prepared to meet the literacy challenges of the 21st century.

Our students will need to be highly literate in order to succeed in school and in the workplaces of tomorrow (NGA & CCSSO, 2010). Historically, evidence across the past five decades indicates that literacy achievement has not been equal for all children in U.S. schools (Morrow, Rueda, & Lapp, 2009; National Assessment of Educational Progress [NAEP], 2013). There is considerable evidence of a growing gap in literacy achievement between (1) minority and nonminority students; (2) students from poorer and richer families; (3) students who are native English speakers and those who are English language learners; and (4) students identified for special education services and those in general education (Morrow et al., 2009).

There are a number of compelling reasons for these achievement gaps in the United States. Consider that by age 2, children who are read to regularly by an adult have greater language comprehension, larger vocabularies, and higher cognitive skills than children read to less often (Raikes et al., 2006). In middle-income neighborhoods, the ratio of books per child is 13 to 1, while in low-income neighborhoods, the ratio is 1 age-appropriate book for every 300 children (Dickinson & Neuman, 2006). Perhaps of most consequence is that so many children now live in poverty. According to the Southern Education Foundation (2013), 48% of the children in the United States are living in poverty. Poverty places children at higher risk for a number of problems, including those associated with brain development and social and emotional development (Every Child Matters, 2013).

National and international reports of achievement continue to reveal concerns about the literacy performance of U.S. students. While the 2013 NAEP report revealed that both 9- and 13-year-olds scored higher in reading in 2012 than students in the early 1970s, this finding did not hold for 17-year-olds. Furthermore, the 2012 NAEP report on students' writing performance revealed that 24% of students in grades 8 and 12 performed at the proficient level, while 54% performed at the basic level, denoting partial mastery of the knowledge and skills that are fundamental for proficient work at each grade level. Only 3% of students in grades 8 and 12 performed at the advanced level, indicating superior writing performance. These statistics reflect the many challenges teachers face in today's classrooms, as well as the importance of providing effective literacy instruction for all students.

The authors of the chapters in this volume are among the educators who recognize the need for accommodation and differentiation to enhance literacy development for all students, many of whom struggle because of life circumstances. Any serious effort to meet the CCSS and close the reading and writing achievement gap will require attention to all aspects of literacy teaching and learning. This challenge can only be met with instruction and assessments that are grounded in evidence-based best practices and principles of learning (Garcia & Wiese, 2009; U.S. Department of Education, 2012).

Evidence-Based Best Practices

While no single instructional program, approach, or method has been found to be effective in teaching all students to read, evidence-based best practices that promote high rates of achievement have been documented. An *evidence-based best practice* refers to an instructional practice that has a record of success in improving reading achievement and is both trustworthy and valid. Evidence indicates that when this practice is used with a particular group of students, they can be expected to make gains in reading achievement (International Reading Association, 2002a, 2002b). Providing comprehensive literacy instruction in the increasingly diverse classrooms of today requires teachers to assess skillfully in order to design appropriate instruction to meet the individual needs of all students. In addition, the classroom teacher must be adept at identifying student needs through ongoing formative assessments and providing appropriate whole-class, small-group, and individual instruction.

What counts as evidence of reliable and trustworthy practice? Evidence-based best practices are established in two ways: by data collected according to rigorously designed studies and by expert consensus among practitioners who monitor student outcomes as part of their practice (U.S. Department of Education, 2012). A position paper published by the International Reading Association (2002b) asserts that such evidence provides:

- *Objective* data that any evaluator would identify and interpret similarly.
- *Valid* data that adequately represent the tasks that children need to become successful readers.
- *Reliable* data that will remain essentially unchanged if collected on a different day or by a different person.
- *Systematic* data that were collected according to a rigorous design of either experimentation or observation.
- *Refereed* data that have been approved for publication by a panel of independent reviewers.

According to a U.S. Department of Education (2012) report, research has produced the following findings that form the basis of evidence-based literacy practices:

- Instruction that focuses on students' strengths and needs in the five core elements of reading: phonemic awareness, phonics, fluency, vocabulary, and comprehension;
- Instruction that is systematic and sequenced;
- Instruction that uses materials that are engaging and relevant to the students' needs;
- Instruction that is continuously monitored to gauge effectiveness.

In our view, evidence-based instruction involves teachers making decisions using "professional wisdom integrated with the best available empirical evidence" (Allington, 2005, p. 16). This definition of evidence-based instruction honors the wisdom and evidence derived from professional experience while at the same time recognizes the important role of empirical research. Furthermore, no single investigation or research study ever establishes a practice as effective. When evaluating claims of evidence for best practices, we must determine whether the research was data-based, rigorous, and systematic (Bogdan & Biklen, 1992; International Reading Association, 2002b). It is important to note that it is the *convergence of evidence* from an array of research studies, using a variety of research designs and methodologies, that allows us to determine best practices.

In order to provide instruction using best practices, as well as to make appropriate instructional and assessment decisions, teachers need a strong knowledge of good evidence, drawn from both professional wisdom and the research. One of the most important questions a teacher can ask is "What evidence is available that suggests that using this practice in my classroom will support comprehensive literacy instruction and increase reading achievement for my students?"

We must acknowledge that some students are at risk of academic failure because of their life conditions. Furthermore, we need to acknowledge that school cultures require specialized academic abilities. Life conditions and experiences that do not support and encourage the development of those specialized academic abilities "tend to produce children who are deficient in the ability to handle academic work" (Gordon, 2009, p. ix). We think Gordon has it right when he states, "We know in the 21st century that the absence of a certain developed ability because of the absence of opportunity to learn should not be interpreted as absence of ability to learn, and the recognition of the fact of diverse human characteristics demands accommodation and differentiation in pedagogical treatment" (p. x).

Comprehensive Literacy Instruction

For literacy instruction to be *comprehensive*, an all-encompassing definition of literacy needs to be considered. Literacy is, after all, the means by which we communicate, whether by comprehending the thoughts, ideas, and intentions of others, or in communicating our own thoughts, ideas, and intentions *to* others. While the traditional view of literacy addresses primarily reading and writing, a *comprehensive view* of literacy encompasses three reciprocal modes of communicating: *speaking/listening, reading/writing,* and *viewing/representing.* Just as oral skills precede and continue to support reading and writing activities, the signs, symbols, and images that are present in the environment are valued literacies in terms of comprehending the messages that exist around us. In our increasingly digital and online communicative context, we are remiss as educators if we fail to support and integrate these modes into our literacy instruction.

Comprehensive literacy instruction addresses these three reciprocal modes of communication, building both receptive skills (listening, reading, viewing) and expressive skills (speaking, writing, visually representing). It is formed around high expectations for continued student growth based on future-looking standards of what students know and are able to do involving these three modes. Literacy instruction should support students in using these communicative modes to develop and solidify knowledge, and to sharing what they think and know, thus preparing them for continued education and productive adult lives. For this reason, comprehensive literacy instruction involves using oral, aural, written, and visual modes to learn. In order for students to become independent communicators, instruction should be provided to each student in his or her zone of proximal development (Vygotsky, 1978) such that he or she is supported in moving from what he or she can do with support to what he or she can do on his or her own. Comprehensive literacy instruction, therefore, needs to involve appropriately targeted guided and individual instruction in addition to whole-class instruction. Instruction that involves a gradual release of responsibility (Pearson & Gallagher, 1983) moves students toward continual improvement as literate beings who communicate effectively for real-world purposes.

The goal of comprehensive literacy instruction is to ensure that all students achieve their full literacy potential. Instruction should prepare our students to enter adulthood with the skills they will need to participate fully in a democratic society that is part of a global economy. Comprehensive literacy instruction, then, can be summarized as instruction that supports and prepares students to independently use listening and speaking, reading and writing, and viewing and representing as a means to effectively comprehend and communicate for authentic and personal reasons. The best practices that are described in this chapter, and throughout this volume, are designed to prepare educators to strive for that worthy end.

The Role of Differentiated Instruction in Comprehensive Literacy Instruction

There is no doubt that as contemporary student populations become increasingly more diverse, teachers and administrators are focused on honing literacy practices that prove to be effective for all students (Guild, 2001; Hall, 2002; McCoy & Ketterlin-Geller, 2004; Tomlinson, 2004). Indeed, the reminders can be heard in almost any professional development gathering: "One size does not fit all" and "We should resist teaching to the middle." Now part of our educational nomenclature, these phrases have become synonymous with the inarguable imperative to differentiate literacy instruction.

For more than three decades, literacy professionals have recognized the need to study our students in order to determine their strengths and needs. However, this careful examination is now taking place in classrooms welcoming students with disabilities, students who are culturally and linguistically diverse, and students with a wide variety of print experiences, interests, and motivation (Guild, 2001; Stronge, 2007). In addition, in order to deliver comprehensive literacy instruction for all students, it is important to use pedagogically sound assessment techniques to support differentiated literacy instruction.

The Role of Assessment in Differentiated Instruction

The goal of assessment is to obtain useful and timely information about desired goals as literacy learning evolves. To capture the dynamic nature of students becoming more proficient, teachers need to use tools and practices that reflect the complexities of reading and writing (Lipson, Chomsky-Higgins, & Kanfer, 2011). In other words, obtaining authentic information about literacy performance should not be sacrificed for the efficiency of contrived texts and tasks created specifically for assessment purposes. Such contrived assessments may misrepresent a student's profile, resulting in instruction that is narrowly focused and limiting.

Teachers can obtain an accurate profile of students' needs and growth with less frequent but more authentic diagnostic tools and/or practices. Performance-based measures such as running records and writing samples are assessment practices so closely aligned to daily practice that they are virtually indistinguishable from instruction.

The first step in arriving at a shared understanding of differentiated instruction is to accept the reality that learners are all essentially different and that instruction matters (Brighton, 2002; Tomlinson, 2001). As Allington wrote in 1983, "Good and poor readers differ in their reading ability as much because of differences in instruction as variations in individual learning styles or attitudes" (p. 1). Differentiation seeks to accommodate the differences in students' learning needs in light of theory, research, and common sense (Tomlinson & Allan, 2000). It is an approach to teaching that includes active planning for student differences. In other words, when teachers differentiate, they are meeting the individual needs of their students without diminishing expectations or sacrificing curricular rigor.

According to Tomlinson (1999), content, process, product, and the learning environment can be differentiated using flexible grouping that is informed by ongoing assessments. *Content* is what the student needs to learn or how the student will get access to the information. *Process* includes the activities in which the student engages in order to make sense of or master the content. *Products* are culminating projects that ask the student to rehearse, apply, and extend what he or she has learned in a unit. And *learning environment* refers to the way the classroom works and feels (Tomlinson, 1999). Meeting the needs of struggling readers using a response-to-intervention (RTI) model, including students with disabilities, and creating a culturally responsive classroom will undoubtedly require teachers to differentiate literacy instruction.

Current Initiatives Influencing Literacy Instruction

During the past 5 years, the CCSS has become a hot topic in education, in the media, and with politicians at every level of government. As we move into the next decade, it is clear that the following initiatives will continue to influence literacy research, policy, and practice: the CCSS for English Language Arts (National Governors Association Center for Best Practices, Council of Chief State School Officers, 2010), RTI (*NASDSE. org*), inclusion, culturally responsive teaching (CRT), and the Partnership for 21st Century Skills (*www.p21.org*). Clearly, these initiatives reflect the need for differentiated instruction that will equip our students with the literacy skills they will need to be successful in the 21st century.

CCSS for English Language Arts

In our view, there are some promising and compelling aspects of the CCSS. These new standards clearly place *comprehension* at the center of literacy learning and place *reading* and *writing* at the center of academic achievement. The ultimate goal of literacy instruction is to nurture students who are able to read and write with deep understanding. We have known for a long time that students who are proficient readers and writers are more likely to be successful in terms of achievement across all academic areas.

There is general agreement that the CCSS place a greater emphasis on higher-level comprehension skills than previous standards (Calkins, Ehrenworth, & Lehman, 2012). In addition, the CCSS place a greater emphasis on writing than have standards in the past. In the new CCSS, equal weight is given to reading and writing, and there is an emphasis on the connections across reading and writing for both instruction and assessment.

The effort to develop common core state standards for the United States was guided by the NGO and CCSSO, in collaboration with content experts, states, teachers, school administrators, and parents. The CCSS, released in the spring of 2010, articulate a vision of what it means to be "a literate person in the twenty-first century" (Common Core State Standards Initiative, 2010). According to the CCSS mission statement, the standards provide a consistent, clear understanding of what students are expected to learn so that teachers and parents know what to do to help them. The standards are designed to be robust and relevant to the real world, reflecting the knowledge and skills that our young people need for success in college and careers. With U.S. students fully prepared for the future, our communities will be best positioned to compete successfully in the global economy (Common Core State Standards Initiative, 2010).

Fostering higher achievement for our students so that they can compete successfully in our global society is a worthy goal. The CCSS set a high bar for our students, but it is one that we should achieve, particularly for literacy skills that provide the very foundation for all academic learning. There will be a number of challenges as we move toward implementation of the CCSS. During 2014–2015, it is anticipated that current state assessments will, in most states, be replaced by assessments from two consortia: Smarter Balanced Assessments and Partnership for Assessment of Readiness of College and Careers (PARCC). Sample items for these assessments can now be viewed on their websites. They include new methods of assessment and have higher expectations for student achievement. While these standards and assessments will "demand more from teachers and far more from students, they are essential if we are to enable students to be successful in developing 21st century skills" (Neuman & Gambrell, 2013, p. 1).

Response to Intervention

RTI is a federally funded program designed to integrate assessment and intervention within a multilevel prevention system to maximize student achievement. RtI has two purposes. First, it can be used for the identification of a specific learning disability in lieu of the IQ–achievement discrepancy model—a model that has resulted in the overidentification of disaggregated students (low socioeconomic status, ethnicity, English as a second language, and poverty) (Fuchs & Fuchs, 2006). Second, RtI is a strategy for reducing the number of students identified with learning disability by providing intervention to all children at risk for school failure (Johnston, 2010).

While there are no mandates for the structure of RtI, there are those who advocate for a system of increasingly more intensive tiers (Fuchs & Fuchs, 2006; McEneaney, Lose, & Schwartz, 2006). In these models, Tier 1 is usually core instruction, Tier 2 is a first level of intervention usually delivered in small groups several times a week, and Tier 3 is more intensive, sometimes daily, intervention. In some situations, the tiers of RTI may result in overidentifying children for intervention and/or preventing differential diagnosis of students with special education needs; therefore, some school districts are rethinking the tiered approach (Dorn & Soffos, 2011). More flexible, collaborative models that blur the lines between core instruction and reading intervention are being used in schools. These efforts allow struggling readers to double or triple the amount of reading instruction they receive, unhindered by label or classification (Poparad, 2010).

Inclusion

The National Center on Educational Restructuring and Inclusion (1995) suggests that inclusion is providing all students, including those with significant disabilities, with equitable opportunities to receive effective instruction in age-appropriate classrooms in their neighborhood schools. More broadly defined, inclusive education refers to "the commitment to educate each child, to the maximum extent appropriate, in the school and classroom he or she would otherwise attend. It involves bringing the support services to the child and requires only that the child will benefit from being in the class (rather than having to keep up with the other students)" (Rogers, 1993, p. 1).

Research indicates that both students with disabilities and their non-disabled peers benefit from well-planned and delivered inclusive instruction. Several studies have found that students without disabilities grew in their understanding and acceptance of students with disabilities while all students, those with and without disabilities, experience increased self-esteem related to socialization and communication (Kochhar, West, & Taymans, 2000; Ritter, Michel, & Irby, 1999). Academically, when differentiated instruction and collaborative strategies are combined, all students in inclusive classrooms grew in social skills, communication skills, and problem-solving skills (Barnitt, 2002; Farlow, 1994).

Culturally Responsive Teaching

CRT is defined as using the cultural knowledge, prior experiences, and performance styles of students to make learning more appropriate and effective. It teaches *to* and *through* the strengths of students (Gay, 2002). Therefore, in order to engage in CRT, teachers need to be culturally aware in addition to possessing pedagogical and content knowledge. Cultural awareness includes understanding the cultural characteristics that have direct implications for teaching and learning, including a group's cultural values, traditions, communication, learning styles, contributions, and relational patterns (Hollins, King, & Hayman, 1994; King, Hollins, & Hayman, 1997; Pai, 1990; Smith, 1998). In addition, teachers should be aware that visible and invisible cultures are present in their classrooms. Visible culture includes literature, crafts, music, art, and technology. Values, beliefs, feelings, opinions, and assumptions comprise the invisible culture. And though visible culture is important, CRT cannot be fully realized without an awareness of the invisible culture (Gay, 2002).

Teachers who engage in CRT are cultural "bridge builders," helping students connect their lived cultural experiences with the expectations of classrooms and content. Culturally responsive teachers possess important characteristics that enhance their ability to differentiate instruction. They see cultural heritages as worthy content to be taught in the formal curriculum; build bridges between academic abstractions and sociocultural realities; use a wide variety of instructional strategies to nurture all students; and teach students to know and support each other's strengths.

Highly effective, differentiated literacy instruction includes opportunities to read, write, listen, speak, view, and represent in classrooms that: (1) are characterized by high expectations; (2) are socially inclusive; (3) engender feelings of competence; and (4) ensure full participation. Classrooms characterized by high expectations value the prior knowledge that all students contribute to the meaning-making process. They are communities where students discuss, debate, and reconcile ambiguity by interacting respectfully with each other. In classrooms where teachers reject "one size fits all" instruction, differences become the ties that bind.

Partnership for 21st Century Skills

The Partnership for 21st Century Skills (*www.p21.org*) is a national organization dedicated to preparing students for the innovative and critical thinking skills required for success in a global economy. To this end, the organization provides resources and support for educators to integrate the three R's with the four C's. The four C's include critical thinking and problem solving, communication, collaboration, and creativity and innovation, as they are essential to successful participation in an ever-changing technological and global society. The organization advocates for integrating these skills in all core subjects through their Framework for 21st Century Learning. Thinking critically and communicating effectively are the primary student outcomes, and the website provides tools and resources for implementation of the framework and professional development in designing 21st-century learning environments.

Best Practices in Action

Literacy researchers have converged on a word to describe the driving force that guides teachers in coordinating and integrating practices effectively: *vision*. Although this is not a word you might expect to see in a discussion of evidence-based practices, the teacher's vision of literacy achievement has long been heralded as the crucial factor in ensuring that the goal of improving literacy instruction for all students is met. According to Calfee (2005), ensuring that "children have the opportunity to acquire the level of literacy that allows them full participation in our democratic society depends on a corps of teachers who possess extraordinary minds and hearts" (p. 67).

Calfee asserts that teachers not only must possess a domain of skills and knowledge to lead students to acquire this level of literacy success but also must acquire a sensitivity to student needs and be passionate in their willingness to make their vision work. Duffy (2003, 2005) describes the teachers' ultimate goal as that of *inspiring students to be readers and writers*—to engage students in "genuinely literate activities" where they are doing something important with literacy. This engagement should reflect the teachers' instructional vision—the reason they are passionate about teaching reading and writing.

Teachers who are visionary decision makers are empowered to identify and select evidence-based literacy practices to create an integrated instructional approach that adapts to the differentiated needs of students. A teacher's vision should clearly be knowledge-based and should encompass what he or she wishes to achieve for each student. How detailed one's vision becomes is certainly an individual matter and subject to personal experiences and situations, but without a vision, the teacher is left to sway and sputter as a candle facing the winds of curricular change and federal-, district-, and school-level impositions. It is the teacher with vision who is able to stand firm in the belief that with knowledge and heart, evidence-based best practices can be selected and adapted to meet the needs of each student every day.

Ten Evidence-Based Best Practices for Comprehensive Literacy Instruction

In keeping with our understanding of comprehensive literacy instruction, we present the following 10 evidence-based best practices that are generally supported by experts in the field (Table 1.1). These practices are based on a broad view of the reading and writing processes, one that

TABLE 1.1. Ten Evidence-Based Best Practices for Comprehensive Literacy Instruction

1. Create a classroom culture that nurtures literacy motivation by integrating choice, collaboration, and relevance into literacy tasks.
2. Provide students with scaffolded instruction in phonemic awareness, phonics, fluency, and vocabulary to support the development of deep comprehension.
3. Provide students with opportunities to engage with texts across a wide range of narrative and informational genres.
4. Provide students with opportunities to engage in close reading for deep comprehension.
5. Provide students with literacy instruction using appropriately leveled texts to support the reading of increasingly complex materials.
6. Teach literacy within and across all content areas for authentic purposes.
7. Balance teacher- and student-led discussions.
8. Use formative and summative assessments that reflect the complex and dynamic nature of literacy.
9. Promote literacy independence by providing time for self-selected reading and writing.
10. Integrate technologies that link and expand concepts and modes of communication.

incorporates the full range of experiences that students need in order to reach their literacy potential. We believe that best practices are characterized by meaningful literacy practices that support students in becoming proficient, persistent, passionate, and prepared to meet the literacy challenges of the 21st century.

The chapter authors throughout this book address and expand on the broad research consensus that supports the following 10 evidence-based best practices.

1. Create a classroom culture that nurtures literacy motivation by integrating choice, collaboration, and relevance into literacy tasks. Most classroom teachers can readily identify students who are highly motivated to engage in literacy tasks and activities. These students are typically the ones who have developed strong reading and writing habits and find reading and writing to be rewarding and valuable. On the other hand, teachers can also readily identify those students who have become frustrated with literacy tasks and rarely choose to engage in reading and writing activities, and may even try to avoid doing so. These are the students we worry the most about because we realize that reading and writing are the gateways to success in academics and careers.

Literacy motivation often makes the difference between superficial and shallow learning and learning that is deep and internalized (Gambrell, 1996). Clearly, students need both the *skill* and the *will* to become competent and motivated literacy learners (Guthrie, McRae, & Klauda, 2007; Guthrie & Wigfield, 2000; Paris, Lipson, & Wixson, 1983). Best practices include ways that teachers support students in their literacy development by creating classroom cultures that foster literacy motivation, such as providing opportunities for choice, collaboration, and engagement in relevant literacy tasks. The most basic goal of any literacy program should be the development of a student who *can read and write* and who *chooses to read and write*. We must keep in mind that we can provide instruction in the most essential literacy skills, but if our students are not intrinsically motivated to engage in reading and writing, they will never reach their full literacy potential.

There is congruence across theoretical perspectives, research findings, and literacy experts (Malloy & Gambrell, 2011b) that a number of classroom characteristics promote and enhance literacy motivation. Three classroom characteristics have emerged as powerful and influential factors in fostering literacy motivation: choice, collaboration, and relevance.

a. *Choice.* Having access to rich and abundant materials to read is critical to the development of literacy motivation. Access to reading materials supports and encourages students to engage in reading and writing in a voluntary and sustained manner (Edmunds & Bauserman, 2006; Guthrie et al., 1996; Neuman & Roskos, 1993). Access to reading materials provides the foundation for students to choose what they want to read (Edmunds & Bauserman, 2006; Guthrie et al., 2007; Turner, 1995). A number of studies have reported that students' intrinsic motivation increased when teachers supported student choice of literacy tasks (Guthrie et al., 2007; McCombs, 2003; Skinner & Bellmont, 1993; Turner, 1995). Research supports the notion that opportunities for choice promote students' intrinsic motivation and independence as literacy learners.

b. *Collaboration.* Current theories of motivation recognize that learning is enhanced by collaborative social interactions with others (Guthrie et al., 1998, 2007). Evidence suggests that a classroom environment that provides opportunities for engagement in collaborative literacy tasks is more likely to foster intrinsic motivation than are more individualized, solitary learning tasks (Almasi, O'Flahavan, & Arya, 2001; Deci & Ryan, 1991; Edmonds & Bausemann, 2006; Gambrell, Hughes, Calvert, Malloy, & Igo, 2011; Guthrie et al., 1998). Guthrie and colleagues (1998) found that students who engaged in collaborative literacy tasks and activities were more intrinsically motivated to read and they read more widely and more frequently than students who were less socially interactive. There is a strong and compelling evidence base in the literature supporting the notion that students should be encouraged to talk about and share their literacy experiences with others.

c. *Relevance.* Relevant literacy activities are reading and writing events like those that occur in people's everyday lives, as opposed to reading and writing solely to learn (Purcell-Gates, 2002, 2005; Purcell-Gates, Duke, & Martineau, 2007). We know that as young children learn and use their developing oral language, they do so for real reasons and purposes (Halliday, 1975). Therefore, in order for literacy learning to be meaningful to students, teachers need to be mindful of the reasons and purposes they establish for reading and writing tasks.

Relevant and more authentic literacy activities are often designed to focus on communicating ideas for shared understanding rather than simply to complete assignments or answer teacher-posed questions. Relevant literacy events include activities such as authoring or recommending books, reading to discover how to do or make something, and collaborating on a report of group findings. It is more likely that students will transfer their classroom literacy learning to real life and future applications when they engage in relevant literacy learning in the classroom (Gambrell et al., 2011; Guthrie et al., 2007; Teale & Gambrell, 2007; Teale & Sulzby, 1986; Teale, Zolt, Yokota, Glasswell, & Gambrell, 2007).

Assor, Kaplan, and Roth (2002) found that when teachers emphasized the relevance of reading tasks and activities, the students rated classroom tasks as important and worthy of their best cognitive effort. Relevant literacy tasks enable students to see the connection between school literacy tasks and "real-life" literacy tasks (Duke, Purcell-Gates, Hall, & Tower, 2006–2007; Gambrell et al., 2011; Guthrie et al., 2007; Guthrie & McPeake, 2013; Guthrie, Wigfield, & You, 2012).

Teachers can raise the value of literacy learning by making reading, writing, speaking, and listening authentic tools for learning in their classrooms. Students who see literacy as a means to understanding their world and gaining both knowledge and pleasure will be more engaged in the types of collaborative, meaning-making, and problem-solving activities that mirror those of their future workplaces.

2. Provide students with scaffolded instruction in phonemic awareness, phonics, fluency, and vocabulary to support the development of deep comprehension. Current literacy research, theories, and policies place a strong emphasis on deep comprehension as the ultimate goal of reading instruction. Students are expected to engage in critical thinking about text and to be able to analyze multiple accounts of an event, note similarities and differences in points of view represented in the text, assess the warrant behind people's ideas, integrate information across several texts, and explain the relationships between ideas and the author's craft (Calkins et al., 2012).

The National Reading Panel (National Institute of Child Health and Human Development, 2000) identified phonemic awareness, phonics, vocabulary, fluency, and comprehension as critical to the development of the reading process and provided research support for instruction in these areas. Students often need concentrated instructional support in these areas in order to learn important foundational skills and strategies that they might have difficulty discovering on their own. The gradual-release-of-responsibility model provides such scaffolded instruction.

In general, the gradual-release model describes a process in which students gradually assume a greater degree of responsibility and independence for a targeted learning outcome. During the first stage, the teacher assumes most of the responsibility by modeling and describing a particular skill or strategy. In the second stage, the teacher and students assume joint responsibility: students practice applying a particular skill or strategy, and the teacher offers assistance and feedback as needed. As students are ready, instruction moves into the third stage, in which students assume all, or almost all, of the responsibility by working in situations where they independently apply newly learned skills and strategies. This gradual withdrawal of instructional support is also known as scaffolded instruction because "supports" or "scaffolds" are gradually removed as students demonstrate greater degrees of proficiency.

We view the gradual-release-of-responsibility model as consistent with the notion of explicit instruction. During each phase of the gradual-release model, teachers can—and should—be explicit in their instruction and feedback. For example, during the first phase, teachers should provide clear explanations and modeling for a specific skill or strategy. As responsibility is gradually released, feedback to students should be specific and understandable. Small-group and one-on-one configurations can be particularly effective in differentiating the scaffolding of strategies for students with similar learning needs. The gradual-release-of-responsibility model and scaffolded instruction are in keeping with constructivist principles when they are used within meaningful, authentic contexts (Graham & Harris, 1996; Harris & Graham, 1994). Indeed, many authors in this book provide examples of how to integrate these models within meaningful reading and writing programs that include use of literature, technology, authentic writing experiences, choice, and collaborative learning.

3. Provide students with opportunities to engage with texts across a wide range of narrative and informational genres. The 2009 NAEP Reading Framework (National Assessment Governing Board, 2009) focuses on two types of texts: literary texts (fiction, literary nonfiction, poetry) and informational texts (exposition, argumentation, persuasive texts, procedural texts, and documents). These text types are important in educational settings as they comprise different purposes for reading (to be entertained or informed) as well as differing sets of strategies for accessing and comprehending them. The recommendations for best practices for these two text types are addressed in specific chapters of this volume.

In providing comprehensive literacy instruction, it is important to note that the teaching of specific text types must mirror the academic needs of students as they move through the grades. In the early years, narrative texts are often privileged (Duke, 2000), as they are sometimes believed to be more engaging and accessible. However, considering the need to read for information that is required in the later elementary grades, reading informational texts must be introduced in the earlier grades so that strategic reading skills can be developed (Duke, 2004; Yopp & Yopp, 2006). Realizing the trend toward reading for information in the later grades, the NAEP Reading Framework suggests that the balance between literary informational texts move toward the following recommended guidelines: a 50/50 balance in fourth grade; 45% literary and 55% informational in eighth grade; and 30% literary and 70% informational in 12th grade (National Assessment Governing Board, 2009, p. 11).

Choosing texts for instruction in the comprehensive literacy classroom should provide both access and targeted instruction across a wide range of texts, beginning in the early elementary grades and moving forward. Narrative texts can be used to support content-area understandings, such as with stories and novels that accurately describe cultures or scientific discoveries. Similarly, informational texts can be used to buttress the background knowledge of topics required to understand literary works. Teachers who become proficient in blending the purposes and strategies for reading across a wide variety of genres support their students in gaining skill in reading and writing through a wide variety of enjoyable and authentic endeavors.

4. Provide students with opportunities to engage in close reading for deep comprehension of text. Comprehension and close reading are clearly aligned in that close reading requires the student to uncover layers of meaning that lead to and support deep comprehension of text. Close reading requires students to understand what the text communicates, make logical inferences, and cite specific textual evidence to support claims and conclusions drawn from the text. Ultimately, close reading is intended to foster analytical thinking and to deepen comprehension.

Close reading involves having students engage with a text of sufficient complexity, examine the meaning of the text thoroughly and methodically, and read and reread deliberately, resulting in deep comprehension of the text (Robb, 2013). When students direct their attention to the text, it empowers them to understand the central ideas and key supporting details, as well as to "reflect on the meanings of individual words and sentences; the order in which sentences unfold; and the development of ideas over the course of the text, which ultimately leads students to arrive at an understanding of the text as a whole" (Partnership for Assessment of Readiness for College and Careers, 2011, p. 7). According to Frey and Fisher (2013), the goal of close reading is to drive students deeper into the text in order for them to engage in critical thinking and not simply draw on surface or superficial comprehension.

Frey and Fisher (2013) offer three assumptions about close reading that we should consider in terms of implementing best practices. First, the practice of close reading assumes that the text is worthy; not every text requires this kind of inspection. Second, the thinking skills needed for close reading should begin in kindergarten, with a range of literacy tasks that focus on close listening and reading. Third, students must be given time to read and reread a text, time to respond to questions that require them to return to text to provide evidence for their answers, and time to engage in discussions with their peers about the meaning of the text.

5. Provide students with literacy instruction using appropriately leveled texts to support the reading of increasingly complex materials. When students are faced with reading materials that are too difficult, reading is typically word-by-word, disfluent, and regarded as an unpleasant experience to be avoided. According to research, when students avoid reading, their reading skills decline instead of increase (Allington, 2009; Kim, 2004). Students need scaffolded instruction with texts that are at the appropriate instructional level, not too easy and not too difficult, in order to develop the skills and strategies needed for proficient reading. Texts that are at the appropriate instructional level offer just the right level of support and challenge.

In addition, appropriately scaffolded reading instruction should support students in reading increasingly complex text. The Common Core State Standards provide guidelines for determining a text's complexity that fall into three categories: quantitative measures, qualitative measures, and reader and task considerations. The quantitative measures examine characteristics of a text that are easily analyzed by a computer, such as sentence length and word frequency. Qualitative measures focus on content of the text and concepts and includes levels of meaning, structure, language conventions, clarity, and knowledge demands. The third category, reader and task considerations, includes motivation, knowledge, and the experience of the reader, as well as task variables such as the purpose and complexity of the reading task. The teacher must keep all three of these elements in mind in planning literacy instruction that incorporates complex texts.

Hiebert (2013) offers three rules for helping students become proficient in reading complex texts: *Read often. Mostly silent. Focus on knowledge.* First, getting good at something is a function of practice, thus students need to have time to read. Second, proficient reading is primarily an internal silent process. This doesn't mean that we ask beginning readers to read silently; however, as reading proficiency increases, silent reading needs to be the dominant mode for reading texts. When students have opportunities to read often and silently, they develop the stamina that underlies the progression of reading increasingly complex texts. Third, the primary reason we read is to acquire the knowledge that resides in texts. According to Hiebert (2013), in order to

> become proficient readers of complex texts, students need to be immersed in learning—some topics about which they are curious, some topics about which communities deem to be important, and some topics that are simply for enjoyment of language and human interaction. Citizens of the digital-global age of the 21st century have the knowledge and know how to acquire knowledge. Knowing how to negotiate texts is fundamental to the process of knowledge acquisition and engagement. Membership in the knowledge generation depends on schools involving students in extensive amounts of reading independently in

the pursuit of knowledge. (*http://textproject.org/frankly-freddy/reading-rules-for-becoming-proficient-with-complex-texts*)

6. Teach literacy within and across all content areas for authentic purposes. One way to encourage and support students' literacy development is to view every subject or content-area lesson as an opportunity to teach reading and writing. According to a study conducted by Hattie (2009), when teachers use effective vocabulary and comprehension strategies in the content areas, student learning of subject matter information increases. Other studies have reported that having students engage in writing activities, on a regular basis, during content-area lessons increases their learning of content information (Bangert-Drown, Hurley, & Wilkinson, 2004; Graham & Perin, 2007).

Cunningham and Allington (2011) suggest that we engage students in reading or writing for 30 minutes twice each week during science and social studies and once each week during math, resulting in students having an additional 150 minutes of literacy engagement each week. As students increase their volume of reading, they also increase their world knowledge. Calkins and colleagues (2012) suggest that when planning units in social studies, science, and math, it is important to plan which units will be writing-intensive, reading-intensive, and media-intensive.

One important consideration when reading and writing across the content areas is the notion of having students engage in literacy tasks and activities for authentic purposes. The dreaded "hoop-jump" of completing a worksheet that will be graded by the teacher and then tossed in a wastebasket is rarely as engaging as creating a product that demonstrates knowledge in a creative and "real-world" way. Students who study the requirements for plants to live can express their understandings just as clearly by creating a "how to" video of green-thumb skills for taking care of plants in the home. Moving up the rungs of Bloom's Taxonomy of Learning Domains (Krathwohl, 2002), content-area lessons and units that result in students *creating* products (as opposed to completing them) encourage higher-order thinking skills and provide opportunities to demonstrate a deep understanding of a topic.

7. Balance teacher- and student-led discussions. The type of discussion that occurs in classrooms speaks volumes about the roles of the teacher and students in the classroom context as well as the opportunities provided for promoting deep understanding of content and the development of language skills. In classrooms where teachers view themselves as the "holders of knowledge," discussions typically follow an *initiation–response–evaluation* model (IRE). The teacher asks a question, the student responds, and the teacher evaluates the response (Alexander, 2008;

Cazden, 2001). While this approach is a traditional one, it often impedes engagement and learning (Alexander, 2008; Galton, 2007) by privileging only the students who know the answer and diminishing opportunities for students to explore or think through what they are learning.

As an alternative to this *monologic* approach to classroom discussion, a body of research is growing to support *dialogic* discussions in which teachers serve as facilitators of knowledge who guide students in developing understandings of text and content (Mercer & Littleton, 2007; Reznitskaya, 2012; Reznitskaya et al., 2012; Sandora, Beck, & McKeown, 1999). In dialogic classrooms, teachers do not focus on questions that have a single answer, but guide students in thinking through the texts they read or content they are learning with open-ended questions that target "thinking through." Teachers who facilitate knowledge model how to include others in a discussion and follow up on each other's responses, look for evidence from text to support claims, and make connections to other texts and personal experiences. In this, more students can be involved and engaged because the onus of understanding is a collaborative venture where knowing a correct answer is no longer a required point of entry; rather, *thinking* and supporting one's thoughts become the driving force toward comprehension and consensus (Malloy & Gambrell, 2011a).

Dialogic classrooms necessitate the negotiation of roles regarding who holds the knowledge and how this knowledge is constructed. These classrooms also are built around context where risk taking is encouraged. Students need to be secure participating and sharing their thinking without embarrassment or retribution. The establishment of such a collaborative and collegial learning context requires thoughtful management on the part of the teacher but has the potential to reap benefits in terms of engagement, thinking skills, and language and communicative growth.

8. Use formative and summative assessments that reflect the complex and dynamic nature of literacy. When selecting assessment tools and/or practices, we should keep in mind the old adage "What gets tested, gets taught." And more importantly, according to Johnston and Costello (2005), what gets assessed and how it gets assessed has implications for literacy learning. Literacy is complex. It involves competencies, strategies, and beliefs, as well as dispositions about print, symbols, images, and the spoken word that transcend the classroom. Literacy prepares students for life. Hence, it is critical that literacy assessments reflect the dynamic and reciprocal nature of listening/speaking, reading/writing, and viewing/representing. In other words, as Carr and Claxton (2002) assert, there must be "a willingness to engage in joint learning tasks, to express uncertainties and ask questions, to take a variety of roles in joint learning enterprises and to take others' purposes and perspectives into account" (p. 16).

Subscribing to the belief that literacy assessment should be as complex as literacy instruction means utilizing a wide variety of formative and summative assessments.

The goal of *formative assessment* is to engage in tasks that allow teachers to monitor student learning and provide ongoing feedback to students. Formative assessments that are closely aligned to instruction yield valuable data that can be used to differentiate text and practices. They also help students identify their strengths and weaknesses and allow teachers to adjust instruction in real time. Formative assessments are referred to as *low stakes* because the evaluative consequences of adequate yearly progress are not attached to such data. Running records, writing samples, and constructed responses are examples of formative assessments.

On the other hand, *summative assessments* are used to evaluate student learning at the end of an instructional unit by comparing student performance to a standard or benchmark. Summative assessments include more traditional evaluative tasks such as midterms, finals, research papers, and so forth. Running records, writing samples, and constructed responses could also be used as summative assessments if grade-level, building, and/or district standardization has occurred. This might include standardizing scoring rubrics, text passages, or administration schedules. Many districts also use data from informal reading inventories in a summative fashion to benchmark student progress.

Some summative assessments, often termed *terminal assessments*, are synonymous with the phrase *high stakes*. These literacy assessments are given at the end of the school year under very strict testing conditions that do not often reflect day-to-day literacy learning. In addition, data from these high-stakes terminal assessments are usually not available to teachers and reading specialists until the following school year.

The International Reading Association suggests that rather than debating the merits of formative versus summative assessments, our efforts are better spent implementing *quality assessments* in whatever form necessary to inform instruction. Quality literacy assessment is defined by the International Reading Association (2013) as a process of inquiry: "It requires gathering information and setting conditions so that the classroom, school, and community become centers of inquiry where students, teachers, and other stakeholders can examine their learning—individually and collaboratively—and find ways to improve their practice" (p. 1). The best practice of choosing and using quality formative and summative assessments can be realized by keeping in mind the complex and dynamic nature of literacy.

9. Promote literacy independence by providing time for self-selected reading and writing. "Practice makes perfect" is an old adage that rings true. Practice may not make you a *perfect* reader and writer, but the consensus among researchers is that practice will make you a *better* reader and writer (Allington, 2009; Cunningham & Allington, 2011; Gambrell, 2009; Heibert & Martin, 2009). The *opportunity* to read and write is a critical component of the literacy curriculum. The effectiveness of these opportunities to read is influenced by a number of variables including time, text difficulty, genre, and dimensions of the task, as well as the readers' engagement and task proficiency (Cunningham & Allington, 2011; Heibert & Martin, 2009). We know it takes much more than just providing students with time to read and write. The role of the teacher is critical in motivating students to read for their own reasons and purposes by assuring an appropriate student–book match so that time spent reading is both profitable and enjoyable for the reader.

There is clear evidence from reading research that the amount of time spent reading (i.e., reading volume) is a major contributor to increased vocabulary and comprehension (Allington, 2009; Hayes & Ahrens, 1988; Nagy & Anderson, 1984; Stanovich, 1986). In a classic study, Anderson, Wilson, and Fielding (1988) found a significant relationship between the amount of reading schoolchildren do and their reading achievement. In this study of 155 fifth graders, the amount of book reading that students reported was the best predictor of performance on several measures of reading achievement. In addition, other studies have supported the inclusion of time to read during the school day (Linehart, Zigmond, & Cooley, 1981; Reutzel & Hollingsworth, 1991; Reutzel, Jones, Fawson, & Smith, 2008).

According to Cunningham and Stanovich (1998), lack of reading practice delays the development of fluency and word recognition skills. Thus, struggling readers may be hindered in comprehending, frustrated in the reading experience, and avoid further practice. Time for reading and writing is important, but it is especially important for struggling readers and writers. Good readers and writers tend to have more practice in reading and writing. Consequently, they become more and more proficient, while less proficient readers and writers spend less time engaged in reading and writing, and thus have fewer experiences with appropriately leveled reading materials or writing tasks (Allington, 2009; Cunningham & Allington, 2011).

During independent reading and writing, students practice and consolidate the skills and strategies they have been taught and thereby come to "own" them. According to Allington (2009), such practice provides students with the opportunity to develop the autonomous, automatic, and appropriate application of literacy skills and strategies *while actually reading and writing*. Adequate time for reading and writing is essential so that students have the experience that is needed to increase proficiency.

10. Integrate technologies that link and expand concepts and modes of communication. Increasingly, teachers are using technology-enhanced instruction as interactive and projected display boards are becoming more commonplace in the classroom. Technology that provides varied displays of knowledge, ways to manipulate knowledge for encoding, or opportunities to locate and communicate knowledge may provide exciting new avenues for teaching and learning. Aside from the possible instructional benefits, students must learn to be proficient in working with and learning from these technology resources, while also becoming adept and competent in working with conventional print documents (Pressley, 2007).

While the integration of Internet use and other computer mediated instruction in the K–12 classroom is increasing, the empirical evidence to support instructional strategies for using these technologies is just beginning to emerge (Azevedo & Cromley, 2004; Coiro & Dobler, 2007; Malloy, Castek, & Leu, 2010). Recommendations from teachers and researchers who focus on these "new literacies" are available for teachers to adapt to their classrooms (Eagleton & Dobler, 2007; Karchmer, Mallette, Kara-Soteriou, & Leu, 2005; Leu, Castek, Henry, Coiro, & McMullan, 2004). What we are coming to understand is that reading on the Internet requires different skills than reading traditional text and that it is important that we understand these differences in order to provide appropriate instruction for our students (Coiro, 2003; Malloy et al., 2010). It is incumbent on teachers, therefore, to become acquainted with new research as it emerges and to incorporate this new knowledge into their classrooms to suit their particular instructional needs. Our students are entering an age when knowledge of technology is a necessity and not a luxury. As educators, we are obligated to prepare them for that reality.

If, as the CCSS (2010) suggest, literacy instruction should be focused on preparing students for college and career, then 21st-century technologies are the tools of our new and evolving trade. Web content including art, music, scripts, podcasts, and video are text sources that should complement and extend more traditional forms of print. For example, any book about animals comes to life because audio and video are valued text sources. And by monitoring live cams (panda, elephant, or Curiosity on Mars), students can view and discuss the world in real time. Is there a more effective way to experience primary and secondary source documents?

However, perhaps the most powerful aspect of new technologies is the seemingly infinite possibilities for communicating and creating. Students can interact with their teachers, classmates, schoolmates, and indeed the world using a fascinating array of tools and platforms. Twitter, Facebook and Edmoto, and blogs can be used for discussion. Wiki, Nings, and Google Docs are user-friendly venues for digital collaboration. A host of programs such as iMovie, Playpod, and Soundcloud are participatory media that encourage students to create digital products. New technologies and media have the potential to remove barriers to reading, writing, learning, communicating, and creating. Assistive and adaptive technologies from the past are replaced with iPad apps. All students, regardless of ability, disability, or language proficiency can participate fully in literacy conversations. And when children are valued, heard, encouraged, and understood, they will be successful.

Teachers as Visionary Decision Makers

Researchers who have entered classrooms in the past few years to observe and record the types of instruction that are occurring in high-achieving learning environments found that, beyond a carefully orchestrated integration of skills and strategies, content, and literature, successful classrooms are led by teachers who motivate and support individual students in ways that cannot be prescribed by any one program, method, or practice (Pressley, 2007; Pressley, Allington, Wharton-McDonald, Block, & Morrow, 2001; Wharton-McDonald, Pressley, & Hampston, 1998). What has become increasingly clear through research that probes more deeply into the inner workings of effective classrooms is that *the teacher* is the crucial factor in the classroom. In fact, study after study points to teacher expertise as the critical variable in effective litearcy instruction. The teacher who is knowledgeable and adept at combining and adjusting various methods, practices, and strategies to meet the needs of a particular set of students with a differentiated set of needs is most likely to lead students to higher levels of literacy achievement and engagement. Effective teachers are able to differentiate and contextualize their instruction and to support the practices they choose through evidence provided by research and through discussions and collaborations with colleagues in their schools and districts.

Michael Pressley, one of the editors of the first volume of *Best Practices* (1999), devoted the last decade of his career to studying and documenting the practices of highly effective literacy educators. In an article that focused on the body of Pressley's research efforts, Mohan, Lundeberg, and Reffitt (2008) identified the following elements of these expert teachers that emerged from Pressley's findings:

• *Effective literacy teachers provide complexity and balance.* Cited as the most notable finding across the research conducted, effective teachers are successful in blending skills and strategy instruction within holistic literacy activities. This integration of targeted development within contextualized uses of text results in a high *instructional density*, meaning that the time devoted to using literacy to learn is very high. Explicit whole-class instruction is followed by small-group and partner work where differentiated literacy support can aid students in their particular areas of need. While explicitly addressing skills and strategies, these classrooms are also highly literature-based and included authentic purposes for using literacy throughout the school day.

• *Effective literacy teachers are adept at scaffolding and individualizing instruction.* A second feature of highly effective literacy teachers is that they know the individual needs of each one of their students and choose practices to address these needs. Using guided reading and writing groups as well as individual instruction and conferencing, these teachers provide targeted instruction to each student in their zone of proximal development (Vygotsky, 1978), where progress can best be expected. Maintaining high expectations for student growth and individualized support is a recipe for ensuring that all students progress as readers and writers throughout the academic year.

• *Effective literacy teachers manage the classroom well and encourage self-regulated learning.* Teachers who establish and maintain positive and clear management procedures from the first days of school experience fewer instructional interruptions due to disciplinary problems, and thus can spend more effort on instruction. Providing a secure and predictable environment where students are clear on the expectations and acceptable behaviors provides the background for encouraging growth in self-regulation and individual growth, both socially and academically. Ideally, students become involved in setting goals and determining areas for improvement, taking more responsibility for their learning as they are successful in achieving goals.

• *Effective literacy teachers create a positive learning environment.* Effective teachers create motivating contexts that engage and sustain students through appropriately challenging instruction. Pressley (2005) found that "engaging primary-grade teachers do something every minute of every hour of every school day to motivate their students, using every conceivable motivational mechanism to do so" (p. 141). By using specific and justified praise, attention to effort and process, and a focus on improvement and achievement, effective teachers plan instruction that will keep students interested and on-task, while maintaining levels of challenge that support but don't frustrate.

Students who are taught in these classrooms are engaged, strategic, and see a clear path between instruction and real-life literacy tasks. The instruction provided for students in these classrooms is both differentiated and contextualized to address all aspects of literacy required of students as they progress through the grades. Teachers are ultimately the instructional designers who implement best practices in relevant, meaningful ways for their particular community of learners. In other words, best practices can be *described*–but not *prescribed*.

Teachers who provide comprehensive literacy instruction have a broad vision of literacy that is continually informed by evidence-based best practices. They understand literacy learning well enough to adapt the learning environment, materials, and methods to particular situations and students. Packaged program approaches typically lack such adaptability. Thus, in the final analysis, comprehensive literacy instruction rests on the shoulders of teachers who make informed decisions about the instructional and assessment approaches and practices that are most appropriate for each student.

Summary

Once teachers are empowered by their vision and have at their disposal a plethora of practices and instructional methods from which to choose, they are free to orchestrate an integration of evidence-based practices to provide comprehensive literacy instruction. No matter how well a particular practice is shown to be effective by research, *optimal literacy teaching and learning can only be achieved when skillful, knowledgeable, and dedicated teachers are given the freedom and latitude to use their professional judgment to make instructional decisions that enable students to achieve their full literacy potential.*

As we increase our understanding of effective literacy instruction, our conceptions of best practices will continue to broaden and deepen. Our students need and deserve instruction that embraces the richness and complexity of literacy processes as well as instruction that is both evidence-based and comprehensive. This is no easy task. It requires commitment, time, and knowledge. It begins with a teacher who is a visionary decision maker, one who can identify the strengths and needs of each individual child and plan instruction accordingly. It begins with a commitment to provide comprehensive, differentiated literacy assessment and instruction for all our students. While the challenge is daunting, the rewards are great as we nurture and support students in becoming engaged lifelong readers and writers.

ENGAGEMENT ACTIVITIES

1. Articulate your vision for literacy teaching and learning. Commit to writing what you wish to accomplish as a literacy teacher as well as what you wish for each of your students to achieve. Refer to this vision statement often as you teach or as you learn more about teaching. Be certain to adjust and enhance your vision statement as new knowledge and expertise dictate.

2. We have suggested that a best practice in literacy includes integrating technologies that link and expand concepts and modes of communication. The CCSS emphasize the use of complex text. Consider how you might invite students into complex text by exploring 21st-century technologies. How can you extend traditional print with digital content? How might you increase text complexity by broadening the definition of print to include websites, song lyrics, and media scripts? How might you challenge students to explore perspective by combining traditional print with Web text such as e-mail, social media, video, blogs, and live cams?

3. Consider the main findings of Pressley's research on highly effective literacy teachers. How does your practice compare to these recommendations? Which practices do you wish to maintain and which would you like to develop?

4. In this chapter, the authors listed 10 evidence-based best practices for comprehensive literacy instruction (p. 14); however, this list is not meant to be exclusive or exhaustive. Consider the literacy instructional practices that you think should be added to this list and give reasons why you, as a literacy professional, think they should be included. Provide evidence to support your decision.

REFERENCES

Alexander, R. J. (2008). *Essays on pedagogy.* New York: Routledge.

Allington, R. L. (1983). The reading instruction provided readers of differing reading abilities. *Elementary School Journal, 83*(5), 548–559.

Allington, R. L. (2005). What counts as evidence in evidence-based education? *Reading Today, 23*(3), 16.

Allington, R. L. (2009). If they don't read much . . . 30 years later. In E. H. Hiebert (Ed.), *Reading more, reading better* (pp. 30–54). New York: Guilford Press.

Almasi, J. F., O'Flahavan, J. F., & Arya, P. (2001). A comparative analysis of student and teacher development in more proficient and less proficient peer discussions of literature. *Reading Research Quarterly, 36*(2), 96–120.

Anderson, R. C., Wilson, P. T., & Fielding, L. G. (1988). Growth in reading and how children spend their time outside of school. *Reading Research Quarterly, 23*(3), 285–303.

Assor, A., Kaplan, H., & Roth, G. (2002). Choice is good, but relevance is excellent: Autonomy-enhancing and suppressing teacher behaviours predicting students' engagement in schoolwork. *British Journal of Educational Psychology, 72*, 261–278.

Azevedo, R., & Cromley, J. G. (2004). Does training on self-regulated learning facilitate students' learning with hypermedia? *Journal of Educational Psychology, 96*(3), 523–535.

Bangert-Drown, R. L., Hurley, M. M., & Wilkinson, B. (2004). The effects of school-based writing to learn interventions on academic achievement. *Review of Educational Research, 74*, 29–58.

Barnitt, V. (2002). Partial list of accomplishments and outcomes reported by the Florida Inclusion Network, fiscal year 2001–2002. Cocoa: Florida Inclusion Network.

Bogdan, R. C., & Biklen, S. K. (1992). *Qualitative research for education: An introduction to theory and methods* (2nd ed.). Boston: Allyn & Bacon.

Brighton, C. M. (2002). Straddling the fence: Implementing best practices in an age of accountability. *Gifted Child Today, 25*(3), 30–33.

Calfee, R. (2005). The mind (and heart) of the reading teacher. In B. Maloch, J. V. Hoffman, D. L. Schallert, C. M. Fairbanks, & J. Worthy (Eds.), *54th yearbook of the National Reading Conference* (pp. 63–79). Oak Creek, WI: National Reading Conference.

Calkins, L., Ehrenworth, M., & Lehman, C. (2012). *Pathways to the Common Core: Accelerating achievement.* Portsmouth, NH: Heinemann.

Carr, M., & Claxton, G. (2002). Tracking the development of learning dispositions. *Assessment in Education: Principles, Policy and Practice, 9*(1), 9–37.

Cazden, C. B. (2001). *Classroom discourse: The language of teaching and learning.* Portsmouth, NH: Heinemann.

Coiro, J. (2003). Exploring literacy on the Internet. *The Reading Teacher, 56,* 458–464.

Coiro, J., & Dobler, E. (2007). Exploring the online comprehension strategies used by sixth-grade skilled readers to search for and locate information on the Internet. *Reading Research Quarterly, 42,* 214–257.

Common Core State Standards Initiative. (2010). Retrieved October 25, 2013, from *www.corestandards.org.*

Cunningham, A. E., & Stanovich, K. E. (1998). What reading does for the mind. *American Educator, 22*(1), 8–15.

Cunningham, P. M., & Allington, R. L. (2011). *Classrooms that work: They can all read and write.* Boston: Pearson.

Deci, E. L., & Ryan, R. M. (1991). A motivational approach to self: Integration in personality. In R. Dienstbier (Ed.), *Nebraska Symposium on Motivation: Vol. 38. Perspectives on motivation* (pp. 237–288). Lincoln: University of Nebraska Press.

Dickinson, D. K., & Neuman, S. B. (2006). Introduction. In D. K. Dickinson & S.

B. Neuman (Eds.), *Handbook of early literacy research* (Vol. 2, pp. 1–10). New York: Guilford Press.

Dorn, L. J., & Soffos, C. (2011). *Interventions that work: A comprehensive intervention model for preventing reading failure in grades K–3.* Upper Saddle River, NJ: Pearson Higher Ed.

Duffy, G. G. (2003). *Explaining reading: A resource for teaching concepts, skills, and strategies.* New York: Guilford Press.

Duffy, G. G. (2005). Developing metacognitive teachers: Visioning and the expert's changing role in teacher education and professional development. In S. E. Isreal, C. C. Block, K. L. Bauserman, & K. Kinnucan-Welsch (Eds.), *Meta-cognition in literacy learning: Theory, assessment, instruction and professional development* (pp. 299–314). Mahwah, NJ: Erlbaum.

Duke, N. K. (2000). 3.6 minutes a day: The scarcity of informational texts in first grade. *Reading Research Quarterly, 35*(2), 202–224.

Duke, N. K. (2004). The case for informational text. *Educational Leadership, 61*(6), 40–44.

Duke, N. K., Purcell-Gates, V., Hall, L. A., & Tower, C. (2006–2007). Authentic literacy activities for developing comprehension and writing. *The Reading Teacher, 60,* 344–355.

Eagleton, M. B., & Dobler, E. (2007). *Reading the Web: Strategies for Internet inquiry.* New York: Guilford Press.

Edmunds, K. M., & Bauserman, K. L. (2006). What teachers can learn about reading motivation through conversations with children. *The Reading Teacher, 59*(5), 414–424.

Farlow, L. (1994, June). *Cooperative learning to facilitate the inclusion of students with moderate to severe mental retardation in secondary subject-area classes.* Paper presented at the annual conference of the American Association on Mental Retardation, Boston.

Frey, N., & Fisher, D. (2013). *Rigorous reading.* Thousand Oaks, CA: Corwin Press.

Fuchs, D., & Fuchs, L. S. (2006). Introduction to response to intervention: What, why, and how valid is it? *Reading Research Quarterly, 41*(1), 93–99.

Galton, M. (2007). *Learning and teaching in the primary classroom.* London: Sage.

Gambrell, L. B. (1996). Motivating contexts for literacy learning. In L. Baker, P. Afflerbach, & D. Reinking (Eds.), *Developing engaged readers in school and home communities.* Mahwah, NJ: Erlbaum.

Gambrell, L. B. (2009). Creating opportunities to read more so that students read better. In E. H. Hiebert (Ed.), *Reading more, reading better* (pp. 251–266). New York: Guilford Press.

Gambrell, L. B., Hughes, E., Calvert, W., Malloy, J., & Igo, B. (2011). Authentic reading, writing, and discussion: An exploratory study of a pen pal project *Elementary School Journal, 112*(2), 234–258.

Garcia, E. E., & Wiese, A.-M. (2009). Policy related to issues of diversity and literacy: Implications for English learners. In L. M. Morrow, R. Rueda, & D. Lapp (Eds.), *Handbook of research on literacy and diversity* (pp. 32–54). New York: Guilford Press.

Gay, G. (2002). Preparing for culturally responsive teaching. *Journal of Teacher Education, 53*(2), 106–116.

Gordon, E. W. (2009). Foreword: Every child must be visible if we are to succeed as a world-class nation. In L. M. Morrow, R. Rueda, & D. Lapp (Eds.), *Handbook of research on literacy and diversity* (pp. ix–xi). New York: Guilford Press.

Graham, S., & Harris, K. R. (1996). *Making the writing process work: Strategies for composition and self-regulation.* Cambridge, MA: Brookline Books.

Graham, S., & Perin, S. (2007). A meta-analysis of writing instruction for adolescent students. *Journal of Educational Psychology, 99,* 445–476.

Guild, P. B. (2001). Diversity, learning style and culture. *New Horizons for Learning* [Online], 1–19. Retrieved from *http://education.jhu.edu/pp/newhorizons/strategies/topics/learning%20styles/diversity.html.*

Guthrie, J. T., & McPeake, J. (2013). Literacy engagement: The missing link. In S. B. Neuman & L. B. Gambrell (Eds.), *Quality reading instruction in the age of Common Core Standards* (pp. 162–175). Newark, DE: International Reading Association.

Guthrie, J. T., McRae, A., & Klauda, S. L. (2007). Contributions of concept-oriented reading instruction to knowledge about interventions for motivations in reading. *Educational Psychologist, 42*(4), 237–250.

Guthrie, J. T., Van Meter, P., Hancock, G., Alao, S., Anderson, E., & McCann, A. (1998). Does concept-oriented reading instruction increase strategy use and conceptual learning from text? *Journal of Educational Psychology, 90*(2), 261–278.

Guthrie, J. T., Van Meter, P., McCann, A. D., Wigfield, A., Bender, L., Poundstone, C. C., et al. (1996). Growth of literacy engagement: Changes in motivations and strategies during concept-oriented reading instruction. *Reading Research Quarterly, 31,* 306–325.

Guthrie, J. T., & Wigfield, A. (2000). Engagement and motivation in reading. In M. L. Kamil, P. B. Mosenthal, P. D. Pearson, & R. Barr (Eds.), *Handbook of reading research* (Vol. 3, pp. 403–422). Mahwah, NJ: Erlbaum.

Guthrie, J. T., Wigfield, A., & You, W. (2012). Instructional contexts for engagement and achievement in reading. In S. Christensen, A. Reschly, & C. Wylie (Eds.), *Handbook of research on student engagement* (pp. 601–634). New York: Springer Science.

Hall, T. (2002). Differentiated instruction: Effective Classroom Practices Report. National Center on Accessing the General Curriculum. Retrieved October 25, 2013, from *www.cast.org/system/galleries/download/ncac/DifInstruc.pdf.*

Halliday, M. A. K. (1975). *Learning how to mean.* London: Arnold.

Harris, K. R., & Graham, S. (1994). Constructivism: Principles, paradigms, and integration. *Journal of Special Education, 28*(3), 233–247.

Hattie, J. (2009). *Visible learning: A synthesis of over 8000 meta-analyses relating to achievement.* New York: Routledge.

Hayes, D. P., & Ahrens, M. (1988). Vocabulary simplification for children: A special case of "motherese"? *Journal of Child Language, 15,* 395–410.

Her Majesty's Government. (2013). Every child matters: Change for children. Retrieved April 30, 2014, from *http://webarchive.nationalarchives.gov.uk/20131401151715/https://www.education.gov.uk/publications/eorderingdownload/DFES10812004.pdf.*

Hiebert, E. H. (2013). Reading rules for becoming proficient with complex text. Retrieved from *http://textproject.org/frankly-freddy/reading-rules-for-becoming-proficient-withcomplex-texts.*

Hiebert, E. H., & Martin, L. A. (2009). Opportunity to read: A critical but neglected construct in reading instruction. In E. H. Hiebert (Ed.), *Reading more, reading better* (pp. 3–29). New York: Guilford Press.

Hollins, E. R., King, J. E., & Hayman, W. C. (Eds.). (1994). *Teaching diverse populations: Formulating a knowledge base* (Vol. 1944). New York: State University of New York Press.

International Reading Association. (2002a). *Evidence-based reading instruction: Putting the National Reading Panel report into practice.* Newark, DE: Author.

International Reading Association. (2002b). *What is evidence-based reading instruction?* (Position statement). Newark, DE: Author.

International Reading Association. (2013). Standards for the assessment of reading. Retrieved April 30, 2014, from *www.reading.org/general/currentresearch/standards/assessmentstandards.aspx.*

Johnston, P. H. (Ed.). (2010). *RTI in literacy: Responsive and comprehensive.* Newark, DE: International Reading Association.

Johnston, P. H., & Costello, P. (2005). Theory and research into practice: Principles for literacy assessment. *Reading Research Quarterly, 40*(2), 256–267.

Karchmer, R. A., Mallette, M. H., Kara-Soteriou, J., & Leu, D. (Eds.). (2005). *Innovative approaches to literacy education: Using the Internet to support new literacies.* Newark, DE: International Reading Association.

Kim, J. (2004). Summer reading and the ethnic achievement gap. *Journal of Education of Students at Risk, 9*(2), 169–189.

King, J. E., Hollins, E. R., & Hayman, W. C. (Eds.). (1997). *Preparing teachers for cultural diversity.* New York: Teachers College Press.

Kochhar, C., West, L. L., & Taymans, J. M. (2000). *Successful inclusion.* Upper Saddle River, NJ: Merrill.

Krathwohl, D. R. (2002). A revision of Bloom's taxonomy: An overview. *Theory into Practice, 41*(4), 212–218.

Leu, D. J. Jr., Castek, J., Henry, L. A., Coiro, J., & McMullan, M. (2004). The lessons that children teach us: Integrating children's literature and the new literacies of the Internet. *The Reading Teacher, 57,* 486–503.

Linehart, G., Zigmond, N., & Cooley, W. (1981). Reading instruction and its effects. *American Educational Research Journal, 18,* 343–361.

Lipson, M. Y., Chomsky-Higgins, P., & Kanfer, J. (2011). Diagnosis: The missing ingredient in RTI assessment. *The Reading Teacher, 65*(3), 204–208.

Malloy, J. A., Castek, J. M., & Leu, D. J. (2010). Silent reading and online reading comprehension. In E. H. Hiebert & D. R. Reutzel (Eds.), *Revisiting silent reading: New directions for teachers and researchers* (pp. 221–240). Newark, DE: International Reading Association.

Malloy, J. A., & Gambrell, L. B. (2011a). The contribution of discussion to reading comprehension and critical thinking. In R. Allington & A. McGill-Franzen (Eds.), *Handbook of reading disabilities research* (pp. 253–262). Mahwah, NJ: Erlbaum.

Malloy, J. A., & Gambrell, L. B. (2011b). Motivation to read. In R. F. Flippo (Ed.), *Reading researchers in search of common ground* (2nd ed., pp. 154–169). Newark, DE: International Reading Association.

McCombs, B. L. (2003). A framework for the redesign of K–12 education in the context of current educational reform. *Theory into Practice, 42*(2), 93–101.

McCoy, J. D., & Ketterlin-Geller, L. R. (2004). Rethinking instructional delivery for diverse student populations serving all learners with concept-based instruction. *Intervention in School and Clinic, 40*(2), 88–95.

McEneaney, J. E., Lose, M. K., & Schwartz, R. M. (2006). A transactional perspective on reading difficulties and response to intervention. *Reading Research Quarterly, 41*(1), 117–128.

Mercer, N., & Littleton, K. (2007). *Dialogue and the development of children's thinking: A sociocultural approach.* London: Routledge.

Mohan, L., Lundeberg, M. A., & Reffitt, K. (2008). Studying teachers and schools: Michael Pressley's legacy and directions for future research. *Educational Psychologist, 43*(2), 107–118.

Morrow, L. M., Reuda, R., & Lapp, D. (Eds.). (2009). *Handbook of research on literacy and diversity.* New York: Guilford Press.

Nagy, W., & Anderson, R. C. (1984). How many words are there in printed school English? *Reading Research Quarterly, 19,* 304–330.

National Assessment Governing Board. (2009). *Reading framework for the 2009 National Assessment of Educational Progress.* Washington, DC: U.S. Department of Education.

National Assessment of Educational Progress. (2013). Report retrieved October 25, 2013, from *http://nces.ed.gov/nationsreportcard.*

National Center on Educational Restructuring and Inclusion. (1995). *National study of inclusive education.* New York: City University of New York.

National Institute of Child Health and Human Development (2000). *Report of the National Reading Panel. Teaching children to read: An evidence-based assessment of the scientific research literature on reading and its implications for reading instruction* (NIH Publication No. 00-4769). Washington, DC: U.S. Government Printing Office.

Neuman, S. B., & Gambrell, L. B. (2013). *Quality reading instruction in the age of Common Core Standards.* Newark, DE: International Reading Association.

Neuman, S. B., & Roskos, K. (1993). Access to print for children of poverty: Differential effects of adult mediation and literacy-enriched play settings on environmental and functional print tasks. *American Educational Research Journal, 30*(3), 95–122.

Pai, Y. (1990). Cultural pluralism, democracy, and multicultural education. In B. Cassara (Ed.), *Adult education in a multicultural society* (pp. 11–27). New York: Routledge.

Paris, S., Lipson, M., & Wixson, K. (1983). Becoming a strategic reader. *Contemporary Educational Psychology, 8,* 293–316.

Partnership for Assessment of Readiness for College and Careers. (2011). PARCC model content frameworks: English language arts/literacy grades 3–11. Retrieved from *www.parcconline.org/sites/parcc/files/PARCCMCFELALiteracy-August2012_FINAL.pdf.*

Pearson, P. D., & Gallagher, M. C. (1983). The instruction of reading comprehension. *Contemporary Educational Psychology, 8,* 317–344.

Poparad, M. A. (2010). *Literacy as leverage for school improvement: Investigating year one implementation of a comprehensive literacy framework.* Unpublished paper.

Pressley, M. (2007). Achieving best practices. In L. B. Gambrell, L. M. Morrow, & M. Pressley (Eds.), *Best practices in literacy instruction* (pp. 397–404). New York: Guilford Press.

Pressley, M. (2005). Oh, the places an educational psychologist can go! . . . and how young educational psychologists can prepare for the trip (apologies to Dr. Seuss). *Educational Psychologist, 40,* 137–153.

Pressley, M., Allington, R. L., Wharton-McDonald, R., Block, C. C., & Morrow, L. M. (2001). *Learning to read: Lessons from exemplary first-grade classrooms.* New York: Guilford Press.

Purcell-Gates, V. (2002). Authentic literacy in class yields increase in literacy practices. *Literacy Update, 11*(1), 9.

Purcell-Gates, V. (2005, December). *What does culture have to do with it?* Oscar S. Causey Research Award address, National Reading Conference, Miami Beach, FL.

Purcell-Gates, V., Duke, N., & Martineau, J. (2007). Learning to read and write genre-specific text: Roles of authentic experience and explicit teaching. *Reading Research Quarterly, 42,* 8–46.

Raikes, H., Luze, G., Brooks-Gunn, J., Raikes, H. A., Pan, B. A., & Tamis-LeMonda, C. S. (2006). Mother–child book reading in low-income families: Correlates and outcomes during the first three years of life. *Child Development, 77,* 924–953.

Reutzel, D. R., & Hollingsworth, P. M. (1991). Investigating topic-related attitude: Effect on reading and remembering text. *Journal of Educational Research, 84*(6), 334–344.

Reutzel, D. R., Jones, C. D., Fawson, P. C., & Smith, J. A. (2008). Scaffolded silent reading: A complement to guided repeated oral reading that works! *The Reading Teacher, 62*(3), 194–207.

Reznitskaya, A. (2012). Dialogic teaching: Rethinking language use during literature discussions. *The Reading Teacher, 65*(7), 446–456.

Reznitskaya, A., Glina, M., Carolan, B., Michaud, O., Rogers, J., & Sequeira, L. (2012). Examining transfer effects from dialogic discussions to new tasks and contexts. *Contemporary Educational Psychology, 37,* 288–306.

Ritter, C. L., Michel, C. S., & Irby, B. (1999). Concerning inclusion: Perceptions of middle school students, their parents, and teachers. *Rural Special Education Quarterly, 18*(2), 10–16.

Robb, L. (2013). *Unlocking complex texts.* New York: Scholastic.

Rogers, J. (1993). The inclusion revolution. *Phi Delta Kappa Research Bulletin.*

Sandora, C., Beck, I. L., & McKeown, M. G. (1999). A comparison of two discussion strategies on students' comprehension and interpretation of complex literature. *Reading Psychology, 20,* 177–212.

Skinner, E. A., & Belmont, M. J. (1993). Motivation in the classroom: Reciprocal effects of teacher behavior and student engagement across the school year. *Journal of Educational Psychology, 85,* 571–581.

Smith, G. P. (1998). *Common sense about uncommon knowledge: The knowledge bases for diversity*. Washington, DC: AACTE.

Southern Education Foundation. (2013). *New majority: Low income students in the south and the nation*. Atlanta, GA: Author.

Stanovich, K. E. (1986). Matthew effects in reading: Some consequences of individual differences in the acquisition of literacy. *Reading Research Quarterly, 21*(4), 360–406.

Stronge, J. H. (2007). *Qualities of effective teachers* (2nd ed.). Alexandria, VA: Association for Supervision and Curriculum Development.

Teale, W. H., & Gambrell, L. B. (2007). Raising urban students' literacy achievement by engaging in authentic, challenging work. *The Reading Teacher, 60,* 728–739.

Teale, W. H., & Sulzby, E. (1986). *Emergent literacy: Writing and reading*. Norwood, NJ: Ablex.

Teale, W. H., Zolt, N., Yokota, J., Glasswell, K., & Gambrell, L. B. (2007). Getting children In2Books: Engagement in authentic reading, writing, and thinking. *Phi Delta Kappan, 88,* 498–502.

Tomlinson, C. A. (1999). Mapping a route toward differentiated instruction. *Educational Leadership, 57,* 12–17.

Tomlinson, C. A. (2001). *How to differentiate instruction in mixed-ability classrooms*. Alexandria, VA: Association for Supervision and Curriculum Development.

Tomlinson, C. A. (2004). Differentiating instruction. *Adolescent Literacy Research and Practice*.

Tomlinson, C. A., & Allan, S. D. (2000). Leadership for differentiating schools and classrooms. In T. L. Jetton & J. A. Dole (Eds.), *Literacy research and practice* (pp. 228–250). New York: Guilford Press.

Turner, J. C. (1995). The influence of classroom contexts on young children's motivation for literacy. *Reading Research Quarterly, 30,* 410–441.

U.S. Department of Education, Office of Vocational and Adult Education. (2012). *Adult education great cities summit: What is evidence-based reading instruction and how do you know it when you see it?* Washington, DC: Author.

Vygotsky, L. S. (1978). *Mind in society*. Cambridge, MA: Harvard University Press.

Wharton-McDonald, R., Pressley, M., & Hampston, J. M. (1998). Literacy instruction in nine first grade classrooms: Teacher characteristics and student achievement. *Elementary School Journal, 99,* 101–128.

Yopp, R. H., & Yopp, H. K. (2006). Informational texts as read-alouds at school and home. *Journal of Literacy Research, 38*(1), 37–51.

CHAPTER 2

Current Issues and Best Practices in Literacy Instruction

Vicki B. Griffo
Christina L. Madda
P. David Pearson
Taffy E. Raphael

This chapter will:

- Offer a reconceptualization of balance in light of current research, insights, and contexts.
- Revisit the research base on best practices in literacy instruction.
- Discuss several dimensions of literacy instruction and how complementary and competing forces surface in the curriculum.
- Consider the role of the teacher as artful orchestrator in enacting balance in a comprehensive literacy program.
- Consider the role of the Common Core State Standards in creating balance in literacy instruction.

Some of education's most enduring and polarizing debates have revolved around questions of what constitutes best practice within the literacy curriculum. When we speak of literacy, we refer to the requisite skills, strategies, and experiences that readers-writers bring to bear when interacting with text in the world. It's no surprise then that such an essential set of skills and practices have attracted so much attention in the education field, given their fundamental role in shaping future citizenry, building the foundation for college and career-readiness, and enhancing one's overall quality of life. As we set out to identify and define a range of best practices for literacy instruction, we begin by revisiting what we believe to be a fundamental construct within the literacy curriculum today: the construct of balance.

As described in earlier editions of this book (Madda, Griffo, Pearson, & Raphael, 2010; Pearson & Raphael, 1999, 2003; Pearson, Raphael, Benson, & Madda, 2007), the notion of a "balanced curriculum" was born out of the 1990s antagonistic "reading wars" debate (Pearson, 2004). This debate pitted those in favor of a whole-language approach to the teaching of reading against proponents of a more phonics-based approach (see Lyon, 1997; McIntyre & Pressley, 1996; Pressley, 2006). Naturally, each side claimed to be advocating for the more effective instructional methodology (see Chall, 1967, 1997, for a historical treatment of this debate).

In today's policy world, however, the tide has changed. The debate is no longer touted as phonics versus whole language. Few in the field contest the necessity of teaching fundamental skills, including phonics and phonemic awareness, from the outset of formal schooling. If the National Reading Panel Report (2000), especially as it was enacted in the Reading First provision of the No Child Left Behind Act of 2002, was the key document shaping policy for the last two editions of this chapter on balance, it has been the Common Core State Standards (CCSS) document of 2010 that has shaped the policy context for this edition (National Governors Association & Council of Chief State School Officers [NGA & CCSSO], 2010). And it is clear that the CCSS for English Language Arts have shifted the terms of the debate. While the foundational skills of early literacy instruction are in the CCSS document, they have been relegated to an appendix-like status. And a range of higher-order processes—close reading of challenging texts to ferret out both essence and nuance, literacy in the disciplines of history and science, writing from text-based sources, and understanding, constructing, and critiquing argument—have rushed in to fill the void. Now the debates (see Pearson, 2013) center on issues of which model of close reading will prevail, how we will support students in meeting the demands of more challenging texts, or how and when we will teach students to cope with the vocabulary demands of these more complex texts.

As we have argued in past editions, regardless of the policy context in which we construct our vision of balance, it must be recognized as a complex and multidimensional construct to be applied across many facets of literacy teaching and learning (Madda, Griffo, Pearson, & Raphael, 2011). Thus, in this chapter, we continue the conversation of what it means to enact a "fully" balanced literacy curriculum that both reflects the demands of 21st-century citizenry and enhances the schooling experience of students. We begin by outlining current issues that frame today's educational context including the presence of 21st-century technologies and the shifting demographics of U.S. schools. Next, we delve into evidence-based best practices, their core components, and tensions that may arise as we strive to achieve balance. We then extend the discussion by addressing balance within a series of dimensions (in previous editions we called these "continua") relevant to issues of content and context within literacy teaching and learning.

Current Issues: A Context for Best Practices

As social, cultural, and technological landscapes continue to evolve and become more complex, so does our notion of what it means to be literate today. While literacy continues to represent a set of shared communicative practices among social/cultural groups, the nature of those practices and the texts involved has changed immensely (National Council of Teachers of English, 2013). Multimodal text forms and the media-driven environments in which they are embedded now accompany print-based literacy practices. Multifaceted and intricate knowledge processes now accompany the more customary ways of meaning making. In other words, to work, live, and contribute to the social and civic fabric of today's increasingly digital and global world, one must possess the skills to critically analyze, deconstruct, and reconstruct meaning across a variety of text types and for myriad purposes (Howland, Jonassen, & Marra, 2013; International Society for Technology in Education, 2012).

As our notions of what it means to be literate change, so must our ideas of what it means to provide literacy instruction in today's classrooms. Full and active participation in 21st-century life requires much more than the acquisition of foundational skills to decipher the printed word. Rather, in order to learn effectively and live productively in the modern age, students must learn to evaluate and think critically about information sources, to organize and manage information, and to communicate and collaborate with others utilizing a variety of tools (International Society for Technology in Education, 2012; Partnership for 21st Century Skills, 2012). These literate competencies are essential to helping students actualize the broader objectives of literacy education such as engaging in lifelong learning, accomplishing personal and professional goals, and living a more fulfilling life.

Indeed, many of the trends we see in education today are reflective of this more transformative view of literacy and literacy instruction (Raphael, Au, & Popp, 2013). For example, the 2010 CCSS in English language arts in many ways represent an effort to embrace a more complex notion of literacy by emphasizing high levels of student thinking among traditional and emerging types of literary and informational texts, and by focusing on the integration of literacy skills within and across the disciplines. This recasting and recontextualizing of literacy instruction according to a disciplinary perspective acknowledges the centrality of the English language arts in learning across subject matter. Moreover, the CCSS stated focus on college and career readiness represents an effort to "lay out a vision of what it means to be a literate person in the twenty-first century" and to ensure that "the skills and understandings students are expected to demonstrate have wide applicability outside the classroom or workplace" (NGA & CCSSO, 2010). However, this emphasis on college and career readiness is also indicative of the ongoing need to address the current state of achievement within U.S. schools.

Results from large-scale assessments of U.S. students' literacy achievement remain a cause for concern. Disparities in performance levels on national assessments persist between students of diverse backgrounds (i.e., from ethnic and racial minority groups, speaking a first language other than English, living in poverty) and their "mainstream" peers (i.e., white, middle-class, native-English-speaking). According to the National Assessment of Educational Progress (NAEP) 2011 Executive Report in Reading, there have been no significant changes in reducing the racial/ ethnic gaps, or social class gaps at either grade 4 or 8 compared with 2009 (National Center of Educational Statistics, 2011). Ongoing disparities in average scores suggest there is still work to be done in terms of meeting students' needs and ensuring that all students are achieving the highest levels of literacy.

The Centrality of Instruction

There are many ways to explain the achievement gap reflected in tests such as the NAEP. These explanations include such factors as economic disparities and related differences in experiential background before entering school, high mobility rates, and so forth—factors that are well beyond the control of a classroom teacher or school staff. Yet, we know from research that there are important factors that we can control within schools and classrooms that influence student achievement levels—those of curriculum that frame instruction (i.e., *what* to teach) and the quality of teaching in implementing the curriculum (i.e., *how* it is taught). For example, a review of research that led to the 2000 National Reading Panel Report suggests that a complete reading program must include instruction in comprehension and fluency as well as basic understanding of the symbol system at the word level (phonics and phonemic awareness); the full report suggests that as important as phonics instruction is, it must always be set within a broader pedagogical context in which it is surrounded by meaning-making activities. These more cautionary themes are also reflected in several of the chapters in the most current *Handbook of Reading Research* (Kamil, Pearson, Moje, & Afflerbach, 2010).

Others have demonstrated the centrality of concept knowledge or vocabulary learning in general and particularly for students who do not speak English as their native language (Carlo et al., 2004). Taylor, Pearson, Peterson, and Rodriguez (2003, 2005) identified a set of classroom practices, dubbed "teaching for cognitive engagement," that support higher levels of achievement; the set includes teacher coaching rather than telling, high levels of questioning, students' active participation in activities that require high levels of thinking (e.g., book club discussions, inquiry groups), and time for students' sustained engagement in reading and writing.

How do these findings connect with the achievement gap? Research has documented that students from diverse backgrounds often have limited exposure to high-quality instruction, even within what teachers believe to be a balanced curriculum. When compared to "mainstream" peers, low-income or minority students tend to receive a great deal of instruction in lower-level skills and little instruction in reading comprehension and higher-level thinking about text (see Amendum & Fitzgerald, 2010; Amendum et al., 2009; Darling-Hammond, 1995, 2004; Kong & Fitch, 2002). It may be a conspiracy of good intentions—one that might be labeled "first things first," where the logic is something like "Let's get the words right and the facts straight before we get to the 'what ifs' and 'I wonders' of classroom instruction." And, of course, the conspiracy is that many lower-performing students spend their entire school careers getting the words right and the facts straight, never reaching that higher-level thinking. One reason for this disparity and conspiracy—lowered expectations for the achievement of students from historically marginalized communities and limited instructional focus areas—is something we can and should change.

Evidence-Based Best Practices: A Research Synthesis

As painful and enduring as the "reading wars" have been, they did help educators and researchers see the shortcomings of unidimensional, dichotomous, "either–or" approaches to literacy instruction (Pearson, 2004). Today, as we have suggested, the old debates have abated in favor of new and productive tensions introduced by the CCSS, and we know that a mix of literacy dimensions is essential to a comprehensive literacy program (Pearson, 2004). Moreover, we are now armed with strong evidence to ensure this sort of balance, for we know—by virtue of the work of the National Reading Panel (NRP; 2000) and a long tradition of research curriculum and pedagogy stemming back into the 1980s (e.g., Anderson, Hiebert, Scott, & Wilkinson, 1984), the 1960s (e.g., Chall, 1967), and even earlier (e.g., Gray, 1948)—that the research confirms the importance of uniting methodologies by putting lower-level processes (e.g., phonics, phonemic awareness) to work within the pursuit of higher-order goals (e.g., comprehension, composition, critique).

Phonemic Awareness

The research (NRP, 2000) suggests that explicit instruction in various elements of phonological awareness, such as rhyming, phonemic segmentation (breaking a word into its phonemic units: *bat* → /buh/aa/tuh/)— and phonemic blending (putting the parts together: /buh/ /aa/ /tuh/ → *bat*)—pays dividends in the long run in terms of its transference to beginning-reading achievement. But we also know that instruction can include many engaging oral language games (see Snow, Burns, & Griffin, 1998) and even invented spelling (see Adams, 1990; Clarke, 1988). As such, there is no need to privilege dense skill-oriented programs over engaging and more authentic language activities.

Phonics

With regards to phonics, we know that the NRP report, its narrow sample of subject populations notwithstanding, concluded that what mattered was early emphasis on the code, not an emphasis on any particular approach to phonics. We know from other work (e.g., Ehri, Nunes, Stahl, & Willows, 2001; Gaskins, Ehri, Cress, O'Hara, & Donnelly, 1997) that approaches to word reading are complementary and that students need a full repertoire of tools to do justice to the challenge of pronouncing unknown words encountered in text.

Ehri (1995) talks about four strategies that we find particularly useful as ways of conceptualizing the curricular goals of teachers and the learning needs of students. Ehri suggests that students need to learn to read words using these four approaches: sequential decoding, analogy, contextual analysis, and sight-word recognition. Sequential decoding, or letter-by-letter decoding, is the stuff of which the time-honored ABC approach is made. And students can indeed sound out words in this way. Analogy should be focused on word families or phonograms—words that are spelled and pronounced similarly, such as *cat, fat, sat, bat,* and the like. Gaskins (2005) found, in building the Benchmark School curriculum, that analogy instruction was much more effective after sequential decoding has been established among readers. Contextual analysis is an ad hoc form of problem solving—what you do when you come to a word you cannot pronounce, and it involves both intraword (morphological analysis) and extraword (the surrounding context) analysis in order to work. Finally, there is immediate sight-word recognition, and it plays two roles in word reading. First, some words, such as *give, have, the*, and *break*, must be learned as sight words because they violate the principles one learns from instruction in sequential decoding and analogy. Second—and this is the really important face of sight word reading—the goal of the other three approaches is to move words from students' repertoire of "arduously analyzable" ("I can figure these out if I work at it") to "immediately recognizable" ("I know that word; it's *irrefutable*"). In short, the goal of phonics and context instruction is to get to the point where readers need them only minimally, freeing up their thinking skills for higher-level processes. Balanced phonics instruction—or, more accurately, balanced word reading instruction—is essential to skilled reading.

Comprehension and Vocabulary

We know from the NRP (2000) that comprehension can be improved by explicit strategy instruction and by a variety of approaches to vocabulary instruction. We also know from previous work (see Murphy, Wilkinson, Soter, Hennessey, & Alexander, 2008; Pearson & Fielding, 1991) that rich conversations about text can improve comprehension of both the texts within which the instruction is embedded and new texts that students subsequently read on their own. Hence, we are prepared to conclude that all three of these approaches—strategy instruction, rich talk about text, and semantically rich conversations about word meanings (see Beck, McKeown, & Kucan, 2002; Blachowicz & Fisher, 2009)—should all be a part of a balanced literacy curriculum. At this point in our research history, there seems to be no basis for privileging any one of the three over the other two, and they do seem to relate well to one another as a complementary set.

Writing

While the role of writing was not within the scope of the NRP Report, we know that writing is a core component of any literacy program and that reading and writing are mutually supportive and interactive processes. Just as with reading, the area of writing has also seen its share of polarizing debates. Mutually exclusive dichotomies—those between *product* versus *process* approaches—have lingered for years. While the *product* contingency emphasizes attention to form and grammar of the text produced, the *process* side focuses on meaning making by emphasizing the stages of writing such as brainstorming, drafting, revising, and editing—with little attention to convention. Whereas the product side is too heavily focused on mechanics, the process side too often relies on familiar registers, such as personal narratives, rather than more complex registers that better prepare students for future academic demands (Schleppegrell, 2004). But just as with debates in reading, these methodologies are complementary, so both are needed. Focus on product alone can lead to formulaic writing whereas process orientations may not equip students either with the necessary conventions to adequately communicate their ideas or with enough knowledge to possess something worth writing about.

Literacy, however, is too complex a process to think of as simply coordinating a balance between linguistic conventions and meaning. Rather, students must be armed with a toolkit of skills and strategies that can be flexibly deployed across the complex settings that characterize today's literacy environment. As students traverse myriad texts, language and comprehension demands vary accordingly—and tools deemed effective within a particular content or context may vary greatly in the next. Thus, balanced instruction requires not only a *rich knowledge base* but also the ability to *adapt and orchestrate a range of classroom experiences* that will provide students with authentic opportunities to exercise and grow their literacy toolkit.

For the remainder of this chapter, we build a case for the rich knowledge base teachers must possess to implement comprehensive literacy instruction that is truly balanced. In so doing, we demonstrate just how far the field has moved beyond the code versus meaning debate (i.e., balance in the past) to argue that there are many content and contextual elements of literacy that must be simultaneously and artfully balanced (i.e., balance today) in order to equip students with the depth and breadth of proficiencies to meet a wide array of literacy challenges. We describe each of the content and contextual aspects of the literacy curriculum as located within continua to illustrate the competing demands and priorities at work within a comprehensive literacy program. In previous versions of this chapter, we have used the term *continua* to refer to these important aspects of literacy. However, continua imply polar opposites that often inadvertently indicate tensions that the research no longer supports. Rather, we believe that there are aspects of the curriculum—both competing and complimentary—that are critical for teachers to consider in shaping pedagogy in their classrooms, a concept that is captured more effectively through the language of dimensions.

Best Practices in Action

Content Dimensions

In the following section we describe several content dimensions that teachers must balance to build, challenge, and refine students' core skills across a wide range of texts. These dimensions underscore the fact that not all texts are created equal; with changes in structure, format, and purpose come associated shifts in linguistic, comprehension, and cultural demands. Thus, students need the chance to learn and grow their core linguistic and comprehension skills and strategies across a diverse platform of texts. Content dimensions are (1) text difficulty, (2) genre, and (3) disciplinary emphasis (see Table 2.1).

Text Difficulty

One area of balance that is gaining currency in education is that of balancing *text difficulty*. Prior to the appearance of the CCSS, the issue in text difficulty was whether kids should be reading level–appropriate or what we have always called "just-right" texts versus age- or grade-appropriate texts. Just-right texts are matched to each student's reading achievement level quite irrespective of their age or grade level in school. The underlying logic is that each individual makes the most progress when she is reading right in her zone of individual comfort (Pearson, 2013). But the CCSS bring a new logic to the curricular table. All students are expected to read texts that are appropriate for their grade level *plus* read at least some texts that are at least a grade beyond their grade-level diet. In other words, in the CCSS world, challenge is calibrated for the entire class, not for each individual. This change places a whole new burden on teachers, who will be required to find classroom-level scaffolds that will help all

TABLE 2.1. Balancing Content Dimensions

Dimension	Competing forces	
Text difficulty	Matched to individual	Stretching limits
Genre	Explicit instruction	Inductive learning
Disciplinary emphasis	Literacy as a skill	Literacy as a tool

Note. Content dimensions consist of three areas: (1) text difficulty, (2) genre, and (3) disciplinary emphasis. Each dimension has two competing forces: text difficulty—(a) matched to individual and (b) stretching limits; genre—(a) explicit instruction and (b) inductive learning; disciplinary emphasis—(a) literacy as a skill and (b) literacy as a tool.

of their students meet even greater challenges than they have ever been asked to meet.

Providing students with a strict diet of texts that fall only within the range of their reading level would rob students of invaluable exposure and opportunity for developing the skills and strategies for accessing texts beyond their reading level—a likely scenario all readers are sure to encounter. Thus, if complex texts are withheld until students are deemed "ready" to receive them, the risk is that some may have little occasion to challenge and stretch their repertoire of literacy skills. Over the past 100 years, a steady decline in the difficulty of classroom texts at the secondary level means that, realistically today, many students will be taught using texts that are far below the difficulty of those they will encounter in college and the workplace (Pearson, 2013). But teachers can counter the growing discrepancy in text difficulty by complementing a healthy diet of appropriately leveled texts used for skill development with access and exposure to more complex texts that are chosen based on students' interests and goals.

With adoption of the newly released CCSS we see a push for balance in text difficulty. The standards recommend greater student exposure to and support in reading a high proportion of challenging text at every grade level. The rationale for this approach is based on the sobering observation that when students finish secondary school (in grade 12 in the United States) the average level of challenge of the texts they are reading is about a whole grade-level below what they will be expected to read as freshmen in college. The authors of the standards point to, and we think rightly so, the tremendous amount of resources devoted to remedial education in the first year of college—not only in community colleges (where one might expect less-well-prepared students to comprise a significant proportion of the population) but also in regional and even research intensive universities. Their solution to closing this text complexity/text challenging gap is to gradually increase the expectations (and instructional support) at every grade level from the primary years onward, so that by 12th grade the gap stands a chance of being closed altogether. While more research is needed in this area, it is our contention that making more difficult texts accessible to students requires a good deal of teacher support and scaffolding to assist comprehension through use of reading strategies and text discussion.

Genre

A second notable dimension of instructional balance with the CCSS is the incorporation of a wide range of *genre pedagogies* into the literacy curriculum (e.g., Duke & Purcell-Gates, 2003; Hicks, 1998; Nodelman, 1992; Pappas & Pettegrew, 1998). *Genre* refers to the evolving classification of texts that form the basis of the curriculum—most notably narrative (e.g., stories, personal narratives), poetry, and informational texts that employ a range of structures (e.g., essays, descriptions, persuasion). Readers encounter a wide span of genres as they read across topics and for various purposes within all forms of printed and online texts. Even as readers take up a single field of study, relevant information can be accessed across a variety of genres that offer varied information and perspective such as textbooks, scientific reports, personal narratives, or the myriad of Web-based texts.

The consideration of genre variation is an important instructional factor because of textual properties that range across a host of features such as structure, word choice, style, and purpose (Graesser, McNamara, & Kulikowich, 2011). The more familiar readers are with the conventions of genre types, the better off they are in comprehending and even composing their own texts. For example, by the time students leave elementary school, they are keenly aware that narrative text structures are organized around characters, setting, and plot; similarly, they are familiar with common expository structures, such as sequence, comparison, description, cause–effect, and problem–solution.

Teaching students to deconstruct the conventions of various genres has proven productive in supporting comprehension, such as attending readers to linguistic and other discourse markers commonly used to communicate important ideas and signal text interconnectivity. For example, to demonstrate a comparison of ideas texts may utilize words such as *however, nevertheless*, and *similarly*, whereas a text showing sequence will contain words like *first, then*, and *previously* (see Almasi, 2003, for more information). Even within a single text, it is common to find different text structures. Today's information age often requires students to navigate multiple, overlapping, and blended genres characteristic of Web-based multimedia text formats. Thus, attending to a range of genres within the literacy curriculum often means transcending traditional notions that contrast narrative with informational texts. The complex, varied, and sophisticated literate actions that accompany new(er) Web-based genres and text formats reiterate the need for exposing students to a full scope of genres in order to develop proficiency and versatility in accessing information across varied contexts and for myriad purposes.

Disciplinary Emphasis

Toolkits of literacy skills and strategies not only vary across text and genre, but across *disciplinary or subject-matter emphasis*. Literacy today is envisioned as a versatile tool central to learning that has application and utility across disciplines, but not necessarily as meaningful in and of itself as a subject area. When we read and when we write, we read and write about something in particular and for a particular purpose. Certainly, literacy skills must be learned and practiced, but earlier, we made an argument for applying reading and writing skills and strategies to contexts in which they were put to service in "real-world" reading and writing tasks for a greater purpose—such as in the service of learning. The benefits of reading and writing are rendered transparent when they are viewed as tools for the acquisition of knowledge and insight typically found in subject-matter learning. Indeed, much has been written (e.g., Cervetti, Pearson, Bravo, & Barber, 2006; Magnusson & Palincsar, 2005; Palincsar & Magnusson, 2001) about the efficacy of reading and writing as tools to support inquiry-based science learning.

Indeed, the CCSS represent an attempt to bring balance to the curriculum by integrating the language arts with other disciplines as a means to helping students "acquire a wide range of ever more sophisticated knowledge and skills" (CCSSO & NGA, 2010, p. 1). Literacy integration across the disciplines offers students myriad contexts in which to genuinely apply their literacy strategies, and ensures a steady source of knowledge to fuel the comprehension and composition processes. As Cervetti and colleagues (2006) put it in the wake of the No Child Left Behind Act of 2001 and the Reading First Act of 2002, it is time to transform literacy from being a curricular "bully" into serving as a curricular "buddy" to enhance both the learning of disciplinary knowledge and its own application in that learning. As we move further down this path of integrating literacy within the disciplines, we still have a lot to learn about characterizing the unique literacy demands of differing content areas (Moje, Stockdill, Kim, & Kim, 2011; Shanahan & Shanahan, 2008). Thus, to prepare students for a life in and beyond school, it is important to equip them with a proficient set of skills through reading and writing across a variety of texts used for different purposes.

Contextual Dimensions

Achieving a balanced literacy curriculum is not only benefited by varying literacy content, but is also dependent on managing the contextual aspects that set the stage for what gets taught. These contextual aspects described here are factors related to the instructional surround. Over the past 30 years, the definition of effective literacy instruction has broadened beyond what needs to get taught (i.e., developing an ability to decode and comprehend many types of texts) to consider how it gets taught. As a field, we now recognize that the effective participation in literate practices is deeply embedded within the society and culture where they are enacted. As students interact with multiple literacies, meaning is not merely constructed via the proficient act of assembling a collection of words and phrases on a page into a prescribed conclusion—as if it were something embedded within a text that needed unearthing. Rather, texts are constructed and deconstructed by individuals who have unique capabilities, motivations, knowledge, and experiences that shape their perspectives, agendas, and biases—all of which contribute to multifaceted layers of meaning. Thus, as students engage with literacy, interpretation can vary from participant to participant and even from event to event. Given the intersection of core skills, text variation, and the influential role of the participant, teachers invite students to play an intricate role in the construction and composition of literacy through balancing the following contextual dimensions of literacy: (1) authenticity, (2) text discussion, (3) teacher control, and (4) professional prerogative (see Table 2.2).

Authenticity

Authenticity has been identified as important to students' literacy learning (Florio-Ruane & Raphael, 2004; Purcell-Gates, Duke, & Martineau, 2007). Balance in authenticity lies between the reality that students need to develop a set of conventional skills that enables them to access texts, while too often school tasks are inauthentic, disembedded and, by implication, not useful for engaging in real-world literacy activities. The content students read, write, and talk about, and the activity settings in which students work, should be grounded in authentic tasks and goals. These tasks and goals should map to the purposes for which we as a society use literacy: to communicate, to learn, and to enjoy.

Many literacy educators proclaim the numerous benefits of reading and responding to authentic literature—books, for example, that are written for the purpose of entertaining, informing, persuading, or

TABLE 2.2. Balancing Context Dimensions

Dimension	Competing forces	
Authenticity	Skill decontextualization	Real-world relevance
Text discussion	Culturally sanctioned	Personal interpretation
Teacher control	Minimal	Maximal
Professional prerogative	Distant	Local

Note. Context dimensions consist of four areas: (1) authenticity, (2) text discussion, (3) teacher control, and (4) professional prerogative. Each dimension has two competing forces: authenticity—(a) skill decontextualization and (b) real-world relevance; text discussion—(a) culturally sanctioned and (b) personal interpretation; teacher control—(a) minimal and (b) maximal; professional prerogative—(a) distant and (b) local.

inspiring—that reflects purposeful use of language, complex natural language, and compelling story lines (e.g., Dyson, 2003). Even our youngest students must be given opportunity to read (even if it's "pretend-read") and respond to high-quality literary texts that demonstrate the many rewards and pleasures of reading. Other authentic practices include writing for real audiences and purposes (e.g., Cappello, 2006), writing to make sense of their lives (Dyson, 2003; Genishi & Dyson, 2009; Schultz, 2006, 2009), and reading to engage in book club or other discussions with teachers and peers (e.g., Raphael, Florio-Ruane, George, Hasty, & Highfield, 2004).

The reality of the digital world and the ubiquitous influence of globalization bear strong implications for literacy and authenticity in a 21st-century context. We need to think beyond the printed page and national boundaries to find "authentic" literacy. Featured prominently in this global digital literacy will be more multimodal features of texts (those in which print is inextricably linked with visual, audio, and/or spatial patterns of meaning) and to multinational audiences for everything we read and write. Based on the CCSS and what the world is like today we have to be mindful of the demands of Web-based multimedia that call for readers to critically analyze, deconstruct, and reconstruct meaning across a variety of texts for various purposes (Howland, Jonassen, & Marra, 2012). In other words, literate competencies have become increasingly more about one's ability to access information, think critically about "text," analyze and evaluate sources, organize information, communicate information, and collaborate utilizing a variety of tools. These "information literacy" skills, necessary for participation in 21st-century citizenry, should be at the heart of school-based literacy activities. Authentic learning in classrooms today therefore should not narrowly focus on students acquiring information via traditional text types, but rather on students seeking out, managing, transforming, and applying information utilizing multiple forms of media (Howland et al., 2012) and learning to find and to share information around the world.

On the face of it, it might seem hard to disagree with an emphasis on authenticity. But, if pursued in too single-minded a fashion, there might be little occasion for treating formal features of language (e.g., its structure, sound–symbol system, punctuation) as objects of study, meaning where useful skills get practiced and acquired. One way of labeling what might be lost under a regime of "hyperauthenticity" is knowledge *about* language and how it works in different contexts.

Text Discussion

Another important contextual dimension of any balanced literacy program is nurturing a classroom environment rich in *text discussion*. Texts are written for a variety of purposes: to inform, to persuade, and to enter-tain. Within these texts language embeds ideological positions that can obscure the nature of interpretation. Literacy development greatly ben-efits from ongoing student opportunities to build on prior knowledge, ideas, and experiences, as well as to voice and refine understandings through substantive discussion (Nystrand, 2006).

The use of oral language has long been linked to supporting both the development of comprehension and the composition of literacy (Gee, 2002, 2007). In the service of supporting reading comprehension, sev-eral discourse routines have been developed that feature varied teacher talk and discussion parameters to help readers co-construct the meaning of texts, such as Reciprocal Teaching (Palincsar & Brown, 1984), Ques-tioning the Author (Beck, McKeown, Sandora, Kucan, & Worthy, 1996; Sandora, Beck, & McKeown, 1999), and Literature Circles, to name a few. Many of these practices have been recommended by the NRP (2000) due to their power to contextualize reading in student experience and understanding. Discussion has also been shown to be a powerful device for developing cognition such as in building persuasive ability. For exam-ple, peer discussions offer opportunity to prompt students to state their positions, challenge thinking through counterarguments, acknowledge examples of good arguments, and model sound reasoning processes. Therefore, text discussions have been demonstrated to enhance student engagement, understanding, and internalization of the knowledge and skills necessary to engage in challenging literacy tasks they encounter on their own (Applebee, Langer, Nystrand, & Gamoran, 2003).

Teacher Control

A third dimension of contextual balance that must be sought in a balanced literacy program is the *degree of teacher control* of the activity within a given pedagogical context. While it is mistaken to assume that literacy learning is limited only to situations when the teacher is providing explicit instruc-tion, it is also erroneous to assume that learning is only meaningful when the teacher is out of the picture. Depending on the goal of the literacy event, activity, or lesson, different levels of teacher and student input are appropriate and necessary. Rodgers's (2004) observations of teaching and learning over time illustrated that effective teachers varied the amount of support and the related degree of teacher control and levels of student activity according to their perceptions of student need. Au and Raphael (1998) characterize variations in teachers' roles in terms of the amount of teacher control and student activity. They define five teacher roles: (1) explicit instructing, (2) modeling, (3) scaffolding, (4) facilitating, and (5) participating. These roles reflect a gradual release of responsibility

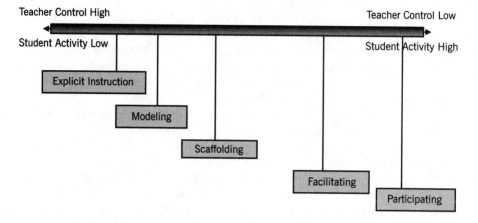

FIGURE 2.1. Teachers' roles.

(Pearson & Gallagher, 1983) where there is decreased control by the teacher and increased activity on the part of the student (see Figure 2.1). That is, teachers don't just start out with greater control and steadily move to lesser, but rather teachers cycle back and forth between these roles in response to student performance and understanding.

In a range of studies, researchers have demonstrated that teacher–student discussions predominately follow a more limiting pattern of teacher question, student response, and teacher evaluation of the response (Cazden, 2001; Mehan, 1979). This I-R-E (initiation–response–evaluation) pattern is grounded in the transmission model of learning that places a premium on recitation and correct answers. Yet, at the other extreme, classroom discussion can suffer from too little structure where discussion is too open-ended and students flounder in the absence of set purpose, structure, and support. Ideally, discussions are most effective when teachers play a supporting role in student-driven topic selection, turn taking, and interpretation.

Professional Prerogative

A fourth and final contextual dimension we offer is that of *professional prerogative*—who, or what, "calls the shots" in terms of how teachers and students spend their time in classrooms. At the one extreme, teachers may rely on a predetermined curriculum of skill instruction, often tied to a curricular scope and sequence that operates within and across grade levels. At the other extreme, the texts and the tasks that arise in the course of instruction, or, even more commonly, the needs that a given student or set of students demonstrate, are the determining force behind what is taught. In the latter view, the curriculum is unveiled as teachable moments occur, with the text, the tasks, and the students functioning as springboards to skill or strategy instruction. Teachers will find many moments when it's necessary to deviate from materials to adhere to their basic professional responsibility to adapt to individual differences.

We suggest the need for teachers to operate flexibly between these two poles. Standards are undoubtedly an important staple within education of which teachers must be knowledgeable and conscientious. They provide educators with a standardized baseline from which to teach by creating an expectation of what content will be covered prior to students entering and exiting the classroom. Yet, there is no predetermined formula that will support the variation that comes our way when we meet the constellation of kids and environments in each and every classroom. Effective literacy instruction is not simply about teachers possessing a good bag of tricks that, if designed well enough, can be applied successfully by any novice. Rather, literacy instruction is the art of knowing how to assemble the tools in concert with each other to make worthwhile instruction that is particular to the students and purposes in a given classroom.

Reflections and Future Directions

In thinking about balance in past iterations of this chapter and considering balance in today's educational environment, we are more convinced than ever before that the scholarly evidence and the world in which our students today will live and work requires attention regarding multiple facets of literacy. The research suggests appropriating the metaphor of "ecological balance" as it has unfolded in our understanding of ecosystems from environmental science. Most appealing about this metaphor is the idea that various elements do their part to support both their own survival and the survival of all of the other elements in the system. So it is in a comprehensive literacy curriculum. The content and contextual dimensions that we described are to be held in harmony. In doing so, they prepare their students for a future that we may not even be able to imagine today, of continually evolving forms for accessing information as well as evolving forms for literate practice for personal growth and satisfaction.

The sheer number of crucial dimensions, not to mention the differences among them, means that effective instruction is entirely dependent on the artful orchestration skills of the teacher. What we are asking teachers is to do what might seem to be impossible—a thorough job of teaching literacy—one that nurtures and grows a rich set of literacy skills and strategies across a wide variety of texts, used for a variety of purposes that map to real-world challenges. The inherent complexity is that teachers have to orchestrate broad knowledge to act adaptively because students and situations are always in flux. Thus, a balanced, comprehensive literacy curriculum can only be realized through artful orchestration by teachers who achieve balance by weighing their professional knowledge with their intimate knowledge of their students and environment.

ENGAGEMENT ACTIVITIES

1. *Redefining our goals for 21st-century teaching of the English language arts.*

   a. We promote the definition of teaching literacy in a 21st-century context as supporting students' abilities to access information; think critically about a wide array of texts that vary in content, format, and platform; analyze and evaluate sources; organize information; communicate information; and collaborate using a variety of tools. How does this definition align with your current thinking, practice, and curricular goals?

   b. How would you emphasize the role of information and communication technologies in helping your students develop 21st-century competencies within the classroom? For example, what are some authentic applications of 21st-century technologies that could support your curricular goals and the advancement of information literacy?

   c. Create a plan for how you and your colleagues can utilize technology in your classroom or school. Consider ways in which the use of technology is consistent with helping students to achieve the information literacy skills cited above.

2. *A close look at our current practices.* The Common Core State Standards (NGA & CCSSO, 2010) emphasize the integration of the English language arts within and across disciplines to support student college and career readiness. After reviewing Common Core documents, reflect on the following questions: What practices (curriculum, instructional materials, or instructional methods) are currently in place within your classroom or school that reflect or support the goals of the CCSS? How can you build on these practices? For example, what changes to these practices can you enact to bring a strong(er) disciplinary focus to your instruction in the English language arts? What challenges do you anticipate and how can you prepare to address them? What

additional preparation will you seek in your role as educator or administrator to implement a disciplinary perspective within literacy teaching and learning?

3. *Bringing professional development into our educational institutions.* In arguing for balance in this chapter, we underscore the central role of the classroom teacher. Teachers make professional decisions about how to support students with diverse needs, determine specific curriculum and instructional support to achieve particular goals, as well as manage competing demands of the curricula. What professional support would be helpful to you or could you put into place to support achieving balance across the content and context dimensions addressed in this chapter?

RESOURCES FOR FURTHER LEARNING

Books

Brock, C. H., Goatley, V. J., Raphael, T. E., Trost-Shahata, E., & Weber, K. (2014). *Engaging elementary students in disciplinary learning and literacy.* New York: Teachers College Press.

Connelly, F. M., He, M. F., & Phillion, J. (Eds.). (2008). *The Sage handbook of curriculum and instruction.* Thousand Oaks, CA: Sage.

Hoffman, J. V., & Goodman, Y. M. (2009). *Changing literacies for changing times: An historical perspective on the future of reading research, public policy, and classroom practices.* New York: Routledge.

Li, G., & Edwards, P. A. (Eds.). (2010). *Best practices in ELL instruction.* New York: Guilford Press.

Morrow, L. M., Rueda, R., & Lapp, D. (Eds.). (2009). *Handbook of research on literacy and diversity.* New York: Guilford Press.

Websites

www.ciera.org—Center for the Improvement of Early Reading Achievement
www.corestandards.org—Common Core State Standards Initiative
www.SchoolRiseUSA.com—School Rise: Enlightened Teaching

REFERENCES

Adams, M. J. (1990). *Beginning to read: Thinking and learning about print.* Cambridge, MA: MIT Press.

Almasi, J. F. (2003). *Teaching strategic processes in reading.* New York: Guilford Press.

Amendum, S., & Fitzgerald, J. (2010). Reading instruction research for

English-language learners in kindergarten through sixth grade: The last 15 years. In R. Allington & A. McGill-Franzen (Eds.), *Handbook of reading disabilities research* (pp. 373–391). Mahwah, NJ: Erlbaum.

Amendum, S., Li, Y., Hall, L., Fitzgerald, J., Creamer, K., Head-Reeves, D. M., et al. (2009). Which reading lesson instruction characteristics matter for early reading achievement? *Reading Psychology, 30(2)*, 119–147.

Anderson, R. C., Hiebert, E. H., Scott, J. A., & Wilkinson, I. A. G. (1984). *Becoming a nation of readers: The report of the Commission on Reading.* Washington, DC: U.S. Department of Education.

Applebee, A. N., Langer, J. A., Nystrand, M., & Gamoran, A. (2003). Discussion-based approaches to developing understanding: Classroom instruction and student performance in middle and high school English. *American Educational Research Journal, 40(3)*, 685–730.

Au, K. H., & Raphael, T. E. (1998). Curriculum and teaching in literature-based programs. In T. E. Raphael & K. H. Au (Eds.), *Literature-based instruction: Reshaping the curriculum* (pp. 123–148). Norwood, MA: Christopher-Gordon.

Beck, I. L., McKeown, M. G., & Kucan, L. (2002). *Bringing words to life: Robust vocabulary instruction.* New York: Guilford Press.

Beck, I. L., McKeown, M. G., Sandora, C., Kucan, L., & Worthy, J. (1996). Your use of the JSTOR archive indicates your acceptance of JSTOR's terms and conditions of use. *Elementary School Journal, 96(4)*, 385–414.

Blachowicz, C., & Fisher, P. (2009). *Teaching vocabulary in all classrooms* (4th ed.). Columbus, OH: Prentice-Hall.

Cappello, M. (2006). Under construction: Voice and identity development in writing workshop. *Language Arts, 83(6)*, 482–491.

Carlo, M. S., August, D., McLaughlin, B., Snow, C. E., Dressler, C., Lippman, D. N., et al. (2004). Closing the gap: Addressing the vocabulary needs of English-language learners in bilingual and mainstream classrooms. *Reading Research Quarterly, 39(2)*, 188–215.

Cazden, C. B. (2001). *Classroom discourse: The language of teaching and learning.* Portsmouth, NH: Heinemann.

Cervetti, G., Pearson, P. D., Bravo, M. A., & Barber, J. (2006). Reading and writing in the service of inquiry-based science. In R. Douglas, M. Klentschy, & K. Worth (Eds.), *Linking science and literacy in the K–8 classroom* (pp. 221–244). Arlington, VA: National Science Teachers Association Press.

Chall, J. S. (1967). *Learning to read: The great debate.* New York: McGraw-Hill.

Chall, J. S. (1997). *Learning to read: The great debate* (3rd ed.). New York: McGraw-Hill.

Clarke, L. K. (1988). Invented versus traditional spelling in first graders' writings: Effects on learning to spell and read. *Research in the Teaching of English, 22(3)*, 281–309.

Darling-Hammond, L. (1995). Inequality and access to knowledge. In J. A. Banks & C. A. M. Banks (Eds.), *Handbook for research on multicultural education* (pp. 465–483). New York: Macmillan.

Darling-Hammond, L. (2004). What happens to a dream deferred?: The continuing quest for equal educational opportunity. In J. A. Banks & C. A. M.

Banks (Eds.), *Handbook of research on multicultural education* (pp. 607–630). San Francisco: Jossey-Bass.

Duke, N., & Purcell-Gates, V. (2003). Genres at home and at school: Bridging the known to the new. *The Reading Teacher, 57*(1), 30–37.

Dyson, A. H. (2003). *The brothers and sisters learn to write: Popular literacies in childhood and school culture.* New York: Teachers College Press.

Ehri, L. C. (1995). Phases of development in reading words. *Journal of Research in Reading, 18,* 116–125.

Ehri, L. C., Nunes, S., Stahl, S., & Willows, D. (2001). Systematic phonics instruction helps students learn to read: Evidence from the National Reading Panel's meta-analysis. *Review of Educational Research, 71*(3), 393–447.

Florio-Ruane, S., & Raphael, T. E. (2004). Reconsidering our research: Collaboration, complexity, design, and the problem of "scaling up what works." *National Reading Conference Yearbook, 54,* 170–188.

Gaskins, I. W. (2005). *Success with struggling readers: The Benchmark School approach.* New York: Guilford Press.

Gaskins, I. W., Ehri, L. C., Cress, C., O'Hara, C., & Donnelly, K. (1997). Procedures for word learning: Making discoveries about words. *The Reading Teacher, 50*(4), 312–327.

Gee, J. P. (2002). A sociocultural perspective on early literacy development. In S. B. Neuman & D. K. Dickinson (Eds.), *Handbook of early literacy research* (Vol. 1, pp. 30–42). New York: Guilford Press.

Gee, J. P. (2007). *Social linguistics and literacies: Ideology in discourses* (3rd ed). London: Routledge.

Genishi, C., & Dyson, A. (2009). *Children, language, and literacy: Diverse learners in diverse times.* New York: Teachers College Press.

Graesser, A. C., McNamara, D. S., & Kulikowich, J. M. (2011). Coh-metrix providing multilevel analyses of text characteristics. *Educational Researcher, 40*(5), 223–234.

Gray, W. (1948). *On their own in reading: How to give children independence in attacking new words.* Chicago: Scott Foresman.

Hicks, D. (1998). Narrative discourses as inner and outer word. *Language Arts, 75*(1), 28–34.

Howland, J. L., Jonassen, D., & Marra, R. M. (2012). *Meaningful learning with technology* (4th ed.). Boston: Pearson.

International Society for Technology in Education. (2012). National educational technology standards for students. Retrieved September 1, 2013, from *www.iste.org/docs/pdfs/nets-s-standards.pdf?sfvrsn=2.*

Kamil, M. L., Pearson, P. D., Moje, E. B., & Afflerbach, P. (Eds.). (2010). *Handbook of reading research* (Vol. 4). London: Routledge.

Kong, A., & Fitch, E. (2002). Using book club to engage culturally and linguistically diverse learners in reading, writing, and talking about books. *The Reading Teacher, 56*(4), 352–362.

Lyon, G. R. (1997). *Report on learning disabilities research.* (Adapted from testimony by Dr. Reid Lyon before the Committee on Education and the Workforce in the U.S. House of Representatives on July 10, 1997.) Retrieved January 2, 2002, from *www.ldonline.org/ld_indepth/reading/nih_report.html.*

Madda, C. L., Griffo, V. B., Pearson, P. D., & Raphael, T. E. (2011). Balance in comprehensive literacy instruction: Evolving conceptions. *Best Practice in Literacy Instruction, 4*, 37–63.

Magnusson, S. J., & Palincsar, A. S. (2005). Teaching and learning inquiry-based science in the elementary school. In J. Bransford & S. Donovan (Eds.), *Visions of teaching subject matter guided by the principles of how people learn.* Washington, DC: National Academy Press.

McIntyre, E., & Pressley, M. (1996). *Balanced instruction: Strategies and skills in whole language.* Boston: Christopher–Gordon.

Mehan, H. (1979). "What time is it, Denise?": Asking known information questions in classroom discourse. *Theory into Practice, 18*(4), 285–294.

Moje, E. B., Stockdill, D., Kim, K., & Kim, H. (2011). The role of text in disciplinary learning. In M. Kamil, P. D. Pearson, P. Mosenthal, P. Afflerbach, & E. B. Moje (Eds.), *Handbook of reading research* (Vol. 4, pp. 453–486). Mahwah, NJ: Erlbaum/Taylor & Francis.

Murphy, P.K., Wilkinson, I.A.G., Soter, A.O., Hennessey, M. N., & Alexander, J. F. (2009). Examining the effects of classroom discussion on students' comprehension of text: A meta-analysis. *Journal of Educational Psychology, 101*(3), 740–764.

National Center of Educational Statistics. (2011). The Nation's Report Card: Reading 2011 (Publication No. NCES 2012–452). Retrieved September 12, 2013, from *http://nces.ed.gov/nationsreportcard/pdf/dst2011/2012455.pdf.*

National Council of Teachers of English. (2013). The NCTE definition of 21st century literacies. Retrieved August 15, 2013, from *www.ncte.org/positions/statements/21stcentdefinition.*

National Governors Association & Council of Chief State School Officers. (2010). Common Core State Standards Initiative. Retrieved August 17, 2013, from *www.corestandards.org/ELA-Literacy.*

National Reading Panel. (2000). *Teaching children to read: An evidence-based assessment of the scientific research literature on reading and its implications for reading instruction* (National Institute of Health Pub. No. 00-4769). Washington, DC: National Institute of Child Health and Human Development.

No Child Left Behind Act of 2001. Public Law No. 107-110 (2002). Available at *www.ed.gov/policy/elsec/leg/esea02/index.html.*

Nodelman, P. (1992). *The pleasures of children's literature.* New York: Longman.

Nystrand, M. (2006). Research on the role of classroom discourse as it affects reading comprehension. *Research in the Teaching of English, 40*, 392–412.

Palincsar, A. S., & Brown, A. L. (1984). Reciprocal teaching of comprehension-fostering and comprehension-monitoring activities. *Cognition and Instruction, 1*(2), 117–175.

Palincsar, A. S., & Magnusson, S. J. (2001). The interplay of firsthand and text-based investigations to model and support the development of scientific knowledge and reasoning. In S. Carver & D. Klahr (Eds.), *Cognition and instruction: Twenty-five years of progress* (pp. 151–194). Mahwah, NJ: Erlbaum.

Pappas, C., & Pettegrew, B. S. (1998). The role of genre in the psycholinguistic guessing game of reading. *Language Arts, 75*(1), 36–44.

Partnership for 21st Century Skills. (2012). Framework for 21st century learning.

Retrieved September 1, 2013, from *http://p21.org/storage/documents/1.__p21_ framework_2-pager.pdf.*

Pearson, P. D. (2004). The reading wars: The politics of reading research and policy—1988 through 2003. *Educational Policy, 18*(1), 216–252.

Pearson, P. D. (2013). Research foundations for the Common Core State Standards in English language arts. In S. B. Neuman & L. B. Gambrell (Eds.), *Reading instruction in the age of Common Core State Standards* (pp. 237–262). Newark, DE: International Reading Association.

Pearson, P. D., & Fielding, L. (1991). Comprehension instruction. In R. Barr, M. L. Kamil, P. Mosenthal, & P. D. Pearson (Eds.), *Handbook of reading research* (Vol. 2, pp. 819–860). New York: Longman.

Pearson, P. D., & Gallagher, M. C. (1983). The instruction of reading comprehension. *Contemporary Educational Psychology, 8*(3), 317–344.

Pearson, P. D., & Raphael, T. E. (1999). Toward an ecologically balanced literacy curriculum. In L. B. Gambrell, L. M. Morrow, S. B. Neuman, & M. Pressley (Eds.), *Best practices in literacy instru*ction (pp. 22–33). New York: Guilford Press.

Pearson, P. D., & Raphael, T. E. (2003). Toward a more complex view of balance in the literacy curriculum. In L. M. Morrow, L. B. Gambrell, & M. Pressley (Eds.), *Best practices in literacy instruction* (2nd ed., pp. 23–39). New York: Guilford Press.

Pearson, P. D., Raphael, T. E., Benson, V. L., & Madda, C. L. (2007). Balance in comprehensive literacy instruction: Then and now. In L. M. Morrow, L. B. Gambrell, & M. Pressley (Eds.), *Best practices in literacy instruction* (3rd ed., pp. 30–54). New York: Guilford Press.

Pressley, M. (2006). *Reading instruction that works: The case for balanced teaching* (3rd ed.). New York: Guilford Press.

Purcell-Gates, V., Duke, N., & Martineau, J. (2007). Learning to read and write genre-specific text: Roles of authentic experience and explicit teaching. *Reading Research Quarterly, 42*(1), 8–45.

Raphael, T. E., Au, K. A., & Popp, J. (2013). Transformative practices for literacy teaching and learning: A complicated agenda for literacy researchers. In S. Szabo, L. Martin, T. Morrison, L. Haas, & L. Garza-Garcia (Eds.), *Annual Yearbook of the Association of Literacy Educators and Researchers, 35*, 9–32.

Raphael, T. E., Florio-Ruane, S., George, M., Hasty, N. L., & Highfield, K. (2004). *Book club plus: A literacy framework for primary grades.* Littleton, MA: Small Planet Communications.

Reading First Act, 2002—No Child Left Behind Act of 2001. Public Law No. 107-110. (2002). Available at *www.ed.gov/policy/elsec/leg/esea02/index.html.*

Rodgers, E. M. (2004). Interactions that scaffold reading performance. *Journal of Literacy Research, 36*(4), 501–532.

Sandora, C., Beck, I., & McKeown, M. (1999). A comparison of two discussion strategies on students' comprehension and interpretation of complex literature. *Reading Psychology, 20*(3), 177–212.

Schleppegrell, M. J. (2004). *The language of schooling: A functional linguistics perspective.* Mahwah, NJ: Erlbaum.

Schultz, K. (2006). Qualitative research on writing. In C. A. MacArthur, S.

Graham, & J. Fitzgerald (Eds.), *Handbook of writing research* (pp. 357–373). New York: Guilford Press.

Schultz, K. (2009). *Rethinking participation: Listening to silent voices.* New York: Teachers College Press.

Shanahan, T., & Shanahan, C. (2008). Teaching disciplinary literacy to adolescents: Rethinking content-area literacy. *Harvard Educational Review, 78*(1), 40–59.

Snow, C. E., Burns, M. S., & Griffin, P. (Eds.). (1998). *Preventing reading difficulties in young children.* Washington, DC: National Academy Press.

Taylor, B. M., Pearson, P. D., Peterson, D. P., & Rodriguez, M. C. (2003). Reading growth in high-poverty classrooms: The influence of teacher practices that encourage cognitive engagement in literacy learning. *Elementary School Journal, 104*(2), 3–28.

Taylor, B. M., Pearson, P. D., Peterson, D. P., & Rodriguez, M. C. (2005). The CIERA school change framework: An evidenced-based approach to professional development and school reading improvement. *Reading Research Quarterly, 40*(1), 40–69.

CHAPTER 3

Best Practices for Motivating Students to Read

John T. Guthrie

This chapter will:

- Convey the research evidence for the importance of motivation and classroom practices to foster motivation and engagement in reading.
- Relate the Common Core State Standards to motivation and engagement
- Present the prevailing motivations that impact students' reading including interest, confidence, and dedication.
- Portray classroom practices such as assuring relevance, providing choices, generating success, arranging collaborations, setting up thematic units, and emphasizing importance to build valuing.

What Do We Mean by *Motivation*?

Many teachers think of a motivated reader as a student who is having fun while reading. While this is often true, motivation is diverse. What we mean by motivation are the values, beliefs, and behaviors surrounding reading. Some productive values and beliefs may lead to excitement, yet other values may lead to determined hard work. We talk about three powerful motivations that drive students' reading. They operate in school and out of school, and they touch nearly every child. Some students may have all of these motivations and some may have only one. For some students, these motivations appear in the positive form, driving students toward reading. Other motivations are negative and push students away from books. When we talk about reading motivations we refer to (1) interest, (2) dedication, and (3) confidence. An interested student reads because he enjoys it, a dedicated student reads because he believes it is important, and a confident student reads because he or she can do it.

Relating Motivation to the Common Core State Standards

The Common Core State Standards (CCSS) map a new terrain for reading proficiency. This landscape goes beyond previous perspectives that reading was mainly based on word recognition and listening comprehension. To meet the CCSS, students have to grapple with complex text and reason deeply to understand this text. They are expected to make meaningful connections within and across texts. But the CCSS not only presents new cognitive demands. The CCSS raises the bar for higher motivation. Complex texts are challenging. Reasoning with text is daunting. To meet these aims successful students must be motivated. They need the confidence to keep trying in the face of difficulty; they need the reading interests to make their effort worthwhile; they need the social belief that they can give and receive help from peers effectively; and they will have to read more widely and deeply than ever. The CCSS implicitly mandates teachers to motivate.

Key Motivations to Read: Interest, Confidence, Dedication

Interest

When we think of motivation our mind first turns to interest. Motivation is enjoying a book, being excited about an author, or being delighted by new information. Researchers refer to interest as "intrinsic motivation," meaning something we do for its own sake. On a rainy day, we might rather read our favorite book than do anything else. We are not trying to get a reward when falling into a novel.

Motivation also brings to mind the reward for success. Who doesn't like to win a trinket for hitting the target with a dart at the state fair? Who doesn't want to earn serious money for working hard in a career? These are extrinsic rewards because someone gives them to us. We do not give them to ourselves, and these rewards do propel us to put out effort, focus energy, and get up in the morning. Yet extrinsic rewards do not motivate reading achievement in the long term. Students who read only for the reward of money, a grade, or a future job are not the best readers. The reason is that if you read for the reward of a good quiz score, what happens after the quiz is that you stop reading. If the test score is the only thing that matters, it is okay to take shortcuts, not really understand, or cheat. It encourages students to become more interested in the reward than the learning. None of these goals generate long-term achievement. Sometimes a reward, such as candy or early recess, will jump-start a group of students to read in *this* moment for *this* purpose. But if the motivation is not intrinsic, it will not increase achievement in the long term. (Wigfield & Guthrie, 1997).

Confidence

Believing in yourself is more closely linked to achievement than any other motivation throughout school. The reason is that confidence, which is belief in your own capacity, is tied intimately to success. This link occurs for simple, daily reading tasks. A student who reads one page fluently thinks he or she can read the next page in the same book proficiently. The link is also forged for reading in general. A student who reads fluently and understands well is also sure of him- or herself as a reader. In and out of school, people like the things they do well.

Conversely, students who struggle begin to doubt their abilities. They expect to do poorly in reading, writing, and talking about text. The real dilemma is that lower-achieving students often exaggerate their limitations. Believing they are worse than they really are, they stop trying completely. Retreating from all text interactions, they reduce their own opportunity to do what they want to do more than anything—to be a good reader. Their low confidence undermines them even further in a cycle of doubt and failure. By middle school, breaking this cycle is a formidable challenge for teachers.

Dedication

Although intrinsic motivation is desirable, this type of motivation is not always possible in school. There are assignments that are not desirable to a student, yet are part of the curriculum. There are books that do not appeal to some individuals, yet at a given moment in a given school, it is necessary to read them. What motivation enables students to read in this situation? The reason to read in this case is the students' belief that reading is important, and the students' persistence in reading, whatever the assignment. We call this "dedication" and researchers call it "behavioral engagement" (Skinner, Kindermann, & Furrer, 2009).

Every student has the potential to be dedicated. Skills are hard for some students to develop, but dedication is related to will. It is up to a student to decide whether to be dedicated or not. Students are either avoidant, dedicated, or somewhere in between the two. Students who value reading are dedicated in the sense that they devote effort, time, and persistence to their reading. These are the three key signs of dedication in students.

Persisting

One of the most important distinctions between dedicated and avoidant students is that avoidant students do not make the connection between their efforts and the outcomes. A fourth-grade teacher, Taysha Gateau-Barrera, told us that "dedicated students know that they don't improve by mistake. They make continued efforts to try hard and be well organized because they want to be successful in school." Avoidance is a particularly powerful sign because it stops all learning abruptly. If a student wants to read and tries to read well, he or she may learn. If another student refuses to interact with text, all hope for gaining skill, knowledge, or experience from text is dashed.

Valuing Knowledge from Reading

Dedicated students read to attain information that expands their knowledge of their perceived world. Reading is a vehicle to take them to the knowledge they want. Unlike the kids who are reading for practice, these students are reading to know. In our interview study (Guthrie, Klauda, & Morrison, 2010), one middle school student said reading was important because "it informs us because we read about the *Titanic*, and it happened on April 12. It's not boring, it's more like fun because they give you information and stuff about the past." Others remarked, "Reading actually teaches you things and makes you really think about life that's going on this Earth." Another said, "In science [we read about] this bacteria that I didn't know about and it's called hiking disease. When you're hiking and you get some water from the pond, and it's this little bug that if it hits you too long it can make you very sick."

Values for the Future

Dedicated middle school students think about their future. Here is one example: "Well I guess if you are a good student and get a good education then you can go somewhere in life." Another said, "By being a good student you get in good colleges, and that's what I'm trying to do." One claimed, "Being a good reader will help you in the future because like if you got a job, you read a lot, like, even if you didn't like it. If you didn't read in school, you wouldn't know the meaning of it." A fourth said, "I sort of want to be a vet when I get older, so readings in science and learning about chemicals help me. Learning how to write things and all that stuff will help me later on." Belief in the importance of reading fuels dedication to wide and frequent reading (Guthrie, Klauda, & Ho, 2013).

Evidence-Based Practices in Classroom Motivation

Evidence for the Power of Motivation and Engagement Is Expanding Rapidly

Evidence that motivation is vital to achievement is now expressed not in a few studies, but in many reviews and handbooks. The *Handbook of Research on Student Engagement* contains more than 800 pages of literature reviews by more than 55 authors (Christensen, Reschly, & Wiley, 2012). In the *Reading Research Quarterly*, reading motivation and its roles in building proficient and dedicated readers was comprehensively documented (Schiefele, Schaffner, Moller, & Wigfield, 2012). Classroom practices that energize motivated students have been systematically reviewed (Guthrie, Wigfield, & You, 2012). Reading motivation has come of age as in indispensible ingredient of teacher preparation. The International Reading Association's Literacy Research Panel was charged to identify the central issues in reading education. Following extended debate, the panel proclaimed that "IRA's vision . . . is that schools must be transformed into places where students at all levels of schooling are actively engaged in personally and socially meaningful learning and inquiry."

Most teachers and the IRA aim to nurture lifelong readers. Motivation is an end goal. At the same time motivation is a means. It stands as a vital link to attainment of the CCSS. As the research shows, and the Literacy Research Panel has articulated, motivation is imperative in progressing toward 21st-century literacy.

Intervention Research in Reading Motivation

Following a meta-analysis of motivation studies involving text interaction, Guthrie and Humenick (2004) concluded that a variety of positive motivations were increased by experimental conditions related to relevance, content goals, choices, and collaborations. Contributions of these practices to middle school students' reading engagement and proficiency with information text in Concept-Oriented Reading Instruction (CORI) has been demonstrated (Guthrie et al., 2013).

Although interventions are rare in motivation research, a few studies can be identified. Vansteenkiste, Lens, and Deci (2006) compared experimental groups who received either intrinsically motivating goals for reading or extrinsically motivating goals for reading the same text. In the intrinsic condition, students who were obese were asked to read a text on nutrition for their own purposes. In the extrinsic condition, similar students were asked to read the same text for the extrinsic goal of memorizing facts to score well on a test. The students with intrinsic goals recalled the text more fully and reported more involvement in the reading than students with the extrinsic goals (Vansteenkiste et al., 2006). Furthermore, when a brief computer-based instructional unit was embellished with personalized features and inconsequential choices, students showed more intrinsic motivation for the activity than if the program did not have the embellishments (Cordova & Lepper, 1996).

In summary, a variety of correlational, experimental, and qualitative research confirms the positive impacts of motivational practices on students' interest, confidence, and dedication in reading. This body of research affirms the effectiveness of specific practices that will be described next including making reading relevant, affording choices, assuring success, arranging for collaborations, emphasizing the importance of reading, organizing thematic units, and integrating multiple motivation supports during instruction.

From K–12, teachers can and do use motivational practices in their classrooms. Each practice described here has been afforded to students across the age range. For example, kindergartners can be given the choice of which story they want the teacher to read aloud; and secondary students can be given a choice of which two or three subtopics to pursue in a long-term multigenre inquiry. In this chapter, we often provide examples for middle elementary-age students. You can generate how to apply the practice for students of the age, ethnicity, background, ability, and currently existing motivation in your own classroom.

Best Practices in Action

Relevance

Appealing to students' interest is a popular motivational approach. In a book-length treatment on building reading motivation for boys, Brozo (2002) found that boys respond when teachers become aware of their students' personal interests and needs. Some boys may want to read about heroes, adventurers, magicians, or tricksters. If their curiosities can be identified through interest inventories, they may become engrossed in a book or a topic and learn to find satisfaction through literacy. Although this suggestion is useful for book clubs or free reading activities, it is not easily used for instruction with information books and is not easy to relate to curriculum-connected, academic accountabilities that are widespread in middle schools.

Real-World Materials

When it is possible to bring media based in the real world into classroom instruction, the text becomes relevant. For example, in a social studies class studying civil rights, the teacher found a poignant newspaper article. It described an elderly female protester who was on a picket line objecting to racist policies. Although she was a civil rights activist she behaved hypocritically by owning a segregated grocery store. The article captivated students' attention and through their critical analysis of the text and the historical situation, they developed keen insights about the economic and moral pressures surrounding racism (Johnson & Cowles, 2009).

Relevant texts are commonplace in vocational schools or courses. One vocational school's students worked in shops that were run like real jobsites. Students were presented many opportunities to participate in work-related scenarios. As well as providing services to the community such as changing the oil or repairing people's car brakes, they read texts on auto mechanics, construction, electricity, plumbing, graphic design, and computer technology. The school did not have to stretch to provide students with authentic tasks or reading materials. Because of their relevance, the students valued these reading tasks. The vast majority of students dedicated themselves to mastering these texts despite their complexity (Darvin, 2006). Whether they are newspapers, job-related texts, or part of the popular culture, texts from the real world are relevant in themselves.

For elementary school students in urban settings, a team of teachers built relevance by forming linkages between students in the upper elementary grades and adult pen pals in local businesses, nonprofit organizations, and government agencies in the area. Adult pen pals read the same books as the students and wrote questions and commentaries guided by a website. Teachers selected grade level books from five domains: fiction, social studies, biography, folk tales, and science. In a final look at the program, the authors stated:

> A key to active student engagement was the series of literacy activities reflective of real life experiences. Students interacted purposefully above all with their adult pen pals. They read to answer real questions, compose responses to their pen pals' questions, and to build conceptual knowledge. The pen pal context provided powerful motivation for students to read and write strategically and learn skills in order to make their letters as good as possible for the real person to whom they

wrote. For many students the motivation extended beyond the particular book and the particular letter. They were motivated enough to read many other books at their grade level on the same topic or the same genre. (Kelley & Clausen-Grace, 2009, p. 736)

In this case, it was not the real-world materials, but the real-world members of their community and authentic questions that inspired reading dedication.

Poignant Topics

A powerful source of relevant texts for young adolescents is novels or biographies on the theme of freedom. As Bean and Harper (2006) showed, young adolescents are captivated by *The Breadwinner* (2001), a novel about Parvana, a 12-year-old girl living in Afghanistan under Taliban rule. In an act of survival, Parvana poses as a boy selling goods to earn money for her family. She achieves some freedom by making her femininity invisible, but she loses some of her ethnic identity. Reading this book, students became immersed in her loses of religious identity as she gained economic freedoms. Many of them discovered they had paid a price for freedoms as well. Relevance of this text to their lives generated dedicated reading.

The quickest way to locate topics relevant to students' interests is to enable them to select a topic for project-based activities. In one example, students in an upper elementary school class selected topics on social justice, which was new to them. In the media center and on the Internet they found books and articles on injustices in housing, employment, and access to healthcare. Reading these multiple self-selected texts, students composed five-panel comic strips using computer software to explain their particular topic. They read deeply and wrote sharply to portray and explain the injustice they unearthed.

In a study at the elementary school level, students volunteered that their personal interests were the main factor that made them want to read a narrative text. In asking why they chose certain books, students replied:

- "I like dolphins. I think they are cool because they live in the ocean and I like oceans."
- "It was important because I like different cultures."
- "Because it was about an Indian and I am interested in Indians."

Identifying students' topical interests through a conversation or a questionnaire can enable teachers to heighten the relevance of books and entice students into dedicated reading.

Teachers Create Relevance

It is often impossible to locate real-world materials. On many occasions, the teacher needs to create relevance by designing events that enable students to see connections of text to themselves. For example, a middle school class was reading *Night* by Elie Wiesel, an account of the author's experiences during the Holocaust. Since it took place on another continent in an earlier generation, the scene in which Jewish individuals were herded like cattle into a railroad car did not engage the students. To render the scene more personal, the teacher made a large rectangle of red tape on the classroom floor. He asked the class to crowd into this limited space. After students' giggling and complaining subsided, the teacher explained that this is how Jews stood for days at a time on a moving train. Following this weak simulation, students began to ask about the people and their circumstances, and their reading was reignited.

A teacher-guided event that is relevance-generating consists of enabling students to create their own questions about text. In one social studies class, students wrote their questions about the freedoms of religion, speech, assembly, petition, and the press. Students were expected to learn about the five basic freedoms embodied in the Constitution. They read for definitions, historical origins, and limits of all these freedoms and prepared a 6- to 8-minute oral report. Their report centered on a single person, event, battle, or place during the Civil War that was connected to one of these freedoms. By enabling students to be guided by their own questions, as well as the curriculum framework, students bring their knowledge, interests, and idiosyncrasies into their reading activities. As a consequence, their willingness to spend time and effort grows and their products display the benefits of dedicated reading.

For students at many ages, the teacher may set up situations involving a discrepant event, a reality that conflicts with what the students might expect to see. For example, as Duke, Purcell-Gates, Hall, and Tower (2006) reported in a study on light, one teacher set up a prism on the overhead projector while her class was out of the room. This caused rainbows to appear on the ceiling. When the students returned there were many oohs and aahs and a rush of questions about how the rainbow effects occurred. The teacher led students to find and read information text on light to help them answer their own questions. Such discrepant events may be created for literature and fiction as well. If students are asked to predict the outcome of a chapter or what a character will do in a scene, the teacher can create a discrepancy between the students' expectations and the events in the book. Exploring and explaining the discrepancies between students' predictions and the actual events can lead to teachable moments that deepen students' comprehension and enhance their reading dedication.

Relationships of teachers and students in elementary school can often be built around finding the right books for students. If teachers use an interest inventory to determine topics that students enjoy, they can often find great books based on this information. Highlighting these books in book talks, book commercials, or other means helps build students' faith in teachers' ability to find relevant materials for them. In teacher–student conferences during independent reading, teachers can help students find and stick with a good book. As students gain trust in the teacher as an ally in finding and enjoying books, students' all-important time spent in reading grows.

Relevance is an instructional practice central to CORI activities (Guthrie et al., 2013). In this context, "relevance" refers to linking books and reading activities to the students' personal experiences. These connections to "me" as a person are especially poignant for adolescents who are centered on thinking about who they are. Such links to self can be tied to long-term history, such as students' cultural experiences in their ethnic group, to a personal interest such as skateboarding, or to a recent personal experience. In CORI for middle school students, we give context through videos related to the conceptual theme. For example, in week 1, we present a video on predation in which a cheetah captures a gazelle on the Serengeti Plain. After watching the 3-minute video, students make observations about it, draw inferences, and make connections between the events. The students then read a paragraph of text to learn more about predation in cheetahs and other animals. They draw inferences from the text and share their observations with peers.

In this 20-minute activity, reading informational text is made relevant by connecting it to a vivid personal encounter with the phenomenon through video. Needless to say, the color, audio effects, and drama rivet the students' attention and arouse their interest. Asking students to perform the processes with the video that we later ask them to perform with the text brings a linkage not only in content, but in the process of learning across the media. Thus, relevance is formed through the immediacy of experience with video and text. It is relevance situated in a disciplinary domain and information texts on the subject matter. We believe that this level of relevancy is effective as a starting point for learning the relevance of other texts on other topics in the future.

When students view a video on predation in the Serengeti the experience is effortless, eye-opening, and interesting. It activates what they already know and arouses natural curiosities. Watching the video is intrinsically motivating, which means that students will do it for their own enjoyment. Students often ask to see the video many times. Linking a readable trade book to this interesting event projects the qualities of the video enjoyment into the text interaction. For this moment, in this situation, reading becomes interesting. Thus, the students' interest in reading is scaffolded by creating situated interest in an extremely concrete situation. Then we extrapolate outward from it. Students are weaned from the relevance-generating event and learn to find interest in other texts and other topics.

Choices

The most widespread recommendation for motivation is providing choices. In the classroom, students are often thrilled to have a choice in their reading. They rise to it with enthusiasm, at least temporarily. A theoretical framework for choice in the classroom is self-determination theory (Vansteenkiste et al., 2006), which argues that students' development of autonomy, or being in charge of their lives, is central to their academic achievement and emotional adjustment. After reviewing Self-Determination Theory, Reed, Schallert, Beth, and Woodruff (2004) stated, "When it comes to addressing specifically the motivational processes of adolescents in literacy-focused classrooms, the single, most powerful suggestion we can make is to encourage teachers to develop learning environments that are autonomy-supportive" (p. 274).

"Autonomy support" in this context refers to enabling students to become self-directing and self-controlling of their literacy and academic work. Reeve (1996) explained autonomy support in the classroom in a book-length treatment entitled *Motivating Others: Nurturing Inner Motivational Resources.* As Reeve said:

> Autonomy support refers to the amount of freedom a teacher gives a student so the student can connect his or her behavior to personal goals, interests, and values. The opposite of autonomy support is coercion or being controlled. Teacher autonomy support expresses itself when teachers allow students choices, respect their agendas, and provide learning activities that are relevant to personal goals and interests. (p. 206)

Among the proposals for instructional practices described in this section, autonomy support may enjoy the largest amount of empirical verification, which has been reviewed in Guthrie and Humenick (2004).

Providing choice is a motivational support system in CORI for middle school that enables students to develop self-direction in the classroom. Teachers provide the following kinds of choices within the 6-week CORI program: self-selection of books or sections of books, student input into topics or sequence of topics, student suggestions for strategy use for comprehension, options for demonstrating learning from text, and selecting partners for teams. As these examples show, we are not affording students open opportunity to take complete charge of everything they do for a week in reading/language arts. These are mini-choices during literacy lessons. Yet as small as these choices may appear, they enable students to feel a stronger sense of investment and to commit larger amounts of effort to their reading work. We have given many examples of the roles and ranges of choices that are possible in middle school elsewhere (McRae & Guthrie, 2009).

On a daily basis effective teachers can give mini-choices. They empower students to increase their investment in learning. When appropriate, in every lesson have students do at least one of the following:

1. Select a story.
2. Select a page to read.
3. Select sentences to explain.
4. Identify a goal for the day.
5. Choose three of five questions to answer.
6. Write questions for a partner exchange.

Success

Support for students' self-efficacy in reading and other subjects is crucial. Without the belief in themselves, students in the upper elementary and middle school grades often retreat from books. As portrayed by Schunk and Zimmerman (2007), several explicit teaching practices increase students' self-efficacy. The self-efficacy-fostering framework consists of providing students' process goals. These are steps for performing reading tasks successfully. Teachers provide feedback for success in the process goals rather than feedback for the students' products or outcomes. That is, teachers give specific direction to students about the effectiveness of their strategy for performing work. They help students set realistic goals for reading. Also beneficial to students' self-efficacy is their perception of coherence in the texts and tasks of instruction. When students can identify the links across contents of reading, and perceive themes in the substance of their reading materials, they gain a belief that they can succeed in reading and writing about text (Guthrie et al., 2013).

To afford your students practices that boost success, assure that at least one of the following is very prominent in every lesson:

1. Text matched to students' reading levels
2. Frequent feedback for reading
3. Authentic reading merged with skills

4. Multiple opportunities for reading
5. Sharing competency with peers
6. Student goal setting
7. Rewarding effort

Collaboration

Collaboration is a central process in CORI. Teachers implementing collaboration are initiating the following activities: (1) reading with partners or in small groups, (2) exchanging ideas and sharing expertise, (3) student-led discussion groups (4) book talks, (5) team projects such as a poster-making activity, and (6) peer feedback. As with the other motivation supports, these activities are contextualized within the conceptual theme and books on the theme. For example, partners may be given 5 minutes to discuss the inferences they generated from reading three pages of text on the conceptual question of the day. In each 90-minute lesson, teachers arrange for students to work in whole-class, partnerships, small-team interactions, and individually. The structure for small-team interaction is collaborative reasoning, based on research from Chinn, Anderson, and Waggoner (2001). In this interactive structure, students make claims about the text, add to each other's interpretations, raise clarifying questions, and attempt to synthesize their own brainstorming. Shown to impact higher order thinking about text, collaborative reasoning is not merely a social break from learning or an open discussion, but a scaffolded process of cumulative contributions based on reading about a topic. The outcome is a collective understanding about text.

Collaboration can occur in every lesson. It may be a broad plan or a brief event. Each lesson can include one of the following:

1. Partners read aloud together
2. Partners exchange questions to answer over text
3. Team summarizes a chapter
4. Literature circles
5. Collaborative reasoning
6. Organize a jigsaw
7. Set up peer editing about text

Emphasizing Importance

Too many students avoid reading because they believe it is not important to them now or in the future. They do not value reading and do not think it will benefit them. To address this dilemma, we believe in providing students with a concrete experience rather than an abstract principle.

Rather than attempting a global strategy of persuading students that reading will enable them to go to college or enter a career of their choice, we attempt to situate the benefit of literacy in a concrete situation. For example, have students view a video of plant–animal relationships. Then have them read a related text and share their new learning with a partner. After the lesson, ask the question, "What were your sources of new learning today?" Students will respond by saying "the video" or "my partner" or "my writing." Soon they will discover that it was the text that enabled them to gain knowledge most effectively on this topic on this day. This recognition is an awareness of the value of reading. It often comes as a surprise to the students. The teacher may also ask how a choice made during the lesson benefitted them. Students' awareness of how well they enjoyed the choice, and how it helped them focus cognitively, raises their estimate of the value of reading.

Valuing literacy is the motivational process we attempt to facilitate with the practice of emphasizing importance. When the students begin to reflect on how the text helped them speak effectively with their team or write effectively, they begin to view the book reading process as beneficial in a new way. Obviously, a single event is limited to one topic in one day in one classroom. This cannot create a lifelong value. However, it is a starting point for the journey of finding literacy to be important. It is a first step in working hard because reading is valuable. If 5 minutes of concentrated effort paid off in today's activity, the ethic of hard work in reading activities can be acquired and applied to broader reaches of schooling.

For each lesson you can ask students to show the importance of reading. Have them:

1. Identify the portion of text they used to answer a question.
2. Point to a text that was most informative about a character in literature.
3. Identify a text that enabled them to explain a concept in information text.
4. Compare what they learned from a text versus what they learned from a video on the topic.
5. Contrast the content they learned from reading, writing, or discussing in a lesson.
6. Explain how the content of a text could help them in an out-of-school situation.

Thematic Units

Thematic units can be taught on many topics. First, you begin with a main theme, or "big idea." Next, identify supporting concepts to explain the big idea. Then, identify texts that contain the concepts. Texts should also afford you the opportunities to teach reading strategies, such as concept mapping. In one unit of CORI for grade 7, the theme is the diversity of plants and animals in community interactions. The superordinate idea of the unit is *symbiosis*, including such forms as mutualism and parasitism. To accentuate the conceptual theme, teachers give students a big question for each week, as well as daily questions related to the week's big question. This does not preclude student questioning, but sets a frame for the topic. In Week 1, the following four questions were presented on the first 4 days of instruction:

1. What are the characteristics of an ecosystem?
2. How does predation contribute to balance in an ecosystem?
3. How do different species of animals rely on their environment for feeding?
4. In what ways do animals adapt to their environment for survival?

To provide resources for literacy in this theme all books are unified around it for the 6 weeks. Texts for whole-class instruction, individual guided reading, and individual books for group projects are selected to be theme-relevant. Strategies that are taught for comprehension, including summarizing and concept mapping, are placed within the context of the conceptual theme. For example, student summaries represent their reading related to a particular question on a given day. Motivation supports, such as choice, are provided in the context of thematic learning. For example, the teacher may provide a choice for which chapter in a selected book to read on a given day. Students make their selection based on their view of what will enable them to learn about the question of the day and to discuss it effectively with a peer. Thus, motivational support of choice is not global, but is framed by the content question of the day and undergirded by the content learning of yesterday.

Build in the following qualities to your thematic units:

1. Instructional units have conceptual complexity and duration.
2. Students learn big ideas of survival, war and peace, discovery, oppression.
3. Topics persist over days and weeks.
4. Students write concept maps of pages, chapters, books, and units.
5. Connect diverse genre (stories, nonfiction, poems) to each other.
6. Have overarching guiding questions that link texts.

Teacher Support

Vital to the classroom is the quality of teacher–student relationships. When teachers emphasize positive interpersonal relationships, student motivation increases. Believing that their teachers think they are important, students participate more socially in the classroom (Furrer & Skinner, 2003). According to both teachers and students, the quality of teacher–student relationships enhances engagement (Decker, Dona, & Christenson, 2007). For African American students in particular, collaborative learning environments enhance students' recall of stories and their desire to participate in similar activities in the future (Dill & Boykin, 2000).

In this line of research, teacher support represents student-centeredness of instruction. It contrasts with a domineering or controlling approach by the teacher. Teacher support refers to students' perceptions of teacher involvement (warmth, knowledge, and dependability), and classroom structure (clarity of goals and expectations) (Skinner et al., 2009). Furrer and Skinner (2003) found that teacher support was associated with increases in students' engagement in classroom activities from fall to spring for students in grades 4 to 7. Students' engagement referred to their self-reported effort, attention, and persistence while participating in classroom learning activities. In contrast, students' behavioral disaffection decreased from fall to spring as a consequence of teacher support. This decrease consisted of a reduction in students' lack of effort or withdrawal from learning activities. Although teacher support is not a specific practice, but rather a broad attribute that may be associated with a number of specific practices such as assuring success, providing relevance, offering choices, arranging collaborations, and providing themes for learning, it was strongly associated with students' increases in behavioral engagement and decreases in behavioral disaffection.

The findings on the favorable effects of emotional support range from grade 1 (Hamre & Pianta, 2005) to college classrooms (Filaka & Sheldon, 2008). For example, teacher support was found to increase competence in reading words and passages in the middle of first grade, especially for at-risk students. In fact, the benefits of emotional support were stronger than the benefits of excellent pedagogy for cognitive learning in beginning reading (Hamre & Pianta, 2005).

Social relationships and teacher support in the classroom are pivotal in middle schools. In overviewing the literature on social motivation, Juvonen (2007) stated:

> Of school-based social relationships, teacher support is probably the most salient. When students feel supported and respected by their teachers they are presumed to comply with the expectations and norms set by instructors and engage in the behaviors endorsed by these authority figures. When students lack a bond or do not get along with a teacher, students are presumed to disengage themselves from school-related activities and the institution. (p. 200)

Juvonen continues: "Perceptions of positive teacher regard at seventh grade have been shown to predict improved academic competence, mental health, and higher academic values in eighth grade" (p. 200). Likewise, lack of sense of belonging in school frequently predicts adolescents' dropout rates (Finn & Rock, 1997).

Teacher caring is central to teacher support (Wentzel, 2009). Students who say "The teacher cares about me" are higher achievers than those who do not feel that the teacher cares. Teachers can learn the practices we have presented, which are ways of expressing that they care about students.

Integration of Motivational Practices

It is entirely possible to integrate multiple motivation practices into a coherent teaching unit. Following are two examples, one at the elementary level and one at the primary level. We and our colleagues have examined how CORI influences third-, fourth-, fifth-, and seventh-grade students' reading comprehension and engagement in reading (Guthrie et al., 2004). CORI includes the classroom practices of providing relevance, choices, collaboration, leveled texts, and thematic units. This cluster of practices is designed to increase intrinsic motivation, self-efficacy, social motivation, and valuing for reading (Guthrie, Wigfield, & Perencevich, 2004). Guthrie, McRae, and Klauda (2007) performed a meta-analysis of CORI's effects across 11 experiments with 75 effect sizes. CORI was found to surpass comparison treatments in increasing students' competence according to standardized tests of reading comprehension, 2-day reading and writing tasks, passage comprehension, reading fluency, and word recognition. CORI also fostered students' reading motivation and engagement in reading. This confirms the theory that an integrated cluster of motivational practices over extended time can increase students' performance on educationally significant measures of reading comprehension. The bulk of the evidence shows that CORI impacted reading comprehension outcomes, although one study also showed that this instructional effect was mediated by behavioral engagement (Wigfield et al., 2008; see further discussion below). Furthermore, these effects were confirmed by investigators who showed that an intervention that added motivational supports to instruction in self-regulation increased students' self-regulated reading more effectively than instruction that did not include motivational practices (Souvignier & Mokhlesgerami, 2006).

Integration is also shown to be effective at the primary level. For example, in Hamre and Pianta's (2005) study of reading instruction in kindergarten, classroom quality was assessed in terms of teachers' provision of effective instruction while building warm, emotional connections with students, which included support for students' self-regulation, a balance of activities for children's diverse skill levels, and sensitivity to students' interests. Classrooms with high global quality induced high levels of student behavioral engagement, which consisted of attending to tasks, completing reading activities, following rules, persisting in the face of difficulty, and exercising control. Students with high behavioral engagement showed higher gains in reading competencies than students with lower behavioral engagement and lower global quality of instruction (Ponitz, Rimm-Kaufman, Grimm, & Curby, 2009). What motivating teachers were doing was being responsive to students' interests (reading a story the students preferred), providing abundant praise, giving students time to complete their work, showing their appreciation for individual students, and expressing confidence in students' ability to learn. At the same time, motivating teachers were not too teacher-centered, authoritative, or controlling.

Instructional Practices That May Decrease Motivation

Some instructional practices are demotivating for students. For example, negative feedback from teachers may be devaluing for students. When teachers consistently scold or make students feel badly for having the wrong answers, students respond by devaluing academic work, as indicated by their expressions that they do not care about learning or grades (Strambler & Weinstein, 2010). In addition, students who experience no choices or limited choices in reading in language arts or science classes show losses of intrinsic motivation for reading. Likewise, when books are extremely difficult to read, students report declines in self-efficacy for reading. When books are irrelevant, as indicated by students' failure to connect the content to their prior knowledge or their life experiences, they report low levels of interest or dedication to reading (Mason-Signh & Guthrie, 2012).

What this evidence shows is that classroom practices are swords that cut in two directions. Affirming practices may foster motivational growth. But undermining practices, such as negative feedback, controlling instruction, and irrelevance, may generate losses in motivation. These findings are consistent with the correlational findings reported by Assor, Kaplan, and Roth (2002) and reciprocal relationships between classroom instruction and student motivations found by Skinner and Belmont (1993). In sum, almost all teaching practices have either positive or negative effects on motivation. Effective teachers can use and sustain the positive ones outlined in this chapter.

Concluding Reflections

Every teacher is a motivator. Teachers empower students to become active with print. Otherwise reading never happens. On the other side of the coin, motivating students to their fullest is rare. Not often do teachers put motivation first. But when they do, students become interested, confident, and dedicated. And almost every teacher is rewarded by having motivated readers.

ENGAGEMENT ACTIVITIES

1. *Reflection.* To grapple with the ideas in this chapter, first make an appraisal of where you are. Many teachers support motivation— some more than others. Where are you? For each motivational practice, such as providing relevance, ask the following questions. You might do it alone or in a grade-level school team. Take a few notes on each question and share your perceptions. Almost certainly, you, especially along with your colleagues, can take steps forward.

   a. Do I do this practice already?
   b. How often do I do this?
   c. When do I do this?
   d. How well does it work?
   e. How can I do this more?
   f. How can I do this better?
   g. How can I connect this practice to my teaching more deeply?

2. *Appraisal.* To understand how your students experience your classroom, ask them. You can give a brief questionnaire with statements such as "The teacher relates the reading to my interests." You may be surprised at what they say. Some questionnaires for students and teachers are available in the appendix of *Engaging Adolescents in Reading* (Guthrie, 2008). They are easily used or adapted for students in grades 3 to 12.

3. *Application.* Select a lesson coming up in the next week. Ask yourself, "What choice am I going to give during the lesson?" Give that small choice. Then compare how the lesson went with a lesson where you did not give any choice. How did the students respond? Do this application for each motivational practice including relevance and so on. Then enrich your lessons by giving two motivation supports, say, choice and relevance, in the

same lesson. How do your students respond, and how can you improve those supports? Your students will become a bit more dedicated to reading. Build momentum.

REFERENCES

Assor, A., Kaplan, H., & Roth, G. (2002). Choice is good, but relevance is excellent: Autonomy-enhancing and suppressing teacher behaviours predicting students' engagement in schoolwork. *British Journal of Educational Psychology, 72,* 261–278.

Bean, T. W., & Harper, H. J. (2006). Exploring notions of freedom in and through young adult literature. *Journal of Adolescent and Adult Literacy, 50,* 96–104.

Brozo, W. G. (2002). *To be a boy, to be a reader: Engaging teen and preteen boys in active literacy.* Newark, DE: International Reading Association.

Chinn, C. A., Anderson, R. C., & Waggoner, M. A. (2001). Patterns of discourse in two kinds of literature discussion. *Reading Research Quarterly, 36,* 378–411.

Christensen, S., Reschly, A., & Wylie, C. (Eds.). (2012). *Handbook of research on student engagement.* New York: Springer Science.

Cordova, D. I., & Lepper, M. R. (1996). Intrinsic motivation and the process of learning: Beneficial effects of contextualization, personalization, and choice. *Journal of Educational Psychology, 88,* 715–730.

Darvin, J. (2006). "Real-world cognition doesn't end when the bell rings": Literacy instruction derived from situated cognition research. *Journal of Adolescent and Adult Literacy, 49,* 10–18.

Decker, D. M., Dona, D. P., & Christenson, S. L. (2007). Behaviorally at-risk African American students: The importance of student–teacher relationships for student outcomes. *Journal of School Psychology, 45,* 83–109.

Dill, E. M., & Boykin, A. W. (2000). The comparative influence of individual, peer tutoring, and communal learning contexts on the text recall of African American children. *Journal of Black Psychology* [Special issue: African American culture and identity: Research directions for the new millennium], *26,* 65–78.

Duke, N. K., Purcell-Gates, V., Hall, L. A., & Tower, C. (2006). Authentic literacy activities for developing comprehension and writing. *The Reading Teacher, 60,* 344–355.

Ellis, D. (2001). *The breadwinner.* Toronto: Groundwood Books.

Filaka, V. F., & Sheldon, K. M. (2008). Teacher support, student motivation, student need satisfaction, and college teacher course evaluations: Testing a sequential path model. *Educational Psychology, 28,* 711–724.

Finn, J. D., & Rock, D. A. (1997). Academic success among students at risk for school failure. *Journal of Applied Psychology, 82,* 221–234.

Furrer, C., & Skinner, E. (2003). Sense of relatedness as a factor in children's academic engagement and performance. *Journal of Educational Psychology, 95,* 148–162.

Guthrie, J. T. (Ed.). (2008). *Engaging adolescents in reading.* Thousand Oaks, CA: Corwin Press.

Guthrie, J. T., & Humenick, N. M. (2004). Motivating students to read: Evidence for classroom practices that increase reading motivation and achievement. In P. McCardle & V. Chhabra (Eds.), *The voice of evidence in reading research* (pp. 329–354). Baltimore: Brookes.

Guthrie, J. T., Klauda, S. L., & Ho, A. (2013). Modeling the relationships among reading instruction, motivation, engagement, and achievement for adolescents. *Reading Research Quarterly, 48,* 9–26.

Guthrie, J. T., Klauda, S. L., & Morrison, D. A. (2010). Motivation, achievement, and classroom contexts for information book reading. In J. T. Guthrie, A. Wigfield, & S. L. Klauda (Eds.), *Adolescents' engagement in academic literacy.* Retrieved July 2, 2014, from *http://corilearning.com/research-publications/2012_adolescents_engagement_ebook.pdf.*

Guthrie, J. T., McRae, A., & Klauda, S. L. (2007). Contributions of Concept-Oriented Reading Instruction to knowledge about interventions for motivations in reading. *Educational Psychologist, 42,* 237–250.

Guthrie, J. T., Wigfield, A., & Perencevich, K. C. (Eds.). (2004). *Motivating reading comprehension: Concept-oriented reading instruction.* Mahwah, NJ: Erlbaum.

Guthrie, J. T., Wigfield, A., & You, W. (2012). Instructional contexts for engagement and achievement in reading. In S. Christensen, A. Reschly, & C. Wylie (Eds.), *Handbook of research on student engagement* (pp. 601–634). New York: Springer Science.

Hamre, B. K., & Pianta, R. C. (2005). Can instructional and emotional support in the first-grade classroom make a difference for children at risk of school failure? *Child Development, 76,* 949–967.

Johnson, A. S., & Cowles, L. (2009). Orlonia's "literacy-in-persons": Expanding notions of literacy through biography and history. *Journal of Adolescent and Adult Literacy, 52,* 410–420.

Juvonen, J. (2007). Reforming middle schools: Focus on continuity, social connectedness, and engagement. *Educational Psychologist, 42,* 197–208.

Kelley, M. J., & Clausen-Grace, N. (2009). Facilitating engagement by differentiating independent reading. *The Reading Teacher, 63,* 313–318.

Mason-Singh, A., & Guthrie, J. (2012). *Situated reading motivations as mediators between perceptions of reading instruction and general reading motivations.* Paper presented at the annual convention of the American Education Research Association, University of Maryland, College Park.

McRae, A., & Guthrie, J. T. (2009). Beyond opportunity: Promoting reasons for reading. In E. H. Hiebert (Ed.), *Reading more, reading better: Are American students reading enough of the right stuff?* Newark, DE: International Reading Association.

Ponitz, C. C., Rimm-Kaufman, S. E., Grimm, K. J., & Curby, T. W. (2009). Kindergarten classroom quality, behavioral engagement, and reading achievement. *School Psychology Review, 38,* 102–120.

Reed, J. H., Schallert, D. L., Beth, A. D., & Woodruff, A. L. (2004). Motivated reader, engaged writer: The role of motivation in the literate acts of adolescents. In T. L. Jetton & J. A. Dole (Eds.), *Adolescent literacy research and practice* (pp. 251–282). New York: Guilford Press.

Reeve, J. (1996). *Motivating others: Nurturing inner motivational resources.* Boston: Allyn & Bacon.

Schiefele, U., Schaffner, E., Moller, J., & Wigfield, A. (2012). Dimensions of reading motivation and their relation to reading behavior and competence. *Reading Research Quarterly, 47,* 427–463.

Schunk, D. H., & Zimmerman, B. J. (2007). Influencing children's self efficacy and self-regulation of reading and writing through modeling. *Reading and Writing Quarterly: Overcoming Learning Difficulties, 23,* 7–25.

Skinner, E. A., & Belmont, M. J. (1993). Motivation in the classroom: Reciprocal effects of teacher behavior and student engagement across the school year. *Journal of Educational Psychology, 85,* 571–558.

Skinner, E. A., Kindermann, T. A., & Furrer, C. J. (2009). A motivational perspective on engagement and disaffection: Conceptualization and assessment of children's behavioral and emotional participation in academic activities in the classroom. *Educational and Psychological Measurement, 69,* 493–525.

Souvignier, E., & Mokhlesgerami, J. (2006). Using self-regulation as a framework for implementing strategy instruction to foster reading comprehension. *Learning and Instruction, 16,* 57–71.

Strambler, M. J., & Weinstein, R. S. (2010). Psychological disengagement in elementary school among ethnic minority students. *Journal of Applied Developmental Psychology, 31,* 155–165.

Vansteenkiste, M., Lens, W., & Deci, E. L. (2006). Intrinsic versus extrinsic goal contents in self-determination theory: Another look at the quality of academic motivation. *Educational Psychologist, 41,* 19–31.

Wentzel, K. R. (2009). Students' relationships with teachers as motivational contexts. In K. R. Wentzel & A. Wigfield (Eds.), *Handbook of motivation at school* (pp. 301–322). New York: Routledge/Taylor & Francis Group.

Wiesel, E. (1960). *Night.* New York: Bantam Books.

Wigfield, A., & Guthrie, J. T. (1997). Relations of children's motivation for reading to the amount and breadth of their reading. *Journal of Educational Psychology, 89,* 420–432.

Wigfield, A., Guthrie, J. T., Perencevich, K. C., Taboada, A., Klauda, S. L., McRae, A., et al. (2008). Role of reading engagement in mediating effects of reading comprehension. *Psychology in the Schools, 45,* 432–445.

PART II

BEST PRACTICES FOR ALL STUDENTS

CHAPTER 4

Best Practices in Early Literacy

Preschool, Kindergarten, and First Grade

Diane H. Tracey
Lesley Mandel Morrow

This chapter will:

- Provide an overview of the primary theories underlying best practices in early literacy education.
- Present a brief summary of the major governmental initiatives, including the Common Core State Standards for English language arts that have significantly affected early literacy education in the United States.
- Offer a research synthesis and research-based instructional strategies related to early literacy best practices.
- Examine special issues related to early literacy instruction including digital literacies, English language learners, and response to intervention.
- Illustrate best practices in early literacy through the presentation of a case study embedded with connections to the Common Core State Standards for English language arts.

Evidence-Based Best Practices: A Research Synthesis

There has been much controversy regarding best practices for early literacy instruction. We often question how much of young children's education should be child-centered versus how much should be curriculum-based. We wonder if our teaching methods should be formal and explicit, or play- and discovery-oriented. We ponder how to make optimal use of technology in early childhood classrooms. We want to know how to best help children who are learning English as a second language, and others for whom literacy learning seems unusually challenging. To answer these questions, we share theory, policy, and research that have helped to shape best practices in early literacy education. Then, we conclude with a case study of an exemplary early childhood classroom and ideas for engagement activities.

Theoretical Influences

Historically, many theorists have addressed early childhood learning from child-centered theoretical perspectives. Child-centered approaches suggest that it is best to provide children with motivating opportunities that stimulate exploration in playful environments. Rousseau (1712–1778) believed that children's learning evolved naturally as a result of their innate curiosity. Pestalozzi (1746–1827) also believed in natural learning, but felt that children needed adult facilitation to enhance their development. Froebel (1782–1852) emphasized the importance of play as a vehicle for learning, and coined the term *kindergarten*, which literally means "children's garden." Piaget (1896–1980) emphasized that children acquire knowledge by interacting with objects and experiences, and subsequently change and reorganize their knowledge in response to those objects and experiences (Piaget & Inhelder, 1969). Dewey's (1916) philosophy of early childhood education led to the concept of a child-centered curriculum built around the interests of children and a problem-based learning approach.

In contrast to child-centered theoretical approaches, Vygotsky (1978, 1986) put forth the theory of social constructivism. Vygotsky recognized that children learn as a result of their social interactions with others. He particularly emphasized the idea that children learn from interacting with others who are more developed than they are—linguistically, cognitively, socially, and emotionally.

Skills-based instructional models involve the systematic explicit teaching of literacy. Skills-based instruction has its roots in *behaviorism* that suggests complex cognitive activities, such as reading and writing, can be broken down into their composite skills that are taught one at a time (Tracey & Morrow, 2012). Direct reading instruction is a skills-based approach. In direct instruction, teachers explicitly focus students' attention on specific, isolated reading skills and provide information to students about those topics. Reading readiness is another kind of skills-based instruction. In a reading readiness approach, educators focus on facilitating reading development through the direct instruction of skills identified as prerequisites for reading, such as letter naming.

The term *emergent literacy* refers to the period in a child's life between birth and the time when the child can read and write conventionally, usually at about the third-grade level. In emergent literacy theory, literacy is viewed as beginning at birth and growing through authentic learning experiences at home and in school. Emergent literacy theory is based on the beliefs that children's development in the areas of listening, speaking, reading, and writing are all interrelated, and that the strengthening of any one of these four areas will have positive effects on the others.

Policy Influences

In addition to theoretical influences, governmental policies have shaped early literacy instructional practices. In 1965, President Johnson authorized the first federal policy directed at preschool education by creating Head Start. The goal of the initiative was to prepare low-income children to become ready for kindergarten. Head Start is still in operation today and grants are made directly to public and private nonprofit organizations. Consistent with a child-centered model of early literacy education, Head Start services address children's cognitive, physical, emotional, and social needs.

In 1997, Congress requested that the National Institute of Child Health and Human Development (NICHD) establish the National Reading Panel (NRP) to determine the most effective practices for teaching reading. Made up of a group of distinguished scholars, the panel reviewed scientifically based reading research and then published *The National Reading Panel Report: Teaching Children to Read* (NICHD, 2000). From the research, five key areas were identified as essential for effective reading instruction: (1) phonemic awareness, (2) phonics, (3) vocabulary, (4) comprehension, and (5) fluency. The five key areas identified by the NRP then became central to the *Reading First* and *Early Reading First* initiatives. These programs provided competitively based, large grants to at-risk school districts that revised their language arts curricula to address the five key areas identified by the NRP.

Another influential policy group has been the National Early Literacy Panel (NELP). The NELP was charged with conducting a synthesis of the scientific research specifically related to early literacy development from birth through kindergarten. The variables identified as essential to early literacy success include (1) expressive and receptive oral language development, (2) knowledge of the alphabetic code, (3) phonological and phonemic awareness, (4) use of invented spelling, (5) print knowledge including environmental print, and (6) other skills such as rapid naming of letters and numbers, visual memory, and visual perceptual abilities (McGill-Frazen, 2010).

The recent, widespread adoption of the Common Core State Standards (CCSS) has also significantly affected the landscape of education in the United States. At the time of writing the present chapter, 45 states, the District of Columbia, and four territories of the United States have all adopted the CCSS. Embedded within the K–12 CCSS are the English language arts (ELA) standards for kindergarten and first-grade students. The ELA standards for kindergarten and first grade contain seven main standards, each containing a number of substrands. These main standards are (1) *Reading: Literature*, (2) *Reading: Informational Text*, (3) *Reading: Foundational Skills*, (4) *Writing*, (5) *Speaking and Listening*, (6) *Language*, and (7) *Text Range, Quality, and Complexity*. For a comprehensive listing of the standards, including their substrands, see *www.corestandards.org*.

Research Influences

While the CCSS for ELA provide widely adopted guidelines for what students need to learn and master to be successfully prepared for the worlds of college and work upon graduation from high school, theoretical frameworks and research show that there is no single method or approach to teaching language arts that is universally effective with all young children. In contrast, teachers need to possess a broad repertoire of theories and instructional strategies, and draw from this repertoire to address students' individual needs. This is known as a *balanced approach* to early literacy instruction. Below, we present research-based ideas to foster balanced literacy instruction in early childhood classrooms. The ideas are organized according to the CCSS for ELA for young learners.

Reading

LITERATURE

A primary goal of an early literacy education is to help young children comprehend and enjoy stories. Comprehension and enjoyment are facilitated when teachers engage their students in prereading, during reading, and postreading activities. Prior to reading or listening to stories, prereading activities build young children's background knowledge and strengthen their vocabulary, both of which contribute positively to text comprehension (van Kleek, 2008). A "picture walk" is an example of an effective prereading activity. During picture walks, children and teachers talk about the pictures in the book prior to reading it. This activity helps prepare the students' minds for the upcoming text, thus enhancing story comprehension. Another effective prereading strategy is using a graphic organizer, whether digital or paper-based. During reading, visualizing can assist with comprehension (Dougherty-Stahl, 2004). Students can close their eyes and try to picture aspects of the story such as the characters and the settings. After reading, students benefit from experiences that help them to better recall the story. Story retelling, especially with storytelling props, is therefore an important skill for children to develop (Curenton, 2011; Morrow, 2009). Research on motivation indicates that students are most engaged with reading tasks when offered opportunities that include choice of activity, social collaboration with peers, appropriate levels of challenge, and experiences of success (Morrow, 2009).

INFORMATIONAL TEXT

In addition to the ability to comprehend and enjoy literature, young students' ability to comprehend and enjoy informational text is an important component of their early literacy development. Informational text includes genres such as expository text (e.g., science and social studies textbooks, books about science and social studies content areas, biographies, and autobiographies) and procedural (how-to) texts.

Research has demonstrated that PreK and kindergarten children are able to learn content from informational texts, learn about different types of informational texts, and learn about how informational texts are organized (Duke, Bennett-Armistead, & Roberts, 2003). Duke, Halladay, and Roberts (2013) recommend that informational texts be used throughout the day in early childhood classrooms. They note that these texts are ideal for whole-class read-alouds, small-group guided reading lessons, independent reading, and as supplements to content-area lessons. Duke, Halladay, and Roberts suggest that classroom teachers provide students with topic choices of the informational texts, and pay close attention to the difficulty level of the texts used in lessons. These researchers also remind classroom teachers to carefully craft the questions they ask young students during discussions of informational texts. Questions recommended are: (1) "What can we learn from this picture that the words did not tell us?," (2) "Why did the author/illustrator choose to put this picture here?," (3) "How does this picture help us understand the words better?," and (4) "What pictures could be added to help explain the words I just read?" (Duke, Halladay, & Roberts, 2013, pp. 55–56).

Guthrie (2004) has spent a great deal of his professional life researching how to engage and motivate students, especially in the use of informational text. He calls his program the Concept-Oriented Reading Instruction (CORI). CORI has five central parts: (1) thematic-based instruction, (2) an emphasis on student choice for both what students read and how they respond, (3) the use of hands-on activities for responding to readings, (4) the availability of a wide variety of text genres at different reading levels chosen to interest students, and (5) the integration of social collaboration into reading response activities. Research on the effects of CORI indicates that students increased motivation for reading, increased use of metacognitive skills, and increased gains in conceptual knowledge (Tracey & Morrow, 2012).

FOUNDATIONAL SKILLS

Consistent with the CCSS, key foundational skills for emergent readers include print concepts, phonological awareness, phonics and other word recognition strategies, and fluency.

Print concepts demonstrate how print works. Print concepts include (1) the relationship between spoken and written language; (2) concepts of words, letters, and sounds; and (3) the directionality of print (in English, left to right and top to bottom). Children learn print concepts via informal storybook readings and exploratory activities at home and school, and through explicit instruction addressing these topics (Gehsmann & Templeton, 2013).

"Phonological awareness" refers to the ability to hear individual words within spoken language, and sounds within spoken words, such as syllables. Phonemic awareness is a subarea of phonological awareness and refers to the ability to hear and manipulate the smallest units of sounds in the English language: phonemes. Both phonological and phonemic awareness are solely auditory processes, and mastery of both is critical to reading success (Cardoso-Martins & Pennington, 2004). Presenting young children with rhyming texts and activities, games that require them to change and move sounds within words to create new words, and small objects to sort according to their beginning, middle, and ending sounds will help strengthen their phonological and phonemic awareness abilities.

Phonics, the ability to correctly associate letters with their corresponding sounds, is an essential word recognition skill for young children (Shaywitz et al., 2004). Of course, the ability to correctly associate letters with their corresponding sounds (phonics) is dependent on the subskills of (1) letter recognition and (2) knowing the sounds that letters make. Some common phonics activities include having children sort pictures or small items based on their initial, medial, or final *letter* (note: in the phonemic awareness activity recommended above, students sorted pictures and items based on their initial, medial, or final *sound*). If young students are having difficulty mastering phonics, it is important to determine if their weakness is a consequence of a visual (letter recognition) deficit or an auditory (phonological processing) deficit (or both), and to intervene accordingly.

Another essential word recognition skill is sight-word acquisition (Gehsmann & Templeton, 2013). *Sight words* are those words that we want students to be able to automatically identify without having to "sound out." Words that occur with great frequency in the English language (e.g., *the, is, was*) are often taught as sight words, as are those associated with thematic instruction. *The Reading Teachers' Book of Lists* (Fry & Kress, 2006) is an excellent resource for sight words and sight-word activities.

Children learn the relationships between letters and their corresponding sounds, and between printed and spoken words, via a system of developing neural connections in their brains between these items (Adams, 1990). Theses connections become stronger and faster with practice, eventually contributing to automatic and fluent reading. The development of fluency is a third key foundational skill for young readers. Fluency develops as a function of practice, often in the form of repeated readings. Activities ideal for promoting fluency are shared reading (teacher-led instruction typically with a big book), paired reading (students in homogeneous or heterogeneous pairs), choral reading (the teacher and students all read aloud at the same time), rereading (reading a text multiple times in order to develop fluency), and Readers' Theater (children are assigned parts in a play and reread to develop proficiency to present the play).

Since young readers learn to read via a system of connections in the brain that become stronger and faster with practice, one of the most effective approaches to teaching word identification is through the use of word families (e.g., the *"at"* family, the *"in"* family, the *"et"* family). The use of word families strengthens the brain's ability to perceive these groups of letter as single chunks, eliminating the need for letter-by-letter reading, and strengthening automaticity and fluent reading. Again, *The Reading Teachers Book of Lists* (Fry & Kress, 2006) is a great resource for creating word family activities.

Writing

Since the 1970s, educators have included writing as an integral part of best practices in early literacy (Morrow, 2009). Writing ability begins in a child's first year of life and is developed through authentic learning activities. Young children begin writing when they make their first scribbles on a page. Later, scribbles become random letters and next, children engage in *invented spelling*—writing without concern for correct spelling or punctuation. Eventually, children's writing and spelling become conventional.

As with reading, writing development is best supported through authentic experiences. Examples of authentic activities include writing notes and letters that are actually mailed (electronically or through the postal service), writing recipes that will be shared, writing in journals or sending e-mails that will be read and responded to, and writing stories and poetry that will be listened to by others. Writing instruction in the classroom includes the use of a writing center, and whole-class and small-group writing lessons in which teachers explicitly teach skills and mechanics.

Speaking and Listening

Children's oral language, both expressive (speaking) and receptive (listening) provides the foundation upon which their reading and writing skills are built (Gillam & Reutzel, 2013). Therefore, helping young children to develop their listening and speaking skills is one of the most important jobs of early childhood educators.

Children's speaking and listening skills are enhanced through experiences that provide language opportunities for progression (Isbell, Sobol, Lindauer, & Lowrance, 2004). Gillam and Reutzel (2013) emphasize the point that teachers do not need to create isolated lessons to address children's listening and speaking skills in classrooms. Rather, Gillam and Reutzel advocate that teachers embed interactions that support language growth into storybook reading and content-based lessons by (1) encouraging children to always speak (and answer questions) in full sentences; (2) helping children learn conversational rules such as listening to each other, taking turns when speaking, staying on topic, and responding to others' comments; and (3) supporting students as they learn to fully describe their experiences, perceptions, and opinions on a wide variety of topics.

Language

Vocabulary development is a special area of importance for young children. However, children come to school with a wide range of vocabulary knowledge. In seminal research on vocabulary development, Hart and Risley (1995, 1999) found that within a year, children from professional homes are exposed to 11.2 million words, children from working-class homes are exposed to 6.5 million words, and children in homes on public assistance are exposed to 3.2 million words. Based on these figures, children from professional homes enter kindergarten with exposure to approximately 30 million more words than do children from economically disadvantaged homes.

Jalongo and Sobolak (2011) determined that in order to become proficient readers, children should know approximately 10,000 words by age 6. According to Byrnes and Wasik (2009), this can be accomplished during the early childhood years if children learn approximately five to six new words per day, which is the same as approximately 38 new words per week and approximately 2,000 new words per year. In order to reach these goals, students need to be exposed to instruction that includes questioning, clarifying, repeating, pointing to words, providing examples, and defining words in terms that young children can understand. There is a positive correlation between how often children listen to storybook read-alouds and the size of their vocabulary (Walsh & Blewitt, 2006). Furthermore, when teachers read with expression, ask open-ended questions, and model language expansion, vocabulary will improve (Beck & McKeown, 2001). Vocabulary will also improve when teachers ask children to chant rhymes in the story and repeat phrases in the book (Beck & McKeown, 2001; Brabham & Lynch-Jackson, 2002; Justice, Meier, & Walpole, 2005).

Text Range, Quality, and Complexity

An important dimension in supporting young children's literacy development is providing a wide variety of high-quality texts that are at the appropriate levels of listening and reading difficulty, and of high interest. The CCSS addresses these issues. A wonderful support website to help educators who are interested in learning more about text complexity is *TextProject.org.*

Special Issues in Early Literacy Instruction

Digital Literacies in Early Childhood Classrooms

To be successful in the 21st century, young learners must become proficient in both traditional (print) and digital literacies (McKenna, Conradi, Young, & Jang, 2013). Although the CCSS for ELA do not have a separate strand for technology, the importance of digital literacy is integrated. McKenna, Conradi, Young, and Jang note that there are often similarities between traditional and digital literacies. For example, both types of texts may have page numbers, a table of contents, headings, and an index. However, the differences between the two types of text may be greater than their similarities. While traditional text is almost always read from the top of the page to the bottom, and from the left to the right, digital texts are often navigated in a nonlinear manner as the reader clicks on links to move through a variety of pages and websites. Additionally, digital texts often contain hyperlinked resources such as on-demand pronunciations, dictionaries, audio texts, and video clips (McKenna et al., 2013). These additional resources, which can be considered scaffolds for learning, may be the reason that digital texts have been found to be at least as effective as traditional texts in supporting literacy achievement, and sometimes more so (Korat & Shamir, 2012; Moody, Justice, & Cabell, 2010; Tracey & Young, 2007).

McKenna and colleagues (2013) suggest three ways that the interactions between young children and the use of technology in the classroom can be conceptualized and implemented. First, young children must learn to comprehend digital texts. Using an LCD projector, teachers can model how to read e-books, navigate websites, and engage in software activities. Virtual field trips can also be taken (McKenna, Labbo, Conradi, & Baxter, 2011). Second, young children must learn to generate digital creations (drawn, spoken, and written). A Digital Language Experience Approach (D-LEA) has been found to be effective with young children (Labbo, Eakle, & Montero, 2002). Another great digital literacy activity is conducting the morning message via a computer and LCD projector (McKenna et al., 2011). Third, young children must learn to use and navigate the unique scaffolds offered in digital environments (e.g., hyperlinks to supports both internal and external to the target text). Again, teacher modeling followed by students' paired and independent practice is the route to learning success.

English Language Learners in Early Childhood Classrooms

Another critical area of importance in early childhood classrooms is addressing the needs of English language learners (ELLs). While all young children are, in reality, ELLs, those for whom English is a second language, face greater risk in mastering listening, speaking, reading, and writing in English than their peers for whom English is their native tongue (Carlo & Bengochea, 2011). Since it is estimated that ELLs will comprise more than 40% of the U.S. elementary and secondary school populations by 2030 (Thomas & Collier, 2002), addressing the particular needs of these students is paramount to the future success of education in the United States

While ELLs must master phonological awareness and word identification strategies like their native, English-speaking peers, *The Report of the National Literacy Panel on Language and Minority Children and Youth* (August & Shanahan, 2006) demonstrated that ELLs' greatest areas of instructional need are "English vocabulary, English proficiency, and other higher-level text processing skills" (Carlo & Bengochea, 2011, p. 118). Of particular importance to this group of students is the mastery of academic vocabulary, those words that are essential to successfully following directions in school such as, "circle, underline, sentence, page, syllable, paragraph, capitalize, and indent" (Carlo et al., 2004). Some ideas for early childhood educators working with ELLs are (1) include print in the classroom in ELLs' first language, such as labels on objects; (2) assign an English-speaking child as a buddy for the ELL to help with that child's oral language development, reading, and writing; (3) provide daily, extensive, and explicit vocabulary instruction; (4) have children collect "Very Own Word" (VOW) cards for new English vocabulary; and (5) use visuals and manipulatives to support instruction.

At-Risk Early Childhood Students and Response to Intervention

Despite the best efforts of educators, some students still struggle to master literacy skills. To respond, many school districts are implementing response-to-intervention (RTI) programs. RTI was created with the goal of reducing the need to classify students through early diagnosis and treatment of young children's learning difficulties. RTI suggests that educational initiatives in schools should be organized in three tiers. The first tier of instruction is offered to all students in general education classrooms. This is typically whole-class instruction, and is usually based on grade-level curriculum using grade-level texts. For nonclassified students who have difficulty mastering grade-level concepts and texts, small-group, in-class instruction addresses their needs. This small-group, in-class instruction is the second tier of RTI. Some nonclassified students still struggle at the second level of RTI, so a third tier of support is available. The third tier is intensive, small-group instruction that is sometimes inside the classroom and other times organized as a pullout program.

Best Practices in Action

The Physical Environment

A classroom's physical environment sets the foundation for literacy learning. The classroom should be inviting, with well-defined centers around the room. Ideally, displays on the walls reflect a theme being studied and demonstrate evidence of the children's growing literacy development. In the whole-class area (a large carpeted space), there should be an interactive whiteboard for the morning message and other computer-based activities, a calendar, weather chart, helper chart, daily schedule, classroom rules, and a pocket chart for assembling cut-up words into sentences.

The literacy center should contain a rug for independent reading and multiple bookshelves for storing books. There should be baskets of books grouped by level of difficulty. Other shelves can hold baskets organized by topics and authors. Colored stickers on the books and baskets assist students in returning them to the correct spot. Books about the current theme can be placed on a special open-faced shelf, and rotated monthly as the class theme changes. Ideally, the literacy center has a flannel board and flannel board characters, puppets, and props for storytelling. There is a rocking chair for the teacher and other adults to read to the class. The listening area in the center can have a CD player for listening to stories and multiple headsets. There are manipulatives for learning about print. These include magnetic letters, puzzles, rhyme cards, and letter chunks on small tiles for making words.

The writing center is an extension of the literacy center. There is a round table for children to meet with the teacher for guided writing instruction and individual conferencing. At least one computer should be a part of the writing center. There are many types of paper, a stapler, markers, crayons, colored pencils, dictionaries, alphabet stamps, and ink stamp pads. A word wall has each of the letters of the alphabet taped on horizontally. When the children learn a new word, it is taped under the letter it begins with on the word wall. Children use the words when they need help spelling or to practice reading. Other classroom centers include science, math, dramatic play, and art.

Classroom Management and Affective Climate

Best practices in literacy instruction take place in classrooms that are well managed. *1-2-3 Magic for Teachers* (Phelan & Schonour, 2004) offers a highly effective approach to classroom management. The approach differentiates between *starting behaviors* and *stopping behaviors*. Starting behaviors are those that students need, such as engaging in schoolwork, cooperating with others, and successfully transitioning between activities. Stopping behaviors are those that must end. Examples of stopping behaviors are calling out, inattention, and off-task activities. *1-2-3- Magic for Teachers* helps educators apply appropriate strategies depending on whether teachers want to start or stop student behavior. When consistently applied, the above-described classroom management approach leads to smoothly run classrooms and positive affective classroom climates.

Case Study

Kim Jackson has been teaching kindergarten for the past 7 years. She recently completed a master's degree with a reading specialist certification. She teaches in a working-class community and has 22 students of diverse backgrounds in her all-day kindergarten class. Ms. Jackson's philosophy of teaching includes integration of the curriculum so that students can build connections between content areas. She implements whole-class, small-group, and center-based instruction in her classroom. She focuses on explicit skills instruction embedded within meaningful, authentic contexts.

Center Management

Ms. Jackson uses daily center-based instruction. To ensure that students visit two specific centers a day, Ms. Jackson has designed a contract for her students. The contract has the name of each center and an icon representing the center. These same labels and icons are visible at the actual centers. When children complete their center work, they check it off on their contracts. The completed work is placed in the basket labeled "Finished Work." After children complete their two assigned centers, they can work at any center they choose. At the end of each day, Ms. Jackson reviews the children's completed work. Any incomplete work, or work that indicates a child needs additional help with a concept, is placed in the "Unfinished" folder. There is a time during the next day for addressing these tasks. This system is consistent with Ms. Jackson's commitment to differentiate instruction based on her students' needs.

Assessing Students to Determine Instructional Needs

In order to provide instruction that meets the varied levels of her students, Ms. Jackson spends considerable time assessing them with formal and informal measures. This is particularly critical for students who are learning English as a second language and other at-risk students. In September, January, March, and June, Ms. Jackson assesses students' knowledge about print and book concepts, phonological and phonemic awareness, letter recognition, phonics, sight words, vocabulary, listening comprehension, and writing ability. As children begin to read conventionally, she takes monthly running records for each child. This system of recording each child's reading behavior assesses the types of reading errors made, the word identification strategies used, and the students' reading comprehension ability. Kim also takes anecdotal notes about her students' behaviors that indicate both progress and points of difficulty. She collects samples of children's writing, analyzes them, and places them in student portfolios. Kim also monitors the students' social, emotional, and physical development.

Small-Group Reading Instruction

As stated above, in addition to whole-class lessons, Ms. Jackson works with small groups of children for reading instruction. With the assessment information she collects, she places students with similar levels of ability and need together. As she works with her students, she takes careful notes regarding literacy progress, and adjusts the group members as needed. Kim presently has four small groups and meets with each group three times a week. If time permits, she will meet with her most at-risk students for additional guided reading sessions.

A Typical Day in Kim Jackson's Classroom (with CCSS Connections)

CHILDREN ARRIVE AT SCHOOL (8:45 A.M.)

It is a Monday morning, and chatter begins to fill the classroom as Kim's students arrive. Quiet music plays in the background as children complete their morning routines. Children move their nametags on the attendance board from the side labeled "Not Here" to "Here," and they place their name sticks into the "Buy Lunch" and/or " Buy Milk" can.

Students know it is time for writing in their journals. Ms. Jackson circulates among the writers, reminding some children to use spaces between words, and suggesting others use classroom tools such as the word wall for their spelling needs. As she listens to completed entries, she has the opportunity to chat with the children about their weekend. When the 2-minute warning bell rings, the children begin to put away their writing journals and transition to the morning meeting on the carpet. (*CCSS Connections: Writing, Language, Speaking, and Listening*).

THE MORNING MEETING (9:00 A.M.)

Using an interactive whiteboard, Ms. Jackson draws the students' attention to the text on the screen. Since it is the month of May, the students echo-read a poem called "May" from *Chicken Soup with Rice* (Sendak, 1962), and then individual students are invited to the board to locate target letters, sight words, and punctuation marks within the text. Ms. Jackson then distributes copies of the text to all of the children, and leads them in an activity in which they circle letters, sight words, and punctuation marks previously learned.

Continuing to use the whiteboard, Ms. Jackson draws her students' attention to an e-book related to the class monthly theme of animals, which she has downloaded from the Internet called *Animals Should Definitely Not Wear Clothing* (Barrett, 1988). Kim reads the humorous book to the class. After the first reading, Kim has the children echo-read each page with her. She then uses the whiteboard to take her students on a virtual field trip to the Bronx Zoo, via the zoo's website (*www.bronxzoo. com*). Kim asks the students questions, encouraging them to answer in full sentences, and responds to her students' inquiries about the zoo and its animals. Kim encourages each child to choose an animal about which he or she would like to learn more. (*CCSS Connections*: *Reading: Literature, Reading: Foundational Skills, Language, Speaking and Listening, Text Range, Quality, and Complexity*)

CENTER TIME (9:30–10:30 A.M.)

Ms. Jackson spends a few minutes reviewing the center activities. A description of what has been added to each center relating to the animal theme is below.

- *Writing Center*: Books about farm, jungle, and forest animals. Animal stickers, an animal dictionary, and paper to make animal books. Two computers are embedded that can be used either for composing or for revisiting the Bronx Zoo website.
- *Literacy Center*: Fiction and nonfiction animal books, animal books with accompanying CDs, an animal puzzle with word labels, an animal concentration memory game, and an animal lotto game.
- *Computer Center*: There is software for printing animal stationery, postcards, and animal masks, and a website bookmarked for visiting the Museum of Natural History's animal exhibits.
- *Science*: Pictures and small figures of farm, forest, and jungle animals are available to promote discussion of the characteristics of these animals and why they live where they do. There are also animal cards to sort into farm, jungle, and forest categories, and recording sheets for all activities.
- *Math*: Little plastic animals in an estimation jar are placed in the Math Center, with a sheet on which students can record their estimation. There is also a basket containing 50 little animals numbered from 1 to 50, the task being to put the animals into sequential order.
- *Blocks*: In addition to the regular blocks, there is an area called *the farm*, one called *the jungle*, and one called *the forest*. Each has been decorated with plastic foliage and other items to represent its habitat. Toy animals of the appropriate type are placed in the farm, jungle, or forest.
- *Art Center*: Animal stencils and animal stamps are added to the art center. There are pictures of farm, forest, and jungle animals, and Play-Doh for children to make models of an animal of their choice.

- *Dramatic Play.* The dramatic play area is transformed into a veterinarian's office. There is a phone and calendar for taking appointments, paper and folders for the doctor's records, a stethoscope, and a prescription pad.

- *(CCSS Connections: Reading: Literature, Reading: Informational Texts, Reading: Foundational Skills, Writing, Language, Speaking and Listening, Text Range, Quality, and Complexity)*

SMALL-GROUP READING INSTRUCTION (9:30–10:30 A.M.)

The first group with which Ms. Jackson meets is reviewing a book they have read before, *We Went to the Zoo* (Sloan & Sloan, 1995). Kim provides a picture walk as the children look through each page and discuss what they see. During this book introduction, the students are asked to find the words *saw* and *many*, since these words caused some difficulty during the first reading. They also discuss the names of the animals in the book. As the group reads, Kim notices that one student makes no errors in reading and finishes quickly. Kim makes a note to possibly move this student to a more advanced guided-reading group. During guided reading, Kim was able to complete a running record on one child. She noted that this student reads *seals* instead of *otters* and said "pander bears" instead of "bears." Kim decides that she will help this child to pay more attention to the print in the words as he reads. Ms. Jackson also calls two more small reading groups in the remaining time. *(CCSS Connections: Reading Literature, Reading: Foundational Skills, Language, Speaking and Listening, Text Range, Quality, and Complexity)*

SNACK AND PLAY (10:30–10:45 A.M.)

By midmorning everyone needs a break. The snack is animal crackers and what Kim calls "animal juice." The children relax and socialize with each other. *(CCSS Connections: Speaking and Listening)*

WRITING WORKSHOP (10:50–11:45 A.M.)

The children gather for writing in the whole-class meeting area. Using the whiteboard again, Ms. Jackson introduces the writing activity for the week. The children will be writing informational texts about an animal of their choice. Students have the option of working with a partner, which is particularly beneficial for students who are learning English as their second language and for other at-risk learners. The students are told to select an animal they like and brainstorm about their animals, including what the animal looks like, what it eats, and where it lives. The students produce writing reflective of different developmental levels such as pictures, scribble writing, letter strings, invented spelling, and conventional writing. Kim will take everyone's writings and make a class book. (*CCSS Connections: Reading: Informational Text, Reading: Foundational Skills, Writing, Language, Speaking and Listening, Text Range, Quality, and Complexity*)

PLAY, LUNCH, AND REST (11:45 A.M.–1:00 P.M.)

Children play either inside or outside depending on the weather, eat lunch, and then rest. Ms. Jackson plays a CD of the story *Barnyard Banter* (Fleming, 2010) during rest time. (*CCSS Connections: Reading: Literature, Language, Speaking and Listening*)

MATH (1:30–2:15 P.M.)

There is a specific math curriculum followed in Ms. Jackson's kindergarten. Since the class is working on counting and categorizing, the students brainstorm as many farm, forest, and jungle animals as they can. They then count which category has the greatest number of species. (*CCSS Connections: Language, Speaking and Listening*)

ART, MUSIC, PHYSICAL EDUCATION, OR LIBRARY (12:15–2:45 P.M.)

The class goes to special teachers for art, music, physical education, and library. Kim has coordinated with these teachers about the theme being studied, so the art teacher is working on paper-mache animal sculptures, the music teacher has found some great animal songs, and the physical education teacher has thought of animal movements to help the students run like chickens on the farm, swing like monkeys in the jungle, and lumber like bears in the forest. The librarian features informational books and storybooks related to animals in her read-alouds. (*CCSS Connections: Reading: Literature, Reading: Informational Text, Language, Speaking and Listening, Text Range, Quality, and Complexity*)

CLOSING CIRCLE WITH READ-ALOUD (2:50–3:00 P.M.)

At closing time, the kindergartners clean up and gather in the meeting area for their closing circle and a read-aloud. Today Kim has chosen an informational book titled *Animal Babies* (Hamsa & Dunnington, 1985), which she reads aloud using a traditional big book. Finally, she and the children review the activities of the day and plan for the next day. (*CCSS*

Connections: Reading: Informational Texts, Language, Speaking and Listening, Text Range, Quality, and Complexity)

Family Involvement

Before the animal unit began, Ms. Jackson sent home a short note about the activities that would be done in school, the skills being taught, and suggestions for activities for parents to do at home. During the unit she asked for volunteers to come into the classroom to read animal books, and she asked for artifacts about animals that parents might share with the class. Kim also asked for parent volunteers to help her students during writing workshop and for help during center time to assist children with activities while she worked with small groups of children for guided reading instruction. Ms. Jackson offered multiple options and time slots for parent participation. At the end of the unit, parents were invited to school to see all the work done about animals. She also put many of the projects on the class website. (*CCSS Connections: Reading: Literature, Reading: Informational Text, Reading: Foundational Skills, Writing, Language, Speaking and Listening, Text Range, Quality, and Complexity)*

Reflections and Future Directions

This is the fifth edition of *Best Practices in Literacy Instruction*, and with each new edition of this chapter we have tried to update, synthesize, and refine the most important aspects facilitating young children's literacy development. In this chapter, we have (1) provided an overview of the primary theories that underlie best practices in early literacy education; (2) presented a brief summary of the major governmental initiatives, including the CCSS for ELA, that have significantly affected early literacy education in the United States; (3) offered a research synthesis and research-based instructional strategies related to early literacy best practices; (4) examined special issues related to early literacy instruction including digital literacies, ELLs, and RTI; and (5) illustrated best practices in early literacy through the presentation of a case study embedded with connections to the CCSS for ELA. Reflecting on the past, we find that the most significant new influence on early literacy education since the fourth edition of this text has been the widespread adoption of the CCSS in the United States. Reflecting forward, we predict that meeting the needs of ELLs and continuing to optimize the potential of digital technologies to support students' literacy growth will be the two most pressing educational issues of the future.

ENGAGEMENT ACTIVITIES

1. After reading the case study in Ms. Jackson's room, compare it to your own early childhood classroom or one that you observe. In what ways are your classrooms similar? In what ways are they different? Are there aspects of Ms. Jackson's classroom that you would like to incorporate into your own (or the one you are observing)? If so, what are they? Are there additions or changes that Ms. Jackson should make in her room?

2. Record the lessons and activities that you implement for your students (or students that you observe) for a full day. At the end of the day, review what you have recorded and add connections to the CCSS, as done for the case study in Ms. Jackson's classroom. Which areas of the CCSS are you most and least addressing? How can your planning and instruction be strengthened based on your findings?

3. We have predicted that meeting the needs of ELLs and continuing to optimize the potential of digital technologies to support students' literacy growth will be the two most pressing educational issues in the future. Choose one of these two topics, and locate and review 10 related websites. Describe each website and report its strengths and weaknesses. Then share what you have found with at least 10 other educators.

CHILDREN'S LITERATURE

Barrett, J. (1988). *Animals should definitely not wear clothing.* New York: Simon & Schuster.
Fleming, D. (2010). *Barnyard banter.* New York: Holt.
Sendak, M. (1962). *Chicken soup with rice.* New York: Harper & Row.
Sloan, P., & Sloan, S. (1994). *We went to the zoo.* Boston: Sundance.

WEBSITES

Common Core State Standards—*www.corestandards.org*
TeacherTube—*www.teachertube.com*
Teach Children ESL—*www.teachchildrenesl.com*
ESL Kid Stuff—*www.eslkidstuff.com*
Everything ESL—*www.everythingesl.net*

REFERENCES

Adams, M. J. (1990). *Beginning to read*. Cambridge, MA: MIT Press.

August, D., & Shanahan, T. (2006). *Developing literacy in second-language learners: Report of the National Panel on Language Minority Children and Youth*. Mahwah, NJ: Erlbaum.

Beck, I. L., & McKeown, M. G. (2001). Text talk: Capturing the benefits of read-aloud experiences for young children. *The Reading Teacher, 55*, 10–20.

Brabham, E., & Lynch-Jackson, C. (2002). Effects of teachers' reading-aloud styles on vocabulary acquisition and comprehension of students in the early elementary grades. *Journal of Educational Psychology, 94*(3), 465–473.

Byrnes, J. P., & Wasik, B. A. (2009). *Language and literacy development: What educators need to know*. New York: Guilford Press.

Cardoso-Martins, C., & Pennington, B. F. (2004). The relationship between phoneme awareness and rapid naming skills and literacy acquisition: The role of developmental period and reading ability. *Scientific Studies of Reading, 8*(1), 27–52.

Carlo, M. S., Aigust, D., Mclaughlin, B., Snow, C. E., Lippman, D., Lively, T. J., et al. (2004). Closing the gap: Addressing the vocabulary needs of English-language learners in bilingual and mainstream classrooms. *Reading Research Quarterly, 39*(2), 188–215.

Carlo, M. S., & Bengochea, A. (2011). Best practices for literacy instruction for English language learners. In L. M. Morrow & L. B. Gambrell (Eds.), *Best practices in literacy instruction* (4th ed., pp. 117–113). New York: Guilford Press.

Curenton, S. M. (2011). Understanding the landscapes of stories: The association between preschoolers' narrative comprehension and production of skills and cognitive abilities. *Early Child Development and Care, 181*(6), 791–808.

Dewey, J. (1916). *Democracy and education*. New York: Macmillan.

Dougherty-Stahl, K. A. (2004). Proof, practice, and promise: Comprehension strategy instruction in the primary grades. *The Reading Teacher, 57*(7), 598–609.

Duke, N. K., Bennett-Armistead, V. S., & Roberts, E. M. (2003). Filling the great void: Why we should bring nonfiction into the early-grade classroom. *American Educator, 27*(1), 30–35.

Duke, N. K., Halladay, J. L., & Roberts, K. L. (2013). Reading standards for informational text. In L. M. Morrow, T. Shanahan, & K. K. Wixson (Eds.), *Teaching with the Common Core standards for English language arts, PreK–2* (pp. 46–66). New York: Guilford Press.

Fry, E. B., & Kress, J. E. (2006). *The reading teacher's book of lists* (5th ed.). San Francisco: Jossey-Bass.

Gehsmann, K. M., & Templeton, S. (2013). Reading standards: Foundational skills. In L. M. Morrow, T. Shanahan, & K. K. Wixson (Eds.), *Teaching with the Common Core standards for English language arts, preK–2* (pp. 67–84). New York: Guilford Press.

Gillam, S. L., & Reutzel, D. R. (2013). Speaking and listening standards. In L. M. Morrow, T. Shanahan, & K. K. Wixson (Eds.), *Teaching with the Common Core standards for English language arts, preK–2* (pp. 107–127). New York: Guilford Press.

Guthrie, J. (2004). Teaching for literacy engagement. *Journal of Literacy Research, 36*(1), 1–29.

Hart, B., & Risley, T. R. (1995). *Meaningful differences in the everyday experience of young American children.* Baltimore: Brookes.

Hart, B., & Risley, T. R. (1999). *The social world of children: Learning to talk.* Baltimore: Brookes.

Isbell, R., Sobol, J., Lindauer, L., & Lowrance, A. (2004). The effects of storytelling and story reading on the oral language complexity and story comprehension of young children. *Early Childhood Education Journal, 32*(3), 157–163.

Jalongo, M. R., & Solobak, M. J. (2011). Supporting young children's vocabulary growth: The challenges, the benefits, the evidence-based strategies. *Early Childhood Education Journal, 38*, 421–429.

Jeong, J. S., Gaffney, J. S., & Choi, J. O. (2010). Availability and use of informational text in second, third, and fourth grades. *Research in the Teaching of English, 44*, 435–456.

Justice, L., Meier, J., & Walpole, S. (2005). Learning new words from storybooks: An efficacy study with at-risk kindergarteners. *Language, Speech, and Hearing Services in Schools, 36*, 17–32.

Korat, O., & Shamir, A. (2012). Direct and indirect teaching: Using e-books for supporting vocabulary, word reading, and story comprehension for young children. *Journal of Educational Computing Research, 46*(1), 135–152.

Labbo, L. D., Eakle, A. J., & Montero, K. M. (2002, May). Digital language experience approach: Using digital photographs and creativity software as a language experience approach innovation. *Reading Online, 5*(8). Available at *www.readingonline.org/electronic/elec_index.asp?HREF=labbo2/index.html.*

McGill-Frazen, A. (2010). The National Early Litercy Panel Report: Summary, commentary, and reflections on policies and practices to improve children's early literacy. *Educational Researcher, 39*(4), 275–278.

McKenna, M. C., Conradi, K., Young, C. A., & Jang, B. G. (2013). Technology and the Common Core standards. In L. M. Morrow, T. Shanahan, & K. K. Wixson (Eds.), *Teaching with the Common Core Standards for English language arts, preK–2* (pp. 152–169). New York: Guilford Press.

McKenna, M. C., Labbo, L. D., Conradi, K., & Baxter, J. (2011). Effective use of technology in literacy education. In L. M. Morrow & L. B. Gambrell (Eds.), *Best practices in literacy education* (4th ed., pp. 361–394). New York: Guilford Press.

Moody, A. K., Justice, L. M., & Cabel, S. Q. (2010). Electronic versus traditional storybooks: Relative influence on preschool children's engagement and communication. *Journal of Early Childhood Literacy, 10*, 294–313.

Morrow, L. M. (2009). *Literacy development in the early years: Helping children read and write* (7th ed.). Needham, MA: Allyn & Bacon/Pearson.

National Institute of Child Health and Human Development. (2000). *Teaching children to read: An evidence-based assessment of the scientific research literature on reading and its implications for reading instruction* (NIH Publication No. 00-4769). Washington, DC: U. S. Government Printing Office.

Phelan, T. W., & Schonour, S. J. (2004). *1-2-3 magic for teachers: Effective classroom discipline pre-k through grade 8.* Glen Ellyn, IL: Parent Magic.

Piaget, J., & Inhelder, B. (1969). *The psychology of the child* (H. Weaver, Trans.). New York: Basic Books.

Shaywitz, B. A., Shatwitz, S. E., Blachman, B. A., Pugh, K. R., Fulbright, R. K., Skudlarski, P., et al. (2004). Development of left occipitotemporal systems for skilled reading in children after a phonologically-based intervention. *Biological Psychiatry, 55*(9), 926–933.

Thomas, W., & Collier, V. (2002). *A national study of school effectiveness for language minority students' long-term academic achievement.* Santa Cruz, CA, and Washington, DC: Center for Research on Education, Diversity, and Excellence.

Tracey, D. H., & Morrow, L. M. (2012). *Lenses on reading: An introduction to theories and models* (2nd ed.). New York: Guilford Press.

Tracey, D. H., & Young, J. W. (2007). Technology and early literacy: The impact of an integrated learning system on high-risk kindergartners' achievement. *Reading Psychology, 28,* 443–467.

van Kleek, A. (2008). Providing preschool foundations for later reading comprehension: The importance of, and ideas for, targeting inferencing in storybook-sharing interventions. *Psychology in the Schools, 45*(7), 627–643.

Vygotsky, L. S. (1978). *Mind in society: The development of higher psychological processes.* Cambridge, MA: MIT Press.

Vygotsky, L. S. (1986). *Thought and language.* Cambridge, MA: MIT Press (Original work published 1962)

Walsh, B., & Blewitt, P. (2006). The effect of questioning style during storybook reading on novel vocabulary acquisition of preschoolers. *Early Childhood Education Journal, 33*(4), 273–278.

CHAPTER 5

Best Practices to Change the Trajectory of Struggling Readers

Victoria J. Risko
Doris Walker-Dalhouse

This chapter will:

- Discuss current issues related to assessment and instruction of struggling readers.
- Present evidence-based practices for K–12 instruction, with attention to directives of the Common Core State Standards.
- Describe how these practices are implemented within authentic instruction.
- Recommend future directions for assessment and instruction of struggling readers.

This chapter focuses on evidence-based assessment and instructional best practices for struggling readers. The best practices we identify (1) are supported by a convergence of evidence, often outcomes of divergent research methodologies; (2) provide a comprehensive and balanced view of students and literacy learning; (3) have a history of demonstrated effectiveness in classrooms and authentic settings; and (4) hold potential, as demonstrated in instructional settings, to be sustainable and to support optimal learning going beyond short-term testing of impact.

A comprehensive and balanced view of students' literacy processes is particularly needed to change the trajectory of students who experience reading difficulties (Risko & Walker-Dalhouse, 2012). Too often assessment and instructional practices for struggling readers are narrow in conception and implementation, frequently aligned with deficit views of students who are experiencing reading difficulties (Bryan & Atwater, 2002). And even within a broader conception of students and instruction, there is a tremendous gap between what is intended and what actually is implemented in classrooms (Schmidt & McKnight, 2012).

Rich contexts for learning benefit all students, but are particularly effective for struggling readers across the grades (Alvarez & Risko, 2010; Camburn & Wong, 2011; Guthrie, 2004; Portes & Salas, 2009), including beginning and young readers (Sharp et al., 1995). Students who need the most support with contextual and conceptual learning are those who often receive it the least. Rich contexts and accelerated learning opportunities are typically situated in high-socioeconomic-status (SES) and higher achieving schools, while students in low-SES receive more of a focus on basic and isolated skill instruction that is less effective for low-achieving students (Camburn & Wong, 2011).

The goal to "play catch up" by teaching a wide array of skills out of authentic reading and writing contexts might provide short-term gains but not lasting ones; students can become skilled but not strategic or thoughtful about their reading. The rush to teach basic skills minimizes comprehension of complicated texts and deep learning of academic content (Willingham, 2009). Instruction that minimizes comprehension instruction, especially for students in the upper grades, has small-to-moderate effects as compared to much larger effects for comprehension interventions (Lipson & Wixson, 2012).

Redirecting instruction requires recognizing the multiple layers of knowledge, languages and language interactions, interests, and experiences that all students need to draw on as they engage in new learning. Higher-order skills and strategies, taught within students' zone of proximal development and sensitive to students' cultural and linguistic histories, can offset low expectations for students' literacy development (Portes & Salas, 2009). Redefining literacy and literacy assessment and instruction to build on students' diversity (Varelas & Pappas, 2013) is central to advancing high-quality instruction for all students.

Some practices we identify elaborate on how to address stated purposes and standards of the Common Core State Standards (CCSS; National Governors Association & Council of Chief State School Officers [NGA & CCSSO], 2010). We believe the CCSS hold promise for changing the trajectory of struggling readers, providing access to disciplinary knowledge, promoting higher levels of thinking, and engaging in authentic learning events. Additionally, these standards will have a significant impact on response-to-intervention (RTI) legislation, which focuses on identifying students who struggle with reading and providing appropriate interventions to reduce the number of students identified as learning-disabled (Lipson & Wixson, 2012) and the requirement of classroom teacher expertise when implementing the first tier of intervention for struggling readers. These standards, however, are *not* a curriculum; ensuring that all students have broad and deep learning, they embrace evidence-based best practices designed to promote equity in literacy learning and achievement.

Evidence-Based Best Practices

High-quality best practices require the expertise of classroom teachers and reading specialists. These practices all share the following characteristics.

Are Informed by Continuous and Multiple Assessments

There is widespread agreement that appropriate and differentiated instruction is informed by continuous and multiple assessments. Both summative and formative assessments are needed to capture the "many interacting abilities" (Spear-Swerling, 2011, p. 152) that develop over time, in different trajectories, and across contexts of school and life experiences. Assessments that are grounded in simple views of literacy (e.g., cognitive processes as the sole indicators of students' literacy performance) fail to capture the range of abilities, social interactions, linguistic and cultural histories that influence literacy development (McIntyre, 2011). Allington and McGill-Franzen (2010), for example, found that an overemphasis on the word-reading skills of young readers skews representation of students' literacy development, not attending to areas (e.g., concept and vocabulary knowledge) that will affect comprehension. In contrast, directives for the CCSS (NGA & CCSSO, 2010, p. 5) advocate for assessments that are coherent and applied in broad strokes, assessing more than one standard simultaneously.

To inform instruction, assessments must identify students' capabilities and needs, individual differences, and literacy profiles (Valencia & Buly, 2004). This involves observations of students' performance in a variety of literacy activities, including open-ended formats. The goal is to identify the knowledge students bring to their reading and writing and if and how this is activated, strategies and skills that they are using confidently and with flexibility, and those that are in process and require further attention (Lipson & Wixson, 2012). Representation of knowledge should be captured in multiple formats, including multimodal assessments. These could include drawings and graphic organizers and computer software to create digital texts and illustrations (Risko & Walker-Dalhouse, 2010).

Formative assessments, which are classroom-based and teacher-designed, capture students' engagement and performance *during* learning activities and are associated with large and meaningful student gains (Popham, 2008). Assessing students when they are given more challenging tasks and texts to determine their response and level of support that may be needed to help them succeed is particularly useful for charting a specific direction for instruction (McIntyre, 2011).

Provide Rich Contexts for Learning

Classrooms with rich learning contexts support active learning and engagement, use of strategies for making sense of words and text ideas, and comprehension of academic content. These classrooms have the following elements.

Use of Knowledge as Analytical Tools

Rich contexts for learning provide a content focus for identifying and resolving real-world problems. Broad, central themes (e.g., challenges faced by explorers, resettlement efforts of immigrants and refugees) are examined from different disciplinary perspectives, and in depth. Students, often in collaboration with peers, are invited to think analytically (e.g., pose problems, hypothesize and generate questions, challenge conventional understandings) as they participate in disciplinary inquiry (Windschitl & Thompson, 2006). Students need to gather evidence and build arguments to address their inquiry- and content-relevant questions, and students are accountable for accurate, comprehensive, and disciplinary-specific representation of information (e.g., graphing survey data, pictorial displays for interview information) (Resnick & Hall, 2001).

Such engagement is associated with gains in academic and conceptual knowledge, and increased strategic and problem-solving engagement (Cognition and Technology Group at Vanderbilt University, 2003; Tracey & Morrow, 2006). When students' interests direct their goals for learning and problem solving, there is a likelihood of increased motivation, finding relevance and connections to content goals, choosing to read more widely, higher confidence in their abilities (Guthrie & Humenick, 2004), understandings and appreciation of disparate disciplinary perspectives (Bransford & Vye, in press), and critical thinking and use of information for problem solving and explaining text meanings (Pianta, Belsky, Houts, Morrison, & the NICHD Early Child Care Research Network, 2007).

Anchor Texts Ground Disciplinary Learning

Rich learning contexts are typically organized around anchor texts, which are sufficiently dense to "seed" interest and enable prolonged examination of complex content. Anchor texts represent students' lived experiences in and out of school. In school, they might include the text shared during a teacher read-aloud, a science experiment, or the study of a film viewed by the class. A basic requirement, though, is that the anchor is accessible to all students; thus, a reading level is not required to access its content.

Anchor texts set up the major concepts to be investigated and reinforced through additional texts that will deepen knowledge and provide reasons to revisit concepts, reread texts, and access resources online; for verifying literal and inferential understandings; and to advance analytical and critical thinking (Cognition and Technology Group at Vanderbilt, 2003). Videos are particularly strong anchors for setting up the examination of complex concepts. They, like other texts, require guided instruction for alerting students to organizational features and important information. An emphasis on the analysis of visual texts, including video material, is embedded in the CCSS (NGA & CCSSO, 2010). Videos are dynamic and embedded with several levels of information with much to notice and examine with each reviewing, and to explore for accuracy of disciplinary knowledge (Bransford & Vye, in press).

Sufficient Time and Resources Support Intensity

Resources include a wide array of texts and interactive technologies, and students' firsthand experiences. These resources are impactful when used coherently and with sufficient time for developing knowledge in depth (Windschitl & Thompson, 2006). Needed are multiple occasions to revisit content, expand on understandings through guided instruction and dialogic conversations, and engage in multiple reading and writing activities. Coherence and focus on content provides prolonged engage and instructional intensity.

Multiple Organizational Formats Support All Learners, Especially Struggling Readers

Rich learning classrooms have multiple organizational formats to support differentiated instruction. There may be large-class instruction to initiate themes around the study of the anchor, small-group instruction that is teacher-led, small and large groups where students collaborate in shared learning activities, and one-to-one instruction. This flexible formatting for learning opportunities allows for additional time for teachers to organize small groups or individual instruction to support struggling readers.

Provide Explicit Instruction

Struggling readers benefit from additional explicit instruction to help them acquire and apply tools to gain success in reading (Cantrell & Wheeler, 2011). These tools include providing students with strategies and skills, and facilitating understanding and use of the academic discourse necessary to respond to and understand text (Wharton-McDonald, 2011). Skills and strategies address all areas of literacy development (e.g., word learning, comprehension monitoring, composing texts, supporting arguments with evidence). Additionally, flexible use of strategies and choosing those that are most appropriate for the genre and content comes with teacher guidance (Shanahan, 2009).

Because the CCSS (NGA & CCSSO, 2010) are focused on outcomes and not teaching of specific strategies to reach those outcomes, teachers' expertise is vital for supporting students' strategic abilities. Thus, teachers, guided by their assessment data, are responsible for articulating and demonstrating the metacognitive work of choosing and applying strategies to aid comprehension. This is especially the case when students are reading texts across disciplines that require increased use of inferential and abstract thinking, and the use of academic language.

Additionally, guided reading instruction supports students' learning with increasingly difficult concepts and texts (Sandoval & Morrison, 2003). And while there are different formats for guiding reading instruction, it typically engages students in previewing, careful reading, use of strategies, and interpretive and critical analysis before, during, and after reading a text (including digital and video texts). And it includes dialogic discussions, and students' generative productions (e.g., written, digital, artistic, or dramatic projects) (Risko & Walker-Dalhouse, 2012).

Previewing and guided text discussions engage students' curiosity and interest in the texts' central concepts while building new knowledge. Previews are designed to invite curiosity and questions and, if needed, to expand knowledge on central, complex concepts that may otherwise remain distant from the students. Central text concepts provide the conceptual glue for related details and facts (Alvarez & Risko, 2010). Text content is more comprehensible when students are reading with knowledge that is relevant to central concepts and related high-level text content; knowledge development "levels the playing field" for struggling readers (Snow & O'Connor, 2013, p. 4).

Revisiting texts to confirm accurate recall, to search for evidence supporting claims, to confirm and expand on interpretations, and more, are characteristics associated with strategic reading, and they are associated with close reading, as described in the CCSS. These actions occur in tandem with activation and extension of prior knowledge. Guided instruction that neglects to engage students' prior knowledge is attempting to build comprehension in a vacuum, in the absence of a foundation that is needed to anchor new learning.

Teach to Students' Capabilities and Cultural and Linguistic Histories While Targeting Specific Areas of Difficulties

Instruction that is well matched to both optimize students' capabilities and target areas of need can change the trajectory of reading disabilities (Wharton-McDonald, 2011). For example, students may know how to search for details and facts during close reading but require guidance and strategies for mapping these around central concepts and main ideas. Reteaching skills and strategies already mastered by students holds them in place rather than advancing their literacy development. Additionally, culturally responsive teaching is closing achievement gaps (McIntyre, Hulan, & Layne, 2011).

There are multiple examples of effective culturally responsive instruction. For instance, there are benefits to developing social justice themes to study world and community problems (Morrison, Robbins, & Rose, 2008) or teachers sharing their own histories to reify the importance of ones' experience for building positive identities in classroom communities (Milner, 2011). May (2011) demonstrated that animated text talk (e.g., interpreting, paraphrasing, and or modeling expressions and meaning of text ideas) around informational multicultural texts engaged students in comprehending complex life experiences and drawing on their "insider" knowledge and comprehension skills to make connections and draw inferences to address culturally relevant issues and events. Irvine and Armento (2001) and Siddle Walker (2001) describe culturally specific teaching styles that promote academic success of African American and other racially diverse groups of children. Intentional and focused interactions between teachers and students and positive teacher feedback are important for student achievement and academic engagement (Dolezal, Welsh, Pressley, & Vincent, 2003).

Cultural modeling, as an example of culturally responsive instruction, seeks to bridge lived experiences and academic content (Lee, 2007; Orellana, Reynolds, & Martinez, 2011). One form of cultural modeling invites students to paraphrase and translate text excerpts into their home languages, moving back and forth across languages using syntactic and lexical clues to derive meaning (Orellana & Reynolds, 2008).

Carol Lee and colleagues implemented a form of cultural modeling to support the learning of African American middle school and high school students. The instructional framework involves analyzing the content to be addressed, requiring generative tasks (e.g., interpretation of symbolism), and making connections to students' routine literacy practices (listening to music, digital composing) and students' conversational patterns. Implementations of this instruction impacted increased comprehension, student-generated questions and comprehension monitoring, writing performance, and engagement (Lee, Rosenfeld, Mendenhall, Rivers, & Tynes, 2004). Students' use of their African American vernacular and rhetorical patterns and prior knowledge and experiences were key elements for scaffolding connections between cultural and linguistic resources and instructional goals.

Provide Multiple Opportunities to Build Students' Identities as Readers and Writers, Problem Solvers, and Producers of Knowledge

Students thrive in classrooms that involve students in multiple opportunities to read and write engaging texts (Spear-Swerling, 2011), and where multiple dimensions of students' identities are made visible. Building students' confidence with positive student–teacher and student–student relationships enables engagement and feelings of self-worth (Triplett, 2007), and persistence in tasks where they feel they can succeed.

Time during the day (i.e., at school and home) to engage in multiple literacy activities during and across the year, including summers, is fundamental to the depth and breadth of reading growth and development. Achievement gaps are persistent in the development of literacy skills between young children in low-income neighborhoods compared to those in more affluent neighborhoods during the elementary grades (Dyson, 2010). Research documenting summer reading loss for low-income children (Allington & McGill-Franzen, 2012) and children whose parents speak languages other than English supports the need for student reading engagement that extends across the calendar versus the academic year and involves classroom and home interventions (Kim & Quinn, 2013).

Embed Skills and Strategies

There are compelling arguments for teaching struggling readers skills within larger contexts. For example, phonemic awareness can be taught as a separate skill or in combination with other skills, such as associating sounds with printed letters simultaneously (see Morris, 2011). The advantage for the latter is that students can learn several skills simultaneously, such as the knowledge of sounds *and* the alphabetic principle of reading English (Perfetti, 1992). Similarly, interactive phonemic awareness (Morris, 2011) provides students with the opportunity to use the context of reading to help them complete parts of words that may be unfamiliar to them (e.g., students may know beginning sounds and fill in the rest of the word). Use of multiple cues allows students to cross-check their hypotheses about word choice, drawing on language, meaning, and sound cues to confirm their hypotheses, fostering adaptability and independence (Clay, 1993; Morris, Tyner, & Penney, 2000).

Instruction that addresses multiple components, not only in word learning, but also comprehension strategies, appears to be more effective than instruction of single strategies (Gelzheiser, Scanlon, Vellutino, & Hallgren-Flynn, 2010), especially for older students whose reading difficulties are influenced by several factors (Wanzek, Wexler, Vaughn, & Ciullo, 2010). Vocabulary learning also benefits from instruction of multiple strategies (e.g., identifying vocabulary critical to text meanings, attending to word parts, use of context to confirm hypotheses about word meanings) (Graves & Silverman, 2011).

Draw on Multiple Forms and Complexity Levels of Texts to Afford Access to New Knowledge and Academic Learning

Struggling readers have a long history of being held in place with limited trajectories in achievement gains, due partly to instruction with texts that are too easy, the use of difficult texts without appropriate instructional supports, and too few opportunities to read texts with success (Allington, 2012). Limited access to a wide range of genre and more challenging texts can restrict struggling readers' trajectory in attaining academic content and accelerating their learning (Chall & Jacobs, 2003).

The CCSS address this issue by recommending a "staircase" metaphor for building students' capacity to read and comprehend increasingly more complex texts. This direction holds potential for designing instruction to support struggling readers' access to challenging texts. The CCSS, however, do not provide guidance on how to tackle the issue of advancing students' success with complicated texts when these texts are often the culprit contributing to students' reading difficulties.

Struggling readers need volumes of practice with easy texts that have varying organizations and genres (e.g., narrative, informational, digital, pictorial texts) and instruction with texts matched to students' instructional reading levels. Allington (2013), for example, recommends multiple opportunities to read texts at a 98% accuracy level. Ehri, Dreyer,

Flugman, and Gross (2007) reported reading gains for primary students, when tutored, with reading texts at 98–100% accuracy. And for upper grades, instructional-level (not grade-level) texts were optimal for advancing the development of struggling readers (O'Connor et al., 2002).

Instruction should occur with texts that are moderately challenging and provide high success rates (Wharton-McDonald, 2011), gradually moving students to more difficult texts with deliberate instructional support. One powerful instructional support is "just-in-time scaffolding" (Frankel, Pearson, & Nair, 2011, p. 227), in which teachers provide timely cues and demonstrations to advance students' strategic work and text understandings followed by repeated practice with the goal of students' independence. Another is dialogic conversations occurring around texts, with advantages for lower-achieving students. Dialogic conversations are most effective when discourse expectations (e.g., norms for supporting claims) are taught and accessible to all students (Michaels, O'Connor, & Resnick, 2007), and when they occur in small groups in which students feel comfortable exchanging ideas (Applebee, Langer, Nystrand, & Gamoran, 2003).

Texts provide scaffolds for other texts. For example, less challenging texts (e.g., videos, wordless picture books or highly illustrated texts, graphic novels that introduce concepts with pictorial or graphic support) can scaffold more complex texts while building concepts and extending students' prior knowledge. Similarly, text sets that have overlapping concepts and vocabulary can couple easier texts with more challenging ones, or video texts with print texts, to advance learning of content and academic knowledge and ease transition to more complex texts.

Differentiate Instruction to Support Identities as Readers and Writers and Literacy Success

Changing the trajectory of struggling readers requires differentiated instruction, provided by highly knowledgeable teachers, and coordinated efforts and guidance from the specialized knowledge that reading specialists can provide (Allington, 2013). Differentiated instruction gives readers access to the same curriculum as their classmates, multiple opportunities to participate in mixed-ability grouping, learning outcomes commensurate with the students' skill and ability, and learning assignments designed to meet students' needs (Hall, Strangman, & Meyer, 2003). Additional instruction provided for small groups and individuals is significantly more effective than instruction for large groups; and when compared, individual instruction is associated with greater acceleration than instruction for small groups (Wanzak & Vaughn, 2007).

Effective teachers consider their instructional practices, materials, assessment, and grouping arrangements, especially in efforts to meet the mandates of the Response to Intervention (RTI) legislation (Watts-Taffe et al., 2012). Consistent with planning for all students, RTI places the first level of intervention for struggling readers in the classroom. Classroom teachers have control over the *process* (i.e., how we plan for and instruct students, establish the learning environment) and the *products* (i.e., assessments of learning). Specific instruction for struggling readers should implement instruction and planning carefully with the reading specialists. This coordinated effort ensures that expert teachers instead of less qualified support staff are providing the instruction for struggling readers (Allington, 2013).

Best Practices in Action

Ms. George, a fifth-grade classroom teacher of a heterogeneous group of middle school students, two Sudanese, four Bosnian, 10 white, and eight African American, is beginning her school year with challenges that face her and other teachers each year. She realizes that she has little knowledge of her students' home literacies and cultural backgrounds, so she plans to communicate with each of her students' families. To do this, Ms. George contacts each child's parents and invites them to share family stories (Kidd, Sanchez, & Thorp, 2005) about their lives and experiences, and their child's development as a reader and writer. Ms. George also listens to the parents as they describe their expectations for their child and their beliefs about his or her progress in reading, and for ways to collaborate with them during the school year.

Ms. George has devoted weeks to planning for alignment of her instructional goals, preliminary assessment information, and district and state standards. As in the past, she will continue to teach thematically, integrating the English language arts across the curriculum while ensuring that each student is achieving progress and feels successful. She is confident that her goals complement the directives of the CCSS (e.g., interdisciplinary teaching, accessing multiple text levels and genre to support knowledge development, engaging students in hands-on experiences and productions representing their knowledge development).

Ms. George realizes that she must differentiate instruction to accommodate the needs of all students, and in particular her struggling readers and English language learners. As a classroom teacher, she is responsible for providing the first level of intervention and progress monitoring of her struggling readers based on the requirements for Tier 1, high-quality classroom based instruction, of the RTI model used in her school district. Ms. George will engage in collaborative planning with the reading specialist in her school, who will both work with struggling readers within

Ms. George's classroom and also provide intensive instruction outside of the classroom for students identified as needing Tier 2, supplementary reading instruction.

Ms. George begins by reviewing the data about her students' performance on standardized measures of achievement administered the previous spring. She uses the scores to make preliminary plans for adapting her instruction and to identify additional assessments to identify specific students' capabilities and needs, and to plan appropriate differentiation.

Dynamic Assessment

During the first week of school, Ms. George meets with students in small groups and during individual conferences to implement the first of multiple formative assessments that will occur throughout the year. Students are asked to choose their favorite texts to read and topics for writings that will be shared with peers. Ms. George is an eager and active participant, recording data on her electronic tablet organized within folders for each student. She is listening to oral readings, text retellings, discussion of purpose and style of writings, and expressions of interests and aspirations. She is analyzing miscues and distinguishing those that affect meaning from those that don't; she is recording word and comprehension monitoring strategies; she is noticing English usage of English learners and records students' use of home languages that may provide hints of language cues she can incorporate into her own language repertoire; she records students' questions and accounts of experiences. She is beginning to gather a wealth of data, including information about the students' cultural and linguistic histories that can be leveraged for instruction. She has information about strategies that struggling readers in her class use to identify unknown multisyllabic words and monitor their reading comprehension. And she identifies difficulties that include limited understandings of novel vocabulary, overattention to memorizing details and facts, low comprehension of main ideas, and limited attention to use and critique evidence for forming arguments.

Ms. George knows that motivation is central to learning. She administers the Reader Self-Perception Scale (Henk & Melnick, 1995), and the Motivation to Read Profile (Gambrell, Palmer, Codling, & Mazzoni, 1996) to learn more about her students' feelings about themselves as readers and their attitudes toward reading.

Because block scheduling is used in Ms. George's middle school, she is confident that the 90 minute block for language arts instruction will provide her with the time for explicit instruction, independent reading and writing in response to reading by students, and monitoring of students' progress and engagement using formative assessment (i.e., conferences, projects, teacher-constructed tests, and observation).

Rich, Anchored Instruction with Explicit Teaching

Ms. George's vision of thematic teaching is not the thematic teaching of past decades; it is not the form of thematic instruction that she experienced during student teaching where themes were shallow and content connections were vague. Instead, her themes are grounded in informational-loaded concepts that invite multiple real-world connections, opportunities to examine and respond to problematic situations, and provisions for academic learning.

Ms. George has assembled a set of materials that relate to a social studies topic of immigration that is part of the fifth-grade curriculum. She chooses texts based on the Lexile scale that uses quantitative measures (i.e., sentence length and word frequency) to match readers to text. In addition to easier texts, she includes instructional-level and complex texts that will be introduced to her struggling readers with guided instruction to increase their conceptual understanding of the content. Among her texts are *Faraway Home* (Kurtz, 2000), the graphic novel *The Arrival* (Tan, 2007), *Journal of Otto Peltonen–A Finish Immigrant* (Durbin, 2002), biographies of refugees, and primary sources (e.g., oral histories recorded at Ellis Island). Additional texts will come from the students and families who will generate brief stories about their families' immigration history. Ms. George plans evening meetings during potluck suppers, hosted by the school principal, to assist the students and their parents in sharing their experiences and beliefs about immigration.

Ms. George attends to both content- and standards-based goals. This instruction is culturally based and rich with activities, building content knowledge and strategies to support enhanced word knowledge and text comprehension. Her content goals focus on building understandings of immigrants and refugees and conditions favoring and challenging immigration, laws that regulate immigration, and the history of immigration cycles and demographics. The central concept for her unit of instruction is "leaving home for a new life—the reasons, the challenges, the laws, and potential contributions." This central concept will ground the choice of texts, discussions, and learning activities.

Ms. George starts the school year with the study of this content because related concepts were currently discussed in the school and neighborhoods, and by state and national legislators. Most recently, community leaders and legislators have argued for and against a new refugee settlement project that is proposed for their city.

While several standards-based goals from the CCSS for English language arts, grade 5 (NGA & CCSSO, 2010), will be addressed in her unit, she includes three that are specifically targeted for those struggling readers who are experiencing difficulty in identifying main ideas (both stated explicitly and inferred) (CCSS RI.5.1., *Key Ideas and Details*); determining meanings of academic words (CCSS RI.5.4., *Craft and Structure*); and identifying and comparing different points of view with supporting evidence (CCSS RI.5.8., *Integration of Knowledge and Ideas*).

Her anchor text is a set of school-approved digital videos that appeared on the local public education channel and that display interviews with refugees who have settled in this city and in other national communities and interviews with church leaders and legislators who state their arguments for and against resettlement programs. This anchor seeds connections to historical information on immigration and refugee status and laws, statistics of refugee relocation programs, decisions that affect allocation of public and private funds supporting resettlement programs and affect city budgets, and challenges refugees face in their home and new country.

Differentiated Instruction

The anchor will be viewed by the entire class followed by small-group discussions and guided instruction, using graphic organizers, to identify main ideas, different points of view and supporting evidence, and generate arguments that are substantiated with text details. Both Ms. George and the reading specialist will join the small groups and conference with individuals to provide guided instruction to meet the goals for understanding the anchor content and the related texts. The reading specialist, with the chosen texts, provides intensive tutoring for those students requiring additional support. Instruction will acknowledge strategies that students are using appropriately and provide intense practice in use of strategies that aid students' ability to identify main ideas, make connections to details to support evidence for building arguments about different perspectives, define new vocabulary and nuanced text meanings, and draw conclusions.

Teacher-guided reading lessons will assist students' transition to and comprehension of increasingly more complex texts. Ms. George plans to guide students through the development of a digital text with hypertext commentaries (Dalton, 2013) as one way to demonstrate their close reading and knowledge acquisition. Students will have multiple opportunities (often guided by the classroom teacher or reading specialist) to read, write, dramatize, and develop digital products (e.g., a graphic novel with selected illustrations and captions) that enhance their literacy identities and their developing expertise of content (Bransford & Vye, in press).

Reflections and Further Directions

In this chapter we have attempted to identify current issues related to the assessment and instruction of struggling readers. We have also sought to contextualize these practices in research and authentic classrooms. However, it is clear to us that the number and depth of documented accounts of teacher practices in urban and rural settings, across multiple grade levels, and in national and international school settings, along with research on the assessment and instruction of struggling readers, must become an even greater educational priority.

ENGAGEMENT ACTIVITIES

1. Examine one of the Anchor Standards in the CCSS for students at your respective grade level. Develop a separate chart for each standard on which you record the *frequency* and *type* of instruction that you have provided for students on a weekly or biweekly basis. Include a column for recording the type of assessment used to denote student progress.

2. Think about your current knowledge of the ethnic, cultural, and linguistic background of *one* specific student in your class who struggles with reading and/or writing. Identify five ways that you can use this information to differentiate reading materials, methods, and instruction for this particular student. Later complete the activity with other students who struggle in these areas.

3. Discuss with others in your professional learning community the extent to which staff and students in your school and classroom reinforce a negative identity as "struggling readers" for students with reading difficulties. To what extent are they isolated socially and in learning experiences from more successful students? How might you foster positive changes in student identity development in your classroom?

4. Examine your school and/or district's literacy plan to determine the provisions made for supporting students who have literacy difficulties. Assess your individual and school progress in implementing the plan. Identify obstacles.

5. Interview a member of the local school board about the literacy program in your district. How does it meet the needs of linguistic, ethnic, and culturally diverse students in the district? How does it meet the needs of students who struggle in reading and writing? Are literacy support personnel (i.e., literacy coaches or

reading specialist) available and utilized effectively to support classroom teachers? Are their community groups supporting children and their parents?

CHILDREN'S AND ADOLESCENT LITERATURE

Durbin, W. (2002). *The journal of Otto Peltonen–A Finnish immigrant*. New York: Scholastic.

Kurtz, J. (2000). *Faraway home*. Orlando, FL: Harcourt Brace.

Tan. S. (2007). *The arrival*. New York: Arthur A. Levine Books.

REFERENCES

Allington, R. L. (2012). *What really matters for struggling readers: Designing research-based programs* (3rd ed.). Boston: Allyn & Bacon.

Allington, R. L. (2013). What really matters when working with struggling readers. *The Reading Teacher, 66*(7), 520–530.

Allington, R. L., & McGill-Franzen, A. (2010). Why so much oral reading? In E. H. Hiebert & D. R. Reutzel (Eds.), *Revisiting silent reading: New directions for teachers and researchers* (pp. 45–56). Newark, DE: International Reading Association.

Allington, R. L., & McGill-Franzen, A. (2012). *Summer reading: Closing the rich/poor reading achievement gap*. New York: Teachers College Press.

Alvarez, M. C., & Risko, V. J. (2010). What comes before matters in the end: Directions for reading comprehension instruction. In S. Szabo, T. Morrison, L. Martin, M. Boggs, & L. Raine (Eds.), *Yearbook of the Association of Literacy Educators and Researchers: Vol. 32. Building literacy communities* (pp. 32–46). Commerce: Texas A & M University.

Applebee, A. N., Langer, J. A., Nystrand, M., & Gamoran, A. (2003). Discussion-based approaches to developing understanding: Classroom instruction and student performance in middle and high school English. *American Educational Research Journal, 40*(3), 685–730.

Bransford, J. D., & Vye, N. J. (in press). Anchored instruction: Then and now. In J. Michael Spector (Ed.), *Encyclopedia of education technology*. Thousand Oaks, CA: Sage.

Bryan, L. A., & Atwater, M. M. (2002). Teacher beliefs and cultural models: A challenge for teacher preparation programs. *Science Education, 86*, 821–839.

Camburn, E., & Wong, S. (2011). Two decades of generalizable evidence on U. S. instruction from national surveys. *Teachers College Record, 113*(3), 561–610.

Cantrell, S. C., & Wheeler, T. (2011). Pedagogy/instruction: Beyond "best practices." In R. Powell & E. C. Rightmyer (Eds.), *Literacy for all students: An instructional framework for closing the gap* (pp. 152–189). New York: Routledge.

Chall, J. S., & Jacobs, V. A. (2003). Poor children's fourth-grade slump. *American Educator, 27*(1), 14–15, 44.

Clay, M. M. (1993). *Reading recovery: A guidebook for teachers in training.* Portsmouth, NH: Heinemann.

Cognition and Technology Group at Vanderbilt. (2003). Connecting learning theory and instructional practice: Leveraging some powerful affordances of technology. In H. F. O'Neil Jr. & R. S. Perez (Eds.), *Technology applications in education* (pp. 173–209). Mahwah, NJ: Erlbaum.

Dalton, B. (2013). Engaging children in close reading: Multimodal commentaries and illustration remix. *The Reading Teacher, 66*(8), 642–649.

Dolezal, S. E., Welsh, L. M., Pressley, M., & Vincent, M. M. (2003). How nine third-grade teachers motivate student academic engagement. *Elementary School Journal, 103*, 239–269.

Dyson, L. (2010). The trend of literacy development during the early years of children living in low-income neighborhoods: A cross-sectional study. *International Journal of Learning, 16*(12), 53–65.

Ehri, L. C., Dreyer, L. G., Flugman, B., & Gross, A. (2007). Reading Rescue: An effective tutoring intervention model for language minority students who are struggling readers in first grade. *American Educational Research Journal, 44*(2), 414–448.

Frankel, K. K., Pearson, P. D., & Nair, M. (2011). Reading comprehension and reading disability. In A. McGill-Franzen & R. L. Allington (Eds.), *Handbook of reading disability research* (pp. 219–231). New York: Routledge.

Gambrell, L. B., Palmer, B. M., Codling, R. M., & Mazzoni, S. A. (1996). Assessing motivation to read. *The Reading Teacher, 49*(7), 518–533.

Gelzheiser, L., Scanlon, D., Vellutino, F., & Hallgren-Flynn, L. (2010). Interactive strategies approach—extended: A responsive and comprehensive intervention for intermediate-grade struggling readers. *Elementary School Journal, 112*(2), 280–306.

Graves, M. F., & Silverman, R. (2011). Interventions to enhance vocabulary development. In A. McGill-Franzen & R. L. Allington (Eds.), *Handbook of reading disability research* (pp. 315–328). New York: Routledge.

Guthrie, J. T. (2004). Teaching for literacy engagement. *Journal of Literacy Research, 36*(1), 1–30.

Guthrie, J. T., & Humenick, N. M. (2004). Motivating students to read: Evidence for classroom practices that increase reading motivation and achievement. In P. McCardle & V. Chhabra (Eds.), *The voice of evidence in reading research* (pp. 329–254). Baltimore: Brookes.

Hall, T., Strangman, N., & Meyer, A. (2003). *Differentiated instruction and implications for UDL implementation.* National Center on Accessing the General Curriculum. Retrieved July 4, 2013, from *http://aim.cast.org/sites/aim.cast.org/files/DI_UDL.1.14.11.pdf.*

Henk, W. A., & Melnick, S. A. (1995). The Reader Self-Perception Scale (RSPS): A new tool for measuring how children feel about themselves as readers. *The Reading Teacher, 48*(6), 470–482.

Irvine, J., & Armento, B. (2001). *Culturally responsive teaching: Lesson planning for elementary and middle grades.* New York: McGraw-Hill.

Kidd, J. K., Sanchez, S. Y., & Thorp, E. K. (2005). Cracking the challenge of changing dispositions: Changing hearts and minds through stories, narratives, and direct cultural interactions. *Journal of Early Childhood Teacher Education, 28*(4), 347–359.

Kim, J. S., & Quinn, D. M. (2013). The effects of summer reading on low-income children's literacy achievement from kindergarten to Grade 8: A meta-analysis of classroom and home interventions. *Review of Educational Research, 83*(3), 386–431.

Lee, C. D. (2007). *Culture, literacy, and learning: Taking bloom in the midst of the whirlwind.* New York: Teachers College Press.

Lee, C. D., Rosenfeld, E., Mendenhall, R., Rivers, A., & Tynes, B. (2004). Cultural modeling as a frame for narrative analysis. In C. Dauite & C. Lightfoot (Eds.), *Narrative analysis: Studying the development of individuals in society* (pp. 39–62). Thousand Oaks, CA: Sage.

Lipson, M. Y., & Wixson, K. K. (2012). RTI: To what interventions are students responding? *The Reading Teacher, 66*(2), 111–115.

May, L. (2011). Animating talk and texts: Culturally relevant teacher read-alouds of informational texts. *Journal of Literacy Research, 48*(1), 3–38.

McIntyre, E. (2011). Sociocultural perspectives on children with reading difficulties. In A. McGill-Franzen & R. L. Allington (Eds.), *Handbook of reading disability research* (pp. 45–56). New York: Routledge.

McIntyre, E., Hulan, N., & Layne, V. (2011). *Reading instruction for diverse classrooms: Research-based, culturally responsive practice.* New York: Guilford Press.

Michaels, S., O'Connor, C., & Resnick, L. (2007). Deliberate discourse idealized and realized: Accountable talk in the classroom and in civic life. *Studies in Philosophy and Education, 27*(4), 283–297

Milner, H. R. IV. (2011). Culturally relevant pedagogy in a diverse urban classroom. *Urban Review, 43,* 66–89.

Morris, D. (2011). Interventions to develop phonological and orthographic systems. In A. McGill-Franzen & R. L. Allington (Eds.), *Handbook of reading disability research* (pp. 279–288). New York: Routledge.

Morris, D., Tyner, B., & Penney, J. (2000). Early steps: Replicating the effects of a first-grade reading intervention program. *Journal of Educational Psychology, 92,* 681–693.

Morrison, K. A., Robbins, H. H., & Rose, D. G. (2008). Operationalizing culturally relevant pedagogy: A synthesis of classroom-based research. *Equity and Excellence in Education, 41*(4), 433–452.

National Governors Association Center & Council of Chief State School Officers. (2010). *Common Core State Standards (CCSS).* Washington, DC: Author.

O'Connor, R. E., Bell, K. M., Harty, K. R., Larkin, L. K., Sackor, S. M., & Zigmond, N. (2002). Teaching reading to poor readers in the intermediate grades: A comparison of text difficulty. *Journal of Educational Psychology, 94*(3), 474–485.

Orellana, M. F., & Reynolds, J. F. (2008). Cultural modeling: Leveraging bilingual skills for school paraphrasing tasks. *Reading Research Quarterly, 43*(1), 48–65.

Orellana, M. F., Reynolds, J. F., & Martinez, D. C. (2011). Cultural modeling: Building on cultural strengths as an alternative to remedial reading approaches. In A. McGill-Franzen & R. L. Allington (Eds.), *Handbook of reading disability research* (pp. 273–278). New York: Routledge.

Pianta, R. C., Belsky, J., Houts, R., Morrison, F., & the NICHD Early Child Care Research Network. (2007). Opportunities to learn in America's elementary classrooms. *Science, 315,* 1795–1796.

Perfetti, C. (1992). The representation problem in reading acquisition. In P. Gough, L. Ehri, & R. Treiman (Eds.), *Reading acquisition* (pp. 145–174). Hillsdale, NJ: Erlbaum.

Popham, W. J. (2008). *Transformative assessment.* Alexandria, VA: Association for Supevision and Curriculum Development.

Portes, P., & Salas, S. (2009). Poverty and its relation to development and literacy. In L. M. Morrow, R. Rueda, & D. Lapp (Eds.), *Handbook of research on literacy and diversity* (pp. 97–113). New York: Guilford Press.

Resnick, L. B., & Hall, M. W. (2001). The principles of learning: Study tools for educators (version 2.0) [CD-ROM]. Pittsburgh, PA: Institute for Learning, University of Pittsburgh.

Risko, V. J., & Walker-Dalhouse, D. (2010). Making the most of assessment to inform instruction. *The Reading Teacher, 63*(5), 420–422.

Risko, V. J., & Walker-Dalhouse, D. (2012). *Be that teacher!: Breaking the cycle for struggling readers.* New York: Teachers College Press.

Sandoval, W., & Morrison, K. (2003). High school students' ideas about theories and theory change after a biological inquiry unit. *Journal of Research in Science Teaching, 40,* 369–393.

Schmidt, W. H., & McKnight, C. C. (2012). *Inequality for all: The challenge of unequal opportunity in American schools.* New York: Teachers College Press.

Shanahan, C. (2009). Disciplinary comprehension. In S. E. Israel & G. G. Duffy (Eds.), *Handbook of research on reading comprehension* (pp. 240–260). New York: Routledge.

Sharp, D. L. M., Bransford, J. D., Goldman, S. R., Risko, V. J., Kinzer, C. K., & Vye, N. J. (1995). Dynamic visual support for story comprehension and mental model building by young, at risk children. *Educational Technology Research and Development, 43*(4), 25–41.

Siddle Walker, V. (2001). African American teaching in the South: 1940–1960. *American Educational Research Journal, 38*(4), 751–779.

Snow, C., & O'Connor, C. (2013). Close reading and far-reaching classroom discussion: Fostering a vital connection. A policy brief from the Literacy Research Panel of the International Reading Association. Retrieved September 13, 2013, from *www.reading.org.*

Spear-Swerling, L. (2011). Patterns of reading disabilities across development. In A. McGill-Franzen & R. L. Allington (Eds.), *Handbook of reading disability research* (pp. 149–161). New York: Routledge.

Tracey, D. H., & Morrow, L. M. (2006). *Lenses on reading: An introduction to theories and models.* New York: Guilford Press.

Triplett, C. F. (2007). The social construction of "struggle": Influences of school literacy contexts, curriculum, and relationships. *Journal of Literacy Research, 39*(1), 95–126.

Valencia, S. W., & Buly, M. R. (2004). Behind test scores: What struggling readers *really* need. *The Reading Teacher, 57*(6), 520–531.

Veralas, M., & Pappas, C. C. (2013). *Children's ways with science and literacy:*

Integrated multimodal enactments in urban elementary classrooms. New York: Routledge.

Wanzak, J., & Vaughn, S. (2007). Research-based implications from extensive early reading interventions. *School Psychology Review, 36,* 541–561.

Wanzak, J., Wexler, J., Vaughn, S., & Ciullo, S. (2010). Reading interventions for struggling readers in the upper elementary grades: A synthesis of 20 years of research. *Reading and Writing: An Interdisciplinary Journal, 23*(8), 889–912.

Watts-Taffe, S., Laster, B. P., Broach, L., Marinak, B., Connor, C. M., & Walker-Dalhouse, D. (2012). Differentiated instruction: Making informed teacher decisions. *The Reading Teacher, 66*(4), 303–313.

Wharton-McDonald, R. (2011). Expert classroom instruction for students with reading disabilities. In A. McGill-Franzen & R. L. Allington (Eds.), *Handbook of reading disability research* (pp. 265–272). New York: Routledge.

Willingham, D. T. (2009). *Why don't students like school?: A cognitive scientist answers questions about how the mind works and what it means for the classroom.* San Francisco: Josey-Bass.

Windschitl, M., & Thompson, J. (2006). Transcending simple forms of school science investigation: The impact of preservice instruction on teachers' understandings of model-based inquiry. *American Educational Research Journal, 43*(4), 783–835.

CHAPTER 6

Best Practices for Teaching Dual Language Learners

Design Principles for Leveraging Everyday Literacies

Michael Domínguez
Kris D. Gutiérrez

This chapter will:

- Provide background information relevant to understanding the demographic, social, cultural, and policy context surrounding instruction for English Language learners.

- Draw attention to the special considerations at work for English language learners in literacy instruction.

- Highlight the important role of thoughtfully constructed, situated literacy practices that draw on students' everyday repertoires of practice to enhance their learning.

Who Is the English Language Learner?

We begin this chapter by helping readers understand English language learners (ELLs) and their contexts for learning. As Rumbaut and Massey (2013) elaborated in their report, *Immigration and Language Diversity in the United States*, the United States has always been a multilingual nation. Yet policies and practices continue to ignore this history, and the linguistic variability of this nation's population, particularly in its youth. Youth who are learning English differ along a number of dimensions, including their country of origin, immigration status and length in the United States, home language, and access to teachers with experience and preparation in the areas of bilingualism, biliteracy, and second language acquisition. Despite this heterogeneity, ELLs are too often misunderstood and taught as if they were a homogenous population. The larger and more relevant question, then, is How can we develop evidence-based best practices and design effective interventions for ELLs through understanding students' linguistic repertoires, their histories, and their contexts of development?

We argue that an evidenced-based and more principled approach to ELL instruction involves identifying how these youth differ from one another, as well as from native English speakers. Toward that end, we discuss how developing a better understanding of the ELL can help the literacy educator, even novice educators, develop effective practices that are consistent with what research tells us about supporting the teaching and learning of ELLs. In particular, we focus on language and literacy practices organized around expansive and consequential forms of learning (Engeström, 1987) that recognize the powerful mediating role of students' linguistic and sociocultural repertoires in developing language and literacy skills, including the appropriation of disciplinary content knowledge.

Evidence-Based Best Practices: A Research Synthesis

The Demographic and Educational Imperative

The changing demographic in the United States and the increasing inequity and lack of access to meaningful instruction in the nation's poorest schools is further acerbated by the decrease in instructional models available to teach ELLs. At a time when there is an increased need for more robust pedagogical models, there remains institutionalized and informal resistance to bilingual and biliteracy approaches, despite evidence to the contrary about their effectiveness (August & Shanahan, 2006). Language ideologies about languages other than English remain a legal and public deterrent to developing a rich menu of approaches for ELLs (Razfar, 2005).

Within this sociopolitical context, the demographic reality of this nation's schools is one defined by the bicultural nature of its students' lives. According to the Pew Foundation (Passel & Cohn, 2009), approximately 73% of children of immigrant families are United States–born, 76% of elementary age and 56% of secondary age, respectively. At the same time, the number of U.S.-born children living in mixed-status households has increased significantly from 2.7 million in 2003 to 4 million in 2008. Yet in contrast to public perception, the number of children who are unauthorized immigrants themselves has remained constant since 2005 (p. ii). Home language and home language practices, then, indicate little about nationality, citizenship, or country of origin (Capps et al., 2005). While Spanish is the first language of the majority of ELLs in the United States (62%), there are significant numbers of youth speaking other languages, including Chinese, Vietnamese, Haitian Creole, Hindi, Korean, Tagalog, Russian, and Arabic, with many of these other languages growing in prominence at significant rates (U.S. Census, 2011). Several states have ELL populations in which Spanish is not the first language of the majority of the ELL student population: North and South Dakota, Alaska, and Montana (First Nation languages), Vermont (Bosnian), and Maine (Somali), for example (Batalova & McHugh, 2010a, 2010b).

The most recent estimates from the National Clearinghouse for English Language Acquisition and Language (NCELA) and the National Center for Education Statistics (NCES) report that the total PreK–12 student enrollment for ELLs is 5,208,247, representing 10% of the total PreK–12 student population (NCELA, 2009; NCES, 2011). If we consider that ELL student enrollment increased by 53.2% from 1997–1998 and 2007–2008 (compared to 10.7% growth for the PreK–12 student population as a whole), ELLs will be commonplace rather than the exception in the classroom. Furthermore, the need to develop literacy practices that create new academic and career pathways for ELLs is no longer an issue limited to western states that hold the largest concentration of ELLs in the country. States in the Midwest and on the Southeast coast are undergoing the most rapid growth in the ELL student population, with Virginia, Kentucky, Indiana, Alabama, and South Carolina experiencing greater than a 200% growth in the last decade (NCELA, 2011). Estimates suggest that by 2025, one in four public school students will be designated as an ELL student (NEA, 2008).

What's In a Name?: Situating Best Practices and the Policy Contexts

These changing demographics and diversity of the ELL student population help push on monolithic views of ELLs and, in doing so, present a significant challenge for policymakers and state educational institutions and agencies, as well as practitioners. For example, despite this demographic group's linguistic and demographic diversity, the term "English learner" has come to be synonymous and used interchangeably with the immigrant student, particularly the Latina/o immigrant, or to imply an equivalency between language use/ability, and race, ethnicity, or national origin. As a consequence, youth who are ELLs are too often characterized in ways that do not capture their linguistic repertoires or the important differences that distinguish learners of English from other student learners, including the complex and varying nature of bilingualism (Gutiérrez, Zepeda, & Castro, 2010).

As Wong-Fillmore and Snow (2005) have noted, there are currently many students developing English as a second language; thus, understanding the trajectory of second language acquisition can support teachers in developing more effective communicative and pedagogical practices (p. 6). To do so, educators and policymakers need to understand the difference between sequential and simultaneous bilingualism. *Sequential bilingualism* refers to youth who are monolingual and who are developing their home language with little to no knowledge of English (Peña & Kester, 2004); *simultaneous bilinguals* have had access to both their first and second languages in the home/community and school contexts from an early age, and thus have some proficiency with both their first and second languages. Recent research suggests that as more ELLs are born in the United States, more of these youth will fall into this latter, simultaneous bilingual category (Almanza de Schoenwise & Klingner, 2012). These demographics underscore the point that nearly all ELLs, regardless of their exposure to English, arrive in schools with some literacy knowledge. However, school policies and practices often assess and label entering students solely based on their proficiency in English, rather than their broader language and literacy abilities. Current labels such as limited-English-proficient (LEP) students, ELLs, or non-English proficient (NEP), for example, are problematic and not very useful in terms of developing robust teaching strategies, as they do not account for students' fuller capacities and experiences, particularly their linguistic repertoires. And while classifications can be useful for particular purposes, the danger here is that focusing on perceived regularities in the group makes it easier to rely on one-size-fits all approaches to language and literacy learning—approaches that ignore the significant variance across members of categories. Furthermore, putting ELLs into a "black box" makes it difficult to develop teaching practices that account for students' extant literacy strengths, abilities, and skills. Robust language and literacy practices should be oriented toward leveraging students' complete linguistic and literacy toolkit, that is, their home, everyday, and school language practices.

The ELL "box problem" is exacerbated if not created by federal, state, and local policies related to the teaching and funding of ELLs. Consider, for example, the lack of consistency across districts and states about what counts as an ELL, as the assessment and classification systems are highly variable and of differing quality. Students who are newcomers to schools in the United States and to the English language, as well as students who have been in U.S. schools for a number of years and who have considerable proficiency with English, can be classified as ELLs and can receive services. However, once students have been reclassified as English-proficient, they become part of a system that no longer focuses on their ongoing needs as ELLs working to develop more expansive forms of literacy across subject matter areas. Such policies belie the amount of time it takes to learn a second language and develop robust forms of language and literacy practices. As discussed in Wong-Fillmore and Snow (2005), "although it used to take them from five to seven years to learn English (Cummins, 1981; Klesmer, 1994), recent studies suggest it is now taking seven to ten years (Ramirez, Pasta, Yuen, Billings, & Ramey, 1991)."

These findings have important implications for practice, especially for practitioners who can be mislead or confused about how to best address the needs of the ELL. ELLs need a range of ongoing forms of assistance regardless of their classification, to negotiate the ongoing and varying language and literacy demands across their academic trajectories. As researchers have pointed out, students who may be at the same level of proficiency with their English-speaking peers at one point in their learning trajectories may fall behind at another time because of the increasingly complex language demands of disciplinary content (Carlo & Bengochea, 2011; Nakamoto, Lindsey, & Manis, 2007). Thus, to ratchet up students' learning, robust forms of language and literacy support need to continue beyond students' reclassification and must be aligned with programs of instruction designed to build a broad range of literacy skills beyond English language development; moreover, they should be aligned with programs of instruction oriented toward creating new learning pathways and trajectories for youth in the academy and beyond.

At the same time, providing strategic forms of assistance also requires appropriate rules for reclassifying students based on their English proficiency, as measured by high-quality language proficiency assessments. These assessments should be built around rigorous English language proficiency standards that are themselves related to the language demands of the state's academic achievement standards or the Common Core (Working Group on ELL Policy, 2011). High-quality assessments sensitive to the range of skills students' possess should help educators better understand ELLs' linguistic repertoires, assets, and potential.

With all this in mind, we argue that fuller and more accurate descriptions of young students helps challenge deficit explanations for their schooling performance and are more accurate in understanding their potential. In short, discourse matters to our practice and labels and narrow descriptors can shape how we see our students' learning and their possibilities. We believe the term *dual language learners (DLLs)*, although not designed to represent the range of all ELLs' experiences, more accurately captures the complex and developmental character of English language learning; it is an asset-based conception of these students and their potential. We use the term in this spirit.

Dual Language Learners and Language Socialization

We know from research on cultural communities and the cultural dimensions of learning that there is both regularity and variance within and across groups of people, including those who share a common language or country of origin (Gutiérrez & Rogoff, 2003; Rogoff, 2003). From a teaching and learning perspective, these differences among students learning a language are best attributed to youths' participation in the practices that constitute everyday family and community life. Language socialization studies (Ochs, 1993; Ochs & Schiefflin, 2011, 2008; Schiefflin & Ochs, 1986) have long argued that children are socialized to particular language practices through their participation in the valued practices of the home and community. Such studies help us to challenge simplistic and overly general conceptions of youth and their linguistic practices, as there is no monolithic view of DLLs, nor is there a particular learning style that they embody. The language practices of DLL youth are as diverse and dynamic as are other cultural practices of which they are a part. However, youth who are learning English as a second language are too often characterized in ways that do not capture their linguistic repertoires or the important differences that distinguish learners of English from other student learners (Gutiérrez et al., 2010).

More often, we fail to recognize that the linguistic demands of DLLs' everyday practices are far more complex than often acknowledged (Faulstich Orellana, 2009). As an example, children who are learning English or who have bilingual capacities often serve as language and sociocultural brokers for their non-English-speaking family members across a range of financial, medical, and educational institutions. Yet these children's classroom experiences neither recognize nor make use of such important cognitive literacy activities and sociocultural accomplishments. There are economic, sociopolitical, and educational consequences to failures of leveraging and extending students' linguistic toolkits.

Given the broader economic and sociopolitical goals articulated in the Common Core Standards (e.g., economic competitiveness), we call attention to research that shows the cognitive, sociopolitical, and economic benefits to bilingualism and biliteracy. As sociologists Rumbaut and Massey (2013) have noted, the loss of dual and immigrant languages would in fact come at a significant cost to the nation:

> In a very real way the progressive death of immigrant tongues repre-
> sents a costly loss of valuable human, social, and cultural capital—for
> in a global economy, speaking multiple languages is a valuable skill.
> Certainly the economy of the Americas would function more fluidly
> and transparently if more people spoke at least two of the hemisphere's
> three largest languages: English, Spanish, and Portuguese. A recent
> report by the Council of Europe makes the case that plurilingualism is
> an advantage in the globalized marketplace of the future. (p. 13)

This recognition of bilingualism, biliteracy, and biculturalism as valuable resources is foundational to designing more expansive literacy
environments—environments that reflect the polylingual and polycultural character of youths' lives and the practices in which they participate
(Gutiérrez, Bien, & Selland, 2011).

Best Practices in Action

Teachers and other practitioners are designers of both curricula and
practices. More important, we think practitioners should be prepared to
be designers of new futures, of possible futures for all youth, particularly
DLLs and youth from nondominant communities for whom literacy is
key (Gutiérrez, 2008). In this section, we highlight approaches to teaching DLL youth that focus on the importance of meaning making and on
the role of everyday knowledge and practices in developing consequential
forms of literacy. From this perspective, a premium is placed on understanding and leveraging students' practices, not just in school but across
the settings of everyday life—from youth interest-driven practices, to those
organized by family and other adults, to disciplinary practices in more
formalized learning settings.

This focus on youths' practices and what youth actually do routinely,
including their regularity of involvement with literacy practices, helps us
understand the linguistic repertoires youth develop as they move within
and across practices. Recognizing that youth are socialized to particular
linguistic practices through their participation in a wide variety of social
practices is useful in shifting the focus from deficit perspectives about
youth and communities' language practices toward the design of learning
environments that leverage students' history of involvement with literacy.
We present a set of design principles to help educators leverage everyday practices toward more expansive forms of literacy production. These
principles underscore the point that developing English language skills
should not replace the need for leveraging students' full linguistic toolkit
to develop consequential and expansive forms of literacy.

Design Principles

- Recognize the variability and regularity in any group of DLLs as central to understanding students' educational strengths and potential.
- Understand the kind of cognitive activity and sociocultural knowledge that DLLs are leveraging, as they navigate a range of contexts with differing language demands.
- Identify and employ strategic and appropriate forms of assistance that are embedded into meaningful practices.
- Recognize the language demands of the practices in which DLLs participate, in the classroom and beyond.
- Extend support for DLLs who are developing capacities in two languages simultaneously and the resulting demands.
- Draw on the existing toolkits that all children bring to the classroom (e.g., even preschool children who are developing their home language but who have little to no knowledge of English have linguistic repertoires that can be leveraged).
- Design literacy practices that utilize everyday linguistic and sociocultural practices, as these are key to building academic and disciplinary knowledge.
- Design literacy practices that socialize youth to and through their participation in robust and consequential learning activity.

With these principles in mind, we outline a number of considerations that should help teachers organize rich learning environments for DLL youth across grade levels who are also learning to read and write in English, as well as appropriating disciplinary content knowledge.

Rising to the Concrete: Leveraging Everyday Knowledge and Linguistic Practices

Today's youth move across a range of contexts and produce artifacts that reflect the intercultural, hybrid, and multimodal practices of which they are part. These repertoires, developed across the ecologies of interest and everyday life, should be cultivated as an important dimension to learning. In terms of supporting the development of robust and consequential forms of learning, we underscore the importance of understanding the everyday in developing expansive forms of language and literacy learning that account for both everyday and school-based forms of learning. Leveraging the everyday includes home language practices and involves more than making learning more relevant and engaging; it also means situating literacy learning in the particular sociocultural and linguistic histories of students.

Learning from a sociocultural perspective (Vygotsky, 1978) suggests that learning is made consequential by grounding abstract knowledge in the everyday. From this view, expansive learning involves bringing the future into the present for learners (Cole, 1992). To help struggling readers, for example, Cole (1992) organized reading in ways that brought versions of the mature forms of reading for children who had not yet developed these aspects of reading into their present practice. In this way, students are engaged in practices that actually imitate or model the rich literacy skills and practices that are the endpoint or object of the activity, instead of participating in narrow and reductive low-level practices.

To accomplish such a goal, high-leverage practices should be situated in learning ecologies oriented toward consequential forms of learning that challenge assumptions that intellectual operations of language and literacy learning can be divided into levels from simple/rote to complex/meaningful or that in order to teach "higher forms of learning" one must first master the simple, "basic"-level skills in order to acquire the higher-order skills. Taken as a whole, the approaches to developing DLLs' literacy practices we discuss reject the view that there is a "lower, 'Level 1' kind of learning/thinking that precedes higher, 'Level 2' learning/thinking both ontogenetically and in the mastery of school" (Laboratory for Comparative Human Cognition, 1989, p. 75)—approaches that reflect a kind of "cognitive reductionism" (Rose, 1988) in the theories of teaching and learning of DLLs themselves (Gutiérrez, 2012). Such conclusions are supported by insights from the National Literacy Panel's meta-analysis of studies of literacy development for DLLs that found that these youth rarely struggle or lack basic alphabetic skills (August & Shanahan, 2006). Rather, learning a language and learning to be literate in both the first and second language involves both discrete skills and higher-level strategies, as well as acquiring the sociocultural knowledge of how and when to use language and literacy practices. Emphasis in instruction, then, must be placed on higher-level text skills and their sociocultural meanings and uses; a blend of "top-down" and "bottom-up" instruction helps to ensure that students' future literacy practices are modeled and are present in their daily practices.

To illustrate how to bring the future into the present and the role of the everyday in literacy learning, we highlight a classic study by Moll and Diaz (1987) that documented how a combination of institutional, ideological, and pedagogical forms worked to constrain the learning of bilingual Spanish-English speakers. Employing a sociocultural methodology with observer–participant accounts, Moll and Diaz examined the consequences of instruction and its social organization on the reading development of two groups of children who were assessed to be bilingual in spoken English and Spanish.

The researchers observed children in two different classrooms—one with a fully bilingual teacher, the other with a monolingual English-speaking teacher. The children in each of the classes were grouped by reading ability: high, medium, and low. And although the children could speak English, their instruction was designed to "remediate" their reading deficiency with lessons organized around an assumption that they could not read and comprehend English. Through their observations, Moll and Diaz found that the reading instruction in the English-language classroom was organized around decoding the text phonetically, with significant attention to repeated practice in word/sound pronunciation. Even children in the highest level reading group had limited opportunity to engage in elaborated talk, as comprehension questions required limited responses from the children.

To better understand how children who could read for meaning in Spanish could be in the early processes of learning to decode in English, Moll and Diaz designed an intervention in which children would read the English texts to themselves but were allowed to discuss the meaning of the texts in Spanish, English, or a combination of the two—a practice common in their own speech community. Children across all three reading groups participated in comprehension-directed activities, and with attention focused on what children could understand from what they had read, rather than on simplistic decoding skills, children's estimated grade level for comprehension significantly increased. Because they had learned to read for comprehension (a higher-order skill) in Spanish, the comprehension results were considerably more positive. "Such gains in comprehension and making sense of texts should not be surprising, as mature reading and mathematical thinking require both top down (Level 2) and bottom-up (Level 1) processes" (Laboratory for Comparative Human Cognition, 1989, p. 75)—the kind of back-and-forth we see in Moll and Diaz's intervention. Such work argues what many in this research community believe: a "'bottom-up,' 'Level 1/Level 2' theory of learning and instruction is wrong in principle and pernicious in practice" (Gutiérrez, 2012, p. 20).

These findings have been supported in subsequent work with DLLs. Researchers (Iddings, Combs, & Moll, 2012) have noted that when instruction and policy restricts the role of home language in learning, particularly content knowledge, learning is constrained. Specifically, reductive English-only literacy programs eliminate students' linguistic repertoires—powerful mediators in students' learning. As Iddings and colleagues (2012) argue, restricting students' use of their own social, cultural, and linguistic resources, as well as those of their peers, creates what they term an "arid zone," where meaningful learning opportunities "dry up," further marginalizing the DLLs' and truncating their opportunities to expand learning and new identities.

As an alternative to creating an "arid zone," Pacheco (2012), for example, incorporated the unique learning, thinking, and knowledge DLLs develop in home–community spaces into a curriculum. In this work, she drew on the notion of "everyday resistance" to illustrate a particular set of enacted political actions and practices that Latina/o students develop to negotiate the demands of their politically charged contexts. As these students came together to develop coordinated and strategic challenges to particular social and educational policies, they engaged in joint sense making, problem solving, and social analysis. This everyday resistance involved practices related to designing, planning, and carrying out collective actions and activities. Over time, these practices foment critical dispositions, social analyses, worldviews, and other sociocultural resources that can serve as thinking and analytic tools for learning in school contexts. Thus, practices of everyday resistance emerge in the course of learning how to address, make sense of, and counter inequities experienced both individually and collectively.

Designing Instruction to Reflect the Everyday Linguistic and Sociocultural Practices of Dual Language Learning

Following Moll and Diaz (1987), we include several additional examples of approaches that illustrate design principles that engage youth in mature literacy activities to leverage and build skills for future literacy practices. One such example is found in the work of Razfar (2010). In a study of the common, everyday literacy practice of corrective feedback and repair with DLL youth, Razfar found that the design and philosophy guiding the deployment of this practice was integral to its success. Traditionally, Razfar notes, corrective feedback is cognitively and individually based; student utterances and attempts at growth are evaluated by the instructor for their form and content, and an individual assessment is given to students based on the accuracy of their response. The impulse of the practice is positive—to provide constructive feedback—but the effect can serve to undermine the DLL student's confidence and ownership of learning, as well as their very identity as a user of English, as the correction is likely to be felt as deeply personal, causing the student emotional stress. Thus, this often naturalized use of immediate and direct corrective feedback around language use can function as a language socialization practice that shapes how language is used, in what contexts, and by whom. The cultural dissonance that DLL youth often experience in this practice can push them toward an *identity* as someone who can*not* use the language correctly.

However, as Razfar (2010) explores, when instructional designs account for the multilayered challenges of dual language learning, alternative discourse practices become possible. In a year-long ethnographic study of a second grade class of DLLs, Razfar traced the ways in which the focal teacher constructed her discourse around moments of corrective feedback. He observed that when the teacher's practices were aimed toward the construction of teacher–student relationships based on *confianza*, or sustained mutual trust, inviting corrective feedback emerged. Feedback, rather than individual and error-centered, was constructive, communal, and caring in nature, and focused on growth and meaning rather than strictly on form; furthermore, the discourse through which it was delivered displayed empathy and care for students (e.g., purposeful and honest use of endearing terms of address), as well as employed and permitted the use of native language to support student's nascent attempts at English usage.

The result was a classroom culture founded on *confianza*, in which both students and teacher understood that the use of corrective feedback was aimed at broadening and supporting all participants' linguistic repertoires of practice. Because the design of the practice of corrective feedback was responsive to their burgeoning language usage, and the anxiety associated with these initial attempts at a new language identity, students were able to see themselves as valuable and important language users, and more easily accessed and engaged with critical thinking tasks. In this environment students were able to build positive peer relationships as they participated in academic tasks and skills, and gained an improved sense of ownership and agency in their language usage. In short, the corrective feedback, rooted in mutual *confianza* and the recognition of the challenges DLLs experience, supported students to take on more opportunities to critique and expand their own English language and literacy skills.

Hybrid Language Practices: Drawing on the Existing Toolkits That All Children Bring to the Classroom

Similar to Razfar, Martínez (2013) offers evidence of the pedagogical and learning benefits of drawing on the existing toolkits that all children bring to the classroom. This participant observation study in an East Los Angeles middle school focused on the role students' language ideologies played in students' learning and identities. He found that the practices of this English-only school had consequences for the ways students viewed their own first-language practices. Consequently, they saw little benefit or value in using their home language and everyday linguistic practices, including viewing code-switching practices as intellectually demanding and complex; instead, they viewed English as normative and qualitatively better.

Recognizing bilingualism as a resource to be valued, the focal teacher in Martinez's study encouraged sense making and self-expression through

Spanish and Spanglish (in which English and Spanish were blended). While home languages remained subordinated in the classroom—English literacy and expression remained the object of the course—providing opportunities to view the home language as a meaningful and productive tool in learning allowed students to recognize Spanglish as a means toward "cultural maintenance." This shift in language ideology opened up opportunities for students to increase their comprehension and to begin to cultivate a critical language awareness that fostered more agency and ownership in their learning; in challenging deficit interpretations of themselves and their linguistic abilities that had limited their investment in learning and language acquisition.

Explicit Skill Instruction in Sociocultural Practice: Intentional Support Embedded into Meaningful Practices

As we noted earlier, consequential instruction for DLLs involves much more than direct instruction around isolated, segmented aspects of literacy (e.g., phonics, decoding); however, we certainly do not discount the importance of employing explicit instruction in meaningful, contextually embedded practices. Moreover, we agree that preparing DLL youth and other nondominant students to deal with such "gatekeeping" tasks as required by standardized and other discrete assessments is a professional and ethical imperative (Delpit, 1986). As articulated by one of our design principles, practitioners need to identify areas for explicit support and employ strategic and appropriate forms of assistance to support the development of skills in meaningful practices. This is key. Learning discrete skills out of the context of meaningful and rigorous practices only helps to "encapsulate schooling" (Engeström, 2004) in ways that make literacy, and particularly language learning, inert and disconnected.

Let us consider vocabulary instruction, a seemingly narrow unit of instructional focus. Research has shown word development to be hugely important for DLL youth, as limitations in vocabulary create one of the largest barriers toward higher-level thinking objectives of DLL youth and to subsequent academic success and progress (August, Carlo, Dressler, & Snow, 2005; August & Shanahan, 2006; McKeown & Beck, 2004; Scarcella, 2003). However, we know from this research that to be effective for DLL youth, vocabulary instruction must be rooted in everyday practices and build from students' knowledge of their first-language (e.g., employing cognates), while attending in explicit ways to complex understandings of foundational words (August et al., 2005; Beck, McKeown, & Kucan, 2002; Carlo et al., 2004; Lesaux, Kieffer, Faller, & Kelley, 2010; Vaughn et al., 2009). Thus, carefully designed vocabulary instruction can serve as an illustrative practice, both because of its importance to the development of

DLL students' linguistic repertoires and because productive and engaging vocabulary instruction involves thoughtful design of ways to situate vocabulary learning in meaningful, rigorous, complex, and rich literacy practices.

A stellar example of how explicit instruction can be organized in thoughtful and relevant ways is illustrated in a mixed-methods, quasi-experimental study of the ALIAS vocabulary intervention by Lesaux and colleagues (2010). In this study, Lesaux and her team deployed an 18-week, daily intervention program in seven urban middle school classrooms serving roughly 500 students, of which 346 were DLLs. The intervention included several units organized around highly engaging, interest-driven informational text, and a limited number (eight to nine words every 2 weeks) of thoughtfully selected, high-utility academic words. At the conclusion of the program, the researchers found significant positive effects for students in meanings of taught words, morphological awareness, and definitions in text, as well as marginally significant gains in depth of word knowledge and at least one measure of reading comprehension. While DLL students still lagged behind their peers, these were promising results. We highlight this study both because it aligns with our design principles but also because it identifies an area of future, consequential research and practice.

One of the features that made this vocabulary intervention successful is how it situated vocabulary instruction into meaningful social literacy practices. First, the program was organized as a routine daily practice in these classrooms, structured such that students were continually exposed to vocabulary words across multiple contexts, with multiple definitions, and in a range of authentic ways. Second, the instruction engaged students with meaningful texts, and in whole-class and small-group discussions, including oral discussion, game play, artifact creation, and in writing activity around the themes and ideas of the texts. These rich, engaging practices served as the context for the use of focal, high-utility words across a range of social and interactional contexts. Third, because the words were present and embedded in many different contexts and media, explicit instruction around topics such as morphology, prefixes and suffixes, varied definitions, and decoding particular word parts, could be targeted and made relevant in their engagement in meaningful activity.

Of relevance to practice, teachers initially skeptical of their students' ability to complete the higher-level tasks embedded in the program were surprised to find that within the context of interest-driven, social practice, the youth participants were able to complete these rigorous tasks with ease. An important implication here is that when skills are embedded within rich, meaningful, and well-designed literacy practices, youth can engage with and master these skills far more quickly and in more compelling ways than through isolated skill, direct instruction.

Of import, the researchers designed a space in which both word learning and learning how to learn words became valued and meaningful practices, as students' active participation in richer and meaningful literacy practices gave meaning to the importance and function of learning and acquiring relevant vocabulary. By modeling how vocabulary learning could function in their own everyday activity and through participation in valued literacy and interactional practices, students not only appropriated new vocabulary, but also learned the sociocultural value of these new literacy skills. This rich example of socializing students to and through rich practices makes it is easier to see how explicit instruction around various discrete, seemingly reductive tasks (e.g., vocabulary, grammar) might be made consequential when organized around evidenced-based design principle. This intervention is also aligned with Cole's (1992) use of the sociocultural proposition of engaging youth in the mature endpoint activity as a way to model the future in the present.

As a final note, while we believe this study was an excellent example of designing intentional instruction into meaningful practices, we would note that the Lesaux study did not make any direct mention nor seem to make any intentional use of students' first languages. We refer back to the Moll and Diaz (1987) study to discuss the ways in which leveraging the children's everyday language practices and their home language repertoire could augment consequential and high-level reading skills. For example, leveraging students' understandings of cognates and exploring translated meanings in texts in their home language are key features of enriched learning for DLL youth. Furthermore, as in the Moll and Diaz study, the organization of such practices does not require any expertise in the second language by the practitioner; instead, the social organization of learning can be designed so that students of varied linguistic backgrounds might share and explore understandings and build new vocabulary across their languages in valued interactions with peers.

The Common Core Standards and Dual Language Learners

In the current academic climate, we note that meeting the special needs of DLLs—the majority of whom are in mainstream, literacy classrooms with students with a range of English language proficiency—are congruent with the demands of the Common Core State Standards (CCSS). The National Governors Association and the Council of Chief State School Officers—the leaders of the CCSS implementation—strongly argue that all students should be held to the same standards. We are in agreement with this ideal, and argue that the Common Core standards present an opportunity to engage youth in robust and consequential literacy practices; using the standards as tools that mediate instruction and learning rather than as the object of instruction, should allow educators to employ the standards reflexively and flexibly in ways that address the additional developmental demands experienced by learning a second language, as well as other sociocultural factors. We have presented research and design principles that strongly concur with the CCSS statement on the Application of CCSS for ELLs: "Teachers should recognize that it is possible to achieve the standards for reading and literature, writing and research, language development and speaking and listening without manifesting native-like control of conventions and vocabulary." We believe this statement implicitly underscores the diversity of the DLL and the complexity of second language acquisition processes. Moreover, it accounts for the time and support it takes to develop literacy, particularly academic literacy. This developmental and dynamic view of language and literacy learning is essential to developing rigorous, culturally sustaining, and future-oriented practices and language ideologies that value youths' linguistic and sociocultural histories.

Reflections and Future Directions

All youth have the right to participate in meaningful and consequential learning activity. In line with our sociocultural view of learning and development (Vygotsky, 1978), learning must be *made* to become consequential. By definition, then, practices are not static and unchanging. They are dynamic, and co-constituted by the people and tools participating in them. From this perspective, best practices are not implemented per se. Rather, evidenced-based practices should be situated in carefully designed learning ecologies in which the everyday is leveraged toward important ends and whose rigorous literacy practices push for complexity while providing the right kind and amount of support to extend students' learning. Rich practices are employed respectfully, thoughtfully, and strategically, and in ways that recognize variability in language learning and in human activity. Finally, as our nation's demographics change, so to must our pedagogies, ideologies, and instructional designs shift to ensure our literacy practices differentiate, accommodate, sustain, and extend the linguistic repertoires of DLLs.

Today's youth, particularly youth from nondominant communities, are increasingly disconnected from school and its practices. We argue for connected forms of learning (Ito et al., 2013) that leverage interest-driven and culturally and socially relevant practices in new designs that connect the everyday with school, work, and interest-driven activity to provide a variety of opportunities to use communicative and written language, and to try out how language is used across social contexts, and from different identity positions. Our own work engaging DLLs in new media, computational, and making and tinkering activity serves as an example of work that studies youth across contexts and leverages existing repertoires to build new learning pathways and trajectories (Schwartz & Gutiérrez, in press).

ENGAGEMENT ACTIVITIES

As we look toward practices that can be applied expediently in classrooms, we reiterate the importance of teachers thinking of and positioning themselves as designers. Teachers need rich understandings of the social context and everyday practices of DLLs in general, as well as their own students in particular. This knowledge helps teachers thoughtfully adapt and create a variety of practices and strategies that can enhance and enrich student learning. This rising to the concrete is praxis—the fusion of theory and practice.

Here, we identify three examples of professional practices that exemplify the best-practice design principles and praxis we have advanced. We hope educators who take up these practices will situate them in ways that have resonance for local contexts and student populations.

1. *Classroom discussion.* Encourage discussion to help DLLs develop communicative skill, oral fluency, and social–contextual uses of language. To encourage DLLs to participate "safely" in classroom discourse, employ *preheated* "cold calling." This practice involves letting students know ahead of time (rather than surprising students and demanding on-the-spot answers—a practice high in anxiety for DLL youth), that they will be asked to respond to a particular question. By giving students the opportunity to write down thoughts or converse in their first language with their peers to formulate what and how they might respond, students have multiple opportunities to produce more thoughtful responses as they develop higher-level skills of meaning making and comprehension. Additionally, slowing the pace of conversations and ensuring that space is provided for DLLs to participate and to use their oral language skills helps to ensure that all students are participating and developing important language

skills. Finally, the activity provides teachers the opportunity to reflect on the nature of their feedback and its alignment with the purpose of the learning activity: Is the goal grammatical correctness or the ongoing opportunity to use language toward a meaningful end? All classroom practices should build *confianza* (trust) with students and extend opportunities for them to engage in ways that do not isolate, alienate, or shut down their attempts to experiment with structuring and vocalizing ideas in English.

2. *Grammar/vocabulary dictionaries.* Employ grammar/vocabulary dictionaries as an ongoing practice in the literacy classroom, embedding grammar or vocabulary discussion into larger, meaningful activities. To do so, students should record new or interesting grammar/sentence structures or vocabulary words in an ongoing journal or notebook as they encounter them. This student artifact can function as an ongoing reference manual and resource as students seek new ways to express a concept or idea they learn in the course of engaging in culturally responsive and interest-driven units. Allowing these grammatical structures and vocabulary words to be chosen by the youth themselves in the context of meaningful social literacy practices helps bring relevance to the content the students select, and motivates their engagement with mastering their use. Teachers can supplement the students' list with high-utility academic words and new syntactic structures to ensure that vocabulary acquisition and grammatical and syntactic knowledge are both relevant and extended. Over the course of instruction, and as these reference manuals grow, activities can be designed to engage students in decoding their own words or identifying parts of speech of interest to them. Students can also be asked to translate their words into one or more languages, find parallel syntactical structures or cognates, and practice using them these words and structure in multiple ways and contexts. Because of the interest-driven, reflexive nature and ownership of the practice, students can participate in self-assessment, as well as more formal assessment, allowing the educator to monitor students' skill development, as evidenced in the grammar/vocabulary notebook that they create.

3. *Personal second language learning.* As Snow, Burns, and Griffin (1998) note, knowledge about language is crucial to helping teachers perform effectively in the classroom. Wong-Fillmore and Snow (2005) argued, "Oral language functions as a foundation for literacy and as the means of learning in school and out. However, despite its importance for learning, many teachers know much less about oral language than they need to know"

(p. 14). Furthermore, most teachers of students learning a second language do not themselves know a second language or the sociocultural contexts of their students' language development. With this in mind, we recommend teachers, particularly those who teach large populations of DLLs, challenge themselves to learn a second language, particular one that many of your students speak. This endeavor has important pedagogical and sociocultural possibilities, as the experience of learning a second language, particularly in an immersive environment, permits teachers to develop a deeper appreciation of the complexity and the demands of learning a second language, as well as the importance of using one's linguistic toolkit as a resource for learning and meaning making. Of significance, knowing the language of the community—even at a rudimentary level—holds significant potential for opening up lines of communication and trust with students and families, and new appreciation for the economic, cognitive, and sociocultural benefits of bilingualism.

ACKNOWLEDGMENTS

We wish to acknowledge Ashley Cartun, PhD student at the University of Colorado Boulder, who provided some research assistance in the development of this chapter.

REFERENCES

Almanza de Schoenwise, E., & Klingner, J. (2012). Linguistic and cultural issues in developing disciplinary literacy for adolescent English language learners. *Topics in Language Disorders, 32*(1), 51–68.

August, D., Carlo, M., Dressler, C., & Snow, C. (2005). The critical role of vocabulary development for English language learners. *Learning Disabilities Research and Practice, 20*(1), 50–57.

August, D., & Shanahan, T. (2006). *Developing literacy in second-language learners: Report of the National Literacy Panel on Language Minority Children and Youth.* Mahwah, NJ: Erlbaum.

Batalova, J., & McHugh, M. (2010a). *States and districts with the highest number and share of English language learners.* Washington, DC: Migration Policy Institute.

Batalova, J., & McHugh, M. (2010b). *Top languages spoken by English language learners nationally and by state.* Washington, DC: Migration Policy Institute.

Beck, I., McKeown, M., & Kucan, L. (2002). *Bringing words to life.* New York: Guilford Press.

Capps, R., Fix, M., Murray, J., Ost, J., Passel, J., & Herwantoro, S. (2005). *The new *demography of America's schools: Immigration and the No Child Left Behind Act.* Washington, DC: Urban Institute.

Carlo, M., August, D., McLaughlin, B., Snow, C., Dressler, C., Lippman, D., et al. (2004). Closing the gap: Addressing the vocabulary needs of English language learners in bilingual and mainstream classrooms. *Reading Research Quarterly, 39*(2), 188–215.

Carlo, M. S., & Bengochea, A. (2011). Best practices in literacy instruction for English language learners. In L. M. Morrow & L. B. Gambrell (Eds.), *Best practices in literacy instruction* (pp. 117–137). New York: Guilford Press.

Cole, M. (1992). Culture and cognitive development: From cross-cultural comparisons to model systems of cultural mediation. In A. F. Healy, S. M. Kosslyn, & R. M. Shiffrin (Eds.), *From learning theory to cognitive processes: Essays in honor of William K. Estes* (pp. 2279–306). Hillsdale, NJ: Erlbaum.

Cummins, J. (1981). Age on arrival and immigrant second language learning in Canada: A reassessment. *Applied Linguistics, 2*, 132–149.

Delpit, L. (1986). Skills and other dilemmas of a progressive black educator. *Harvard Educational Review, 56*(4), 379–386.

Engeström, Y. (1987). *Learning by expanding: An activity–theoretical approach to developmental research.* Helsinki: Orienta-Konsultit.

Engeström, Y. (2004). Non scolae sed vitae discimus: Toward overcoming the encapsulation of school. *Learning and Instruction, 1*, 243–259.

Faulstich Orellana, M. (2009). *Translating childhoods: Immigrant youth, language and culture.* New Brunswick, NJ: Rutgers University Press.

Gutiérrez, K. (2008). Developing a sociocritical literacy in the third space. *Reading Research Quarterly, 43*(2), 148–164.

Gutiérrez, K. (2012). Re-mediating current activity for the future. *Mind, Culture, and Activity: An International Journal, 19*, 17–21.

Gutiérrez, K., Bien, A., & Selland, M. (2011). Polylingual and polycultural learning ecologies: Mediating emergent academic literacies for dual language learners. *Journal of Early Childhood Literacy, 11*(2), 232–261.

Gutiérrez, K., & Rogoff, B. (2003). Cultural ways of learning: Individual traits or repertoires of practice. *Educational Researcher, 32*, 19–25.

Gutiérrez, K., Zepeda, M., & Castro, D. (2010). Advancing early literacy learning for all children: Implications of the NELP report for dual language learners. *Educational Researcher, 39*(4), 334–339.

Iddings, A. C, Combs, M. C., & Moll, L. (2012). In the Arid Zone: Drying out educational resources for English language learners through policy and practice. *Urban Education, 47*(2), 495–514.

Ito, M., Gutiérrez, K., Livingstone, S., Penuel, W., Rhodes, J, Salen, K., et al. (2013). *Connected learning: An agenda for research and design.* Irvine, CA: Digital Media and Learning Research Hub Reports on Connected Learning.

Klesmer, H. (1994). Assessment and teacher perceptions of ESL student achievement. *English Quarterly, 26*(3), 8–11.

Laboratory for Comparative Human Cognition. (1989). Kids and computers: A positive vision of the future. *Harvard Educational Review, 59*(1), 73–86.

Lesaux, N. K., Kieffer, M. J., Faller, S. E., & Kelley, J. G. (2010). The effectiveness and ease of implementation of an academic vocabulary intervention for linguistically diverse students in urban middle schools. *Reading Research Quarterly, 45,* 196–228.

Martínez, R. (2013). Reading the world in Spanglish: Hybrid language practices and ideological contestation in a sixth-grade English language arts class-room. *Linguistics and Education, 24,* 276–288.

McKeown, M. G., & Beck, I. L. (2004). Direct and rich vocabulary instruction. In J. F. Baumann & E. J. Kame'enui (Eds.), *Vocabulary instruction: Research to practice* (pp. 13–27). New York: Guilford Press.

Moll, L. C., & Diaz, E. (1987). Change as the goal of educational research. *Anthropology and Educational Quarterly, 18,* 300–311.

Nakamoto, J., Lindsey, K. A., & Manis, F. R. (2007). A longitudinal analysis of English language learners word decoding and reading comprehension. *Reading and Writing: An Interdisciplinary Journal, 20,* 691–719.

National Center for Education Statistics. (2011). *The nation's report card: Reading 2011* (NCES 2012-457). Washington, DC: Institute of Education Sciences, U.S. Department of Education.

National Clearinghouse for English Language Acquisition (NCELA). (2009). *State Title III directors and 2007–2008 state consolidated state performance reports (CSPR); State Title III information system.* Washington, DC: Author. Retrieved October 10, 2013, from *www.ncela.gwu.edu/t3sis.*

National Clearinghouse for English Language Acquisition (NCELA). (2011). *The growing number of English learner students, 1997/98–2007/08.* Washington, DC: Author. Retrieved October 10, 2013, from *www.ncela.us/files/uploads/9/growing_EL_0910.pdf.*

National Education Association (NEA). (2008). *English language learners face unique challenges: Policy brief.* Washington, DC: Author. Retrieved October 15, 2013, from *www.weac.org/Libraries/PDF/ELL.sflb.ashx.*

National Governors Association & Council of Chief State School Officers. (2012). *Application of Common Core State Standards for English language learners.* Retrieved October 1, 2013, from *www.corestandards.org/assets/application-for-english-learners.pdf.*

Ochs, E. (1993). Constructing social identity: A language socialization perspective. *Research on Language and Social Interaction, 26*(3), 287–306.

Ochs, E., & Schieffelin, B. (2008) Language socialization: An historical overview. In P. A. Duff & N. H. Hornberger (Eds.), *Encyclopedia of language education: Vol. 8. Language socialization* (2nd ed., pp. 3–16). New York: Springer.

Ochs, E., & Schieffelin, B. (2011). The theory of language socialization. In A. Duranti, E. Ochs, & B. Schieffelin (Eds.), *The handbook of language socialization* (pp. 1–22). Malden, MA: Wiley-Blackwell.

Pacheco, M. (2012). Learning in/through everyday resistance: A cultural-historical perspective on community resources and curriculum. *Educational Researcher, 41*(4), 121–132.

Passel, J., & Cohn, D. (2009). *A portrait of unauthorized immigrants in the United States.* Washington, DC: Pew Hispanic Center.

Peña, E., & Kester, E. S. (2004). Semantic development in Spanish-English bilinguals. In B. A. Goldstein (Ed.), *Bilingual language development and disorders in Spanish-English speakers* (pp. 105–128). Baltimore: Brookes.

Ramirez, J. D., Pasta, D. J., Yuen, S., Billings, D. K., & Ramey, D. R. (1991). *Final report: Longitudinal study of structural immersion strategy, early-exit, and late-exit transitional bilingual education programs for language minority children*. San Mateo, CA: Aguirre International.

Razfar, A. (2005). Language ideologies in practice: Repair and classroom discourse. *Linguistics and Education, 16*, 404–424.

Razfar, A. (2010). Repair with *confianza*: Rethinking the context of corrective feedback for English learners (ELs). *English Teaching: Practice and Critique, 9*(2), 11–31.

Rogoff, B. (2003). *The cultural nature of human development*. New York: Oxford University Press.

Rose, M. (1988). Narrowing the mind and page: Remedial writers and cognitive reductionism. *College Composition and Communication, 39*, 267–302.

Rumbaut, R., & Massey, D. (2013). Immigration and language diversity in the United States. *Daedalus, 142*(3), 141–154.

Scarcella, R. (2003). *Academic English: A conceptual framework*. Los Angeles: University of California Language Minority Research.

Schieffelin, B., & Ochs, E. (1986). Language socialization. In B. Siegel (Ed.), *Annual review of anthropology: Vol. 15* (pp. 163–191). Palo Alto, CA: Annual Reviews.

Schwartz, L., & Gutiérrez, K. (in press). Literacy studies and situated methods: Exploring the social organization of household activity and family media use. In J. Rowsell & K. Pahl (Eds.), *The Routledge handook of literacy studies*. New York: Routledge.

Snow, C. E., Burns, M. S., & Griffin, P. (1998). *Preventing reading difficulties in young children*. Washington, DC: National Academy Press.

U.S. Census Bureau. (2013). Table 1: Detailed languages spoken at home by English proficiency. In C. Ryan (Ed.), *Language in the United States: 2011*. Washington, DC: Author. Retrieved from *www.census.gov/prod/2013pubs/acs-22.pdf*.

Vaughn, S., Martinez, L. R., Linan-Thompson, S., Reutebuch, C. K., Carlson, C. D., & Francis, D. J. (2009). Enhancing social studies vocabulary and comprehension for seventh-grade English language learners: Findings from two experimental studies. *Journal of Research on Educational Effectiveness, 2*, 297–324.

Vygotsky, L. S. (1978). *Mind in society*. Cambridge, MA: Harvard University Press.

Wong-Fillmore, L., & Snow, C. (2005). What teachers need to know about language. In C. T. Adger, C. E. Snow, & D. Christian (Eds.), *What teachers need to know about language* (pp. 7–54). Washington, DC: Center for Applied Linguistics.

Working Group on ELL Policy. (2010). *Improving educational outcomes for English language learners: Recommendations for the reauthorization of the Elementary and Secondary Education Act*. Washington, DC: Author.

CHAPTER 7

Best Practices in Adolescent Literacy Instruction

Douglas Fisher
Nancy Frey

This chapter will:

- Explore the theory, research, and best practices related to disciplinary literacy.
- Identify and explain effective approaches for teaching content areas other than English language arts.
- Analyze close reading practices, including annotation, text-based discussions, and writing with evidence.
- Examine ways to foster transformation of texts in the mind and on paper.

The adoption of the Common Core State Standards (CCSS) has spurred renewed debate about literacy instruction for adolescents. Many secondary educators reacted positively to its emphasis on the critical role of disciplinary literacy in grades 6–12; others have viewed this goal with some bewilderment about what it means for teachers of science, history, and the technical subjects. Even if you work in a territory not directly responsible for the implementation of the Common Core standards, these are shaping discussions about the direction of literacy research itself.

For the past several decades, content teachers were told, "Every teacher is a teacher of reading." Unfortunately, this isn't accurate when you consider the complexity of reading acquisition as identified in this book. Reading instruction requires a deep knowledge of language structure and function (Schleppegrell, 2004). In addition, the focus on reading alone is limiting. Adolescents are engaged in reading, writing, speaking, listening, and viewing; in other words, they are employing the full range of literacies. The message that "every teacher is a reading teacher" confounded reading with literacy, while at the same time it diminished the importance of the discipline. This is more than an issue of semantics. Knowledge of a discipline is built through the use of all aspects of literacy. The written, spoken, and visually constructed information of a discipline becomes increasingly specialized from grades 6 to 12 and in postsecondary education. An understanding that all learning is based in language helps content teachers structure their instructional time such that students read, write, speak, listen, and view in the classroom. Providing students time to use language as part of their content-area instruction has the power to significantly improve achievement (Greenleaf et al., 2011), especially for English language learners (ELLs) (Schleppegrell, 2013).

In order for students to learn the concepts of the discipline, they must be able to cognitively transform the information. Educators have long known that learning is an active process that requires the student to manipulate information in order to make it his or her own (Bransford, Brown, & Cocking, 1999). Inadequate instructional practices rely on transmission rather than the transformation of knowledge. A transmission model of instruction is a retreat from a commitment to foster transformation of information.

In this chapter, we discuss emerging practices in adolescent literacy instruction in the disciplines that promote transformation, rather than transmission of content. We begin with an examination of the growing knowledge base of disciplinary literacy. We then spotlight four instructional practices that can contribute to the parallel advancement of content learning and literacy knowledge: close reading, annotation, discussion, and writing with evidence.

Evidence-Based Best Practices

Shanahan and Shanahan (2008) describe three stages of literacy development: the basic literacy of the primary grades, the intermediate literacy of late elementary school, and the disciplinary literacy of middle and high school (see Figure 7.1). Basic literacy represents the foundational and generalizable skills that are needed for all reading tasks: decoding

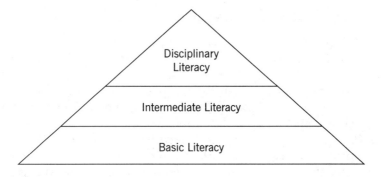

Basic Literacy: Literacy skills such as decoding and knowledge of high-frequency words that underlie virtually all reading tasks.

Intermediate Literacy: Literacy skills common to many tasks, including generic comprehension strategies, common word meanings, and basic fluency.

Disciplinary Literacy: Literacy skills specialized to history, science, mathematics, literature, or other subject matter.

FIGURE 7.1. The increasing specialization of literacy development. From Shanahan and Shanahan (2008, p. 44). Copyright 2008 by the President and Fellows of Harvard College. Reprinted by permission.

skills, comprehension of print and literacy conventions, recognition of high-frequency words, and usual fluency routines.

As students progress beyond this stage, they move into intermediate literacy. This stage involves the development of skills that allow students to use some generic skills to understand their literacy tasks. At this stage, students are better able to employ various cognitive comprehension strategies and can utilize procedures to monitor and address misunderstandings. Additionally, they are able to take notes, activate background knowledge, summarize their thinking, and so on.

Beyond this stage, disciplinary literacy becomes the focus. The skills involved in this stage have not traditionally been formally taught and are difficult to acquire due to the abstract nature of many discipline-specific texts. Moreover, disciplinary literacy is constrained in terms of its applicability to a wide range of reading materials. Specifically, an English teacher who is proficient in teaching literacy skills related to reading classic and contemporary novels may not be so skilled at guiding students to comprehend a technical biology article from a professional journal. The disciplines of history/social studies and the sciences have been most thoroughly explored in the research literature.

Disciplinary Literacy in History

Discipline-specific literacy in social studies and history demands that students are able to read, discuss, and write critically about historical events and documents. Wineburg's (1991) comparative analysis of high school history students and historians exposed a glaring gap in the use of analytic thinking by the two groups. High school students were much more vulnerable to simply accepting the content of the documents at face value, while historians routinely interrogated the text. Stahl and Shanahan (2004) identified three essential literacy practices of historians, namely, that they identify the source of the information, corroborate the contents through other reliable sources, and contextualize the information within the milieu of the time. Monte-Sano and De La Paz (2012) have researched how the construction of document-based questioning prompts influence whether students use or fail to use these practices. They found that prompts written to spur thinking about sourcing ("What was happening in the world that motivated them to give these speeches?"), causation ("Why did they speak out?"), or corroboration ("What are the similarities and differences between these two documents?") resulted in higher-quality writing (p. 279). On the other hand, situated prompts that asked students what they would do ("Write a letter to the secretary-general") resulted in lower-quality historical reasoning because students wrote from a contemporary perspective, rather than from a historical one.

Discipline-Specific Literacy in Science

In contrast, scientific literacy requires students to apply knowledge across texts and science fields in order to understand concepts. For example, understanding the process of osmosis requires knowledge of biology, chemistry, and physics. Faggella-Luby, Sampson Graner, Deshler, and Valentino Drew (2012) state that "novice readers often ignore, discount, or compartmentalize information," unlike scientists who "deeply engage with concepts across science genres" and fields (p. 71). The inability to think across science content limits their ability to create scientific texts, such as reporting on results of lab experiments. Nam, Choi, and Hand (2011) recommend use of a science writing heuristic to promote such critical thinking. Throughout the lab, the science teacher pauses to promote written student inquiry:

- *Question*: What are my questions I hope to answer through this experiment?
- *Test*: What tests can I conduct?
- *Observe*: What are my observations?

- *Inquiry*: What are my data?
- *Claim and Evidence*: What do I claim? What is my evidence?
- *Collaboration*: How do my claims compare to others?
- *Reflection*: How have my ideas changed from the beginning?

In this model, science writing isn't viewed as a single element of literacy, but rather as the convergence of all. Students read and discuss the work of others, make observations, analyze data, and write about them. In comparative studies of middle school science students, the researchers found that public discussion and negotiation of the investigation resulted in higher levels of application of scientific argumentation in their summary writing (Nam et al., 2011).

In order for students to gain discipline-specific literacies necessary for content learning, they must be able to transform texts and information in their minds and on paper. In the next section, we explore four instructional practices necessary for this transformation to occur. However, these hinge on assumptions about text complexity. In the absence of these assumptions, best practices for transforming texts have limited effectiveness.

Best Practices in Action

Assumptions about Text Complexity

In discussing best practices, it is useful to identify assumptions on which these practices are predicated. Our assumption is related to text complexity. As Allington (2002) emphatically states, "You can't learn much from books you can't read" (p. 16). In fact, there is no evidence that an 11th-grade learner reading at the fifth-grade level will benefit from reading 11th-grade texts without fairly extensive supports. Secondary-content teachers have long faced this dilemma, but without the tools to provide such support they replaced text-based sources with lectures. A student reading well below grade level is going to need access to texts such that will allow him or her to extract information in a meaningful way. However, confining him or her to texts that are at his or her independent reading level will not result in gains in content knowledge. We have decades of evidence about that problem. Secondary students need complex texts, and they need to be adequately supported to understand them. In the next section, we discuss four instructional approaches that provide meaningful access to complex texts and content. These text-based supports allow struggling readers to benefit more fully from transformational instruction by lowering the barriers presented by texts that are too difficult to read. Importantly, these supports—close reading, annotation, discussion, and writing with evidence—require the use of all facets of literacy. We'll follow Kim Elliot, a high school biology teacher, as she leads her students through lessons featuring these practices.

Four Instructional Approaches

Close Reading

The practice of close analytic reading of complex text is not new, having been applied for nearly a century in college classrooms across the world. High school educators have relied for many years on the works of Adler and Van Doren (*How to Read a Book*, 1972) and Elder and Paul (*The Thinkers Guide to How to Read a Paragraph*, 2008) to guide students through careful inspection of a text. Having said that, not all texts deserve this kind of attention. Elder and Paul (2008) advise that the first step is determining the purpose of the reading (Reading for a Purpose, ¶ 5):

1. *Sheer pleasure*: requires no particular skill level.
2. *To figure out a simple idea*: which may require skimming the text.
3. *To gain specific technical information*: skimming skills required.
4. *To enter, understand, and appreciate a new worldtview*: requires close reading skills in working through a challenging series of tasks that stretch our minds.
5. *To learn a new subject*: requires close reading skills in internalizing and taking ownership of an organized system of meanings.

When a sufficiently complex text does warrant careful inspection, close reading instruction is in order. In our experience, we have found that short passages, be they wholly self-contained or excerpted from a longer reading, work best. This allows students to zoom in on a particularly challenging text, one rich with disciplinary knowledge, in order to deeply understand its content. High school biology teacher Kim Elliot did just that during a unit on evolution. She selected a passage from *The Panda's Thumb: More Reflections in Natural History* (Gould, 1980). "I chose this reading as part of a larger study of contrivances, or imperfect but functional adaptations, in organisms," she said. "My students will also reading and discussing other examples, like Darwin's work on the study of floral diversification." She determined the purpose of the reading—to learn a new subject—and identified the main points. "I want them to understand that these adaptations are the product of whatever the organism had available, and how these resulting contrivances are a bit of evolutionary 'make do.' What I mean by that is that although it isn't perfect, it's functional and pretty clever," she said.

Her close reading consists of a minimal amount of frontloading. Students had previously learned about the basic elements of evolution earlier in the week. "They need some prior knowledge to draw upon if they're going to understand this article," Ms. Elliot remarked. A hallmark of a novice learner is that they are not good at knowing what information they will need for a task, and therefore they frequently overlook existing knowledge they possess when learning something new (Billingsley & Wildman, 1990; Bransford et al., 1999). "In the past I probably would have spent 20 minutes reteaching them what they had previously learned before we ever got to the article," she said. "But that's not what scientists do. They have to consolidate what is known and what is unknown. I realized that when I do all the frontloading they didn't have to think about what they need. It's like packing for a trip. It's more challenging when you have to decide what goes in the suitcase yourself, as opposed to having someone pack it for you."

Students first begin to transform information in their minds by making connections to what they already know. This requires them to leverage the *right* prior knowledge in order to begin building a schema for new information. "That's tough for them," said the science teacher. "But I need for them to consider and either discard or select relevant information for themselves," she said. "I can't always be the one doing all the thinking for them."

Ms. Elliot usually has students read the passage once to themselves "to get the flow of the information" and "if it's really tough I'll read it aloud to them while they follow along." Students who need more support might listen to an audio recording, or read the text in shorter chunks. Ms. Elliot said, "When I first started I thought I would really have a hard time with my students who read below grade level," she said. "In practice that hasn't been the case because there's so much rereading and discussion that the kids who don't get it the first time begin to understand it better as we proceed."

Ms. Elliot often thinks aloud about a portion of the passage to model scientific thinking. "I added a labeled diagram of a panda's paw to the reading," said Ms. Elliot. "The part I chose to model was how I drew on the anatomy unit we had completed a few months ago to understand the terms in the article and the diagram. I thought aloud about the adductor and abductor muscles in order to show them how I was drawing on knowledge from a previous unit to understand."

Annotation

The practice of annotating a text, that is, marking and writing on the text in a meaningful way, is as old as books themselves. Even centuries ago when a monastery's library might only hold 10 or 20 books, monks made annotations on sacred texts. There are several reasons for annotating text, first and foremost because it promotes cognitive interaction and metacognitive thinking. It can also contribute to discipline-specific understanding of texts. Monte-Sano (2011) described the efficacy of annotations to support the development of historical reasoning in high school. Initially students annotated little or not at all, but with practice and feedback from their teacher on the annotations, students in the study were increasingly adept at using multiple, contrasting pieces of evidence to support claims and interpretations.

Science students must locate and construct valid arguments based on evidence (Driver, Newton, & Osborne, 2000). However, novice science students often simply consume texts whole without noticing the evidence forwarded to support a claim. Annotation practices invite students to slow down, reread, and interact with texts. During Ms. Elliot's close reading of the passage from *The Panda's Thumb* (Gould, 1980), students were required to annotate. "The second time they read through the text, I tell them to annotate," she said. "We've done quite a bit of work as a school on annotation so that students are comfortable doing this."

Her school has developed guidelines for doing so, and encourages students to customize their annotations as they become more skilled. Schoolwide annotation practices, derived from the work of Adler and Van Doren (1972) include:

- Underline the major points using your pen or pencil.
- Circle keywords or phrases that are confusing or unknown to you.
- Write a question mark (?) for areas you are wondering about during the reading. Be sure to write your question!
- Use an exclamation mark (!) for things that surprise you and briefly note what it was that caught your attention.

"Some teachers use highlighters as well, although I don't because I want them to spend more of their attention on making notes to themselves, rather than filling the page with bright colors. I know when I look back at some of my old college textbooks I have no idea why I highlighted something. I wasn't annotating," she said. Student annotations also give her insight into what a student is noticing and not noticing. "When I have a student who is struggling with understanding and interpreting a complex text, I ask her to show me her annotations," Ms. Elliot said. "Sometimes it's practically blank, which tells me she wasn't reading for detail. Other times I see the questions they have written and places where they have marked their confusion. It helps me laser-in on what the roadblock might be." In the case of this passage, the main idea was in the second sentence, and easily overlooked by most of her students during the early phase of the close reading lesson:

> Our textbooks like to illustrate evolution with examples of optimal design—nearly perfect mimicry of a dead leaf by a butterfly or of a poisonous species by a palatable relative. But ideal design is a lousy argument for evolution. (Gould, 1980, p. 20)

Ms. Elliot observed the annotative behaviors of her students, making notes to herself about who noticed and who did not. Rather than correct this immediately (a temptation to be sure), she used this information to guide discussion of the main idea and key details, reminding students to continue to annotate throughout the discussion phase of the close reading lesson.

Discussion

Meaningful talk about complex text drives close reading lessons. As noted earlier, students engage in repeated readings and annotate in order to transform thoughts and questions onto paper. But without discussion, these practices are far less effective. It also requires a skilled teacher to lead the discussion, not just host an extended question-and-answer session. The use of accountable talk practices (Michaels, O'Connor, Hall, & Resnick, 2010) ensures that students practice the three principles of discussion: accountability to the classroom community, to the knowledge base, and to the practice of reasoning and logic as an intellectual pursuit. In practice, it is common to consider the student side of accountable talk; in truth it begins with the teacher's consistent use of these same principles. Michaels and colleagues (2010) recommend that teachers use the following conversational moves to promote accountable talk and avoid regressing to a "chalk and talk" session (italics are direct quotes from pp. 27–32):

- *Marking:* "That's an important point." By marking student comments, you alert others to key points that you want to forward.
- *Challenging students:* "What do *you* think?" This is an effective conversational move for turning the conversation back to them. Remember, you already know the content. They're the ones who need to discover it.
- *Keeping the channels open*: "Did everyone hear that?" Large classrooms can make it difficult for students to follow discussions. By asking questions like this from time to time, you mark important points and moderate sound levels.

- *Keeping everyone together*: "Who can repeat . . .?" This invites students to expand on the comments of others, and reminds them about the importance of listening in discussion.
- *Linking contributions:* "Who wants to add on . . .?" Many people refer to it as "piggybacking." Adolescents need to acquire the ability to link and synthesize commentary.
- *Verifying and clarifying*: "So, are you saying . . .?" The teacher is not only a facilitator, but also a guide who elevates the conversation. Restatements such as this can expand academic language and highlight where gaps in knowledge or logic still need to be addressed by the group.
- *Pressing for accuracy*: "Where can we find that?" We use this frequently, especially with text-based discussion, to guide listeners about how evidence is located. At other times, it can help a speaker discern between hearsay and evidence.
- *Building on prior knowledge*: "How does this connect?" Link the concepts and texts under current discussion to those that have been read and discussed in previous lessons.
- *Pressing for reasoning*: "Why do you think that?" The intent of a question like this is to move the conversation from opinion to argument. This encourages the speaker to provide facts, cite textual evidence, or identify when the circumstance is ambiguous.
- *Expanding reasoning*: "Take your time; say more." The teacher delivers this message to signal the class about the importance of hearing every voice. Some students are quick to answer and can easily dominate. This conversational move validates those who arrive at conclusions as they speak.
- *Recapping:* "What have we discovered?" Extended discussions can end too abruptly and leave participants wondering about larger ideas. This conversational move invites summary and synthesis.

Many secondary students wrongly view the teacher as the primary source; he or she is not. These conversational moves keep the discussion going and challenge students to collectively locate answers within and across texts and experiences. While these conversational moves are generalizable across readings, text-dependent questions are developed with a specific reading in mind. Text-dependent questions cause students to engage in meaningful rereading, and advance their comprehension beyond surface-level comprehension. Shanahan (2013) lays down a three-part cognitive path that works for us: *What does the text say? How does the text work? What does the text mean?* The first path through a reading invites discussion about the main ideas and details, while the second path asks students to look at the structure. The third path—What does the text mean?—requires students to infer across the text and make intertextual comparisons. Unfortunately, too often students never progress beyond the first cognitive path and therefore have little experience at deepening their comprehension.

Biology teacher Kim Elliot designs text-dependent questions in advance of the close reading in order to guide students' thinking. Their initial readings of the text involve the entire passage; as they examine structure and deeper meaning their rereadings sometimes consist of a few sentences or paragraphs:

- *What the text says–General understandings and key details*: How did the panda's thumb evolve? Is this a perfect design or an imperfect one?
- *How the text works–Structure and vocabulary*: How does the author vacillate between posing questions and furnishing information? To what effect? What is an "opposable thumb"? What are the similarities and differences between the panda's paw and the human hand?
- *What the text means–Author's purpose*: How does Gould demonstrate his progression in understanding imperfect design? What is his stance regarding imperfect design?
- *What the text means–Inferencing across the text:* How does the last paragraph of the reading compare and contrast with the first?
- *What the text means–Intertextual connections:* Reexamine the section on evolutionary design in our textbook. Should it be expanded to include examples of imperfect design? Why or why not?

"I don't always use all the questions I prepare, and I don't follow them in a lockstep order," said Ms. Elliot. "It really varies by class period. At times the group comes together very early on in arriving at conclusions or anticipating a point before I have even posed the question. Other times I need to lead them a bit more," she said. "But I'm finding that by having my questions ready, I am much better at listening for learning and inquiry, and not just 'correct answers.' I'm clearer on what I want them to learn from the piece," she offered.

Writing with Evidence

While taking notes is a strong predictor of test performance (Peverly, Ramaswamy, & Brown, 2007), students often do not know how to take good notes. In a study of the implementation of several content-literacy instructional routines, teachers noted that students had difficulty with identifying main ideas and summarizing, and that their instruction in taking and making notes improved student performance (Fisher, Frey, & Lapp, 2009). At the same time, secondary students find the volume of information they must acquire and process each day challenging.

Another major challenge for secondary students is the increased emphasis on writing to inform, explain, and persuade. Students in middle school may find this especially difficult, given the diminished attention to writing personal responses. The Common Core standards describe three text types—narrative, informational, and argumentative—that are mixed and matched for a variety of purposes. Rather than writing a one-dimensional piece, they are more often required to combine these in a variety of ways. For example, the passage read by Ms. Elliot's biology class included narrative paragraphs (the author's recounting of a visit to a zoo as a child), informative paragraphs (devoted to the anatomy of the panda paw), and argumentative paragraphs (statements linking claims to evidence). However, without good notes to draw upon, students are not adequately prepared to write using evidence. Instead, they rely too heavily on what they have personally experienced, or what they recall from a text read days or weeks ago. In both cases, the result is vague, weakly constructed information.

A third challenge to writing with evidence is that many secondary students write infrequently. A national survey of high school science, social studies, and English teachers found that 47% did not assign a multiparagraph essay even once a month, and 71% did not assign one weekly (Kiuhara, Graham, & Hawken, 2009). We would be appalled if reading assignments were so paltry, and yet the dearth of writing that occurs in high school classrooms is somehow more acceptable to some. It is hard to imagine how students will ever become stronger writers when they engage in writing so infrequently.

Ms. Elliot knows that science students need to write regularly. Many of their science writing assignments are text-based. "We call them science weeklys at my school," she explained. Students must summarize and synthesize readings drawn from close readings in the classroom and their own outside readings. At the conclusion of the close readings she conducts, she asks her students to use their annotations to create collaborative graphic organizers, another means for transforming the text on paper. Venn diagrams, concept maps, semantic webs, compare-and-contrast charts, cause-and-effect charts, and the like, allow students to create visual representations of what they have read.

Transforming a piece of text into a graphic and visual form requires students to reread and engage in critical thinking about what they read. Graphic organizers have been used with students of all ages and across the disciplines (Fertig, 2008; Struble, 2007). They have been used with students with disabilities (Gajria, Jitendra, & Sood, 2007), English language learners (Rubinstein-Ávila, 2006), and students identified as gifted and talented (Cassidy, 1989). In sum, graphic organizers are an effective way for students to learn and remember content. Unfortunately, sometimes graphic organizers are simple photocopies and function more like worksheets rather than thinking tools.

The misapplication of a graphic organizer occurs when students are asked to copy information onto the tool, often while the teacher does all of the work and thus all of the thinking. For example, the students in another teacher's class were each provided with a photocopy of a Venn diagram. Following a reading of an informational text that compared cuttlefish and squid, the students copied the information that she wrote and projected with a document camera. By the end of the lesson, each student had an exact replica of the teachers' graphic organizer but they did none of the analysis or thinking. While the product is impressive, the students in the class are not benefiting from the use of graphic organizers as a tool for transforming text. They are no more likely to use a Venn diagram when confronted with a text that compares and contrasts information. And they are not very likely to remember the specific information about cuttlefish and squid.

The students in Ms. Elliot's class have a very different experience with graphic organizers. They were taught various tools at the beginning of the year and are encouraged to select a tool that fits with the information presented. After the close reading, students convened in small collaborative groups to expand their annotations using graphic organizing tools. Rather than decide for them, and thus do the critical thinking for them, Ms. Elliot made a variety of graphic organizers available for them to use. Students worked together to ensure that key points were recorded. At the end of the week, they will be writing a summary and critique of this reading for their science weekly, equipped with evidence to draw from the text.

Graphic organizers do not have to be two-dimensional. Three-dimensional and manipulative graphic organizers are called Foldables™ (Fisher, Zike, & Frey, 2007). In essence, students fold paper in specific configurations to represent the content or concept. For example, a flip-book made from three pieces of paper provides students with a tool to take notes about the Five Pillars of Islam. A piece of paper held in portrait position and folded in half on the vertical axis, and then cut three times to make four tabs, is used to take notes about the four ways that heat can be transferred. A similar three-tab fold was used by a student in a biology class to take notes about the digestive system (see Figure 7.2). These interactive graphic organizers provide students with a structure that they use to store information, building their schema for later recall and use.

Reflections and New Directions

A common objection we field from content teachers is that these practices take too much time. "How will I cover all my content?," they argue. We contend that they are correct *if they presume to leave everything else as is.* A close reading is hard to squeeze in to a 60-minute period that has always featured 45 minutes of lecture each day. To be sure, the process of teaching students to think, not just consume, is a daunting one. Many students in our classrooms today have relatively little experience at engaging in

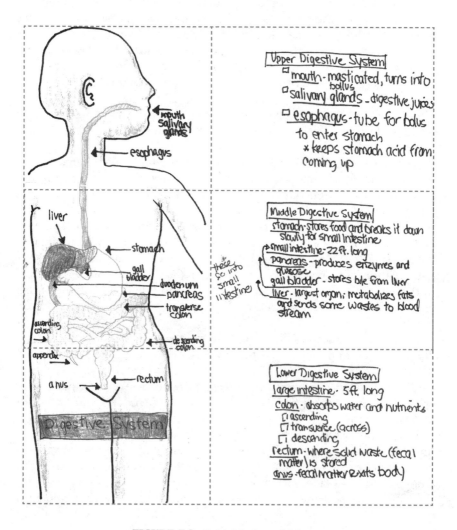

FIGURE 7.2. Foldable from biology.

inquiry; they have become accustomed to being taught exactly what will be on the test and not much more. But our goal is to turn out thinkers, not encyclopedias. That spirit of inquiry, the ability to question and probe texts, and with it, the thinking of others, is where we are setting the bar for ourselves as a profession. And we can't achieve a higher goal simply through maintaining the status quo.

A second concern we have, and that we hear from others, is that independent reading will disappear from schools. Students must read widely, and for a variety of reasons, including reading for pleasure. Adolescents need opportunities to discover their identities through text, and without heavy accountability (Ivey & Johnston, 2013). A steady diet of daily reading does wonders for building background knowledge about the range of topics needed across the curriculum (Fisher, Grant, & Ross, 2010). A study of educational success among students in 27 countries found that coming from a home with 500 books was the strongest predictor of a child's level of educational attainment—stronger than parents' occupation, education, or demographics (Evans, Kelley, Sikora, & Treiman, 2010). And while it may not be feasible to stock home libraries, the use of daily opportunities to read from an array of texts has a positive effect on content learning (Francois, 2013). When these two assumptions are in place—a move from lecture to inquiry, with daily opportunities to read, discuss, and write for a variety of purposes—the effects of these practices will be magnified.

Concluding Remarks

Discipline-specific literacy is an important consideration for adolescent learners. As we have noted, there are a number of best practices for helping students learn content, all of which have a basis in language. While we no long think of all teachers as teachers of reading, teachers can use reading, writing, speaking, listening, and viewing to ensure student understanding. Discipline-specific literacy draws on each of the literacy components addressed in this book from vocabulary to comprehension, to enable readers to make sense of the complex and amazing world around them.

ENGAGEMENT ACTIVITIES

1. Identify the differences in the ways different content areas approach reading and writing. How is it that scientists read or write and how is that different from other disciplines?

2. Use any of the transforming-text approaches to summarize this chapter. You might engage in a close reading, annotate the pages,

engage in an extended discussion about the text, create a graphic organizer, take notes, or summarize your understanding in writing. Share your transformations with others and talk about the differences and similarities you identified.

3. Consider an upcoming lesson. How might you change that lesson to include the evidence-based practices discussed in this chapter? Is there a piece of text that students could read closely?

4. Select a piece of text worthy of instruction. Develop a series of text-dependent questions that require students to return to the text to determine the answers. Review the questions to ensure that they are not limited to recall, right there, questions.

RESOURCES FOR FURTHER LEARNING

For additional information on instructional approaches for transforming texts, see the following:

Fisher, D., Frey, N., & Alfaro, C. (2013). *The path to get there: A Common Core road map for higher student achievement across the disciplines.* New York: Teachers College Press.

Graham, S., & Perin, D. (2007). *Writing next: Effective strategies to improve writing of adolescents in middle and high schools* (Carnegie Corporation Report). Washington, DC: Alliance for Excellent Education.

Michaels, S., O'Connor, M. C., Hall, M. W., & Resnick, L. B. (2010). *Accountable Talk® sourcebook: For classroom conversation that works* (v.3.1). Pittsburgh, PA: University of Pittsburgh Institute for Learning. Retrieved from *http://ifl.lrdc. pitt.edu.*

REFERENCES

Adler, M. J., & Van Doren, C. (1972). *How to read a book.* New York: Touchstone.

Allington, R. L. (2002). You can't learn much from books you can't read. *Educational Leadership, 60*(3), 16–19.

Billingsley, B. S., & Wildman, T. M. (1990). Facilitating reading comprehension in learning disabled students: Metacognitive goals and instructional strategies. *Remedial and Special Education, 11*(2), 18–31.

Bransford, J. D., Brown, A. L., & Cocking, R. C. (Eds.). (1999). *How people learn: Brain, mind, experience, and school.* Washington, DC: National Academy Press.

Callison, D. (2003). Note-taking: Different notes for different research stages. *School Library Media Activities Monthly, 19*(7), 33–37, 45.

Cassidy, J. (1989). Using graphic organizers to develop critical thinking. *Gifted Child Today, 12,* 34–36.

Driver, R., Newton, P., & Osborne, J. (2000). Establishing the norms of scientific argumentation in classrooms. *Science Education, 84*(3), 287–312.

Evans, M. D. R., Kelley, J., Sikora, J., & Treiman, D. J. (2010). Family scholarly culture and educational success: Books and schooling in 27 nations. *Research in Social Stratification and Mobility, 28*(2), 171–197.

Faggella-Luby, M., Sampson Graner, P., Deshler, D., & Valentino Drew, S. (2012). Building a house on sand: Why disciplinary literacy is not sufficient to replace general strategies for adolescent learners who struggle. *Topics in Language Disorders, 32*(1), 69–84.

Fertig, G. (2008). Using biography to help young learners understand the causes of historical change and continuity. *Social Studies, 99*(4), 147–154.

Fisher, D., Frey, N., & Lapp, D. (2009). Meeting AYP in a high need school: A formative experiment. *Journal of Adolescent and Adult Literacy, 52*, 386–396.

Fisher, D., Grant, M., & Ross, D. (2010). Building background knowledge. *The Science Teacher, 77*(1), 23–26.

Fisher, D., Zike, D., & Frey, N. (2007, August). Foldables: Improving learning with 3-D interactive graphic organizers. *Classroom Notes Plus*, pp. 1–12.

Francois, C. (2013). Reading in the crawl space: A study of an urban school's literacy-focused community of practice. *Teachers College Record, 115*(5), 1–35.

Gajria, M., Jitendra, A., & Sood, S. (2007). Improving comprehension of expository text in students with LD: A research synthesis. *Journal of Learning Disabilities, 40*(3), 210–225.

Gould, S. J. (1980). *The panda's thumb: More reflections in natural history.* New York: Norton.

Greenleaf, C. L., Litman, C., Hanson, T. L., Rosen, R., Boscardin, C. K., Herman, J., et al. (2011). Integrating literacy and science in biology: Teaching and learning impacts of reading apprenticeship professional development. *American Educational Research Journal, 48*(3), 647–717.

Ivey, G., & Johnston, P. (2013). Engagement with young adult literature: Outcomes and processes. *Reading Research Quarterly, 48*(3), 255–275.

Kiuhara, S. A., Graham, S., & Hawken, L. S. (2009). Teaching writing to high school students: A national survey. *Journal of Educational Psychology, 101*(1), 136–160.

Michaels, S., O'Connor, M. C., Hall, M. W., & Resnick, L. B. (2010). *Accountable Talk® sourcebook: For classroom conversation that works* (v.3.1). Pittsburgh, PA: University of Pittsburgh Institute for Learning. Retrieved from *http://ifl.lrdc.pitt.edu*.

Monte-Sano, C. (2011). Beyond reading comprehension and summary: Learning to read and write in history by focusing on evidence, perspective, and interpretation. *Curriculum Inquiry, 41*(2), 212–249.

Monte-Sano, C., & De La Paz, S. (2013). Using writing tasks to elicit adolescents' historical reasoning. *Journal of Literacy Research, 44*(3), 273–299.

Nam, J., Choi, A., & Hand, B. (2011). Implementation of the science writing heuristic (SWH) approach in 8th grade science classrooms. *International Journal of Science and Mathematics Education, 9*(5), 1111–1133.

Paul, R., & Elder, L. (2008). *The thinker's guide to how to read a paragraph* [Kindle version]. Tomales, CA: Foundation for Critical Thinking.

Peverly, S., Ramaswamy, V., & Brown, C. (2007). What predicts skill in lecture note taking? *Journal of Educational Psychology, 99*(1), 167–80.

Rubinstein-Ávila, E. (2006). Connecting with Latino learners. *Educational Leadership, 63*(5), 38–43.

Schleppegrell, M. J. (2004). *The language of schooling: A functional linguistics perspective.* Mahwah, NJ: Erlbaum.

Schleppegrell, M. J. (2013). The role of metalanguage in supporting academic language development. *Language Learning, 63,* 153–170.

Shanahan, T. (2013). Meeting the Common Core challenge: Planning close reading. Retrieved from *https://sites.google.com/site/tscommoncore/home/close-reading.*

Shanahan, T., & Shanahan, C. (2008). Teaching disciplinary literacy to adolescents: Rethinking content-area literacy. *Harvard Educational Review, 78*(1), 40–59.

Stahl, S. A., & Shanahan, C. (2004). Learning to think like a historian: Disciplinary knowledge through critical analysis of multiple documents. In T. L. Jetton & J. A. Dole (Eds.), *Adolescent literacy research and practice* (pp. 94–115). New York: Guilford Press.

Struble, J. (2007). Using graphic organizers as formative assessment. *Science Scope, 30*(5), 69–71.

Wineburg, S. S. (1991). On the reading of historical texts: Notes on the breach between school and academy. *American Education Research Journal, 28,* 495–519.

PART III

EVIDENCE-BASED STRATEGIES FOR LITERACY LEARNING AND TEACHING

CHAPTER 8

Best Practices in Teaching Phonological Awareness and Phonics

Patricia M. Cunningham

This chapter will:

- Describe the role of phonemic awareness in learning to read.
- Explore what research says about the best way to teach phonics.
- Summarize what we know about multisyllabic word decoding.
- Depict classroom practices consistent with what we know about phonemic awareness, phonics, and multisyllabic word decoding.
- Connect the activities to the reading foundation standards in the Common Core State Standards for the English language arts.

Phonics is and has been the most controversial issue in reading. Since 1955, when Rudolph Flesch's book *Why Johnny Can't Read* became a national best-seller, educators and parents have debated the role of phonics in beginning-reading instruction. A variety of published phonics programs have been touted as the "cure-all" for everyone's reading problems. Enthusiasm for these programs has lasted just long enough for everyone to relearn the truth that thoughtful reading requires much more than just the ability to quickly decode words. As the chapters of this book demonstrate, the most effective literacy frameworks include a variety of instruction and activities that provide children with a balanced literacy diet. This chapter focuses on phonemic awareness and phonics. When the knowl-edge from this chapter is combined with that from all the other chapters, good balanced research-based literacy instruction will result.

Evidence-Based Best Practices

To become good readers and writers, children must learn to decode words. In the beginning stages of learning to read, phonemic awareness is crucial to success. As children move through the primary grades, they must develop phonics strategies. Successful reading in the intermediate grades requires children to have strategies for decoding multisyllabic words. The Common Core State Standards (CCSS) for the English lan-guage arts (ELA) recognizes the importance of phonemic awareness, phonics, and morphemic knowledge by focusing on these in the Reading Foundations strand of the CCCSS for the ELA (National Governors Asso-ciation & Council of Chief State School Officers [NGA & CCSSO], 2010) We can use these foundational standards and research to guide us as we ourselves guide children through all stages of successful decoding.

Phonemic Awareness

One of the understandings that many children gain from early reading and writing encounters is the realization that spoken words are made up of sounds. These sounds (phonemes) are not separate and distinct. In fact, their existence is quite abstract. Phonemic awareness has many levels and includes the concept of rhyme, the ability to blend and seg-ment words, and the ability to manipulate phonemes to form different words. Phonemic awareness standards for kindergarten require that stu-dents demonstrate understanding of spoken words, syllables, and sounds including the ability to:

- Recognize and produce rhyming words.
- Count, pronounce, blend, and segment syllables in spoken words.
- Blend and segment onsets and rimes of single-syllable spoken words.
- Isolate and pronounce the initial, medial vowel, and final sounds in three-phoneme words.
- Add or substitute individual sounds in simple, one-syllable words to make new words.

Phonemic awareness is one of the best predictors of success in learn-ing to read (Ehri & Nunes, 2002; National Reading Panel [NRP], 2000). Upon learning that phonemic awareness is such an important concept, some people have concluded that phonemic awareness is all we need to worry about in preparing children to read. Phonemic awareness training programs have been developed and mandated for every child every day for 30–40 minutes. The classroom reality is that there are only so many minutes in a day, and if something gets 30–40 minutes, other important things get less time. In addition to phonemic awareness, children who are going to learn to read successfully must develop print-tracking skills and begin to learn some letter names and sounds. They need to develop cognitive clarity about what reading and writing are for, which you can only learn when you spend some of your time each day in the presence of reading and writing. Yopp and Yopp (2000) argue for phonemic awareness instruction as only *one* part of a beginning literacy program:

> Our concern is that in some classrooms phonemic awareness instruction will replace other crucial areas of instruction. Phonemic awareness supports reading development only if it is part of a broader program that includes—among other things—development of students' vocabulary, syntax, comprehension, strategic reading abilities, decoding strategies, and writing across all content areas. (p. 142)

Phonics

While there is general agreement on the need to develop children's decoding strategies, there is little agreement on which methods are most successful for doing this. Stahl, Duffy-Hester, and Stahl (1998) reviewed the research on phonics instruction and concluded that there are several types of good phonics instruction and that there is no research base to support the superiority of any one particular type. The NRP (2000) reviewed the experimental research on teaching phonics and determined that explicit and systematic phonics is superior to nonsystematic or no phonics but that there is no significant difference in effectiveness among the kinds of systematic phonics instruction:

> In teaching phonics explicitly and systematically, several different instructional approaches have been used. These include synthetic phonics, analytic phonics, embedded phonics, analogy phonics, onset-rime phonics, and phonics through spelling. . . . Phonics-through-spelling programs teach children to transform sounds into letters to write words. Phonics in context approaches teach children to use sound–letter correspondences along with context clues to identify unfamiliar words they encounter in text. Analogy phonics programs teach children to use parts of written words they already know to identify new words. The distinctions between systematic phonics approaches are not absolute, however, and some phonics programs combine two or more of these types of instruction. (p. 2-89)

Several studies published since the NRP report suggest that effective phonics instruction might include a variety of approaches. Davis (2000) found that spelling-based decoding instruction was as effective as reading-based decoding instruction for all her students, but more effective for children with poor phonological awareness. Juel and Minden-Cupp (2000) noted that the most effective teachers they observed of children who entered first grade with few literacy skills combined systematic letter–sound instruction with onset/rime analogy instruction and taught these units for application in both reading and writing. McCandliss, Beck, Sandak, and Perfetti (2003) investigated the effectiveness of Isabel Beck's instructional strategy, Word Building, with students who had failed to benefit from traditional phonics instruction. They found that the children who received this word-building instruction demonstrated significantly greater improvements on standardized measures of decoding, comprehension, and phonological awareness.

The CCSS do not specify how phonics is to be taught. Rather, they specify that children should know and apply grade-level phonics and word analysis skills in decoding words. Kindergarteners are expected to know the most frequent sound for each consonant and the long and short sounds for the five vowels. First graders learn the common sound for the consonants digraphs (*sh, ch, th, wh*); the sounds for final-*e* vowels, vowel teams, inflectional endings (*s, ed, ing*); and are expected to decode regularly spelled one- and two-syllable words. In addition to the kindergarten and first-grade expectations, second graders are expected to decode words with common prefixes and suffixes.

Multisyllabic Word Decoding

Little research has been conducted on multisyllabic word decoding, but what we do know leads us to believe that morphemes—prefixes, suffixes, and roots—are the building blocks of big words. In 1984, Nagy and Anderson published a landmark study in which they analyzed a sample of 7,260 words found in books commonly read in grades 3–9. They found that most of these words were polysyllabic words and that many of these big words were related semantically through their morphology. Some of these relationships are easily noticed. The words *hunter, redness, foglights,* and *stringy* are clearly related to the words *hunt, red, fog,* and *string.* Other, more complex, word relationships exist between such words as *planet/planetarium, vice/vicious,* and *apart/apartment.* Nagy and Anderson hypothesized that if children knew or learned how to interpret morphological relationships, they could comprehend six or seven words for every basic word known. McCutchen, Green, and Abbott (2008) examined the development of morphological knowledge among older elementary students and the relationship of their morphological knowledge to decoding. They found that morphological awareness continued to develop from fourth to sixth grade and that children's skill with morphology made a unique contribution to decoding ability. Carlisle (2010) analyzed 16 studies to determine the value of morphological awareness instruction and concluded that morphological analysis has the potential to contribute to students' literacy development in phonology, orthography, and word meanings. Goodwin, Gilbert, and Cho (2013) investigated the ability of 213 middle-school students to read 39 morphologically complex words. They found that students' ability to read a root word such as *isolate* did predict their ability to read a derived word such as *isolation*. Students were less able to use their root word knowledge when there was a change in pronunciation in the derived word, as there is in the words *discrete* and *discretionary*. The Common Core standards recognize the importance of morphemes in decoding big words, and morphemic analysis is the principal reading foundations goal for children in third, fourth, and fifth grades.

Best Practices in Action

While research does not tell us what kind of phonemic awareness and phonics instruction is most effective, we can use some research-based findings to evaluate classroom activities. Activities designed to develop phonemic awareness should be done in the context of reading and writing so that children develop the other concepts necessary for successful beginning reading. Because children vary in their level of phonemic awareness, phonics activities for young children should include opportunities to develop phonemic awareness. Because it is not clear how phonics is best taught (and because all children might not learn best with any single method), phonics instruction should include a variety of activities, including letter–sound, spelling, and analogy instruction. As children encounter more big words in their reading, they should learn to use morphemes to unlock the pronunciation, spelling, and meaning of polysyllabic words. The remainder of this section describes activities to teach phonemic awareness, phonics, and multisyllabic word decoding in ways that are consistent with research. These activities can all be used to teach the specific phonemic awareness, phonics, and morphemic knowledge specified in the CCSS for the ELA.

Focus on Rhymes and Sound Substitution to Develop Phonemic Awareness

Children who come to school with well-developed phonemic awareness abilities have usually come from homes in which rhyming chants, jingles, and songs were part of their daily experience. These same chants, jingles, and songs should be a part of every young child's day in the classroom.

There are many wonderful rhyming books, but because of their potential to develop phonemic awareness, two deserve special mention. Along with other great rhyming books, Dr. Seuss wrote *There's a Wocket in My Pocket* (1974). In this book, all kinds of Seusssian creatures are found in various places. In addition to the wocket in the pocket, there is a vug under the rug, a nureau in the bureau and a yottle in the bottle! After several readings, children delight in chiming in to provide the nonsensical word and scary creature that lurks in harmless-looking places. After reading the book a few times, it is fun to decide what creatures might be lurking in your classroom. Let children make up the creatures, and accept whatever they say as long as it rhymes with their object:

> "There's a pock on our clock!"
> "There's a zindow looking in our window!"
> "There's a zencil on my pencil!"

Another wonderful rhyming book for phonemic awareness is *The Hungry Thing* by Jan Slepian and Ann Seidler. In this book, a large, friendly, dinosaur-looking creature (You have to see him to love him!) comes to town, wearing a sign that says "Feed Me." When asked what he would like to eat, he responds, "Shmancakes." After much deliberation, a clever little boy offers him some pancakes. The Hungry Thing eats them all up and demands, "Tickles." Again, after much deliberation the boy figures out he wants pickles. As the story continues, it becomes obvious that The Hungry Thing wants specific foods and that he asks for them by making them rhyme with what he wants. He asks for *feetloaf* and gobbles down the meatloaf. For dessert, he wants *hookies* and *gollipops*!

The Hungry Thing is a delightful book, and in many classrooms teachers have made a poster-size Hungry Thing, complete with his sign that reads "Feed Me" on one side and "Thank You!" on the other. Armed with real foods or pictures of foods the children try to feed The Hungry Thing. Of course, he won't eat the food unless they make it rhyme. If they offer him spaghetti, they have to say "Want some bagetti?" (or "zagetti," or "ragetti"—any silly word that rhymes with *spaghetti*!) To feed him Cheerios, they have to offer him "seerios," "theerios," or "leerios"!

Focus on Blending and Segmenting to Develop Phonemic Awareness

In addition to hearing and producing rhymes and substituting sounds to create new words, the ability to put sounds together to make a word—blending—and the ability to separate out the sounds in a word—segmenting—are critical components of phonemic awareness. Blending and segmenting are not easy for many children. In general, it is easier for them to segment off the beginning letters—the onset—from the rest of the word—the rhyme—than it is to separate all the sounds. In other words, children can usually separate *bat* into /b/ and /at/ before they can produce the three sounds /b/ /a/ and /t/. The same is true for blending. Most children can blend /S/ and /am/ to produce the name Sam before they can blend /S/ /a/ and /m/. Most teachers begin by having children blend and segment the onset from the rime and then move to blending and segmenting individual letters.

There are lots of games children enjoy that can help them learn to blend and segment. The most versatile is a simple riddle-guessing game. The teacher begins the game by naming the category and giving the clue: "I'm thinking of an animal that lives in the water and is a /f/ /ish/ [or /f/ /i/ /sh/, depending on what level of blending you are working on]." The child who correctly guesses "fish" gives the next riddle: "I'm thinking of an animal that goes quack and is a /d/ /uck/ [or /d/ /u/ /ck/]." This sounds simplistic but children love it, and you can use different categories to go along with units you are studying.

A wonderful variation on this guessing game is to put objects in a bag and let children reach in the bag and stretch out the name of an object they choose and then call on someone to guess "What is it?" Choose small common objects you find in the room—a cap, a ball, chalk, a book—and let the children watch you load the bag and help you stretch out the words for practice as you put them in.

Children also like to talk like "ghosts." One child chooses an object in the room to say as a ghost would—stretching the word out very slowly—"dddoooorrr." The child who correctly guesses "door" gets to ghost-talk another object—"bbbooookkk." The ghost-talk game and the guessing game provide practice in both segmenting and blending as children segment words by stretching them out and other children blend the words together to guess them.

Encourage Writing with Invented Spelling

When young children write, they need to spell many words that they have not yet learned to spell. If teachers demonstrate how you can stretch out words and put down letters for the sounds you hear, young children will write a lot more than if they think they have to spell all the words correctly or wait for someone to spell the words for them. As they stretch out words, they are segmenting those words into their component sounds. Segmenting is an important—and difficult—phonemic awareness ability that will develop more quickly if children are encouraged to stretch out words while writing.

How Emphasizing Rhyme, Sound Substitution, Segmenting, and Blending Reflects What We Know

Rhyme awareness—the ability to make and recognize rhymes—is one of the earliest developed phonemic awareness abilities. Many children come to kindergarten with developed rhyme awareness. These children were not given any direct instruction in rhyme, but they were immersed in an environment of songs, jingles, and books in which rhyme played a large role. Including rhyming songs, jingles, and books as part of every early-childhood day allows all children to begin developing their phonemic awareness. Sound substitution is more complex but requires the ability to rhyme. Children who can rhyme and substitute sounds know that if you change the last sound of *ham* into a *t* sound you have changed a *ham* into a *hat*!

Segmenting and blending words are two of the more difficult phonemic awareness abilities. Children need lots of practice with oral activities in which they put sounds together to create words and pull words apart into their component sounds. When children are encouraged to stretch out words while writing, they get a lot of practice with segmenting. Writing also gives students a way to apply the letter–sound knowledge they are learning. Many children can read their own writing before they can read the same words in books.

Make Words to Include a Variety of Phonics Approaches

Making Words (Cunningham, 2013) is a popular activity with both teachers and children. Children love manipulating letters to make words and figuring out the secret word that can be made with all the letters. While children are having fun making words, they are also learning important information about phonics and spelling. As children manipulate the letters to make the words, they learn how small changes, such as changing just one letter or moving the letters around, result in completely new words. Children develop phonemic awareness as they stretch out words and listen for the sounds they hear and the order of those sounds. Making Words lessons are an example of a type of instruction called "guided discovery." In order to truly learn and retain strategies, children must discover them. But some children do not make discoveries about words on their own. In Making Words lessons, children are guided toward those discoveries.

Every Making Words Lesson has three parts. First, children manipulate the letters to make words. This part of the lesson uses a spelling approach to help children learn letter sounds and how to segment words and blend letters. In the second part of the lesson, children sort words according to rhyming patterns. We end each lesson by helping children transfer what they have learned to reading and spelling new words. Children learn how the rhyming words they sorted help them read and spell lots of other rhyming words.

Each Making Words lesson begins with short easy words and moves to longer more complex words. The last word is always the secret word—a word that can be made with all the letters. As children make the words, a child who has made it successfully goes to the pocket chart and makes the word with big letters. Children who don't have the word made correctly quickly fix their word to be ready for the next word. The small changes between most words encourages even those children who have not made a word perfectly to fix it because they soon realize that having the current word correctly spelled increases their chances of spelling the next word correctly.

In Step 2 of a Making Words lesson, children sort the words into patterns. Many children discover patterns just through making the words in the carefully sequenced order, but some children need more explicit guidance. This guidance happens when all the words have been made and teachers guide children to sort them into patterns. Children sort the words into rhyming words and notice that words that rhyme have the same spelling pattern.

Many children know letter sounds and patterns but do not apply these to decode an unknown word encountered during reading or spell a word they need while writing. This is the reason that every Making Words lesson ends with a transfer step. Once words are sorted according to beginning letters, children apply these beginning letter sounds to new words. Once words are sorted according to rhyme, children use these rhyming words to spell new words. Here is an example of how you might conduct a Making Words lesson and cue the children to the changes and words you want them to make.

A Sample Making Words Lesson

BEGINNING THE LESSON

The children all have the letters: *a e u c c k p s*. These same letters—big enough for all to see—are displayed in a pocket chart or on the active board. The vowels are in a different color and the letter cards have lowercase letters on one side and capital letters on the other side.

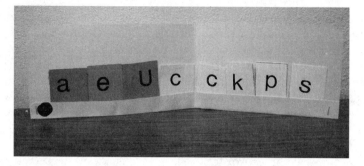

The words the children are going to make are written on index cards. These words will be placed in the pocket chart as the words are made and will be used for the Sort and Transfer steps of the lesson.

The teacher begins the lesson by having the children hold up and name each letter as the teacher holds up the big letters in the pocket chart.

"Hold up and name each letter as I hold up the big letter. Let's start with your vowels. Show me your *a*, your *u*, and your *e*. Now show me your two *c*'s, *k*, *p*, and *s*. Today you have eight letters. In a few minutes, we will see if anyone can figure out the secret word which uses all eight letters."

STEP 1: MAKING WORDS

"Use two letters to spell the word *up*. I got *up* at 6:30."

Find someone with *up* spelled correctly and send that child to spell *up* with the big letters.

"Change one letter to spell *us*. The fifth graders put on a play for *us*."
"Add a letter you don't hear to spell *use*. We *use* our letters to make words."
"Move the same letters to spell the name *Sue*. Do you know anyone named *Sue*?"

Find someone with *Sue* spelled with a capital *S* to spell *Sue* with the big letters.

"Change one letter to spell *cue*. When you are an actor, you listen for your *cue*."

Quickly send someone with the correct spelling to make the word with the big letters. Keep the pace brisk. Do not wait until everyone has *cue* spelled with their little letters. It is fine if some children are making *cue* as *cue* is being made with the big letters. Choose your struggling readers to go to the pocket chart when easy words are being spelled and your advanced readers when harder words are being made.

> "Change one letter in *cue* to spell *cup*. The baby drinks from a sippy *cup*."
>
> "Change the vowel to spell *cap*. Do you ever wear a *cap*?"
>
> "Add a silent letter to change *cap* into *cape*. Batman wore a *cape*."
>
> "Change one letter to spell *cake*. Do you like chocolate *cake*?"
>
> "Change one letter to spell *sake*. I hope for your *sake* that it doesn't rain during the game."
>
> "Change the last two letters to spell *sack*. A *sack* is another name for a bag."
>
> "Change one letter to spell *pack*. *Pack* your clothes for the sleepover."
>
> "Change the last letter to spell another four-letter word, *pace*. The racers ran at a very fast *pace*."
>
> "Add one letter to spell *space*. When we write, we leave a *space* between words."
>
> "I have just one word left. It is the secret word you can make with all your letters. See if you can figure it out."

Give the students 1 minute to figure out the secret word and then gives clues if needed. Let someone who figures it out go to the big letters and spell the secret word—*cupcakes*.

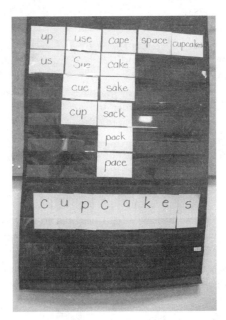

STEP 2: SORTING THE WORDS INTO PATTERNS

Put the index cards with words you made in the pocket chart having children pronounce and chorally spell each. Give them a quick reminder of how they made these words:

> "First, we spelled a two-letter word, *up, u-p.*
>> We changed the last letter to spell *us, u-s.*
>> We added the silent *e* to spell *use, u-s-e.*
>> We used the same letters with a capital *S* to spell *Sue, S-u-e.*
>> We changed the first letter to spell *cue, c-u-e.*
>> We changed the last letter to spell *cup, c-u-p.*
>> We changed the vowel to spell *cap, c-a-p.*
>> We added the silent *e* to spell *cape, c-a-p-e.*
>> We changed one letter to spell *cake, c-a-k-e.*
>> We changed one letter to spell *sake, s-a-k-e.*
>> We changed two letters to spell *sack, s-a-c-k.*
>> We changed one letter to spell *pack, p-a-c-k.*
>> We changed the last letter to spell *pace, p-a-c-e.*
>> We added a letter to spell *space, s-p-a-c-e.*
>> Finally, we spelled the secret word with all our letters, *cupcakes, c-u-p-c-a-k-e-s.*"

Next, have the children sort the rhyming words. Take one of each set of rhyming words and place them in the pocket chart.

Sue	*cake*	*pace*	*sack*	*cup*

Have three children come and find the other words that rhyme and place them under the ones you pulled out.

Sue	*cake*	*pace*	*sack*	*cup*
cue	*sake*	*space*	*pack*	*up*

Have the children chorally pronounce the sets of rhyming words.

STEP 3: TRANSFER

Tell the children to pretend it is writing time and they need to spell some words that rhyme with some of the words we made today. Have children use whiteboards or half-sheets of paper to write the words. Say sentences that children might want to write that include a rhyming word. Work together to decide which words the target word rhymes with and to decide how to spell it.

"Boys and girls, let's pretend it is writing time. Terry is writing about what he likes to eat for a *snack* and he is trying to spell the word *snack*. Let's all say *snack* and stretch out the beginning letters. What two letters do you hear at the beginning of *snack*?"

Have the children stretch out *snack* and listen for the beginning letters. When they tell you that *snack* begins with *sn,* write *sn* on an index card and have the children write *sn* on their papers or whiteboards.

Take the index card with *sn* on it to the pocket chart and hold it under each column of words as you lead the children to chorally pronounce the words and decide if *snack* rhymes with them:

"Sue, cue, snack"	Children should show you "thumbs down."
"Cake, sake, snack"	Children should again show you "thumbs down."
"Pace, space, snack"	Children should again show you "thumbs down."
"Sack, pack, snack"	Children should show you "thumbs up."

Finish writing *snack* on your index card by adding *ack* to *sn* and place *snack* in the pocket chart under *sack* and *pack.*

Make up sentences and use the same procedure to demonstrate how you use *pace* and *space* to spell *brace, Sue* and *cue* to spell *due, up* and *cup* to spell *pup,* and *sack* and *pack* to spell *track.*

We hope this sample lesson has helped you to see how a Making Words lesson works and how Making Words lessons help children develop phonemic awareness, phonics, and spelling skills. Most important, we hope you see that in every lesson children will practice applying the patterns they are learning to reading and spelling new words.

Teach Children to Use the Words They Know to Decode and Spell Other Words

Another activity that includes a variety of approaches to phonics is called Using Words You Know (Cunningham, 2013). To plan a Using Words You Know lesson, pick three or four words that your children can read and spell and that have many rhyming words spelled the same way. You can use any words your students know that have lots of rhyming words. *Play*, for example, will help you decode and spell many other words, including *stray, spray, clay, delay* and *betray. Rain* helps you decode and spell *brain, Spain, chain, sprain*, and *complain*. You can also use brand names that have lots of rhyming words. Bring in packages with the product names, and then use those names as the known words. Children are highly motivated by these products and are fascinated to see how many other words these products can help them read and spell. Here is a sample lesson using ice cream and Cool Whip.

Begin the lesson by displaying the products, and let the children talk a little about them. Draw the children's attention to the names, and tell them that these names will help them spell and read a lot of other words. Using the board, chart, or overhead projector, make columns and head each with one of the key words, underlining the spelling pattern. Have your students do the same on a sheet of paper. At the beginning of the lesson, their papers look like this:

ice   cr<u>eam</u>   c<u>ool</u>   wh<u>ip</u>

Show the students words that rhyme with *ice, cream, cool,* or *whip*. Do not say these words and do not allow them to say the words but rather have them write them in the column with the same spelling pattern. Send one child to write the word on the chart, board, or overhead. When everyone has the rhyming word written under the original word that will help them read it, have them say the known word and the rhyming word. Help them to verbalize the strategy they are using by saying something like "If *c-r-e-a-m* is *cream, d-r-e-a-m* must be *dream*." "If *c-o-o-l* is *cool, d-r-o-o-l* is *drool*." After showing them eight to 10 words and having them use the known word to decode them, help them practice using known words to spell unknown words. To help them spell, don't show them a word. Instead, say a word, such as *twice*, and have them say the word and write it under the word that it rhymes with. Again, help them verbalize their strategy by leading them to explain:

"If *ice* is spelled *i-c-e, twice* is probably spelled *t-w-i-c-e*."
"If *whip* is spelled *w-h-i-p, strip* is probably spelled *s-t-r-i-p*."

To show children how they can decode and spell bigger words based on rhyming words, end the lesson by showing them a few longer words and having them write them under the rhymes and use the rhymes to decode them. Finally, say a few longer words, help them with the spelling of the first syllables, and have them use the rhyme to spell the last syllable. Here is what their papers would look like with at the end of the lesson:

ice	cream	cool	whip
nice	dream	drool	tip
mice	stream	pool	skip
slice	scream	fool	trip
twice	gleam	spool	strip
dice	beam	stool	clip
sacrifice	mainstream	whirlpool	equip
device	downstream	preschool	spaceship

It is very important for Using Words You Know lessons that you choose the rhyming words for them to read and spell rather than ask them for rhyming words. In English, there are often two spelling patterns for the same rhyme. If you ask them what rhymes with *cream*, or *cool*, they may come up with words with the *e-e-m* pattern such as *seem* and words with the *u-l-e* pattern such as *rule*. The fact that there are two common patterns for many rhymes does not hinder us while reading. When we see the word *drool*, our brain thinks of other *o-o-l* words such as *cool* and *school*. We make this new word *drool* rhyme with *cool* and *school* and then check out this pronunciation with the meaning of whatever we are reading. If we were going to write the word *drool* for the first time, we wouldn't know for sure which spelling pattern to use, and we might think of the rhyming word *rule* and use that pattern. Spelling requires both a sense of word patterns and a visual checking sense. When you write a word and then think "That doesn't look right!" and then write it using a different pattern, you are demonstrating that you have developed a visual checking sense. Once children become good at spelling by pattern, you can help them develop their visual checking sense. During Using Words You Know lessons, we are trying to get them to spell based on pattern, and we "finesse" the problem of two patterns by choosing the words we present to them.

Using Words You Know lessons are easy to plan if you use one of the many rhyming word sites on the Internet. Children enjoy Using Words You Know, especially if the words you use are popular products such as *Coke, Crest,* and *Cat Chow.*

How Making Words and Using Words You Know Reflect What We Know

Making Words and Using Words You Know are examples of lesson formats that teach phonics in a variety of ways. When the children are making words with their letters, they are engaging in a spelling approach to phonics. They are told the word, and they must figure out which of their letters to use to spell it. This spelling approach is also used in Using Words You Know when the teacher says a word that rhymes with the key words and the children decide how to spell them based on their known rhyming words.

Both lesson formats also teach children to decode words based on pattern and analogy. In a Making Words lesson, there are always several sets of rhymes with the same spelling pattern. Children sort out these rhyming words and then use these words to decode two new words and spell two new words with the same pattern. Analogy and pattern instruction is also obvious in Using Words You Know lessons in which children use known words to decode and spell rhyming words with the same pattern.

While not the focus of the lesson, both Making Words and Using Words You Know provide opportunities for children to develop phonemic awareness and firm up their beginning letter knowledge if they still need to do that. Teachers encourage the children to stretch out words as they are making them. In the transfer step, children blend the beginning letters with the rhyming patterns to read the new words.

Sorting rhyming words is included in every Making Words lessons, but there are also opportunities to sort for beginning letter patterns if children still need their attention focused on those. Whenever possible, we include words such as *cup* and *cupcakes*, which share the same base word to provide opportunities for children to begin to develop morphemic awareness. In Using Words You Know lessons, we always include some words with two or more syllables to help children extend their decoding strategies to longer words.

Making Big Words

You can use the Making Words lesson format to help your older students discover the morphemic patterns they can use to decode, spell, and build meaning for big words. The Making Big Words (Cunningham, 2013) lesson format has three steps. In the first step, the students make words. Rather than little letter cards, they are given a letter strip with the appropriate letters (in alphabetical order so as not to give away the secret word). Once they have made words, they sort the words according to morphemic patterns and then use these patterns to spell other words. Here is a sample Making Big Words lesson.

A Sample Making Big Words Lesson

The students all have a letter strip with these letters: *a a e i u l m n p r t*. One student is assigned the job of "letter manipulator" for today's lesson.

As students make each word at their desks, the teacher calls on a student who has the word made correctly to spell aloud the letters in that word. The letter manipulator moves the letters on the overhead or active board so that everyone has a visual image against which to check their spelling. Students tear the letters apart and arrange them in alphabetical order—vowels first and consonants next.

The words the students are going to make are written on index cards. These words will be placed in the pocket chart or along the chalk ledge and will be used for the Sort and Transfer steps of the lesson.

STEP 1: MAKING WORDS

The teacher begins the lesson by telling students what word to make and how many letters each word requires. She gives a sentence for each word to clarify meaning.

> "Use four letters to spell the word *real*. The creatures in the movie were animated but they looked very *real*."

Find someone with *real* spelled correctly and have that student spell *real* aloud so that the letter manipulator can spell *real* with the transparency or active board letters.

> "Use four letters to spell *ripe*. We pick strawberries when they are *ripe*."
> "Spell another four-letter word, *mine*. Would you like to work deep down under the earth in a coal *mine*?"
> "Let's spell one more four-letter word, *time*. What *time* do we go to lunch?"

"Add one letter to *time* to spell *timer*. I put the cookies in the oven and set the *timer* for 15 minutes."

"Use five letters again to spell *miner*. I am claustrophobic so I would not be a good coal *miner*."

Quickly call on someone with the correct spelling to spell the word aloud for the letter manipulator. Keep the pace brisk. Choose your struggling readers to spell words aloud when easy words are being spelled and your advanced readers when harder words are being made.

"Use five letters to spell *ripen*. The strawberries are just beginning to *ripen*."

"Use five letters to spell *paint*. We all love to *paint* in art class."

"Use five letters to spell *plant*. In the spring we will *plant* flowers in our garden."

"Add one letter to *plant* to spell *planet*. Mars is called the red *planet*."

"Use six letters to spell *unreal*. Everyone said that watching the tornado touch down felt very *unreal*."

"Use six letters to spell *unripe*. Strawberries do not taste good when they are *unripe*"

"Use seven letters to spell *planter*. I plant spring flowers in a hanging *planter*.

"Use the same letters in *planter* to spell *replant*. Every year I *replant* the shrubs that die during the winter.

"Change the first two letters in *replant* to spell *implant*. If your heart does not have a steady beat, doctors can *implant* a pacemaker into your body to regulate your heartbeat."

"Use seven letters to spell *painter*. The *painter* is coming next week to paint the house."

"Use the same seven letters in *painter* to spell *repaint*. After the storm, the roof leaked and we had to *repaint* the kitchen.

"I have just one word left. It is the secret word you can make with all your letters. Move your letter and see if you can figure out the word that can be spelled with all the letters. You have 1 minute to try to figure out the secret word and then I will give you clues."

Give the students 1 minute to figure out the secret word and then gives clues if needed. "Our secret word today is related to the word *planet*. Start with the word *planet* and add your other letters to it." Let someone who figures it out go to the overhead and spell the secret word—*planetarium*.

STEP 2: SORTING THE RELATED WORDS

Put the words on index cards in the pocket chart and have the words pronounced. Remind students that related words are words that share a root word and meaning. Choose a set of related words and model for students to use related words in sentences to show how they are related. (Choose the most complex set of words to model.)

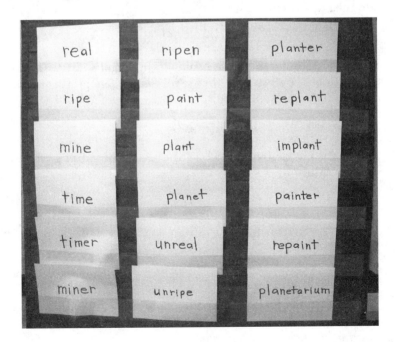

plant   planter   replant   implant

"A *planter* is a container you plant things in. When you *replant* something, you *plant* it again. When you *implant* something, you plant it in something or somebody. The *er* suffix can be a person or a thing. *Re* is a prefix that sometimes means *again*. *Im* is a prefix that sometimes means *in*."

Let volunteers choose other sets of related words and help them construct sentences and explain how the prefixes and suffixes change the root words.

paint   painter   repaint

"A *painter* is a person who *paints*. When you *repaint* something, you *paint* it again. *Er* is a suffix that sometimes means the person who does something. *Re* is a prefix that sometimes means *again*."

ripe   ripen   unripe

"The strawberries are starting to *ripen* and will soon be *ripe* enough to eat. *Unripe* strawberries taste terrible! The suffix *en* changes how a word can be used in a sentence. The prefix *un* often turns a word into the opposite meaning."

real   unreal

"When you see something this is actually happening it is *real* but sometimes things are so strange they seem *unreal*. The prefix *un* changes *real* into the opposite meaning."

time   timer

"To *time* the cookies baking, we set the *timer*. The suffix *er* sometimes means a thing."

mine   miner

"A *miner* is a person who works in a *mine*. The suffix *er* sometimes means a person."

planet   planetarium

"You can see all the different *planets* and how they move at a *planetarium*. Other words that end in *ium* and mean places are *aquarium, terrarium, auditorium, gymnasium,* and *stadium*."

Sorting the related words, using sentences that show how they are related, and explaining how prefixes and suffixes affect meaning or change how words can be used in a sentence is a crucial part of each Making Words lesson in fifth grade. Students often need help in explaining how the prefixes and suffixes work. For less common prefixes and suffixes such as *ium*, it is helpful to point out other words students may know (*auditorium, stadium*) that begin or end with that word part.

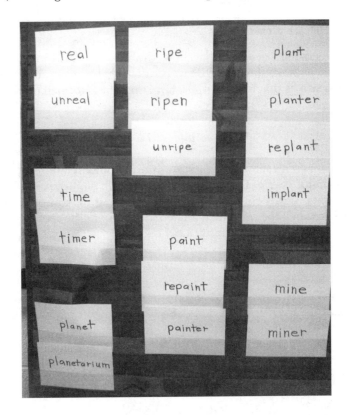

STEP 3: TRANSFER

The transfer step is the most important step of the lesson because it is when we teach students how the prefixes, suffixes, and roots they are learning help them read and spell lots of other words. Once we have sorted all the words into related word sets, we say five or six new words and have students decide which word parts these words share with our related words and how they will help them spell them. It is very important to make this a learning experience, rather than a test. Make sure everyone knows how to spell the new part of the transfer word and which related words will help before letting anyone write the word. Have students number a sheet of paper 1–6. Pronounce a word that follows the pattern of some of the related words.

unripe   unreal

Have students use *unripe* and *unreal* to spell other words that begin with *un*. Give them help to spell the root word if needed.

unfair   unpainted

Let volunteers tell a sentence that shows the meaning relationship between *fair, unfair; painted, unpainted.* Have students use *repaint* and *replant* to spell other words that begin with *re*. Give them help to spell the root word if needed.

rebuild   refill

Let volunteers tell a sentence that shows the meaning relationship between *build, rebuild; fill, refill.* Have students use *painter, planter, miner,* and *timer* to spell other words that begin with *er,* meaning person or thing. Give them help to spell the root word if needed. Point out the spelling change—drop *e*—if necessary.

leader   driver

Let volunteers tell a sentence that shows the meaning relationship between *lead, leader; drive, driver.*

1. unfair
2. unpainted
3. rebuild
4. refill
5. leader
6. driver

Word Detectives

Word Detectives is another activity that helps students learn how to use morphemes to decode, spell, and build meaning for big words. When introducing big words to our students, we teach them to ask themselves two questions to "solve the mystery of big words."

"Do I know any other words that look and sound like this word?"
"Are any of these look-alike/sound-alike words related to one another?"

The answer to the first question helps students with pronouncing and spelling the word. The answer to the second question helps them discover what, if any, meaning relationships exist between this new word and others words they know. To be most effective, students need to be word detectives throughout the school day in every subject area. Imagine that during math your students encounter the new word *equation*. You demonstrate and give examples of equations and help build meaning for the concept. Finally, you ask your students to pronounce *equation* and to see whether they know any other words that look and sound like *equation*. Students think of words that end like *equation* such as *addition, multiplication, nation*, and *vacation*. For the beginning chunk, they think of *equal* and *equator*.

You list these words, underlining the parts that are the same and having the students pronounce the words, emphasizing the part that is pronounced the same. Then you point out to students that thinking of a word that looks and sounds the same as a new word will help you quickly remember how to pronounce the new word and will also help you spell the new word.

Next you explain that words, like people, sometimes look and sound alike but are not related. Since this is the first time this analogy is used, you spend some time talking with the students about people with red hair, green eyes, and so on who have some parts that look alike but are not related and others who are.

"Not all people who look alike are related, but some are. This is how words work too. Words are related if there is something about their meaning that is the same. After we find look-alike, sound-alike words that will help us spell and pronounce new words, we try to think of any ways these words might be in the same meaning family."

With help from you, the students discover that *equal, equator,* and *equation* are related because the meaning of *equal* is in all three. An *equation* has to have *equal* quantities on both sides of the *equal* signs. The *equator* is an imaginary line that divides the earth into two *equal* halves.

Later, during science time, your students are doing some experiments using thermometers and barometers. At the close of the lesson, you point to these words and ask your students to once again be word detectives. They notice that the *meters* chunk is pronounced and spelled the same. You ask the students if they think these words are just look-alikes or are related to one another. The students conclude that you use them both to measure things and the *meters* chunk must be related to measuring, as in *kilometers*. Students also notice that *thermometer* begins like *thermostat* and decide that *thermometer* and *thermostat* are related because they both involve heat or temperature.

Throughout their school day, children encounter many new big words. Because English is such a morphologically related language, most new words can be connected to other words by their spelling and pronunciation, and many new words have meaning-related words already known to the student. Children who use clues from other big words to figure out the decoding, spelling, and meaning of new big words are being "word detectives."

How Making Big Words and Word Detectives Reflects What We Know

Both Making Big Words and Word Detectives help students become sensitive to morphology. They learn how prefixes, suffixes, and roots provide links to the spelling, pronunciation, and meanings of big words. In Word Detectives, because the words chosen always come out of the context of what is being studied, students learn to use morphology and context together as clues to solve the mysteries of big words.

Conclusions and Looking to the Future

This chapter has summarized what we know from research about how to teach phonemic awareness and phonics. The key conclusion of this research is that children do need systematic phonics instruction but there is no one best way to teach phonics. This conclusion is disturbing to those who would like for there to be a specified best way so that everyone could be mandated to do it in that way. In many schools, one approach to phonics has been mandated despite the lack of proof that that approach is any better than others teachers might favor.

In order to improve reading instruction for all children, we need to look to the research on effective literacy instruction (Allington & Johnston,

2002; Pressley, Allington, Wharton-McDonald, Block, & Morrow, 2001). These nationwide studies identified effective first- and fourth-grade classrooms and analyzed the literacy instruction that occurred in those classrooms. They found that there were many differences in these classrooms but also many commonalities. The classrooms of the most effective teachers were characterized by high academic engagement, excellent and positive classroom management, explicit teaching of skills, large amounts of reading and writing, and integration across the curriculum. Within these commonalities, there were huge differences in the way the components were orchestrated. How we teach phonics has not been demonstrated to have a huge effect on achievement, but how we orchestrate classrooms has shown that effect. To improve beginning literacy achievement, we need to continue our efforts to research how to create, maintain, and support excellent classroom teachers.

ENGAGEMENT ACTIVITIES

1. Consider the three activities suggested to teach phonemic awareness. How will rhyming books, blending and segmenting games, and writing with inventive spelling help children achieve the phonemic awareness goals specified in the Common Core?

2. Consider the activities suggested to teach phonics. How can you use Making Words and Using Words You Know activities to help students achieve the first- and second-grade phonics goals specified in the Common Core?

3. Consider the activities suggested to teach morphemic awareness. How can you use Making Big Words and Word Detectives lessons to help third, fourth, and fifth graders develop morphemic awareness as specified in the Common Core?

CHILDREN'S LITERATURE

Seuss, Dr. (1974). *There's a wocket in my pocket*. New York: Random House.
Slepian, J., & Seidler, A. (1967). *The hungry thing*. New York: Scholastic.

REFERENCES

Allington, R. L., & Johnston, P. H. (2002). *Reading to learn: Lessons from exemplary fourth-grade classrooms*. New York: Guilford Press.
Carlisle, J. F. (2010). Effects of instruction in morphological awareness on

literacy achievement: An integrative review. *Reading Research Quarterly, 45,* 464–487.

Cunningham. P. M. (2013). *Phonics they use: Words for reading and writing* (6th ed.). Boston: Pearson Education.

Davis, L. H. (2000). The effects of rime-based analogy training on word reading and spelling of first-grade children with good and poor phonological awareness. *Dissertation Abstracts International, 61,* 2253A

Ehri, L. C., & Nunes, S. R. (2002). The role of phonemic awareness in learning to read. In A. E. Farstrup & S. J. Samuels (Eds.), *What research has to say about reading instruction* (pp. 110–139). Newark, DE: International Reading Association.

Flesch, R. (1955). *Why Johnny can't read.* New York: Harper & Row.

Goodwin, A. P., Gilbert, J. K., & Cho, S. (2013). Morphological contributions to adolescent word reading: An item response approach. *Reading Research Quarterly, 48,* 39–60.

Juel, C., & Minden-Cupp, C. (2000). Learning to read words: Linguistic units and instructional strategies. *Reading Research Quarterly, 35,* 458–492.

McCandliss, B., Beck, I. L., Sandak, R., & Perfetti, C. (2003). Focusing attention on decoding for children with poor reading skills: Design and preliminary tests of the Word Building intervention. *Scientific Studies of Reading, 7,* 75–104.

McCutchen, D., Green, L., & Abbott R. D. (2008). Children's morphological knowledge: Links to literacy. *Reading Psychology, 29,* 289–314.

Nagy, W., & Anderson, R. C. (1984). How many words are there in printed school English? *Reading Research Quarterly, 19,* 304–330.

National Governors Association & Council of Chief State School Officers. (2010). *Common Core State Standards for English language arts and literacy in history/ social studies, science, and technical subjects.* Washington, DC: Authors.

National Reading Panel. (2000). *Teaching children to read: An evidence-based assessment of the scientific research literature on reading and its implications for reading instruction* (National Institute of Health Publication No. 00-4769). Washington, DC: National Institute of Child Health and Human Development.

Pressley, M., Allington, R. L., Wharton-McDonald, R., Block, C. C., & Morrow, L. M. (2001). *Learning to read: Lessons from exemplary first-grade classrooms.* New York: Guilford Press.

Stahl, S. A., Duffy-Hester, A. M., & Stahl, K. A. (1998). Everything you wanted to know about phonics (but were afraid to ask). *Reading Research Quarterly, 33,* 338–355.

Yopp, H. K., & Yopp, R. H. (2000). Supporting phonemic awareness development in the classroom. *The Reading Teacher, 54,* 130–143.

CHAPTER 9

Best Practices in Vocabulary Instruction

Camille L. Z. Blachowicz
Peter J. Fisher

This chapter will:

- Present five research-based guidelines for vocabulary instruction.
- Share the research that underpins each of the guidelines and give examples of instruction reflecting the targeted guideline along with their Common Core State Standards connections.
- Describe a classroom that utilizes this type of instruction.
- Share resources for vocabulary instruction.

Evidence-Based Best Practices

The term *vocabulary instruction* can encompass a number of activities that occur in a classroom. We often ask teachers to make a list of word study activities that normally occur during a single day in their classroom. A typical list from a fourth-grade teacher included the following:

- Teach the suggested words prior to the reading selection from a literary selection.
- Brainstorm synonyms for the word *said* as part of a mini-lesson in writing.
- List word families as part of spelling instruction.

- Teach the meaning of *quadrant* for word problems in math class.
- Have the Mexican American and Arab American students teach the rest of the students the Spanish and Arabic words for *plains, rivers, clouds, mountains,* and *rain* as part of social studies on the Great Plains.
- Develop a semantic web for the Great Plains in social studies class, including words learned so far in the unit.
- Talk about *honesty* in relation to one student's having "borrowed" a marker from another without permission.
- Clarify the meanings of some difficult words in the teacher read-aloud at the end of the day.

Clearly, for each of these teaching events, the nature of the learning task was somewhat different. In some cases, students were learning unfamiliar words (the Spanish and Arabic words) for familiar concepts (plains, rivers, etc.), whereas in others they were learning new concepts as well as leaning new vocabulary (*quadrant*). In addition, we might expect that students would remember some general vocabulary words and use them almost immediately (synonyms for *said*), whereas students might recognize other words in a reading selection but not choose to use them in their own writing. Other words might be used in writing to answer questions related to their unit of study.

The Common Core State Standards (CCSS) distinguish between domain-specific vocabulary—the concepts in a content area (*topic, point on a graph*)—and general academic vocabulary—words that can be applied across content areas (*consist of, analyze*). However, we believe it is not easy to classify academic words in this way. For example, although the word *analyze* shares a common meaning across subject areas—*to resolve or separate a whole into its elements or component parts*—its application differs across standards. In the English language arts standards, students are expected to analyze how the author develops a theme and how specific words shape meaning and tone. In math, to solve problems, students must analyze givens, constraints, and relationships. In science, they must analyze and interpret data as well as alternative explanations and predictions. What does this mean for instruction? Simply put, teachers will need to teach the meaning of words like *analyze* in the context of how those words are applied in a domain and not assume that just because students may have encountered the word in language arts, this understanding will transfer to math and science. In addition, we hope that with the focus on teaching academic vocabulary, we will not lose the excitement of learning words for general vocabulary knowledge.

Vocabulary instruction occurs in our classrooms every day at a variety of levels and for a variety of purposes. After all, words are the currency of education. However, teachers are increasingly faced with a diverse group of learners in terms of current word knowledge, linguistic background, learning styles, and literacy abilities. It is up to us as teachers to make word learning enjoyable, meaningful, and effective.

How, then, does a teacher meet all these needs in a classroom of diverse learners? Like much in education, there is no simple answer. There are two important research-grounded assumptions about vocabulary that underpin effective vocabulary instruction. First, word learning is incremental—learning a word is not like an on–off switch, it's more like a dimmer switch that keeps strengthening what we know (Baker, Simmons, & Kame'enui, 1995). Think about little kids who first learn *cat* and then proceed to call the dog *cat*, the bird *cat*, and so forth, until they come to realize that *cat* refers to furry, whiskered, meowing animals only . . . and until they go to the zoo and see the *cats* that roar and learn more about the word and what it can apply to. So, many meaningful exposures build the depth and breadth of our word knowledge. The specific number of exposures needed to learn a word varies widely (McKeown, Beck, Omanson, & Pople, 1985; Schwanenflugel, Stahl, & McFalls, 1997), and is dependent on the nature of the word to be learned, the helpfulness of the contexts in which it appears, and the purpose for reading. Most of the research in this area has looked at word learning from storybooks or novels; clearly, when reading this type of text, the number of exposures needed will be very different from when reading a science or social studies textbook.

Second, students learn many more words than we can teach them, roughly 3,000–4,000 a year from kindergarten to 12th grade (D'Anna, Zechmeister, & Hall, 1991; Nagy, Herman, & Anderson, 1987). This number suggests that learning happens incidentally from all kinds of contexts: books and other written media (Cunningham, 2005), conversation around school tasks (Stahl & Vancil, 1986), and conversations at home, in the park, or on the playing fields with friends (Hart & Risley, 1995; Snow, 1991b). Moreover, television, music, social media, and movies all build vocabulary.

These assumptions underpin the orchestration of effective instruction, which needs to be multifaceted and approach vocabulary learning and instruction from many angles. It also must be comprehensive, reflecting best practice research on the effective components necessary. The National Reading Panel (2000) report highlighted the fact that there was a dearth of instructional research on exemplary vocabulary instruction in real classrooms and the U.S. Office of Education began funding projects to address this issue. In response, the Multifaceted Comprehensive Vocabulary Instruction Program (MCVIP; Baumann, Blachowicz, Manyak, Graves, & Olejnik, 2009–2012) was conceived. MCVIP was stimulated by conversations around Michael Graves's (2006; Graves & Silverman,

2010) four-component curriculum model for integrating vocabulary into the curriculum, which reflected the same research base as much of our own work (Baumann, Ware, & Edwards, 2007; Blachowicz & Fisher, 2015; Cobb & Blachowicz, 2014; Manyak, 2007). This research base gives teachers clues to the important dimensions of an effective elementary vocabulary program that integrates vocabulary into the overall curriculum rather than considering it as a free-standing element (see Figure 9.1). In this model, the teacher:

- Provides and engages students in rich and varied language activities.
- Teaches individual general academic and domain-focused vocabulary.
- Develops students' independent word-learning strategies.
- Stimulates and develops word consciousness.

Fourth- and fifth-grade teachers in three states participated in the formative development of the MCVIP model, which produced both significant standardized and performance gains on vocabulary measures for their students (Baumann, Blachowicz, Manyak, Graves, & Olejnik,

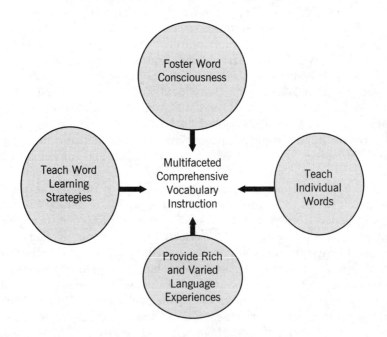

FIGURE 9.1. MCVIP components of effective vocabulary instruction.

2009–2012). They helped us develop examples of instruction that ensured that the four components of good vocabulary instruction could be integrated into the school curriculum.

The Teacher Provides and Engages Students in Rich and Varied Language Activities

We have a three-word mnemonic for vocabulary teaching—*flood, fast, focus*—to help our teachers consider the choices they have to make.

Flood

First, not all learning requires intentional teacher-directed instruction; you should *flood* your classroom with words related to your topic of study, not all of which you want your students to learn to the same depth. Nagy, Herman, and Anderson (1985) point out that there is no way we can intentionally teach all the words students learn each year. An enriched environment that increases the meaningful and interesting encounters students have with words can increase this incidental learning (Cunningham, 2005). Students can create word blasts or semantic maps (Pittelman, Heimlich, Berglund, & French, 1991), and engage in sorting and other activities, to begin building a relational set of terms connected to your topic of study (Blachowicz & Fisher, 2010). Research on self-selection (Fisher, Blachowicz, & Smith, 1991; Haggard, 1985) reveals that students can select their own words for personal word books or word walls/wizards to begin recording their own interesting words for study, often choosing words more difficult than the teacher or text list would suggest. Self-selection allows your students with more prior knowledge to stretch their knowledge, but it also allows students who are just building a basic vocabulary to choose the words that are right for them. You can have as many Flood words as you want in a class to enrich the environment, but these are not assigned to all or tested in traditional ways. Rather, they form a backdrop of topically related terms for incidental learning.

Fast

You can use *fast* instruction for terms where an easy definition or analogy will build on knowledge the students already have. We know that short definitional word explanations can do the trick when the concept is familiar but the term is not (Baumann, Edwards, Boland, Olejnik, & Kame'enui, 2003; Kame'enui, Carnine, & Freschi, 1982; McKeown et al., 1985; Pany, Jenkins, & Schreck, 1982). Fast paced instruction identifies the word, provides a synonym, gives an example of use, and then asks students to provide their own connection or synonym. When words are *almost* alike, a short feature analysis, word laddering, or semantic decision question ("Would you be more scared by a big or a gigantic monster?") can help establish these word nuances.

Focus

Use *focused* instruction for words where deeper, semantically rich teaching of a new concept is required. This type of instruction involves both definitional and contextual information, multiple exposures, and deep levels of processing so that students develop a rich base for word meaning (Graves, 1986; Mezynski, 1983; Nagy & Scott, 2000; Stahl & Fairbanks, 1986) and reading comprehension (Baumann, 2009; Elleman, Endia, Morphy, & Compton, 2009). This is the type of conceptual instruction that takes time and energy, but it pays off with deep learning of those less familiar words, often ones that are less concrete.

These three dimensions can help you fine-tune instruction. You need to choose whether a word can be taught easily or whether it needs more instruction. Imagine a group of fourth-grade students who are well familiar with the word *crown*. Teaching the meaning of the word *diadem* won't be too difficult. They already have the concept of a crown and are learning only a new label for a related term. Little, if any, instruction, might be needed, though repetition through reading and use can help the word "stick." For the same students, in the same selection, the word *irony*, however, would probably be harder to teach. This is an abstract concept that might not be too familiar to most 9-year-olds and the teacher would have to help the student establish a rich network of related concepts, such as understanding how emphasis and tone can affect meaning, "Yeah, you're *really* cute." So it makes sense to look at "knowing" a word as a continuous process that can be affected by meaningful encounters with words and by instruction aimed at helping the learner develop a network of understanding. This involves developing learners who are active, who personalize their learning and look for multiple sources of information to build meaning, and who are playful with words.

Good learners are active. As in all learning situations, a hallmark of good instruction is having the learners actively attempt to construct their own meanings. Learning new words as we have new experiences is one of the most durable and long-lasting ways to develop a rich vocabulary. For example, the words *thread, needle, selvage, pattern,* and *dart* may be learned naturally in the context of learning to sew, just as *hit, run, base,* and *fly* take on special meanings for a baseball player. This is particularly important with students whose primary language is not English. They may need the additional contextual help of physical objects and movement to internalize English vocabulary. Another way for students to become actively involved in discovering meaning is by answering questions that ask them to evaluate different features of word meaning (McKeown, Beck, & Worthy, 1993). For example, answering and explaining one's answer to the question "Would a recluse enjoy parties?" helps students focus on the important features of the word *recluse*, a person who chooses to be alone rather than with others.

Vocabulary and Emergent Readers

The variance in vocabulary knowledge of young children is well established. In 1995 Betty Hart and Todd Risley, two researchers at the University of Kansas who looked at parent–child interactions among different social groups, found some striking differences among preschoolers. On average, professional parents talked to their toddlers more than three times as much as parents of families on welfare did. Not surprisingly, that difference resulted in a big discrepancy in the children's vocabulary size. The average 3-year-old from a welfare family demonstrated an active vocabulary of around 500 words, whereas a 3-year-old from a professional family demonstrated a vocabulary of over 1,000 words.

Those differences become more pronounced as children get older—by the time the low-income children get to school and start to learn to read, they're already at an enormous disadvantage. It is estimated that children from economically privileged homes enter kindergarten having heard some 30 million more words than students from economically disadvantaged homes. Furthermore, the difference in time spent in "lap reading"—sitting in the lap of an adult and listening to a book being read—may be of the magnitude of 4,000–6,000 hours.

Read-alouds, reading aloud to children—sometimes also referred to as "shared storybook reading"—is a productive means for giving students opportunities to develop new-meaning vocabulary. Because children's books present more advanced and less familiar vocabulary than everyday speech (Cunningham & Stanovich, 1998), listening to books that are read helps students to go beyond their existing oral vocabularies and presents them with new concepts and vocabulary. Discussions after shared storybook reading also give students opportunities to use new vocabulary in the more decontextualized setting of a book discussion.

Numerous studies have documented the fact that young students can learn word meanings incidentally from read-aloud experiences (Blachowicz & Obrochta, 2005, 2007; Eller, Pappas, & Brown, 1988; Elley, 1988; Robbins & Ehri, 1994). In school settings, the effect is large for students age 5 and older and smaller for those under age 4. Involving students in discussions during and after listening to a book has also produced significant word learning, especially when the teacher scaffolds this learning by asking questions, adding information, or prompting students to describe what they heard. Whitehurst and his associates (Whitehurst et al., 1994, 1999) have called this process "dialogic reading."

However, teachers are amazed when they hear that storybook reading with young children is not always a positive experience. Some reading situations are less optimal than others, and research also suggests that this scaffolding (providing explanations, asking questions, clarifying) may be more essential to those students who are less likely to learn new vocabulary easily. Children with less rich initial vocabularies are less likely to learn new vocabulary incidentally and need a thoughtful, well-designed scaffolded approach to maximize learning from shared storybook reading (Robbins & Ehri, 1994; Senechal, Thomas, & Monker, 1995).

De Temple and Snow (2003) draw the contrast between talk around shared storybook reading that is cognitively challenging and talk that is not. There has been substantial research on the nature and effects of storybook reading in both home and school settings that supports their view and suggests ways in which read-alouds can maximize student vocabulary learning (Neuman & Dickinson, 2001). Some of the findings include:

- Children can learn the meaning of unknown words through incidental exposure during storybook reading.
- With traditional storybook readings, in the absence of scaffolding for those with less rich initial vocabularies, the vocabulary differences between children continue to grow over time.
- Children learn more words when books are read multiple times.
- Children do not benefit from being talked *at* or read *to*, but from being talked *with* and read *with* in ways requiring their response and activity.
- Natural scaffolded reading can result in more learning than highly dramatic "performance" reading by the adult.
- Children learn more words when books are read in small groups.

In sum, most researchers agree on several principles related to developing vocabulary with read-aloud storybook reading in schools. First, there should be some direct teaching and explanation of vocabulary during storybook reading in school settings. Second, adult–child discussion should be interactive, and discussion should focus on cognitively challenging ways to interact with the text rather than literal one-word or yes/no questions. The students need to be able to contribute to the discussion in a substantial way; smaller groups of five or six allow for this type of interaction. Third, the rereading of texts in which vocabulary is repeated can maximize learning; informational texts and text sets can both capitalize on children's interest in "real" things (trucks, dinosaurs, pandas) and provide satisfaction on thematically related words. Lastly, the nature of the learning that occurs is different with familiar versus unfamiliar books. In an initial reading the children may focus on the plot or storyline. In subsequent readings the reasons for characters' actions, and especially unfamiliar vocabulary, may become the focus of their interest. Read-alouds can be a potent tool in exposing students to new vocabulary in a meaningful and pleasurable way.

Wide Reading

Wide reading is another hallmark of word learning, with many studies suggesting that word learning occurs normally and incidentally during normal reading (Herman, Anderson, Pearson, & Nagy, 1987; Nagy, Herman, & Anderson, 1985). The psychological research also strongly supports the effect of wide reading on vocabulary growth (Cunningham, 2005). Furthermore, discussion in the classroom (Stahl & Vancil, 1986) is another correlate of incidental word learning. Although this type of learning through exposure cannot guarantee the learning of specific vocabulary words, it does develop a wide, flexible, and usable general vocabulary.

The Teacher Teaches Individual, General Academic, and Domain-Focused Vocabulary

Although contextualized word learning in wide reading, discussion, listening, and engaging in firsthand learning provides a great deal of word learning, explicit instruction can also contribute to vocabulary development (Biemiller, 2001), and is important in relation to learning academic vocabulary. This is most appropriate where students need a shared set of vocabulary words to progress in their learning. It is hard to have a discussion about phototropism if the words *plant, sun, bend,* and *light* have not already been established in the learner's vocabulary. We teach words for so many different purposes and require varying levels and types of understanding according to the task, the word, and the subject area. Baker and colleagues (1995) have argued that an important principle of vocabulary instruction is that it should be aligned with the depth of word knowledge required in any setting. We understand this to mean that teachers should decide how much students need to know about a word's meaning before teaching it.

    Depth refers to how much is known about a particular word: Can you recognize the meaning in text or conversation, can you use it appropriately, or can you define it? We all have the experience of being asked "What does *energetic* mean?" and replying "Well, Lassie is energetic when she runs all over the house and barks at everything." We tend to sup- *and example:* ply examples to illustrate meaning rather than to give a definition. This is probably appropriate in many situations and relies on the questioner's ability to use the context we provide to elaborate on the basic meaning of the word. We often do this even when we could give a definition, but on many occasions we do it because we know how to use a word, perhaps *calligraphy*, but are unsure of the precise meaning. Other times we can understand some of the meaning of a word when we hear or see someone use it—and yet not feel comfortable about using it ourselves. We learn more about words each time we see or hear them; that is, we increase our depth of understanding. In relation to classrooms, it is helpful to consider what level of understanding is needed for successful completion of the task. Perhaps, when reading a particular selection, it is enough to know that a *pallet* is a form of bed, or maybe it is necessary to know what distinguishes it from other beds (it is made of straw) because it is part of a social studies unit that connects living styles to the environment.

Breadth of knowledge of a word is related to depth insofar as it can add layers of understanding, but breadth is concerned primarily with how a word is connected to other words in a domain of learning. For example, do students understand the relations among the words *plains, rivers, mountains, foothills*, and *erosion*? Students in the fourth grade may need to see how each relates to the other when studying a unit on the Great Plains. However, their depth of understanding of *erosion* may be limited as compared to that of a high school geography student or a geomorphologist.

Numerous studies comparing definitional instruction with incidental learning from context or with no-instruction control conditions support the notion that teaching definitions results in learning. However, students who received instruction that combined definitional information with other active processing, such as adding contextual information, writing contextual discovery, or rich manipulation of words, all exceeded the performance of students who received only definitional instruction (see Blachowicz & Fisher, 2000, for a review of this research). A meta-analysis of studies that compared different types of instruction (Stahl & Fairbanks, 1986) concluded that methods with multiple sources of information for students provide superior word learning. In effective classrooms, students encounter words in context and work to create or understand appropriate definitions, synonyms, and other word relations.

For a simple, individual word lesson (Baumann et al., 2009–2012; Beck, McKeown, & Kucan, 2013), to introduce students to new words, we know that it is important to:

- Make sure the students see the word and can pronounce it.
- Give or generate a "kid-friendly" definition for the term.
- Present an oral or written context using visuals or objects when possible to flesh out the context.
- Ask students for a semantic response ("Would you invite a burglar into your home? Why or why not?").
- Have students use words in speech and writing.

This process can work for an efficient way to teach vocabulary that can be handily connected to students' prior knowledge. Ideally this is only a first step, followed by connecting the individual word to a network of related words within their content area or thematic unit area of study.

Teachers can model mature word-learning strategies by helping students gather information across texts and sources. Students should keep looking for different types of information that will flesh out the meaning they need to understand. Students benefit from the following:

- Definitional information
- Contextual information
- Usage examples

They also profit from manipulating words in many contexts.

Definitional information can be provided in many ways. Giving synonyms and antonyms provides information on what a word is or is not. Creating definitions using frames or other models helps students understand what a dictionary can provide. Example sentences clue students into nuance as well as usage. Semantic maps (as exemplified earlier), webs, feature analysis, and comparing and contrasting are good activities to organize information about sets of related words.

Care must be taken that the students see the words in context and have chances to use the words with feedback. Teachers often present usage sentences for choice and discussion. For example, for the word *feedback*, the teacher might present the following and ask students to choose the correct usage.

We gave him feedback on his choices.
We were feedbacked by the teacher.

As in all vocabulary activities, **discussion is the key**. After choice and discussion, the teacher could ask each student to do two things: (1) locate a sentence or paragraph in the text where the word is used and explain the meaning, and/or (2) write and illustrate an original sentence.

Graphic Organizers

Making word meanings and relationships visible is another way to involve students actively in constructing word meaning. Semantic webs, maps, organizers, or other relational charts, such as the one on *steam* in Figure 9.2, not only graphically display attributes of meanings but also provide a memory organizer for later word use. Many studies have shown the efficacy of putting word meaning into a graphic form such as a map or web (Heimlich & Pittelman, 1986) or a semantic feature chart (Pittelman et al., 1991), an advanced organizer, or other graphic form. It is critical to note, however, that mere construction of such maps, without discussion, is not effective (Stahl & Vancil, 1986).

Clustering Techniques

Other approaches that stress actively relating words to one another are clustering strategies that call for students to group words into related sets, brainstorming, grouping and labeling (Marzano & Marzano, 1988), designing concept hierarchies (Wixson, 1986), constructing definition maps related to conceptual hierarchies (Bannon, Fisher, Pozzi, & Wessell,

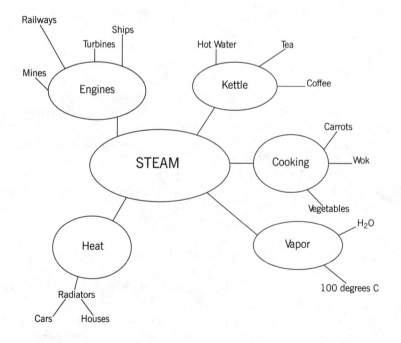

FIGURE 9.2. Graphic web/map on *steam*.

1990–1991; Schwartz & Raphael, 1985), or mapping words according to their relation to story structure categories (Blachowicz, 1986). All these approaches involve student construction of maps, graphs, charts, webs, or clusters that represent the semantic relatedness of words under study to other words and concepts. Again, discussion, sharing, and use of the words are necessary components of active involvement, as are feedback and scaffolding on the part of the teacher.

Teaching Domain-Specific Vocabulary

Clustering techniques work well with teaching domain-specific vocabulary since the words in a unit of study may be semantically related or even defined in opposition to each other. For example, learning the meaning of *reflex angle* is easy once the meanings of *acute, obtuse*, and *right angles* are known. We suggest four principles that are particularly relevant to academic vocabulary, although they could apply to most vocabulary instruction (Blachowicz, Fisher, Ogle, & Watts-Taffe, 2013).

1. *Link manipulation to language.* For example, we watched a fifth-grade special needs teacher teach angles in math to her students by having them show the types of angles with their arms using their heads as the vertex.
2. *Include visual representations.* Charts and graphs are an important part of content-area instruction, and students can learn vocabulary by reading and making them.
3. *Teach morphemes.* Specific morphemes can be useful, particularly in science—for example, when teaching students about the four types of symbiosis: *parasitism, mutualism, commensalism*, and *amensalism*.
4. *Use meaningful and varied repetition and review.* For example, we watched a second-grade teacher with her students as they reviewed the difference between insects and spiders. Over a 3-day period, they read about it, watched brief videos, sorted examples, and made charts.

The Teacher Develops Students' Independent Word-Learning Strategies

Control of Learning

Good learners take control of their own learning. They can select words to study and use context, word structure, and word references to get information about important vocabulary they need to know. Studies that focus on self-selection of vocabulary suggest that when students choose words that they need to learn, they learn the word meanings more successfully and retain the meanings longer than when a teacher chooses the words. Haggard (1982) interviewed adults and secondary school learners about their memories of learning new words and found that these learners most easily retained words that were usable in their peer groups—popular among peers, occurring frequently in their readings, buzzwords in the media. Her subsequent teaching studies involving self-selection of words to be learned (Haggard, 1982, 1985; Ruddell & Shearer, 2002) suggested that the control offered by self-selection is an important factor in building a generalized vocabulary. Moreover, for students for whom English is a second language, some self-selection is critical to getting a true picture of words that confound learning (Jiminez, 1997).

With the popularity of wide reading approaches and cooperative group models of classroom instruction, Fisher and colleagues (1991) examined the effects of self-selection in cooperative reading groups on word learning. The fourth-grade groups analyzed in this study were highly successful in learning a majority of the words chosen for study. In a later study with fifth- and seventh-grade readers (Blachowicz, Fisher, Costa, & Pozzi, 1993) the results were repeated and new information was added. The teachers who were coresearchers in the study were interested not only in whether the words were learned but also in whether the students chose challenging words for study. In all groups studied, the students consistently chose words at or above grade level for study. These and other studies indicate that self-selection and self-study processes can work effectively in the classroom. Collaborative word choice, with the students selecting some words to be learned and the teacher also contributing words for study, may be called for in content-area learning and with new difficult conceptual topics (Beyersdorfer, 1991). Combined with teacher selection and support, helping students learn to select words for self-study is a powerful tool for independent learning.

Context

Researchers suggest that learning words from context is an important part of vocabulary development, but point out that it is unreasonable to expect single new contextual exposures to do the job (Baldwin & Schatz, 1985). Students need to understand context and how to use it. (See CCSS Language Standard 4 starting in grade 2 which calls upon students to "Use sentence-level context as a clue to the meaning of a word or phrase.")

Although several studies have provided intensive instruction in contextual analysis with mixed results, recent instructional studies suggest that successful context-use instruction involves explicit instruction, good planning, practice and feedback, scaffolding that leads to more student responsibility, and a metacognitive focus (Blachowicz & Fisher, 2000; Buikema & Graves, 1993; Kuhn & Stahl, 1998). For example, a teacher might choose particular words from students' reading to teach how to predict meaning and look for clues. Similarly, instruction focusing on structural analysis or morphology (the learning of word parts, such as the Greek roots *tele-* and *graph*) can be helpful in learning new words while reading, as long as a teacher emphasizes problem solving. A specific type of morphological analysis that allows English language (EL) students to draw on their first language skills is the use of cognates. *Cognates* are words that are similar in their native languages to English forms of words (e.g., *excelente* [Spanish] and *excellent* [English]) (Scott, Miller, & Flinspach, 2012). In their review of the research, Dressler and Kamil (2006) argue: "In summary, transfer between cognates occurs optimally between closely related first and second languages, and in learners possessing high levels of reading proficiency, cognitive flexibility and metalinguistic awareness" (p. 215). Much of the research has been done with Spanish–English cognates. They share many common etymologies in terms of Latin roots. In English, these multisyllable words occur in academic more than in conversational English. It is posited, therefore, that use of cognates is a more effective strategy in the later grades. We know that native English speakers are more likely to use morphology as an aid to word learning as they become older and more proficient readers. Jimenez, Garcia, and Pearson (1996) found that poorer readers view languages as more dissimilar than alike, and so are less likely to look for cognates. However, several studies have found cognate instruction to be effective (Kieffer & Lesaux, 2007; Lesaux, Kieffer, Faller, & Kelley, 2010).

Dictionary

Students also need supportive instruction in learning how to use the dictionary—an important word-learning tool (See CCSS Language Standards on Conventions of Standard English, which call on students to "resolve issues of complex or contested usage, consulting references [e.g., *Merriam-Webster's Dictionary of English Usage, Garner's Modern American Usage*] as needed.") Every teacher who has watched a student struggle to look up a word knows that using a dictionary can be a complex and difficult task. Stories of dictionary use often take on a "kids say the darndest things" aura: the student whose only meaning of *sharp* has to do with good looks feels vindicated by finding "acute" as one meaning for *sharp* in the dictionary ("That sure is acute boy in my class"). Another, noting that *erode* is defined as "eats out," produces the sentence "Since my mom went back to work my family erodes a lot" (Miller & Gildea, 1987). Aside from providing humorous anecdotes for the teacher's room, dictionaries and dictionary use are coming under closer scrutiny by those involved in instruction. Students do not automatically understand how dictionaries work or how they can most effectively take information from them.

The use of morphology, word parts such as prefixes, suffixes, roots, and the other elements needed to break a word's meaning apart, is also an important strategy. Breaking words apart not only helps students learn and remember those specific words but also supplies them with the building blocks to understand new words they encounter (Carlisle, 2000). For morphology instruction, contextual analysis, and work with dictionaries, it is wise to remember to work from the known to the unknown. As students engage in learning any one of these processes, it is important for them to understand the underlying rationale. This is best achieved through exploration of the "how-to" with familiar words and phrases. Once they have mastered easy words, they can practice with more and more difficult words until the process becomes automatic.

The Teacher Stimulates and Develops Word Consciousness

Word consciousness can be thought of as an interest in and awareness of words (Graves & Watts-Taffe, 2002). It can include how words make meaning, the nuances of word meaning, morphology, syntax, and beliefs about word learning. This seems a lot to teach, but students become conscious of words as they manipulate, explore, and experiment with them. Students learn by playing with words, and watching teachers model their own learning about words.

Models

Teachers should also be models of word learning. We all remember the year we learned many new words in school. We had a teacher who was an avid punster, crossword puzzle aficionado, or otherwise involved in wordplay. Teachers can be sure that they and their classrooms are models of best practices by being good models of enthusiastic and pleasurable word learning. Using word games such as Hinky Pinkies, puns, puzzles, contests, and other playful activity develops this awareness in an enjoyable and motivating way (Blachowicz & Fisher, 2004). In a detailed study of word learning in the middle elementary grades, Beck, Perfetti, and McKeown (1982) found one classroom in which the students outperformed others in word learning. Looking around the classroom, they saw a 79¢ piece of poster board on the wall, with words entered on it by different students. When the researchers asked about this, they were told by the teacher, "Oh, that's just a little something we do each day. If the kids encounter a new and interesting word, they can tell the rest of the class about it, put it on the chart, and earn points for their team." The students became attuned to listening for new and interesting words, and this interest was validated in the classroom on a regular basis. Techniques such as "word of the day" and "mystery word" are easy, low-maintenance, inexpensive, and time-effective ways of making sure that kids are intentionally exposed to words each day and motivated to do their own word learning.

When the goal is to have students gain control of vocabulary to use for their own expression, students need many experiences that allow them to use words in meaningful ways. Use in writing and conversation, where feedback is available, is essential to durable and deep learning. Creating personal word books and dictionaries is a good first step toward ownership; use in many situations is a second step. Using new words in discussion, writing, independent projects, and wordplay develops real ownership and moves new words into students' personal vocabularies.

Wordplay

Wordplay is also an important part of the word-rich classroom. The ability to reflect on, manipulate, combine, and recombine the components of words is an important part of vocabulary learning. (See CCSS which call on students to "Determine the meaning of words and phrases as they are used in the text, including figurative and connotative meanings; analyze the impact of specific word choices on meaning and tone, including words with multiple meanings or language that is particularly fresh, engaging, or beautiful.") This type of manipulation develops metalinguistic reflection on words as objects to be manipulated intelligently and for humor (Nagy & Scott, 2000; Tunmer, Herriman, & Nesdale, 1988). Phonemic awareness (being able to segment phonemes, such as the *am* in *ambulance*), morphological awareness (of word part meanings), and syntactic awareness (how a word functions in language) all play important parts in word learning (Carlisle, 1995; Willows & Ryan, 1986). There is also evidence that this type of learning is developmental over the school years (Johnson & Anglin, 1995; Roth, Speece, Cooper, & De La Paz, 1996).

Part of creating a "positive environment for word learning" involves having activities, games, materials, and other resources that allow students to play with words. Who would not enjoy spending a few minutes each day figuring out a *wuzzle* or word puzzle? Wuzzles and other word games and puzzles call on students to think flexibly and metacognitively about words. Much of the fun stems from the fact that words can be used in multiple ways with humorous results (see Figure 9.3).

jobsinjobs

Q. Can you tell what phrase this Wuzzle (Word Puzzle) represents?

A. In between jobs

FIGURE 9.3. Wuzzle example.

So, our students need "word-rich" and "word-aware" classrooms, where new vocabulary is presented in rich listening and personal reading experiences, time is taken to stop and discuss new words, language is a part of all activities, and words, dictionaries, puzzles and word games, word calendars, books on riddles, and rhymes round out the environment for enthusiastic word learning.

Best Practices in Action

You can tell that Angela, a fourth-grade teacher, loves words and wordplay from the moment you walk into her classroom. A poster headed "New Words We Like" is displayed prominently on the front wall. It is filled with entries from students, with some words spilling over onto the wall on index cards. For each word, there is an entry, a description of where the student encountered the word, such as the one for *vile*, which the student illustrated with a drawing and verbal description of her sister's shoes (see Figure 9.4). Each student who used the word during the week could add his or her initials to the picture with another example.

In the library area, a shelf of riddle, joke, and pun books holds many well-thumbed volumes, and a "joke of the day" is posted on the wall. The bookcase also has a multitude of dictionaries—sports dictionaries, animal dictionaries, dictionaries of tools, and others. On the bottom shelf, a number of word games are stored, including Boggle, Scrabble, Pictionary, and their junior versions. There is also a basket of crossword books nearby and blank forms for making crossword puzzles. The nearby computer has a crossword puzzle program that is well used. There is also a box of discs called "Personal Dictionaries" on which students keep their own word lists. For some, a simple list in table form is used. These can be easily alphabetized and realphabetized with each addition. Other students like to use spreadsheets to keep their word files, so that they can resort them in different ways.

Rather than having a set of dictionaries stored on her bookshelf, Angela has dictionaries in convenient locations around the room. These range from hardbound collegiate dictionaries to more accessible softbacks at a range of levels. She also has several "learner's dictionaries" (e.g., *American Heritage Dictionary*, 2000), which are intended for students who are learning English. These define words functionally instead of classically, and Angela finds that many of her students like to use them, not just the students for whom English is a second language.

Angela's day starts with a word of the week, in which she poses a puzzle such as "Would a *ruthless* person be a good social worker?" If some students have a view, they answer and explain their reasoning. If no one has anything to offer, Angela presents the word in a few context sentences and then provides a definition. No more than 5 minutes are spent on this activity, and she varies the format. Sometimes she presents a word as a puzzle, sometimes as a guessing game, and so forth.

Today the class is starting a new unit on whales, so Angela begins with a vocabulary frame (Blachowicz, Bates, & Cieply, 2012) brainstorming. In this case, it is the grammar/structure of an informational piece on animal description that organizes the frame. She puts up a piece of chart paper (see Figure 9.5) and begins by having students brainstorm the words they already know about whales and enter these words on the

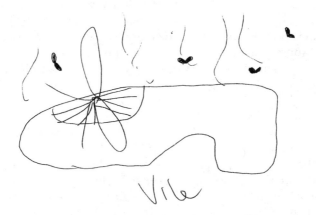

FIGURE 9.4. Personal word record: *vile*. "My brother says my sister's shoes smell vile. *Vile* = really bad, nasty."

Habitat/home	Description/types	Food
Predators/prey	Life/cycle	Other interesting words

FIGURE 9.5. Vocabulary frame for an informational article on whales.

chart in the categories related to the "grammar" of the selection, in this case the structure of a narrative animal description. (See CCSS, which call on students to "Use precise words and phrases, telling details, and sensory language to convey a vivid picture of the experiences, events, setting, and/or characters.")

As the unit progresses, more and more words will be added, and new categories will be drawn out of the "Other interesting words" category. Because she has many ESL students in her class, Angela uses the "Vocabulary Visit" (Blachowicz & Obrochta, 2005) model of scaffolding, recording, and revisiting thematic content material over the course of the unit.

In math class, students are busy working on their graphic dictionary of math terms, showing types of angles labeled with their names. During literature time, students are engaged in self-selection words for study from *The Castle in the Attic* (Winthrop, 1986), their core book for the unit. As they read their self-selected books on medieval life, they add to their personal lists.

At the end of each school day, Angela reads from a chapter book that her class has chosen. She asks the students to choose from a list of conceptually rich books that are too difficult for most of the children to read on their own. Each day, at the end of the reading, she asks students to pick a "wonderful word" the author used from that day's reading, and they add it to their wonderful word list. The day ends, as it began, with the wonder of words.

Reflections and Future Directions

In 2003, Hispanic students represented 19% of public school enrollment, up from 6% in 1972 (National Center for Educational Statistics, 2005). This is only part of the increase in English language learners in the schools system. While we know all children are language learners, educating an increasingly diverse student population whose first language is not English presents a special challenge, particularly in the area of vocabulary development (Blachowicz & Fisher, 2000). Finding creative and effective means for developing the vocabularies of diverse learners will be a major challenge of this decade. This is a critical issue for equity as well as for instruction.

Concluding Comments

All of us are vocabulary teachers when we work with students in class-rooms. We teach them new ways of looking at the world and, in doing so, develop new concepts and understandings. Every day, we teach words in a variety of ways. Our obligation to the students is not just to be vocabulary teachers but to be the best vocabulary teachers that we can be. Following the five evidence-based guidelines will make our classrooms homes for motivated word learners whose interest and skill in learning new words will grow along with their vocabularies.

ENGAGEMENT ACTIVITIES

1. Choose a vocabulary word from a text selection you will use with students. Construct a vocabulary frame for that word (see Figure 9.3 for an example). Then develop three contextual sentences, each of which gives a clue to the meaning. Lastly, develop two usage-choice sentences. Try them out with a classmate or with students in class. Write a reflection on what worked and what did not. How would you modify what you did?

2. Choose a vocabulary website below to use with your students. Describe the directions you would give them to use it (see the Reading Center website—*www2.nl.edu/reading_center*—for some other sites to start with or search in your browser).

3. Develop a Vocab-O-Gram for a selection. Use it to select the words you would teach. Try it out with a classmate or with students in class. Write a reflection on what worked and what did not. How would you modify what you did?

RESOURCES FOR FURTHER LEARNING

Books

Beck, I. L., McKeown, M. G., & Kucan, L. (2013). *Bringing words to life: Robust vocabulary instruction* (2nd ed.). New York: Guilford Press.
Baumann, J. F., & Kame'enui, E. J. (Eds.). (2012). *Vocabulary instruction: Research to practice* (2nd ed.). New York: Guilford Press.

Blachowicz, C., Fisher, P. J., Ogle, D., & Watts-Taffe, S. (2013). *Teaching academic vocabulary K–8: Effective practices across the curriculum.* New York: Guilford Press.

Blachowicz, C., & Fisher, P. (2013). *Teaching vocabulary in all classrooms* (5th ed.). Boston: Pearson, Allyn & Bacon.

Graves, M. F. (2006). *The vocabulary book: Learning and instruction.* New York: Teachers College Press.

Websites

National Center to Improve the Tools of Educators (NCITE) Research Synthesis: Reading and Diverse Learners—*http://idea.uoregon.edu/~ncite/documents/teachrep/reading.html.* NCITE staff reviewed reading research on the design of instructional materials for diverse learners in six general areas: vocabulary acquisition, word recognition, text organization, emergent literacy, fluency, and comprehension.

The Text Project—*http://textproject.org.* Many ideas related to vocabulary as a factor in text complexity.

Vocabulary Improvement Project (VIP)—*mind.ucsc.edu/vip.* The VIP is a national research program funded by the U.S. Department of Education. Its main goal is to develop intervention strategies aimed at helping children who are learning English.

Media, Games, Apps, and More

learninggamesforkids.com. Vocabulary games include analogies, antonyms, compound words, contractions, context and definitions, parts of speech, suffixes and prefixes, homophones, idioms, and syllables. First to fifth grade.

pbskids.org. Over 20 different games to build language and vocabulary in young students. Preschool to first grade.

sheppardsoftware.com. Games to practice nouns, verbs, and adjectives. Second to fourth grade.

spellingcity.com. Twenty-five games with over 42,000 words, to play online or in print, including parts of speech and vocabulary test. Kindergarten to high school.

vocabulary.co.il. Games to enhance vocabulary and practice skills. Kindergarten to high school.

Bluster! This word matching game develops vocabulary and word understanding. Includes over 800 vocabulary words. First to fifth grade.

Dabble. Given 20 letters, you have 5 minutes to make five different words. Second grade and up.

Enchanted Dictionary 4–6th or 7–12th. Helps students learn core vocabulary for science, social studies, math, or English/language arts. Select the words you wish to practice and press "play." Fourth grade and up.

ESL Interactive Audio–Picture English Lessons—*www.web-books.com/Language.* Offers interactive ESL with pronunciation and pictures.

EnglishCLUB.net—*www.englishclub.net.* Features grammar and vocabulary activities, word games, pen pal listings, and question-and-answer service. Includes free classroom handouts for ESL teachers.

Learn English—Have Fun—*www.englishday.com.* Offers online English crosswords, ESL word games, jokes, tests, and word-search puzzles. New games and crosswords added regularly.

Interesting Things for ESL Students—*www.aitech.ac.jp/˜itesls.* Free Web-based textbook and fun study site. Daily Page for English, proverbs, slang, anagrams, quizzes, and more.

REFERENCES

American Heritage Dictionary for Learners of English. (2000). Boston: Houghton Mifflin.

Baker, S. K., Simmons, D. C., & Kame'enui, E. J. (1995). *Vocabulary acquisition: Curricular and instructional implications for diverse learners* (Technical Report No. 14). Eugene: National Center to Improve the Tools of Educators, University of Oregon.

Baldwin, R. S., & Schatz, E. I. (1985). Context clues are ineffective with low frequency words in naturally occurring prose. In J. A. Niles & R. V. Lalik (Eds.), *Issues in literacy: A research perspective* (34th yearbook of the National Reading Conference, pp. 132–135). Rochester, NY: National Reading Conference.

Bannon, E., Fisher, P. J. L., Pozzi, L., & Wessel, D. (1990–1991). Effective definitions for word learning. *Journal of Reading, 34,* 301–303.

Baumann, J. F. (2009). Intensity in vocabulary instruction and effects on reading comprehension. *Topics in Language Disorders, 29,* 312–328.

Baumann, J. F., Blachowicz, C. L. Z., & Manyak, P. C., Graves, M. F., & Olejnik, S. (2009–2012). *Development of a multi-faceted, comprehensive, vocabulary instructional program for the upper-elementary grades* (R305A090163). Washington, DC: U.S. Department of Education, Institute of Education Sciences, National Center for Education Research (Reading and Writing Program).

Baumann, J. F., Edwards, E. C., Boland, E., Olejnik, S., & Kame'enui, E. W. (2003). Vocabulary tricks: Effects of instruction in morphology and context on fifth-grade students' ability to derive and infer word meanings. *American Educational Research Journal, 40,* 447–494.

Baumann, J. F., Ware, D., & Edwards, E. C. (2007). "Bumping into spicy, tasty words that catch your tongue": A formative experiment on vocabulary instruction. *The Reading Teacher, 62*, 108–122.

Beck, I. L., & McKeown, M. G. (1983). Learning words well—a program to enhance vocabulary and comprehension. *The Reading Teacher, 36*, 622–625.

Beck, I. L., & McKeown, M. G. (1991). Conditions of vocabulary acquisition. In R. Barr, M. Kamil, P. Mosenthal, & P. D. Pearson (Eds.), *Handbook of reading research* (Vol. 2, pp. 789–814). New York: Longman.

Beck, I. L., McKeown, M. G., & Kucan, L. (2013). *Bringing words to life: Robust vocabulary instruction* (2nd ed.). New York: Guilford Press.

Beck, I., Perfetti, C., & McKeown, M. (1982). The effects of long-term vocabulary instruction on lexical access and reading comprehension. *Journal of Educational Psychology, 74*, 506–521.

Beyersdorfer, J. M. (1991). *Middle school students' strategies for selection of vocabulary in science texts.* Unpublished PhD dissertation, National-Louis University, Evanston, IL.

Biemiller, A. (2001). Teaching vocabulary: Early, direct, and sequential. *American Educator, 25*(1), 24–28, 47.

Blachowicz, C. L. Z. (1986). Making connections: Alternatives to the vocabulary notebook. *Journal of Reading, 29*, 643–649.

Blachowicz, C. L. Z., Bates, A., & Cieply, C. (2012, April 30). *Vocabulary framing: Supporting student vocabulary learning and language use in a multifaceted vocabulary instruction project.* Paper presented at the annual conference of the International Reading Association, Chicago.

Blachowicz, C. L. Z., & Fisher, P. J. L. (2000). Vocabulary instruction. In R. Barr, M. L. Kamil, P. B. Mosenthal, & P. D. Pearson (Eds.), *Handbook of reading research* (Vol. 3, pp. 503–523). New York: Longman.

Blachowicz, C. L. Z., & Fisher, P. J. L. (2012). Keep the "fun" in *fun*damental: Encouraging word consciousness and incidental word learning in the classroom through wordplay. In E. J. Kame'enui & J. F. Baumann (Eds.), *Vocabulary instruction: Research to practice* (2nd ed., pp. 189–209). New York: Guilford Press.

Blachowicz, C. L. Z., & Fisher, P. J. L. (2015). *Teaching vocabulary in all classrooms* (5th ed.). Boston: Pearson.

Blachowicz, C. L. Z., Fisher, P. J. L., Costa, M., & Pozzi, M. (1993, November). *Researching vocabulary learning in middle school cooperative reading groups: A teacher–researcher collaboration.* Paper presented at the Tenth Great Lakes Regional Reading conference, Chicago.

Blachowicz, C. L. Z., Fisher, P. J. L., Ogle, D., & Watts-Taffe, S. (2013). *Teaching academic vocabulary K–8: Effective practices across the curriculum.* New York: Guilford Press.

Blachowicz, C. L. Z., & Obrochta, C. (2005). Vocabulary visits: Developing content vocabulary in the primary grades. *The Reading Teacher, 59*, 262–269.

Blachowicz, C. L. Z., & Obrochta, C. (2007). "Tweaking practice": Modifying read-alouds to enhance content vocabulary learning in grade 1. In D. Dickinson (Ed.), *National Reading Conference Yearbook* (pp. 111–121). Oak Creek, WI: National Reading Conference.

Buikema, J. L., & Graves, M. F. (1993). Teaching students to use context clues to infer word meanings. *Journal of Reading, 36*, 450–457.

Carlisle, J. (1995). Morphological awareness and early reading achievement. In L. Feldman (Ed.), *Morphological aspects of language processing* (pp. 189–209). Hillsdale, NJ: Erlbaum.

Carlisle, J. F. (2000). Awareness of the structure and meaning of morphologically complex words: Impact on reading. *Reading and Writing: An Interdisciplinary Journal, 12*, 169–190.

Cobb, C., & Blachowicz, C. (2014). *No more "look up the list" vocabulary instruction.* Portsmouth, NH: Heinemann.

Cunningham, A. E. (2005). Vocabulary growth through independent reading and reading aloud to children. In E. H. Hiebert & M. L. Kamil (Eds.), *Teaching and learning vocabulary: Bringing research to practice* (pp. 45–68). Mahwah, NJ: Erlbaum.

Cunningham, A. E., & Stanovich, K. E. (1998, Spring/Summer). What reading does for the mind. *American Educator*, pp. 8–17.

D'Anna, C. A., Zechmeister, E. B., & Hall, J. W. (1991). Toward a meaningful definition of vocabulary size. *Journal of Reading Behavior, 23*, 109–22.

De Temple, J., & Snow, C. (2003). Learning words from books. In A. V. Kleeck, S. A. Stahl, & E. B. Bauer (Eds.), *On reading books to children: Parents and teachers* (pp. 16–36). Mahwah, NJ: Erlbaum.

Dressler, C. & Kamil, M. L. (2006). First- and second-language literacy. In D. August & T. Shanahan (Eds.), *Developing literacy in second-language learners: Report of the National Literacy Panel on Language-Minority Children and Youth* (pp. 197–238). Mahwah, NJ: Erlbaum.

Elleman, A. M., Endia, J. L., Morphy, P., & Compton, D. L. (2009). The impact of vocabulary instruction on passage-level comprehension of school-age children: A meta-analysis. *Journal of Research on Educational Effectiveness, 2*, 1–44.

Eller, R. G., Pappas, C. C., & Brown, E. (1988). The lexical development of kindergartners: Learning from written context. *Journal of Reading Behavior, 20*, 5–24.

Elley, W. B. (1988). Vocabulary acquisition from listening to stories. *Reading Research Quarterly, 24*, 174–187.

Fisher, P. J. L., Blachowicz, C. L. Z., & Smith, J. C. (1991). Vocabulary learning in literature discussion groups. In J. Zutell & S. McCormick (Eds.), *Learner factors/teacher factors: Issues in literacy research and instruction* (40th yearbook of the National Reading Conference, pp. 201–209). Chicago: National Reading Conference.

Graves, M. F. (1986). Vocabulary learning and instruction. *Review of Research in Education, 13*, 49–89.

Graves, M. F. (2006). *The vocabulary book: Learning and instruction.* New York: Teachers College Press.

Graves, M. F., & Silverman, R. (2010). Interventions to enhance vocabulary development. In R. L. Allington & A. McGill-Franzen (Eds.), *Handbook of reading disabilities research* (pp. 312–328). Mahwah, NJ: Erlbaum.

Graves, M. F., & Watts-Taffe, S. M. (2002). The place of word consciousness in a research-based vocabulary program. In A. E. Farstrup & S. J. Samuels (Eds.),

What research has to say about reading instruction (3rd ed., pp. 140–165). Newark, DE: International Reading Association.

Haggard, M. R. (1982). The vocabulary self-selection strategy: An active approach to word learning. *Journal of Reading, 26,* 634–642.

Haggard, M. R. (1985). An interactive strategies approach to content reading. *Journal of Reading, 29,* 204–210.

Hart, B., & Risley, T. R. (1995). *Meaningful differences in the everyday experience of young American children.* Baltimore: Brookes.

Heimlich, J. E., & Pittelman, S. D. (1986). *Semantic mapping: Classroom applications.* Newark, DE: International Reading Association.

Herman, P. A., Anderson, R. C., Pearson, P. D., & Nagy, W. E. (1987). Incidental acquisition of word meaning from expositions with varied text features. *Reading Research Quarterly, 22,* 263–284.

Jiminez, R. J. (1997). The strategic reading abilities and potential of five low-literacy Latina/o readers in middle school. *Reading Research Quarterly, 32,* 224–243.

Jimenez, R. T., Garcia, G. E., & Pearson, D. P. (1996). The reading strategies of bilingual Latina/o students who are successful English readers: Opportunities and obstacles. *Reading Research Quarterly, 31,* 90–112.

Johnson, C. J., & Anglin, J. M. (1995). Qualitative developments in the content and form of children's definitions. *Journal of Speech and Hearing Research, 38,* 612–629.

Kame'enui, E. J., Carnine, D. W., & Freschi, R. (1982). Effects of text construction and instructional procedures for teaching word meanings on comprehension and recall. *Reading Research Quarterly, 17,* 367–388.

Kieffer, M. J., & Lesaux, N. K. (2007). Breaking down words to build meaning: Morphology, vocabulary, and reading comprehension in the urban classroom. *The Reading Teacher, 61,* 134–144.

Kuhn, M., & Stahl, S. (1998). Teaching children to learn word meanings from context: A synthesis and some questions. *Journal of Literacy Research, 30,* 119–138.

Lesaux, N. K., Kieffer, M. J., Faller, S. E., & Kelley, J. G. (2010). The effectiveness and ease of implementation of an academic English vocabulary intervention for linguistically diverse students in urban middle schools. *Reading Research Quarterly, 45,* 196–228.

Manyak, P. (2007, March). Character trait vocabulary: A schoolwide approach. *The Reading Teacher, 60,* 574–577.

Marzano, R. J., & Marzano, J. S. (1988). *A cluster approach to elementary vocabulary instruction.* Newark, DE: International Reading Association.

McKeown, M. G., Beck, I. L., Omanson, R. C., & Pople, M. T. (1985). Some effects of the nature and frequency of vocabulary instruction on the knowledge and use of words. *Reading Research Quarterly, 20,* 522–535.

McKeown, M. G., Beck, I. L., & Worthy, M. J. (1993). Grappling with text ideas: Questioning the author. *The Reading Teacher, 46,* 560–566.

Mezynski, K. (1983). Issues concerning the acquisition of knowledge: Effects of vocabulary training on reading comprehension. *Review of Educational Research 53,* 253–279.

Miller, G. A., & Gildea, P. M. (1987). How children learn words. *Scientific American, 257,* 94–99.

Nagy, W. E., Herman, P. A., & Anderson, R. C. (1985). Learning words from context. *Reading Research Quarterly, 20,* 233–253.

Nagy, W. E., & Scott, J. A. (2000). Vocabulary processes. In M. L. Kamil, P. B. Mosenthal, P. D. Pearson, & R. Barr (Eds.), *Handbook of reading research* (Vol. 3, pp. 269–284). Mahwah, NJ: Erlbaum.

Nagy, W. [E.], & Scott, J. (2001). Vocabulary processes. In M. L. Kamil, P. B. Mosenthal, P. D. Pearson, & R. Barr (Eds.), *Handbook of reading research* (Vol. 3, pp. 269–283). New York: Longman.

National Center for Educational Statistics. Retrieved August 11, 2005, from *nces. ed.gov/programs/coe/2005/section1/indicator04.asp.*

National Reading Panel. (2000). *Report of the National Reading Panel: Teaching children to read.* Washington, DC: National Academy Press.

Neuman, S. B., & Dickinson, D. K. (Eds.). (2001). *Handbook of early literacy research* (Vol. 1). New York: Guilford Press.

Pany, D., Jenkins, J. R., & Schreck, J. (1982). Vocabulary instruction: Effects on word knowledge and reading comprehension. *Learning Disabilities Quarterly, 5,* 202–15.

Pittelman, S. D., Heimlich, J. E., Berglund, R. L., & French, M. P. (1991). *Semantic feature analysis: Classroom applications.* Newark, DE: International Reading Association.

Robbins, C., & Ehri, L. C. (1994). Reading storybooks to kindergarteners helps them learn new vocabulary words. *Journal of Educational Psychology, 86,* 54–64.

Roth, F., Speece, D., Cooper, D., & De La Paz, S. (1996). Unresolved mysteries: How do metalinguistic and narrative skills connect with early reading? *Journal of Special Education, 30,* 257–277.

Ruddell, M. R., & Shearer, B. A. (2002). "Extraordinary," "tremendous," "exhilarating," "magnificent": Middle school at-risk students become avid word learners with the vocabulary self-collection strategy (VSS). *Journal of Adolescent and Adult Literacy, 45,* 352–363.

Schwanenflugel, P. J., Stahl, S. A., & McFalls, E. L. (1997). *Partial word knowledge and vocabulary growth during reading comprehension* (Research Report No. 76). Athens: University of Georgia, National Reading Research Center.

Schwartz, R. M., & Raphael, T. E. (1985). Concept of definition: A key to improving students' vocabulary. *The Reading Teacher, 39,* 198–205.

Scott, J. A., Miller, T. F., & Flinspach, S. L. (2012). Developing word consciousness: Lessons from highly diverse fourth-grade classrooms. In E. J. Kame'enui & J. F. Baumann (Eds.), *Vocabulary instruction: Research to practice* (2nd ed., pp. 169–188). New York: Guilford Press.

Senechal, M., Thomas, E., & Monker, J. (1995). Individual differences in 5-year olds' acquisition of vocabulary during storybook reading. *Journal of Educational Psychology, 87,* 218–229.

Snow, C. E. (1991). *Unfulfilled expectations: Home and school influences on literacy.* Cambridge, MA: Harvard University Press.

Stahl, S. A., & Fairbanks, M. M. (1986). The effects of vocabulary instruction: A model-based meta-analysis. *Review of Educational Research, 56*, 72–110.

Stahl, S. A., & Vancil, S. (1986). Discussion is what makes semantic maps work in vocabulary instruction. *The Reading Teacher, 40*, 62–69.

Tunmer, W. E., Herriman, M. L., & Nesdale, A. R. (1988). Metalinguistic abilities and beginning reading. *Reading Research Quarterly, 23*, 134–158.

Whitehurst, G. J., Epstein, J. N., Angell, A. L., Payne, A. C., Crone, D. A., & Fischel, J. E. (1994). Outcomes of an emergent literacy intervention in Head Start. *Journal of Educational Psychology, 86*, 542–555.

Whitehurst, G. J., Zevenberg, A. A., Crone, D. A., Schultz, M. D., Velting, O. N., & Fischel, J. E. (1999). Outcomes of an emergent literacy intervention from Head Start through second grade. *Journal of Educational Psychology, 91*, 261–272.

Willows, D. M., & Ryan, E. B. (1986). The development of grammatical sensitivity and its relationship to early reading achievement. *Reading Research Quarterly, 21*, 253–266.

Winthrop, E. (1986). *The castle in the attic.* New York: Yearlong Books.

Wixson, K. K. (1986). Vocabulary instruction and children's comprehension of basal stories. *Reading Research Quarterly, 21*, 317–329.

CHAPTER 10

Best Practices in Narrative Text Comprehension Instruction

Janice F. Almasi
Susan J. Hart

This chapter will:

- Describe the role of social context in comprehension instruction.
- Discuss the importance of scaffolding during comprehension instruction.
- Discuss the importance of teaching readers to be strategic versus teaching strategies.
- Assert that metacognition is crucial as readers become transformed into strategic learners.
- Explain the links between comprehension instruction and the Common Core State Standards

---

The first section of this chapter reviews what the current research has to say about comprehension, while the second section describes the fundamental changes that need to take place to recontextualize comprehension as a means of cultivating strategic and reflective learners. The third section describes adjustments that can be made within literacy classrooms to foster an environment that is conducive to a "transformational view" of strategy instruction.

Evidence-Based Best Practices: A Research Synthesis

Two issues have been at the forefront of comprehension research and practice. The first issue concerns the role of word recognition in instruction aimed at improving comprehension, and the second issue relates to the role of knowledge in instruction aimed at improving comprehension.

The Role of Word Recognition in Instruction Aimed at Improving Comprehension

Many researchers and practitioners subscribe to the notion that the ability to decode words is central to successful comprehension. The logic underlying this perspective is that decoding skills alone, or at least in large part, are sufficient to lead to high levels of comprehension. This perspective is based on automaticity theory (Fleisher, Jenkins, & Pany, 1979; LaBerge & Samuels, 1974; Samuels, 2004). Hoover and Gough's (1990) "simple view" of reading followed a similar theoretical premise, arguing that skilled reading consisted simply of decoding and linguistic comprehension.

These theories are most evident in emergent literacy practices and instruction with struggling readers where much of the instruction focuses on word recognition and fluency and little, if any, instruction focuses on comprehension. The logic in this practice is "students need to learn to read the words first, we will focus on comprehension afterward."

If these theories were accurate, then it would be inconceivable that readers could decode words accurately and struggle with comprehension. Valencia's research (Riddle Buly & Valencia, 2002; Valencia, 2011) indicated that readers who struggle vary greatly. Nearly 20% of all struggling readers in their research were able to decode words accurately and read fluently; however, their comprehension was weak. Leach, Scarborough, and Rescorla's (2003) research found that nearly half of the fourth graders in their study had late-emerging comprehension difficulties (i.e., comprehension difficulty emerged after third grade). Of those students, one-third had comprehension difficulty, but were able to decode words accurately. These studies dispel the notion that accurate decoding alone guarantees comprehension. A significant number of readers who struggle with comprehension do so despite having adequate word recognition skills.

Programs and legislation that aim to teach all children to read by grade three often focus on teaching children to read words accurately and with fluency. Reading First programs of the 2000s were an example of such legislation. Reading First was intended to provide explicit instruction in phonics, phonemic awareness, fluency, vocabulary, *and* comprehension; however, ensuing instructional practice focused largely on phonics, phonemic awareness, and fluency. Ultimately, when the final report of Reading First's impacts was released, findings indicated that these code-based interventions had no significant impact on comprehension for children in grades 1, 2, or 3 (Gamse, Jacob, Horst, Boulay, & Unlu, 2008).

Almasi, Palmer, Madden, and Hart's (2011) review of research on interventions that foster narrative comprehension for struggling readers found similar results. Those interventions focused solely on decoding and/or fluency were not as successful at enhancing comprehension as interventions that included both decoding and comprehension instruction. Furthermore, interventions that focused exclusively on comprehension were consistently successful at enhancing comprehension. In a more quantitative analysis of research, Edmonds and colleagues (2009) examined studies in which three types of interventions were used to enhance comprehension: (1) fluency/word-study interventions, (2) comprehension interventions (e.g., teaching single strategies, multiple strategies, or using graphic organizers), and (3) multicomponent interventions, which included either word study and comprehension or fluency and comprehension. Their analysis found that comprehension interventions were superior to all other types of intervention for enhancing comprehension, and the most effective interventions were those that taught multiple strategies. In particular, teaching multiple strategies was effective for struggling readers and students with disabilities.

These recent reviews of research confirm the conclusion that while the ability to decode words and read with fluency is necessary for successful reading, and vital *for* comprehension, the ability to decode by itself is not sufficient to ensure successful comprehension. These research findings should put to rest the notion that an instructional emphasis on decoding (i.e., phonics, phonemic awareness) by itself, or even in large part, leads to significant impacts on comprehension—it does not.

The Role of Knowledge in Comprehension

The issue the field is currently grappling with concerns the relative contributions of content knowledge and process knowledge to comprehension. Some have argued (e.g., Hirsch, 2006; McKeown, Beck, & Blake, 2009; Neuman, 2006) that having relevant content knowledge (e.g., domain knowledge, prior knowledge, vocabulary) is critical to comprehension. Others contend that it is essential that readers possess process knowledge related to what comprehension strategies to use, and procedural and conditional knowledge related to where, when, and how to use those strategies (e.g., Duke & Pearson, 2008–2009; Pressley, 2000; Pressley et al., 1992). The relevant question here is, "Does a reader have difficulty comprehending because he or she lacks knowledge of the words and concepts in the text, or does he or she lack knowledge of the process of knowing when/how to access that knowledge?"

Beginning with the National Reading Panel (2000), government-issued reports regarding research-based comprehension practice have consistently found that there is strong research evidence to support teaching comprehension strategies to both young readers (e.g., Shanahan et al., 2010) and adolescent readers (Kamil et al., 2008). Unfortunately, the Common Core State Standards (CCSS; National Governors Association & Council of Chief State School Officers [NGA & CCSSO], 2010) do not mention strategy instruction, choosing instead to focus on the resulting products of comprehension that are most closely aligned with literal interpretations and close readings of the text that emphasize literal recall, making logical inferences, citing textual evidence to support conclusions, and analyzing the structure of texts. Each of these standards can be met by providing strategy instruction; however, the specific language of strategy instruction is not used.

Those arguing on behalf of content knowledge suggest that a focus on teaching comprehension strategies has undermined comprehension because the curriculum has neglected content knowledge and the vocabulary that is gained when learning content (Hirsch, 2006). The argument is predicated on the notion that "if you can't understand what the words mean or the concepts in the text, then comprehension is impossible." The instructional implications are that teachers need to build vocabulary and provide core knowledge to enhance comprehension. Unfortunately, many times those who struggle to comprehend do so regardless of whether they have content knowledge. As well, those who argue in favor of the content knowledge position are often long on rhetoric and short on empirical evidence. McKeown and colleagues (2009) is often cited as a study that supports the content knowledge position in that the fifth graders in the content knowledge condition were more successful at oral recall of narrative text than students in the strategies condition. However, all students did equally well on another measure of comprehension, the sentence verification technique. Thus, the results are mixed, and unfortunately there were several issues with the quality of the study. The study was not conducted with struggling readers (or poor comprehenders), did not control for variations in content knowledge, and used intact classrooms but did not analyze results in a way that would control for the problems of using intact classrooms. Most importantly, the strategy instruction condition did not consist of instruction that most experts in strategy instruction would call "authentic strategy instruction." Thus, the study that is most often cited as evidence in support of the content knowledge position produced mixed results and had several methodological issues that render the findings suspect.

Although there is little substantive evidence to support the content knowledge position, there is, however, evidence that refutes the content knowledge position, and there are decades of research that support strategies instruction. The remainder of this review will focus on that body of research.

Nation's (2005) review of the research suggested that, while poor comprehenders tend to have weak expressive and receptive vocabularies, and that this lack of word-level knowledge contributes to poor comprehension, it is not likely that weak vocabulary entirely accounts for comprehension difficulties. For example, 7- and 8-year-old poor comprehenders continued to struggle to make inferences and understand text in studies where great care was taken to make sure all students had relevant content knowledge and vocabulary (Cain & Oakhill, 1999; Cain, Oakhill, Barnes, & Bryant, 2001). These findings suggest that something beyond vocabulary and content knowledge accounts for successful comprehension. Poor comprehenders in these studies understood relevant vocabulary, had the requisite content knowledge, and could find the location of the pieces of information they needed in the text to make an inference; yet they still could not make accurate inferences. In other words, this study was able to rule out the possibility that lacking content knowledge did not cause these students' comprehension failure. The instructional implication based on this research is that poor comprehenders need to learn *how* to access knowledge and integrate it to make inferences. Simply having content knowledge was insufficient for comprehension. These readers needed the process knowledge of how, when, and where to integrate knowledge across sentences in order to make inferences. These poor comprehenders needed strategy instruction.

Those who argue in favor of strategy instruction do not deny that content knowledge is important; instead, they argue that strategy instruction is needed for many learners to become independent, self-regulated readers so they can learn relevant content from text. Palincsar and Schultz (2011) suggested that strategy instruction is intended to teach readers a "repertoire of thinking tools that should be used in opportunistic ways, determined by the demands of the text and the goals of the reader" which are to taught "in the service of advancing knowledge building" (p. 91).

Strategies are cognitive and metacognitive processes that are deliberately and consciously employed as a means of attaining a goal (Almasi & Fullerton, 2012; Paris, Lipson, & Wixson, 1983; Pressley, Borkowski, & Schneider, 1989). Afflerbach, Pearson, and Paris (2008) distinguished strategies from skills by noting that intentionality, awareness, and goal-directedness are the hallmarks of strategic action.

The key aspect of this definition is that strategic behaviors are actions employed by an agentic individual. Often educators speak of strategies as if they are nouns rather than actions. This may be because much of the early research on strategy instruction focused on identifying what good and poor readers did while reading to enhance their comprehension. These "good and poor reader studies" helped the field understand what good readers were thinking and doing while reading. Instructional practice based on these findings attempted to teach struggling readers to engage in those strategies that good readers did while reading. Typically, these strategies were taught in isolation and they were taught quickly—sometimes over the course of a few lessons or a few weeks.

Reviews of these studies identified a number of powerful strategies that had significant impacts on comprehension, including comprehension monitoring, constructing mental images, identifying story grammar components, generating questions while reading, making inferences, and summarizing (e.g., Almasi et al., 2011; Gersten, Fuchs, Williams, & Baker, 2001; National Reading Panel, 2000; Pressley, 2000). Inadvertently, these studies may have led to current instructional practice in which strategies are often taught one at a time and in isolation. The other inadvertent outcome that may have emerged is that, due to the isolated nature of the instruction, teachers often prompted students to employ the specific strategy, rather than encouraging students to make their own decisions about whether to use the strategy or not. The results of these studies have shown that students are able to learn how to use a strategy to improve short-term comprehension, but over time these comprehension gains were not sustained.

These practices may have also led to the unintended practice in which students are taught that there is only one "right" way to use strategies or that there are "better" strategies to use to construct meaning (Aukerman, 2013). Aukerman (2013) referred to strategy instruction as "comprehension-as-procedure pedagogy" (p. A4), and suggested that readers are taught a "prespecified," or correct, way of using strategies to construct meaning. Wilkinson and Son (2011) acknowledged the plethora of studies that support strategy instruction; however, they argued that research on strategy instruction has been unable to find particular combinations of strategy use that are effective and that research has been unable to determine whether the strategies that are taught are actually what causes the increases in comprehension. Both of these criticisms are valid; however, they reflect unintended consequences from the early research. Instead, instruction is intended to assist readers in *becoming* strategic. That is, instruction should help readers learn how to become metacognitively aware so that they can actively make decisions on their own about how to make sense of the text. It does not mean that they should be taught a prescribed pattern of strategy use, or combinations of strategies, aimed at making sense of text. It means teaching students to become independent decision makers while they are reading.

Furthermore, research has also shown that the ability of such short-term, isolated strategy instruction to yield long-term benefits and transfer to all reading contexts is questionable (Almasi et al., 2011; Pressley, 2000). Many of these early studies did not provide students with the type of explicit instruction that enables them to internalize the strategic processing necessary to transfer what they learned to other contexts. Instruction that fosters transfer includes opportunities for readers to talk not only about the strategies they use, but also about the conditions under which they may or may not use them. That is, readers must think about and consider where, when, and why they might use a strategy as they make decisions about whether to use a particular strategy to meet their reading goal.

In short, these early studies focused on teaching students the "strategy" rather than teacher students "to be strategic." Subsequently teachers have come to focus on strategies as things to be taught, rather than as actions to be fostered. The difference is that strategic actions require intentionality—they require a reader who is actively processing the text and making decisions (Afflerbach et al., 2008; Paris, Wasik, & Turner, 1991; Pressley et al., 1989). Such readers continually monitor the reading experience and consciously make decisions as to where, when, how, and why they should apply strategic behaviors and actions (e.g., activating background knowledge to make connections, visualizing, making predictions, making inferences, identifying text structure, monitoring comprehension, summarizing) as warranted by the conditions surrounding the reading event. Thus, teaching readers to be strategic not only involves teaching them about the strategy, but also about the conditions under which one might actually *use* the strategy.

The ability to use a reading strategy to improve comprehension is thus far more difficult when the ultimate goal is to teach students to be strategic. It involves not only teaching students about the strategy, but also teaching them about the subtle nuances related to analyzing the reading task and making decisions about which strategies might best be suited for particular purposes, at particular times, and under particular circumstances. Such instruction takes time. Thus, researchers developed interventions that taught readers how to use *sets* of strategies rather than individual strategies. These interventions focused on teaching students how to recognize where and when they should use strategies, how to select from a variety of strategies, and how to determine whether their choices were moving them toward their goal: comprehension. Reciprocal teaching (Palincsar & Brown, 1984), Informed Strategies for Learning (e.g., Paris, Cross, & Lipson, 1984), and Transactional Strategies Instruction (TSI) (Anderson, 1992; Pressley et al., 1992) are examples of interventions that not only teach students how to flexibly use a cohesive set of strategies, but also how to develop metacognitive awareness of the task and self that fosters self-initiated and self-regulated strategy use. Research has shown that each of these interventions has proven successful with readers at various age levels, and some studies have shown that they lead to sustained and significant growth in comprehension over time (Brown, Pressley, Van Meter, & Schuder, 1996; Van Keer, 2004). Recent research has also indicated that teaching strategies one at a time was not as effective as teaching them as a set, as in Transactional Strategies Instruction (Reutzel, Smith, & Fawson, 2005).

As a result of these research findings core reading programs (i.e., basal reading programs) published in the past decade have incorporated much of the research related to comprehension strategies instruction (Pilonieta, 2010). However, as Dewitz, Jones, and Leahy (2009) found, the five most widely used commercial core reading programs do not provide the type of explicit instruction or the gradual release of responsibility that is foundational to comprehension strategies instruction. Furthermore, Dewitz, Leahy, Jones, and Sullivan (2010) found these publications woefully inadequate in their attempt to provide students with the procedural and conditional knowledge associated with strategy use. What continues to be problematic is that teachers tend to misunderstand what strategic processing involves, focus on isolated strategy use rather than strategic processing, and focus on activities rather than strategies. Teachers may engage students in an activity, but they do not provide the requisite instructional elements to teach *strategic processing*. Very often, the teacher him- or herself actually performs the strategies rather than teaching their students how to use the strategy independently. That is, a teacher may set a purpose for reading rather than teaching the students how, when, and why they should set their own purposes while reading. Thus, students are not actively engaged in the decision-making process regarding what strategies to use and when to use them. As a result, they do not learn to become planful, self-regulated readers who possess a repertoire of strategies to assist them as they read. Struggling readers in particular are at a disadvantage in this scenario.

In summary, the previous review of reading comprehension research provided an overview of two generations of comprehension strategies research that has led to two different perspectives on instruction. The first perspective is what we will call the "isolation view" in which strategies are taught in isolation and their use is often prompted by teachers. A common metaphor is that readers acquire a "toolbox" of different strategies (Almasi & Fullerton, 2012). From this perspective the strategies, or "tools," used by the reader are outside of the reader (kept in a metaphorical toolbox) and accessed when needed. A more knowledgeable other, such as a teacher, might let you know which tool to select and when to use it: "Today we're going to learn about the parts of a story. Stories include setting, characters, plot, and a solution. Here is a story map for you to fill out after you read the story. It will help you remember what you have read."

The "transformational view," which is what this chapter seeks to encourage, emphasizes the importance of teaching strategies in a manner that enables students to *become* strategic. Just as a Transformer action figure can morph from a car to a robot whose body parts can change into a variety of mechanical tools and weapons, a reader engages with strategies until the strategies become part of the reader. The reader no longer reaches for a tool from a toolbox that is outside of him or her; the reader actually *is* the tool. The tools are within the reader, and the reader must consider reader factors, textual factors, and contextual factors to determine what strategy works best in a given situation. The reader actually embodies the tools/strategies. That is, the reader becomes the tools/strategies and the tools/strategies become the reader. The reader is transformed by using the strategies. Teachers from this perspective do not tell readers when to use a strategy, instead they say things like "Today we are going to read a story. What strategies or tools might we use as we are reading to help us understand the story?" This is followed by a discussion among the students as to different types of strategies that they might use to help them as they read. The section that follows will provide further explanation of what these best practices look like in action.

Best Practices in Action

The lack of coherence between reading programs and research-based strategies instruction has led to a disconnect between content and learning. Core reading programs like those that Dewitz, Jones, and Leahy evaluated, establish a precedent as to how comprehension instruction will occur within classrooms. Within the environments perpetuated by such reading programs, strategy instruction is prescriptive in nature. It removes the social context of learning and expects all students to use the same strategies, in the same way, for the same outcome. Learners are separate from the context of learning. Separating content and learning leads to a different understanding of how people conceptualize the nature of knowledge and learning.

Some would argue that the goal of comprehension is to extract the meaning from the text. This perspective implies that there is only one correct interpretation of a text and the reader must discover it. From this perspective, knowledge is located outside of the learner, and the learner must acquire that knowledge to successfully comprehend text.

An alternate perspective is that there are multiple ways of knowing, or understanding a text, and the reader's job is to construct meaning in a manner best suited to his or her goals as a reader and the context. From this perspective, knowledge is located within the learner, and the learner must actively construct meaning to successfully comprehend text.

The viewpoint that students are products, detached from their own learning processes has dominated our schools. As No Child Left Behind Act of 2001 (No Child Left Behind Act, 2001) embraced the "Big Five": (1) phonemic awareness, (2) phonics, (3) fluency, (4) vocabulary, and (5) comprehension (National Reading Panel, 2000), core reading programs followed in-line and perpetuated a decontextualized nature of teaching strategies in isolation (Dewitz et al., 2009). In terms of comprehensive literacy instruction, this perspective brought with it a mindset that emphasized "the simple view" of reading comprehension (Hoover & Gough, 1990). Such a developmental perspective stresses individual skills such as decoding, listening, fluency, and vocabulary/content knowledge as steps to achieve comprehension. Hoffman (2009) stated that such a perspective might work for literacy growth if literacy instruction and literacy learning were not such complex processes. The remainder of this chapter extends the conversation about comprehensive literacy instruction to recognize the social context of literacy learning as it relates to reading comprehension. As the research synthesized above has shown, teaching strategies as skills in isolation has not yielded long-term effects on comprehension. Rather than focusing on strategies research has shown are most critical to comprehension and perpetuating the notion that strategies should be taught in isolation, this chapter attempts to change the conversation by focusing on how to teach readers to be strategic, while recognizing the social nature of learning. Figure 10.1 depicts a more comprehensive and contextual view of how strategies can be implemented within a literacy environment so that students can become strategic and reflective within a classroom culture that values the learning process. Figure 10.1 illustrates how four elements work together to create a learning environment that fosters independent, self-regulated comprehension: (1) context, (2) explicit instruction, (3) agency/metacognition, and (4) scaffolding.

The following ideas, based on Almasi and Fullerton's (2012) critical elements of strategy instruction model, will help classroom teachers and interventionists to identify critical features necessary to help readers become strategic.

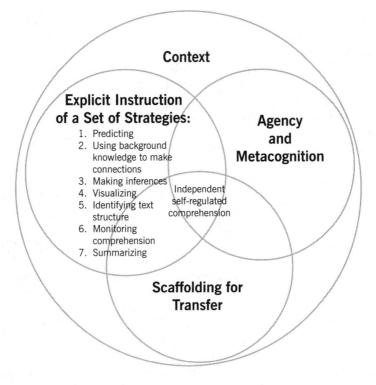

Context

Explicit Instruction of a Set of Strategies:
1. Predicting
2. Using background knowledge to make connections
3. Making inferences
4. Visualizing
5. Identifying text structure
6. Monitoring comprehension
7. Summarizing

Agency and Metacognition

Independent self-regulated comprehension

Scaffolding for Transfer

FIGURE 10.1. Key elements in a transformational view of comprehension strategy instruction.

Context

The instructional context in Figure 10.1 represents the overall instructional environment and everything contained within that environment. Context is critical for solid comprehension strategy instruction because it is through context that students become acculturated into the language of strategies, observe strategic behaviors and actions, and participate in strategic processing firsthand. Sociocultural perspectives on learning (e.g., Vygotsky, 1978) suggest that learning is a "cognitive apprenticeship" that occurs when learners are able to interact socially with others who might guide, support, or stretch their thinking so that they can learn how to use and implement the "tools of culture" (Rogoff, 1990, p. i) that will be needed. In an instructional context focused on comprehension, this means that students learn how to be strategic. The "tools" needed to be strategic in one context or culture might differ from those needed in another. For example, a reader might need different "tools" or act in a different manner when reading in an online environment than when reading traditional text (Coiro & Dobler, 2007; Leu et al., 2008), or when reading in a Western society that places greater value on "school literacy" or "written literacy" than in a society that values "oral literacy," where a higher demand is placed on memory. Johnston (2004) has noted that classrooms are sites where "children are *becoming* literate" (p. 22). It is where they are developing social and personal identities about who they are as readers, writers, and thinkers. It is where they explore, try out, and try on various ways of being, acting, and thinking as they negotiate their own identities. In this sense, then, the classroom instructional context is a space in which readers author themselves (Holland, Lachicotte, Skinner, & Cain, 1998), which means that there is a great deal of playful experimentation needed, particularly as readers attempt new or different ways of accomplishing tasks and goals. This is not a space where there are "right" or "wrong" ways of "doing" reading or comprehending. It is a space where readers construct and build their own understanding of themselves and of what works for them and under what conditions. Thus, the instructional context must be a safe space that is free of the hazards that lead children to become cautious, fearful, anxious, and passive participants in their own learning. Often such hazards arise when children are assessment-focused or performance-oriented, as Prawat (1989) described them. Their goal might be to "get done," which might lead them to rush through or skim a text so they finish, rather than engage in strategic behaviors that would assist their comprehension but cause them to take longer.

Creating a "safe" environment means creating a space in which it is "okay" to be uncertain or wrong, and in fact, it is celebrated when students say "I don't get it" or "I'm confused." The teacher's response, in a safe space, would be, "Wonderful! Owen I'm so glad you were able to recognize when your reading doesn't make sense! That shows you are a good reader because you know when the text doesn't make sense! What didn't make sense to you?" In these classrooms, the teacher creates a safe space where students can openly discuss what they don't understand and test new or different ways of making sense of text. These safe spaces include many opportunities for readers to talk with other readers about the texts, what they understood (or did not understand), and how they went about making sense of the text (e.g., what strategic processes they used, when they used them, where they used them, and why they used them). Teachers in these classrooms are not asking comprehension questions or noting who understood and who did not. Instead, teachers who create safe spaces make note of students' strategic processing and under what circumstances.

In the above scenario, the teacher might ask other students if they had a similar problem, "Did anyone else have difficulty understanding that part? Let's talk about what strategies we can use to help ourselves when the text doesn't make sense." The teacher might then use the teachable moment to begin a very brief explanation of "fix-up strategies" that we might use when the text doesn't make sense, such as rereading, reading ahead to clarify meaning, or discussing the difficult part with another person.

Explicit Instruction

Another critical feature of context focuses on the nature of the instruction itself. Explicit instruction is represented in Figure 10.1 as a key element within the context. It is an aspect that is often heralded as being vital to best practice, but in reality does not occur. Explicit instruction involves teacher modeling, explanation, and think-alouds that help children understand what strategic processes are, how to use them, under what conditions they might be used, and why they might be used. In the research literature, this is known as declarative, procedural, and conditional knowledge (Paris et al., 1983). In Figure 10.1 seven research-based comprehension strategies are represented within explicit instruction as a list, but they should be thought of as a flexible and interconnected set of strategies. Teachers should teach this set of strategies using explanation, modeling, thinking aloud, and long-term guided practice in a variety of settings.

Brown (2008) found that the teachers trained to use transactional strategies instruction (TSI) provided much richer explanations of the processes involved in strategic thinking. The TSI teachers described the reasons for using particular strategies at particular times and the processes underlying their use. They also provided a great deal of modeling and verbalized about the thought processes they used while reading, whereas non-TSI teachers did not. In addition, TSI teachers provided commentary on and elaborated students' thought processes to take advantage of teachable moments.

In the example above, the teacher might provide an explanation of various fix-up strategies and then think aloud about how to use one of them in the context:

> "Okay, so Owen said that he didn't understand what the author, Stephen Mooser, meant in the sentence, 'Happy HICCUP Halloween.' That is confusing and it doesn't seem to make sense. When we are reading and the text doesn't make sense we can use our fix-up strategies. So, I might think, 'Wait a second that doesn't make sense. I'd better stop and use a fix-up strategy.' One fix-up strategy we can use is to read ahead slowly and see if the meaning clears up. That just

means reading ahead a little farther and being very alert and cautious while I read. So, as I read ahead slowly I'm going to keep trying to think of that HICCUP in the middle of the sentence that didn't make sense and see if the next couple of sentences help clarify the meaning. I'm going to try that."

The teacher would then continue by reading aloud from the text (in this example, the text was Stephen Mooser's *The Ghost with the Halloween Hiccups*):

[Teacher reading aloud] "Oh my," said Laura. "You have the hiccups." "All HICCUP day," said Mr. Penny." [Teacher thinking aloud] "Okay, now I've read ahead a little further to see if the meaning cleared up. I noticed that Laura told Mr. Penny that he had the hiccups. So I guess that means Mr. Penny has the hiccups. Then there is another odd sentence with HICCUP in the middle of it. I noticed that there are quotation marks around the sentence 'All HICCUP day' and that usually means someone's talking. So, if he has the hiccups and he's talking . . . well, that reminds me of when I have hiccups. Sometimes if I have hiccups and I try to talk, I hiccup in the middle of the sentence I'm trying to say. Maybe that's it! Could it be that the author, Stephen Mooser, is trying to show us how Mr. Penny was actually talking by inserting an actual HICCUP right in the middle of his sentence? Let me go back and reread that sentence and make a pretend HICCUP in the place where the word hiccup is capitalized, 'All [makes a hiccup sound] day.' Does that make sense now?"

In this think-aloud the teacher fluidly integrated several aspects of strategy instruction. She provided a *think-aloud* of what she might think while she was reading if that same sentence didn't make sense to her. Then she included an *explanation* of what one fix-up strategy, reading ahead, is and how to do it. She then *modeled* the fix-up strategy by reading ahead from the spot where Owen had difficulty. After she read aloud she actually used several comprehension strategies: she *summarized* what she read, *made a connection to her background knowledge* about what happens to her when she has the hiccups, and then she used the *rereading fix-up strategy* to check (*monitor*) her comprehension.

Ultimately she is showing the students how to weave together a variety of strategies to make sense of the text—the "read ahead slowly" fix-up strategy gets linked to two of the seven comprehension strategies, "summarization" and "using background knowledge to make connections to bring meaning to the sentence," before she goes back to use the "rereading fix-up strategy" to check her understanding, which is yet another one of the seven comprehension strategies (monitoring comprehension). In this small example we can see how complicated the reading process actually is. When we read successfully we never use just one strategy. Instead, we integrate the entire set of strategies together in different combinations as in the example above.

After the think-aloud, the teacher might turn the conversation back to the students to ask them if they interpreted the sentence in a different way or used different strategies: "Did anyone understand that sentence in a different way?" "Did anyone use other strategies to help them make sense of that sentence?" By doing this the teacher opens the door to a safe environment where different combinations of strategies can be used and different interpretations of the text are valued. What we see in this example is a teacher who is providing explicit instruction, but she is grounding it in authentic reading experiences and continually turns the context back over to the students.

Another aspect of explicit instruction includes providing lots of guided practice for readers to use and try out ways of recognizing and using strategic behaviors in varied contexts. This guided practice should take place over time and should gradually shift the responsibility for strategic thinking, actions, and behaviors to students so that over time students are able to engage in these processes independently and of their own volition. This is where Dewitz and colleagues (2009) found that core reading programs lagged in their attempts at reproducing research-based best practices in comprehension strategy instruction. These programs simply did not provide sufficient opportunities for students to use what they had learned in multiple contexts and under varying conditions. As well, too much teacher guidance did not enable students to assume responsibility for their own learning.

Explicit instruction should also occur in authentic reading contexts. That is, readers need to practice being strategic using authentic texts of all sorts: books, informational texts, comic books, magazines, online texts, newspapers, etc. Transfer will not occur unless readers have the opportunity to think about how they might be strategic in different contexts (e.g., in school, out of school, in church) and under different circumstances (e.g., when they are fatigued, unmotivated, stressed).

Unlike direct instruction, explicit instruction does not break the reading process down into separate parts or subskills. Each time reading occurs it should reflect the entire reading process with authentic texts. That is, strategic reading requires students to read whole texts—not chunks of texts, or a couple of sentences, or sentences with blanks in them, or words (or parts of words) in isolation. In order for readers to truly understand what it means to be strategic, they must encounter the reading process in its complex entirety. It is similar to learning to drive a car. Imagine if we taught teenagers how to drive by having steering practice using fake steering wheels in a classroom. After steering practice, imagine the teacher providing braking practice by having students pumping imaginary brakes followed by acceleration practice using imaginary accelerator pedals. Inauthentic sites of practice do not provide learners with the realities they will encounter when they have to coordinate all of those separate pieces into a coherent whole while also making decisions about where and when to brake and under what conditions you might need to brake more quickly. So it is with reading and learning to be strategic. We must provide authentic learning contexts in which readers learn to negotiate and manage the entire process all at once. This means being an active participant in the process and learning to make decisions.

Pearson and Dole (1987) have also noted that during explicit instruction there are no "correct" answers. There are multiple sets of strategies, combinations of strategies, and strategic behaviors that can be used to accomplish a given reading task. If we use the driving scenario again, it is similar to using multiple or different routes to arrive at the same place for a meeting. Everyone can arrive at the same place by using different paths. So it is with strategic processes in reading. Different readers can use different strategies, combinations of strategies, and strategic behaviors to accomplish the same goal: comprehension of text.

The final feature of explicit instruction is that the feedback that teachers offer should be suggestive rather than corrective. If there are no "correct" answers, then the feedback we offer students should provide alternate suggestions or different ways of approaching the task. As well, we can provide opportunities for students to share the different strategies they use with each other so they can see how other readers approach and accomplish tasks.

Agency/Metacognition

"Agency" refers to the notion that people are active participants in their life events, not simply a product of those events (Bandura, 2008). In reading, this means that the reader plays an active role in, and influences, the manner in which the reading event occurs. That is, the reader is an agent who has an influence on how the reading event will proceed and what strategic behaviors and actions will be used. In many classrooms that teach "strategies," however, it is often the teacher who takes on a great deal of authority in terms of making decisions about what strategies will be taught, to whom, with what texts, and when. At times teachers determine what graphic organizers will be used, with what texts, and when they will be filled out. In a classroom that fosters agency, the teacher enables and empowers students to make such decisions themselves. At the heart of agentic behavior is metacognition. That is, students are able to influence and make decisions about the reading process when they are able to evaluate their progress to determine whether their reading is successful or unsuccessful and then to make adjustments as needed so that they can reach their goal.

Johnston (2004) suggested ways in which teachers' language can enable agentic behaviors. He noted that teachers foster agency by providing opportunities for students to stop and talk about their thinking. For example, during a read-aloud teachers might stop at points that are particularly thought-provoking or that are prime opportunities for predicting and say, "What are you thinking? Share your thoughts with a partner." These stopping points provide an opportunity for children to verbalize their thought processes. This is not simply "sharing." The goal is for students to actually verbalize the thought processes that are going through their minds during the reading process. In this way, metacognitive awareness is built.

Instructional opportunities that foster verbalization also occur when students are able to figure out something while reading. For example, if a young reader recognizes a word such as "laundry" that he or she ordinarily would not recognize, the teacher might say, "You figured that out. How did you do that?" As Johnston (2004) has noted, the teacher's question does not have a "correct" answer. Instead, it is an invitation to tell a narrative about how the student solved a problem. The story is a process-oriented story in which the student shares the strategy or combination of strategies that he or she used to solve the problem "Well, I looked at the picture and saw dirty laundry on the floor. Then I noticed a slot in the wall with a word that began with L on it. I figured the word must be laundry." By verbalizing these thought processes, students see a variety of ways they can solve similar problems.

Thus, teachers can encourage metacognitive behaviors by asking open-ended questions that encourage students to share their own thought processes. Other examples include, "Why doesn't that make sense to you?", "What did you do to figure that out?", and "How did you know that?" Brown's (2008) study showed that TSI teachers tended to ask students to explain their thinking whereas non-TSI teachers did not. Such questions led the students in the TSI classrooms to clarify and justify their thinking and they were able to draw upon their personal experiences and evidence from the text to do so.

The language that students use to respond to such questions brings awareness to what are typically "covert" or hidden thought processes (Prawat, 1989). The thoughts become an object for others to reflect upon and evaluate. Vygotsky (1978) has noted that such "egocentric" speech is the basis for inner speech. When this type of language is in its external and public form, it becomes available for everyone to ponder. During that thinking, some individuals may think about how that process might be helpful to them, such as "Oh, I never thought about doing it that way. I'll have to try that." Such reflection then opens the doors for the individual to try it on his or her own. When a person attempts such behaviors on his or her own it shows that he or she is beginning to internalize the process. These attempts, however, also illustrate the need (as mentioned above) for creating a safe space because these initial attempts are just that—initial— and we want students to be willing to take risks to try new ways of thinking and processing text. As students become more metacognitive, they are able to recognize when text doesn't make sense, which means they recognize the need for strategic action. Such recognition leads to action, which leads to agency. Students determine *whether* they need to be strategic, *when* they need to be strategic, *where* they need to be strategic, and *how* to be strategic. Such agentic behavior is necessary to help students transform from passive to active participants in the reading process.

Scaffolding That Leads to Transfer

Decades of research have shown that strategy instruction improves reading comprehension; however, the troublesome aspect is helping readers transfer such instruction to different contexts. Providing sufficient guided practice under varying conditions is critical to transfer. One way to provide such guided practice is by incorporating strategies instruction into every aspect of the classroom, in every content area. This includes creating a safe context and providing opportunities for student verbalization that lead to agency in *every* learning opportunity—during read-alouds, during shared reading, during guided reading, and after independent reading. This form of scaffolding is flexible and might occur during whole-class, small-group, or individualized instruction. TSI is a model of instruction that incorporates these principles into every reading event because the teacher–student and student–student conversations that characterize TSI can occur during the reading of any text, including online reading. The type of teacher scaffolding that occurs during TSI is not preplanned. It requires a trained teacher who is able to identify opportune, teachable moments as students are reading text in authentic contexts. Brown (2008) has noted that teachers gradually release responsibility to students by engaging in think-alouds in which they explain and model their own thought processes to students. TSI teachers grab teachable moments during the course of authentic reading experiences to demonstrate the type of strategic thinking and behaviors they engage in naturally.

At other times, particularly with struggling readers, scaffolding that leads to transfer needs to be planned more deliberately. During this type of scaffolding, the teacher might select a strategy, a combination of strategies, or a strategic behavior on which to focus instruction. These preplanned lessons might be conducted during guided reading groups so that students can practice using the focal strategies with texts at their independent or instructional reading level. This type of instruction should not occur with texts that are at a frustrational level for students.

Almasi and Fullerton's (2012) critical elements of strategy instruction model describes a means of planning instructional lessons so that teacher-scaffolded support is gradually reduced. In this model, two dimensions of scaffolded support are considered: (1) the amount of cognitive effort a reader must expend, and (2) the nature of the instructional tasks and texts used during the lesson. The amount of cognitive effort a reader must expend is greater when the reader must complete the reading tasks independently because all of the burden for reading and enacting strategic behaviors belongs to the reader; however, the amount of cognitive effort diminishes when the reader can complete the reading task with a partner, a small group, or with the whole class. By using various grouping patterns, the teacher can provide guided practice and scaffolding in different ways.

The amount of scaffolded support can also be varied by teaching students how to engage in strategic behaviors using different types of tasks and texts in lessons. If we define "text" broadly so that it includes any sign or symbol that communicates a message, then texts would include movies, cartoons, pictures, wordless picture books, texts that are read aloud, texts read during shared reading, and texts read independently. This broad conceptualization of "text" means that initial strategy lessons can introduce readers to difficult strategies such as comprehension monitoring without requiring them to actually decode the text. In this manner, struggling readers can learn very high-level cognitive strategies at a young age. By introducing readers to strategic processing in this manner it helps them learn the language of being a strategic reader.

Focal lessons aimed at teaching students new strategies or strategic behaviors (e.g., making predictions, monitoring comprehension, summarizing, visualizing, making connections, making inferences) that they did not know about previously might begin with very concrete lessons using video excerpts from movies or television programs. In this type of lesson, teachers can provide explicit instruction for students using "texts" where the reader can focus solely on the strategic processing rather than having to bear the additional burden of decoding. For example, Mrs. Macklin noticed that her second graders often made "wild" predictions that were based more on their background knowledge and didn't use the text to help form the prediction. She decided to model how to predict by using a video clip from a TV show in which she could stop the video at a highly predictable, or "cliff hanger" point and think aloud about the thoughts going through her mind as she formed a prediction, "Well, I'm really excited to see the next part because I noticed _____ and that makes me think that _____ is going to happen next." At this point she might open the discussion up for the students to share their thoughts: "Does anyone else have a prediction about what might happen next in the show?" As students share their ideas, Mrs. Macklin will try to encourage them to verbally share the thought processes they are using as they form their predictions and link those ideas to some evidence in the show that they have already seen, "Oh, you think _____ is going to happen? What did you notice in the show so far that makes you think that?" Mrs. Macklin would then continue using the think-aloud with whole-class input during this lesson in which the "text" is a TV show.

After teaching this type of lesson, follow-up guided practice lessons can be planned that vary either the type of text or task (e.g., teaching students how to make predictions with a wordless picture book or during a read-aloud while keeping it as a whole-class or small-group activity so cognitive effort needed will still be low) and/or the amount of cognitive effort needed (e.g., making predictions from a video with a partner or independently). The goal in this form of scaffolding is to alter the types of texts, tasks, and grouping arrangements during follow-up guided practice sessions so that over time we are releasing the responsibility for strategic processing to students. Eventually students will be using the strategy with text written at their instructional level independently. By planfully mapping out these two dimensions of scaffolding during instruction, responsibility is gradually released to students, which leads to transfer.

In summary, the four key ingredients to support an environment that cultivates strategic and reflective learning are (1) context, (2) explicit instruction, (3) agency/metacognition, and (4) scaffolding. These four components are essential within a setting that values the learning process because they provide a space where students' prior experiences, individual perceptions, and own pace of learning are valued.

It is within such an environment that we begin to recognize it is not just about the strategy you teach: environment matters. Research has shown that teaching strategies in isolation is not effective—we must provide a space for students that cultivates their transformation into independent, agentic learners who recognize that context matters as they decide when and how to use strategies that best meet their needs.

Reflections and Future Directions

This chapter aimed to change the discourse surrounding comprehension strategy instruction from ideas about how to teach the seven research-based strategies to ideas about how to teach students to be strategic. This focus will help teachers achieve the most elusive aspect of comprehension instruction: transfer. Transfer happens when students become agentic. They see the value of thinking strategically and use it to make decisions about how to solve problems as they read.

The benefit of this approach to comprehension instruction is that we know it works. The research reviewed in this chapter is quite conclusive that teaching readers to be strategic results in long-term gains in comprehension. There are several limitations to consider, however. One is that learning to teach in this manner is difficult and can take years to learn how to do well (Brown & Coy-Ogan, 1993; Duffy 1993a, 1993b; El-Dinary & Schuder, 1993). Research that is more recent has begun to tackle that issue using technology-based methods of teacher training (Graves, Sales, Lawrenz, Robelia, & Richardson, 2010). Another issue is that most assessments of comprehension focus on the product of comprehension, which often relies on memory and recall of text and the ability to make inferences. The reliance on literal and inferential questions as the primary ways of assessing comprehension means that instruction tends to approximate the text. Assessments that focus more on the processes used to make sense of text would be better aligned with an emphasis on teaching students to be strategic. Currently, we rely on self-reports of strategy use (which are not always reliable) or think-aloud protocols (which are time-consuming to administer and labor-intensive to code) as the primary ways of assessing strategic processing. Developing new ways to assess strategic processing (and valuing them) would begin to change the instructional emphasis in our schools and classrooms.

Concluding Remarks

For decades, we have emphasized the importance of teaching students comprehension strategies. However, shifting the emphasis from "the strategy" to "the student" is critical. This shift requires teachers to move from focusing on the strategies that are taught to *focusing on the context in which they are taught*. The focus on context ensures that we create learning opportunities that make it safe for readers to try on new ways of thinking and acting. A safe space accompanied by explicit instruction means that the context is ripe for readers to explore their own identity as readers and construct meaning. When we also includes lots of opportunities for students to verbalize and share the thought processes they use while reading, this enables them to become more metacognitively aware while reading. Such metacognitive awareness enables readers to evaluate their reading progress and make decisions about what strategic processes may be needed to successfully attain their goals. When readers are active participants who make their own decisions about the reading process, they possess agency, which is the key to transformation.

This chapter suggests that by recognizing the underlying belief systems that are perpetuated by various programs, change can begin to occur in educational environments. If learners are valued within their own comprehension instruction, positive change will be reflected in the way in which these learners negotiate/identify themselves as learners. By cultivating an environment that values the learner as inextricably linked to his or her own learning process, learners' agency will improve and positively impact their able to transform into lifelong learners who are strategic and reflective.

ENGAGEMENT ACTIVITIES

1. Develop a list of ideas for creating a safe environment for strategy use.

2. Discuss the importance of teaching students to be strategic readers who determine when and where strategic action should take place as they read.

3. The CCSS related to literal recall, making logical inferences, citing textual evidence to support conclusions, and analyzing the structure of texts are long-term goals. Discuss how comprehension strategy instruction provides the means of attaining those goals.

RESOURCES FOR FURTHER LEARNING

Almasi, J. F., & Fullerton, S. K. (2012). *Teaching strategic processes in reading* (2nd ed.). New York: Guilford Press.

Dewitz, P., Leahy, S., Jones, J., & Sullivan, P. M. (2010). *The essential guide to selecting and using core reading programs.* Newark, DE: International Reading Association.

Johnston, P. H. (2004). *Choice words: How our language affects children's learning.* Portland, ME: Stenhouse.

REFERENCES

Afflerbach, P., Pearson, P. D., & Paris, S. G. (2008). Clarifying differences between reading skills and reading strategies. *The Reading Teacher, 61*(5), 364–373.

Almasi, J. F., & Fullerton, S. K. (2012). *Teaching strategic processes in reading* (2nd ed). New York: Guilford Press.

Almasi, J. F., Palmer, B. M., Madden, A., & Hart, S. (2011). Interventions to enhance narrative comprehension. In R. Allington & A. McGill-Franzen (Eds.), *Handbook of reading disability research* (pp. 329–344). New York: Routledge.

Anderson, V. (1992). A teacher development project in transactional strategy instruction for teachers of severely reading-disabled adolescents. *Teaching and Teacher Education, 8*(4), 391–403.

Aukerman, M. (2013). Rereading comprehension pedagogies: Toward a dialogic teaching ethic that honors student sensemaking. *Dialogic Pedagogy: An International Online Journal, 1*, A1–A30.

Bandura, A. (2008). Reconstrual of "free will" from the agentic perspective of social cognitive theory. In J. Baer, J. C. Kaufman, & R. F. Baumeister (Eds.), *Are we free?: Psychology and free will* (pp. 86–127). New York: Oxford University Press.

Brown, R. (2008). The road not yet taken: A transactional strategies approach to reading comprehension instruction. *The Reading Teacher, 61*(7), 538–547.

Brown, R., & Coy-Ogan, L. (1993). The evolution of transactional strategies instruction in one teacher's classroom. *Elementary School Journal, 94*(2), 221–233.

Brown, R., Pressley, M., Van Meter, P., & Schuder, T. (1996). A quasi-experimental validation of transactional strategies instruction with low-achieving second-grade readers. *Journal of Educational Psychology, 88*(1), 18–37.

Cain, K., & Oakhill, J. V. (1999). Inference making ability and its relation to comprehension failure in young children. *Reading and Writing Quarterly: An International Journal, 11*, 489–503.

Cain, K., Oakhill, J. V., Barnes, M. A., & Bryant, P. E. (2001). Comprehension skill, inference-making ability, and their relation to knowledge. *Memory and Cognition, 29*(6), 850–859.

Coiro, J., & Dobler, E. (2007). Exploring the online comprehension strategies used by sixth-grade skilled readers to search for and locate information on the Internet. *Reading Research Quarterly, 42*, 214–257.

Dewitz, P., Jones, J., & Leahy, S. (2009). Comprehension strategy instruction in core reading programs. *Reading Research Quarterly, 44*(2), 102–126.

Dewitz, P., Leahy, S., Jones, J., & Sullivan, P. M. (2010). *The essential guide to selecting and using core reading programs.* Newark, DE: International Reading Association.

Duffy, G. G. (1993a). Rethinking strategy instruction: Four teachers' development and their low achievers' understandings. *Elementary School Journal, 93*(3), 231–247.

Duffy, G. G. (1993b). Teachers' progress toward becoming expert strategy teachers. *Elementary School Journal, 94*(2), 109–120.

Duke, N. K., & Pearson, P. D. (2008–2009). Effective practices for developing reading comprehension. *Journal of Education, 189*(1–2), 107–122.

Edmonds, M. S., Vaughn, S., Wexler, J., Reutebuch, C., Cable, A., Tackett, K. K., et al. (2009). A synthesis of reading interventions and effects on reading comprehension outcomes for older struggling readers. *Review of Educational Research, 79*(1), 262–300.

El-Dinary, P. B., & Schuder, T. (1993). Seven teachers' acceptance of transactional strategies instruction during their first year using it. *Elementary School Journal, 94*(2), 207–219.

Fleisher, L. S., Jenkins, J. R., & Pany, D. (1979). Effects on poor readers' comprehension of training in rapid decoding. *Reading Research Quarterly, 15*(1), 30–48.

Gamse, B. C., Jacob, R. T., Horst, M., Boulay, B., & Unlu, F. (2008). *Reading First Impact Study Final Report Executive Summary* (NCEE 2009–4039). Washington, DC: National Center for Education Evaluation and Regional Assistance, Institute of Education Sciences, U.S. Department of Education.

Gersten, R., Fuchs, L. S., Williams, J. P., & Baker, S. (2001). Teaching reading comprehension strategies to students with learning disabilities: A review of research. *Review of Educational Research, 71*(2), 279–320.

Graves, M., Sales, G. C., Lawrenz, F., Robelia, B., & Richardson, J. (2010). Effects of technology-based teacher training and teacher-led classroom implementation on learning reading comprehension strategies. *Contemporary Educational Technology, 1*(2), 160–174.

Hirsch, E. D. (2006). Building knowledge: The case for bringing content into the language arts block and for a knowledge-rich curriculum core for all children. *American Educator, 30*(1), 8–17.

Hoffman, J. V. (2009). In search of the "simple view" of reading comprehension. In S. E. Israel, & G. G. Duffy (Eds.), *Handbook of research on reading comprehension* (pp. 54–66). New York: Routledge.

Holland, D., Lachicotte, W., Skinner, D., & Cain, C. (1998). *Identity and agency in cultural worlds.* Cambridge, MA: Harvard University Press.

Hoover, W. A., & Gough, P. (1990). The simple view of reading. *Reading and Writing: An Interdisciplinary Journal, 2,* 127–160.

Johnston, P. H. (2004). *Choice words: How our language effects children's learning.* Portland, ME: Stenhouse.

Kamil, M. L., Borman, G. D., Dole, J., Kral, C. C., Salinger, T., & Torgesen, J. (2008). *Improving adolescent literacy: Effective classroom and intervention practices: A practice guide* (NCEE No. 2008-4027). Washington, DC: National Center for Education Evaluation and Regional Assistance, Institute of Education Sciences, U.S. Department of Education. Retrieved from *http://ies.ed.gov/ncee/wwc.*

LaBerge, D., & Samuels, S. J. (1974). Toward a theory of automatic processing in reading. *Cognitive Psychology, 6*(2), 293–323.

Leach, J. M., Scarborough, H. S., & Rescorla, L. (2003). Late-emerging reading disabilities. *Journal of Educational Psychology, 95*(2), 211–224.

Leu, D. J. Jr., Coiro, J., Castek, J., Hartman, D. K., Henry, L. A., & Reinking, D. (2008). Research on instruction and assessment in the new literacies of online reading comprehension. In C. C. Block & S. R. Parris (Eds.), *Comprehension instruction: Research-based best practices* (2nd ed., pp. 321–346). New York: Guilford Press.

McKeown, M. G., Beck, I. L., & Blake, G. K. (2009). Rethinking reading comprehension instruction: A comparison of instruction for strategies and content approaches. *Reading Research Quarterly, 44*(3), 218–253.

Nation, K. (2005). Children's reading comprehension difficulties. In M. J. Snowling & C. Hulme (Eds.), *The science of reading: A handbook* (pp. 248–266). Malden, MA: Wiley Blackwell.

National Governors Association & Council of Chief State School Officers. (2010). Common Core State Standards. Retrieved from *www.corestandards.org.*

National Reading Panel. (2000). *Teaching children to read: An evidence-based assessment of the scientific research literature on reading and its implications for reading instruction* (Report of the Subgroups). Washington, DC: U.S. Department of Health and Human Services, Public Health Service, National Institutes of Health, and the National Institute of Child Health and Human Development.

Neuman, S. B. (2006). How we neglect knowledge—and why. *American Educator, 30*(1), 24–27.

No Child Left Behind Act of 2001, Pub. Law 107-110, 115 Stat. 1425.

Palincsar, A. S., & Brown, A. L. (1984). Reciprocal teaching of comprehension-fostering and comprehension-monitoring activities. *Cognition and Instruction, 1,* 117–175.

Palincsar, A. S., & Schultz, K. M. (2011). Reconnecting strategy instruction with its theoretical roots. *Theory into Practice, 50,* 85–92.

Paris, S. G., Cross, D., & Lipson, M. Y. (1984). Informed strategies for learning: A program to improve children's reading awareness and comprehension. *Journal of Educational Psychology, 76,* 1293–1252.

Paris, S. G., Lipson, M. Y., & Wixson, K. K. (1983). Becoming a strategic reader. *Contemporary Educational Psychology, 8,* 293–316.

Paris, S. G., Wasik, B. A., & Turner, J. C. (1991). The development of strategic readers. In R. Barr, M. L. Kamil, P. Mosenthal, & P. D. Pearson (Eds.), *Handbook of reading research* (Vol. 2, pp. 609–640). New York: Longman.

Pearson, P. D., & Dole, J. A. (1987). Explicit comprehension instruction: A review of research and a new conceptualization of instruction. *Elementary School Journal, 88*(2), 151–165.

Pilonieta, P. (2010). Instruction of research-based comprehension strategies in basal reading programs. *Reading Psychology, 31,* 150–175.

Prawat, R. S. (1989). Promoting access to knowledge, strategy, and disposition in students: A research synthesis. *Review of Educational Research, 59*(1), 1–41.

Pressley, M. (2000). What should comprehension instruction be the instruction of? In M. L. Kamil, P. B. Mosenthal, P. D. Pearson, & R. Barr (Eds.), *Handbook of reading research* (Vol. 3, pp. 545–561). Mahwah, NJ: Erlbaum.

Pressley, M., Borkowski, J. G., & Schneider, W. (1989). Good information processing: What it is and how education can promote it. *International Journal of Educational Research, 13,* 857–867.

Pressley, M., El-Dinary, P. B., Gaskins, I., Schuder, T., Bergman, J. L., Almasi, J., et al. (1992). Beyond direct explanation: Transactional instruction of reading comprehension strategies. *Elementary School Journal, 92*(5), 513–555.

Recht, D. R., & Leslie, L. (1988). Effect of prior knowledge on good and poor readers' memory of text. *Journal of Educational Psychology, 80*(1), 16–20.

Reutzel, D. R., Smith, J. A., & Fawson, P. C. (2005). An evaluation of two approaches for teaching reading comprehenaion strategies in the primary years using science information texts. *Early Childhood Research Quarterly, 20,* 276–305.

Riddle Buly, M., & Valencia, S. W. (2002). Below the bar: Profiles of students who fail state reading assessments. *Educational Evaluation and Policy Analysis, 24*(3), 219–239.

Rogoff, B. (1990). *Apprenticeship in thinking: Cognitive development in social context.* New York: Oxford University Press.

Samuels, S. J. (2004). Toward a theory of automatic information processing in reading, revisited. In R. B. Ruddell & N. J. Unrau (Eds.), *Theoretical models and processes of reading* (5th ed., pp. 1127–1148). Newark, DE: International Reading Association.

Shanahan, T., Callison, K., Carriere, C., Duke, N., Pearson, P. D., Schatschneider, C., et al. (2010). *Improving reading comprehension in kindergarten through 3rd grade: A practice guide* (NCEE 2010-4038). Washington, DC: National Center for Educational Evaluation and Regional Assistance, Institute of Education Sciences, U. S. Department of Education. Retrieved from *whatworks.ed.gov/publications/practiceguides.*

Valencia, S. W. (2011). Reader profiles and reading disabilities. In A. McGill-Franzen & R. L. Allington (Eds.), *Handbook of reading disability research* (pp. 25–35). New York: Routledge.

Van Keer, H. (2004). Fostering reading comprehension in fifth grade by explicit instruction in reading strategies and peer tutoring. *British Journal of Educational Psychology, 74,* 37–70.

Vygotsky, L. S. (1978). *Mind in society.* Cambridge, MA: Harvard University Press.

Wilkinson, I. A. G., & Son, H. (2011). A dialogic turn in research on learning and teaching to comprehend. In M. L. Kamil, P. D. Pearson, P. Afflerbach, & E. Moje (Eds.), *Handbook of reading research* (Vol. 4, pp. 358–387). New York: Routledge.

CHAPTER 11

Best Practices in Informational Text Comprehension Instruction

Nell K. Duke
Nicole M. Martin

This chapter will:

- Explain the need to teach informational text comprehension across genres, tasks, and grade levels.
- Identify research-supported strategies for scaffolding comprehension and developing strategic comprehenders of informational text.
- Describe a unit that enacts research-supported practices and supports development of many key Common Core State Standards related to informational text comprehension.

Evidence-Based Best Practices: A Research Synthesis

We believe that a long-term and situated view of informational text comprehension instruction is important. Rather than expecting students to learn solely from generic approaches to instruction or from one lesson or unit of study, we, basing our conclusions on decades of research, suggest that students are more likely to learn how to comprehend complex informational text well when they experience carefully designed informational text comprehension instruction across genres, tasks, and grade levels; when their teachers seek to develop strategic readers; and when they have many scaffolded opportunities to comprehend informational text.

Teaching Informational Text Comprehension across Genres, Tasks, and Grade Levels

We begin our discussion of evidence-based best practices by highlighting three characteristics of comprehension with important implications for instruction. These characteristics suggest that we need to teach informational text comprehension across genres, tasks, and grade levels.

First, comprehension is genre-specific to a significant degree (Duke & Roberts, 2010). That is, the processes involved in comprehending one genre are not isomorphic with those involved in comprehending another; the ability to comprehend one genre well does not guarantee proficiency at comprehending another genre. The purpose and characteristics of the genre influence the processes involved in successfully comprehending it. For example, informative/explanatory genres often present large amounts of information about topics that are unknown or less familiar to readers; may be designed to develop understanding of abstract and complex ideas and relationships; and may use specialized vocabulary, text structures, and text features (e.g., Dickson, Simmons, & Kame'enui, 1998; Duke & Tower, 2004; Pappas, 2008). Perhaps as a result, readers read informative/explanatory text differently than, for example how they read, narrative text (e.g., Kucan & Beck, 1996; Olson, Mack, & Duffy, 1981). They elaborate on the author's ideas, make more of particular kinds of connections, notice interesting details, and attend to the informational text structures used by authors—a distinct contrast to the processes that readers use to comprehend narrative text (such as predicting what will happen next, making more inferences of particular kinds, and attending closely to specific story elements). Even within the broad category of "informational text," readers may read different genres differently. For example, Martin (2011) found that second- through fifth-grade students used different processes when reading procedural text (i.e., text with the primary purpose of telling someone how to do something) than when reading biographies or persuasive texts. These findings imply that the type of text used during lessons can affect what students do and learn, and that teaching comprehension of any particular kind of text means using that specific kind of text during instruction.

Second, multiple factors—not only the text genre—can influence students' comprehension. Reader factors—including the reader's word identification skills, fluency, prior knowledge, interests, and vocabulary—can affect what is understood and learned from text (e.g., Alexander, Kulikowich, & Jetton, 1994; Riddle Buly & Valencia, 2002). These reader factors intersect with text, task, and contextual factors (e.g., RAND Reading Study Group, 2002; Common Core State Standards Initiative, 2010). For example, a student who possesses knowledge that the author of a text assumes the reader has will have a different comprehension experience than a student who does not possess that knowledge. The context of the comprehension, such as whether it occurs in a quiet space or one full of distractions, is also influential, and differentially for different readers. Finally, the reading task—including how much support is involved (see later in this section), how motivated the learner is to engage in that specific task, and the demands of the task itself—all influence comprehension. For example, with informational text sometimes we have the task of comprehending within and across a set of texts on a common topic, other times our task is to comprehend a single text. Sometimes our task involves reading for general edification, other times there is a specific need to apply what is learned from the text. If we want comprehenders to manage a broad range of tasks, our instruction must provide that broad range within and across school years.

Finally, comprehension develops over time (Duke & Carlisle, 2011). Based on available evidence, a federal panel determined that comprehension instruction should occur with intensity even in the primary grades of schooling (Shanahan et al., 2010). Researchers have found that children can develop knowledge of informational text language and structures, specifically, even when they have not yet learned to read words (e.g., Duke & Kays, 1998; Pappas, 1993). However, students' comprehension appears to increase throughout elementary and high school. For instance, Barbara Taylor (1980) found that sixth graders who read informational text tended to recall more than fourth graders but less than adults. Also, Judith Langer (1986) discovered that ninth graders more competently reproduced informational text they read than third graders, recalling on average 19% more of the text and including more informational text language and structures. Interventions designed to improve informational text comprehension have been effective from at least as early as first grade (e.g., Kelly, Moore, & Tuck, 1994; Kraemer, McCabe, & Sinatra, 2012) through adulthood (e.g., Caverly, Mandeville, & Nicholson, 1995; Kauffman, Zhao, & Yang, 2011). This suggests that informational text comprehension instruction should be a focus of instruction across multiple grades, perhaps at every grade.

These three characteristics of text comprehension—that comprehension is genre-specific to a significant degree; that multiple factors, including text, reader, and contextual factors can influence students' comprehension; and that comprehension develops over time—suggest that students are most likely to develop informational text comprehension when lessons focus specifically on comprehending particular types of informational text, entail, over time, a broad range of reading tasks, and occur frequently throughout schooling.

Developing Strategic Readers of Informational Text

The evidence base calls for teaching students to become strategic readers of informational text (e.g., Almasi & Hart, 2011; Block & Pressley, 2007). It is now widely understood that readers flexibly use a range of mental processes when reading text (Duke & Pearson, 2002; Pressley & Afflerbach, 1995). For example, readers may preview, activate background knowledge, and set reading purposes before reading. To comprehend informational text, this means that students need to learn "to be active in the way that good comprehenders are active" (Block & Pressley, 2007, p. 225). Students need to learn to be strategic readers (Almasi & Hart, 2011) of informational text—a goal that can be addressed through comprehension strategy instruction and text structure instruction, particularly when set in the context of authentic purposes and tasks.

Comprehension Strategy Instruction

Researchers have consistently observed that students who participate in comprehension strategy instruction learn comprehension processes and exhibit higher levels of informational text comprehension than their peers (Duke, Pearson, Strachan, & Billman, 2011; Gersten, Fuchs, Williams, & Baker, 2001; Shanahan et al., 2010). Moreover, a direct comparison of an approach that involves teaching a single strategy at a time versus multiple comprehension processes within a short time has hinted that teaching multiple processes may better support students' informational text comprehension development (e.g., Reutzel, Smith, & Fawson, 2005), perhaps because students can see how readers select, use, and coordinate more than one process at a time and practice doing the same. These studies suggest that students can become more strategic readers when they are explicitly taught the processes that other readers use to comprehend informational text, such as those listed in Table 11.1.

Text Structure Instruction

Researchers have repeatedly provided evidence that readers use informational text structures—organizational patterns such as *cause and effect, comparison and contrast, description, problem and solution,* and *sequence*—to comprehend informational text (e.g., Meyer, 1975; Meyer & Poon, 2001). Teaching students to identify and use these text structures has also been found to improve students' abilities to comprehend informational text (e.g., Taylor, 1982; Williams et al., 2005). For example, Joanna Williams and her colleagues (2005) investigated the effects of teaching the compare/contrast text structure to second graders. For nine lessons, the

TABLE 11.1. Ten Processes Used to Comprehend Informational Text

Name	Description	Sample guiding questions
Setting reading purposes	Readers think about what they want to accomplish with the reading and make decisions about how they will read.	*What is my goal? Do I need to read the whole text or just part of it? Do I need to study it or just search for information?*
Connecting to prior knowledge	Readers think about what they already know and how this knowledge might connect with the text.	*Have I read or learned about this before? What have other authors or people said about this? Am I familiar with the way this text is structured, and what does this mean for my reading?*
Predicting	Readers think about what will come next in the text. They check and revise their previous predictions and generate new ones.	*What will I learn next? Did the author talk about what I expected? Given what I just read, does my prediction still make sense?*
Inferring	Readers draw conclusions about information not stated or shown in the text.	*For this to make sense, what needs to be true? What has the author left out that might be important?*
Interpreting graphics and text features	Readers think about the meanings of the text's graphics and other features, as well as how these connect to the text's words and main ideas.	*What does this show? What is most important about it? What can I learn from it?*
Evaluating content	Readers think about their reactions to the text's words, graphics, ideas, and implications.	*What do I think about this? Do I agree or disagree, and why?*
Monitoring (and fixing up) comprehension	Readers think about their reading and comprehension processes. Whenever they encounter problems while they are reading, they take action until the problems are solved.	*Does this make sense? Am I understanding this well? What can I do to help myself understand this better?*
Questioning	Readers ask questions about the text, authors' ideas, and their own thinking.	*Why is this true? What does that mean?*
Summarizing	Readers think about what they have read or learned. They may focus on recalling the text, paragraphs, and/or sentences.	*What has the author said so far? What did I learn in this paragraph?*

teachers and students in the study reviewed the lesson objective, studied words used by authors to signal the compare/contrast text structure, and read aloud and discussed an informational text with a compare/contrast structure. Then they discussed key vocabulary concepts, analyzed the structure of the text, and recorded ideas on graphic organizers. They also responded to three short-answer comprehension questions, wrote summaries, and reviewed what they had learned. Later, with texts they had never seen before, the students who participated in these text structure lessons were more able to remember, find, and use the compare/contrast text structure and signal words than their peers (who had participated in business-as-usual instruction or lessons focused on learning science content). Williams and her colleagues (2005) concluded that "students who received the Text Structure program not only learned what they were taught but were also able to demonstrate transfer of what they had learned to content beyond that used in instruction" (p. 546). In this study, second graders learned to use the compare/contrast text structure to comprehend informational text. Studies such as these suggest that text structure instruction may help students to become more strategic readers of informational text.

Authentic Texts and Purposes

There is also evidence to suggest that students' comprehension development is accelerated when they are asked to read authentic texts for authentic purposes during instruction. By this, we mean asking students to read texts "that occur outside of [only] a learning-to-read-and-write context" and are read and written "for the purposes for which they are read or written outside of a learning-to-read-and-write context and purpose" (Purcell-Gates, Duke, & Martineau, 2007, p. 14).

We have observed the power of reading authentic texts for authentic purposes in our own work. Consider, for example, a study that one of us (Nell K. Duke) conducted with colleagues a few years ago (Purcell-Gates et al., 2007). In the study, the second- and third-grade teachers were encouraged to incorporate authentic reading and writing activities—such as creating brochures for a local nature center or writing procedural texts to teach neighboring classes how to conduct physics experiments—into science lessons. While students were working on these tasks, some of these teachers also explicitly taught the features of informational and procedural texts. When students' growth was measured throughout the 2 years of the study, it became clear that "students in classrooms with more authentic reading and writing of science informational and procedural texts grow at a faster rate than those with less authenticity" (p. 30). Students who had more opportunities to read (and write) authentic texts for authentic purposes grew more than their peers in second and third grade. Neither the teacher's explicit text feature instruction (except, in the case of one measure, in combination with authentic texts and purposes), nor the amount of time that students spent reading and writing text, nor students' socioeconomic backgrounds were associated with students' accelerated growth. Instead, teachers' uses of authentic reading and writing activities during instruction was linked to students' informational comprehension development.

Other researchers have also provided evidence of the value of situating comprehension strategy and text structure instruction in students' reading of authentic texts for authentic purposes. For example, John Guthrie and his colleagues have studied Concept-Oriented Reading Instruction (CORI; e.g., Guthrie, Anderson, Alao, & Rinehart, 1999; Guthrie et al., 2004, 2009). In CORI, students learn and "perform strategies within a meaningful context" (p. 407). Over the course of 12 weeks, teachers teach multiple comprehension processes (activating background knowledge, creating graphic organizers, identifying text structures, questioning, searching for information, and summarizing), while students conduct scientific inquiries, read informational text, and participate in hands-on activities in order to develop expertise in scientific content (e.g., "Survival of Life on Land and Water"; Guthrie et al., 2004, p. 407) to share with others. Guthrie and his colleagues (2004) found that CORI students outperformed their peers who received "strategy instruction" [SI] and "traditional instruction" [TI] on measures of comprehension and motivation. The researchers concluded that "CORI students were more motivated than SI and TI students and were more strategic readers than SI students" (p. 415). In this study, teaching comprehension processes while students read authentic texts for authentic purposes helped them to become more strategic readers. (See Guthrie, McRae, & Klauda, 2007, for a meta-analysis of CORI research.)

Additionally, Nancy Romance and Michael Vitale have tested an interdisciplinary instructional model, Science IDEAS, in elementary classrooms. In IDEAS, teachers teach comprehension processes such as activating prior knowledge and summarizing while students work to solve problems and develop scientific expertise. Students complete hands-on science activities; read informational text; take notes, create concept maps, and write summaries in student journals; collaborate on projects and real-world application activities; and review their learning. (For more information, see *www.scienceideas.org*.) In a recent summary of over a decade of research, the researchers reported significant increases in first through fifth graders' scientific knowledge and reading comprehension from Science IDEAS instruction. Romance and Vitale (2012) concluded that "increasing time for integrated science instruction in grades K–5 will not only result in stronger preparation of students for secondary science; but also concurrently improve student proficiency in reading comprehension (in general) and content-area reading comprehension (more specifically) across grades 3–8" (p. 513). In Science IDEAS, teaching comprehension processes while asking students to read for authentic purposes and tasks helped students to learn and use comprehension processes to read informational text.

In short, researchers have found that teaching students to become strategic readers—to select and use specific mental processes—will help them to comprehend informational text. Studies have suggested that text structure instruction, as well as comprehension strategy instruction, may encourage students to become more effective readers of informational text, especially when teachers also ask students to read authentic texts for authentic purposes.

Offering Students Scaffolded Opportunities to Read Informational Text

Finally, the evidence base calls for offering students scaffolded opportunities to read informational text. We are using the term "scaffolded opportunities" to refer to lessons in which language and materials are used to mediate students' thinking as they comprehend text. Researchers have found that teacher read-alouds, discussions, prereading activities, and visual aids can improve students' informational text comprehension.

Read-Alouds

Teacher read-alouds may support students' informational text comprehension development. We have long known that read-alouds can help students to become acquainted with the language and other features of text, to understand how adults and their peers think about text, and to develop content-area knowledge (e.g., Anderson, Hiebert, Scott, & Wilkinson, 1985; Wan, 2000). Researchers have also shown that read-alouds can increase students' informational text knowledge and comprehension. For example, Linda Kraemer and her colleagues (2012) recently examined the effects of informational text read-alouds on students' listening comprehension and book preferences. The researchers focused on four first-grade classrooms (77 students). All four teachers continued their normal read-aloud routines during the study, but in two of the classrooms a researcher also read informational texts three times a week for a month. Kraemer and her colleagues observed that students' listening comprehension (but not book preferences) changed over the course of the study. The students who participated in the informational text read-alouds demonstrated increased growth in their ability to comprehend informational text when compared to their peers.

Discussions

Text discussions have also been linked to students' comprehension development (e.g., Gambrell & Almasi, 1996; Murphy, Wilkinson, Soter, & Hennessey, 2009). For instance, in a recent review of research, Karen Murphy and her colleagues (2009) concluded that text discussions have "the potential to increase student comprehension, metacognition, critical thinking, and reasoning, as well as students' ability to state and support arguments" (p. 743). Researchers have tested several discussion approaches with informational text and have noted their positive effects on students' comprehension. Table 11.2 describes three approaches involving discussion that can support students' informational text comprehension development.

Prereading Activities

Prereading activities, or instructional routines that teachers use to prepare students for reading, have also led to increases in students' informational text comprehension. For instance, Sandra McCormick (1989) studied the effects of previewing social studies texts with 76 fifth graders for 2 weeks. For 10 minutes, students participated in discussions of their background knowledge, a summary of the text-to-be-read, and key vocabulary. Students' informational text comprehension was judged to be "superior" to their unaided reading. Similarly, the six graders in David Memory's (1983) study were given a question that signaled the text's main idea and text structure before reading. After three lessons, he found that the prequestion helped struggling readers (but not those classified as skilled) to comprehend informational text. Both of these studies testify to the value of teacher-directed prereading activities for helping students to comprehend the informational text being used in the lesson. However, because students' comprehension of future texts is so important, we believe that the use of prereading activities needs to involve and be accompanied by instruction in strategies that will help students to engage in their own, independent prereading of future texts.

Visual Aids

Visual aids, or concrete tools that may be used to structure readers' thinking, are another support that has led to increased informational text comprehension. Researchers have found that asking students to create mental

TABLE 11.2. Three Approaches to Discussion of Informational Text

Name	Overview	Central tenets
Collaborative Strategic Reading (CSR) (e.g., Klingner & Vaughn, 1999; Klingner et al., 2001)	Students take on roles and work together in small groups to use four comprehension strategies while reading informational texts.	The discussion format includes comprehension strategy instruction and cooperative learning. Teachers preteach CSR in whole-group lessons. They model and think aloud, and students role play. Students learn to (1) activate their prior knowledge and make predictions (*previewing*), (2) find words and ideas that are unknown or confusing to them and apply "fix-up" strategies (*click and clunk*), (3) summarize (*get the gist*), and (4) construct questions about what they read (*wrap up*).
Questioning the Author (QtA) (Beck & McKeown, 2006; McKeown, Beck, & Worthy, 1993)	Teachers lead discussions focused on understanding authors' messages.	Teachers and students co-construct meaning during the first reading of a text. Teachers encourage students to view their text as the product of writers who have knowledge and opinions but are also capable of error and bias. Teachers use questions such as "What is the author trying to say?" "How does that fit in with what the author already told us?" and "Did the author explain that clearly? Why or why not?" (Beck et al., 1996, p. 390).
Reciprocal Teaching (RT) (e.g., Palincsar & Brown, 1984; Rosenshine & Meister, 1994)	Students discuss the text together in small groups. They collaborate to apply comprehension strategies in informational text.	Teachers teach four comprehension processes (*predicting, questioning, clarifying,* and *summarizing*) and gradually release responsibility for the discussions to students. Teachers tell students when, how, and why each process may be useful, as well as paraphrase, clarify, and extend students' comments and questions when needed. In small-group discussions, students add onto summaries, ask additional questions, seek and offer help with confusing sections, and/or respond to each other's thoughts.

images, construct or complete graphic organizers, and to study instructional graphics have helped to improve their comprehension of informational text (e.g., Armbruster, Anderson, & Meyer, 1991; Boothby & Alvermann, 1984; Griffin & Tulbert, 1995). For example, Bonnie Armbruster and her colleagues (1991) examined the effects of framing—using graphic organizers that depict a text's structure and capture its main ideas—while reading social studies textbooks. Twelve fourth- and fifth-grade classes (or 365 students) participated. Teachers variously (1) completed frames in front of students while they discussed texts, (2) asked students to complete and discuss their own frames, or (3) followed the lessons in the teachers' manuals. The researchers found that the students who studied or completed the frames outscored their peers. Although the fifth graders appeared to benefit more than the fourth graders, the combined results of four rounds of instruction showed that framing was "more effective than the discussion and questioning practices recommended by the teachers' editions" (p. 411). The use of a visual aid supported students' comprehension of informational text.

In summary, researchers have shown that read-alouds, discussions, prereading activities, and visual aids can help students to comprehend the informational texts being used in reading and content-area lessons. As one part of an instructional agenda that also includes comprehension strategy and text structure instruction with authentic texts for authentic purposes, scaffolded opportunities to read informational text may support students' informational text comprehension development.

Best Practices in Action

In this section, we describe a single unit that employs the evidence-based best practices described in the previous section.[1] This unit could be taught at any grade level. The unit integrates reading and writing, as research suggests is well advised (Graham & Hebert, 2011). The unit also involves a great deal of science content, which the studies reviewed earlier suggest will enhance informational comprehension development as well as motivation.

The teacher begins by reading aloud a magazine article about a senior center where seniors are engaged in a great deal of physical activity. Students are impressed by a photo of a senior doing bicep curls and the description of a senior whose goal is to swim 50 miles a year! During the read-aloud, the teacher asks questions to engage students in specific

---

[1]This unit description is based on a first-grade unit developed by one of us (Nell K. Duke) in conjunction with Scholastic, Inc., as part of the *Information in Action* project.

comprehension processes, such as asking students "What are we learning about these seniors?" to encourage summarizing. She also asks about key details in the text, such as the specific activities in which the seniors are engaged. After reading, the teacher leads children in a discussion, based on the reading and their prior knowledge, about why it's important for seniors to be active.

Common Core Connection–The activities described in the previous paragraph support development toward Reading Anchor Standards 1 and 2:

1. *Read closely to determine what the text says explicitly and to make logical inferences from it; cite specific textual evidence when writing or speaking to support conclusions drawn from the text.*
2. *Determine central ideas or themes of a text and analyze their development; summarize the key supporting details and ideas.*

Next, the teacher tells students that based on the discussion, she thinks they would be great at persuading other seniors to exercise! After a brief conversation about past situations in which students have attempted to persuade or convince someone of something, the teacher shares some exciting news . . . there is a senior center just down the road from them! She looks it up on the Internet and reads portions of the site information to students. She asks students whether they would like to try to persuade seniors at this center to exercise, if they don't already, and keep exercising if they do. Students turn and talk with one another about this possibility. The teacher pulls the group back together and learns that students are very interested in trying to persuade seniors to exercise.

Over the next several days, the teacher shares with students a range of pamphlets designed to persuade people to act in a certain way, such as to eat healthy, use proper car restraint systems for children, and get regular medical checkups. These pamphlets serve as models and inspiration for students for the pamphlets they plan to write. Students analyze the pamphlets (at least those that they are able to read themselves) using a graphic organizer for persuasive text (see Figure 11.1). With prompting from the teacher, they also notice specific strategies the authors use to persuade—not only providing reasons for their opinions, but also using persuasive photographs, presenting graphs and statistics, and appealing to readers' emotions.

Common Core Connection–The activities described in the previous paragraph support development toward Reading Anchor Standards 5 and 8:

5. *Analyze the structure of texts, including how specific sentences, paragraphs, and larger portions of the text (e.g., a section, chapter, scene, or stanza) relate to each other and the whole.*

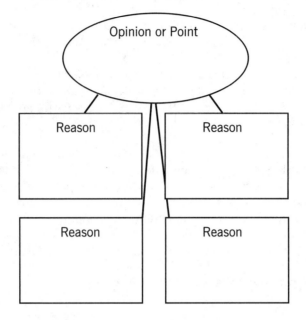

FIGURE 11.1. Graphic organizer supporting CCSS (for reading and writing) regarding opinion/point and reasons.

8. *Delineate and evaluate the argument and specific claims in a text, including the validity of the reasoning as well as the relevance and sufficiency of the evidence.*

With a sense now of what a persuasive pamphlet contains, students embark on conducting research to inform the writing of their own pamphlets. This includes hands-on experiences, such as graphing their heart rate before and after exercise and interviewing personnel from the senior center, as well as the use of written text to gather information. The teacher ensures that there are many books, magazine articles, and websites available in the classroom that provide information about the effects of exercise and encourages students to make use of a range of these resources. She briefly preteaches some key vocabulary related to exercise and physiology that students might encounter in their reading. Students meet in student-led small groups in which they use the four strategies of the Collaborative Strategic Reading approach (Klingner & Vaughn, 1999; Klingner, Vaughn, Dimino, Schumm, & Bryant, 2001) to tackle reading some of the more difficult sources. During this time, the teacher meets with small groups to compare the information presented in different sources and to assist students in synthesizing information across sources.

Common Core Connection–The activities described in the previous paragraph support development toward Reading Anchor Standards 7 and 9:

7. *Integrate and evaluate content presented in diverse media and formats, including visually and quantitatively, as well as in words.*
9. *Analyze how two or more texts address similar themes or topics in order to build knowledge or to compare the approaches the authors take.*

At this point, students begin detailed planning of the pamphlets they will write, using the same graphic organizer they used for the reading (Figure 11.1). In addition to an opinion/reasons structure, each pamphlet is to include photographs or illustrations and at least one graph, such as a graph some students read on the number of years that different amounts of exercise add to your life. The teacher helps students to think carefully about what information might be most persuasive and appropriate for seniors. Arguing that exercise will help seniors get in shape for football is not very appropriate; arguments that exercise can improve balance and longevity are.

Common Core Connection–The activities described in the previous paragraph support development toward Writing Anchor Standards 8, 9, 1, and 4 (though termed writing standards, *some of these standards also call for reading/ comprehension):*

8. *Gather relevant information from multiple print and digital sources, assess the credibility and accuracy of each source, and integrate the information while avoiding plagiarism.*
9. *Draw evidence from literary or informational texts to support analysis, reflection, and research.*
1. *Write arguments to support claims in an analysis of substantive topics or texts, using valid reasoning and relevant and sufficient evidence.*
4. *Produce clear and coherent writing in which the development, organization, and style are appropriate to task, purpose, and audience.*

After students have completed their drafts, they read one another's work and provide feedback. Students are eager to revise to make their pamphlets as persuasive as possible to seniors. Some students turn back to the informational texts available on exercise in order to gain yet more information to enhance their pamphlet. The teacher is pleased to see this additional informational text reading, as she is working toward the Common Core State Standards' expectation of 50% informational reading over the course of the school day in the elementary grades. Excitement is palpable as the day arrives for students to deliver their pamphlets to the senior center. The results reflect their hard work in comprehending and composing informational text (see Figure 11.2).

Do you want to stay helthy? If you do then, read this pamphlet and it will tell you about why exercise is important.

I think exercise is important for senos so you can be strong and feel good. It will also make your heart go faster!

The first reson is you will feel good and keep alert. It will keep your muscles strong.

2   3   4

FIGURE 11.2. Excerpts from a first grader's pamphlet persuading senior citizens to exercise.

Reflections and Future Directions

Research offers many insights and practices that support a complex, integrated unit such as the one described in this chapter. At the same time, there are areas in need of additional research and development activity. For example, research on how to help students comprehend graphical devices like those described in the unit is relatively scarce. Similarly scarce are studies on how to best help younger children to engage in the kind of synthesis of sources that writing the exercise pamphlets required. Another important—perhaps the most pressing—direction for future work lies in how to help teachers to design and implement units such as the one described. We know that project-based units like this are educationally promising but also difficult to implement without a high degree of support (e.g., Halvorsen et al., 2012). Yet the research reviewed in this chapter and elsewhere suggests that such units provide a rich context for the development of informational comprehension. We wish readers of this volume success in this difficult but rewarding endeavor.

ENGAGEMENT ACTIVITIES

1. Return to the section on Best Practices in Action. Try to identify within the unit the instructional strategies and insights described in the section on Evidence-Based Best Practices: A Research Synthesis.

2. Work to design your own unit modeled after the one described in the Best Practices in Action unit and informed by the findings in the section on Evidence-Based Best Practices: A Research Synthesis.

3. Take a careful look at a typical school day in your or another's classroom. How much opportunity to read informational text do students have? Does it reach the target amounts identified in the Common Core State Standards? Are students supported in learning *how to* read information text? How might best practices and the unit described in this chapter serve to enhance informational text exposure and instruction?

REFERENCES

Alexander, P. A., Kulikowich, J. M., & Jetton, T. L. (1994). The role of subject-matter knowledge and interest in the processing of linear and nonlinear texts. *Review of Educational Research, 64,* 201–252.

Almasi, J. F., & Fullerton, S. K. (2012). *Teaching strategic processes in reading* (2nd ed.). New York: Guilford Press.

Almasi, J. F., & Hart, S. J. (2011). Best practices in teaching comprehension. In L. M. Morrow & L. B. Gambrell (Eds.)., *Best practices in literacy instruction* (3rd ed., pp. 250–275). New York: Guilford Press.

Anderson, R. C., Hiebert, E. H., Scott, J. A., & Wilkinson, I. A. (1985). *Becoming a nation of readers: The report of the Commission on Reading.* Washington, DC: National Institute of Education.

Armbruster, B. B., Anderson, T. H., & Meyer, J. L. (1991). Improving content-area reading using instructional graphics. *Reading Research Quarterly, 26,* 393–416.

Beck, I. L., & McKeown, M. G. (2006). *Improving comprehension with questioning the author: A fresh and expanded view of a powerful approach.* New York: Scholastic.

Beck, I. L., McKeown, M. G., Sandora, C., Kucan, L., & Worthy, J. (1996). Questioning the author: A yearlong classroom implementation to engage students with text. *Elementary School Journal, 96,* 385–414.

Block, C. C., & Pressley, M. (2007). Best practices in teaching comprehension. In L. B. Gambrell, L. M. Morrow, & M. Pressley (Eds.), *Best practices in literacy instruction* (3rd ed., pp. 220–242). New York: Guilford Press.

Boothby, P. R., & Alvermann, D. E. (1984). A classroom training study: The effects of graphic organizer instruction on fourth graders' comprehension. *Reading World, 23,* 325–339.

Caverly, D. C., Mandeville, T. F., & Nicholson, S. A. (1995). Plan: A study-reading strategy for informational text. *Journal of Adolescent and Adult Literacy, 39,* 190–199.

Common Core State Standards Initiative. (2010). Common Core State Standards for the English language arts and literacy in history/social studies, science, and technical subjects. Retrieved from *www.corestandards.org.*

Dickson, S., Simmons, D. C., & Kame'enui, E. J. (1998). Text organization: Research bases. In D. C. Simmons & E. J. Kame'enui (Eds.), *What reading research tells us about children with diverse learning needs: Bases and basics* (pp. 239–277). Mahwah, NJ: Erlbaum.

Duke, N. K., & Carlisle, J. F. (2011). The development of comprehension. In M. L. Kamil, P. D. Pearson, E. B. Moje, & P. Afflerbach (Eds.), *Handbook of reading research* (Vol. 4, pp. 199–228). London: Routledge.

Duke, N. K., & Kays, J. (1998). "Can I say 'once upon a time'?": Kindergarten children developing knowledge of information book knowledge. *Early Childhood Research Quarterly, 13,* 295–318.

Duke, N. K., & Pearson, P. D. (2002). Effective practices for developing reading comprehension. In A. E. Farstrup & S. J. Samuels (Eds.), *What research has to say about reading instruction* (3rd ed., pp. 205–242). Newark, DE: International Reading Association.

Duke, N. K., Pearson, P. D., Strachan, S. L., & Billman, A. K. (2011). Essential elements of fostering and teaching reading comprehension. In S. J. Samuels & A. E. Farstrup (Eds.), *What research has to say about reading instruction* (4th ed., pp. 51–93). Newark, DE: International Reading Association.

Duke, N. K., & Roberts, K. M. (2010). The genre-specific nature of reading comprehension. In D. Wyse, R. Andrews, & J. Hoffman (Eds.), *The Routledge international handbook of English language and literacy teaching* (pp. 74–86). London: Routledge.

Duke, N. K., & Tower, C. (2004). Nonfiction texts for young readers. In J. V. Hoffman & D. L. Schallert (Eds.), *The texts in elementary classrooms* (pp. 111–128). Mahwah, NJ: Earlbaum.

Gambrell, L. B., & Almasi, J. F. (Eds.). (1996). *Lively discussions!: Fostering engaged reading.* Newark, DE: International Reading Association.

Gersten, R., Fuchs, L. S., Williams, J. P., & Baker, S. (2001). Teaching reading comprehension strategies to students with learning disabilities: A review of research. *Review of Educational Research, 71,* 279–320.

Graham, S., & Hebert, M. (2011). Writing to read: A meta-analysis of the impact of writing and writing instruction on reading. *Harvard Educational Review, 81,* 710–744.

Griffin, C. C., & Tulbert, B. L. (1995). The effect of graphic organizers on the comprehension and recall of expository text: A review of the research and implications for practice. *Reading and Writing Quarterly, 11*(1), 73–89.

Guthrie, J. T., Anderson, E., Alao, S., & Rinehart, J. (1999). Influences of concept-oriented reading instruction on strategy use and conceptual learning from text. *Elementary School Journal, 99,* 344–366.

Guthrie, J. T., McRae, A., Coddington, C. S., Lutz Klauda, S., Wigfield, A., & Barbosa, P. (2009). Impacts of comprehensive reading instruction on diverse outcomes of low- and high-achieving readers. *Journal of Learning Disabilities, 42*, 195–214.

Guthrie, J. T., McRae, A., & Klauda, S. L. (2007). Contributions of concept-oriented reading instruction to knowledge about interventions for motivations in reading. *Educational Psychologist, 42*(4), 237–250.

Guthrie, J. T., Wigfield, A., Barbosa, P., Perencevich, K. C., Taboada, A., Davis, M. H., et al. (2004). Increasing reading comprehension and engagement through concept-oriented reading instruction. *Journal of Educational Psychology, 96*, 403–423.

Halvorsen, A., Duke, N. K., Brugar, K. A., Block, M. K., Strachan, S. L., Berka, M. B., et al. (2012). Narrowing the achievement gap in second-grade social studies and content area literacy: The promise of a project-based approach. *Theory and Research in Social Education, 40*, 198–229.

Kauffman, D. F., Zhao, R., & Yang, Y. (2011). Effects of online note taking formats and self-monitoring prompts on learning from online text: Using technology to enhance self-regulated learning. *Contemporary Educational Psychology, 36*, 313–322.

Kelly, M. U., Moore, D. W., & Tuck, B. F. (1994). Reciprocal teaching in a regular primary school classroom. *Journal of Educational Research, 88*, 53–61.

Klingner, J. K., & Vaughn, S. (1999). Promoting reading comprehension, content learning, and English acquisition through collaborative strategic reading (CSR). *The Reading Teacher, 52*, 738–747.

Klingner, J. K., Vaughn, S., Dimino, J., Schumm, J., & Bryant, D. (2001). *From clunk to click: Collaborative strategic reading*. Longmont, CO: Sopris West.

Kraemer, L., McCabe, P., & Sinatra, R. (2012). The effects of read-alouds of expository text on first graders' listening comprehension and book choice. *Literacy Research and Instruction, 51*, 165–178.

Kucan, L., & Beck, I. L. (1996). Four fourth graders thinking aloud: An investigation of genre effects. *Journal of Literacy Research, 28*, 259–287.

Langer, J. A. (1986). *Children reading and writing: Structures and strategies*. Norwood, NJ: Ablex.

Martin, N. M. (2011). *Exploring informational text comprehension: Reading biography, persuasive text, and procedural text in the elementary grades*. Unpublished PhD dissertation, Michigan State University, East Lansing.

McCormick, S. (1989). Effects of previews on more skilled and less skilled readers' comprehension of expository text. *Journal of Reading Behavior, 21*, 219–239.

McKeown, M. G., Beck, I. L., & Worthy, M. J. (1993). Grappling with text ideas: Questioning the author. *The Reading Teacher, 46*, 560–586.

Memory, D. (1983). Main idea prequestions as adjunct aids with good and low-average middle grade readers. *Journal of Reading Behavior, 15*, 37–48.

Meyer, B. (1975). *The organization of prose and its effect on memory*. Amsterdam, Holland: North Holland.

Meyer, B., & Poon, L. W. (2001). Effects of structure strategy training and signaling on recall of text. *Journal of Educational Psychology, 93*(1), 141–159.

Murphy, P. K., Wilkinson, I. A. G., Soter, A. O., & Hennessey, M. N. (2009).

Examining the effects of classroom discussion on students' comprehension of text: A meta-analysis. *Journal of Educational Psychology, 101,* 740–764.

Olson, G. M., Mack, R. L., & Duffy, S. A. (1981). Cognitive aspects of genre. *Poetics, 10,* 283–315.

Palincsar, A. S., & Brown, A. L. (1984). Reciprocal teaching of comprehension-fostering and comprehension-monitoring activities. *Cognition and Instruction, 1,* 117–175.

Pappas, C. C. (1993). Is narrative "primary"?: Some insights from kindergartners' pretend readings of stories and information books. *Journal of Reading Behavior, 25,* 97–129.

Pappas, C. C. (2008). The information book genre: Its role in integrated science literacy research and practice. *Reading Research Quarterly, 41,* 226–250.

Pressley, M., & Afflerbach, P. (1995). *Verbal protocols of reading: The nature of constructively responsive reading.* Hillsdale, NJ: Erlbaum.

Purcell-Gates, V., Duke, N. K., & Martineau, J. A. (2007). Learning to read and write genre-specific text: Roles of authentic experience and explicit teaching. *Reading Research Quarterly, 42,* 8–45.

RAND Reading Study Group. (2002). *Reading for understanding: Toward an R & D program in reading comprehension.* Santa Monica, CA: Author.

Reutzel, D. R., Smith, J. A., & Fawson, P. C. (2005). An evaluation of two approaches for teaching reading comprehension strategies in the primary years using science information texts. *Early Childhood Research Quarterly, 20,* 276–305.

Riddle Buly, M., & Valencia, S. W. (2002). Below the bar: Profiles of students who fail state reading assessments. *Educational Evaluation and Policy Analysis, 24,* 219–239.

Romance, N. R., & Vitale, M. R. (2012). Expanding the role of K–5 science instruction in educational reform: Implications of an interdisciplinary model for integrating science and reading. *School Science and Mathematics, 112,* 506–515.

Rosenshine, B., & Meister, C. (1994). Reciprocal teaching: A review of the research. *Review of Educational Research, 64,* 479–530.

Shanahan, T., Callison, K., Carriere, C., Duke, N. K., Pearson, P. D., Schatschneider, C., et al. (2010). *Improving reading comprehension in kindergarten through 3rd grade: A practice guide* (NCEE 2010-4038). Washington, DC: National Center for Education Evaluation and Regional Assistance, Institute of Education Sciences, U.S. Department of Education. Retrieved from *whatworks. ed.gov/publications/practiceguides.*

Taylor, B. M. (1980). Children's memory for expository text after reading. *Reading Research Quarterly, 15,* 399–411.

Taylor, B. M. (1982). Text structure and children's comprehension and memory for expository material. *Journal of Educational Psychology, 74,* 323–340.

Wan, G. (2000). Reading aloud to children: The past, the present, and the future. *Reading Improvement, 37,* 148–160.

Williams, J. P., Hall, K. M., Lauer, K. D., Stafford, B., DeSisto, L. A., & deCani, J. S. (2005). Expository text comprehension in the primary grade classroom. *Journal of Educational Psychology, 97,* 538–550.

CHAPTER 12

Best Practices in Fluency Instruction

Melanie R. Kuhn
Timothy Rasinski

This chapter will:

- Discuss the role of fluency in the reading process and in reading achievement.
- Clarify reading fluency's place in the Common Core State Standards.
- Present effective approaches to fluency instruction.
- Suggest future directions for research.

Fluency is an integral component in reading development and text comprehension and, over the past decade or so, it has become central to the literacy curriculum of many primary and elementary schools. In fact, the Common Core State Standards (CCSS; National Governors Association & Council of Chief State School Officers [NGA & CCSSO], 2010) have identified reading fluency as a foundational skill, or a competency that should be acquired early since it lays the foundation for further growth in reading. During this same period, however, fluent reading has come to be equated with accurate, automatic word recognition in the minds of many educators (Applegate, Applegate, & Modla, 2009).

This (mis)understanding has been driven, in large part, by a system of assessments that bases student competency on the number of correct words read in a minute. Indeed, improvements in reading rate seem to be the primary goal of numerous fluency programs (e.g., Kuhn, Schwanen-flugel, & Meisinger, 2010; Rasinski, Reutzel, Chard, & Linan-Thompson, 2011). Unfortunately, an exclusive, or even a primary, focus on accurate and automatic word recognition can lead students to a skewed view of what skilled readers do. Additionally, many educators view fluency as a primarily oral reading activity, and since most reading at the college and career level is done silently, reading fluency instruction is often seen as inappropriate beyond the primary grades (Rasinski et al., 2011). The dominance of these perspectives has led to a demotion in the perceived importance of fluency in the reading process, a reflection of which can be seen in the failure to list reading fluency as a topic in the most recent surveys of "What's Hot, What's Not" in reading (Cassidy & Grote-Garcia, 2012; Cassidy, Ortlieb, & Shettel, 2011).

From our perspective, none of the above positions accurately portrays fluency's role in the reading process. We would instead argue that fluency is one of many important components in skilled reading, and its instruction is a valuable element of the literacy curriculum when placed in the proper perspective. Moreover, research has found that a lack of proficiency in reading fluency is a factor in a significant percentage of students' who experience difficulty in reading (Rasinski & Padak, 1998; Valencia & Buly, 2004). To determine the appropriate role of fluency instruction, it is important to remember there are *two* aspects of fluent reading that are integral to literacy development, automaticity (LaBerge & Samuels, 1974) and prosody (Benjamin & Schwanenflugel, 2010; Schreiber, 1991). Critically, this understanding is built upon the recognition that fluency is not only characterized by both elements, but that both aspects contribute to a learner's ability to construct meaning from text (Benjamin, Schwanenflugel, & Kuhn, 2009).

Our goals for this chapter include a discussion of what we consider to be a more appropriate role for fluency instruction in the classroom; how fluency connects to the CCSS; the provision of several effective instructional approaches, some of which expand the ways in which fluency can be developed; and how future research may inform both theory and practice.

Evidence-Based Best Practices: A Research Synthesis

To understand why instruction in reading fluency should involve more than simple speeded word recognition, it is important to consider how both automaticity and prosody contribute to its development. Here we will discuss the role of both.

Contribution of Automatic Word Recognition to Comprehension

When it comes to word recognition, skilled readers identify the vast majority of words both accurately and effortlessly. As a result, they do not need to spend a great deal of time determining the words in a text. This is important because, as with any cognitive task, individuals have a limited amount of attention available while reading (e.g., Adams, 2011; Samuels, 2006). Therefore, whatever attention they spend on one task (word recognition) is attention that is unavailable for another task (comprehension).

Beginning readers find themselves experiencing the reverse (Adams, 2011). Since they are just developing their decoding skills, they need to focus a great deal of their attention on word recognition, leaving them little attention for comprehension. One of our roles as educators is to help students move from purposeful decoding to word identification that is effortless or automatic. There is a general consensus that this can best occur through practice—practice that consists not only of work on word recognition, but also on the supported reading of a wide variety of connected text (e.g., Kuhn et al., 2010; Rasinski, 2011). As a learner repeatedly encounters words, she or he embeds them in memory, such that less attention is required to decode them accurately. Eventually the words become part of a reader's sight word vocabulary, generally over the course of three to eight repetitions (e.g., Torgesen, 2005).

Contribution of Prosody to Reading Fluency

While automaticity has a central role in the development of fluent reading, it is critical to stress that fluency consists of more than simply reading words quickly and accurately; it also involves prosodic reading, or those melodic elements of language that, when taken together, constitute expressive reading (e.g., Kuhn et al., 2010). These include intonation, stress, tempo, and appropriate phrasing. When learners apply these elements correctly, oral reading should take on the qualities of fluent speech. Furthermore, readers who incorporate prosody provide evidence of an otherwise invisible process, that of comprehension. This is because prosody contributes to shades of meaning and a richer understanding of what is written.

Recent research also indicates that prosody contributes to comprehension above and beyond that made by automatic word recognition (Benjamin et al., 2009; Benjamin & Schwanenflugel, 2010). While we know that prosody is closely tied to comprehension, the exact nature of the relationship is a matter of additional research (e.g., Does understanding the text allow for prosody, Does prosody lead to better comprehension, or Is the relationship reciprocal?; Kuhn et al., 2010). No matter what the relationship, however, the use of expression contributes to learners' engagement with text, helping to bring text to life and adding nuance to their reading.

Best Practices in Action

The CCSS confirm that fluency is a critical foundational skill (NGA & CCSSO, 2010). The Standards across the elementary grades (with the exception of kindergarten) state that students should "read with sufficient accuracy and fluency to support comprehension" (CCSS Initiative, 2012, pp. 16–17). At the same time, the standards argue that there is a

> need for college and career ready students to be proficient in reading complex informational text independently in a variety of content areas. Most of the required reading in college and workforce training programs is informational in structure and challenging in content; post-secondary education programs typically provide students with both a higher volume of such reading than is generally required in K–12 schools and comparatively little scaffolding. (p. 4)

Fortunately, the approaches we present in this chapter will not only help your students become more fluent readers, they also provide you with a way to support them as they read the kinds of challenging texts that the CCSS require.

Fluency Instruction and the Literacy Curriculum

Given that fluency is an important contributor to comprehension, it is critical that effective instructional approaches are used for its development. Such approaches need to go beyond simply asking students to read text rapidly; they must present learners with a richer and more nuanced understanding of skilled, fluent, and meaning-filled reading (Kuhn et al., 2010; Rasinski, Samuels, Hiebert, Petscher, & Feller, 2011). Importantly, several principles underlie effective fluency instruction (Rasinski, 2005), qualities that can be integrated across a range of literacy curricula, depending on the needs of your learners.

In this section, we present several approaches that can be implemented as part of your regular classroom instruction; these are designed for flexible groups (Fluency-Oriented Oral Reading; Kuhn, 2004–2005), synthesized fluency routines (Fluency Development Lesson; e.g., Rasinski, Padak, Linek, & Sturtevant, 1994), shared reading approaches (Fluency-Oriented Reading Instruction; Kuhn & Schwanenflugel, 2008), or simply as authentic, rehearsed, and enjoyable oral reading activities (e.g., poetry, readers theater; e.g., Young & Rasinski, 2009). These approaches can serve as regular components of your lesson plans for younger readers who are making the transition to fluency, or they can be integrated into your literacy curriculum as needed for older readers who have not achieved fluency to date. Importantly, they all have a focus on comprehension and prosody, as well as accuracy; as such, we feel they better represent the type of instruction that leads to the development of skilled reading than does instruction that focuses only on rate and accuracy.

Principles of Fluency Instruction

One of this chapter's authors, Timothy Rasinski (2005), has outlined four basic principles that can help you develop effective fluency instruction. While you do not need to implement all four principles simultaneously, you will find one or more of them underlying effective instructional approaches. To begin with, students should have the opportunity to listen to you, or another skilled reader, model fluent reading for them. Such modeling, even if consists of only a few minutes of oral reading a day, provides students with a better sense of what their own reading should sound like, something that is especially important for students whose reading is choppy or staccato.

Next, it is critical that you provide students with support while they themselves are reading aloud; this can involve listening to a fluent rendering of the text while reading it themselves. Support of this type can come in the form of choral reading with a group, paired reading with a partner, or reading while listening to a prerecorded rendering of the text. Third, you should help focus students' attention on reading in meaningful phrases. As with modeling, a focus on phrasing helps students develop a more complete understanding of the importance of prosody while simultaneously helping them move beyond reading that is word by word or that uses phrasing in ways that fail to replicate language.

Finally, and most importantly, it is essential that your students have ample opportunities to read. As with most skills, students become better at reading through practice (Allington, 2009; Samuels, 2006), although the nature and purpose of practice—and how much support is required—will vary depending on the needs of the individual learner and the difficulty of the text. Practice can take two different forms. In wide reading, students read a given passage or text once; this is often followed by discussion or follow-up activities to ensure comprehension. Deep or repeated reading, on the other hand, involves students reading a text several times until they are able to read and understand it well before moving on to a new passage.

The four principles outlined above can be used independently, or they can be combined to create synergistic instructional routines. However, there is one aspect of most fluency instruction, that of repetition, that needs to be reconsidered in light of some recent findings (Kuhn et al., 2010; Mostow & Beck, 2005). First, it is important to stress that repetition does, indeed, help students develop their automaticity—as well as their prosody; this, in turn, helps ensure learners become fluent readers. What needs to be reconsidered is not the repetition, per se, but instead how that repetition occurs. That is, repetition can occur through a traditional repeated reading format in which a given text is read several times. Alternatively, it can occur through the single reading of multiple texts.

Because of the number of shared words and syntactic constructions in many texts, especially those designed for young readers (Adams, 1990), it is possible for repetition to occur across a range of reading materials. In this scenario, students are likely to see the same words and grammatical patterns in multiple contexts, for example, words like *the, ran,* and *cat,* and sentence structures such as noun phrase + verb phrase + prepositional phrase (e.g., *The dog ran quickly after the cat*). Furthermore, there is evidence indicating that readers may learn words faster when the words are encountered in a variety of contexts rather than when they are seen repeatedly in the same context (Mostow & Beck, 2005). As a result of this expanded understanding, we present several approaches to fluency instruction that are based on the above principles as well as both the wide and repeated reading of text.

Fluency-Oriented Oral Reading/Wide Fluency-Oriented Oral Reading

As was discussed above, for many years, repetition was considered a key element in fluency development. However, when reviewing the research on fluency interventions, Melanie Kuhn and Steven Stahl (2003) found something surprising. They noticed that students using a repeated readings approach and students who read equivalent amounts of text with support made similar gains in fluency. In order to explore this finding further, Kuhn (2004–2005) compared two types of small-group fluency instruction with striving second-grade readers: one used repeated readings while the other used the wide reading of a number of texts. Additionally, she included a group that listened to, but did not read, the texts used by the fluency groups and a control group.

Both approaches are designed for small groups of students (up to six per group) and involve reading for 15–20 minutes per session three times a week. Since the goal is to scaffold, or support, your students, they should read material slightly beyond their instructional level; for example, students reading at the primer level can read texts ranging from a late first- to an early third-grade reading level. The first procedure is a modified repeated readings technique, Fluency Oriented Oral Reading (FOOR). In this version, you should echo- or choral-read a single trade book three times over the course of a week. For the second approach, Wide Fluency Oriented Oral Reading (Wide FOOR), you should echo- or choral-read a different text for each of the three sessions. While discussion of the material should occur naturally as part of the lessons, comprehension and vocabulary instruction are not the primary focus of these lessons.

In the initial study, both the FOOR and the Wide FOOR groups outperformed their peers (who either listened to the stories or did no extra reading) in terms of word recognition in isolation, prosody, and correct words per minute. Additionally, the students in the Wide FOOR group made greater growth on comprehension than their peers in all the groups. This finding may be due to the differences in the approaches; since one text was read repeatedly in the FOOR approach, the students may have focused on improving word recognition and prosody, whereas the use of multiple texts in the Wide FOOR may have led readers to focus on comprehension. However, you could further assist learners in their understanding of the material being read by incorporating vocabulary and comprehension instruction into these approaches (e.g., see Stahl, 2008).

Fluency Development Lesson

The Fluency Development Lesson (FDL) (Rasinski et al., 1994) also integrates several of the principles of effective fluency instruction mentioned earlier into a coherent classroom routine. In the FDL, students work daily with a brief text. First, you read a relatively short passage (50–200 word poem or selection taken from a longer prose piece) to your students two or three times as they follow along silently or listen to your oral reading. After the modeling component, you should discuss the meaning of the text as well as the quality of your oral reading with your students. Next, students read the selection chorally as a group; this allows each student to provide oral support for their classmates. Students then divide into partners and engage in paired repeated reading; at this point, each student reads the selection two or three times while their partner follows along silently and provides support and encouragement. After completing this practice, students are offered the chance to perform the daily text for their classmates either as individuals or in small groups. Finally, you and your students choose words from the text for word study and analysis. As an option, students may also take the assigned passage home for further practice with family members.

An early implementation of the FDL in a self-contained second-grade classroom found significant gains in overall fluency and a trend for improved overall achievement in reading (Rasinski et al., 1994). More recently, Belinda Zimmerman, Timothy Rasinski, and Maria Melewski (2013) reported substantial gains in word recognition, reading fluency, and comprehension among first- through fourth-grade struggling readers who were receiving FDL instruction as part of a 5-week summer reading clinic.

Fast Start (Padak & Rasinski, 2005) is a variation of the FDL designed for home involvement. In Fast Start, students work with a skilled reader (parent, caregiver, or even an older sibling) on a daily rhyme or other short text. The skilled reader reads the passage to his or her child two or three times while pointing to the words; next, the skilled reader and the child read the passage together two or three times; then the skilled reader listens to the child read the passage to him or her a couple of times. Finally, the skilled reader and the child engage in a brief word study activity using one or more words from the passage (e.g., if the word *wall* was found in the passage, the skilled reader and the child may write and read other words within the same word family—*ball, call, stall, mall*, and so on).

In an implementation of Fast Start with first-grade students, Rasinski and Stevenson (2005) found that it had a profound and positive impact on the reading development of the most at-risk students—Fast Start students made nearly double the gains in word recognition fluency than their peers who received the same instruction in school but did not participate in the program at home. In another school-based study of first graders, parents' use of Fast Start at home with their children over a 3-month period resulted in significant improvements in students' reading fluency (Crosby, Rasinski, Padak, & Yildirim, 2013). Moreover, the same study found that most of the participating parents and children found value and enjoyment in Fast Start. Over the course of 5 years, the number of parents and frequency of use of Fast Start has progressively increased.

Fluency-Oriented Reading Instruction/Wide Fluency-Oriented Reading Instruction

Fluency-Oriented Reading Instruction (FORI) and Wide Fluency-Oriented Reading Instruction (Wide FORI) are designed for the shared reading component of your literacy curriculum. However, both can be easily modified for small-group instruction or used for tutoring one or two struggling readers. FORI (Stahl & Heubach, 2005) involves a weekly lesson plan that consists of rereading a single, challenging selection (see Figure 12.1). On the first day, you should introduce the week's selection using your typical prereading activities; for example, you may choose to

	Monday	Tuesday	Wednesday	Thursday	Friday
Fluency-oriented reading instruction					
Basal lesson	**Teacher introduces story.** Teacher reads story to class; class discusses story. Option: Teacher develops graphic organizers. Option: Class does activities from basal.	**Students practice story.** Teacher and students echo-read story.	**Students practice story.** Teacher and students choral-read story.	**Students practice story.** Students partner-read story.	**Students do extension activities.** These may include writing in response to story, etc. Option: Teacher does running records of children's reading.
Home reading	Children read 15–30 minutes in a book of their own choosing.	Students take story home and practice reading basal story aloud to someone.	Students who need more practice take home the basal story—others take book of their own choosing.	Students who need more practice take home the basal story—others take book of their own choosing.	Children read 15–30 minutes in a book of their own choosing.

FIGURE 12.1. FORI weekly lesson plan.

highlight important vocabulary, build background knowledge, or preview the text. At this point, you should read the material aloud to your students while they follow along in their own copies of the text. This both provides your students with the pronunciation of any unknown words and allows them to focus on meaning. After reading the selection for the first time, you should discuss the material with your learners. Such a discussion further reinforces the notion that your primary goal is comprehension.

On Day 2, you should echo-read the selection; this approach can be made even more effective by integrating comprehension questions at natural stopping points throughout the selection (Stahl, 2008). The third day's lesson is the shortest of the week, consisting of a simple choral reading of the material with your students. Depending on the amount of time you can allocate to your shared reading on this day, you may want to integrate a second choral reading of the material into your instruction. The fourth day involves asking your students to partner-read alternating pages of the text. By Day 4, the students should be fairly comfortable with the text, having encountered it at least three times previously. Furthermore, having partners provides additional support for reading the text successfully. Depending on how quickly the partners complete their first reading, you may have time for them to reread the selection again; for this second reading, the partners should read the pages opposite those they read initially. You should implement your usual postreading extension activities on Friday, the last day of the FORI procedure; for example, you might ask students to summarize the selection, to complete graphic organizers of the material, or to write in response to the reading.

The FORI program provides your students with modeling, support or assistance, a focus on appropriate phrasing, and, perhaps most importantly, ample opportunities to read substantial amounts of connected text. While it is the case that some teachers find the format to be a bit tedious, the vast majority of the students actually enjoyed the predictable and consistent routine. What is critical, however, is that the material being used is long enough for your students to read for an extended period of time (between 20 and 40 minutes per day) and that the texts being used are sufficiently challenging for your learners (e.g., grade-level texts if the majority of your students are reading below grade level and texts that are above grade level if the majority of your students are reading at grade level). When these conditions are in place, FORI has been shown to help students make significant gains in terms of their reading ability.

The original FORI intervention took place with second graders who were reading below grade level, and the approach was developed in response to a mandate that teachers use only grade-level texts for their literacy instruction. It was hoped that the repetition and scaffolding would help readers' access what were clearly challenging texts for these learners.

While the FORI procedure was originally used as a way of covering a selection from a basal reader or literature anthology, it can be used with any text that is part of your literacy curriculum, including trade books. However, it is essential that the selection is somewhat challenging for the learners and that each of your students has his or her own copy of whatever material is being read.

In many classrooms, there is particular story or expository piece that is a required as part of your weekly literacy curriculum. As a result, you may feel a corresponding sense of accountability attached to these selections. In practice, this can mean that you dedicate a greater proportion of your class time to their instruction. The FORI procedure allows you to develop meaningful lessons around such selections. At the same time, the approach provides room for integrating additional reading materials—and instructional approaches—into your literacy curriculum as well. In fact, FORI should not be viewed as the only component of your literacy instruction; instead, it is important that you include multiple types of literacy learning, such as small-group and individual reading instruction, opportunities to write, and a focus on word study, as part of a balanced curriculum. Although the procedure is quite straightforward, it has been shown to be successful with students who are using complex material; as such, it can go hand-in-hand with the CCSS.

Since the use of multiple texts may also be part of the CCSS requirements, there is a wide-reading alternative, Wide FORI, that could be used as the basis of your weekly lesson plans. Importantly, this approach has also been shown to be at least as effective as FORI at improving students' reading ability. Wide FORI incorporates the reading of three texts over the course of a week (see Figure 12.2), thereby ensuring that your learners encounter a large number of words in multiple contexts. Furthermore, by reading multiple texts, your students who are exposed to Wide FORI experience a broader range of concepts, helping them develop the breadth, as well as the depth, that is central to the CCSS as well as the development of their fluency (Logan, 1997).

The primary text for the Wide FORI lessons is usually the basal or literature anthology selection that may be required as part of your literacy curricula, but you can use any shared reading text. Since the approach involves three texts over the course of a week, you will need to spend less time on the first selection than is the case in the FORI approach (i.e., 3 as opposed to 5 days). However, the first day parallels Day 1 for FORI. You should begin by introducing the text using prereading activities (e.g., building background knowledge or discussing vocabulary). Day 1 continues by reading the selection aloud to your class as your students follow along, and concludes with a discussion of the material with your learners. Day 2 consists of echo reading the selection, followed by a choral or

	Monday	Tuesday	Wednesday	Thursday	Friday
Wide fluency-oriented reading instruction	**Teacher introduces story.** Teacher reads story to class; class discusses story. Option: Teacher develops graphic organizers. Option: Class does activities from basal (Story 1).	**Students practice story.** Teacher and students echo-read Story 1. Option: Students do partner-reading.	**Students do extension activities.** These may include writing in response to story, etc. Option: Teacher does running records of children's reading.	**Teacher and students echo- or choral-read trade book (Story 2).** Option: Students partner-read Story 2. Option: Students do extension activities (writing, etc.).	**Teacher and students echo- or choral-read trade book (Story 3).** Option: Students partner-read Story 3. Option: Students do extension activities (writing, etc.).
Home reading	Children read 15–30 minutes per day in a book of their own choosing.	Students take story home and practice reading basal story aloud to someone.	Children read 15–30 minutes per day in a book of their own choosing.	Children read 15–30 minutes per day in a book of their own choosing.	Children read 15–30 minutes per day in a book of their own choosing.

FIGURE 12.2. Wide FORI lesson plan.

279

partner reading of the text if time allows. Day 3 involves your implementing any extension activities you feel are appropriate for the material.

The remaining lessons, on Days 4 and 5, incorporate the reading of a second and third selection. You should echo-read these texts with your students and follow up by discussing them with your class. Furthermore, if time allows, have your students undertake a second reading of the material; whether you decide to have your learners echo-, choral-, or partner-read at this point should depend on your students' comfort with the material, the text difficulty, and the amount of time available. Again, it is essential that the texts be substantive enough to ensure students are spending between 20 and 40 minutes actually engaged in reading. When using Wide FORI as described here, students have made gains not only in terms of their word recognition and fluency, but on their comprehension as well.

Fluency through Authentic Rehearsal and Performance

Although readers theater is often thought of as the rehearsal and eventual performance of a script (e.g., Rasinski et al., 2011), we enlarge our definition of readers theater here to include the authentic reading performance of any text for the purpose of eliciting both efferent and aesthetic responses from the audience. While "recitation" is another term that has been used in place of "readers theater," we prefer the term readers theater since recitation implies a memorization and performance of a text from memory. In readers theater, the final performance is read by the performer.

When employing a readers theater approach to fluency instruction, you should assign (or have your students choose) texts that are meant to be performed and will be performed by your learners (e.g., poems, speeches, plays). Your students can work individually, in pairs, or in small groups to practice and perform their assigned text. Once a text is assigned, your students should rehearse (engage in repeated readings of) their text over a period of time (usually several days). The goal of the rehearsal is not fast reading, but a prosodic and meaningful oral interpretation of the text. During this rehearsal time you should engage in modeling the readings, coach and provide feedback to your students, and set the stage for the performance. After an appropriate period of rehearsal (depending on the length and complexity of the text), your students can perform their selections for an audience usually made up of classmates, teacher, parents, and other guests. The cycle of practice and performance should become a classroom routine that is repeated over the following days, weeks, and months.

Readers theater, as we describe it here, incorporates the elements or principles of effective fluency instruction that we described earlier—modeling fluent reading, assisted reading, and repeated reading—within an authentic and purposeful framework. Classroom-based research has found that a readers theater approach to fluency instruction leads to significant improvements in reading fluency and overall reading achievement (Solomon & Rasinski, 2011; Worthy & Prater, 2002; Young & Rasinski, 2009). Moreover, the same research has also shown that students, teachers, and parents view readers theater as a highly motivating and engaging reading activity.

Reflections and Future Directions

While we know much about fluency's role in the reading process as well as ways to develop fluency in our learners (including the approaches outlined above; e.g., Kuhn et al, 2010; Rasinski et al., 2011), there are still a number of questions that need to be answered.

As was discussed in the *Best Practices in Action* section, recent research (Kuhn et al., 2006; Mostow & Beck, 2005) indicates that improvements in fluency do not result specifically from the repetition of text, but instead from a more generalized increase and repeated exposure to the amount of challenging words and connected text students are responsible for reading with appropriate support. If it is the case that fluency development can occur simply by increasing the amount of text students read with support, than there may be a range of approaches that are as effective as those discussed here. Continuing research in this area may allow us to create additional instructional approaches while simultaneously developing a better understanding of how fluency contributes to learners' overall reading development.

Along these same lines, the appropriate level of text difficulty used in fluency instruction is an issue worth further consideration. Research by Steven Stahl and Kathleen Heubach (2005), as well as by ourselves and others (e.g., Hollingsworth, 1970, 1978; Kuhn, 2004–2005; Rasinski et al., 2011), has found that greater progress was made when students were given more challenging materials for repeated or scaffolded wide readings. Given that the CCSS (NGA & CCSSO, 2010) advocates the use of more complex and challenging text, it is intriguing to consider that elements of fluency instruction may provide some key insights into how students can successfully negotiate the more complex texts they will be encountering.

The nature of the texts provided for fluency instruction is also an issue that requires further study (Hiebert, 2006; Rasinski et al., 2011).

Some scholars (and many commercial fluency programs) argue that the texts for fluency instruction should contain academic content and be specifically designed to include words that students need to learn to recognize automatically. Other scholars suggest the use of texts that have a strong voice in order to provide opportunities to work on prosody and that are meant to be performed (e.g., poetry, readers theater scripts, songs) in order to provide students with a natural context for repeated readings (i.e., rehearsal).

Fluency is most often thought of as an oral reading phenomenon most appropriate for the primary grades. Yet most reading done by adults and students beyond the initial stages of reading is silent. Studies have found strong correlations between oral reading fluency and silent reading comprehension (Daane, Campbell, Grigg, Goodman, & Oranje, 2005). And, more recently, promising attempts have been made to develop instructional methods for developing silent reading fluency (Rasinski et al., 2011; Reutzel, Jones, Fawson, & Smith, 2008). Still, future research needs to explore further the nature of silent reading fluency and how it may best be taught in classroom and clinical settings.

Additionally, a growing body of research suggests that fluency concerns may be impacting students' reading proficiency beyond the primary grades (Rasinski, Rikli, & Johnston, 2009). Research needs to explore why significant numbers of students emerge from the primary grades without sufficient proficiency in fluency, how it may be more effectively taught to primary-grade students, and how students beyond the primary grades who still struggle in fluency may receive appropriate instruction in this key area.

Finally, while the role of the teacher in fluency instruction is clearly important, it has not been thoroughly investigated. While wide and repeated readings may seem to be primarily activities students engage in independently, we feel that the teacher must play a significant role in fluency instruction by choosing appropriate texts, modeling fluent reading, encouraging and providing feedback and support for students, and setting the stage for performance (e.g., Rasinski, 2005). Clearly the appropriate role of the teacher during fluency instruction needs further examination and clarification.

Concluding Remarks

In recent years, there has been a renewed focus on approaches that assist learners with their fluency development. However, we strongly believe that certain forms of assessment, along with their corresponding practices, have skewed conceptualizations of reading fluency. This, in turn, has negatively affected the way in which fluency is taught. We believe the approaches and principles presented here provide an alternative that will help you begin to integrate effective fluency instruction into your classroom. By doing so, your students will not only develop automatic word recognition and integrate expression into their oral reading, they will be better able to read challenging text with understanding, thereby helping them achieve the ultimate goal of reading instruction.

Although several issues related to reading fluency still need to be resolved, we feel strongly that appropriate fluency instruction offers a key to success in reading for many developing and struggling readers. We hope you agree and are willing to give fluency instruction a try!

ENGAGEMENT ACTIVITIES

1. How would you respond to a school administrator or parent who notes that since reading speed (a indicator of reading fluency) is associated with reading proficiency, you should emphasize students improving their reading rate through timed reading activities?

2. Think about the CCSS that were designed specifically for reading fluency as well as the importance of using challenging texts within the CCSS framework. How do these two understandings complement each other? How can fluency-oriented instructional approaches help your learners achieve both your goals for fluent reading and provide your learners with access to complex material? And how do these approaches help ensure students are able to successfully read—and learn from—such texts?

3. Consider a challenging but brief text that you want your students to read as a way of developing both their fluency and their understanding. How could you use the FDL to achieve your goals? What type of selection would be appropriate for your learners? Would you consider using this method with a poem or a passage from lengthier material?

4. Finally, think about several challenging texts that you would like to implement as part of the shared reading component of your literacy curriculum. Which of the two whole-class approaches— FORI or Wide FORI—would be most appropriate for your students? How would you go about implementing these approaches with a specific text or texts? How might you adapt the lessons for small-group instruction? How would these help you meet your overall, as well as specific, instructional goals?

RESOURCES FOR FURTHER LEARNING

Professional Books

Johns, J., & Berglund, R. (2010). *Fluency: Differentiated interventions and progress monitoring assessments* (4th ed.). Newark, DE: International Reading Association.

Kuhn, M. R. (2008). *The hows and whys of fluency instruction.* New York: Allyn & Bacon.

Kuhn, M. R., & Levy, L. (2015). *Developing fluent readers: Teaching fluency as a foundational skill.* New York: Guilford Press.

Kuhn, M. R., & Schwanenflugel, P. J. (2007). *Fluency in the classroom.* New York: Guilford Press.

Rasinski, T., Blachowicz, C., & Lems, K. (Eds.). (2012). *Fluency instruction: Research-based best practices* (2nd ed.). New York: Guilford Press.

Rasinski, T. V. (Ed.). (2009). *Essential readings in fluency.* Newark, DE: International Reading Association.

Rasinski, T. V. (2010). *The fluent reader* (2nd ed.). New York: Scholastic.

Samuels, S. J., & Farstrup, A. (Eds.). (2006). *What research has to say about fluency instruction.* Newark, DE: International Reading Association.

Children's Book Recommendations for Building Fluency

Rasinski, T. V. (2008). *Tim Rasinski presents fabulously famous books for building fluency, Library A (grades K–2).* New York: Scholastic.

Rasinski, T. V. (2008). *Tim Rasinski presents fabulously famous books for building fluency, Library B (grades 3–5).* New York: Scholastic.

Rasinski, T. V. (2008). *Tim Rasinski presents fabulously famous books for building fluency, Library C (grades 6–8).* New York: Scholastic.

REFERENCES

Adams, M. J. (1990). *Beginning to read: Thinking and learning about print.* Cambridge, MA: MIT Press.

Adams, M. J. (2011). The relationship between alphabetic basics, word recognition, and reading. In S. J. Samuels & A. E. Farstrup (Eds.), *What research has to say about reading instruction* (4th ed., pp. 4–24). Newark, DE: International Reading Association.

Allington, R. L. (2009). If they don't read much . . . 30 years later. In E. H. Hiebert (Ed.), *Reading more, reading better* (pp. 30–54). New York: Guilford Press.

Applegate, M. D., Applegate, A. J., & Modla, V. B. (2009). "She's my best reader; she just can't comprehend": Studying the relationship between fluency and comprehension. *The Reading Teacher, 62,* 512–521.

Benjamin, R., & Schwanenflugel, P. J. (2010). Text complexity and oral reading prosody in young readers. *Reading Research Quarterly, 45*(4), 388–404.

Benjamin, R., Schwanenflugel, P. J., & Kuhn, M. R. (2009, May). *The predictive value of prosody: Differences between simple and difficult texts in the reading of 2nd graders.* Paper presented at the College of Education Research conference, University of Georgia, Athens.

Cassidy, J., & Grote-Garcia, S. (2012). Defining the literacy agenda: Results of the 2013 What's Hot, What's Not Literacy Survey. *Reading Today, 30*(1), 9–12.

Cassidy, J., Ortlieb, E., & Shettel, J. (2011). What's hot for 2011. *Reading Today, 28(3),* 1, 6, 7, 8.

Common Core State Standards Initiative (2012). English Language Arts Standards. Retrieved from *www.corestandards.org/ELA-Literacy.*

Crosby, S. A., Rasinski, T., Padak, N., & Yildirim, K. (2013). *A three year study of a school-based parental involvement program in early literacy.* Unpublished manuscript, Kent State University, Kent, OH.

Daane, M. C., Campbell, J. R., Grigg, W. S., Goodman, M. J., & Oranje, A. (2005). *Fourth-grade students reading aloud: NAEP 2002 Special Study of Oral Reading.* Washington, DC: U.S. Department of Education, Institute of Education Sciences.

Hiebert, E. H. (2006). Becoming fluent: What difference do texts make? In S. J. Samuels & A. E. Farstrup (Eds.), *What research has to say about reading fluency* (pp. 204– 226). Newark, DE: International Reading Association.

Hollingsworth, P. M. (1970). An experiment with the impress method of teaching reading. *The Reading Teacher, 24,* 112–114.

Hollingsworth, P. M. (1978). An experimental approach to the impress method of teaching reading. *The Reading Teacher, 31,* 624–626.

Kuhn, M. R. (2004–2005). Helping students become accurate, expressive readers: Fluency instruction for small groups. *The Reading Teacher, 58,* 338–344.

Kuhn, M. R., & Schwanenflugel, P. J. (2008). *Fluency in the classroom.* New York: Guilford Press.

Kuhn, M. R., Schwanenflugel, P. J., & Meisinger, E. B. (2010). Review of research: Aligning theory and assessment of reading fluency: Automaticity, prosody, and definitions of fluency. *Reading Research Quarterly, 45,* 230–251.

Kuhn, M. R., Schwanenflugel, P. J., Morris, R. D., Morrow, L. M., Woo, D., Meisinger, B., et al. (2006). Teaching children to become fluent and automatic readers. *Journal of Literacy Research, 38,* 357–387.

Kuhn, M. R., & Stahl, S. A. (2003). Fluency: A review of developmental and remedial practices. *Journal of Educational Psychology, 95,* 3–21.

LaBerge, D., & Samuels, S. J. (1974). Toward a theory of automatic information processing in reading. *Cognitive Psychology, 6,* 293–323.

Logan, G. D. (1997). Automaticity and reading: Perspectives from the instance theory of automatization. *Reading and Writing Quarterly, 13,* 123–146.

Mostow, J., & Beck, J. (2005, June). *Micro-analysis of fluency gains in a reading tutor that listens.* Paper presented at the annual meeting of the Society for the Scientific Study of Reading, Toronto, Canada.

National Governors Association & Council of Chief State School Officers. (2010). Common Core State Standards. Retrieved from *www.corestandards.org.*

Padak, N., & Rasinski, T. (2005). *Fast start for early readers: A research-based, send-home literacy program.* New York: Scholastic.

Rasinski, T. V. (2005). The role of the teacher in effective fluency instruction. *New England Reading Association Journal, 41,* 9–12.

Rasinski, T. V. (2011). The art and science of teaching reading fluency. In D. Lapp, N. Frey, & D. Fisher (Eds.), *Handbook of research on teaching the English language arts* (3rd ed., pp. 23–246). New York: Routledge.

Rasinski, T. V., & Padak, N. D. (1998). How elementary students referred for compensatory reading instruction perform on school-based measures of word recognition, fluency, and comprehension. *Reading Psychology: An International Quarterly, 19,* 185–216.

Rasinski, T. V., Padak, N. D., Linek, W. L., & Sturtevant, E. (1994). Effects of fluency development on urban second-grade readers. *Journal of Educational Research, 87,* 158–165.

Rasinski, T. V., Reutzel, C. R., Chard, D., & Linan-Thompson, S. (2011). Reading Fluency. In M. L. Kamil, P. D. Pearson, B. Moje, & P. Afflerbach (Eds.), *Handbook of reading research* (Vol. 4, pp. 286–319). New York: Routledge.

Rasinski, T. V., Rikli, A., & Johnston, S. (2009). Reading fluency: More than automaticity?: More than a concern for the primary grades? *Literacy Research and Instruction, 48,* 350–361.

Rasinski, T. V., Samuels, S. J., Hiebert, E., Petscher, Y., & Feller, K. (2011). The relationship between silent reading fluency instructional protocol on students' reading comprehension and achievement in an urban school setting. *Reading Psychology: An International Quarterly, 32,* 75–97.

Rasinski, T. V., & Stevenson, B. (2005). The effects of fast start reading, a fluency based home involvement reading program, on the reading achievement of beginning readers. *Reading Psychology: An International Quarterly, 26,* 109–125.

Reutzel, D. R., Jones, C. D., Fawson, P. C., & Smith, J. A. (2008). Scaffolded Silent Reading (ScSR): An alternative to guided oral repeated reading that works! *The Reading Teacher, 62,* 194–207.

Samuels, S. J. (2006). Toward a model of reading fluency. In S. J. Samuels & A. E. Farstrup (Eds.), *What research has to say about fluency instruction* (pp. 24–46). Newark, DE: International Reading Association.

Schreiber, P. A. (1991). Understanding prosody's role in reading acquisition. *Theory into Practice, 30,* 158–164.

Solomon, D., & Rasinski, T. (2011, Spring). Improving intermediate grade students' reading fluency, comprehension, and motivation through the readers' theater club. *Reading in the Middle,* pp. 7–16.

Stahl, K. A. D. (2008). Creating opportunities for comprehension within fluency-oriented reading. In M. R. Kuhn & P. J. Schwanenflugel (Eds.), *Fluency in the classroom* (pp. 55–74). New York: Guilford Press.

Stahl, S. A., & Heubach, K. (2005). Fluency-oriented reading instruction. *Journal of Literacy Research, 37,* 25–60.

Torgesen, J. (2005, September). *Teaching every child to read: What every teacher needs to know.* Paper presented at the Georgia Reading First Pre-Service conference, Atlanta, GA.

Valencia, S. W., & Buly, M. R. (2004). Behind test scores: What struggling readers really need. *The Reading Teacher, 57,* 520–531.

Worthy, J., & Prater, K. (2002). "I thought about it all night": Readers theater for reading fluency and motivation. *The Reading Teacher, 56,* 294–297.

Young, C., & Rasinski, T. (2009). Implementing readers theatre as an approach to classroom fluency instruction. *The Reading Teacher, 63*(1), 4–13.

Zimmerman, B., Rasinski, T., & Melewski, M. (2013). When kids can't read, what a focus on fluency can do. In E. Ortlieb & E. Cheek (Eds.), *Advanced literacy practices: From the clinic to the classroom* (pp. 137–160). Bingley, UK: Emerald Group.

CHAPTER 13

Best Practices in Teaching Writing

Karen Bromley

This chapter will:

- Discuss the role of writing in the Common Core State Standards.
- Synthesize theory and research that supports K–8 writing instruction.
- Present evidence-based practices for teachers of writing.
- Suggest future directions for writing instruction.

Text message: *Hey Glo . . . ty 4 the pb sandwich . . . Wd def <3 his2. Cant w8 2 come back 2mro. Cu then . . . ps . . . I want 2 c the w8 n c tree 2!*

Translation: *"Hey Gloria! Thank you for the peanut butter sandwich. Winn Dixie definitely loved his too. Can't wait to come back tomorrow. See you then! PS . . . I want to see the wait-and-see tree too!"*

This text message and translation from Opal to Gloria Dump, characters in *Because of Winn Dixie*, by Kate DiCamillo (2000), are examples of how April, a fourth-grade teacher, connects her students' digital literacies with traditional literacy. April shared this text message and translation with her students after they read a chapter in *Because of Winn Dixie*. Next she had her students create their own text messages and translations related to a favorite part of the story. Students then shared their work with each other in pairs and April posted their written pieces on a bulletin board in her room. April believes this writing activity meets many of the Common Core State Standards (CCSS; National Governors Association & Council of Chief State School Officers [NGA & CCSSO], 2010) for writing;

- Writing Standards 1–3 (writing arguments, informative/explanatory texts, and narratives). April asked her students to write texts to inform others.
- Writing Standards 4–6 (developing and strengthening writing and using technology to produce and enhance writing). April had students use technology/text messaging language and translate it into standard English.
- Writing Standards 7–9 (engaging in reading, research and writing from sources). April asked students to choose a favorite part of the story and use it as a basis for their writing.
- Writing Standard 10 (writing routinely over different time frames). Although this is only one example, April often has her students complete short writing activities like this. Additionally, she stresses the importance of the writing–reading connection by requiring students to write about literary and informational texts.

April's goal and the goal of the CCSS (NGA & CCSSO, 2010) is to help students produce clear and coherent writing. April believes activities like this further this goal and honor the "out-of-school" literacies many students use today as they practice using traditional English. In this activity, she includes the important components of effective writing instruction: a purpose for writing, choices in how and what to write, a real audience, and a suggested format. Of course there are a variety of other best-practice writing activities that April and teachers like April use to fulfill the CCSS (NGA & CCSSO, 2010) in reading, writing, speaking, listening, and language. You will learn about several more best practices as you continue reading this chapter.

Evidence-Based Best Practices: A Research Synthesis

Writing is a complex interaction of cognitive and physical factors. It is a way to explore thinking and create new knowledge. Writing involves the hand, eye, and both sides of the brain as one makes connections and constructs meaning. It requires knowing the conventions of grammar, spelling, punctuation, and form. It involves small-muscle development and eye–hand coordination to form letters, words, and paragraphs with a pen, pencil, or on a keyboard. It requires having a vocabulary that permits effective self-expression and communication. Writing can be a personal process done solely for oneself or a social process done for and with others.

Writing Theory and Research

Cambourne (1988) suggests that authentic *engagement* accompanied by *immersion* and *demonstration* result in learning. This theory of learning gives us a framework for understanding writing. Students learn to write when they are surrounded with examples and models, given expectations, allowed to make decisions and mistakes, given feedback, and provided with time to practice in realistic ways.

Engagement as well as relevance are basic to Graves's (1983, 1994) theory of the writing process, which includes the recursive steps of *planning, drafting, revising, editing*, and *publishing* for a real audience. The CCSS (NGA & CCSSO, 2010), while focusing on the production of *argumentative, informative*, and *narrative* writing, acknowledge that the writing process is applicable to these types of writing as well (p. 8). This process approach to writing is basic to a writing-workshop format (Fletcher & Portaluppi, 2001) where the teacher sets up the structure and allows students choices in what they write. Atwell's (2002) work with middle-school students also supports the use of writing process in a writing workshop. Other research also indicates that teaching the writing process has a positive effect on quality of writing (Graham & Perrin, 2007).

Oral language is an important contributor to writing because both speaking and writing depend on the same cognitive abilities. Vygotsky (1978) believed that children's early speech is a precursor to inner speech, which results in the ability to think in words. This self-talk is like an inner commentator that develops into a mature writer's voice. Vygotsky theorized that thought and knowledge emerge from oral language that is embedded in social interaction. This co-construction of meaning can support and strengthen students' writing.

Many teachers teach writing before they teach reading. Elbow (2004) and Graves (1983) theorize that since young children can write what they can say, they can then read what they have written more easily than they can read someone else's writing. The process of writing helps children understand written language and prepares them for reading and understanding the writing of others. Additionally, social interaction around a shared experience, part of the language experience approach, can be the basis for writing. When students talk about an experience and that talk is transcribed, they can then read the written story or report. With middle school students, similar substantive discussions or "curricular conversations" focused on content can strengthen their writing as well as their reading, speaking, and thinking abilities (Angelis, 2003). This kind of *demonstration* and *immersion* in talking, writing, and reading as students create meaning together is the *engagement* Cambourne (1988) puts at the heart of all learning.

Grammar, Spelling, and Other Conventions

Research shows grammar instruction to have little positive effect on writing. Studies over time indicate that teaching formal grammar to students has "a negligible or even harmful effect on improving students' writing" (Routman, 1996, p. 119). In fact, "a heavy emphasis on mechanics and usage results in significant losses in overall quality" (Hillocks, 1987, p. 74). Thus, the National Council of Teachers of English (NCTE) published a resolution urging teachers to discard traditional school grammar instruction (Brozo, 2003). However, an approach called "sentence combining" is a useful alternative to teaching formal grammar. "Sentence combining provides mindful practice in manipulating and rewriting basic phrases or clauses into more varied and syntactically mature forms" (Saddler, 2013, p. 240). The CCSS (NGA & CCSSO, 2010) identify sentence construction and sentence combining as directly related to clear and coherent writing.

As well, mandated tests often require identifying and correcting errors, which is another practice to teach students rather than formal grammar. Alerting students to the pattern of errors in their writing is one way to do this. Finding and correcting errors gives students a window into learning about standard grammar and conventions.

Research suggests a strong relationship between spelling and writing (Cunningham & Cunningham, 2010). Good writing depends on the automatic use of spelling skills. When students struggle with spelling, they use up valuable cognitive resources they might otherwise use for other aspects of writing (Singer & Bashir, 2004). Students who try to use standard spelling but do not possess this skill often labor over every word and use words they can readily spell rather than words that are more difficult. Thus, accurate and automatic spelling can improve fluency (McCutcheon, 2006) and have a positive effect on the quality and length of a written piece as well as a writer's confidence.

While spelling and handwriting seem to "occupy an ever-smaller portion of the elementary school curriculum," automatic knowledge of spelling and other conventions is important (Schlagal, 2013, p. 257). In fact, Moats (2005–2006) believes that writing, even more than reading, depends on being able to automatically use "basic skills such as handwriting, spelling, grammar, and punctuation so that the writer can focus on topic, organization, word choice, and audience" (p. 12). This knowledge is important whether students write with pencil and paper or use a computer keyboard. While grammar checkers may find grammar problems and spell checkers may correct misspellings of commonly used words, these devices do not catch all errors, and students still need knowledge of standard grammar and spelling.

Berninger and Winn (2006) report that students produce better writing when they use a word processor, since it corrects some spelling and grammar. Baker (2000) found that word processors eased the difficulties many young children have with fine motor control and helped them better understand revision. Baker also found that, through student interaction with the Internet and the digital world, their writing abilities improved. Students found support for their writing efforts, increased their awareness of audience, and gained useful feedback.

Vocabulary is also an important contributor to good writing and one of the focus areas of the CCSS (NGA & CCSSO, 2010). Word knowledge and using appropriate language at all levels is key to clear and coherent writing. Thus, vocabulary instruction impacts how well students write. Zarry (1999) found that students who received vocabulary instruction that engaged them in playful activities were able to use the words they learned more often in writing and wrote narratives of a higher quality than students who did not receive such instruction.

Special Populations

On the National Assessment of Educational Progress (NAEP; 2011) writing tests given in eighth and 12th grades (no tests were given to fourth graders), approximately 80% of students performed at or above the "basic" level, 27% scored at or above the "proficient" level, and 3% scored at the "advanced" level. Gender made a difference in scores and girls outperformed boys in persuasive, informative, and narrative writing. But many students from diverse cultural and language backgrounds do not always do well on the NAEP and other standardized tests. These English learners need additional time and instruction in order to meet the new writing standards (Olson, Scarcella, & Matuchniak, 2013). Asian, black, Hispanic, Native American, and other ethnic groups often come from urban schools in poor communities that lack the resources of more affluent schools. In an analysis of 50 studies of K–12 writing with racial or ethnic minorities, Ball (2006) found that balance between process and product writing that reflects cultural understandings and influences on writing helped these students meet the demands of school and work.

Studies of students with learning disabilities indicate these students possess limited metacognitive awareness of the knowledge, skills, and strategies necessary to be good writers (Troia, 2006). So, writing instruction that incorporates self-monitoring, goal setting, and self-evaluation is important for these students. Troia reports that these students may skip the planning stage, have problems generating and transcribing ideas, and often do not revise. He notes that students with learning disabilities need more time provided for writing, and they need intensive, individualized, and explicit instruction in self-regulation skills and writing strategies.

This brief discussion examines some of the theory and research evidence that supports writing instruction. In the next section, the classroom practices of several K–8 teachers provide examples of some best practices for sound writing instruction.

Best Practices in Action

What other effective writing practices does April follow, besides the text messaging and translation activity described earlier? April uses writing workshop as often as she can even though time pressures to cover required curriculum and prepare students for the state tests make it difficult. She tries to use writing workshop at least three times a week. She finds it difficult, though, because she has varied ability levels in her class of 28 students and she rarely has classroom support from the reading team or other professionals.

April explains writing workshop this way:

> "At the beginning of the school year I provide each student with a Writer's Workshop Notebook. Then we brainstorm a list of ideas that students can write about. They put this list in their notebook and they can add to it during the year. Each student chooses a topic to write about and they use the writing process to draft, revise, proofread, and edit their piece. Students keep all their work in writing folders." She teaches mini-lessons about the writing process when she sees a pattern in students' work. "In lessons at the beginning of the year, we focus on capitalization, punctuation, and paragraphing. As the year continues, I teach mini-lessons on dialogue, the use of quotation marks, how to revise writing, poetry, and past, present, and future tenses. When I teach a mini-lesson, I expect students to reflect the skill we worked on in that lesson in their writing."

April often uses the Smartboard for these lessons. She says students are glued to lessons on the Smartboard because they are physically engaged in the lesson.

April uses peer-partners so students can give each other feedback that promotes revising. She says "Sometimes I pair my 'high-fliers' with less capable students and have them conference with each other. I find that students often work better with each other than I think they will. Students listen when a peer tells them how to make their work better. When they question each other about clarity, I see good revising. I also require students to reread their work before they conference with me because I want them to find their own spelling and punctuation mistakes. Just taking the time to reread, proofread, and edit makes their work better. I try to conference with each student as they finish a writing piece so they can publish their work." Thus, April relies on oral language, writing process, and social interaction to help develop good writers.

April has three computers in her classroom and she has "fancy writing paper" for students to use for their finished work. She says some students use the computer for the final copy and others handwrite the final copy. Students draw their own illustrations or use clip art. They read their final pieces orally to the class, which is hugely popular. We post final pieces on our hall bulletin board or on a classroom bulletin board for others to read.

Overall, most students enjoy writing about a topic of their choice and follow through to the publishing stage. Most students' writing abilities improve during the year, which also contributes to doing better on the writing portion of our mandated state tests. There are always a few students who continue to struggle with generating ideas and drafting. But for the most part, the choices and audience that are a part of writer's workshop help motivate most of my students to produce great writing.

While testing still drives teaching in many classrooms and some teachers dropping writing workshop, there are teachers like April who believe they should help students develop as writers first so achievement on tests is a natural outcome. These teachers use a writing-process approach and direct instruction in skills to develop good writers. They believe that when students can articulate ideas confidently and write in organized, fluent, and clear ways, they will do well on mandated writing tests.

Tracy, a curriculum coordinator, says

"I am opposed to mandated tests since I see the stress they place on teachers and students, and the imbalance in classrooms between 'on-demand' writing and planned, thoughtful writing. The tests require the use of text-based details with little opportunity for independent thinking or use of prior knowledge. They send students mixed messages about what reading and writing are *really* all about."

Tracy works with teachers like April and others who want to make writing interesting and authentic as they teach the skills students need to do well on tests. Many of these teachers want to remain loyal to a writing-process approach because they believe it develops thoughtful and effective writers. Yet, they must also prepare students for "on-demand" writing tasks that include little opportunity for planning and revising. These teachers regularly have students complete "parallel tasks" that mirror the kinds of writing on the tests.

The CCSS (NGA & CCSSO, 2010), mandated assessments, and accountability issues cause some teachers to reduce time for writing, teach writing artificially, and fragment the curriculum. In some classrooms, the focus may be away from the writing process and toward writing skills and the written product. While proponents of a process approach to writing instruction are sometimes criticized for overlooking direct instruction, conventions, and legibility, a skills-product approach is sometimes criticized for its teacher-centeredness and tendency to overlook student motivation, purpose, and voice. However, good writers need *simultaneous* opportunities to engage in the process and to learn the skills of writing. Casey and Hemenway (2001), in a 10-year study of students from third grade to high school graduation, found that a balance between structure and freedom results in "more dynamic writers excited about their abilities" (p. 68). Their study suggests that providing instruction that is intentional, socially interactive, and authentic can build a bridge between structure and freedom that supports good writing.

The following discussion explores three areas to include in a best-practices writing program; *a supportive environment, intentional writing instruction*, and *writing assessment*.

A Supportive Environment

A supportive environment for writing that includes individual, physical, and social aspects is critical to best-practices instruction. A teacher's positive attitude and commitment are basic. For example, when teachers decide to adopt improved student writing as a schoolwide goal, the focus of their professional development can be on writing. Teachers can form study groups, discuss students' writing, examine writing tests, and analyze test results to see what their students do and don't do. Teachers can develop writing curriculum, create a vision of exemplary student performance, and specify criteria for it. Examining present practices with questions like these is a place to begin to teach writing well:

- What choices do my students have in their writing?
- How much and what kind of writing do they do daily?

- Who do my students write for besides me? What other audiences do they have?
- Who gives students feedback on their writing?
- Are they writing in a variety of formats in all content areas?
- How do I use the writing process? What kind of direct instruction do I provide?
- What opportunities do I provide students to use word processors and e-mail?

Creating a supportive environment for writing includes making the classroom rich with words for students to use when they write. In the following classrooms, two teachers recognize the value of environmental print for enhancing reading and writing. In Kelly's first grade, she adds several words to the "word wall" every week so students can use them in their writing. The class composes a daily Morning Message as they convert spoken language to writing and learn to spell, form letters, and use punctuation. These are printed on 5 × 8 labels that identify *wastebasket, pencil sharpener*, and other classroom objects. Kelly has a writing corner with baskets of pencils, felt-tip markers, calligraphy pens, colored pencils, ballpoint pens, and paper. In Sean's sixth-grade classroom, he also has word walls for science and social studies terms that are especially helpful for the five English-language learners in the class. Sean says Lev, who is newly from Russia, and a buddy use the word walls each day as Lev learns English (and his buddy learns some Russian). In both classrooms, each student has a dictionary and thesaurus.

The CCSS (NGA & CCSSO, 2010) state that "reading widely and deeply from among a broad range of high-quality, increasingly challenging literary and informational texts" builds a foundation for school success (p. 10). Thus, having a large classroom library of books of varied reading levels and genres, building in silent reading time, reading orally to students, and engaging in discussions and shared reading are important components of a supportive environment. Reading mentor texts provide students with written models they can emulate in their own writing (Dorfman & Cappelli, 2007; Duke, Caughlan, Juzwik, & Martin, 2012). Since reading plays a central role in students' writing, teachers often use a reading workshop approach with mentor texts to promote better writing.

Many classrooms are wired for Internet access, and students use notebooks or computers regularly to locate information and plan, draft, revise, and publish their stories, poems, and reports using software such as Inspiration and Publisher. In Sean's classroom, his sixth graders also use Blackboard, an online classroom program where he has students discuss books they are reading and respond to each other's postings. His struggling writers often use Dragon Naturally Speaking, a speech-to-print software program that does not require handwriting or keyboarding.

Calkins (1994) suggests writing workshop should include mini-lessons, time for writing, peer conferring and/or response groups, share sessions, and publication celebrations. Teachers who use writing workshop (Atwell, 2002; Fletcher & Portaluppi, 2001) include a brief lesson on a demonstrated need for a group of students. Kelly and Sean set aside blocks of time when students write on topics of their choice during writing workshop. They also spend time sharing and discussing a well-written piece of literature to help students improve their writing and learn to respond to a piece of work. They have students write in science, math, and social studies so students are writing to learn as they learn to write.

Encouraging buddy reading, discussion, and collaborative writing can be helpful for students who have ideas to contribute but do not yet have the language skills, motivation, or confidence to write without this stimulation. Both students who are learning English and those who struggle are supported and encouraged to develop their abilities when they work in pairs with students who possess stronger skills. Kelly and Sean share models with their students of the kinds of writing they expect them to do. They compose reports, poems, and other written forms with the class as a whole so that students have opportunities to learn from one another as they see a piece develop.

Establishing a writing community in the classroom and school is also critical to building a social context and improving student writing. Calling students "authors" and "writers" can have a positive effect on how students view themselves, and whether or not and how they write. Posting the writing of every student in the class validates them as writers as well. Inviting authors and illustrators of children's books to share their work with other students can nudge even the most reluctant writer to write. The entire school can study the work of an author before a visit so students know the author's style and content and can interact in substantive ways with him or her. A visit from an author like Jerry Pallotta (*www. alphabetman.com*), who talks about his writing and shares the many alphabet books he has written, can spark students of all ages to read his work and write like him.

Intentional Writing Instruction

Writers need direct intentional instruction in strategies for becoming better writers as well as time to write (Graham & Harris, 2013). Students need to learn how to effectively use ideas, organization, voice, word choice, fluency, conventions, and presentation (Culham, 2003). They need opportunities for enough instruction, guidance, and practice to allow them to become accomplished. Good writing teachers balance writing process and product as they encourage clear and coherent writing that uses standard English.

NCTE promotes teaching standard conventions and correctness by having students edit their own writing (Brozo, 2003). Other alternatives to isolated grammar instruction include teaching grammar during writing instruction, having grammar debates, teaching students to use style manuals, creating assignments that require writing for real audiences, and studying grammar controversies (Dunn & Lindblom, 2003). When teachers engage students in the writing process, teach and discuss word usage, and teach students to construct sentences using their own work, students can learn to use grammar and improve their writing.

Many teachers incorporate direct instruction in composing and the conventions of grammar, spelling, form, and handwriting into writing workshop (Peterson, 2000). For example, teaching terms like *purpose, audience, form, voice, noun, verb,* and *adjective* gives students a common vocabulary for discussing and improving their writing. Talking about sentence construction, grammar, and usage makes sense to students when they are writing for a real audience. Many teachers use "fix-the-error exercises" to teach specific grammar skills with examples from real literature that students are familiar with (Kane, 1997). Like April, Kelly, and Sean, they teach mini-lessons using their own writing and volunteers' writing to show how quotation marks, commas, and periods should be used.

Carol, a seventh-grade teacher who has used writing workshop for several years, begins with a lesson on one aspect of writing that she knows several students need help with, such as organization, run-on sentences, adjectives, verbs, or punctuation. Recently, Carol taught a mini-lesson on common and proper nouns after noticing the overuse of pronouns in several of her students' narrative stories. Part of the lesson included revising the work of a draft volunteered by a student. On another day she reviewed with the class the function and placement of topic sentences in expository writing and a five-paragraph report (a one-paragraph introduction, three-paragraph body, and one-paragraph conclusion).

Often in a mini-lesson, teachers share a piece of writing as a model so students know what good writing looks and sounds like (Fletcher & Portaluppi, 2007). Reading and listening to literature also helps students think like writers and write with an audience in mind. Good narrative and expository writing lets students see how an author holds the reader's attention and uses conventions. Then students can begin to use this knowledge in their own writing. For example, one third grader had read several of R. L. Stine's books in which "THE END" is used in the final sentence, as in "It doesn't really matter in . . . THE END." The student borrowed this technique and concluded his nonfiction report with "Volcanoes are very cool but when they erupt it's . . . THE END."

To extend her students' writing beyond topics they choose themselves, Carol uses a "genre study" (Calkins, 1994; Duke et al., 2012), where students immerse themselves in a particular kind of literature and then write in this form. For example, during recent writing workshops with a group of struggling writers and in conjunction with a science unit on climate change, Carol's students read nonfiction books about the environment, gathered information from a CD-ROM encyclopedia, took an electronic field trip to a weather station, and then created their own informative reports. She compiled these reports into a book that her students shared with a third-grade class. Carol encourages students to coauthor at least one story or report because she believes collaboration is a catalyst for learning.

Moss (2005) shows how even first and second graders can immerse themselves in a genre, such as informational text for example, and learn to write in that format. Read (2005) found that instructional practices in primary grades underestimate the ability of these students. She says, "Given appropriate instruction in the skills of writing and a topic that they've chosen and find interesting, young students are fully capable of dealing with the complex problems that occur when reading and writing informational texts" (p. 44).

Teachers of writing need to be writers themselves. Tracy, the curriculum coordinator quoted earlier, keeps a personal journal, uses e-mail, and writes curriculum, lesson plans, and grant proposals. She believes that writing regularly is a powerful strategy for learning. She says, "Writing is a process of constructing meaning, and I never realize what I know until I start writing. I come up with ideas I didn't have before I begin writing. For this reason, I believe every teacher should write and writing should be part of every content area."

When students write in a variety of forms in the content areas to explain or share information, they construct new meaning and demonstrate their science and social studies knowledge too. Expository writing across the curriculum can take many forms. In first grade, Kelly linked math, social studies, and language arts in a unit called "Quilt Connections." After students had read and heard stories about quilts, researched other cultures' quilts in the library and on the Internet, visited a museum exhibit, and learned about shapes, equal parts, and fractions, a final activity involved creating a quilt. The finished quilt, made of special fabrics and designs contributed by students, went home each day with a different student along with a journal. Students and parents wrote about the quilt in the journal, giving parents an opportunity for involvement in their child's classroom learning.

Mark had his third-grade students write daily "on-demand" responses to questions he posed during a study of the Cheyenne, Iroquois, Navaho, Sioux, and Seminole tribes. In this on-demand writing, students have only a short time to think, perhaps list a few ideas, and then write. Mark does not grade this work, but he reads it and responds and/or has students read and respond to one another's entries. Mark's students, like Sean's sixth graders, also engage in writing an occasional "parallel task" that mirrors the kind of writing task found on the state tests. For example, at the conclusion of the study of Native Americans, Mark's students read a poem and a short nonfiction article about Native American reservations, compared the information offered in each, and wrote an essay from the perspective of a member of one of the tribes they studied. Students compared and contrasted information from both sources and presented their finished pieces to the class.

Writing to explain is part of many mandated math tests. Colleen's eighth-grade students use journals as a way to explain math concepts. This is a way to explore students' thinking, and it is an example of on-demand writing. Colleen's students also write to her in their journals to explain what they believe they do well, what they don't understand, and, for extra credit, how to correct test items they missed. This kind of expository writing exposes students' reasoning so that Colleen can reteach a concept if needed. For Colleen, writing is an assessment tool that helps to measure math learning and misconceptions.

Because graphic organizers are visual representations of information that show relationships and contain key vocabulary, they make excellent planning tools for writing (Bromley, 2006; Irwin-DeVitis, Bromley, & Modlo, 1999). They also appear on many mandated tests, thus making it important that even young students learn to use them. For students learning English or those with learning disabilities in literacy, graphic organizers are particularly useful because they simplify information, use key words, and help organize ideas before writing. For another parallel task, Mark had his students use Venn diagrams and t-charts to compare and contrast a nonfiction selection and poem before writing.

Graphic organizers also support inquiry. For example, in a study of Mexico, Rebecca's second-grade students gathered information from several sources on data charts before they wrote about what they learned. As part of a sixth-grade unit on immigration, Michele's students took the perspective of a person in the story or focused on relationships among characters in *Esperanza Rising* by Pam Munoz Ryan (2000). Before writing, students used a character map and character relationship map to record evidence and the page numbers where it appeared.

Central to good writing instruction is giving students choices in topics, their own and teacher-provided, because choice in both topic and format builds interest and commitment to writing. For example, to conclude a study of pollution and the environment, Sean and his class identified several writing options. Then students signed up in groups of four for the project they wanted to complete. One group wrote and performed a play, a second group wrote an article for the local newspaper accompanied by digital pictures, two groups created PowerPoint presentations, and another group updated entries on the Internet encyclopedia Wikipedia about the effects of river pollution on local bird life.

Research in K–6 classrooms indicates that teachers report an increase in motivation to write when their work is published on the Internet (Karchmer, 2001). In addition to skills in viewing and analyzing, when students do research on the Internet and write for the Web, they build skills in keyboarding, word processing, and navigating with browsers and search engines (Owens, Hester, & Teale, 2002; Wepner & Tao, 2002). Both students and teachers use the Internet, CD-ROM encyclopedias, and primary sources on the Web such as historical documents or secondary sources like museum or observatory websites. Some examples follow for using the computer to motivate struggling students and develop better writers:

- Establish electronic key pal exchanges with students in other states or countries that can be social and/or related to a content area. This cross-cultural literacy is beneficial to everyone.
- Have students (in pairs or triads) use Publisher or another software program to create items for a monthly classroom newsletter. Have them insert clip art and pictures, format the text, and send the newsletter electronically to parents or take hard copies home.
- Use digital storytelling (Sylvester & Greenidge, 2009–2010), the creation and sharing of a multimedia text consisting of still images, and a narrated soundtrack that tells a story. Visit the Center for Digital Storytelling at *www.storycenter.org* for examples, articles, and resources.
- Alert parents to Internet sites like *www.kidpub.com/kidpub* that publish students' book reviews, poems, and short stories.
- Encourage student use of PowerPoint or other presentation software to share their inquiry-driven projects. Visit "Top 9 tips for students- Create classroom presentations worthy of an A" at *http://presentationsoft.about.com/od/classrooms/tp/student_tips.htmto*.
- Explore other technology like the wiki (meaning "quick" in Hawaiian) that requires writing. Wikis are an easily learned, open-source software program that allow all users to access and edit written pages on an ongoing basis.
- Reconnect with a library-media specialist who can help you and your students learn about podcasting (from the acronym for

*p*ersonal-*on*-*d*emand and broad*casting*) (Smythe & Neufeld, 2010). Podcasting lets students create content quickly and easily.

Writing Assessment

Writing instruction has improved dramatically over the last several decades. Much of this improvement is the result of better writing assessments that inform more effective instruction. Of course, not all writing needs formal assessment, but, whether formal or informal, assessment should be ongoing. Students need to regularly assess their own written products because self-assessment encourages students to take responsibility for their own writing progress (Bromley, 2007). Periodically, asking questions like these can help students reflect and set goals for themselves:

- What do I do well as a writer?
- What is one thing I have learned most recently as a writer?
- What do I need to learn to be a better writer?

This self-assessment should be ongoing because students improve as writers when they regularly examine their work with an eye toward making it more organized, fluent, and clear.

Portfolios, rubrics, and checklists offer opportunities for writing assessment by both students and teachers. Writing folders or portfolios hold a record of student progress and can show a student's growth as a writer. Teachers, students, and parents can examine written work in a folder or portfolio to determine what skills a student possesses and those he or she needs to develop. As well, conversations with parents and assigning grades are more easily accomplished when there is a body of written work from which to make observations.

Rubrics and checklists can also help identify students' strengths and needs (Bromley, 2007). Teams of teachers often develop rubrics and checklists based on the priorities for grading a particular project. Even very young writers need feedback in order to understand their writing strengths and the areas where they need to improve. Just saying "Great job!" or "Need to improve" does not help children know how to be better writers. Young children need feedback on the important aspects of communicating effectively and a basic checklist or rubric can provide this feedback (see Figure 13.1 and 13.2).

More sophisticated rubrics are appropriate for older students. One project sixth-grade teacher Sean uses to develop students' careful reading and to build expository and persuasive writing skills is the "Classic" Inspiration Project (see Figure 13.3). The project introduces the class to books they may not have read yet and integrates reading, writing, and

My Editing Checklist

Title of my work Name Date	Yes	No
1. Did I reread my writing and revise first?		
2. Is my introduction interesting? Does it invite a reader?		
3. Is my writing focused on one idea or topic?		
4. Did I add some words that describe?		
5. Did I delete some unnecessary words?		
6. Did I use complete sentences?		
7. Do my sentences begin with capital letters?		
8. Did I check my spelling and make corrections?		
9. Did I check for periods and commas?		
10. Did I indent each paragraph?		
11. Does my conclusion connect to my introduction?		
12. Does my title fit what I wrote about?		

FIGURE 13.1. An editing checklist for young children helps them self-evaluate.

technology. In this essay students consider whether or not they believe a book is a "classic" (one that reflects quality, a universal theme, and the potential for longevity). Sean wants students to develop arguments based on evidence and share their arguments with the class. Students read a book and either defend it or are critical about it. In their essays, students use Inspiration software and are graded with the rubric in Figure 13.3. They must produce a pleasing and readable visual layout with appropriate computer graphics, and present the finished essays to the class. Sean allocates points for specific components, spelling, layout, and graphics, for a total of 100 points. He often has students give themselves a grade using this rubric. Sean also identifies a grade and conferences with students to determine whether and how they agree with his assessment, which he believes helps improve their writing and accuracy in self-assessment.

When his sixth graders create checklists and rubrics with him "they seem to understand the assignment better and have confidence that they can achieve a higher grade when they have a say in rubric development."

Name _____   Date _____

Rubric for Writing

	Beginning 1	Developing 2	Satisfactory 3	Excellent 4	Points
Content	Random ideas and/or information	A few ideas, some information	Enough ideas/ information to communicate meaning	Communicates meaning clearly and thoroughly	
Order	Ideas not in order	A few ideas in order	Most ideas flow in order from main topic	Ideas flow from main topic to details	
Sentences	Run-ons and fragments	A few complete and some fragments	Mostly complete sentences	Uses complete sentences	
Spelling	Many spelling errors	Some spelling errors	Few spelling errors	No spelling errors	
Punctuation	No punctuation (? , . !)	Some punctuation used correctly	Punctuation is mostly correct	Punctuation used correctly	
Capitals	Uses uppercase letters randomly	Uses some uppercase letters randomly	Begins sentences with uppercase letters	Uses uppercase letters to start names and sentences	
Handwriting	Hard to read, letters formed inconsistently, no spacing	Somewhat legible with some well-formed letters	Mostly legible with spacing and letter forms	Legible, neat, well-formed and spaced letters	
					Total points

FIGURE 13.2. A basic rubric provides feedback to young children on the aspects of good writing.

"Classic" Inspiration Project Rubric

Name _____ Date _____ Period _____

Book Title _____

Author _____

	4	3	2	1
All three components included	• 2 reasons book is a *classic* with examples • 2 exciting or engaging parts • Theme and why it is universal (30 pts.)	3–4 components explained accurately (25 pts.)	1–2 components explained accurately (20 pts.)	1 component explained accurately (10 pts.)
Spelling	All spelling accurate (20 pts.)	All but 1–3 words spelled accurately (17 pts.)	All but 4–5 words spelled accurately (12 pt.)	All but 5 or more words spelled accurately (15 pts.)
Layout	• Flows in a way that is organized and easy to understand • Shows creativity • Graphics do not interfere with information (30 pts.)	• Layout is mostly understandable • Organization is present, but little creativity • Some graphics get in way of info (25 pts.)	• Layout is partly understandable • Weak organization • Little creativity • Graphics interfere with info (20 pts.)	• Layout is confusing • Lacks organization • Graphics interfere with info (15 pts.)
Graphics	• Pictures and graphics used are appropriate • They aid creativity (20 pts.)	• Most pictures and graphics used are appropriate (17 pts.)	• Some pictures and graphics are appropriate (12 pts.)	• Pictures and graphics are not appropriate • Pictures and graphics hinder presentation of info (8 pts.)

Comments:

FIGURE 13.3. This rubric combines criteria for writing using digital and standard English.

First, he explains the project or writing piece and shares an example. He has students brainstorm characteristics or criteria for an excellent paper. Then they group the characteristics into categories and rate them for importance. Lastly, Sean creates a draft, shares it on the Smartboard, and the class edits it as needed and votes to accept it. When students create criteria for a written piece, such as the Descriptive Writing Checklist in Figure 13.4, Sean feels it has a dramatic effect on the final product. When students have finished writing and revising, they check off the presence of each component and then have a peer read the piece and do the same. Based on this feedback, students revise before they hand the paper to Sean. He says, "You can't possibly do this for every checklist or rubric. But once the process is complete, you can use some of the criteria for other projects, as I did to create the rubric for this essay" (see Figure 13.5).

Knowing the key components of a good piece of writing provides students with goals for writing and the characteristics of a good report, essay, letter, PowerPoint presentation, play, or poem, for example, before they write. It also gives the teacher and students an objective way to assess the finished product after writing. Rubrics show teachers what to reteach, and rubrics can help parents understand a student's grade. Of course, teachers don't use them for every piece of writing, but they can improve the quality of writing on key assignments and final projects. Templates found at these websites contain existing criteria that can be used as is or edited:

- Rubistar (*www.rubistar.4teachers.org*)
- Schrock Guide for Educators (*www.school.discovery.com/schrock-guide/assess.html*)

Peers can also assess one another's written work and provide feedback (see Figure 13.3). Besides conferencing with students one-on-one, many teachers use peer conferences to give students real and immediate audience feedback on their work. Often, when a student reads his or her work to a peer or hears it read to him or her, the student discovers what to revise. Kelly uses writing groups of two to three students and has students read each other's work and give feedback on drafts. She uses *TAG* (*Tell, Ask, Give*), in which peers *tell* the writer one thing they like about a piece, *ask* a question about something they don't understand, and *give* a piece of advice. One student's handwriting improved dramatically when a peer wrote "You should write neater so I can read it!" When Carol's third graders work in pairs or small groups to give each other feedback, she uses a different version of *TAG*. She uses the language of *PQS* (*Praise, Question, Suggest*). To help frame constructive feedback, both teachers model

Descriptive Writing Checklist

Name _____ Date _____ Period _____

Title of Essay _____

My Editing Peer _____

Directions: Use this checklist as you work on your essay. Your essay will be scored according to the rubric on the attached sheet.

	Self	Peer
Literary Style		
Includes title	_____	_____
Varies sentence structure and length	_____	_____
Includes at least 2 similes	_____	_____
Includes at least 1 metaphor	_____	_____
Uses adjectives, adverbs, and vivid verbs	_____	_____
Refers to a minimum of 3 senses	_____	_____
Organization		
Introductory paragraph has a clear topic	_____	_____
Introductory paragraph grabs the reader's attention	_____	_____
All paragraphs include a main idea and supporting details	_____	_____
A clear and logical order of information is evident	_____	_____
Details let the reader develop a clear mental picture	_____	_____
Concluding paragraph is a summary and restates the central idea	_____	_____
Mechanics		
Uses capital letters correctly	_____	_____
Uses all punctuation correctly	_____	_____
Essay is free of spelling errors	_____	_____
Essay is free of run-on sentences and fragments	_____	_____

FIGURE 13.4. When students help define the criteria it alerts them to the components of good writing.

Descriptive Writing Rubric

Name _____ Date _____ Period _____

Title of Essay _____

	4	3	2	1	0
Descriptive components	Unique language that engages the senses—2 similes, 1 metaphor, adverbs, adjectives, and vivid verbs (35 pts.)	Language is often precise and appropriate. Vivid vocabulary present with 1 missing component (29 pts.)	Some language is precise and appropriate. Vivid vocabulary minimal with 2–3 missing components (25 pts.)	Limited use of vivid vocabulary and figurative language with 4 or more missing components (21 pts.)	Lacks descriptive components. Not developed as a descriptive writing piece (0 pts.)
Mechanics	Varied sentence structure. All correct grammar, capitals, punctuation (15 pts.)	Most sentences show variety. Correct grammar, capitals, punctuation except 1–2 errors (13 pts.)	Some sentence variety. Correct grammar, capitals, punctuation except 3–4 errors (11 pts.)	Little sentence variety. Correct grammar, capitals, punctuation except 5 or more errors (9 pts.)	No sentence variety. Incomplete sentences. Grammar and other errors hinder message (0 pts.)
Spelling	All spelling correct (15 pts.)	All but 1 word spelled correctly (13 pts.)	All but 2–3 words spelled correctly (11 pts.)	All but 4 or more words spelled correctly (9 pts.)	Many spelling errors that affect message (0 pts.)
Organization	All paragraphs include topic and conclusion sentences with details. Clear connections and smooth transitions (35 pts.)	Most paragraphs include topic and conclusion sentences and details. Some unclear connections and transitions (29 pts.)	Some paragraphs include topic and conclusion sentences and details. Weak organization and sequence of ideas (25 pts.)	Some organization. Transitions and connections not present or weak (21 pts.)	Organization, connections, and transitions not evident (0 pts.)

Comments:

FIGURE 13.5. A rubric that reflects student-created criteria provides feedback on the written product.

responses first by thinking aloud about a draft and then ask students to respond to the draft with three statements.

Conferencing with students during writing workshop using a checklist is a good way to assess and improve writing (see Figure 13.6). April, the fourth-grade teacher who was introduced at the beginning of this chapter, makes conferences a priority. She has a sign-up sheet for conferences, and she tries to see five students for a few minutes every day. To make the most of a conference, April has students come with a question they have about their writing. For example, "This sentence doesn't sound right to me. What do you think?" or "Is my introduction strong enough?" Requiring students to reflect on their own work and wonder about some aspect of it shifts responsibility for improved writing to the student. But April also asks pointed questions to prompt each student to rethink and revise his or her writing as well.

Teachers can also assess student writing with tools like the "The Word Writing CAFÉ" (Leal, 2006), which is a "*C*omplexity, *A*ccuracy, and *F*luency *E*valuation." This group-administered assessment is an inventory of words students know how to write. It does not measure sentence or paragraph creation but rather the ability to write and spell words correctly. It can be used at the beginning, middle, and end of the year to assess growth in the number and type of words students can write how this changes over time. The CAFÉ can also show interests, strengths, and weaknesses (Bromley, Vandenberg, & White, 2007). While the CAFÉ does not measure writing in context, it does show the handwriting, spelling, and number and complexity of vocabulary words students can write.

Reflections and Future Directions

The CCSS (NGA & CCSSO, 2010) provide K–12 teachers with standards for infusing digital skills into the curriculum at every grade level. Thus, *blended learning* that mixes technology and the digital world with traditional reading and writing practices is fast becoming accepted in many classrooms. Many teachers understand the role computers and the Internet increasingly play in writing that occurs out of school and at work. Although the "new" literacies of e-mail, text messaging, and Twitter do not always conform to standard grammar, spelling, or punctuation, students still need to possess basic skills in the conventions of standard English in order to be successful in many aspects of the adult world. Accountability, mandates, and tests will undoubtedly continue to affect what and how writing is taught. Thus, teachers need to be flexible, open to collaboration with others, and creative in blending "out-of-school" literacies with in-school writing. Research is needed that examines technology, writing,

Conference Checklist

NAME	M	T	W	Th	F	M	T	W	Th	F	Comments

Minilessons: _____

_____

_____

_____

_____

✓ Good conference   ☺ Shared today   ☹ Not working

— Weak conference   ★ Publishing conference   **T** Helped find topic

⌇ Not sure   **P** Published today

FIGURE 13.6. A conference checklist can help keep track of individual and class progress in writing.

and best-practices instruction for increasingly diverse classrooms. We need to understand better what sound instruction should look like for students who differ in cultural, ethnic, language, learning backgrounds, and gender.

Concluding Comments

The goal of a best-practices writing program ought to be to develop writers who enjoy and learn from writing as they write clearly and coherently in a range of forms for a variety of purposes and audiences. Vygotsky's (1978) ideas about *thought, knowledge,* and *social interaction,* and Cambourne's (1988) model of *engagement,* through *immersion* and *demonstration,* provide a foundation for this kind of program, as do the CCSS (NGA & CCSSO, 2010) and the research briefly presented here. Establishing a supportive classroom for writing, providing intentional instruction, and regularly assessing writing can help student writers become fluent, competent, and independent.

ENGAGEMENT ACTIVITIES

1. April believes that the writing activity described at the beginning of this chapter for her fourth-grade students meets the CCSS (NGA & CCSSO, 2010). Do you agree? Why or why not?

2. Visit *www.readingonline.org* and bookmark this electronic journal of the International Reading Association for future reading. Read a recent article on the teaching of writing. How does it connect (or not connect) to what you just read in this chapter?

3. Look at the CCSS (NGA & CCSSO, 2010) for writing for first-grade students. How would you support them to "use a variety of digital tools to produce and publish writing, including collaboration with peers"? Remember the importance of purpose, audience, and choice.

REFERENCES

Angelis, J. (2003). Conversation in the middle school classroom: Developing reading, writing, and other language abilities. *Middle School Journal, 34*(3), 57–61.
Atwell, N. (2002). *Lessons that change writers.* Portsmouth, NH: Boynton Cook.
Baker, E. A. (2000). Instructional approaches used to integrate literacy and

technology. *Reading Online, 4*(1). Retrieved from *www.readingonline.org/articles/art_index.asp?HREF=baker/index.html.*

Ball, A. F. (2006). Teaching writing in culturally diverse classrooms. In C. A. MacArthur, S. Graham, & J. Fitzgerald (Eds.), *Handbook of writing research* (pp. 293–310). New York: Guilford Press.

Berringer, V. W., & Winn, W. D. (2006). Implications of achievement in brain research and technology for writing development, writing instruction, and educational evolution. In C. MacArthur, S. Graham, & G. Fitzgerald (Eds.), *Handbook of writing research* (pp. 96–114). New York: Guilford Press.

Bromley, K. (2007). Assessing student writing. In J. Paratore & R. L. McCormack (Eds.), *Classroom literacy assessment: Making sense of what students know and do* (pp. 210–226). New York: Guilford Press.

Bromley, K., Vandenberg, A., & White, J. (2007). What can we learn from the word writing CAFE? *The Reading Teacher, 61*(4), 284–295.

Bromley, K. (2006). From drawing to digital creations: Graphic organizers in the classroom. In D. S. Strickland & N. Roser (Eds.), *Handbook on teaching literacy through the communicative and visual arts* (Vol. 2, pp. 349–354). Mahwah, NJ: Erlbaum.

Brozo, W. (2003). Literary license. *Voices from the Middle, 10*(3), 43–45.

Calkins, L. (1994). *The art of teaching writing.* Portsmouth, NH: Heinemann.

Cambourne, B. (1988). *The whole story: Natural learning and the acquisition of literacy in the classroom.* Auckland, New Zealand: Scholastic.

Casey, M., & Hemenway, S. (2001). Structure and freedom: Achieving a balanced writing curriculum. *English Journal, 90*(6), 68–75.

Culham, R. (2003). *6 + 1 traits of writing: The complete guide: Grades 3 and up.* New York: Scholastic.

Cunningham, P. M., & Cunningham, J. W. (2010). *What really matters in writing: Research-based practices across the elementary curriculum.* Boston: Allyn & Bacon.

DiCamillo, K. (2000). *Because of Winn-Dixie.* Cambridge, MA: Candlewick Press.

Dorfman, L. R., & Cappelli, R. (2007). *Mentor texts: Teaching writing through children's literature, K–6.* Portland, ME: Stenhouse.

Duke, N. K., Caughlan, S., Juzwik, M. M., & Martin, N. (2012). *Reading and writing genre with purpose in K–8 classrooms.* Portsmouth, NH: Heinemann.

Dunn, P. A., & Lindblom, K. (2003). Why revitalize grammar? *English Journal, 92*(3), 43–50.

Elbow, P. (2004). Write first! *Educational Leadership, 62*(2), 8–13.

Fletcher, R., & Portaluppi, J. (2001). *Writing workshop: The essential guide.* Portsmouth, NH: Heinemann.

Fletcher, R., & Portaluppi, J. (2007). *Craft lessons: Teaching writing K–8* (2nd ed.). Portland, ME: Stenhouse.

Graham, S., & Harris, K. R. (2013). Designing an effective writing program. In S. Graham, C. A. MacArthur, & J. Fitzgerald (Eds.), *Best practices in writing instruction* (pp. 3–25). New York: Guilford Press.

Graham, S., & Perrin, D. (2007). *Writing next: Effective strategies to improve writing of adolescents in middle and high schools.* New York: Carnegie Corporation.

Graves, D. (1983). *Writing: Teachers and children at work*. Portsmouth, NH: Heinemann.

Graves, D. (1994). *A fresh look at writing*. Portsmouth, NH: Heinemann.

Hillocks, G. (1987). Synthesis of research in teaching writing. *Educational Leadership, 11*, 71–82.

Irwin-DeVitis, L., Bromley, K., & Modlo, M. (1999). *50 graphic organizers for reading, writing and more*. New York: Scholastic.

Kane, S. (1997). Favorite sentences: Grammar in action. *The Reading Teacher, 51*(1), 70–72.

Karchmer, R. A. (2001). The journey ahead: Thirteen teachers report how the Internet influences literacy and literacy instruction in their K–12 classrooms. *Reading Research Quarterly, 36*(4), 442–480.

Leal, D. J. (2006). The word writing CAFÉ: Assessing student writing for complexity, accuracy and fluency. *The Reading Teacher, 59*(4), 340–350.

McCutcheon, D. (2006). Cognitive factors in the development of children's writing. In C. A. MacArthur, S. Graham, & J. Fitzgerald (Eds.), *Handbook of writing research* (pp. 115–130). New York: Guilford Press.

Moats, L. C. (2005–2006). How spelling supports reading: And why it is more regular and predictable than you may think. *American Educator*, pp. 12–22, 42–43.

Moss, B. (2005). Making a case and a place for effective content area literacy instruction in the elementary grades. *The Reading Teacher 59*(1), 46–55.

My Editing Checklist. (2001). New York: Scholastic.

National Assessment of Educational Progress. (2011). The Nation's Report Card: Writing. Retrieved from *http://nationsreportcard.gov/writing_2011/summary.aspx*.

National Governors Association & Council of Chief State Security Officers. (2010). Common Core State Standards. Retrieved from *www.corestandards.org*.

Olson, C. B., Scarcella, R., & Matuchniak, T. (2013). Best practices in teaching writing to English learners: Reducing constraints to facilitate writing development. In S. Graham, C. A. MacArthur, & J. Fitzgerald (Eds.), *Best practices in writing instruction* (pp. 381–402). New York: Guilford Press.

Owens, R. F., Hester, J. L., & Teale, W. H. (2002). Where do you want to go today?: Inquiry-based learning and technology integration. *The Reading Teacher, 55*(7), 616–641.

Peterson, S. (2000). Yes, we do teach writing conventions! (Though the methods may be unconventional). *Ohio Reading Teacher, 34*(1), 38–44.

Real, S. (2005). First and second graders writing informational text. *The Reading Teacher, 59*(1), 36–44.

Routman, R. (1996). *Literacy at the crossroads: Crucial talk about reading, writing and other teaching dilemmas*. Portsmouth, NH: Heinemann.

Rubric for Writing. (2000). *The reading teacher's book of lists* (4th ed.). New York: Prentice Hall

Ryan, P. M. (2000). *Esperanza rising*. New York: Scholastic.

Saddler, B. (2013). Best practices in sentence construction skills. In S. Graham, C.

A. MacArthur, & J. Fitzgerald (Eds.), *Best practices in writing instruction* (2nd ed., pp 238–256). New York: Guilford Press.

Schlagal, B. (2013). Best practices in spelling and handwriting. In S. Graham, C. A. MacArthur, & J. Fitzgerald (Eds.), *Best practices in writing instruction* (2nd ed., pp. 257–283). New York: Guilford Press.

Singer, B. D., & Bashir, A. S. (2004). Developmental variations in written composition skills. In C. A. Stone, E. R. Silliman, B. J. Ehrren, & K. Apel (Eds.), *Handbook of language and literacy: Development and disorders* (pp. 559–582). New York: Guilford Press.

Smythe, S., & Neufeld, P. (Eds.), Podcast time: Negotiating digital literacies and communities of learning in a middle years ELL classroom. *Journal of Adolescent and Adult Literacy, 53*(6), 488–496.

Sylvester, R., & Greenidge W. (2009–2010). Digital storytelling: Extending the potential for struggling writers. *The Reading Teacher, 63*(4), 284–295.

Top 9 tips for students—Create classroom presentations worthy of an "A." Retrieved from *http://presentationsoft.about.com/od/classrooms/tp/student_tips.htmto*.

Troia, G. A. (2006). Writing instruction for students with learning disabilities. In C. A. MacArthur, S. Graham, & J. Fitzgerald (Eds.), *Handbook of writing research* (pp. 324–336). New York: Guilford Press.

Vygotsky, L. (1978). *Mind in society*. Cambridge, MA: Harvard University Press.

Wepner, S., & Tao, L. (2002). From master teacher to master novice: Shifting responsibilities in technology-infused classrooms. *The Reading Teacher, 55*(7), 642–661.

Zarry, L. (1999). Vocabulary enrichment in composition. *Education, 120,* 267–271.

CHAPTER 14

Best Practices in Reading Assessment

Working toward a Balanced Approach

Peter Afflerbach
Byeong-Young Cho
Maria Elliker Crassas
Jong-Yun Kim

This chapter will:

- Describe the current state of literacy assessment.
- Examine a series of imbalances that influence the usefulness and contributions of literacy assessment.
- Suggest means for achieving balance and best practices in literacy assessment with the advent of the Common Core State Standards.
- Provide examples of balanced approaches and best practices with literacy assessment.

This chapter focuses on classroom-based reading assessment, which we believe is well suited to enhance teaching and learning in the era of the Common Core State Standards (CCSS). Consideration of best practice in reading assessment must account for the contexts (sometimes contentious contexts) in which teaching and learning take place, and where reading assessments are proposed, mandated, developed, conducted, interpreted, and used. The current context of reading assessment is marked by a series

315

of imbalances. A significant portion of this imbalance is attributable to the attention given to high-stakes testing and a resultant lack of focus on classroom-based reading assessment that might help change the teaching and learning of reading. Correcting these imbalances can provide one basis for superior teaching and learning, while ignoring them may diminish the achievements of teachers and their students. The most pressing challenges to best practice in classroom assessment of reading relate to a lack of balance in:

- The assessment of reading processes and reading products.
- The assessment of reading skills and strategies and the assessment of how students use what they understand from reading.
- The assessment of single text reading with reading from multiple sources including Internet/hypertext.
- The assessment of cognitive and affective aspects of reading.
- Formative reading assessment and summative reading assessment.
- The reading assessment that is done to or for students and reading assessment that is done with and by students.
- The assessment of in-school literacies with out-of-school literacies.
- The demands for teacher and school accountability and professional development opportunities that help teachers develop expertise in reading assessment.

Best practices in reading assessment, grounded in the knowledge and insight informed by research related to the classroom-based assessment of reading for students and teachers, address these challenges. This chapter offers an account of effective reading assessments that reflect our most current, evidence-based understandings of reading, and of assessment.

Evidence-Based Best Practices

The promise to meet these reading assessment challenges emanates from the knowledge we possess about reading (National Assessment Governing Board, 2012; Snow, 2002; Stanovich, 1986) and developing effective reading assessments (Darling-Hammond, 2010; Morsy, Kieffer, & Snow, 2010). Never before have we had such detailed understanding of reading and its development, and never before have we possessed as many potentially valid reading assessment options. We view the advent of the CCSS as an opportunity to reorient reading assessment within classrooms, with clear benefits to teaching and learning.

There are rich, evidence-based conceptualizations of reading and its development. For example, the necessary strategies and skills for accomplished reading are well researched (Pressley & Afflerbach, 1995). Successful reading demands readers' use of prior knowledge (Kintsch, 1988), inferential reasoning (Graesser, Mills, & Zwaan, 1997), and evaluative mindsets (Wiley et al., 2009). This research provides detail that should inform both our instruction and our assessment. We also understand how related factors, including motivation and engagement (Guthrie, Wigfield, & You, 2012), self-efficacy (Schunk & Zimmerman, 2007), metacognition (Veenman, in press), and epistemic beliefs (Braten, Britt, Stromso, & Rouet, 2011) influence students' reading and their reading development. Thus, our ability to describe the nature of reading and what student readers need to succeed is greatly enhanced, as is our means to provide instruction and assessment that fosters student readers' growth.

As our knowledge about reading evolves, so too does our understanding of effective reading assessment. Many forms of reading assessment, informed by research in educational measurement, have the potential to positively influence instruction and learning. Pellegrino, Chudowsky, and Glaser (2001) propose that when we carefully chart the territory of what we will assess, we are then in a position to create the assessment materials and procedures that are sensitive to the nature of students' development. As we have confidence in our full account of the construct of reading and we utilize our knowledge from assessment and psychometrics, we should have confidence in the assessments we design and use. In turn, this should give us confidence in the inferences about student accomplishment we make from assessment results. Designing reading assessment while using the knowledge (the collected wisdom) about the construct of reading allows for accurate and useful inferences from reading assessment information.

Consider an example of how this should work. We know from research that successful developing readers must decode printed text, often relying on phonics early in their reading careers. Part of decoding involves learning to identify pairs of consonants, in isolation and as they appear in words, and knowing the unique sounds that these consonant blends make. Allowing for dialect variations, we know that the *ch-* consonant blend makes predictable sounds and we can design assessments that allow us to measure students' ability to recognize *ch-* in print, to determine its sound counterparts, and to correctly pronounce, or "say" the *ch-* blend. As we are careful with our understanding of the *ch-* blend and how we assess students' ability to produce the sounds, we can make accurate inferences about their developing ability to do so. We can examine students' ability to decode the *ch-* blend using assessments that include words that contain the *ch-* blend within meaningful text and the *ch-* blend in isolation. From students' performance on these assessments we infer their phonics skills and decoding strategies. With confidence in our conceptualization of phonics and in the materials and procedures we use to assess phonics, we are afforded confidence in the inferences we draw from assessment results. We can use the results of our assessment in a formative manner, to immediately shape our understanding of the developing reader and subsequent instruction. We can also use the results in a summative manner, as they provide evidence that the student has (or has not) met a key learning goal.

As broad as our understanding of reading is, we must strive to develop assessments that describe the complexity of student reading growth. Davis (1998) reminds us that assessment is always just a sample and an approximation of the thing we want to describe. As well, Davis notes that many of our assessments are "thin": they yield results that describe but a portion of reading, and this limitation should temper the inferences we make about students' growth and learning. For example, performance assessments are developed to help us understand students' increasingly complex strategy use and higher-order thinking in relation to the Common Core. Yet, they are most often silent about students' motivations, or self-efficacy, factors that clearly influence reading, strategy use, and higher-order thinking.

While theoretical and practical knowledge of reading and reading assessment is rich, the realization of useful reading assessment is impoverished. Many states, school districts, and schools use reading measures informed by habit and tradition, rather than by current understanding of reading and assessment. Given the considerable advances in our understanding of reading and reading assessment, shouldn't we find it puzzling that our students' adequate yearly progress is measured by tests much like those we ourselves took in elementary and middle school? In addition, the use of single-test scores to judge students' reading achievement and teachers' accountability skews schools' reading assessment agendas and funding. Despite the fact that using single-test scores to make highly consequential decisions is indefensible (American Educational Research Association/American Psychological Association/National Council on Measurement in Education, 1999), much school capital is invested in testing. The purchasing, training, practicing, administering, scoring, and teaching related to high-stakes tests each take from limited school resources and create a poverty of alternatives and the means to pursue them. While the high-stakes performance assessments created by consortia affiliated with the CCSS hold promise of improving this situation, they do not solve all of the above problems.

Best Practices in Action

Assessment must reflect the evolution of our understanding of the construct of reading, and assessment must be informed by state-of-the-art knowledge of the science of educational measurement. Reading assessment must reflect a series of balances that produces information that is useful to different audiences, designed for their different purposes. And it is within classrooms that the promise of reading assessment must be realized. In spite of the considerable growth in our understanding of how to develop and use classroom-based reading assessments (Calfee & Hiebert, 1996), implementation is generally slow.

Effective reading assessment is that which informs important educational decisions. A first concern for classroom teachers is collecting and using reading assessment information that can be used to shape instruction and learning. Consider the students who populate our classrooms. In a classroom of 25 or 30 students, we expect that each will vary in terms of reading skills and strategies, prior knowledge for texts, motivation, and self-esteem as readers. They will vary in the attributions they make for their reading success or failure and they will vary in terms of their agency, or the degree to which they feel they are in control of the reading they do. These individual differences contribute to varied performances and achievement in reading. We need assessments that describe the characteristics of student readers in diverse classrooms, characteristics that can influence their reading achievement.

Talented teachers use their understandings of each of these student characteristics to shape reading instruction, and careful classroom-based assessment informs teachers and serves as a basis for this instruction. Our assessment focus must be broad enough to focus not only on strategies, skills, and content-area knowledge gain, but also on students' motivations, agency, attributions, and self-esteem. Throughout reading lessons and on a daily basis, over marking periods and across the school year, this is high-stakes assessment, for without it there is not progress to achieve daily, weekly, and annual reading goals.

Best practices in reading assessment are balanced so that they provide teachers with detailed and current information about their students' reading development. Vygotsky (1978) proposes the zone of proximal development as the place in which students learn new things in relation to their knowledge and competencies, and in relation to teachers' instruction and support. If you believe that teacher accountability hinges, in part, on identifying students' zones of proximal development and teaching in these zones, then the centrality of classroom-based assessment is evident. We need formative classroom-based assessments that help us identify teachable moments for each student, that give us the detail we need to effectively teach to students' needs, and that describe the important outcomes of effective reading instruction.

Over the course of a school year, carefully teaching to students' individual needs can obviate the need to teach to the test. We must know where students are in terms of their skill and strategy development, motivation and engagement, prior knowledge for the texts they read, and self-esteem as readers. When reading assessment provides us with this balance of information, we can identify the next steps for student learning and for our teaching. A robust classroom assessment program continually provides detailed information about students' current competencies and next steps: it informs our ongoing work in the zone of proximal development.

Achieving Balance in Reading Assessment

In this section, we describe necessary balances that promote best practices in classroom-based reading assessment. We provide an overview of the specific balance, explain why it is necessary, and describe the means to achieving this balance. In doing so, we refer to specific reading assessments that can provide valid and reliable assessment information. These assessments include reading inventories and miscue analysis, performance assessments, teacher questioning, observations and surveys of student growth, and checklists.

Balancing Assessments That Focus on Reading Processes and Reading Products

All of our reading assessment involves making inferences about students' growth and achievement. We reason about the extent of students' reading development using our assessment of the processes and products of their reading. *Process assessments* focus on students' skills, strategies, and task performances as they are used. In contrast, *product assessments* focus on what students produce as a result of reading. Too much attention is now given to product assessments, especially tests, and this creates an imbalance that favors product assessment at the expense of process assessment. The CCSS provide learning goals as reading products for each grade level but leave much room for teachers concerning how to teach and assess the goals. Therefore, the imbalance between process and product assessments is maintained with the Common Core, unless teachers are supported in their efforts to focus on students' reading processes.

Reading processes are those skills and strategies that readers use when they decode words, determine vocabulary meaning, read fluently, and comprehend. Process-oriented reading assessment focuses on the skills and strategies that students use to construct meaning from text. Such assessment allows teachers to assess in the midst of students' reading. For example, as we listen to the student applying phonics knowledge to sound out the *ch-* consonant blend, we are in the midst of the student using decoding processes. When we observe a student rereading a sentence to clarify meaning, we are in the midst of a metacognitive process. Our process assessment helps us to determine the skills and strategies that work or do not work, as the student attempts to construct meaning. Moreover, assessment of reading processes can be situated in the context of a student actually reading, providing insights into how reading skills and strategies work together.

In contrast, product-oriented reading assessment gives an after-the-fact account of student reading achievement. Typical reading product assessments are quizzes, tests, and questions related to students' comprehension of text. The information provided by product assessments can help us determine students' achievement in relation to important reading goals, such as content-area learning. When we examine test scores, we can make inferences about students' achievement in relation to lesson and unit goals, and curriculum standards, but we must make backward inferences about what worked (or didn't work) as the student read, and as we taught. If we are interested in making inferences about how our instruction contributed (or didn't contribute) to the students' achievement, a similar series of backward inferences is necessary. This is an important fact about product assessments: they are relatively limited in their ability to provide detail on what students can and can't do as they read. An apt analogy is one in which we try to determine why a soccer team won or lost a game by examining the final score. Certainly the final score is important, but it tells us nothing about the means by which it was achieved. There may be very little for us to go on if we are interested in gaining useful information from the assessment about how to do better.

In contrast, a balance of classroom-based assessment of reading processes can provide us with detailed information on how students process text and construct meaning. Here, our inferences are based on our assessment of the processes themselves. A prime example of assessment that focuses on readers' processes is miscue analyses (Clay, 1993; Goodman & Goodman, 1977), in which the teacher focuses on a student's oral reading behaviors. Assessment here is "online" and we get information about students' reading processes as they read. Accordingly, miscue analysis can illustrate how students decode print, engage prior knowledge, read fluently, construct meaning, and monitor the meaning-making process. It can inform the teacher of student strengths or weaknesses in sound–symbol correspondences, or in literal and inferential comprehension.

The inferences we make about students' strengths and needs comes from the actual account of reading processes. With oral reading data, we may observe that a student is not consistently monitoring comprehension, as the student continues to read even when meaning-changing miscues are made. We are able to pinpoint the problem, and we may be able to provide instruction to address a detailed, precise need based on our process-oriented reading assessment information.

Balancing the Assessment of Reading Skills and Strategies with the Assessment of How Students Use What They Understand from Reading

Students must comprehend the texts they read and students must also be able to use the information they gain from reading to perform reading-related tasks. In early grades, a considerable portion of assessment dwells on students' development of the mechanics of reading. This is followed by reading assessment that focuses on the reader's comprehension of text. We can assess students' ability to determine or construct main ideas and we can ask students to locate or identify details in texts. When we ask students to summarize a text, we are continuing a focus on constructing meaning. Each of these assessments focuses on comprehension as the final goal of reading. We must remember that reading to answer comprehension questions, while common school practice, is rarely encountered in the reading done outside of school. Thus, reading assessment should also focus on how students use the meaning they construct from text in reading-related tasks. When students read guidelines for conducting hands-on experiments to help guide their science inquiry, or they read colonists' diaries so that they can create a dramatic presentation on the struggles in Jamestown, reading involves these two goals: to comprehend text and to use what is comprehended in a related task or performance. Of course, such reading is the norm outside of the classroom. So it should be in classrooms.

Performance assessment features in the high-stakes assessments associated with the CCSS and related assessment consortia (Partnership for Assessment of Readiness for College and Careers, 2013; Smarter Balanced Assessment Consortium, 2012) and focuses on the things we expect students to do with knowledge gained from reading (Baxter & Glaser, 1998). For example, fifth-grade students read instructions and guidelines for conducting a hands-on science experiment. Of course, we focus on their comprehension, but we are also very interested in their application of what is learned (or comprehended) in the conducting of the science experiment. This includes the correct sequencing of steps in scientific inquiry, identification of laboratory tools, and following safety procedures. The performance assessment accommodates our need to measure and describe the link between comprehension of text and how students use what they comprehend. Performance assessment has the added attraction of using rubrics that help students conceptualize suitable levels of performance at a specific task: they provide students with a blueprint of what they must do to achieve a superior score, and the performance assessment illustrates for students what is needed. The rubric also provides the means for students to check their progress toward a particular performance level, and to practice self-assessment. Performance assessments and their related rubrics can help students continue to learn how to do assessment for themselves.

Balancing the Assessment of Basic Skills and Strategies with the Assessment of Higher-Order Thinking

Many reading comprehension assessments focus on student understanding of a text, and use multiple-choice items. After students read a given text, they choose the best answer from among alternatives, with questions focusing on identifying the main idea, and inferring vocabulary and sentence meaning. These tests often fail to tap students' higher-order thinking skills and strategies in reading, which include analysis and synthesis, application, and evaluation. The anchor standards for reading in the Common Core now emphasize these higher-order skills and strategies. Students must be able to read complex texts closely by analyzing the language and structure contributing to the meanings in text, integrating the ideas and thoughts from the text, and interrogating the usefulness of the text based on readers' goals.

In order to achieve a balance between the assessment of basic and higher-order skills and strategies in reading, it is important to examine the relationship of reading skills and strategies with higher-order thinking. Bloom's taxonomy (Anderson & Krathwohl, 2001; Bloom, 1956) proposes that establishing a literal understanding of text involves basic comprehension, while related cognitive processes of applying, analyzing, synthesizing, and evaluating represent higher-order thinking in reading. We offer two examples of reading assessment that can provide information about students' higher-level thinking: students' generation of critical questions about their reading, and students' composition of integrative essays when learning from multiple source texts.

In order to create critical questions, a student must identify or construct main ideas, determine the author's intention, and use the meaning so constructed to formulate questions. Consider students who are asked to generate a critical question about a text concerning global warming and climate change. Before engaging in this task, students must first identify the main idea: average temperatures and carbon dioxide levels continue to rise globally. They also must understand the author's intention: for the readers to take action to combat global warming. Students can then ask informed critical questions, such as how persuasive the author was or what sources the author used to make his or her argument. Based on the students' critical questions, teachers can assess the extent to which a student has understood text, and how this understanding is manipulated by the student to create a meaningful question. Second, writing an integrative essay based on the reading of multiple texts helps us to understand a student's comprehension of each text, and the ability to combine information from across texts into a coherent whole (Wolfe & Goldman, 2005). In this task, a well-developed assessment rubric serves two roles: a scaffolded guide for students' higher-order thinking and scoring guidelines for a classroom teacher to assess the student work. We note that our second example involves writing in a major role, and that writing ability may be confounded with reading ability. Such is literacy use outside of the classroom, and determining the relative contribution of reading and writing to student's performance is challenging.

Without basic skills and strategies in reading, higher-order reading skills and strategies cannot occur: the latter are dependent, in part, on the former. It may be difficult to draw a strict boundary between basic and higher-order levels in reading, and the assessment of higher-order thinking necessarily involves some basic skills and strategies. Even so, it is our responsibility to conduct reading assessments that tap students' higher-order thinking skills and strategies. Creating balanced reading assessment that describes the development of basic and higher-order thinking is imperative, as schools move toward the CCSS. Accordingly, we should see movement away from a preponderance of assessments that require students to fill in a short answer or to choose one short answer from several choices.

Balancing the Assessment of Single-Text Reading with Reading from Multiple Sources Including Internet/Hypertext

A predominant goal of reading instruction and assessment is to help readers construct meaning from the text, and most reading assessments of comprehension focus on the understanding of single texts. After reading a single text, students are asked to determine details and main ideas, answer literal and inferential questions, and demonstrate vocabulary knowledge. While this assessment approach focuses on comprehension of single, short passages, success at reading involves more. The CCSS require multiple text reading, and reading assessment must inform the ways in which students "analyze how two or more texts address similar themes or topics in order to build knowledge or to compare the approaches the authors take" (p. 10).

The environment of reading changes based on developments in informational technology and the Internet and hypertext (Cho, 2013; Leu, Kinzer, Coiro, & Commack, 2004). In this dynamic environment, students must be able to comprehend single texts, as well as multiple sources of information from different texts, searching and deciding which sources are more reliable and coherently integrating information taken from various sources. Current reading assessments are limited in their ability to assess this new aspect of reading. The focus on a traditional printed text represents an imbalance in assessment for two reasons. First, in an authentic reading situation, the texts students encounter may be composed of multiple modalities of information. Readers of informational text may encounter verbal and nonverbal information such as graphs, photos, drawings, and maps. Second, reading multiple sources of texts may require additional cognitive skills and strategies that cannot be assessed with tests that dwell on the comprehension of a single text. Stahl and colleagues (1996) showed that high school students had difficulty understanding multiple sources of information about a historical event, not because they lacked comprehension skills, but because they struggled to distinguish and identify the relationships between multiple sources. This difficulty is increased when the texts students read conflict with one other. For example, suppose a student reads a text that argues that human activity is a cause of global warming, while another text refutes the argument. In this situation, reading assessment must describe the student's ability to construct meaning from each text, and to identify the relative strengths and weaknesses of claims and evidence presented in different texts (Rouet, 2006; Wineburg, 1991).

Teachers can assess students' comprehension of multiple texts, and the print and nonprint information contained in texts. Using two approaches sketched below, teachers can determine if students have the knowledge, skills, and strategies to evaluate the information value and credibility of multiple sources, and to integrate the sources for coherent understanding. In the first case, teachers can determine students' source evaluation skills as they think out loud about their reading processes. In this assessment task, teachers can observe whether students can ask questions to judge the source credibility (e.g., Are you familiar with the author? When was this article published? Does the text come from a source that you trust?) and usefulness of the source (e.g., Is this source comprehensible to me? Does this source fit my purpose of reading?). In the second case, teachers can examine the ways students integrate multiple sources of text information through performance assessments. For instance, when students read about the Civil War, teachers can prompt students to write an integrative essay from primary and secondary source texts as related to the topic and judge their responses to measure how they differentiate fact and opinion, make sense of the different roles the source texts play in understanding, and build the linkages between the texts.

Balancing the Assessment of Cognitive and Affective Reading Outcomes and Reader Characteristics

Current high-stakes assessments, early reading screening instruments, and the majority of classroom reading assessments focus on the skills and strategies that contribute to reading comprehension as cognitive achievement. Assessment measures the cognitive development of student readers, but pays little or no attention to other factors that can support and enhance reading development. Experienced classroom teachers and parents know that possession of reading skills and strategies is essential to students' reading success, but does not guarantee this success. A host of factors influence reading development and reading achievement, including motivation and engagement, self-efficacy, epistemic beliefs, and agency (Afflerbach, Cho, Kim, Crassas, & Doyle, 2013). Successful readers are engaged readers (Guthrie & Wigfield, 1997). These readers are motivated to read, they identify themselves as readers, they persevere in the face of reading challenge, and they consider reading to be an important part of their daily lives. When we think of our teaching successes, do we think of students who earned high test scores? Or do we think of students who went from reluctant readers to enthusiastic readers? Do we think of students who evolved from easily discouraged readers to readers whose motivation helped them persevere through reading challenges? Do we remember students who avoided reading at all costs changing to students who learned to love reading? Certainly, we can count such students and our positive influence on them among our most worthy teaching accomplishments. The lesson here is that successful student readers are not just good strategy and skill readers; they are efficacious, they are motivated, and they believe in their ability to read. The affective factors that are essential for successful reading can be taken for granted, as is evident by their scant mention in the CCSS. Educators cannot successfully teach academic skills and strategies in the CCSS, nor can they develop lifelong readers, when students are not motivated and engaged in reading and learning. Accomplished teachers know the great impact of those factors on student reading and reading development. Thus, our assessments must inform us about how these powerful factors are operating in each student.

If we are serious about accountability, we need to have balance in the assessment that demonstrates that high-quality teaching and effective reading programs change student readers' lives. To achieve balance we need assessments that are capable of measuring and describing student growth that is complementary to reading skill and reading strategy development. This growth can include positive motivation, perseverance in the face of difficulty, appropriate attributions made for reading success and failure, and self-esteem as a reader (Afflerbach, in press). We are fortunate to have such measures. For example, we can conduct surveys and inventories of students' reading motivation (Gambrell, Palmer, Codling, & Mazzoni, 1996), attitudes toward reading (McKenna & Kear, 1990), and reading self-concept (Chapman & Tunmer, 1995). These assessments can help us understand and describe growth that is related to the already assessed cognitive development. They move us toward a fuller and fairer measure of the accomplishments of students and their teachers.

Balancing Formative Reading Assessment and Summative Reading Assessment

We are a society enamored with numbers. Schools, school districts, classrooms, states, teachers, and students are all evaluated and ranked in relation to annual series of tests, or summative reading assessments. These assessments report important summary information about students' reading skills and strategies. They summarize reading achievement as a grade-level equivalent, a raw score, or a percentile rank. Summative assessment is important because it helps us to understand if students reach grade-level benchmarks, unit and lesson goals, and standards in classrooms, districts, and states. However, summative assessment is, by its very nature, after-the-fact teaching and learning. We do not have as rich an opportunity with summative assessment, compared with formative assessment, to inform instruction and to address students' individual needs as they are developing.

In spite of this limitation, summative assessment is used to make highly consequential decisions. Accountability, sanction, reward, school success, and school failure are often determined through a process that uses a single summative assessment score. The pressure to focus on such summative assessment creates an imbalance with formative assessment efforts, the very type of assessment that helps teachers and schools demonstrate accountability on a daily basis. Formative assessment, in contrast, is conducted with the goal of informing our instruction and improving student learning. At the heart of effective reading instruction is the classroom teacher's detailed knowledge of each student. This knowledge is constructed through ongoing, formative assessments, conducted across the school day and throughout the school year, like the process-oriented reading assessment discussed earlier in this chapter.

For example, teacher questioning may be tailored so that it provides formative assessment information. The teacher adept at asking questions during instruction develops a detailed sense of how well students are "getting" the lesson. The teacher's questions can focus on the skills and strategies, cognitive and affective influences on reading achievement and content-area learning that are a result of reading. Then, the teacher uses information provided by students' responses to questions to build a detailed sense of how students are progressing toward lesson goals and appropriate instructional foci. Consider a fifth-grade teacher's questions to her students as they read a chapter in a science textbook: What is an ecosystem? On what balances does an ecosystem depend? Can you explain your reasoning? Where do you get the information contained in your explanation? Questions like these evoke responses that demonstrate the degree of student understanding. From students' responses, the teacher constructs her own understanding of their achievement. The degree of detail that is provided by formative assessment may help a classroom teacher to determine a teachable moment, identify the need for reteaching an important concept or skill related to ecosystems, or to move forward to new instruction with confidence that students possess the requisite knowledge to succeed. Creating balance will result in formative assessment describing students' ongoing reading growth as it occurs, and summative assessment providing summary statements about students' literacy achievement. States and school districts should attend to the linkages between summative assessments, such as those provided by the Smarter Balanced Assessment Consortium (2012) and the Partnership for Assessment of Readiness for College and Careers (2013), and the formative assessment used in the classroom. As the CCSS describe grade-level achievement goals, assessment practices are likely to be implemented as summative assessments. However, we know that successful teachers frequently use formative assessments in their classrooms because they know the importance of understanding students' reading development on a daily basis. Understanding whether a student achieves the final goal is different from understanding whether the student progresses smoothly toward the final goal.

Balancing the Reading Assessment That Is Done to or for Students with Reading Assessment That Is Done with and by Students

Many students move through school with reading assessment done to them, or for them. Students read, take a quiz or test, and hand it in. It is evaluated and graded, and then returned to the student. The student earns a score, but gains no understanding of how assessment works. A result is that many students think of assessment as a "black box" (Black & Wiliam, 1998), and a consequence of this approach to reading assessment is that students do not learn to do reading assessment for themselves. Even as we ask questions in class, without our explanation of why we ask these questions or how we arrive at our evaluations of student responses, students will not understand how the evaluation of their reading is made. Across school years there may be lost opportunities for students to learn to conduct reading assessment on their own, and students remain outsiders to the culture of reading assessment.

Our classroom-based assessment should provide students with the means to eventually assume responsibility for assessing their own reading. Accomplished readers regularly assess their ongoing comprehension of text and their progress toward achieving reading-related goals, as they are metacognitive. This ability is not innate: it is learned from models of doing assessment that the students eventually internalize. In fact, a hallmark of the successful reader is the ability to monitor reading and conduct ongoing assessment of reading progress (Pressley & Afflerbach, 1995; Veenman, in press). We note that the CCSS assume high levels of self-assessment from students, but discussion of such self-assessment is largely absent from the Common Core materials.

To create balance, we should provide opportunities in which students learn the value of self-assessment and the means to do accurate and useful assessment for themselves. A good start is modeling straightforward assessment routines, and helping students learn to initiate and successfully complete the routines independently. For example, consider the checklist used by a second-grade teacher. As students read, she regularly asks the students to refer to the checklist and engage in the assessment thinking that it requires. She models using the checklist and expects that her students will learn to use it as they read independently. The checklist includes the following:

- ____ I check to see if what I read makes sense.
- ____ I remind myself why I am reading.
- ____ I focus on the goal of my reading while I read.
- ____ I check to see if I can summarize sentences and paragraphs.
- ____ If reading gets hard, I ask myself if there are any problems.
- ____ I try to identify the problem.
- ____ I try to fix the problem.
- ____ When the problem is fixed, I get back to my reading, making sure I understand what I've read so far.

The teacher also models the use of the checklist by asking related questions of herself when she reads to the students, and thinks aloud about why she asks the questions and her answers to the questions. This predictable presentation of assessment routines can help set developing readers on a healthy path to self-assessment.

Checklists can be adjusted to the content and complexity of instructional goals. For example, if we are interested in fostering students' ability to self-assess their critical reading, we may devise a checklist with the following items:

_____ I check the text to see if the author provides evidence to support claims.

_____ I compare the information in the text with what I already know about the topic.

We do not give up our responsibility to conduct classroom-based reading assessments when we promote student self-assessment. Rather, we look for opportunities when using our assessments to help students learn to do assessment themselves. Creating balance is imperative, for if in all our teaching related to reading students do not begin to learn how to do self-assessment, they will not become truly independent readers.

Balancing the Assessment of In-School and Out-of-School Literacy Practices

Out-of-school, students are constantly involved with text. Whether students are texting, blogging, creating rhymes, journaling, or networking on Facebook, they need and acquire specific literacy skills in order to do these things effectively. Yet, some of these students do not see themselves as capable in-school readers (Alvermann et al., 2007). They may not realize how frequently and how effectively they use their literacy skills. These students may struggle in traditional school literacy tasks, and we, as educators, may not view them as proficient readers, or sufficiently literate.

The lack of knowing and understanding students' out-of-school literacies demonstrates how teacher–student relationships may be " 'thin' and 'single-stranded' " (Moll et al., 1992, p. 134). For example, a teacher might know his student solely by a set number of oral reading performances, written responses to quizzes, and the student's limited classroom interactions. Teachers may only "know" their students through their school performances, which were often in limited classroom contexts. The assessment of out-of-school literacies can help us better understand students' daily literacy practices, and how we might tap into those literacies in which students are most proficient, toward achieving positive school outcomes.

A straightforward means of becoming familiar with students' notions of literacy is to hold conversations about them. Students describe and demonstrate literacy practices, and this allows us to determine the commonalities and idiosyncrasies of in-school and out-of-school literacies. A second approach is to have students keep account of their literacy practices. For example, Alvermann and colleagues (2007) had struggling adolescent readers keep track of their reading outside of school in a daily reading log. Through this documentation, the researchers found that these "struggling readers" looked much more like readers than one would think. Students read and interacted with text in such forms as song lyrics, Internet sites, text in electronic games, and sets of directions. If we become familiar with students reading in and out of school, we may identify those contexts in which they are capable readers.

A means of using assessment to gather information on students' out-of-school literacy is the use of surveys about reading practices. These surveys might include the following questions:

- What do I think a good reader looks like?
- What types of text do I like to read in school or outside of school?
- What types of text do I use outside of school on a regular basis?
- How does text connect me with others?
- Why is it important to be able to read and understand text outside of school?
- How is reading and understanding text outside of school important in my life?

These questions help us to understand students' ideas about reading, and about themselves as readers, which may open up opportunities for us to broaden those ideas and definitions. Even further, their answers may alert us to how students can bring their outside-of-school reading interests into the classroom.

By understanding and acknowledging students' literacy practices, we give value to those practices and we put ourselves in a position to connect them with in-school literacy practices. This yields both cognitive and affective benefits. For example, students' careful analysis of a popular song can have much in common with a school task of interpreting a poem. Our assessment of each can inform our broad understanding of literacy development. By bringing out-of-school literacies into our classrooms and not focusing solely on traditional school-based texts, we gain the ability to capitalize on our students' current literacy interests and strengths and build upon them. We note that the CCSS exclusively focus on reading scenarios with academic texts, tasks, and purposes. However, in order to be college- and career-ready, as the CCSS emphasize, we must appreciate and nurture our students' literate practices both in and out of the classroom.

Balancing the Demands for Teacher and School Accountability with Professional Development Opportunities to Develop Expertise in Reading Assessment

Each of the necessary balances described in this chapter is dependent on teachers' professional development in assessment. Successful classroom-based reading assessment demands teacher expertise, and professional development is the means for helping teachers develop their expertise. Specifically, teachers must be supported in developing effective formative assessments. The complex text and task combinations that comprise the CCSS demand such focused, expert assessment as teachers help their students progress toward attainment of the standards. Teachers as assessment experts examine what aspect of reading to assess, choose the texts and tasks to best capture it, make inferences about the students' reading from the assessment information, and transform the understanding of students' reading into informative feedback for students to use for self-assessment of their strengths and weaknesses.

Teacher and school accountability are commonly associated with the results of high-stakes testing. We believe that this approach is looking for accountability in the wrong place. Unfortunately, in the contest for scarce-school resources, tests win and formative assessment loses. The costs involved in developing, buying, administering, and scoring these assessments are considerable. The school funds spent on high-stakes tests are taken from limited school budgets. This means that money spent on tests cannot be spent on initiatives that would help teachers become better at classroom-based assessment.

Lack of professional development opportunities prevents many teachers from becoming practicing experts in classroom-based reading assessments (Black & Wiliam, 1998). Teachers can develop expertise with classroom assessment when they are supported by their administrators and school districts (Johnston, 1987). Specifically, professional development can help teachers learn and use effective reading assessment materials and procedures that best inform the daily teaching and learning in the classroom (Stiggins, 1999). As we noted earlier, the array of factors that we must assess is large, ranging from reading strategies and skills (the traditional focus of assessment), to motivation, self-efficacy, and metacognition. Just as there are zones of proximal development for students' strategy and skill development, there are zones of proximal development for students' motivation, self-efficacy, and metacognition.

Regular and detailed assessments provide information that helps teachers recognize and utilize the teachable moment. These daily successes sum to the accomplished teaching and learning that is reflected in accountability tests. But accountability is not achieved through testing—it is achieved through the hard work that surrounds successful classroom assessment and instruction. Professional development also helps teachers construct reliable product assessments, such as quizzes, tests, and report cards. Professional development helps teachers become educated consumers and users of the variety of reading assessments that are available.

Summary

Effective reading assessment is necessary for reading program success and balance is necessary for effective reading assessment. Current reading assessment practice is marked by a series of imbalances that influence teaching and learning. We can view the CCSS movement as providing an opportunity to highlight and remedy these assessment imbalances. As teachers we are challenged to provide effective instruction for each and every student. Effective instruction is dependent on assessment that helps teachers and students move toward and attain daily and annual reading goals. This chapter describes the balances that must be attained if reading assessment is to reflect our best, most recent understandings of reading and how to measure reading development. We are not wanting for description and detail of how classroom-based reading assessment helps our teaching and how our teaching helps student readers develop. There must be a concerted effort to bring classroom-based reading assessment into the spotlight and to deliver on its promise.

High-quality classroom assessment of reading is as much a product of teacher expertise and effort as it is of political power, popular will, and continuing education. Many people believe that tests are at best a key to school excellence, and at worst a nuisance. A full accounting of the costs of current reading assessment programs, especially high-stakes tests, may help the general public understand how much school resource is given to reading assessment that yields information that is of relatively little use for teachers. Teachers must earn and maintain the trust that is currently given, by some, to high-stakes standardized tests. If in correcting an imbalance in our school and classroom we are able to demonstrate the superior nature of particular reading assessment information, we may gain converts to classroom assessment.

The imbalances identified in this chapter need our attention. Righting these should lead to assessment programs that are more integral to the daily lives of teachers, students, and classrooms. When we focus on process assessment, we can accurately determine what aspect of a summarization strategy students do and don't understand. When we assess and determine how a student's motivation grows as the result of gaining control of the act of reading, we are describing a compelling success story. And when we share our reading assessment knowledge with our students, we are preparing them to conduct assessment of their own reading, fostering independence. The CCSS demand as much.

Reflections and Future Directions

A balanced approach to classroom reading assessment will be achieved when classroom teachers can conduct assessment in a reliable and valid manner, thus gaining the public trust. Earlier, we sketched the importance of professional development to teachers' growing ability to conduct classroom reading assessments and effectively use their results. However, there is little research that describes how teachers develop as assessment experts, or that demonstrates what type of classroom assessment training most benefits teachers and their students.

A related area for future research and action is the public perception of assessment. We are a society that purports to value scientific inquiry, along with research results and agendas for action that are informed by such inquiry and results. Why, then, do our most consequential reading assessments and their uses appear relatively uninformed by our most recent understandings? Similarly, why do states and school districts spend the bulk of their assessment budgets on test purchasing, administering, scoring, and reporting? This problem is exacerbated by the federal mandate of testing all students in grades 3 through 8 in reading, yet the problem existed prior to the passage of the No Child Left Behind Act.

A final area for future research relates to the effects of reading assessment on student reading achievement. Despite the importance of reading assessment in determining student achievement and related consequences, reading assessment itself is not a common focus of research (Afflerbach, Cho, Kim, & Clark, 2010). Reading assessment is used as the measure of student achievement in many research designs. But few studies describe how assessment can contribute to student learning and achievement, although work in this area is promising (Black & Wiliam, 2006; Crooks, 1988). Research should help us determine the relationship of reading assessment with students' reading achievement. Classroom-based reading assessments, especially those that focus on formative assessment, the assessment of processes, and the application of knowledge gained from reading, should positively impact teaching and learning.

Concluding Comments

Early in this chapter we framed best practices in reading assessment in relation to balance and imbalance. As we conclude this chapter we are balancing concern and optimism. Our concern is fueled by the fact that high-stakes tests continue to monopolize the vocabulary of school success. Test scores are what we talk about when we talk of reading achievement. In addition, the resources that high-stakes tests demand continue to prevent the allocation of needed resources to formative assessment. This is an untenable situation, given the centrality of formative assessment to success at the CCSS. We note that it is simple to infer the need for massive formative assessment in support of students striving to meet the CCSS. In contrast, the mechanisms and funding that are necessary to foment such change are complex, and not well explicated.

In contrast, our optimism is fueled by the fact that eminently useful reading assessment materials and procedures exist and are being developed (PARCC & Smarter Balanced Assessment Consortium), indicating that part of the hard work is already done. We have the means to develop reading assessment that is central to the identification and accomplishment of teachable moments and reading assessment that reflects student achievement in relation to our most recent understanding of reading. This must be complemented by teachers' professional development, public commitment to examine our new conceptualizations of reading and reading assessment, and endorsement of those assessments that best describe and support students' reading achievement.

ENGAGEMENT ACTIVITIES

The following activities are designed to encourage readers of this chapter to investigate balance and imbalance in reading assessment.

1. Conduct task analyses of an CCSS ELA related to the students you teach. Task analyses give us detailed knowledge of the things we ask students to do. This puts us in a position to assess our assessments. Are they sensitive to all the growth that students may exhibit? Do they favor one type of achievement while ignoring others? Task analyses not only help us determine the suitability of the assessment, they prompt our attention to aspects of reading strategies and tasks that may be the focus of instruction. Knowing the assessment in this case helps us think about teaching, assessment, and balance in assessment. As you conduct your

task analysis, determine all the factors that must be operating for student success.

2. Develop an account of all the relevant factors that influence students' growth in reading, focusing on both cognition and affect. Next, compare this account with the reading assessments that you use in the course of a school year. What is the "coverage" of these assessments? Is each and every factor that influences students' reading growth given assessment attention? What factors are underrepresented? What factors are overrepresented?

3. The CCSS "raise the bar" in relation to text and task difficulty. For students to meet these standards, high-quality formative assessment is a must. Consider how you can use formative assessment to identify students' zones of proximal development as students work toward attainment of a specific CCSS. What formative assessment information, focused on student cognition and affect, will inform your daily reading instruction in relation to that standard? How will you use the formative assessment information as students move toward attainment of the standard?

4. Based on your account of the reading assessments mandated in your school, and the coverage of these assessments, create a presentation for teachers and school administrators that advocates for optimal assessment. In the presentation, describe what you believe to be the areas that receive adequate reading assessment coverage, and those that are not sufficiently assessed. Suggest specific reading assessment materials and procedures that can contribute to better balance in reading assessment.

REFERENCES

Afflerbach, P. (in press). *Handbook of individual differences in reading: Reader, text, and context.* New York: Routledge.

Afflerbach, P., Cho, B.-Y., Kim, J.-Y., & Clark, S. (2010). Classroom assessment of literacy. In D. Wyse, R. Andrews, & J. Hoffman (Eds.), *The international handbook of English language and literacy teaching* (pp. 401–412). London: Routledge.

Afflerbach, P., Cho, B.-Y., Kim, J.-Y., Crassas, M. E., & Doyle, B. (2013). Reading: What else matters besides strategies and skills? *The Reading Teacher, 66,* 440–448.

Alvermann, D. E., Hagood, M. C., Heron-Hruby, A., Hughes, P., Williams, K. B., & Yoon, J. (2007). Telling themselves who they are: What one out-of-school time study revealed about underachieving readers. *Reading Psychology, 28*(1), 31–50.

American Educational Research Association/American Psychological Association/National Council on Measurement in Education. (1999). *The standards for educational and psychological testing.* Washington, DC: Author.

Anderson, L., & Krathwohl, D. (2001). *A taxonomy for learning, teaching and assessing: A revision of Bloom's taxonomy of educational objectives.* New York: Addison, Wesley Longman.

Baxter, G., & Glaser, R. (1998). Investigating the cognitive complexity of science assessments. *Educational Measurement: Issues and Practice, 17(3)*, 37–45.

Black, P., & Wiliam, D. (1998). Assessment and classroom learning. *Educational Assessment: Principles, Policy and Practice, 5*, 7–74.

Black, P., & Wiliam, D. (2005). Assessment for learning in the classroom. In J. Gardner (Ed.), *Assessment and learning* (pp. 9–26). London: Sage.

Bloom, B. S. (1956). *Taxonomy of educational objectives: Handbook 1. Cognitive domain.* New York: McKay.

Braten, I., Britt, M. A., Stromso, H. I., & Rouet, J.-F. (2011). The role of epistemic beliefs in the comprehension of multiple expository texts: Toward an integrated model. *Educational Psychologist, 46(1)*, 48–70.

Calfee, R., & Hiebert, E. (1996). Classroom assessment of reading. In R. Barr, M. Kamil, P. Mosenthal, & D. Pearson (Eds.), *Handbook of reading research* (2nd ed., pp. 281–309). Mahwah, NJ: Erlbaum.

Chapman, J. W., & Tunmer, W. E. (1995). Development of young children's reading self-concepts: An examination of emerging subcomponents and their relationship with reading achievement. *Journal of Educational Psychology, 87*, 154–167.

Cho, B.-Y. (2013). Adolescents' constructively responsive reading strategy use in a critical Internet reading task. *Reading Research Quarterly, 48(4)*, 329–332.

Clay, M. (1993). *Reading Recovery: A guidebook for teachers in training.* Portsmouth, NH: Heinemann.

Crooks, T. (1988). The impact of classroom evaluation on students. *Review of Educational Research, 58*, 438–481.

Darling-Hammond, L. (2010). *Performance counts: Assessment systems that support high-quality learning.* Washington, DC: Council of Chief State School Officers.

Davis, A. (1998). *The limits of educational assessment.* Oxford, UK: Blackwell.

Gambrell, L., Palmer, B., Codling, R., & Mazzoni, S. (1996). Assessing motivation to read. *The Reading Teacher, 49*, 518–533.

Guthrie, J., & Wigfield, A. (1997). *Reading engagement: Motivating readers through integrated instruction.* Newark, DE: International Reading Association.

Goodman, K., & Goodman, Y. (1977). Learning about psycholinguistic processes by analyzing oral reading. *Harvard Educational Review, 47*, 317–333.

Graesser, A. C., Mills, K. K., & Zwaan, R. A. (1997). Discourse comprehension. *Annual Review of Psychology, 48*, 163–189.

Guthrie, J. T., Wigfield, A., & You, W. (2012). Instructional contexts for engagement and achievement in reading. In S. L. Christenson, A. L. Reschly, & C. Wylie (Eds.), *Handbook of research on student engagement* (pp. 601–634). New York: Springer.

Johnston, P. (1987). Teachers as evaluation experts. *The Reading Teacher, 40,* 744–748.

Kintsch, W. (1988). The role of knowledge in discourse comprehension: A construction–integration model. *Psychological Review, 95*(2), 163–182.

Leu, D. J. Jr., Kinzer, C. K., Coiro, J. L., & Cammack, D. W. (2004). Toward a theory of new literacies emerging from the Internet and other information and communication technologies. In R. B. Ruddell & N. Unrau (Eds.), *Theoretical models and processes of reading* (5th ed., pp. 1570–1613). Newark, DE: International Reading Association.

McKenna, M. C., & Kear, D. J. (1990). Measuring attitude towards reading: a new tool for teachers. *The Reading Teacher, 43,* 626–639.

Moll, L. C., Amanti, C., Neff, D., & González, N. (1992). Funds of knowledge for teaching: Using a qualitative approach to connect homes and classrooms. *Theory into Practice, 31,* 132–141.

Morsy, L., Kieffer, M., & Snow, C. (2010). *Measure for measure: A critical consumer's guide to reading comprehension assessments for adolescents.* New York: Carnegie Corporation.

National Assessment Governing Board. (2012). *Reading framework for the 2013 National Assessment of Educational Progress.* Washington, DC: American Institutes for Research.

Partnership for Assessment of Readiness for College and Careers. (2013). PARCC task prototypes and new sample items for ELA/literacy. Retrieved September 17, 2013, from *www.parcconline.org/samples/ELA.*

Pellegrino, J., Chudowsky, N., & Glaser, R. (2001). *Knowing what students know: The science and design of educational assessment.* Washington, DC: National Academy Press.

Pressley, M., & Afflerbach, P. (1995). *Verbal reports of reading: The nature of constructively responsive reading.* Hillsdale, NJ: Erlbaum.

Rouet, J.-F. (2006). *The skills of document use: From text comprehension to Web-based learning.* Mahwah, NJ: Erlbaum.

Schunk, D. H., & Zimmerman, B. J. (2007). Influencing children's self-efficacy and self-regulation of reading and writing through modeling. *Reading and Writing Quarterly, 23*(1), 7–25.

Smarter Balanced Assessment Consortium. (2012). Sample items and performance tasks. Retrieved September 17, 2013, from *www.smarterbalanced.org/sample-items-and-performance-tasks.*

Snow, C. (2002). *Reading for understanding: Toward an R & D program in reading comprehension.* Washington, DC: Rand.

Stahl, S., Hynd, C., Britton, B., McNish, M., & Bosquet, D. (1996). What happens when students read multiple source documents in history? *Reading Research Quarterly, 31,* 430–456.

Stanovich, K. (1986). Matthew effects in reading: Some consequences of individual differences in the acquisition of literacy. *Reading Research Quarterly, 21,* 360–407.

Stiggins, R. (1999). Evaluating classroom assessment training in teacher education. *Educational Measurement: Issues and Practices, 18,* 23–27.

Veenman, M. (in press). Metacognition. In P. Afflerbach (Ed.), *Handbook of individual differences in reading: Reader, text, and context*. New York: Routledge.

Vygotsky, L. (1978). *Mind in society: The development of higher psychological processes*. Cambridge, MA: Harvard University Press.

Wiley, J., Goldman, S. R., Graesser, A. C., Sanchez, C. A., Ash, I. A., & Hemmerich, J. A. (2009). Source evaluation, comprehension, and learning in Internet science inquiry tasks. *American Educational Research Journal, 46*(4), 1060–1106.

Wineburg, S. (1991). Historical problem solving: A study of the cognitive processes used in the evaluation of documentary and pictorial evidences. *Journal of Educational Psychology, 83*, 73–87.

Wolfe, M. B. W., & Goldman, S. R. (2005). Relations between adolescents' text processing and reasoning. *Cognition and Instruction, 23*, 467–502.

PART IV

PERSPECTIVES ON
SPECIAL ISSUES

CHAPTER 15

Best Practices in Teaching the New Literacies of Online Research and Comprehension

Donald J. Leu
Lisa Zawilinski
Elena Forzani
Nicole Timbrell

This chapter will:

- Define a dual-level theory of New Literacies, useful to guide instruction, especially in the New Literacies of online research and instruction.

- Explain how we should interpret the Common Core State Standards in reading with both a lens to the future and a lens to the past, integrating instruction in the New Literacies of online research and comprehension with traditional reading comprehension.

- Provide 10 research-based principles that inform instruction in New Literacies and provide two specific ideas to implement each principle in the classroom.

- Provide a glimpse into what New Literacies classrooms may be like in the future.

New Literacies for New Times: Research and Theoretical Perspectives

The Internet is a very disruptive technology (Christensen, 1997), altering traditional elements of our society from newspapers to music. The

Internet is also altering the nature of literacy, generating New Literacies that require additional skills and strategies. Most importantly, it is reshaping the nature of literacy education, providing us with many new and exciting opportunities for our classrooms.

We live during a time in which new technologies continuously appear online, requiring additional skills to effectively read, write, and learn, sometimes on a daily basis. Consider, for example, just a few of these new technologies: Twitter, Facebook, Google+, Siri, Foursquare, Dropbox, Skype, Chrome, iMovie, Contribute, or any of many, many mobile "apps" and ebooks. Each requires additional reading and/or writing skills to take full advantage of its affordances. In addition, new tools for literacy will appear on the Internet tomorrow with additional New Literacies required to use them effectively. Finally, each online tool regularly is updated; each time this happens new affordances appear, requiring additional skills and strategies. It is clear that the nature of literacy regularly and continuously changes in online spaces.

Thus, when we speak of New Literacies in an online age we mean that literacy is not just "new" today; it becomes "new" every day of our lives. Proficiency in these continuously new, online literacies will define our students' success in both school and life. Most importantly, how we adapt to a dynamic definition of literacy in the classroom will define our students' future. One might even suggest that, over a lifetime, learning how to learn New Literacies is more important than learning a specific literacy of reading or writing. Every specific literacy that you know today will change repeatedly and substantially during your lifetime.

Some believe there is little to teach; our students are already "digital natives," skilled in online literacies (Prensky, 2001). It is true that today's students have grown up in an online world and are developing proficiency with gaming, social networking, video, and texting (Alvermann, Hutchins, & DeBlasio, 2012; Zickuhr, 2010). However, this does not necessarily mean they are skilled in the effective use of online information, perhaps the most important aspect of the Internet. Studies show that students lack critical evaluation skills when reading online (Bennet, Maton, & Kervin, 2008; Forzani & Maykel, 2013; Graham & Metaxas, 2003) and that they are not especially skilled with reading to locate information online (Kuiper & Volman, 2008).

New Literacies

As we try to understand these New Literacies we encounter a conundrum: How can we develop adequate understanding when the very object that we seek to study continuously changes? Our field has never before faced an issue such as this, since literacy has generally been static, permitting us, over time, to carefully study and understand it. One way out of this conundrum may be to think about literacy on two different levels, using a dual-level theory of New Literacies (Leu, Kinzer, Coiro, Castek, & Henry, 2013).

A dual-level theory of New Literacies conceptualizes literacy at lowercase (new literacies) and uppercase (New Literacies) levels. Lowercase theories of new literacies explore several types of elements: (1) a set of new literacies required by a specific technology and its social practices such as text messaging (Lewis & Fabos, 2005); (2) a disciplinary base, such as the semiotics of multimodality in online media (Kress, 2003); or (3) a distinctive, conceptual approach such as new literacy studies (Street, 2003). Lowercase theories of new literacy are better able to keep up with the rapidly changing nature of literacy since they are closer to the specific types of changes that rapidly take place. Multiple lowercase theories also permit our field to maximize the lenses we use and the technologies and contexts we study. Every scholar who studies new literacy issues is generating important insights for everyone else, even if we do not share a particular lens, technology, or context. How, though, do we come to understand these insights, taking place in many different fields from many different perspectives? For this, we require a second level of theory, an uppercase theory of New Literacies.

New Literacies, as the broader concept, benefits from work taking place in the multiple, lowercase dimensions of new literacies by identifying the common findings that appear. Leu and colleagues (2013) suggest that this broader New Literacies theory currently includes these common findings:

1. The Internet is this generation's defining technology for literacy and learning within our global community.
2. The Internet and related technologies require new literacies to fully access their potential.
3. New literacies are deictic; they rapidly change.
4. New literacies are multiple, multimodal, and multifaceted, and, as a result, our understanding of them benefits from multiple points of view.
5. Critical literacies are central to new literacies.
6. New forms of strategic knowledge are required with new literacies.
7. New social practices are a central element of new literacies.
8. Teachers become more important, though their role changes, within new literacy classrooms. (p. 1158)

This chapter uses the findings from this broader New Literacies theory to provide the context for understanding one lowercase form, the new literacies of online research and comprehension (Leu et al., 2013).

The New Literacies of Online Research and Comprehension

The new literacies of online research and comprehension frames online reading comprehension as a process of problem-based inquiry involving the skills, strategies, dispositions, and social practices that take place as we use the Internet to conduct research, solve problems, and answer questions. At least five processing practices occur during online research and comprehension, each requiring additional new skills and strategies when they take place online: (1) reading to identify important questions, (2) reading to locate information, (3) reading to evaluate information critically, (4) reading to synthesize information, and (5) reading and writing to communicate information.

How does the nature of reading and writing change online? What, if any, new literacies do we require? We are just discovering some of the answers to these questions (Afflerbach & Cho, 2008). First, it appears that online reading comprehension typically takes place within a problem-solving task (Coiro & Castek, 2010). In short, online reading comprehension is online research. Second, online reading also becomes tightly integrated with writing as we communicate with others to learn more about the questions we explore and as we communicate our own interpretations. A third difference is that new technologies such as browsers, search engines, wikis, blogs, e-mail, and many others are required. Additional skills and strategies are needed to use each of these technologies effectively. Keyword entry in a search engine, for example, becomes an important new literacy skill during online reading because it is required in search engines, an important new technology for locating information. Other online technologies require additional new skills and strategies during online reading. Finally, and perhaps most importantly, online reading may require even greater amounts of higher-level thinking than offline reading. In a context in which anyone may publish anything, higher-level thinking skills such as critical evaluation of source material become especially important online.

There are several reasons why the new literacies of online research and comprehension are important to classroom reading programs. First, they focus directly on information use and learning, so these skills are central to education at all levels. Second, the ability to read and use online information effectively to solve problems defines success in both life and work (PIAAC Expert Group on Problem Solving in Technology-Rich Environments, 2009). Third, these new literacies are not always included in literacy programs (International Reading Association, 2009). Finally, our students often appear to lack these skills (Bennet et al., 2008).

National Standards

New Literacies and the new literacies of online research and comprehension appear to be recognized in recent policy initiatives. Nations have integrated this research into new curriculum and educational standards, seeking to prepare youth for work and life in an online age of information.

Australia

Australia has recently developed the Australian Curriculum (Australian Curriculum, Assessment and Reporting Authority [ACARA], n.d.). This initiative tightly integrates literacy and the Internet within the English curriculum and suggests that online research and communication are essential elements in this area:

> ICT (Information and Communication Technology) capability is an important component of the English curriculum. Students use ICT when . . . they conduct research online, and collaborate and communicate with others electronically. (ACARA, n.d., General Capabilities, Information and Communication Technology Competence section, para. 2)

Canada: Manitoba

The province of Manitoba has developed an educational framework called Literacy with ICT Across the Curriculum (Minister of Manitoba Education, Citizenship, and Youth, 2006). This initiative recognizes that reading has changed and that online reading is a problem-solving task, requiring new skills to locate, evaluate, synthesize, and communicate in online contexts. It describes these new online literacies as

> identifying appropriate inquiry questions; navigating multiple information networks to locate relevant information; applying critical thinking skills to evaluate information sources and content; synthesizing information and ideas from multiple sources and networks; representing information and ideas creatively in visual, aural, and textual formats; crediting and referencing sources of information and intellectual property; and communicating new understandings to others, both face to face and over distance. . . .(Minister of Manitoba Education, Citizenship, and Youth, 2006, p. 18)

The United States

In the United States, the Common Core State Standards (CCSS) Initiative (2012) establishes more uniform standards across states to prepare students for college and careers in the 21st century. One of the key design principles in the CCSS, research and media skills, focuses on the integration of online research and comprehension skills within the classroom such as locating, evaluating, synthesizing, and communicating:

> To be ready for college, workforce training, and life in a technological society, students need the ability to gather, comprehend, evaluate, synthesize, and report on information and ideas, to conduct original research in order to answer questions or solve problems, and to analyze and create a high volume and extensive range of print and nonprint texts in media forms old and new. The need to conduct research and to produce and consume media is embedded into every aspect of today's curriculum. (CCSS, n.d., p. 4)

Three changes are especially noticeable in the English language arts standards of CCSS:

1. There is a greater focus on reading informational texts.
2. Higher-level thinking is emphasized.
3. Digital literacies are integrated throughout the English language arts standards.

Each of these reflects the shift in reading from page to screen that we have described as important to the new literacies of online research and comprehension. While there is more that can be done (Drew, 2012), a number of anchor standards appear to include these new literacies of online research and comprehension if one reads them carefully, with an understanding of how reading changes online.

Reading Our Standards with Dual Lenses: A Lens to the Future and a Lens to the Past

Interestingly, the word *Internet* is never used in the CCSS reading standards (Leu et al., 2011), despite the fact that the writing standards specify the use of *digital sources, technology,* and the *Internet* repeatedly (CCSS, 2010, p. 41). Because of this, many will ignore instruction in online reading, thinking that the CCSS only references traditional, offline reading comprehension. Many may also fail to integrate reading and writing instruction, an important part of any literacy program.

Why? The answer is related to prior knowledge. One of the most consistent patterns in reading research is the finding that the prior knowledge we bring to a text profoundly shapes our interpretation. Given that most of our prior knowledge about reading is derived from an understanding of reading in offline contexts, the U.S. standards are likely to be interpreted in relation to offline reading comprehension, not online reading comprehension. Another way of looking at this issue is to suggest that many educators will read the CCSS only with a lens to our past, and not a lens to our future, failing to include instruction in important online reading skills. Figure 15.1 illustrates the problem in relation to Anchor Reading Standard 1, often referred to as *close reading*: "Read closely to determine what the text says explicitly and to make logical inferences from it; cite specific textual evidence when writing or speaking to support conclusions drawn from the text."

With our extensive prior knowledge derived from offline reading, we naturally interpret this standard, using a lens to our past, and teach inferential reasoning with narrative text offline. On the other hand, when we

Reading with a lens to the past

Reading with a lens to the future

- We would use narrative text.
- We would teach inferential reasoning about setting, events, problems, solutions, characters, etc.
- Typical discussion questions might include:
  o Tell us what you think will happen next?
  o What evidence in your text suggests this answer?

- We would use informational text such as search engine results.
- We would teach how to infer information from search result listings.
- Typical discussion questions might include:
  o Which of these sites is a commercial site?
  o What evidence in the text suggests this?
  o Which of these sites comes from England? Which comes from Minnesota?
  o What evidence in the text suggests this?

FIGURE 15.1. Reading the U.S. CCSS with a lens to the past and a lens to the future.

read this standard using a lens to the future, we would think of the inferential reasoning required to read in different contexts online, perhaps the reading of search engine results. When we read search engine results to select the best site for our needs, we are required to make many inferences about what we would find at each link. Many students do not read search engine results; they simply click and look their way down each list of search results, reviewing each web page, often skipping right past a useful resource (Leu, Forzani, & Kennedy, 2013). Instruction in how to make inferences and use textual evidence to support those inferences would be very useful to students. Educators who read with both a lens to the past and a lens to the future would interpret Reading Anchor Standard 1 by teaching both types of close reading.

These two lenses operate within most of the other Common Core standards in reading, too. Consider, for example, Reading Anchor Standard 6: "Assess how point of view or purpose shapes the content and style of a text." Someone reading this standard with a lens to the past would interpret it by teaching point of view within narratives, engaging students in discussions about the point of view held by different characters. Someone reading this standard with a lens to the future would interpret it by teaching point of view in relation to the evaluation of a website's reliability, where point of view is one of several important elements to consider when evaluating the reliability of information that is found online. Since the words *Internet* or *online* never appear in the reading standards of the United States and since we are only beginning to develop our knowledge of online reading, we run the risk of interpreting nearly all of the standards in reading with a lens to our past, implementing them only within traditional print contexts. Such an outcome will limit instruction, denying important learning opportunities to our students.

Principles That Inform Instruction in New Literacies and the New Literacies of Online Research and Comprehension

How can we begin to think about instruction in the New Literacies, consistent with newly appearing standards? We provide 10 principles and two instructional ideas that you can use to implement each principle.

Begin Teaching and Learning New Literacies as Early as Possible

Schools should begin to integrate online experiences and new literacies instruction as soon as children begin their literacy education program

(Forzani & Leu, 2012). A useful first step is to use *online* resources to teach CCSS foundational *offline* reading skills in PreK, kindergarten, and first grade. A number of locations can be used to teach the foundational skills of CCSS in both reading and writing. These sites teach early offline reading skills while they also provide important early experiences with navigating an online interface. In short, they allow you to combine both an instructional lens to our past and a lens to our future.

Starfall

Starfall (*www.starfall.com*) is an exceptional resource for children that supports the development of early offline reading skills within an online context. Starfall is free, a gift from the CEO of Blue Mountain Greeting Cards, who is dyslexic, to honor all the teachers of reading who helped him on his journey. It includes delightful activities that teach CCSS foundational skills in reading: letter-name knowledge, phonemic awareness, phonics, and sight word recognition. It also develops both early comprehension and advanced comprehension skills.

ReadWriteThink

ReadWriteThink (*www.readwritethink.org*) is another wonderful resource for teachers of young children, but also every K–12 teacher. It provides an extensive set of lessons in the English language arts developed by teachers. It is also free. There are over 142 lessons developed by teachers for grades K–2 that use children's literature to develop foundational CCSS skills, often using online resources.

Use New Literacies to Help the Last Student Become the First

Make it a policy to always teach a new technology, with new literacies, to your weakest reader(s) first. This enables struggling readers and writers to become literate in this new technology before other, higher-performing students in reading. Those who struggle with reading and writing become literate in a new literacy before others and can teach this new literacy to others who are not literate with this new form. This is a powerful principle that positions weaker readers as experts. It should always be used. Unfortunately, the opposite often happens. Struggling readers frequently are denied access to online experiences because their offline literacy skills are thought to be insufficient to permit success (Castek, Zawilinski, McVerry, O'Byrne, & Leu, 2011). Avoid this problem by helping your weakest students become literate in a new technology first.

Teach E-Mail to Struggling Readers First

In the next few years, all classrooms will be using child-safe e-mail systems that are available, and often free, such as ePals. Capitalize on this opportunity by teaching struggling readers the New Literacies required by your student e-mail system and then have them teach their newly acquired e-mail skills to other students. Have them also be available to support those who require assistance.

Teach Blogging and Wiki Skills to Struggling Readers First

When you begin to use wikis and blogs in your classroom, make certain that you use these opportunities, too, to help the last become first with New Literacies. Imagine a first or fifth grader who has been struggling with literacy learning suddenly becoming the class expert on how to create a new blog comment or post. A few minutes of coaching on the necessary steps puts this student in the expert seat. The rest of the class then relies on this student for instruction and coaching. This student's role in the classroom shifts as he or she shares responsibility for teaching important reading and writing skills.

Teach Online Search Skills Since These Are Important to Success in the New Literacies of Online Research and Comprehension

The ability to read and locate online information is a gate-keeping skill. If one cannot locate information online, it becomes very hard to solve a problem with online information and to learn in online spaces.

Additional reading skills and strategies are required to generate effective keyword search strategies (Kuiper & Volman, 2008); to read and infer which link may be most useful among a set of search engine results (Henry, 2006); and to efficiently scan for relevant information within websites (Rouet, Ros, Goumi, Macedo-Rouet, & Dinet, 2011). Each is important to integrate into classroom reading programs.

Use Google's "Inside Search"

Search engines regularly add new search capabilities that are not always known to users. To keep up to date with those that are added to Google, visit Google's "Inside Search" at *www.google.com/insidesearch/searcheducation/index.html*. Here you will find lesson plans, activities to improve your own search skills, daily search challenges for your students, and training webinars for both you and your students. There is a similar page for the

Bing search engine at *http://onlinehelp.microsoft.com/en-us/bing*. Bing integrates closely with Facebook, which provides additional search capabilities.

Play "One Click"

To develop better close reading skills during the reading of search results, play "One Click." Conduct a search for any topic that you are studying in class. If you lack an interactive whiteboard or a projector, print out enough copies of the first page of search results for each student. Distribute these. Then see if students can locate the best link on the search results page for each question that you ask such as, "Which link will take you to a site developed by an Egyptologist?" or "Which site on this page is a commercial site and will probably try to sell you something?" Each question should require students to make an inference from the limited information appearing in the search results list. If you have an interactive whiteboard or a projector, do the same but ask students to come to the projected screen and point to the answer they think is correct, explaining their reasoning and teaching others, showing them the evidence that they used.

Use Online Reading Experiences to Develop Critical Thinking Skills and a Generation of "Healthy Skeptics"

A central objective of any instructional program in the New Literacies is to develop students who read as "healthy skeptics." We seek to raise a generation of students who always question the information they read for reliability and accuracy, always read to infer bias or point of view, and always check the sources they encounter while reading. The Internet demands this.

Critically evaluating online information includes the ability to read and evaluate the level of accuracy, reliability, and bias of information (Center for Media Literacy, 2005). Although these skills have always been necessary with offline texts (Bråten, Strømsø, & Britt, 2009; Bråten, Strømsø, & Salmerón, 2011), the proliferation of unedited information and the merging of commercial marketing with educational content (Fabos, 2008) presents additional challenges that are quite different from traditional print and media sources, requiring new strategies during online reading.

Without explicit training in these new literacy skills, many students become confused and overwhelmed when asked to judge the accuracy, reliability, and bias of information they encounter in online reading environments (Graham & Metaxas, 2003; Sanchez, Wiley, & Goldman, 2006; Sundar, 2008). Your leadership in this area will ensure that students in your district graduate with the critical evaluation skills required in an online age.

Reverse Wikipedia

Typically, Wikipedia is simply used for information. Reverse this and use Wikipedia to make critical evaluation skills the primary focus. Select an entry for any topic being studied in the classroom. For homework, have students find one claim made at the site that is contested by others online and bring the disputed information as well as the sources to class. Have students share their disputed facts and sources and discuss critical evaluation strategies that could be used to help resolve the conflict. This conversation will teach many new online research and comprehension strategies to your students.

Source Plus

Schools increasingly require students to list the sources of any online information that is used in a report. Take this one step further and require students to also indicate how they determined that each source was reputable and reliable.

Integrate Online Communication into Lessons

It is easy to integrate the Internet into classrooms through the use of online communication tools such as e-mail, wikis, and blogs, as well as the child-safe social networks for schools that are now beginning to appear. Each creates a wonderfully natural way in which to develop a culture of effective online information use in classrooms (Zawilinski, 2012). Importantly, they may also be used to keep parents informed about what is taking place in classrooms.

As we begin to integrate these online communication tools into our classrooms, we should not ignore concerns about child safety. We want to restrict communication only to our students and to a community of people whom we can trust, such as parents and other teachers and students. There are many versions of wikis, blogs, and e-mail that can provide these protections. Typically, they do this in three ways. First, most permit you to restrict access. You can often list the addresses of people you wish to be able to view, add, or edit information. Second, many tools, especially child-safe e-mail tools, permit you to approve any message before it is sent. Finally, most prohibit e-mail from outside coming in as well as e-mails going to addresses outside the e-mail system that you use.

Investigate Other Teachers' Use of Blogs, Wikis, and E-Mail in Their Classrooms

To gather ideas about how online communication tools can be used effectively in classrooms simply search online to see how other teachers do this (Zawilinski, 2009). Using Twitter hash tags such as #educhat #engchat or #edtechchat is one way of connecting with teachers and sharing blog and wiki resources. Another is to search online with keywords such as 1st-grade classroom blog, 4th-grade classroom blog, classroom wiki, or classroom e-mail. Send links of good classroom models to other teachers in your school to review and consider.

Child-Safe E-Mail at ePals and Gaggle

Both ePals (*www.epals.com*) and Gaggle (*www.gaggle.net*) provide child-safe e-mail. Many teachers begin classroom e-mail use by choosing settings that limit students to exchanging e-mails with other students in the classroom. Later teachers adjust settings to permit e-mail to students in other classrooms in your school. Finally, they open settings to other students around the world who have been admitted into the system. At each step you can monitor all correspondence if you wish.

When Online Tools Are Blocked, Use the Word Pilot to Create New Instructional Opportunities in Your Classroom

Technology coordinators often place severe restrictions on classroom access to Internet tools for one reason or another. As a literacy educator you should determinedly work to make access to child-safe online tools and resources easier for students in your classroom.

A useful strategy is to meet with your principal and suggest that a "pilot" be implemented in your classroom for an online technology that is blocked by your district. Prepare for this meeting carefully. Describe what the technology does, how it will increase opportunities for students, and how you will ensure child safety. Also suggest that a note be sent to parents to inform them about what will be taking place, why it is important, and to request their permission. Thus, anxieties are reduced and, after a successful pilot, your school may be more receptive to additional innovations.

Conduct a Pilot with Edmodo

Edmodo is an educational tool for online collaboration that uses an interface similar to that of social networks. Should it be blocked by your district, ask to conduct a pilot of this tool in one classroom to evaluate its potential for other classrooms. Edmodo has elements that can be used to support child safety. Access can be limited only to students in a single classroom. Also, teachers can approve student posts before they appear. Help students prepare for face-to-face discussion by asking them to post their initial thinking to Edmodo and then read other classmates' comments before the discussion. They can post their response as an image or text and invite others to respond.

Conduct a Pilot with Google Drive

Google Drive (*https://drive.google.com*) is an online suite of tools. While more and more schools are seeing the usefulness of Google Drive for their students, many still block this tool. Google Drive offers free online tools, including Google Docs for word processing, spreadsheets, forms, presentations, and drawing pages. Word-processing and other files may be used by anyone with permission from the creator. Thus, multiple students and teachers can collaboratively work on a single document at once. Using this tool as part of a pilot is a low-risk way to begin implementing technology into the classroom.

Use Performance-Based Assessments for Evaluating Students' Ability with New Literacies

Good instruction is informed by good assessment. While no assessment is perfect (Darling-Hammond, 2010), some have argued that performance-based assessments do this better than many other forms of assessments (Wiggins, 1998). Performance-based assessments provide more diagnostic information than do many other types of assessments, for they are administered while students perform an authentic task.

Some initial models for assessing the new literacies of online research and comprehension have appeared. For example, the PISA Digital Reading Assessment (Organization for Economic Cooperation and Development [OECD], 2011) evaluated 15-year-olds from a number of different countries. Another approach is the Online Research and Comprehension Assessment, or ORCA (Leu, Kulikowich, Sedransk, & Coiro, 2009). Each online research task in science is directed through chat messages from an avatar student within a social network. Along the way, students are asked to locate four different websites and summarize the central information from each using their notepad. They also evaluate the source reliability of a website and write a short report of their research in either a wiki or an e-mail message. The assessments have demonstrated high levels of both reliability and validity (Leu, Coiro, Kulikowich, & Cui, 2012). This format and the performance-based nature of the assessment may provide a model for others. To gain greater understanding of what performance-based assessments of online research and comprehension will look like in the future, you may view a video of one student completing one of the assessments: *http://neag.uconn.edu/orca-video-ira*.

The extent to which CCSS assessments will focus on offline and online literacies is not yet clear. What does appear to be clear is that to the extent performance-based assessments in new literacies are included in CCSS assessments, teachers are likely to be better informed about instruction.

Use Informal Observation Strategies

While we wait for better formal assessments, you can use informal observations of students conducting online research to gain important diagnostic information about an individual student's ability. Give students a short online research project and carefully observe how they locate, evaluate, synthesize, and communicate information online during their research. Careful observation is a teacher's best instructional friend.

Use Think-Alouds

Another way to gather informal, performance-based assessment data is through think-alouds. As students learn about online research, invite one student to think aloud using the projected screen so the entire class can see online research and comprehension strategies in action. This will provide students with new strategies and provide you with important insights about needed skill development.

Use Internet Reciprocal Teaching in One-to-One Computing Classrooms

As we move to one-to-one computing classrooms (cf. Argueta, Huff, Tingen, & Corn, 2011), we will be challenged to teach new literacies. Teachers may have only a few seconds of their students' attention to teach a new online skill if laptops are open. If laptops are closed, attention may not be substantially greater. A central issue is this: How do you teach a new online research and comprehension skill in the 15 seconds or so that you have students' attention? One way is to embed the skill you seek to teach in a research problem for groups of students to solve. When you see a student use the target skill that you have embedded into the research problem, have that student explain what he or she did on the projected screen so that others can also solve the problem. This approach, a part of Internet Reciprocal Teaching (Leu et al., 2008), has demonstrated efficacy in the classroom for developing online research and comprehension skills (Leu & Reinking, 2010).

Teach Source Evaluation Skills

If you want to teach source evaluation skills, have small groups conduct research to answer a three-part problem such as this:

1. How high is Mt. Fuji in feet?
2. Find a different answer to this same question.
3. Which answer do you trust and why do you trust it?

As you observe students begin work on the third part of the problem, you likely will see a student begin to use the strategy that you have targeted: locating and evaluating the source of the information. When you see someone use this strategy, perhaps by clicking on a link to "About Us," interrupt the other groups and have this student teach the strategy to the class, explaining how he or she evaluates a source for expertise and reliability. There are many inconsistent facts online that can also be used, just like this, to teach source evaluation including: "How long is the Mississippi River?" or "What is the population of San Francisco?"

Monitor Laptop Use

Consider the use of monitoring software on your computer in one-to-one classrooms. Monitoring software places a thumbnail image of each student's computer screen on the teacher's computer. This may be used to observe students to evaluate their strengths and skill needs. It may also be used to display a student's screen when the student is teaching an important new skill that he or she has discovered to the class. There are many different monitoring software programs including Apple Remote Desktop, LanSchool, Netop School, and others.

Prepare Students for Their Future by Using Collaborative Online Learning Experiences with Classroom Partners in Other Parts of the World

Some teachers are beginning to explore the future of classroom instruction. They connect with other classrooms around the world to engage in collaborative classroom learning projects. These classrooms use ePals, Google Drive, blogs, e-mail, wikis, and simple web page development tools to learn, exchange information, and work on collaborative research projects. With these projects, students increase their new literacies skills, develop a richer understanding of content, and a greater understanding of the differences that define our planet. Most importantly, these experiences provide students with preparation for the world they will soon enter, especially in the workplace.

Use Internet Morning Message of the Week

Use e-mail to connect with several teachers at your grade level, possibly in different countries, and set up a weekly e-mail exchange project. Invite each participating classroom to send the other classrooms a weekly e-mail message, describing what took place in their classroom on one day. Thus, each classroom will receive a number of messages from around the world each week. Print copies out for students or display them on a projected screen to help students develop new friends and a richer understanding of the world around them. In younger grades, ask your class to dictate a response each week, while you transcribe it. In older grades, assign the report-writing project to a different group each week. Have another group serve as editors to read, suggest revisions, and edit the work. Then send it out to the other participating classes.

Find an International Classroom and Work on a Common Project

Use tools like "Find a Classroom Match" (*www.epals.com/find-classroom*) to connect with classrooms around the world. Visit "Join a Project" (*www.epals.com/find-project*) to select a classroom learning project. Both sites require you to register in order to access the free, child-safe e-mail. You may need to request that your district provide your classroom with access to these resources. If so, request that you be permitted to conduct a pilot for your school.

Recognize That a New Literacies Journey Is One of Continuous Learning

As new technologies appear on the Internet, new literacies and new opportunities for instruction appear (International Reading Association, 2009). Consider, for example, one student who was reading online about the height of Mount Rainier. She had located the height in feet, 14,410, but wished to know what it was in meters so she could share it with a friend in France. A second student noticed the problem and showed her a strategy that had become possible with an update to this search engine. This second student went to the Google search box in the browser and typed in "14410 ft. to meters." She knew this would produce the conversion immediately and the answer was quickly listed at the top of the search results page. Not only had the first student determined the answer without an additional lengthy search, she also acquired a new literacy skill.

Examples like this take place regularly as we encounter new affordances within older technologies or as new technologies, themselves, appear. They remind us that our New Literacies' future is really a journey, not a destination. The regular appearance of New Literacies requires additional roles for teachers and students.

For teachers, it means bringing both a lens to the future and a lens to the past to each Common Core standard, integrating online literacy experiences into the classroom in a regular and thoughtful fashion. This will require knowing which online reading and writing skills are important to support. It will also mean developing learning experiences for these skills. In addition, it means learning from other colleagues, an important source of information in a world where it is hard for any one person to keep up with all of the changes that are taking place. It also means being on the lookout for new skills and strategies that students in your class manifest so you can then distribute these skills to your other students and to fellow teachers.

For students, it means having regular, consistent, and safe access to online technologies in the classroom and at home. When this is not possible at home, it becomes even more important for it to be available at school.

Build an Online Support System

Keep a running list of the best new online tools and resources that you encounter. Regularly distribute these through your school's social network, e-mail, wiki, or blog, and encourage others to do the same. Consider sharing resources with teachers outside of your school community by using online professional learning networks linked through wikis or Twitter hash tags. This will quickly build a community around the effective integration of online new literacies into classrooms.

Build an Online Expert Board

Keep an Online Expert Board in your classroom or on your class blog or wiki. As you observe students who demonstrate new and useful online reading and writing strategies, add the name of the student and the skill they displayed in an Online Expert Board, where everyone can see it. Students can use this information when they need help, finding another student who might be able to help them.

Reflections and Future Directions

In a world in which change takes place to literacy every single day, it is impossible to accurately predict precisely what literacy instruction will look like in the future. We believe, however, that the new literacies of online research and comprehension will always be central for learning, though these new literacies will continuously evolve. We also believe that the future will include online technologies for literacy that do not exist now, requiring even newer skills and strategies to be developed by our students. These changes will require each of us to always have one lens turned to the future so that we might continuously learn about even newer online tools that we can use in our classrooms, preparing our students for their future.

ENGAGEMENT ACTIVITIES

1. *Develop a lens to the future for the CCSS in reading.* Review the Common Core standards for your grade level. How can you implement each one in a way that uses a lens to the future to develop online reading research and comprehension skills? What activities mentioned in this chapter can you begin to implement now?

2. *Implement lessons in reading and online searching for information.* Visit "Inside Search" at *www.google.com/insidesearch/searcheducation/index.html* and implement one of the many lessons in your classroom. Observe the results. Which online search skills do your students have? Which do they lack? Develop additional lessons to support them in this area of reading to locate information.

3. *During a shared reading activity, model your thinking for students as you read across different websites.* Notice and predict what information lies behind certain links. Look for similarities and differences across information on sites. Demonstrate how readers try to corroborate information between different sources, and show students how you think through aspects of source evaluation.

4. *Use ePals to connect with other classrooms.* Subscribe to ePals. It is free. Then communicate with teachers around the world at your level who are looking to collaborate. Plan a collaborative activity with your students and their students.

REFERENCES

Afflerbach, P., & Cho, B.-Y. (2008). Determining and describing reading strategies: Internet and traditional forms of reading. In H. S. Waters & W. Schneider (Eds.), *Metacognition, strategy use, and instruction* (pp. 201–255). New York: Guilford Press.

Alvermann, D., Hutchins, R. J., & DeBlasio, R. (2012). Adolescents' engagement with Web 2.0 and social media: Research, theory, and practice. *Research in the Schools, 19*(1), 33–44.

Argueta, R., Huff, J., Tingen, J., & Corn, J. (2011). Laptop initiatives: Summary of research across six states. North Carolina State University, College of Education. Retrieved from *www.fi.ncsu.edu/assets/podcast_episodes/white-paper-series/laptopinitiatives-summary-of-research-across-six-states.pdf*.

Australian Curriculum, Assessment and Reporting Authority. (n.d.). The Australian Curriculum, v3.0. Available at *www.australiancurriculum.edu.au/Home*.

Bennet, S., Maton, K., & Kervin, L. (2008). The "digital natives": A critical review of the evidence. *British Journal of Educational Technology, 39*, 775–786.

Bråten, I., Strømsø, H. I., & Britt, M. A. (2009). Trust matters: Examining the role of source evaluation in students' construction of meaning within and across multiple texts. *Reading Research Quarterly, 44*(1), 6–28.

Bråten, I., Strømsø, H. I., & Salmerón, L. (2011). Trust and mistrust when students read multiple information sources about climate change. *Learning and Instruction, 21*(2), 180–192.

Castek, J., Zawilinski, L., McVerry, G., O'Byrne, I., & Leu, D. J. (2011). The new literacies of online reading comprehension: New opportunities and challenges for students with learning difficulties. In C. Wyatt-Smith, J. Elkins, & S. Gunn (Eds.), *Multiple perspectives on difficulties in learning literacy and numeracy* (pp. 91–110). New York: Springer.

Center for Media Literacy. (2005). Literacy for the 21st century: An overview and orientation guide to media literacy education. Part 1 of the CML media lit kit: Framework for learning and teaching in a media age. Retrieved from *www.medialit.org/cml-medialit-kit*.

Christensen, C. M. (1997). *The innovator's dilemma: When new technologies cause great firms to fail*. Boston: Harvard Business School Press.

Coiro, J., & Castek, J. (2010). Assessment frameworks for teaching and learning English language arts in a digital age. In D. Lapp & D. Fisher (Eds.), *Handbook of research on teaching the English language arts* (3rd ed., pp. 314–321). Co-sponsored by the International Reading Association and the National Council of Teachers of English. New York: Rutledge.

Common Core State Standards Initiative. (2012). Common Core State Standards Initiative: Preparing America's students for college and career. Retrieved from *www.corestandards.org*.

Darling-Hammond, L. (2010). Performance-based assessment and educational equity. *Harvard Educational Review, 64*(1), 5–31.

Drew, S. (2012). Open up the ceiling on the Common Core State Standards. *Journal of Adolescent and Adult Literacy, 56*, 321–330.

Fabos, B. (2008). The price of information: Critical literacy, education, and today's Internet. In J. Coiro, M. Knobel, C. Lankshear, & D. Leu (Eds.), *Handbook of research on new literacies* (pp. 839–870). Mahwah, NJ: Erlbaum.

Forzani, E., & Leu, D. J. (2012). New literacies for new learners. *Educational Forum, 76*(4). 421–424.

Forzani, E., & Maykel, C. (2013). Evaluating Connecticut Students' Ability to Critically Evaluate Online Information. *CARReader, 10,* 23–37.

Graham, L., & Metaxas, P. T. (2003). Of course it's true: I saw it on the Internet! *Communications of the ACM, 46*(5), 71–75.

Henry, L. (2006). SEARCHing for an answer: The critical role of new literacies while reading on the Internet. *The Reading Teacher, 59,* 614–627.

International Reading Association. (2009). *IRA position statement on new literacies and 21st century technologies.* Newark, DE: Author. Available at *www.reading. org/General/AboutIRA/PositionStatements/21stCenturyLiteracies.aspx.*

Kress, G. (2003). *Literacy in the new media age.* London: Routledge.

Kuiper, E., & Volman, M. (2008). The Web as a source of information for students in K–12 education. In J. Coiro, M. Knobel, C. Lankshear, & D. Leu (Eds.), *Handbook of research on new literacies* (pp. 241–246). Mahwah, NJ: Erlbaum.

Leu, D. J., Coiro, J., Castek, J., Hartman, D., Henry, L. A., & Reinking, D. (2008). Research on instruction and assessment in the new literacies of online reading comprehension. In C. C. Block & S. R. Parris (Eds.), *Comprehension instruction: Research-based best practices* (pp. 111–153). New York: Guilford Press.

Leu, D. J., Coiro, J., Kulikowich, J., & Cui, W. (2012, December). *Using the psychometric characteristics of multiple-choice, open Internet, and closed (simulated) Internet formats to refine the development of online research and comprehension assessments in science: Year three of the ORCA project.* Paper presented at the annual meeting of the Literacy Research Association, San Diego, CA.

Leu, D. J., Forzani, E., & Kennedy, C. (2013). Providing classroom leadership in new literacies: Preparing students for their future. In S. B. Wepner, D. S. Strickland, & D. Quatroche (Eds.), *The administration and supervision of reading programs* (5th ed., pp. 200–213). New York: Teachers College Press.

Leu, D. J., Kinzer, C. K., Coiro, J., Castek, J., & Henry, L. A. (2013). New literacies: A dual level theory of the changing nature of literacy, instruction, and assessment. In N. Unrau & D. Alvermann (Eds.), *Theoretical models and processes of reading* (6th ed., pp. 1150–1181). Newark, DE: International Reading Association.

Leu, D. J., Kulikowich, J., Sedransk, N., & Coiro, J. (2009). *Assessing online reading comprehension: The ORCA project.* Research grant funded by the U.S. Department of Education, Institute of Education Sciences.

Leu, D. J., McVerry, J. G., O'Byrne, W. I., Kiili, C., Zawilinski, L., Everett-Cacopardo, H., et al. (2011). The new literacies of online reading comprehension: Expanding the literacy and learning curriculum. *Journal of Adolescent and Adult Literacy 55*(1), 5–14.

Leu, D. J., & Reinking, D. (2010). Final report: Developing Internet comprehension strategies among adolescent students at risk to become dropouts. U.S. Department of Education, Institute of Education Sciences Research Grant. Retrieved from *www.newliteracies.uconn.edu/iesproject/researchdocuments.html.*

Lewis, C., & Fabos, B. (2005). Instant messaging, literacies, and social identities. *Reading Research Quarterly, 40*, 470–501.

Minister of Manitoba Education, Citizenship, and Youth. (2006). A continuum model for literacy with ICT across the curriculum: A resource for developing computer literacy. Retrieved from *www.edu.gov.mb.ca/k12/tech/lict/resources/handbook/index.htm.*

National Governors Association for Best Practices & Council of Chief State School Officers. (2010). *Common Core State Standards for English language arts and literacy in history/social studies, science, and technical subjects.* Washington, DC: Author. Retrieved from *www.corestandards.org/assets/CCSSI_ELA%20Standards.pdf.*

Organization for Economic Co-operation and Development. (2011). PISA 2009 results: Students on line: Digital technologies and performance (Vol. 6). Retrieved from *http://dx.doi.org/10.1787/9789264112995-en.*

PIAAC Expert Group on Problem Solving in Technology-Rich Environments. (2009). *Problem solving in technology-rich environments: A conceptual framework* (OECD Education Working Paper No. 36). Paris: OECD. Available at *http://search.oecd.org/officialdocuments/displaydocumentpdf/?cote=edu/wkp(2009)15&doclanguage=en.*

Prensky, M. (2001). Digital natives, digital immigrants. *On the Horizon, 9*(5). 1–6.

Rouet, J.-F., Ros, C., Goumi, A., Macedo-Rouet, M., & Dinet, J. (2011). The influence of surface and deep cues on primary and secondary school students' assessment of relevance in Web menus. *Learning and Instruction, 21*(2), 205–219.

Sanchez, C. A., Wiley, J., & Goldman, S. R. (2006). Teaching students to evaluate source reliability during Internet research tasks. In S. A. Barab, K. E. Hay, & D. T. Hickey (Eds.), *Proceedings of the Seventh International Conference on the Learning Sciences* (pp. 662–666). Bloomington, IN: International Society of the Learning Sciences.

Street, B. (2003). What's new in new literacy studies? *Current Issues in Comparative Education, 5*(2), 1–14.

Sundar, S. S. (2008). The MAIN model: A heuristic approach to understanding technology effects on credibility. In M. J. Metzger & A. J. Flanagin (Eds.), *Digital media, youth, and credibility* (pp. 73–100). Cambridge, MA: MIT Press.

Wiggins, G. (1998). *Educative assessment: Designing assessments to inform and improve student performance.* San Francisco: Jossey-Bass.

Zawilinski, L. (2009). HOT blogging: A framework for blogging to promote higher order thinking. *The Reading Teacher, 62*, 650–661.

Zawilinski, L. (2012). *An exploration of a collaborative blogging approach to literacy and learning: A mixed method study.* Unpublished PhD dissertation, University of Connecticut, Storrs.

Zickuhr, K. (2010). Generations 2010. Pew Internet and American Life project. Retrieved from *www.pewinternet.org/~/media//Files/Reports/2010/PIP_Generations_and_Tech10.pdf.*

CHAPTER 16

Organizing Effective Literacy Instruction

Differentiating Instruction to Meet Student Needs

D. Ray Reutzel
Sarah K. Clark
Michelle Flory

This chapter will:

- Provide an overview of the global and national context in which organizing for classroom literacy instruction is embedded.

- Present the evidence-based elements of effective literacy instruction: Common Core State Standards and response-to-intervention models.

- Discuss the use of assessment data to inform Common Core State Standards and response-to-intervention literacy instruction.

- Describe the use of an array of effective literacy instructional practices to use within the frameworks of Common Core State Standards and response to intervention.

- Offer alternative grouping approaches as a part of effective literacy instruction to use within the frameworks of Common Core State Standards and response to intervention.

- Illustrate the scheduling of a literacy instructional block to support effective literacy instruction in an age of Common Core State Standards and response to intervention.

Evidence-Based Best Practices:
Differentiating Literacy Instruction in a Common Core and Response-to-Intervention Era

Many if not most citizens living in our ever-shrinking, globally connected world would agree that the ability to read is a critical factor in living a healthy, happy, and economically productive life. On the other hand, the inability to read often denies individuals and groups access to many significant educational, social, health care, and economic opportunities. Years ago these facts were widely heralded in a report titled, *Becoming a Nation of Readers* (Anderson, Hiebert, Scott, & Wilkinson, 1985). Unfortunately, more recent U.S. evidence seems to point to a nation of *nonreaders*. We are as a people, by and large, literate but often uninformed. We tend to spend much of our time engaged in almost any other conceivable activity except sustained, deep reading. As a nation we spend less time reading than watching TV or surfing on the Internet. A 2011 national survey revealed that U.S. adults spend 7–12 times more time watching TV than reading books (Bureau of Labor Statistics, 2011). In fact, the National Endowment for the Arts survey in 2004 found about 25% fewer Americans were reading books as compared to previous decades. Jenkins (2008) found in a survey that 58% of U.S. adults don't read a book again after high school graduation and 42% of college graduates never read a book again after college graduation. Eighty percent of U.S. families didn't buy or read a book in the last year and 70% have not been in a bookstore in the last 5 years. These statistics paint a picture of a U.S. population that is able to read, but isn't inclined to do so. This situation does not bode well for a democratic republic such as ours that is highly dependent upon a literate and well-informed populace.

As troubling as these facts are, it is only compounded when national statistics are presented showing a substantial and continuing achievement gap between the rich and the poor, and between Asian and Caucasian students and students of other ethnic and linguistic minorities. And as if that isn't troubling enough, there are international data showing U.S. students' achievement in the bottom half of 30 comparable and competitive nations in literacy, math, and science achievement (Fleishman, Hopstock, Pelczar, & Shelley, 2010). This tale of a nation with increasing numbers of *nonreaders* encumbered by two achievement gaps, one national and one international, has led in the past decade to two important educational reforms that are shaping the literacy instruction of today and tomorrow, as well as influencing the classroom environment that supports literacy instruction. The first of these two educational reforms is the increasing use of response-to-intervention (RTI) models adopted to close the national achievement gap by delivering timely interventions to students who are falling behind their national peers. The second reform is the adoption and implementation of the Common Core State Standards (CCSS) intended to close the international achievement gap between the United States and other developed nations and return the United States to a more advantaged status in the global economy.

Gap 1: The U.S. Achievement Gap

The first achievement gap, which is largely a national concern, has centered on a persistent reading achievement gap. Since 1992, African American, Hispanic, and Native American students have continued to lag significantly behind their Caucasian and Asian peers in reading achievement. By the mid-1990s, political opinions had coalesced around the need for sweeping reforms in literacy instruction and assessment. The politically charged "perfect storm" around literacy was initiated with the National Assessment Educational Progress (NAEP) national report card on reading confirming that the achievement gap between Caucasian and Asian students and those in other economic, ethnic, linguistic, and cultural groups had widened to an all-time high (Williams, Reese, Campbell, Mazzeo, & Phillips, 1995).

The U.S. Congress and the U.S. Department of Education reacted to this devastating news by forming several blue ribbon panels charged with examining research on proven teaching practices and then sharing their findings with the public. The National Reading Panel (NRP; National Institute of Child Health and Human Development, 2000) examined the teaching of reading in elementary and secondary schools; the National Literacy Panel for Language Minority Children and Youth (August & Shanahan, 2006) explored literacy development and instruction for second-language learners; and the National Early Literacy Panel (NELP; 2008) looked at beginning literacy learning for preschoolers and kindergartners. Reports from these three panels have been most influential in reforming public policy and instructional practice in reading. These research findings were not only quickly adopted by commercial reading program publishers, they were also codified into law as a part of the federal government's No Child Left Behind Act (e.g., Reading First, Early Reading First), which included far-reaching policy and legislative changes to federally funded Title I and Head Start programs.

Though there has been modest progress in closing the national reading achievement gap, results of these initiatives have been disappointing. Although the achievement gap narrowed to its lowest measured level since 1992, it is clear that children in specific ethnic groups, often those living in poverty, continue to fail to read at grade level at more than twice the rate of those living out of poverty, and in Asian and Caucasian ethnic groups. Too many students in the most rapidly growing segment of U.S. society, namely African American, Hispanic, and Native American children, continue to perform at levels below their peers nationally in basic reading proficiency.

The RTI model is a recent addition to the special education law titled the Individuals with Disabilities Education Act (IDEA). RTI is a recommended process for schools to follow when working with children who are struggling to learn to read or who are not reading at grade level. The underlying premise of RTI is that the instruction students receive, or have received previously, is not sufficient to meet the needs of the learner. There are three levels, or tiers, of instruction that make up the RTI model. First, there is Tier 1 instruction that consists of the standards and objectives taught at each grade level. Tier 1 instruction is intended for the whole class or heterogeneous small groups with differentiated levels. This instruction is usually from a research-based core literacy program taught with fidelity to the program. In instances where student progress is not being met in Tier 1 instruction there is a pressing need to address the instructional effectiveness and the curriculum materials in use. For those students who lag behind their peers or who lack competence in one or more key literacy skills, Tier 2 is needed. Tier 2 reading instruction provides targeted, small-group literacy instruction to meet the needs of the individual struggling reader. It relies heavily on reading assessments to help determine those needs. Schools often have a district-adopted program for teachers to use in Tier 2 instruction. If the student does not respond to Tier 2 intervention, then a more intensive form of instruction is implemented. The third and final tier is Tier 3 instruction, sometimes referred to as the "double-dose" intervention. Students can be serviced individually, although most Tier 3 instruction continues in small groups and are taught by the teacher, reading specialist, or special educator.

A variety of reading assessments play an important role in assisting the teacher in providing the correct form of instruction to each of the students in the class. Types of reading assessments include screening, diagnostic, progress monitoring, and outcome assessments. Some of these are used before, during, and after the reading process. Teacher observations also provide the necessary information needed to make instructional decisions, as do regular consultations with reading specialists and/or reading coaches who utilize assessment data to inform instructional decisions. The RTI model operates in a functional way to close the national achievement gap between those who typically perform well without supplementary reading instructional attention and those who typically lag behind (Reutzel & Cooter, 2016).

Gap 2: The International Reading Achievement Gap

The second achievement gap, an international concern, has resulted from academic achievement comparisons of U.S. graduating high school seniors with graduates from 34 other highly developed world nations and economies. These comparisons have revealed that U.S. students lag approximately 2 years behind the academic performance levels of similarly aged graduating students in other developed nations. An increasingly influential group of corporate, governmental, and public policy advocacy groups see these two literacy-related achievement gaps as threats to the U.S. economy and even national security (Brill, 2011; Darling-Hammond, 2010; Friedman & Mandelbaum, 2011; Neuman & Celano, 2012; Perry, 2011; Weber, 2010).

The Progress in International Reading Literacy Study (PIRLS), released in 2011, is an international comparative study of fourth-grade student literacy-related achievement (Wagner, 2008). In 2011, 57 educational systems participated in the PIRLS comparison and five nations scored higher than the United States, and others scored significantly higher. As stated in the book *Waiting for "Superman,"* "the steady progress of the American education system has ground to a halt. As countries in the rest of the world have continued to advance, U.S. reading and math scores have frozen in place" (Weber, 2010, p. 17).

There is increasing concern about how U.S. students stack up when compared to the other 34 developed nations in the world on competitive rankings in literacy, science, and mathematics (Wagner, 2008). According to the Programme for International Student Achievement (see Fleischman, Hopstock, Pelczar, & Shelley, 2010), the United States ranks 14th in literacy, 17th in science, and 25th in mathematics among 34 developed comparable nations. These rankings continue to highlight a considerable gap in the nation's student academic outcomes when compared to students in other developed nations. This fact in turn raises concerns about U.S. students' abilities to compete in an increasingly competitive world economy in the future.

Although increased attention given to teaching children the essential or critical components of the literacy process in the past decade has resulted in moderate national effects (Mathes et al., 2005; NAEP, 2011; NELP, 2008; Rathvon, 2004), the detrimental national and international achievement gaps continue to persist. In an effort to "raise the bar" of literacy achievement expectations to assure readiness of U.S. students for career and college upon high school graduation, the National Governors' Association and the Council of Chief State School Officers (NGA & CCSSO, 2010) joined together in the adoption, implementation, and assessment of the CCSS for the English language arts (K–12) (ELA K–12 CCSS).

As of this writing, 45 states, the District of Columbia, four U.S. territories, and the Department of Defense Education Activity have adopted the ELA K–12 CCSS. This state-by-state adoption of learning standards represents the first time in U.S. history that there has been a near border-to-border coordination of learning goals. The vast majority of teachers and students nationally will be using these ELA K–12 CCSS or something closely related now or in the near future.

Not only do the CCSS represent the most extensive basis in history for national agreement on learning standards concerning what students should know and be able to do in literacy, but these new standards are markedly higher than past standards in terms of what they expect teachers to accomplish with their students (Carmichael, Martino, Porter-Magee, & Wilson, 2010; McLaughlin & Overturf, 2013; Morrow, Wixson, & Shanahan, 2013). In the past, educational standards have typically been written using a developmental model from youngest to oldest learners. With the CCSS, the designers seemed to have followed the recommendations of the late Stephen Covey (2004) in his book titled *The Seven Habits of Highly Effective People*; they began with the end in mind. In other words, they reverse-engineered the CCSS by starting with what is expected of college- and career-ready high school seniors, and then reverse-engineered the CCSS from there. As Shanahan (2013, p. 208) wrote, "Past standards have represented what educators thought they could accomplish, while the CCSS are a description of what students would need to learn if they are to leave school able to participate in U.S. society and to compete globally by working or continuing their education."

The CCSS are without a doubt more demanding of both teachers and students. They represent a forward-looking, 21st-century representation of what the high school graduating student needs. In the initial stages of implementation and assessment, it is highly likely that school administrators and teachers will see fewer students meeting these higher literacy standards.

The CCSS elevate the expectations of teachers to teach all children to read and write well enough to succeed in college and career. Thus, using the evidence-based standards of effective literacy instruction from the first decade of the new millennium (NELP, 2008; NRP, 2000), teachers now have an objective clearly in view: helping students achieve the new and more demanding performances outlined in the CCSS (NGA & CCSSO, 2010). The intention of this instruction is to lift all students to international standards' proficiency in reading and writing, which will close the international achievement gap through the offering of evidence-based and standards-based high-quality Tier 1 literacy instruction across the grades as is typically explicated in a RTI model of instructional delivery (Fuchs, Fuchs, & Vaughn, 2008).

If there is one clear message that classroom teachers should take away from this brief recitation of issues related to literacy instruction and assessment, it is the significance that the United States places on the ability of its citizens to read and read well. Consequently, it has been in the past and indeed is today a continuing national priority for our citizens to once again become *A Nation of Readers.* Teachers occupy a unique and important position to positively affect the literacy achievement of the next generation by organizing for and delivering effective literacy instruction that meets the needs of *all* students, preparing them for successful careers and college and becoming lifelong readers.

The next section of this chapter is devoted to best practices in action. We begin with a description of CCSS Tier 1 literacy instruction that incorporates elements of evidence-based reading and writing instruction into three allocated time blocks. Following this description, we discuss how teachers can organize their classrooms to support Tier 2, small-group, targeted literacy instruction, which is derived from administration of progress-monitoring assessments that reveal students' skill, strategy, or conceptual instructional needs. We provide illustrations of how to manage the complexities of the classroom environment where whole-class, small-group, and individual instruction is the new normal, expected practice in literacy instruction.

Best Practices in Action

A Classroom Vignette

It's the first day of school for 27 excited and somewhat frightened third-grade children. Ms. Wilki, third-grade teacher at West Elementary School, greets each child with a warm smile and a friendly handshake as each one enters a clean classroom that has been carefully crafted to support a variety of literacy teaching and learning opportunities to meet the diverse needs of children in today's classrooms.

The classroom is organized and partitioned into several areas including whole-class, small-group, and individual learning centers. The classroom is filled with print—labeled objects, posters, charts, daily schedules, objectives for the day, message centers, books, word walls, word chunks, environmental print collections, signs, work board or classroom routine displays—ready to implement the new CCSS curriculum designed to prepare college- and career-ready students. A multicolored carpet with squares for each student is located at the front of the room near the dry-erase whiteboard. The big open space seems to be the perfect "staging area" for group gatherings, read-alouds, and conversations up close to the soft teacher's chair. Near this location there is an iPod docking station and an easel stocked with large chart paper and an area for big books readied for whole-class instruction. A small horseshoe-shaped table in a distant corner of the classroom awaits teacher-directed, targeted, small-group literacy instruction groups. It is topped with a few colored bins filled with literacy manipulatives like vocabulary cards, mini whiteboards with markers and erasers, word sort cards, and a jar of popsicle sticks with each child's name on it to ensure each child gets a turn.

Around the perimeter of the classroom there are multiple literacy centers focusing on foundational skills (word work and fluency), comprehension, and writing. A publishing center runs along one side of the room opposite the windows; on a cupboard top in this area, a full line of writing tools and materials await anxious but willing hands for writing and publishing. A carpeted reading nook, complete with several comfortable chairs for independent reading, is neatly organized in a quiet area of the room.

Nonfiction books about the science topic that week are on display above the classroom library chidlren's books, which are available to check out on the classroom library clipboard. Near the front of the room is a writing center complete with individual computer tablets with word processors, a computer with Internet access and a printer, telephone, desk, writing tablets, pencils, pens, erasers, markers, rubber stamps, dictionary, speller, and a dry-erase board for business planning and messages. Across the room sits a small center stocked with vocabulary words, definitions, laminated word maps, computer tablets with connections to Wikipedia, *Dictionary.com*, thesaurus, and other word research tools to enable children to study word meanings and meaningful word parts. Near the classroom door is a paired or buddy reading fluency center stocked with digital recorders, headphones, browsing boxes for reading practice, and materials for evaluating self and others' reading fluency. A storage area with 20 large plastic trays is located on the other side of the classroom door. The classroom has desks organized into pods to facilitate group interaction and projects. The light in the room is bright and cheerful with a lamp near Ms Wilki's desk next to a picture of her family and some framed notes from past students. Children are instructed to each find a chair with his or her own nametag. School is ready to start.

If permitted, Ms. Wilki would tell us that much study, reading, planning, thought, and preparation has proceeded this momentous day. It is common knowledge that effective classroom environments include a variety of grouping strategies, effective classroom routines, classroom management that encourages self-regulation, and effective instructional interventions that do not occur by accident. These complex organizational components, like so much of effective literacy instruction, are the products of teacher knowledge, skill, and ingenuity.

As you can tell from the vignette above, Ms. Wilki attends to the individual differences students bring with them to school, and she is well aware that not all students respond to instruction in the same way or with similar enthusiasm. Ms. Wilki also understands that every child needs to be taught, to varying degrees, all of the components of evidence-based literacy Tier 1 instruction that addresses grade-level CCSS (Neuman, Gambrell, & Massey, 2013). This is not meant to imply that a one-size-fits-all instructional approach using the CCSS will be effective with all children. Following such high-quality instruction, teachers will collect and analyze progress monitoring data and design Tier 2 and Tier 3, targeted literacy instruction delivered in small groups and individually to fill gaps and strengthen the acquisition of established standards.

The Daily Literacy Block: Organizing an Effective Instructional Routine

Students develop a sense of security when the events of the school day revolve around a sequence of familiar activities. Although variety is the spice of life, students find comfort in familiar instructional routines and schedules in a well-organized classroom (Holdaway, 1984). There are any number of ways to organize the activities and instruction of the school day. It is important, however, that children experience a variety of interactive settings as a whole class, in small groups, and individually each day. Groups should be flexible, meet the needs of the students, incorporate assessment data to inform instructional decisions, and involve the "best practices" of literacy instruction. It is also important that children receive daily planned, intentional, and explicit instruction in the critical components, strategies, and skills of learning to read and write successfully.

One such approach used to organize the school day is the Daily Literacy Instruction Block, based in part on the recommendations of Shanahan (2004) and also based on the work of Mathes and colleagues (2005) relating to the value of small-group reading instruction. The Daily Literacy Instruction Block (see Figure 16.1) is a functional and flexible instructional scaffolding model used by teachers in classrooms to provide interactive, shared, whole-group, and small-group differentiated reading and writing experiences for children similar to such other organizational plans as the four-block plan by Patricia Cunningham (Cunningham, Hall, & Defee, 1998). Additionally, the Daily Literacy Instruction Block incorporates terminology used in the CCSS to ensure alignment with these national standards. Variety of assessments including screening, diagnostic, progress monitoring, and outcome assessment play key roles in assisting the teacher make instructional decisions that meet the developmental needs of students.

Tier 1

Foundational Skills Instruction (60 minutes)
Small Groups or Whole Class

Word Work (30 minutes)
- Print Concepts
- Phonological Awareness
- Phonics and Word Recognition

Fluency (30 minutes)
Using both literature and information text. . . .
- Rate
- Accuracy
- Expression

Comprehension Strategy Instruction (30 minutes)
Small Groups or Whole Class

Literature *and* Information Text
- Key Ideas and Details
- Craft and Structure
- Integration of Knowledge and Ideas
- Range of Reading and Level of Text Complexity

Vocabulary Acquisition and Use

Writing and Spelling Instruction (30 minutes)
Small Groups or Whole Class

Writing
- Text Types and Purposes
- Production and Distribution of Writing
- Research to Build and Present Knowledge
- Range of Writing

Language
- Conventions of Standard English
- Knowledge of Language

Tier 2 and Tier 3

Targeted Small-Group Instruction (60 minutes)

- Small-group instruction to address gaps in Tier 1 and Tier 2 instruction for-below grade-level students (*RTI*)
- Small-group instruction to *accelerate* Tier 1 instruction for on- and above-grade-level students

Reading Assessment
Assessments used to inform literacy instruction:
- Screening
- Diagnostic
- Progress Monitoring (ongoing)
- Outcome Assessment

FIGURE 16.1. Daily literacy instruction block (180 minutes total).

374

The Daily Literacy Instruction Block is divided into four clearly defined instructional times and activity blocks: (1) foundational skills instruction, (2) comprehension strategy instruction, (3) writing and spelling instruction, and (4) targeted small-group instruction. The Daily Literacy Instruction Block incorporates into its structure the critical components of reading and writing instruction recommended in this chapter and in several national reading research reports, including decoding and word recognition instruction, fluency development, writing, vocabulary and comprehension strategy instruction, and guided oral reading (August & Shanahan, 2006; NELP, 2008; NRP, 2000; Snow, Burns, & Griffin, 1998). The Daily Literacy Instruction Block is designed for 180 minutes of allocated daily instructional time in grades K–6 and incorporates both Tier 1 and Tier 2 instruction. This is an uninterrupted block of time to ensure instructional density and proper pacing with focused attention on the tasks. The structure of the time allocations found in the Daily Literacy Instruction Block is outlined in Figure 16.1.

Tier 1 Literacy Instruction: Meeting the Demands of the CCSS

Tier 1 literacy instruction is grade level–appropriate instruction for *all* students. This means that achieving the CCSS are expected of all students at each subsequent grade level. Students must meet new expectations in reading foundations, literature, informational text, writing, listening and speaking, and language at each grade level and be able to read and write increasingly complex texts. In order to meet these new standards, teachers will need to allocate instructional time and focus to the "just right set" of evidence-based instructional priorities. Many core reading programs adopted by school districts align with the CCSS, but teacher knowledge and instructional approach remain highly important in Tier 1 literacy instruction. In what follows, we outline the priorities for time allocation and instructional focus in Tier 1 reading instruction that is intended to meet the new and higher expectations of the CCSS.

READING FOUNDATIONAL SKILLS INSTRUCTION (60 MINUTES)

The *foundational skills* instructional block is functionally divided into two key components: *word work* (30 minutes) and *fluency* (30 minutes). The purpose of the word work component of the foundational skills instruction is to develop children's (1) phonological and phonemic awareness, (2) concepts about print, (3) letter recognition and production, (4) decoding and word recognition, and (5) spelling concepts, skills, and strategies.

Word Work (30 Minutes). Effective instructional practices used during this time allocation include shared reading of enlarged texts (including charts, posters, use of lessons and text on the smart board, overhead transparencies, and big books), the co-construction of interactive written sentences and brief stories, making and breaking words using manipulative letters, and choral response techniques using such tools as gel, white dry erase, or magna-doodle boards. We cannot overemphasize the importance of providing the whole class with direct, explicit instruction on each of these word-related skills, strategies, and concepts. Children need clear explanations such as "think-alouds" coupled with expert modeling of reading and writing behaviors, and guided application of these concepts, skills, and strategies during this time allocation as well. We also strongly recommend that daily lessons focus on both decoding and spelling—reading and writing processes that help children better understand the reciprocal nature of all reading and writing processes. While explicit instruction and modeling are necessary, games and word play can also be used as an instructional approach during word work to increase student engagement in these foundational literacy skills.

Fluency (30 Minutes). The *fluency* component of the foundational skills instruction begins with explicit explanation, description, and modeling of reading fluency as defined in the research and professional literature: (1) accuracy, (2) rate, and (3) expression, so that children learn how to read fluently using a broad range of texts. Children need to see and hear models of what fluent reading sounds like and what it does not sound like. After explaining, defining, describing, modeling, demonstrating, and discussing fluent reading, teachers use various formats for choral reading, such as echoic (echo chamber), unison (all together), antiphonal (one side against another), line-a-child, and so on. For those who are unfamiliar with these choral reading variations, we recommend reading Opitz and Rasinski's (2008) *Good-Bye Round Robin* or Rasinski's (2003) *The Fluent Reader.* Once children sense their emerging fluency, they want to demonstrate it to others. Children love to perform their practiced oral reading for an audience of either parents or other students in the school building. When preparing an oral reading performance, teachers might use one of three well-known oral reading instructional approaches: (1) readers' theater, (2) radio reading, and (3) recitation (Opitz & Rasinski, 2008). Remember that fluency achieved in just one type of task or text type is insufficient, and that children require instruction and practice with a variety of reading fluency tasks and a variety of text types (literature and informational texts) and levels of challenge. This will teach students that fluency can vary depending on the genre (fictional vs. nonfictional reading), topic of the text (familiar or unfamiliar ideas and vocabulary), and that reading at a comfortable pace, not necessarily a fast pace, to achieve comprehension is a trait of a good reader.

COMPREHENSION INSTRUCTION (30 MINUTES)

The purpose of the *comprehension* instructional block is to develop children's (1) vocabulary and (2) comprehension. Effective instructional practices used within this time segment include explicit instruction of vocabulary concepts, using a variety of methods and requiring a variety of responses (Beck, McKeown, & Kucan, 2013; McKenna, 2002; Stahl & Nagy, 2006), and wordplay (Johnson, 2001).

Vocabulary Instruction. To support the growth of one's vocabulary, it is important to remember that there are four different types of vocabularies (listening, speaking, reading, and writing) and teachers should work to strengthen each of these types during instructional time. Students learn vocabulary at different levels beginning at the unknown, moving to acquainted, and finally a word becomes established within a student's vocabulary (NRP, 2000). Graves (1987) articulated six tasks that should be incorporated during vocabulary instruction: (1) learning to read new words, (2) learning new meanings for old words, (3) learning new words that represent known concepts, (4) learning new words that represent new concepts, (5) clarifying and enriching the meaning of known words, and (6) moving words from receptive to expressive vocabulary. While teachers can use the vocabulary recommended in the core reading program to assist in the comprehension of the current story, that doesn't have to be the only vocabulary instruction that takes place. Additional new words can be introduced to the students, added to the word walls, highlighted during read-alouds, and encouraged in student writing.

Comprehension Instruction. Effective comprehension strategy instruction includes both dialogic collaboration and conversation around a variety of texts and the teaching of a variety of comprehension strategies, including (1) questioning, (2) text structure, (3) graphic organizers, (4) inferences, (5) predicting, (6) monitoring, (7) summarizing, and (8) background knowledge activation or building, etc. (Dole & Liang, 2006; Wilkinson & Son, 2011). Providing the whole class with direct explicit instruction on each of these comprehension skills, strategies, and concepts continues to be considered a "best practice" of literacy instruction. With comprehension, using both literature and informational texts is essential to align with the CCSS as well as to provide opportunities for students to interact with each other and with the teacher around the contents and structure of the texts they are reading—often referred to as "close readings" (Cummins, 2013; Shanahan, 2012a, 2012b). To strengthen comprehension, children need clear explanations, "think-alouds" coupled with expert modeling of comprehension thought processes and behaviors, as well as teacher-guided application of these concepts, skills, and strategies in the reading of many texts at different levels and in many genres. It is also strongly recommend that teachers consider teaching multiple comprehension strategies such as *reciprocal teaching* (Palincsar, 2003), *concept-oriented reading instruction* (Guthrie, 2003; Swan, Coddington, & Guthrie, 2010), and *transactional strategies* (Brown, Pressley, Van Meter, & Shuder, 1996; Reutzel, Smith, & Fawson, 2005) to be used collectively and strategically while interacting with a variety of texts over long periods of time (NRP, 2000; Reutzel et al., 2005).

Additionally, children need to be taught how different texts are organized through close readings of a text (Fisher, Frey, & Lapp, 2012; Shanahan et al., 2010; Shanahan, Fisher, & Frey, 2012). Understanding text structure aids comprehension. The use of retelling, as well as guide sheets or graphic organizers, helps students organize information and understand text more clearly. For example, literature texts typically include the following features: (1) setting, (2) characters, (3) conflict or problem, (4) goal or plot (rising action, climax, falling action), and (5) resolution. The use of story maps supports the comprehension of literature texts because they require students to engage in the text and assist in self-monitoring (Davis & McPherson, 1989; Reutzel & Cooter, 2013). Informational texts are structured differently than literature texts and follow one of five informational text structures: (1) descriptive, (2) sequence, (3) problem/solution or question/answer, (4) compare and contrast, and (5) cause and effect. Helping students learn to navigate informational texts and learn how to use information text features such as the table of contents, the glossary, the index, the graphics (including maps, pictures, and graphs), as well as the inserts and bubble callouts, can support and deepen student comprehension of these types of texts (Roberts et al., 2013).

WRITING AND SPELLING INSTRUCTION (30 MINUTES)

The purpose of the *writing and spelling* instructional block is to develop children's (1) composition skills, (2) spelling, (3) mechanics, (4) grammatical understandings, and (5) literary and writing genre concepts, skills, and strategies.

Writing Instruction. During writing instruction, a variety of emphases should be incorporated including fluency development, exploring writing types and the purposes of writing, producing and distributing writing, researching and presenting knowledge in writing, and experiencing the range of writing experiences (including writing over extended periods of time as well as writing for shorter time periods). Students need to develop the ability to fluently produce letters, words, and sentences in order to allow for thoughts to be efficiently represented (Coker, 2006; Graham et al., 2012). Time should be given in the earliest stages of writing development for helping children acquire handwriting or keyboarding skills that allow them to transcribe thoughts efficiently into words, phrases, and sentences.

Once transcription is fluent, effective instructional practices used within this writing time allocation include modeled writing by the teacher; a writer's workshop with drafting, conferencing, revising, editing, publishing, and disseminating; and explicit whole-class instruction on each of these writing skills, strategies, and concepts. Simply setting up a writer's workshop in the classroom, however, is not sufficient. Most students do not have enough experience with generating ideas for writing, understanding how to select writing topics, utilizing advance planning for writing, understanding how to produce and organize text, understanding writing mechanics, and using the steps of revision or editing (Harris, Graham, Mason, & Friedlander, 2008). Therefore, children need clear explanations, "think-alouds" coupled with expert modeling of writing behaviors, and guided application of these writing concepts, skills, and strategies during this time allocation as well. It is also a "best practice" to learn about writing through reading and studying the styles of the authors of children's literature. Many students can model those authors that use description imagery, sensory details, figurative language, good plot structure, or characterization.

Incorporating writing strategy instruction such as the *Self-Regulated Strategy Development* (SRSD) instructional approach developed by Karen Harris and Steve Graham (Harris et al., 2008) allows teachers to create a personalized writing instruction experience for each student. The SRSD model is organized in progressive stages including: (1) developing background knowledge, (2) discussing it, (3) modeling it—collaborative modeling, (4) memorizing it, (5) supporting it, and (6) independent performance. These stages are not followed in a lock-step manner but rather are designed to be adjusted according to the needs and abilities of each individual student. Incorporating writing instructional strategies such as the SRSD allows the teacher not only to teach a variety of writing types, to address each phase of the writing process, and to utilize the opportunity to teach or reinforce writing strategies and skills, but it also allows the teacher to emphasize and explain the steps of the writing process (Graham & Harris, 1992). We also strongly recommend that daily lessons provide a time allocation for sharing children's writing in an "author's chair" or using some other method of disseminating and sharing children's writing products. Writing instruction is often done at the pace of the writer with different children at different stages of the writing process. Some may be publishing their writings while others may be at the editing stage. Differentiated instruction is especially important in this area, with the teacher constantly aware of the pacing and stages of each child.

Spelling Instruction. Enlisting a variety of spelling instructional strategies is also recommended so as to provide a variety of learning activities and to maintain student interest. An emphasis on helping students to recognize spelling patterns can alleviate confusion about spelling (Helman, Bear, Templeton, Invernizzi, & Johnston, 2013). Using spelling instructional strategies such as the *spelling in parts* (SIP) strategy designed by Powell and Aram (2008) assists students in learning new spelling patterns and provides strategies for students to use when students encounter larger words and need to break them down into smaller, more manageable chunks. While many Tier 1 programs offer spelling lists that focus on a phonics skill each week, teachers should remain purposeful in their practice options for the selected spelling words, rather than relying on the traditional approach of copying words five times each on Monday, sentences on Tuesday, definitions on Wednesday, and so forth. Planning meaningful spelling instruction teaches students about the English language, offers varied ways to practice words with similar word affixes (prefixes, suffices, or word roots), and adds to the student's growing vocabulary.

Tier 2 Literacy Instruction: Closing the Achievement Gap

Tier 2 literacy instruction, in an RTI model of instructional delivery, is intended to close gaps in students' skills, knowledge, or strategies as revealed in regular progress monitoring of instructional effectiveness. If a student is found to be lagging behind his or her peers in literacy growth, then further diagnostic assessment is employed to determine the area(s) of weakness so that the teacher can deliver targeted, small-group instruction to quickly close this gap and return students to Tier 1 instruction. In Tier I instruction, varied grouping is often employed by the classroom teacher to include whole-class, small-group, partners, and individual work time. With Tier 2 literacy instruction, small-group instruction has been found to be most effective, rather than whole group. In what follows, we discuss how to organize the classroom to support targeted small-group reading instruction to support the delivery of Tier 2 literacy instruction.

TARGETED SMALL-GROUP INSTRUCTION (60 MINUTES)

Targeted small-group instruction time is a designated time for the classroom teacher to provide Tier 2 and Tier 3 instruction to struggling readers who need more time and help and are below grade level in their reading skills. This time can also be used to accelerate and enrich literacy instruction for students who are performing on or above grade level. Managing the Tier 2 and Tier 3 small-group instruction time is a complex effort for most teachers. A teacher must be thoughtful concerning the behaviors and active learning of all class members while assessing, teaching, and working with the Tier 2 program or specific lesson for each group that meets. We recommend that the teacher, rather than a parent helper, or teaching assistant work with Tier 2 intervention students because of the teacher knowledge and literacy training that a teacher can offer a student who is struggling. It's important that students clearly understand the expectations for this time so as to use their time wisely in completing literacy tasks, and also to minimize off-task behaviors that can occur when the teacher is working with small groups (Morrow, 2010). We show in Figure 16.2 options for managing the Tier 2 small-group literacy instruction environment. Options provide effective classroom management suggestions and range from simple to increasingly complex management options.

The first option is the most *simple* of the four options. During the simple option, the majority of the students work independently or with a partner doing *daily* assigned literacy tasks that are completed at student desks. These tasks can be listed menu-style where students themselves select the tasks they would like to complete each day, or tasks can be specifically assigned by the teacher. The teacher is stationed in the small-group differentiated reading area of the classroom prepared to offer differentiated reading instruction. The teacher works with small groups of students who are pulled from the whole class and then students rotate back when the next group is called. The classroom has a quiet working noise level to help each student focus on the varied tasks.

The second or the *complex* option looks very similar to the first option except that the majority of the students are working independently or with a partner doing *weekly* assigned literacy tasks that are completed at student desks. The students working on literacy tasks independently or with a partner have a week to complete the assigned tasks so work on each task may spill over from one day to the next. These tasks may be listed menu-style where students select the tasks they would like to complete over the course of the week or tasks can be specifically assigned by the teacher. The teacher is stationed in the small-group differentiated reading area of the classroom prepared to offer differentiated reading instruction.

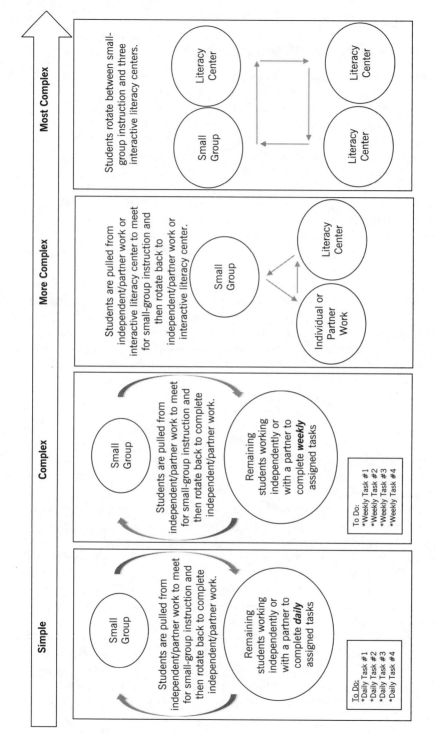

FIGURE 16.2. Four options for managing Tier 2 small-group instruction.

The third option is the *more complex* option. This option is similar to the first two options except that a literacy center has been introduced into the rotation. Students are either working independently or with a partner on their self-selected menu or teacher-assigned literacy tasks, or they are working in a small group with the teacher, or they are working in another small group at the literacy center. Students may be assigned a specific time to go to the literacy center or students may be invited to go to the literacy center after their assigned tasks are completed. This is sometimes called the "workshop model." It is important that the teacher create a way to keep students accountable for the work in each center to ensure that it is not just keeping the students quiet while the intervention groups are meeting, but that the instructional time being spent is valued and connected to the learning plan that week.

The fourth, and *most complex*, option is where the teacher works with small, targeted instruction reading groups and the remaining students are rotating through three or more literacy centers. The teacher is stationed in the small-group differentiated reading area of the classroom prepared to offer targeted small-group reading instruction. The children are called to their small reading group (homogeneous group) from an assigned "center rotation" group (mixed-abilities group). Literacy centers are teacher-selected, -designed, and -provisioned. Literacy centers focus on activities and tasks that reinforce and support Tier 1 and Tier 2 instruction. These activities are centered on word work, fluency, vocabulary, comprehension instruction, and writing and spelling. The fourth and most complex option requires that the literacy center activities and tasks are clearly understood, independent of teacher supervision, and able to be completed within the time allowed. It is also important that tasks completed at literacy centers have a component of accountability and performance. We caution teachers against the creation of too many learning centers. In the early part of the year, fewer centers are easier for both teachers and students to handle. As the year progresses, adding a few new centers, especially optional centers, can add variety to this time block. As time progresses and children acquire more experience with the rotation between learning centers, we have found it better to assign children specific tasks to be completed during this time period rather than a time-controlled rotation through various literacy centers. Many teachers model in detail the literacy centers at the beginning of the week, check for understanding, and then use the remaining time that day and the rest of the week to focus solely on Tier 2 instruction. It is important to note that this option of Tier 2 instruction requires upfront planning and material preparation from the teacher so that students have access to the centers and can remain independent, allowing the teacher to focus on the small-group tasks. Establishing clear procedures for this work time, teaching those expectations, and practicing them with the students initially and again whenever needed will maintain the consistent positive working tone that is needed for *all* students to succeed.

Reflections and Future Directions

Teachers accommodate individual student needs in literacy instruction increasingly by providing high-quality Tier 1 literacy instruction to help all children meet CCSS using literacy progress monitoring, screening, diagnostic and outcomes assessment within a RTI framework to help those who struggle to catch up and keep up with their peers. Throughout the history of classroom literacy instruction, several variations on ability grouping and whole-class instruction and seatwork have persisted despite a large body of relevant research pointing to many negative outcomes for students and teachers related to these grouping strategies (Rupley & Blair, 1987). In recent years, however, research has demonstrated the consistent advantages of providing students small-group, differentiated literacy instruction targeting specific identified needs and teaching to meet those needs.

Concluding Comments

More research is needed to determine the effects of implementing the CCSS on students' reading achievement over time. We also need research to determine the effects that Common Core assessments will ultimately have on literacy instruction. For example, we don't know if this educational reform will yield outcomes similar to previous reforms on the behaviors of teachers, leading them to reduce literacy instruction to a pursuit of test scores. Furthermore, we do not know how the lack of professional development support around implementing the Common Core will affect literacy teachers' instruction and the curricula used or developed in schools (Reutzel, 2013). These are issues that will be determined as the implementation of the CCSS and the accompanying CCSS assessments play out in the years ahead. The years ahead are filled with hope and promise of improved outcomes for U.S. students as CCSS and RTI take hold in classrooms, but whether or not this promise will be realized as hoped has yet to be determined.

ENGAGEMENT ACTIVITIES

1. Discuss why the pursuit of established, grade-level CCSS within an RTI model or framework can lead to successfully differentiating literacy instruction to meet the needs of *all* learners.

2. Observe several targeted, small-group literacy instructional sessions in at least one classroom and take field notes. Then interview four or five children in various groups about their perceptions of the differentiated instruction they receive in Tier 2 small-group settings. Does the instruction look different for each group, or is the level of text the only change observed with the same routine in each group meeting? Do you think that changing the text level is sufficient differentiation to be effective for all children?

3. When given a reading or writing task to perform individually *or* in a cooperative learning group, what is the result on students' performance? Is quality higher or lower? Do individuals or groups use learning time more efficiently? Is the performance or product given by individuals or cooperative learning groups higher or lower? How do children of varying abilities and skill levels feel about the group processes and products?

4. Discuss whether it is important for teachers to know what children are learning from time spent in learning centers. If it is important, how can teachers require accountability from children for learning activities found in typical independent learning centers—like a buddy or paired reading fluency center, for example?

5. Although teachers often want to provide targeted, differentiated small-group literacy instruction in their classrooms, they do not know how to manage the activity of all of the children while teaching a small group. What options are described in this chapter that can be used to accomplish this aim?

REFERENCES

Anderson, R., Hiebert, E., Scott, J., & Wilkinson, I. (1985). *Becoming a nation of readers*. Washington, DC: National Institute of Education.

August, D., & Shanahan, T. (2006). *Developing literacy in second-language learners: A report of the National Literacy Panel on Language-Minority Children and Youth*. Mahwah, NJ: Erlbaum.

Beck, I. L., McKeown, M. G., & Kucan, L. (2013). *Bringing words to life: Robust vocabulary instruction* (2nd ed.). New York: Guilford Pres.

Brill, S. (2011). *Class warfare: Inside the fight to fix America's schools.* New York: Simon & Schuster.

Brown, R., Pressley, M., Van Meter, P., & Schuder, T. (1996). A quasi-experimental validation of transactional strategies instruction with previously low-achieving second-grade readers. *Journal of Educational Psychology, 88,* 18–37.

Bureau of Labor Statistics. (2011). *Time spend in leisure and sports activities for the civilian population by selected characteristics, 2011 annual averages.* Washington, DC: Author. Retrieved December 12, 2012, from *www.bls.gov/news release/ atus.t11.htm.*

Carmichael, S. B., Martino, G., Porter-Magee, K., & Wilson, W. S. (2010). *The state of state standards–and the Common Core–in 2010.* Washington, DC: Thomas B. Fordham Institute.

Coker, D. L. (2006). Impact of first-grade factors on the growth and outcomes of urban school children's primary-grade writing. *Journal of Educational Psychology, 98,* 471–488.

Covey, S. (2004). *The seven habits of highly effective people.* New York: Simon & Schuster.

Cummins, S. (2013). *Close reading of informational texts: Assessment-driven instruction in grades 3–8.* New York: Guilford Press.

Cunningham, P. M., Hall, D. P., & Defee, M. (1998). Nonability-grouped, multi-level instruction: Eight years later. *The Reading Teacher, 51*(8), 652–664.

Darling-Hammond, L. (2010). *The flat world and education: How America's commitment to equity will determine our future.* New York: Teachers College Press.

Davis, Z. T., & McPherson, M. D. (1989). Story map instruction: A road map for reading comprehension. *The Reading Teacher, 43*(3), 232–240.

Dole, J. A., & Liang, L. A. (2006). Help with teaching reading comprehension: Comprehension instructional frameworks. *The Reading Teacher, 59*(8), 742–753.

Fisher, D., Frey, N., & Lapp, D. (2012). *Text complexity: Raising rigor in reading.* Newark, DE: International Reading Association.

Fleischman, H. L., Hopstock, P. J., Pelczar, M. P., & Shelley, B. E. (2010). *Highlights from PISA 2009: Performance of US 15-year-old students in reading, mathematics, and science literacy in an international context* (NCES 2011-004). Washington, DC: National Center for Education Statistics.

Friedman, T. L., & Mandelbaum, M. (2011). *That used to be us: How American fell behind in the world it invented and how we can come back.* New York: Farrar, Straus & Giroux.

Fuchs, D., Fuchs, L. S., & Vaughn, S. (Eds.). (2008). *Response to intervention: A framework for reading educators.* Newark, DE: International Reading Association.

Graham, S., Bollinger, A., Olson, C. B., D'Aoust, C., MacArthur, C., McCutchen, D., et al. (2012). *Teaching elementary school students to be effective writers* (IES practice guide, NCEE 2012-4058). Washington, DC: Institute of Education Sciences, U.S. Department of Education.

Graham, S., & Harris, K. R. (1992). Self-regulated strategy development: Programmatic research in writing. In *Contemporary intervention research in learning disabilities* (pp. 47–64). New York: Springer.

Graves, M. F. (1987). The roles of instruction in fostering vocabulary development. In M. G. McKeown & M. E. Curtis (Eds.), *The nature of vocabulary acquisition* (pp. 165–184). Hillsdale, NJ: Erlbaum.

Guthrie, J. T. (2003). Concept-oriented reading instruction: Practices of teaching reading for understanding. In A. P. Sweet & C. E. Snow (Eds.), *Rethinking reading comprehension* (pp. 115–140). New York: Guilford Press.

Harris, K. R., Graham, S., & Mason, L. H., & Friedlander, B. (2008). *Powerful writing strategies for all students.* Baltimore: Brookes.

Helman, L., Bear, D. R., Invernizzi, M., Templeton, S., & Johnston, F. (2013). *Words their way: Within word pattern sorts for Spanish-speaking English learners.* Boston: Pearson.

Holdaway, D. (1984). *Stability and change in literacy learning.* Portsmouth, NH: Heinemann.

Jenkins, J. (2008). *Dan Poynter's* ParaPublishing.com: *Jerrold Jenkins Survey.* Retrieved August 23, 2013, from *http://parapublishing.com/sites/para/resources/statistics.cfm.*

Johnson, D. D. (2001). *Vocabulary in the elementary and middle school.* Boston: Allyn & Bacon.

Mathes, P. G., Denton, C. A., Fletcher, J. M., Anthony, J. L., Francis, D. J., & Schatschneider, C. (2005). The effects of theoretically different instruction and student characteristics on the skills of struggling readers. *Reading Research Quarterly, 40*(2), 148–183.

McKenna, M. C. (2002). *Help for struggling readers: Strategies for grades 3–8.* New York: Guilford Press.

McLaughlin, M., & Overturf, B. J. (2012). The Common Core: Insights into the K–5 standards. *The Reading Teacher, 66*(2), 153–164.

Morrow, L. M. (2010). Preparing centers and a literacy-rich environment for small-group instruction in early reading first preschools. In M. C. McKenna, S. Walpole, & K. Conradi (Eds.), *Promoting early reading: Research, resources, and best practices* (pp. 124–141). New York: Guilford Press.

Morrow, L. M., Shanahan, T., & Wixson, K. K. (Eds.). (2013). *Teaching with the Common Core standards for English language arts, preK–2.* New York: Guilford Press.

National Assessment of Educational Progress (NAEP). (2011). Department of Education, Institute of Education Sciences, National Center for Education Statistics, Washington, DC. Retrieved September 25, 2013, from *http://nces.ed.gov/programs/digest/d11/tables/dt11_134.asp.*

National Early Literacy Panel (NELP). (2008). *Developing early literacy: Report of the National Early Literacy Panel.* Jessup, MD: National Institute for Literacy.

National Endowment for the Arts. (2004). *Reading at risk: A survey of literary reading in America.* Washington, DC: National Endowment for the Arts, Research Division Report No, 46, XI. Retrieved August 23, 2013, from *http://arts.gov/publications/reading-risk-survey-literary-reading-america-0.*

National Governors Association & Council of Chief State School Officers. (2010). Common Core State Standards for English language arts and literacy in history/social studies, science, and technical subjects. Retrieved September 25, 2013, from *www.corestandards.org.*

National Institute of Child Health and Human Development. (2000). *Report of the National Reading Panel: Teaching children to read: An evidence-based assessment of the scientific research literature on reading and its implications for reading instruction: Reports of the subgroups.* Washington, DC: National Institute of Child Health and Human Development, National Institutes of Health.

Neuman, S. B., & Celano, D. (2012). *Giving our children a fighting chance: Poverty, literacy, and the development of information capital.* New York: Teachers College Press.

Neuman, S. B., Gambrell, L. B., & Massey, C. (Eds.). *Quality reading instruction in the age of Common Core standards.* Newark, DE: International Reading Association.

Opitz, M. F., & Rasinski, T. V. (2008). *Good-bye round robin: 25 effective oral reading strategies* (update ed.). Portsmouth, NH: Heinemann.

Palincsar, A. M. (2003). Collaborative approaches to comprehenaion instruction. In C. E. Snow & A. P. Sweet (Eds.), *Rethinking reading comprehension* (pp. 99–114). New York: Guilford Press.

Perry, S. (2011). *Push has come to shove: Getting our kids the education they deserve– Even if it means picking a fight.* New York: Crown.

Powell, D. A., & Aram, R. (2008). Spelling in parts: A strategy for spelling and decoding polysyllabic words. *The Reading Teacher, 61*(7), 567–570.

Rasinski, T. V. (2003). *The fluent reader: Oral reading strategies for building word recognition, fluency, and comprehension.* New York: Scholastic.

Rathvon, N. (2004). *Early reading assessment: A practitioner's handbook.* New York: Guilford Press.

Reutzel, D. R. (2013). Implementation of the Common Core standards and the practitioner: Pitfalls and possibilities. In S. B. Neuman, L. B. Gambrell, & C. Massey (Eds.), *Quality reading instruction in the age of Common Core standards* (pp. 59–74). Newark, DE: International Reading Association.

Reutzel, D. R., & Cooter, R. B. (2013). *The essentials of teaching children to read: What every teacher should know!* (3rd ed.). Boston: Pearson.

Reutzel, D. R., & Cooter, R. B. (2015). *Strategies for reading assessment and instruction: Helping every child succeed* (5th ed.). Boston: Pearson.

Reutzel, D. R., Smith, J. A., & Fawson, P. C. (2005). An evaluation of two approaches for teaching reading comprehension strategies in the primary years using science information texts. *Early Childhood Research Quarterly, 20*(3), 276–305.

Roberts, K. L., Norman, R. R., Duke, N. K., Morsink, P., Martin, N. M., & Knight, J. A. (2013). Diagrams, timelines, and tables—Oh, my!: Fostering graphical literacy. *The Reading Teacher, 67*(1), 12–24.

Rupley, W. H., & Blair, T. R. (1987). Assignment and supervision of reading seatwork: Looking in on 12 primary teachers. *The Reading Teacher, 40*(4), 391–393.

Shanahan, T. (2004, November). *How do you raise reading achievement?* Paper presented at the Utah Council of the International Reading association meeting, Salt Lake City, UT.

Shanahan, T. (2012a). Planning for close reading. Shanahan on literacy blog: Retrieved August 30, 2013, from *www.shanahanonliteracy.com/2012/07/planning-for-close-reading.html*.

Shanahan, T. (2012b). What is close reading? Shanahan on literacy blog: Retrieved August 30, 2013, from *www.shanahanonliteracy.com/2012/07/planning-for-close-reading.html*.

Shanahan, T. (2013). Common Core State Standards: Educating young children for global excellence. In D. R. Reutzel (Ed.), *Handbook of research-based practice in early education* (pp. 207–221). New York: Guilford Press.

Shanahan, T., Callison, K., Carriere, C., Duke, N. K., Pearson, P. D., Schatschneider, C., et al. (2010). *Improving reading comprehension in kindergarten through 3rd grade: A practice guide* (NCEE 2010-4038). Washington, DC: National Center for Education Evaluation and Regional Assistance, Institute of Education Sciences, U.S. Department of Education. Retrieved September 25, 2013 from *whatworks.ed.gov/publications/practiceguides*.

Shanahan, T., Fisher, D., & Frey, N. (2012). The challenge of challenging text. *Educational Leadership, 69*(6), 58–62.

Snow, C. E., Burns, M. S., & Griffin, P. (1998). *Preventing reading failure in young children*. Washington, DC: National Academy Press.

Stahl, S. A., & Nagy, W. E. (2006). *Teaching word meanings*. Mahwah, NJ: Erlbaum.

Swan, E. A., Coddington, C. S., & Guthrie, J. T. (2010). Motivating silent reading in classrooms. In E. H. Hiebert & D. R. Reutzel (Eds.), *Revisiting silent reading: New directions for teachers and researchers* (pp. 95–111). Newark, DE: International Reading Association.

Wagner, T. (2008). *The global achievement gap: Why even our best schools don't teach the new survival skills our children need–and what we can do about it*. New York: Basic Books.

Weber, K. (Ed.). (2010). *Waiting for "Superman": How we can save America's failing public schools*. New York: Public Affairs.

Wilkinson, I. A. G., & Son, E. H. (2011). A dialogic turn in research on learning and teaching to comprehend. In M. L. Kamil, P. D. Pearson, E. Moje, & P. Afflerbach (Eds.), *Handbook of reading research* (Vol. 4, pp. 359–387). New York: Routledge.

Williams, P. L., Reese, C. M., Campbell, J. R., Mazzeo, J., & Phillips, G. W. (1995). *NAEP 1994 reading: A first look*. Washington, DC: Educational Testing Service for National Center for the Educational Statistics, Office of Educational Research and Improvement, U.S. Department of Education.

CHAPTER 17

Helping Parents Help Children Achieve the Common Core State Standards

Reaching Out in Different Ways

Jeanne R. Paratore
Patricia A. Edwards
Lisa M. O'Brien

This chapter will:

- Explain why parent involvement is important to students' Common Core State Standards for the English language arts.

- Provide a description of the families that populate our schools as a basis for understanding and planning appropriate forms of parent involvement.

- Describe new understandings of productive parent–teacher partnerships.

- Share examples of evidence-based programs that meet the varied needs of the families we serve.

- Provide a list of principles to guide teachers as they plan their work with families.

In the chapters throughout this text, we have learned that implementation of the Common Core State Standards (CCSS) has raised the bar for teachers and students throughout the United States, as students are now expected to achieve literacy standards that, in many cases, surpass those demanded of them in previous years. At its core, the "movement" for the CCSS is grounded in a quest for equity– a quest that is far from new, but one that has been largely out of reach for students in high-poverty urban and rural schools. The promise of the CCSS is that finally equity will be achieved through an educational system that provides all students the same demanding curriculum and rich opportunities to learn.

Most literacy experts believe that for almost all students, realizing this promise will require far more than excellent instruction in school. Rather, students who fully benefit from implementation of the CCSS will do so, at least in part, because of the support they receive from their parents or other caregivers outside of school. In this chapter, our purpose is to examine the foundation for this belief and to translate the evidence into actions that teachers can take to productively engage parents in their children's learning.

Why Is Parent Involvement Important?

The importance of parent involvement in children's academic success has been well documented and widely accepted. Based on a comprehensive research synthesis, Henderson and Mapp (2002) reported that academic effects are demonstrated across broad and varied measures: students of involved parents have higher rates of school attendance, better social skills and behavior, higher grades and test scores, lower rates of retention, and higher rates of high school graduation and postsecondary study. These findings are further strengthened by additional, large-scale studies that postdate Henderson's and Mapp's review. For example, Houtenville and Conway (2008) sought to determine both educational and economic effects of parent involvement. They analyzed a large data set (10,382 eighth-grade students) from the National Education Longitudinal Study (NELS; *http://nces.ed.gov/surveys/nels88*). They found parental effort to have significantly positive effects on student achievement, "along the order of four to six years of parental education or more than $1000 in per-pupil spending" (p. 450).

We also know, however, that some studies have yielded findings of unproductive parental involvement programs (e.g., Mattingly, Prislan, McKenzie, Rodriguez, & Kayzar, 2002; St. Pierre, Ricciuti, & Rimdzius, 2005), and these raise questions about precisely what makes some programs succeed, while others fail. Some studies help answer these questions by examining how various types of parent involvement differentially influence student outcomes. In a meta-analysis of 51 studies (total sample 13,000 students), Jeynes (2012) examined the effects of several forms of parent involvement on the academic achievement of preschool through 12th-grade students. He found that regardless of program type, parent involvement programs were significantly related to students' academic achievement (0.3 *SD*), with slightly greater effects for older students (0.33 *SD*) than younger students (0.31 *SD*). Furthermore, he found that parent involvement programs emphasizing parent–child shared reading (i.e., any program that encouraged parents and their children to read together) and parent–school partnerships (i.e., any efforts that support parent and teacher collaboration as equal partners in enhancing children's academic and/or behavior outcomes) had the largest effects (0.51 *SD*, 0.35 *SD*, respectively) as compared to programs emphasizing checking homework and communication between parents and teachers (0.27 *SD*, 0.28 *SD*, respectively). English as a second language instruction (i.e., efforts to improve parents' English so as to empower their school involvement) or Head Start programs emphasizing parent involvement did not yield a significant effect on students' academic achievement.

In their work, Fan, Williams, and Wolters (2012) focused on school motivation, a key contributor to academic achievement (e.g., Guthrie & Wigfield, 2000), and studied how various aspects of parent involvement influenced school motivation among students of differing ethnic backgrounds (12,721 tenth graders including Asian American, Hispanic, Caucasian, and African American). Fan and colleagues (2012) found that although parent involvement in the form of holding high aspirations enhanced all students' school motivation, differences in effects of other practices were observed across ethnic groups regardless of socioeconomic status. For example, parent–school communication regarding benign or positive issues (e.g., course selection, help with homework) (as opposed to negative issues, e.g., poor behavior or low academic performance) was positively related to Hispanic students' intrinsic motivation for English language arts (ELA), but had no effect on Asian American, Caucasian, or African American students' intrinsic motivation for ELA. Similarly uneven effects were observed when the form of involvement was participation in school functions: it contributed to enhanced intrinsic motivation and self-efficacy for ELA for Caucasian students; for African American students, parent participation in school functions was positively related to students' self-efficacy but negatively related to intrinsic motivation; and parent involvement in school functions had no association with Asian American or Hispanic students' motivation for ELA.

Altschul (2011), too, found that the form of parent involvement mattered. In this study, at-home parent involvement for Mexican American students ($N = 1,609$) was associated with enhanced academic achievement (i.e., according to standardized measures of reading, math, science, and history), while parent involvement in school functions had no effects.

Additional evidence of differences according to families' ethnic backgrounds is found in an earlier study by Jeynes (2003). He conducted a meta-analysis of 20 studies (total sample of 12,000 students) of effects of parent involvement on academic achievement of students of different ethnic backgrounds (African American, Latino, Asian) in grades K–12. In examined studies, parent involvement was represented in various ways, including parent communication with children about school; checking children's homework; holding high expectations for academic success; encouraging outside reading; and attending school functions. Parent involvement had significant positive effects for all racial groups, although these effects were not equal. African American and Latino groups benefited more than Asian Americans. In addition, parent involvement had positive effects on all academic measures (e.g., GPA [grade point average], achievement tests), but effects were greater on achievement tests than on GPA.

Also seeking to understand factors that related to parent involvement effects, Dearing, Kreider, Simpkins, and Weiss (2006) examined the role of parent education. In a longitudinal study of low-income children (N = 281) whose parents were involved in an intervention program with services for children (high-quality preschool) and parents (education and job training) during the children's kindergarten year, Dearing and colleagues found that effects varied by maternal education. That is, there was a relationship between the intervention, higher levels of parent involvement, and higher levels of literacy performance among children whose parents were less educated but no relationship when parents were relatively more educated. Furthermore, when parent involvement in children's schooling increased between kindergarten and fifth grade, children of both high- and low-education families achieved higher literacy performances, suggesting that benefits accrue when involvement is not only sustained, but also heightened. Moreover, despite an achievement gap across children of high- and low-education mothers when parent involvement was low, this gap disappeared when parent involvement levels were high.

In our view, the combined evidence supports a clear claim that parent involvement in their children's learning has noteworthy academic benefits for nearly all children. Moreover, when children have mothers with less education, parent involvement exerts an even more powerful influence on children's literacy performance, even eliminating the achievement gap that typically separates the performance of children of low- and high-education mothers. Furthermore, the evidence that relationships vary depending on the form of parent involvement and by education levels and the race/ethnicity of the family suggests that parents in diverse communities may enact their involvement in differing, yet meaningful ways.

What Is the Teacher's Role in Parent Involvement?

Few teachers reading the evidence about the importance of parent involvement will be surprised—their own observations and experiences confirm the outcomes of formal investigations. However, some teachers—especially those in low-income communities—believe that the parents of the children with whom they work are disengaged and uninterested in their children's learning (e.g., Compton-Lilly, 2003; Edwards, 2009). Studies indicate that some teachers believe so strongly in parents' lack of interest and motivation related to their children's schooling that they even fail to reach out to them, assuming their efforts will meet with resistance (e.g., Edwards, 2009; Lareau, 1989). Some may be surprised, then, by findings that the actions teachers take are instrumental in levels of parent involvement. Based on evidence collected from a sample of over 1,200 parents of elementary school children, Epstein (1986) concluded: "Parents' education did not explain experiences with parent involvement unless teacher practices were taken into account. In the classrooms of teachers who were leaders in the use of parent involvement, parents at all educational levels said they were frequently involved in learning activities at home" (p. 291).

In another study, Sheldon (2003) collected data from 113 public schools in one urban system. He found that high-quality parent involvement programs correlated strongly with the outreach practices, particularly "the depth and breadth of schools' efforts to involve hard-to-reach families and the community in the school and in students' learning" (p. 160).

A study by Cooper (2010) provides additional evidence of teacher effects on parent involvement. In this large-scale investigation (N = 19,375 kindergartners), Cooper sought to determine specific moderators (income status, parental education, teacher education) of the relationship between family poverty and school-based parent involvement. School-based parent involvement was defined as parents who "attended a PTA meeting, attended an open house, attended a parent advisory group or policy council, attended a school or class event, attended a regularly scheduled parent–teacher conference, volunteered at school, participated in fundraising, or contacted teacher or school since the start of kindergarten" (p. 483). Cooper found that among poor parents with little education, school-based involvement was low; however, among poor parents with high levels of education (i.e., a college degree or higher), parents had "slightly higher school-based involvement than their non-poor counterparts" (p. 487). Furthermore, the negative association between poverty and school-based parent involvement was moderated by teachers' level of education—that is, the negative association weakened when teachers held graduate-level degrees. Yet additional analyses indicated that, when teachers initiated school-based parent involvement, high-income parents benefited more than low-income parents, as the gap in levels of involvement between the two groups became wider. Cooper speculated that the types of parental involvement that teachers typically advocate may favor the abilities, experiences, and predispositions about schooling of high-income parents, and as such, prominent outreach efforts may be a better "match" for high-income parents.

Park and Holloway (2013) examined effects of school-outreach efforts on parent involvement. Analyzing data from 3,248 parents of high school students (African American, Caucasian, and Latino), they found that school-outreach efforts were strongly associated with school-based involvement, particularly if efforts were perceived by parents as informative (e.g., how to help child with homework, why child is placed in particular groups or classes, parents' expected role at school). They also found that parents with greater self-efficacy regarding their capacity to support their children's learning believed they had an important role in their child's education, and for high-poverty parents, self-efficacy was a powerful predictor of school involvement. Finally, although Park and Holloway found that ethnicity was not a factor in *whether* parents engaged in their child's education, there were differences in *how* parents of differing ethnic backgrounds were involved (when accounting for mother's educational attainment and family income). For example, African American and Latino parents were less likely to participate in school-based involvement (e.g., attend general school meetings, parent–teacher organization meetings, class events, volunteer in class) than white parents. This finding lends yet more support to the claim that the particular forms of parent involvement advocated by teachers are consequential in engaging all parents.

Walker, Ice, Hoover-Dempsey, and Sandler (2011), too, found evidence that both the forms of parent involvement and the ways teachers support parent involvement matter. They investigated school-based and home-based involvement practices among low-income, immigrant Latino parents of first through sixth-grade children ($N = 147$). Results indicated that home-based involvement was predicted by partnership-focused role construction (i.e., the belief that schools and parents share responsibility for students' educational outcomes) and by specific invitations from the parents' children. School based-involvement was predicted by specific invitations from teachers (as opposed to "a welcoming environment") but was also mediated by parents' perception of time and energy for involvement.

Taken together, these findings indicate that many parents of diverse ethnic and economic backgrounds participate in their child's schooling in ways that enhance their children's achievement; however, the particular ways in which parents become engaged may differ from familiar and predominant forms of parent involvement, making teachers' efforts to engage parents puzzling and complex. In particular, initiatives are generally successful when (1) teachers initiate specific invitations for parent involvement; (2) parents and teachers co-construct roles and responsibilities; (3) the forms of involvement are a "good fit" for parents' schedules and family commitments; and (4) teacher actions support parents' ability (and in turn, self-efficacy) relative to the focal tasks and activities.

Given the evidence of the importance of parent involvement in children's learning and of the power of teachers and schools in establishing high levels of involvement, we next turn our attention to developing an understanding of the families we must be prepared to serve.

Who Are the Families in Our Schools?

As classroom teachers, we see firsthand the changing demographics of our classrooms: our students represent increasingly varied ethnicities and races, countries of origin, first languages, and religions. Also changing, but unseen in the faces and voices of our children, are the structural demographics of the American family, a change so dramatic that Footlick (1990) observed:

> The American family does not exist. Rather, we are creating many American families, of diverse styles and shapes. In unprecedented numbers, our families are unalike: we have mothers working while fathers keep house; fathers and mothers both working away from home; single parents; second marriages bringing children together from unrelated backgrounds; childless couples; unmarried couples, with and without children; gay and lesbian parents. We are living through a period of historic change in American life. (p. 15)

The face of the American family has changed in yet another way: the number of children living in poverty is on the rise. According to a report from the Annie B. Casey Foundation (2013), the number of children living in poverty in 2011 was 23% (over 16 million children), up from 19% in 2005; the rate is even higher (26%) for children under 3 years old. For children of color, the risk is far worse, with African American children (39%) and Latino children (34%) experiencing substantially higher rates than their white (14%) peers. Many inner-city neighborhoods today include almost exclusively the most disadvantaged segments of the urban minority population, families plagued by persistent poverty and welfare dependency, workers who experience long spells of joblessness, and individuals who, in the face of limited opportunities, turn to street crime and other forms of aberrant behavior (Hays, 2004; Iceland, 2006; Shipler, 2005). Furthermore, although poverty is most often associated with urban areas, DeNavas-Walt, Proctor, and Smith (2009) reported a higher percentage of such families in rural areas (15.1%) as compared to urban areas (12.9%).

The continued rise in child poverty is attributed to two primary factors: the failure of hourly wages to keep pace with inflation, particularly for young workers and those with less than a college education; and the increase in the number of families headed by a single parent—usually the mother. Mother-only families are at high risk for poverty due to the absence of a second adult earner and the historically lower earning power of women. Poverty affects children and their school lives in devastating ways. Kozol (1994) poignantly described the lives of homeless children:

> Many of these kids grow up surrounded by infectious illnesses no longer seen in most developed nations. Whooping cough and tuberculosis, once regarded as archaic illness, are now familiar in the shelters. Shocking numbers of these children have not been inoculated and for this reason cannot go to school. Those who do are likely to be two years behind grade level . . . many get to class so tired and hungry that they cannot concentrate. Others are ashamed to go to school because of shunning by their peers. Classmates label them "the hotel children" and don't want to sit beside them. Even their teachers sometimes keep their distance. The children look diseased and dirty. Many times they are. Often unable to bathe, they bring the smell of destitution with them into school. There *is* a smell of destitution, I may add. It is the smell of sweat and filth and urine. . . . (p. 77)

Added to this bleak outlook is the problem of underresourced, underperforming schools in high-poverty communities. In one account, Kozol (1994) described a chilling reality for many urban black children and their families:

> On an average morning in Chicago, about 5,700 children in 190 classrooms come to school only to find they have no teacher. Victimized by endemic funding shortages, the system can't afford sufficient substitutes to take the place of missing teachers. "We've been in this typing class a whole semester," says a 15-year-old at Du Sable High, "and they still can't find us a teacher." . . . In a class of 39 children at Chicago's Goudy Elementary School, an adult is screaming at a child: "Keisha, look at me. . . . Look me in the eye!" Keisha is fighting with a classmate. Over what? It turns out: over a crayon, said *The Chicago Tribune* in 1988. Last January the underfunded school began rationing supplies. . . . The odds these black kids in Chicago face are only slightly worse than those faced by low-income children all over America. Children like these will

be the parents of the year 2000. Many of them will be unable to earn a living and fulfill the obligations of adults; they will see their families disintegrate, their children lost to drugs and destitution. When we later condemn them for "parental failings," as we inevitably will do, we may be forced to stop and remember how we also failed them in the first years of their lives. (p. 75)

There is little reason to believe that this account is outdated. In a report based on school visits conducted between 2000 and 2005 in schools in 11 states, Kozol (2005) found conditions such as these relentlessly persistent in many low-income schools, despite (and, in some cases, Kozol argued, because of) various reform initiatives. Although reports such as these can lead to discouragement and even despair, they should not. There is evidence that excellent schools can make a difference (e.g., Reeves, 2005; Taylor & Pearson, 2002; Teddlie & Stringfield, 1993), especially when teachers add productive parent involvement efforts to the instructional strategies they undertake as part of teaching reform (e.g., Allen, 2007; Chrispeels & Rivero, 2001; McIntyre, 2010). In the section that follows, we describe some of the ways that effective teachers join with parents in partnerships that support children's literacy learning.

Best Practices in Action: Strategies for Working with Parents in the CCSS Era

As we think about parent involvement in the context of the CCSS, it is tempting to believe that the most important task we have as teachers is to convey to parents precisely what students need to learn, and to rely on the standards themselves as content for parent involvement initiatives. This is an approach that has historical roots. For example, in work that long preceded the CCSS, Seefeldt (1985) argued that schools should communicate with parents through the curriculum. She advised teachers to

> capitalize on the curriculum as a means of communicating with parents. It is an ongoing way to keep parents totally informed of their child's day, the school's goals and objectives, and the meaning of early childhood education. It's one way to begin to establish close, meaningful communication with busy parents . . . remember—informed, involved, parents, those who are aware of what their children do in an early childhood program, are also supportive parents. (p. 25)

On the one hand, this is good and important advice. We know that children are likely to do better when parents are informed about their school curriculum. On the other hand, taken at face value, this advice might lead one to believe that involving parents in meetings during which we convey information about the curriculum is, by itself, a worthwhile form of parent involvement. But such an approach lacks the reciprocity and exchange of information that we know marks programs that make a difference.

Both research and practical experience tell us that effective parent involvement initiatives are grounded in attention to both the *how* and the *what* of parent involvement. Hoover-Dempsey and Whittaker (2010) explained that teachers need to consider the forms of involvement (e.g., conveying high expectations, teaching children at home, attending school meetings, volunteering at school) that fit into parents' family time constraints, and they need to consider what parents may need to know (e.g., specific skill knowledge). Shockley, Michalove, and Allen (1995) reminded us that as we think about the forms and content of involvement, we must also think about the joint construction of roles and responsibilities. They called for parent involvement programs that represent a genuine partnership, defined as an enterprise in which "each participant has the responsibility to commit to both individual and shared goals. . . . Families have opportunities to share with teachers their routines, values, and issues, just as teachers have the opportunity to share with families classroom routines, values, and issues" (pp. 92–93). Edwards (2004) cautioned teachers to begin with clear knowledge of the families they serve, and with this knowledge as a backdrop to follow a four-step process as they work with parents to co-construct a meaningful partnership: (1) developing definitions, (2) deciding on types, (3) examining perceptions, and (4) implementing practices.

As we thought about and reflected on the collected evidence, we focused on findings that the success of parent involvement was *not* predicted by parents' income or education levels or by ethnicity or language. Rather, success was tied to the intensity of the school's or teacher's outreach; the match between the particular form of involvement and the parents' schedule and commitments; the extent to which parents viewed themselves as capable of implementing the desired actions; and the extent to which parents and teachers collaborated to determine roles and responsibilities. We used this evidence to identify three categories as central to productive home–school partnerships. The first category, *developing parent–teacher relationships,* was identified over three decades ago by Lawrence-Lightfoot (1978) as a partial solution to improving home–school partnerships; nonetheless, attention to relationship-building remains insufficient (e.g., Greene & Compton-Lilly, 2011; Lawrence-Lightfoot, 2004). Unlike traditional models of parent involvement in which the goal is often to convey to parents information we want them to know, building relationships is grounded in *exchanging*, rather than *giving*, information. Actions focus on learning from parents (e.g., parents' working schedules and other family responsibilities; parents' understandings of their role in their children's learning) as well as on sharing information with parents (e.g., teachers' preferences for how and when parents should contact them; teachers' expectations for parent involvement). As we seek information, we should pay particular attention to the type of information that will help us to understand the child's cultural and social worlds outside of school, as this will help us to identify areas of congruence and also areas of potential conflict. This information may be critical to understanding how to connect home and school learning experiences.

In the second category, *understanding school and classroom programs*, we place actions or events that help parents to understand more fully teachers' (and school or district) academic and behavioral expectations. The central purpose of this category is to build parental background knowledge about schools and classrooms so that they understand their children's daily experiences, the tasks and requirements their children describe in their conversations about their school lives, and the tasks and responsibilities teachers ask parents to engage in at home. In the era of the CCSS, this category may focus, at least in part, on the particular standards at a grade level. The third category is *family learning interventions*, that is, specific actions teachers expect parents to take to support their children's school success (e.g., monitoring homework, teaching specific skills, reading to or listening to children read). This category also is likely to have a clear connection to the CCSS at each grade level. In the next section, we describe examples of successful home–school partnership initiatives related to each of these categories.

Developing Parent–Teacher Relationships

Perhaps the most well-known and thoroughly studied example of an approach to parent–teacher relationship building is the work of Moll and his colleagues (e.g., González, Moll, & Amanti, 2005; Moll & Cammarota, 2010) on identifying *funds of knowledge* present in households of the children we teach. As described by González and colleagues (2005),

> The concept of *funds of knowledge* . . . is based on a simple premise: People are competent, they have knowledge, and their life experiences have given them that knowledge. Our claim is that first-hand research experiences with families allow one to document this competence and knowledge. It is this engagement that opened up many possibilities for positive pedagogical actions. (p. x)

The Fund of Knowledge project is grounded in "respectful talk between people who are mutually engaged in a constructive conversation" (González et al., 2005, p. 8). Participating teachers learn to visit homes not for the purpose of teaching parents what to do, but instead to deepen their understanding of what parents know and do as part of their daily family, community, and work experiences. To do so they observe, question, and discuss, with a focus on gaining a deeper understanding of their children's lives outside of school. In addition, teachers meet as an after-school study group to discuss their observations and the knowledge they have gained and to articulate the ways they can act on the information. That is, how can they make connections between children's family and community lives and what they must learn in school? Participating teachers described their experiences as transformative. One teacher explained:

> Participating in the project helped me to reformulate my concept of culture from being very static to more practice-oriented. This broadened conceptualization turned out to be the key which helped me deveop strategies to include the knowledge my students were bringing to school in my classroom practice. (in González et al., 2005, pp. 99–100)

A second example of an approach designed to support parent–teacher relationship building, the Parent Story approach, is drawn from the work of Edwards, Pleasants, and Franklin (1999):

> Parent stories can provide teachers with the opportunity to gain a deeper understanding of the "human side" of families and children (i.e., why children behave as they do, children's ways of learning and communicating, some of the problems parents have encountered, and how these problems may have impacted their children's views about school and the schooling process. (p. xviii)

Edwards and colleagues (1999) explained that through parent stories, teachers have the opportunity to see and understand the ways home and school cultures may differ and the challenges that the differences create for students; they can learn about individual and social pressures facing families; and they can also learn about parents' aspirations and expectations for their children. Armed with this knowledge, teachers can come to recognize their own strengths and responsibilities in helping parents meet certain challenges, and they can also learn to seek help for issues outside of their expertise.

To collect family stories, Edwards and colleagues (1999) suggest seven major steps. First, teachers seek at least one colleague who is also interested in collecting family stories, so that they can share their experiences—positive and negative—along the way and have a partner with whom to problem-solve. Second, teachers systematically review records of each of the children in their classrooms, and, to start, choose one student about whom they have concerns or questions. Third, teachers prepare questions related to 11 categories: (1) parent–child family routines; (2) child's literacy history; (3) teachable moments (e.g., explicit or implicit home-learning opportunities); (4) home life (e.g., discipline, parent–child relationship, problems); (5) educational experiences (outside of home, e.g., library visits, summer activities); (6) parents' beliefs about their child; (7) child's time with others; (8) parent–child sibling relationships; (9) parents' hobbies, activities, and interests in books; (10) parent–teacher relationship; and (11) parents' school history and ideas about school. (See Edwards et al., 1999, pp. 36–40, for a suggested list of interview questions.) Fourth, teachers identify a time and place to have the conversation with the parent(s), and as they talk, they either tape-record or take written notes to assist them later as they reflect on and consider ways to act on the information they have gathered. Fifth, teachers review and reflect on the information shared by parents. Edwards and colleagues provide specific steps to follow, including composing a list of the positive and negative aspects of the "story," recording facts that "stick out" in your mind, and generating new questions. Sixth, teachers use their notes to develop some instructional ideas to help the child in the classroom and also support learning at home. Seventh, teachers implement their ideas in the classroom and meet with parents to explain how they might help the child at home.

The Funds of Knowledge and Parent Story approaches are especially comprehensive and potentially very instructive. However, building parent–teacher relationships need not be quite as formal a process as each of these requires. Allen (2007), for example, emphasized ways teachers might take advantage of existing daily and weekly routines to create spaces for conversations with parents. In communities in which parents walk their children to school, a teacher positioned at the appropriate location can initiate "handoff chats" (Allen, 2007, p. 71), sharing information about the child's progress, providing parents an opportunity to ask a question about a homework assignment, and so forth. Other examples include "getting-to-know-you" conferences with each parent early in the school year, characterized as a "listening conference" (p. 72) during which parents shared their knowledge and insights about their children; weekly communication about classroom work that includes an envelope containing a sample of children's work, a comment from the teacher about the child's learning progress and a space for parents to write their own response to the child's work and progress.

Understanding School and Classroom Programs

We chose two examples of initiatives that were intended, at least partially, to support parents' understanding of school and classroom programs, and represent a good "match" for CCSS demands. The first, the Family Fluency Program (Morrow, Kuhn, & Schwanenflugel, 2007) was designed to develop parents' understanding of the classroom reading program and to engage parents as partners in support of children's classroom literacy learning. The program comprised two parent workshops. At the first meeting, teachers described the school's reading program and provided a brief demonstration of a typical reading lesson. After hearing a short reading selection, parents observed the ways the teacher prompted children to connect the selection to background experiences and to make predictions or ask questions. They also learned about echo reading, choral reading, and partner reading, and about ways to engage children in a discussion of the story. They discussed the purpose of each of the strategies and the ways each is expected to support children's reading achievement. In addition, parents received a handout (in English and in Spanish) that described how to practice the fluency strategies. Next, parents practiced the strategies with each other; following this activity, their children joined them and they practiced the strategies with their children. As the meeting ended, parents were asked to read (at least twice) the stories that would be sent home each week by the classroom teacher, and to practice the fluency strategies at least three times each week. At the second workshop, teachers focused on developing parents' understanding of "good" fluency. They played audiotapes of children reading the same selection, one with excellent fluency, one with adequate fluency, and one with poor fluency. They provided parents with a recorder and audiotapes and suggested that parents audiotape their children's reading so they could compare earlier and later oral readings and evaluate progress. Children again joined the meeting and parents and children together practiced audiotaping the child's reading. Results indicated that participating parents read with their children more than they had before; learned and used strategies to support reading fluency; and recognized and mentioned improvement they saw as they engaged their children in repeated readings.

A second example, the Parent Institute for Quality Education (PIQE; Chrispeels & Rivero, 2001) was designed to increase parent involvement by helping parents to gain a fuller understanding of expectations for their roles and responsibilities in their children's schooling. Consistent with evidence on effective home–school partnerships, PIQE is based on the underlying principle that the parents served (mostly low-income, recent immigrants) need information about the educational system, about how to interact with the school, and about how to help their children at home.

Parents were invited to attend eight, 90-minute sessions, each of which addresses an issue related to one of the principles. Print materials were translated into parents' first language, and during each session parents talk and interact with each other and with the instructor about the focal topic. Classes were scheduled in both the morning and evening to accommodate the needs of different families, and classes are taught by instructors who are fluent in the dominant language of the group of parents. Outcomes, based on presurvey and postsurvey data (collected from 95 families) and interview data (collected from a subsample of 11 families) were noteworthy: parents' understanding of their roles in their children's education grew as they gained new information and, both at home and at school, they acted on their new understanding. Moreover, absent any change in teachers' invitations or active effort, parents increased school involvement in four particular ways: they initiated more communication with the teacher; they provided more positive support to their children; they increased their engagement in teaching activities at home; and they increased requests for information about their children's academic progress.

In each of these examples, outcome data were focused on changes in parent behaviors rather than changes in children's achievement. However, evidence from other studies (e.g., Houtenville & Conway, 2008; Jeynes, 2003; Sheldon, 2003) of a direct relationship between parent involvement and children's achievement indicates that interventions that build parents' understanding of school and classroom programs, as these did, are an important part of administrators' and teachers' home–school partnerships repertoire.

Supporting Family Learning

Three general findings can be derived from studies of effects of family literacy interventions: first, effective programs not only focus on important literacy content, but they also support parents' self-efficacy by allocating time to explain, model, and guide parents in implementation of the focal literacy activity (Hoover-Dempsey & Sandler, 1995; Hoover-Dempsey & Whitaker, 2010; Hoover-Dempsey et al., 2005). Second, effective programs consider both short- and long-term effects of focal activities and, in turn, focal activities are thoroughly aligned with this understanding (Sénéchal & Young, 2008). In the early grades, a focus on specific code-related skills will support early literacy achievement, but by itself, these skills may have little influence on achievement after grade 1. Across grade levels, a focus on listening to children read will support children's development of word-reading accuracy and fluency (Toomey, 1993), but may have little influence on children's development of vocabulary and concept knowledge.

A focus on reading aloud to children beginning in early childhood will support acquisition of vocabulary, language, and concept knowledge that will, in turn, support children's comprehension in grade 2 and beyond, but these abilities may show few effects prior to grade 2 (Whitehurst & Lonigan, 2002). Third, effective parent involvement programs embed literacy events in engaging, high-quality texts and in motivating, interesting, and playful games and activities, and within contexts that are of social importance for family members (Paratore & Yaden, 2010; Roser, 2010).

There are numerous projects and approaches that meet these three criteria (e.g., Edwards, 1994, 1995; Jordan, Snow, & Porche, 2000; Paratore, 1993, 2001; Rodriguez-Brown, 2010). We have chosen to share two, each of which demonstrates a different type of intervention approach. The first, Project EASE (Jordan, Snow, & Porche, 2000) was designed to focus entirely on supporting the child's literacy learning through parent–child literacy interactions. The second, the Intergenerational Literacy Program (Paratore, 2001), focuses on advancing parents' English language and literacy knowledge, parent–child literacy interactions, and in turn, children's literacy achievement.

Project EASE (Jordan et al., 2000) was developed as a year-long literacy intervention program serving families of children entering kindergarten. Project EASE comprised five parent-training sessions (held during the day when children were in school), each organized around a 1-month unit. Each training session provided parents with background information related to a focal topic (e.g., vocabulary learning) and guided parents in implementation of activities designed to promote development of the particular literacy skill or ability (thereby supporting the development of parental self-efficacy). During each of the remaining 3 weeks, parents received a packet containing scripted activities related to the focal topic. Each packet included a book rich in interesting vocabulary and in opportunities for discussion and conversation and suggestions for the types of parent–child interactions that are associated with children's language and literacy learning. At the end of the program, the children were given a battery of language and literacy tasks, and the children of families who participated in the program showed significant gains in vocabulary, narrative understanding, phonemic awareness, and story sequencing. Moreover, language skills showed the largest effect, a finding that is especially important given the evidence of the strong relationship between early language knowledge and later reading achievement (Sénéchal, Ouellette, & Rodney, 2006; Whitehurst & Lonigan, 2002). Further, the intervention had the greatest effects on children who scored low at pretest, suggesting the potential for programs of this type to close the achievement gap.

The Intergenerational Literacy Project (ILP; Paratore, 2001) was designed to serve three purposes: to help parents develop their own literacy, to support the practice of family literacy in the home, and, in turn, to support children's school-based success. The ILP has served over 2,500 families, almost all new immigrants who journeyed to the United States from 56 different countries. On average, learners have attended school for just over 8 years, although parents' education levels vary widely: over 15% of learners have gone to school for fewer than 4 years and more than 14% have attended at least some college. Classes are held four mornings or three evenings per week for 2 hours each day and for 40 weeks each year. Children's classes are offered in both the morning (for preschool children) and the evening (for preschool and school-age children) as well.

Each of the adult literacy classes follows the same basic guidelines—each focuses about half of class time on reading and writing of adult interest and the other half on texts of importance or of interest to child development and child learning. All teachers and tutors are focused on supporting parents' and children's understanding of strategies to improve their reading and writing and application of those strategies in their daily lives and to support children's school success. This understanding is reinforced through several instructional routines. On a daily basis, adult learners report their previous day's literacy activities on a two-sided literacy log. On one side, parents record literacy activities of personal interest, such as reading recipes, holding conversations in English with coworkers, and writing letters. On the other side, learners detail literacy activities that they engaged in with their children, including storybook reading, homework monitoring, and shared television watching. A few minutes of class time each day is devoted to literacy log sharing, which allows parents to learn from ways in which their peers use literacy at home and helps teachers and tutors to build learners' understanding of what constitutes literacy. (If, for example, a parent reports having gone to the supermarket, teachers will tease out how that learner may have interacted with print while shopping.)

A second instructional routine that promotes parents' metacognitive awareness of their own and their children's learning is the use of graphic organizers. Teachers draw learners' attention to how completing the organizer helps them make sense of the text and its structure; and they explain that their children are learning to use the same strategies and tools in school. Over the years of the project, a diverse collection of assessment practices has been used to monitor and document project outcomes. Short-term outcomes include higher rates of attendance and retention in family literacy classes than those of traditional adult basic education and, in many cases, of other family literacy programs (Paratore, 1993; Paratore, Krol-Sinclair, David, & Schick, 2010; Paratore, Melzi,

& Krol-Sinclair, 1999), indicating that daily instructional practices are effective in maintaining parents' motivation to advance their own and their children's literacy knowledge; increased use of reading and writing outside of class to achieve personal goals, thereby making print literacy a more frequent routine in their daily lives; and increased parent–child storybook reading (at least weekly), a practice that has been found to correlate highly with early reading achievement (e.g., Bus, van IJzendoorn, & Pellegrini, 1995). Long-term effects (Paratore et al., 2010) indicate that when children whose parents participated in the ILP are compared with their general education peers, they have significantly higher rates of school attendance, consistently higher scores on state assessments (in both English language arts and mathematics), higher rates of high school graduation, and higher rates of enrollment in postsecondary education.

Summing It Up: Reaching Out to Parents in Different Ways

It is widely believed that the implementation of the CCSS has the potential to level the playing field for all students, and in turn, to contribute to more equitable learning opportunities in schools across the United States. To realize this potential, however, students will need more than a common curriculum—they will also need the benefit of learning opportunities that extend beyond the ringing of the school bell at the end of each day. Such opportunities are not available to all children, and may be especially absent among students who reside in high-poverty communities with parents who have low levels of education. This is not because their parents have low aspirations or expectations for their children's learning; rather, they may lack clarity or have a different point of view about their roles and responsibilities in their children's learning; or they may lack the ability or knowledge to carry out the activities teachers expect of them.

The evidence is clear: teachers who understand and initiate actions that productively engage parents in their children's learning extend their influence beyond the school day. Edwards (2004) coined two terms, *differentiated parenting* and *parentally appropriate*, to characterize the actions of such teachers. Edwards explained that teachers who understand *differentiated parenting* recognize that parents are different from one another in their perspectives, beliefs, and abilities to negotiate school. Teachers who have an awareness of the need to be *parentally appropriate* know that because parents are different, tasks and activities must be compatible with their capabilities. But let's not let this understanding mislead us—responding to the need for differentiated parenting does not mean that we must limit our expectations of what parents can do. Rather, just as the

CCSS demand a certain amount of instructional scaffolding for many students, forming productive home–school partnerships may require instructional scaffolding for parents, such that we help parents to understand both *what* to do and *how* to do it. Appropriate outreach can support the development of parents' awareness *and* capability, and as such support their realization of self-efficacy relative to desired practices. This type of outreach, in turn, can make a difference for the achievement of children who too often experience school failure.

Our understanding of the evidence, then, leads us to these five principles for development parent–teacher partnerships that work:

1. Contact parents directly (rather than through their children) and invite them to join with you to develop a plan to support their children's literacy learning.
2. Together, determine the "forms" of parent involvement that fit parents' schedule and availability.
3. Together, determine the types of routines and activities that will support children's literacy learning in and out of school and help them achieve the CCSS.
4. Together, determine the types of support parents will need to effectively implement the literacy routines and activities that will help their children achieve the CCSS.
5. Create a plan for providing parental support and "checking in" along the way, maintaining adherence to parents' schedule and availability.

In this chapter, we set out to provide information that would support teachers' efforts to approach parent involvement. We hope that, as you reflect and act on the information we have presented, you will be able to say that we achieved our goal.

ENGAGEMENT ACTIVITIES

1. Edwards (2004) explained that a fundamental step in developing productive parent–teacher partnerships requires that we, as teachers, examine our own perceptions about the parents of the children in our classrooms. Gather one or two colleagues and talk together about perceptions of parents' aspirations for their children's school success and about their dispositions toward parent involvement. Outline steps you might take, individually or together, to "check" perceptions and develop a clear understanding of parents' views and dispositions toward parent involvement.

Implement one or more of the steps and then reflect: How might you use the information you gain to help parents support their children's progress toward the CCSS?

2. Explore the Council of Great City Schools' *Parent Roadmap to the Common Core State Standards* (*www.cgcs.org*). Based on the description at your grade level, choose a few activities that are recommended for parents to do at home. Meet with parents to discuss the selected activities. Together, choose one or two that are a good "fit" for parents and their children. Discuss the types of support parents might need to productively engage their children in the activities. Co-construct a plan to provide necessary support and to check in with each other along the way to monitor children's progress and provide ongoing support.

3. Parents are more involved in parent–child learning activities when they have a clear understanding of what to do and how to do it. Consider an activity that you would like parents to do to support their children's achievement of a particular grade-level CCSS. Building on what you know about the parents of children in your classroom, outline the knowledge or skills parents need to effectively implement the activity and develop a plan for coaching parents toward successful implementation.

REFERENCES

Allen, J. (2007). *Creating welcoming schools: A practical guide to home–school partnerships with diverse families*. New York: Teachers College Press.

Altschul, I. (2011). Parental involvement and the academic achievement of Mexican American youths: What kinds of involvement in youths' education matter most? *Social Work Research, 35*(3), 159–170.

Annie B. Casey Foundation (2013). Kids count data book: State trends in child well-being. Retrieved October 30, 2013, from *http://datacenter.kidscount.org/files/2013KIDSCOUNTDataBook.pdf*.

Arnold, D. H., Lonigan, C. J., & Whitehurst, G. J. (1994). Accelerating language development through picture book reading: Replication and extension to a videotape training format. *Journal of Educational Psychology, 86*, 235–243.

Bus, A. G., van IJzendoorn, M. H., & Pellegrini, A. D. (1995). Joint book reading makes for success in learning to read: A meta-analysis in intergenerational transmission of literacy. *Review of Educational Research, 65*, 1–21.

Chrispeels, J. H., & Rivero, E. (2001). Engaging Latino families for student success: How parent education can reshape parents' sense of place in the education of their children. *Peabody Journal of Education, 76*(2), 119–169.

Compton-Lilly, C. (2003). *Reading families: The literate lives of urban children*. New York: Teachers College Press.

Cooper, C. E. (2010). Family poverty, school-based parental involvement, and policy-focused protective factors in kindergarten. *Early Childhood Research Quarterly, 25*(4), 480–492.

Council of the Great City Schools. (n.d.). Parent roadmap to the Common Core standards—English language arts—K–12. Retrieved October 31, 2013, from *www.cgcs.org.*

Dearing, E., Kreider, H., Simpkins, S., & Weiss, H. B. (2006). Family involvement in school and low-income children's literacy: Longitudinal associations between and within families. *Journal of Educational Psychology, 98*(4), 653–664.

Dearing, E., McCartney, K., Weiss, H. B., Krieder, H., & Simpkins, S. (2004). The promotive effects of family educational involvement for low-income children's literacy. *Journal of School Psychology, 42*(6), 445–460.

DeNavas-Walt, C., Proctor, B. D., & Smith, J. C. (2009). *Income, poverty, and health insurance coverage in the United States: 2008* (No. P60–236). Washington, DC: U.S. Census Bureau. Retrieved October 7, 2009, from *www.census.gov/hhes/www/poverty/poverty08html.*

Edwards, P. A. (1994). Responses of teachers and African-American mothers to a book-reading intervention program. In D. K. Dickinson (Ed.), *Bridges to literacy: Children, families, and schools* (pp. 175–210). Cambridge, MA: Blackwell.

Edwards, P. A. (1995). Empowering low-income mothers and fathers to share books with young children. *The Reading Teacher, 48,* 558–565.

Edwards, P. A. (2004). *Children literacy development: Making it happen through school, family, and community involvement.* Boston: Allyn & Bacon.

Edwards, P. A. (2009). *Tapping the potential of parents: A strategic guide to boosting student achievement through family involvement.* New York: Scholastic.

Edwards, P. A., Pleasants, H. M., & Franklin, S. H. (1999). *A path to follow: Learning to listen to parents.* Portsmouth, NH: Heinemann.

Epstein, J. (1986). Parents' reactions to teacher practices of parent involvement. *Elementary School Journal, 86,* 277–294.

Fan, W., Williams, C. M., & Wolters, C. A. (2012). Parental involvement in predicting school motivation: Similar and differential effects across ethnic groups. *Journal of Educational Research, 105*(1), 21–35.

Footlick, J. K. (1990, Winter–Spring). What happened to the family? [Special issue]. *Newsweek,* pp. 15–20.

González, N., Moll, L. C., & Amanti, C. (2005). *Funds of knowledge: Theorizing practices in households, communities, and classrooms.* Mahwah, NJ: Erlbaum.

Greene, S., & Compton-Lilly, C. (2011). *Connecting home and school: Complexities and considerations in fostering parent involvement and family literacy.* New York: Teachers College Press.

Guthrie, J. T., & Wigfield, A. (2000). Engagement and motivation in reading. In M. L. Kamil, P. B. Mosenthal, P. D. Pearson, & R. Barr (Eds.), *Handbook of reading research* (pp. 403–424). Mahwah, NJ: Erlbaum.

Hays, S. (2004). *Flat broke with children: Women in the age of welfare reform.* Cambridge, UK: Oxford University Press.

Henderson, A. T., & Mapp, K. (2002). *A new wave of evidence: The impact of school, family, and community connections on student achievement.* Austin, TX: National Center for Family and Community Connections with Schools.

Hoover-Dempsey, K. V., & Sandler,H. M. (1995). Parental involvement in children's education: Why does it make a difference? *Teacher's College Record, 97,* 310–331.

Hoover-Dempsey, K. V., Walker, J. M. T., Sandler, H. M., Whetsel, D., Green, C. L., Wilkins, A. S., et al. (2005). Why do parents become involved?: Research findings and implications. *Elementary School Journal, 106*(2), 105–130.

Hoover-Dempsey, K. V., & Whitaker, M. C. (2010). The parental involvement process: Implications for literacy development. In K. Dunsmore & D. Fisher (Eds.), *Bringing literacy home* (pp. 53–82). Newark, DE: International Reading Association.

Houtenville, A. J., & Conway, K. S. (2008). Parental effort, school resources, and student achievement. *Journal of Human Resources, 43*(2), 437–453.

Iceland, J. (2006). *Poverty in America: A handbook* (2nd ed.). Berkeley and Los Angeles: University of California Press.

Jeynes, W. (2003). A meta-analysis: The effects of parental involvement on minority children's academic involvement. *Education and Urban Society, 35*(1), 202–218.

Jeynes, W. (2012). A meta-analysis of the efficacy of different types of parental involvement programs for urban students. *Urban Education, 47*(4), 706–742.

Jordan, G. E., Snow, C. E., & Porche, M. V. (2000). Project EASE: The effect of a family literacy project on kindergarten students' early literacy skills. *Reading Research Quarterly, 35*(4), 524–546.

Kozol, J. (1994). The new untouchables. In J. Krevotics & E. J. Nussel (Eds.), *Transforming urban education* (pp. 75–78). Boston: Allyn & Bacon.

Kozol, J. (2005). *The shame of the nation.* New York: Crown.

Lareau, A. (1989). *Home advantage: Social class and parental intervention.* New York: Falmer Press.

Lawrence-Lightfoot, S. L. (1978). *Worlds apart: Relationships between families and schools.* New York: Basic Books.

Lawrence-Lightfoot, S. L. (2004). *The essential conversation: What parents and teachers can learn from each other.* New York: Random House.

Mattingly, D. J., Prislan, R. A., McKenzie, T. L., Rodriguez, J. L., & Kayzar, B. (2002). Evaluating evaluations: The case of parent involvement programs. *Review of Educational Research, 72*(4), 549–576.

McIntyre, E. (2010). Issues in funds of knowledge teaching and research: Key concepts from a study of Appalachian families and schooling. In M. L. Dantas & P. C. Manyak (Eds.), *Home–school connections in a multicultural society: Learning from and with culturally and linguistically diverse families* (pp. 201–217). New York: Routledge.

Moll, L. C., & Cammarota, J. (2010). Cultivating new funds of knowledge through research and practice. In K. Dunsmore & D. Fisher (Eds.), *Bringing literacy home* (pp. 289–305). Newark, DE: International Reading Association.

Morrow, L. M., Kuhn, M. R., & Schwanenflugel, P. J. (2007). The family fluency program. *The Reading Teacher, 60*(4), 322–333.

Paratore, J. R. (1993). Influence of an intergenerational approach to literacy on the practice of literacy of parents and their children. In C. Kinzer & D. Leu (Eds.), *Examining central issues in literacy, research, theory, and practice* (pp. 83–91). Chicago: National Reading Conference.

Paratore, J. R. (2001). *Opening doors, opening opportunities: Family literacy in an urban community.* Needham Heights, MA: Allyn & Bacon.

Paratore, J. R., Krol-Sinclair, B., David, B., & Schick, A. (2010). Writing the next chapter in family literacy: Clues to long-term effects. In K. Dunsmore & D. Fisher (Eds.), *Bringing literacy home* (pp. 265–288). Newark, DE: International Reading Association.

Paratore, J. R., Melzi, G., & Krol-Sinclair, B. (1999). *What should we expect of family literacy?: Experiences of Latino children whose parents participate in an intergenerational literacy program.* Newark, DE: International Reading Association.

Paratore, J. R., & Yaden, D. B. (2010). Family literacy on the defensive: The defunding of Even Start—Omen or opportunity? In D. Lapp, D. Fisher, & D. Alvermann (Eds.), *Handbook of research on teaching the English language arts* (3rd ed., pp. 90–96). Newark, DE: International Reading Association.

Park, S., & Holloway, S. D. (2013). No parent left behind: Predicting parental involvement in adolescents' education within a sociodemographically diverse population. *Journal of Educational Research, 106*(2), 105–119.

Reeves, D. B. (2005). High performance in high-poverty schools: 90/90/90 and beyond. In J. Flood & P. L. Anders (Eds.), *Literacy development of students in urban schools: Research and policy* (pp. 362–388). Newark, DE: International Reading Association.

Rodriguez-Brown, F. (2010). Latino culture and schooling: Reflections on family literacy with a culturally and linguistically different community. In K. Dusmore & D. Fisher (Eds.), *Bringing literacy home* (pp. 203–225). Newark, DE: International Reading Association.

Roser, N. (2010). Talking over books at home and in school. In K. Dunsmore & D. Fisher (Eds.), *Bringing literacy home* (pp. 104–135). Newark, DE: International Reading Association.

Seefeldt, C. (1985). Communicate with curriculum. *Day Care and Early Education, 13*(2), 22–25.

Sénéchal, M., Ouellette, G., & Rodney, D. (2006). The misunderstood giant: On the predictive role of early vocabulary to future reading. In D. K. Dickinson & S. B. Neuman (Eds.), *Handbook of early literacy research* (Vol. 2, pp. 173–182). New York: Guilford Press.

Sénéchal, M., & Young, L. (2008). The effect of family literacy interventions on children's acquisition of reading from kindergarten to grade 3: A meta-analytic review. *Review of Educational Research, 78*(4), 880–907.

Sheldon, S. B. (2003). Linking school–family–community partnerships in urban elementary schools to student achievement on state tests. *Urban Review, 35*(2), 145–164.

Shipler, D. K. (2005). *The working poor: Invisible in America.* New York: Vintage Books.

Shockley, B., Michalove, B., & Allen, J. (1995). *Engaging families: Connecting home and school literacy communities.* Portsmouth, NH: Heinemann.

St. Pierre, R. G., Ricciuti, A. E., & Rimdzius, T. A. (2005). Effects of a family literacy program on low-literate children and their parents: Findings from an evaluation of the Even Start Family Literacy Program. *Developmental Psychology, 41*(6), 953–970.

Taylor, B. M., & Pearson, P. D. (2002). *Teaching reading: Effective schools, accomplished teachers*. Mahwah, NJ: Erlbaum.

Teddlie, C., & Stringfield, S. (1993). *Schools make a difference: Lessons learned from a 10-year study of school effects* New York: Teachers College Press.

Toomey, D. (1993). Parents hearing their children read: A review: Rethinking the lessons of the Haringey Project. *Educational Research, 35*, 223–236.

Walker, J. M., Ice, C. L., Hoover-Dempsey, K. V., & Sandler, H. M. (2011). Latino parents' motivations for involvement in their children's schooling. *Elementary School Journal, 111*(3), 409–429.

Whitehurst, G. J., & Lonigan, C. J. (2002). Emergent literacy: Development from prereaders to readers. In S. B. Neuman & D. K. Dickinson (Eds.), *Handbook of early literacy research* (Vol. 1, pp. 11–29). New York: Guilford Press.

CHAPTER 18

Best Practices in Professional Development for Improving Literacy Instruction in Schools

Sharon Walpole
Michael C. McKenna

This chapter will:

- Summarize research on the design and effects of professional development.
- Present a rationale for schoolwide specific professional development.
- Recommend a professional development cycle.
- Describe three promising practices: professional learning communities, coaching, and technology-based modules.
- Illustrate current professional development efforts in enacting the Common Core State Standards.

Many readers of this book will resonate with this quite sobering fact: professional development (PD) in schools is often a waste of two most precious resources—time and money. In fact, the failure of PD to change instruction and achievement is well documented. This need not be the case. We will argue that accepting and attending to the growing science of how teachers learn in schools can strengthen those most elusive links, from PD to instruction to achievement. The Common Core State Standards (CCSS; National Governors Association & Council of Chief State School Officers [NGA & CCSSO], 2010) require new student learning and therefore new teaching at a time when many district budgets leave scant resources to commit. This combination of facts makes attention to what works in PD for teachers a national imperative. We will argue that the key to effective PD is the specificity of its target. Unless PD is designed for immediate application in instruction, with particular students and instructional materials in mind, it will not work.

Evidence-Based Best Practices: A Research Synthesis

Although public schools are spending as much as $20 billion a year on PD (Guskey, 2009), there is more evidence that teachers are engaging in PD than that the PD is producing desired results. Hill (2009) describes the current PD system as broken, with most PD provided locally, with very little quality control, by individuals whose content knowledge is limited. School and district leaders have too little time or expertise to plan or administer the necessary PD, and they tend to adopt multiple innovations at the same time (Guskey, 2009; see also Guskey & Yoon, 2009). This tendency may explain the fact that PD continues to be provided with relatively little reflection on whether teachers are actually learning anything (Webster-Wright, 2009).

Consider these facts: (1) teachers are constantly exposed to PD that does not result in changes in their practice, and (2) their underlying beliefs must play a role in this passive resistance. Guskey (1986) claimed that these facts are explained by a lack of attention by professional developers to what motivates teachers to actively engage. Perhaps PD does not routinely influence instruction because teachers do not think that the PD applies to them personally or because they lack the skills or motivation to carry out the instruction recommended in the PD (Gregoire, 2003).

In the area of literacy, these fairly generic descriptors of the failure of PD take on a special importance. Think about the policy context that nearly always places literacy at the heart of accountability for students, teachers, and schools. No Child Left Behind (NCLB) accountability measures have had real consequences for schools and teachers, and response-to-intervention (RTI) initiatives guarantee that this focus will continue regardless of how NCLB is revised or replaced. The CCSS—recently embraced by almost all states and required for Race to the Top funding—set high expectations for reading achievement and will lead to increased pressure on teachers. Given this high-stakes policy context, the demand for new and more effective PD in the area of reading instruction will continue.

Ideally, this high-quality PD in literacy will be aligned with standards and assessments, coherent with other school initiatives, targeted to the needs of diverse learners, and sensitive to the specific organizational environments of schools and districts (Hochberg & Desimone, 2010). It will also acknowledge the ways that teachers learn. Teacher self-efficacy is related to teaching effort, goals, persistence, and resilience (Bandura, 1977), and individual teacher learning is influenced by social interactions with peers and with PD providers (Marrero, Woodruff, Schuster, & Riccio, 2010). When literacy PD does not address all of these issues, it cannot be expected to produce the changes in teacher knowledge, teacher instruction, and student achievement that are at the heart of the PD logic map represented in Figure 18.1.

Much has been made of a list of features of high-quality PD experiences: they must be content-focused, include active learning, be coherent, be of sufficient duration, and include collective participation of teachers (Desimone, 2009). But simply because a PD initiative has all of these features is not enough. It appears that God (or the Devil) is in the details. Some large-scale PD research findings are particularly sobering. Goldschmidt and Phelps (2010) examined the effects of an extensive PD initiative in California. Teachers engaged in a 40-hour summer institute, 40 hours of follow-up PD, and 40 hours of collaborative team meetings—surely a substantial PD initiative in reading. When researchers tested teacher knowledge, they found significant knowledge gains associated with the initial institute, but these knowledge gains were not sustained 6 months later. Classroom practice, even with follow-up PD and team meetings, neither solidified nor extended the knowledge gained from the initial institute. In fact, it appeared to reduce knowledge gains.

Another large and high-profile example also yielded disappointing results. In an experimental study investigating the effects of PD on the knowledge and practice of second-grade teachers and on the reading achievement of their students, researchers tested: (1) a scalable PD model

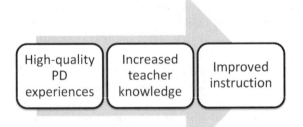

FIGURE 18.1. Basic PD logic map.

that focused on building content knowledge, (2) a combination of that PD and in-class coaching, and (3) a business-as-usual control group. Teachers in both of the experimental treatments increased their knowledge compared to the control condition and also taught more explicitly than control teachers. There was no difference in student achievement, however, and, also disappointing, the coaching condition did not have a greater impact on instruction than the PD alone (Garet, Porter, Desimone, Birman, & Yoon, 2008). In contrast, though, Neuman and Cunningham's (2009) preschool study did find that coaches added value to more traditional PD coursework. These coaches helped teachers to enact the PD targets in their own classrooms.

In addition to the type and amount of support provided after PD, the direct match of PD targets with teachers' instructional materials appears to make a difference. Brady and colleagues (2009) provided what may have been high-quality PD to teachers from multiple schools, but they faced a formidable implementation challenge. Some teachers had materials or other curriculum requirements that contradicted the goals of the PD, circumstances that led to dissonance for those teachers and prevented them from enacting the knowledge they had gained.

Why isn't it a simple causal chain? Substantial PD should change teacher knowledge and beliefs, knowledge and beliefs should change instruction, and instruction should change achievement. Given time and resources, we should be able to build pedagogical content knowledge (PCK). PCK includes both what should be taught and exactly how it can and should be taught (Shulman, 1986). Over a career, a teacher should be engaging in PD that builds PCK, refining it to incorporate new research findings.

But it doesn't really work that way. PD occurs in an incredibly complex environment. Teachers juggle competing (often contradictory) influences. They work with a small set of grade-level or content-area colleagues, in schools with particular cultures, with changing curriculum and testing requirements. They are influenced by school, district, state, and federal initiatives. They serve children from increasingly diverse families. Desimone (2009) proposed that to truly understand PD we must accept this complexity. Her model for studying PD, which we represent in Figure 18.2, sets a very high bar.

The Schoolwide Argument

If a well-articulated model of the multiple influences on teachers is available, why aren't PD efforts always successful? To be fair, although Figure 18.2 may connote a central linear chain from PD to achievement,

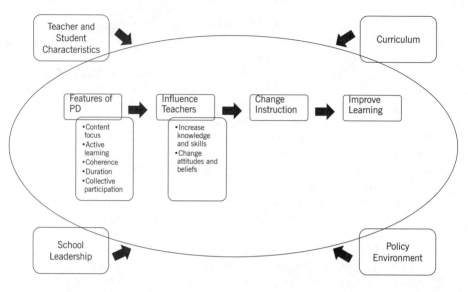

FIGURE 18.2. A representation of Desimone's (2009) call for PD research.

Desimone's argument was about strategies to frame and synthesize research. The large-scale "failed" PD studies we described above have one thing in common: they separate knowledge-building efforts from pedagogy and materials. In essence, they require teachers to make what Salomon and Perkins (1989) called "high-road transfer." Teachers must take ideas from PD into the complex world of their school and classroom. It may be that that goal is unrealistic, especially if the new ideas are very distant from current practice or require different texts and materials. Effective PD design may consequently require a more recursive, nested, repetitive process. And it may need to target instruction first, with knowledge gains a dividend earned later.

A recent cross-case analysis of PD projects in science (Park Rogers et al., 2010) provides a blueprint for continued PD efforts in literacy. The authors argue that effective efforts must integrate content, pedagogy, curriculum, and demonstration. Then they must include individually sensitive opportunities for reflection. To truly link content, pedagogy, curriculum, and demonstration, it is clear that PD must be provided to teachers working together. In essence, the context matters at least as much as the PD design—new ideas must be explored and integrated with the support and input of colleagues and then coordinated within the school's general instructional talk and practice. Although individual teachers may learn individual things, they are influenced powerfully by their colleagues, and that influence may inhibit them from implementing what they have learned. For this reason, we, like Kelcey and Phelps (2013), see the grade-level team nested within the school as the best setting for PD.

Think of it this way: PD can be a sort of ongoing design experiment (Reinking & Bradley, 2008), relying on an iterative, cyclical relationship among instructional practice, improved student achievement, and changes in teacher knowledge and beliefs. In design experiments, the treatment is constantly modified through feedback from the individuals who are applying it. For PD initiatives, that can really only happen if the individual school is the PD site, with positive contextual support from the school's administration, who schedule it, participate in it, and support its application. The cycle of a design experiment is flexible enough to include persuasion, vicarious experience, practice, observation and feedback, and coaching (Mouza, 2009; Timperley & Phillips, 2003; Tschannen-Moran & McMaster, 2009). Figure 18.3 represents our current thinking about how to engage in this kind of schoolwide, cyclical PD.

You can see in Figure 18.3 that we link the initial presentation of new ideas to curriculum supports from the very start. We are trying to avoid the snags that high-road transfer produces. If we begin with a very specific instructional target, providing all materials and lesson plans that teachers need to enact it, teachers are more likely to try out the targeted approach in their classrooms. In essence, we will have enabled initial implementation.

Initial trials will lead teachers to ask very specific questions. Such questions, if asked of others who are also trying the very same new instructional strategy, can lead to reflection and refinement. We believe that it is that process of discussion and experimentation that builds PCK, and that these gains will fuel continued trials of new instructional strategies. Kazemi and Hubbard (2008) call this the "coevolution" of teacher participation in the PD and their experimentation in their classrooms. Over time, teachers will be able to gather data on the effects of their efforts on students. If these are positive, they will build self-efficacy and be encouraged to continue implementation. Then they can begin the cycle anew with another very specific instructional target linked to curriculum supports.

Promising PD Practices

So far, we have proposed that effective PD is a collaborative schoolwide process with ongoing iterative cycles. While we are far from having a science of PD in schools, there are some promising practices to consider as you enact this schoolwide, cyclical PD. You will see that these practices can be used singly or in combination.

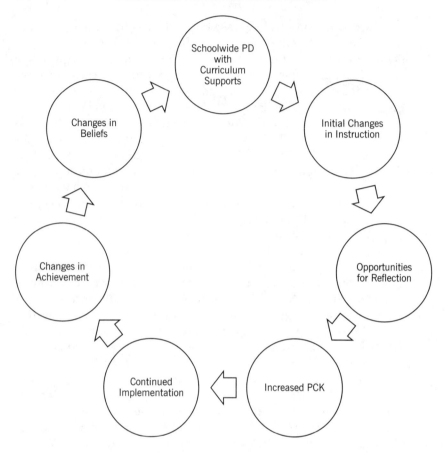

FIGURE 18.3. Schoolwide, cyclical PD.

School-Based Professional Learning Communities

We define professional learning communities (PLCs) as a general structure for an ongoing, site-based, collaborative interaction among a set of teachers. PLCs are localized enactments of the National Staff Development Council (NSDC; 2001) standards, which identified aspects of context, process, and content that contribute to the quality and effects of PD. The NSDC standards recommended that teachers be organized into learning communities, guided by building- and district-level leadership, and supported with adequate resources. The process standards required the use of student achievement data and teacher implementation data as teachers identified evidence-based strategies consistent with their teaching and learning goals. Finally, the content standards demanded attention to the needs of all students, including those who struggle, and attention to the involvement of stakeholders outside the school.

In 2010, NSCD changed its name to Learning Forward and revised its standards to reflect an even more overt commitment to site-based collaboration. The new Standards for Professional Learning (Learning Forward, 2012; *http://learningforward.org/standards/standards-list#.Um_soST-SlNQ*) put learning communities first, followed by leadership, resources, data, learning designs, implementation, and outcomes. The standards are aggressive, but there are very specific resources available to support their enactment.

Although we see the powerful potential of teacher collaboration, we also see a potential peril. Teachers may not have the capacity to identify the very specific instructional strategies ("learning designs," in their new parlance) associated with student achievement. Many schools use PLCs to link teachers to one another, but it may be that Communities of Practice, which link teachers and researchers are necessary to achieve the practice-oriented goals of most PD initiatives (Englert & Rozendal, 2004). Teachers need to wrestle with ideas *in context*; PD providers need to help teachers ground their efforts *in evidence*.

Not all schools have the resources necessary to work directly with researchers, but there are many ways to do so vicariously. Books provide access to new ideas; books chosen well provide access to research in action. Books also ensure that there are always new ideas for the PLC to consider. We recommend that PLCs take their design and process from the Learning Forward standards and their instructional targets from the work of literacy researchers. PD process without very specific content is not likely to yield changes in achievement; PD content without very specific processes is equally risky.

Coaching

Our first foray into the PD literature came as we explored (and supported!) the work of literacy coaches working in federal reforms (see McKenna & Walpole, 2008; Walpole & McKenna, 2004). We define *coaching* as a process in which a coach works only with teachers (rather than students) to design and provide PD. We began our exploration of coaching with four assumptions:

1. The instructional methods teachers employ influence student achievement.
2. Variations in the methods themselves and in the quality of teacher implementation are considerable.

3. Coaching can help teachers implement specific methods and abandon others; coaching can help teachers improve the quality of their work.
4. The effect of coaching can be gauged by changes in student achievement as a result of this altered practice. (Walpole & McKenna, 2009a, p. 25)

We developed a model we call "reform-oriented coaching." In it, the coach works with grade-level teams to build and rebuild a reading program that works for children. Much is demanded of the reform-oriented coach, and a close partnership with the principal is essential. Our reform-oriented coach is a guide to grade-level PLCs described above, locating books for book studies; driving the selection of instructional strategies; participating in the PLC process; providing ongoing observation and formative, nonevaluative feedback; and collecting and analyzing student achievement data.

Not surprisingly, 15 years of research on the roles and effects of coaching have yielded mixed results. Coaches are forced into multiple roles, sometimes with responsibilities far outside the continuous professional support of teachers. Teachers may be influenced by coaches, but they are also influenced by other forces. Taylor (2008) identifies these forces and argues that they exert an influence on teacher knowledge that is independent of coaching and that may actually be inconsistent with the goal of coaching. We re-create his model in Figure 18.4.

While coaching does not always work, it can work. Our own recent review of the coaching literature (Walpole & McKenna, 2013) yielded a set of take-home messages for would-be coaches. We present them in Figure 18.5. Coaching support can be an effective component of a PD initiative.

Use of Technology

Finally, we suggest that technology can be an important resource in PD efforts. Remember that technology is a tool. During PD sessions, technology can provide very concrete examples of ideas in action. It can extend time and transcend distance, allowing teachers to connect with researchers through webinars and websites. If we capture video of instruction, technology can allow teachers to observe themselves and one another remotely; it can facilitate coaching conversations. Like PLCs and coaching models, though, technology does not always enhance PD efforts. In fact, not all teachers access technology equally. Self-directed teacher access of Web-based video demonstrations is highly variable (Downer, Kraft-Sayre, & Pianta, 2009; Downer, Locasale-Crouch, Hamre, & Pianta, 2009). Used

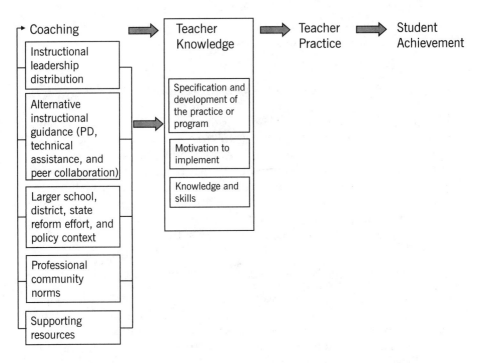

FIGURE 18.4. Multiple influences on teacher knowledge.

1. Coaching does not always change instruction or achievement.
2. Coaches need to use a model to guide their time and activities.
3. Coaches cannot be effective unless their work is integrated into a school's climate.
4. Coaches' goals must be aligned with the goals of other instructional leaders.
5. Coaches must place the needs of teachers ahead of their own needs.
6. Coaches must learn many things on the job.
7. Coaches must differentiate for teachers.
8. Coaches must constantly build their coaching toolbox.
9. Coaches must observe to see whether and how teachers are implementing new practices.
10. Coaches must use multiple assessment measures to gauge the effects of instruction on student achievement.

FIGURE 18.5. Take-home messages for coaches.

wisely and in PLCs, however, technology can extend the reach of teachers outside their own classrooms and beyond the school day.

Best Practices in Action

We do not want you to get the impression that best practices in PD are unreasonable to realize. We just want you to expect them to require long-term hard work. We have been working with schools in two separate initiatives related to CCSS implementation. Both include the formative design elements that we have identified as key for PD initiatives as well as the schoolwide cycle that we presented in Figure 18.3. Both are ongoing and both have included fits and starts that are part of the iterative process. In both cases, the results have been worth the wait.

Redefining Small-Group Foundational Skills Instruction

Our first example of an iterative design of PD is currently in its fourth year. It began with a real-world problem: a school system was experiencing weak achievement in the early primary grades and was also trying to embrace the challenging texts required by the CCSS. In collaboration with district administrators, we agreed to help teachers redesign small-group instruction with the goal of accelerating skill acquisition in grades K–2.

We had an existing set of lesson plans designed for this purpose (Walpole & McKenna, 2009b). They are organized around discrete skills-based targets in phonemic awareness, alphabet knowledge, word recognition, fluency, and open-ended attention to vocabulary and comprehension. Based on a simple set of informal diagnostic tests, teachers can identify student needs, group them, and begin the appropriate lessons. Our goal, then, was very specific: to teach teachers how and when to use this set of lessons and to measure student progress associated with this new practice.

We began *outside* of the classrooms in a series of monthly presentations at each of the three elementary schools in the district. Schools arranged for substitutes so that grade-level teams could meet with us for 2 hours each. We presented an assessment module and four skills-based modules over the course of 4 months. Each session included very brief research references, but mostly demonstration, both live and through video. After the sessions, teachers reviewed our lesson plans and engaged in book study.

Teachers moved *inside* their classrooms to instructional trials during that first semester of PD. Once they had had time to practice the instructional techniques, we came in to observe and coach. We watched every teacher in every school, and met with them in grade-level teams to give overall feedback.

By the fall of Year 2, all teachers could implement these small-group skills lessons. They could also collect informal data to track student progress and regroup. We continued with school visits, but this time they were focused on problem solving. We helped teachers fine-tune their schedules and modify lesson plans when needed. We modeled in some classrooms, where teachers wanted to explore instructional pace. State-mandated literacy screening data revealed impressive gains compared to historical control groups. By spring of Year 2, the teachers were ready to tackle the rest of their reading block.

Since we did not have plans for the rest of the block, we began by developing them. We used the CCSS text-difficulty recommendations to select texts for shared reading for second grade, and we then planned backward for first grade and kindergarten. Then we selected very challenging texts for interactive read-alouds. Once we had texts selected, we chose a very small set of evidence-based instructional strategies that could be used repeatedly in shared and interactive reading. We made lesson plans for every day's reading. This task was much more challenging than anyone could have predicted, so the final plans were not ready until just before the fall of Year 3. We had a relatively brief kick-off session, and gave teachers the new plans. Because of our extensive experience with them, both we and the district administration thought this would be enough.

It wasn't. Not at first. Adding two additional daily instructional components (shared and interactive reading) lessons that had never been piloted was a real challenge. The teachers embraced them, though. We conducted a survey to get implementation feedback and presented the results separately on a release day to each grade level across the three schools. Some teachers were frustrated by the pacing of the lessons. The district formed a committee with representatives from all three schools to repace any sets of lessons that were too long. By the spring of Year 3, teachers were comfortable enough with the new shared and interactive reading lessons that they again allowed us to observe individually and provide feedback to grade-level teams. Surveys redone in fall of Year 4 revealed that a second implementation year was *much* more comfortable. State-level data continue to reveal improvements in achievement.

In this initiative, we were able to design curriculum and then design comprehensive PD to support teacher implementation. We did some of our work outside the classroom, in formal sessions. We did some of it with live observation and feedback. We used what we learned in observations and surveys to direct our sessions outside the classroom. We tested the effects of our work on student achievement. Since these effects were positive, we extended our efforts. As PD providers, we made teachers' planning efforts simpler and used their PD time to help them improve their instruction immediately. This effort took years of consistent contact and commitment.

Designing CCSS Implementation in High School

Similar time and commitment have been required to explore the CCSS in a struggling high school. This time, we did not start with lesson plans. Rather, we started with a short menu of instructional strategies that we presented in large-group, state-sponsored sessions. Participating PLCs consisted of an administrator and a team of teachers who committed one full day out of school each month. They engaged with us in a 3-hour knowledge-building session and then in a 3-hour planning session to decide what to do back at school. They read McKenna and Robinson's (2012) *Teaching through Text: Reading and Writing in the Content Areas.* Frankly, we were surprised at the type and amount of engagement that these teacher leaders exhibited. They were taking the CCSS call for more and harder text in every content area very seriously; they were also very interested to learn how to teach adolescents to write arguments.

As the PD year neared an end, one of the teachers attending asked if we would be interested in a follow-up initiative at his high school. We were reluctant, having never worked schoolwide in a high school. Before we agreed, we met with the principal. He took us on a full-day walk-through, providing extensive and frank descriptions of the struggles his teachers faced. When we were sure that our visions matched, we committed to him.

We needed to link PD directly to curriculum supports, but we were not sure how to do it. The principal decided to assign all of the teachers who had participated in the state PD to one ninth-grade team—they included an English teacher, a history teacher, a science teacher, a math teacher, and a coach. This team committed to trials of a small set of instructional practices. Our shared goal was first to see which practices were actually reasonable to be used repeatedly in high school across content areas and then to collect artifacts that we could eventually use in PD for the rest of the staff.

We had high levels of support from the principal and we developed strong relationships with one another. We used all of the tools in our coaches' toolboxes flexibly. We interacted frequently through e-mail. We conducted walk-throughs of all classrooms and extended observations in others. We engaged in individual and small-group feedback and problem-solving sessions. By the end of that year, we decided that we would make Web-based PD modules to document our work and then to extend it to other teachers at the school.

Technology was a great support here. We taped and edited interviews about what was going well and also about how we were solving problems. We also interviewed students and were surprised to hear them say that they appreciated their teachers' willingness to use the same instructional strategies because it made reading and writing easier for them. By the end of that year, we had Web modules with actual examples from the school and also a short list of strategies that we knew how to teach to teachers and to use with students. Those strategies are listed in the instructional menu in Figure 18.6.

We entered a new year poised for scale-up. The principal's support continued. He was creative in his assignment of teachers to sections, and he was able to free our English teacher to become a full-time coach. His goal was to use the Web-based modules we had created in PLCs with all ninth- and 10th-grade teachers. The other members of our pilot group would be distributed among the PLCs so that he would always have a content-area ally. He and his team worked very hard that year; they experienced both successes and failures. We guided him from the side and engaged in more limited face-to-face work with his teachers.

The principal realized that his teachers were suffering from initiative overload. Competing initiatives were allowing them to dodge the real goal: increased quantity and quality of student reading, writing, and research during school. He decided to link the literacy initiative explicitly

---

Strategies to Build Background Knowledge
- Preview the text, including both content and text structure.
- Teach technical vocabulary.
- Provide visual support with video or pictures.
- Use custom graphic organizers.

Strategies to Engage Students
- Use peer-assisted learning strategies (PALS).
- Use reciprocal teaching groups.
- Write reading guides.
- Assign argumentative writing.
- Employ text sets.
- Assign collaborative research and writing.

Strategies to Share Knowledge
- Engage in a structured whole-class discussion.
- Form jigsaw discussion or writing groups.
- Engage in collaborative summarization.

FIGURE 18.6. Instructional strategies menu for middle school and high school.

with other initiatives—including the teacher evaluation system. Basically, he took on the difficult job of creating coherence.

By the summer of that year, we all had learned enough to make the link between PD and curriculum more concrete. We wrote a book advocating a new method of designing text sets and describing the implementation of the instructional strategies menu (Lewis, Walpole, & McKenna, 2014). The book includes coaching forms meant for the beginning of any PD session. Each form includes two repeated stems, focusing on what the strategy requires and what the coach noticed. When observations are focused in this way, we have found that a coach's notes readily prompt both praise to convey and questions to explore during a postobservation conference. The language of each stem is repeated to capture key aspects of an instructional approach. An example based on semantic feature analysis appears in Figure 18.7.

The strategy requires that you select a group of related terms to compare and contrast. I noticed _____

_____

_____

_____

The strategy requires that you develop a comprehensive list of attributes. I noticed _____

_____

_____

_____

The strategy requires that you indicate the presence or absence of each attribute for each target concept. I noticed _____

_____

_____

_____

The strategy allows you to finish the chart for students before they read or allow them to do it during reading. I noticed _____

_____

_____

_____

FIGURE 18.7. Example of a coaching form for semantic feature analysis.

Notice that both the instructional strategy and the coaching form are so flexible that they can be used in any content setting. And that was exactly the point. Our coach was able to foster common understandings about which strategies teachers implement and how they worked. In the process, he engaged in text selection and unit planning across content areas. By the start of the 2013–2014 school year, the school had used an iterative PD design to create a comprehensive curriculum.

As each of these initiatives makes clear, best practices in PD are cyclical, but they are neither quick nor predictable. Specific targets (lesson plans or instructional strategies) are absolutely essential if you want teachers to engage in new teaching.

Reflections and Future Directions

The approach to PD we have described in this chapter may cause pushback for several reasons. We acknowledge this possibility and conclude by addressing them.

First, our approach is designed to move teachers away from certain instructional strategies in favor of others. The very phrase *best practices* implies a continuum along which various strategies can be placed in terms of their effect on learning. The fact that you are reading a book with this phrase in the title probably suggests that you agree with this idea, but some researchers do not. Our colleague David Reinking (2011) argues that the quantitative studies through which such strategies are determined are too narrow to be implemented with confidence in diverse settings. That is true enough, but when we see the same strategies prove effective in study after study, in a range of classrooms serving a variety of students, we feel comfortable recommending them to teachers. This is not to say that any one strategy will be effective for a given teacher in a particular context. We offer no such guarantee. Nor can we say that researchers will never identify still better practices in the future. In fact we hope they do! For the present, however, we take the phrase *best practices* to mean the best we have—a set of instructional strategies that are more likely than others to produce the results we desire. For this reason, they are worthy targets of PD.

Second, the reform-oriented model of coaching we advocate here is likely to push some teachers out of their comfort zone. It will compel them to take chances, try new approaches, and reflect with candor on their past practice. In describing several well-established coaching models (McKenna & Walpole, 2008), we borrowed the Mohs hardness scale for minerals and applied it to literacy coaching. We placed reform-oriented coaching at the "hard" end of the spectrum because it involves the least compromise and can at times be somewhat confrontational. Such coaching assumes a very clear idea of the instruction that should be occurring, and it defines the task of coaching as moving teachers in the direction of such instruction. As a result, some teachers may feel that their professionalism is challenged; some may resist, passively or overtly. The reform-oriented coach needs a clear vision and a thick skin, a supportive principal, and the ability to let data do the persuading.

Third, the examples of our own work in schools have illustrated the amount of time required to bring about substantive change. It cannot be accomplished in weeks or months. It takes years. We quite understand how the stark reality of such a commitment can give one pause. And yet we have repeatedly seen teachers make such a commitment. It is only possible, however, through a schoolwide effort that embraces a shared goal. It cannot depend on the longevity of a single individual but on shared leadership dedicated to achieving that goal. It means that when a new teacher joins the faculty, a veteran can be expected to say, "This is how we teach reading here."

ENGAGEMENT ACTIVITIES

1. Review the Standards for Professional Learning at *LearningForward.org*. You will see that there is a facilitator's guide available for download (*http://learningforward.org/standards#.UnAz3RYhEdI*) to assist you.

2. Choose a professional text that you can integrate into your existing PLC structure. Be specific about why you chose it and how you would want your colleagues to use it.

3. Choose a Web-based PD module from our open-access PD site (*comprehensivereadingsolutions.com*). Make a schedule with colleagues to specify a date by which each person will have viewed the module and completed its associated tasks. Schedule a PLC meeting to share what you have learned.

4. Choose an instructional strategy to increase student engagement in reading the challenging texts required by the CCSS. Create a PD session that defines and demonstrates the strategy and a set of lesson plans and materials that allows participants to use the strategy immediately in their classrooms. Plan a timeline that permits teachers first to practice and then to meet again to problem-solve.

REFERENCES

Bandura, A. (1977). Self-efficacy: Toward a unifying theory of behavioral change. *Psychological Review, 84*, 191–215.

Brady, S., Gillis, M., Smith, T., Lavalette, M., Liss-Bronstein, L., Lowe, E., et al. (2009). First grade teachers' knowledge of phonological awareness and code concepts: Examining gains from an intensive form of professional development and corresponding teacher attitudes. *Reading and Writing, 22*, 425–55.

Desimone, L. M. (2009). Improving impact studies of teachers' professional development: Toward better conceptualizations and measures. *Educational Researcher, 38*, 181–199.

Downer, J.,Kraft-Sayre, M. E., & Pianta, R. C. (2009). Ongoing, Web-mediated professional development focused on teacher–child interactions: Early childhood educators' usage rates and self-reported satisfaction. *Early Education and Development, 20*, 321–345.

Downer, J., Locasale-Crouch, J., Hamre, B., & Pianta, R. (2009). Teacher characteristics associated with responsiveness and exposure to consultation and online professional development resources. *Early Education and Development, 20*, 431–455.

Englert, C., & Rozendal, M. S. (2004). A model of professional development in special education. *Teacher Education and Special Education, 27*(1), 24–46.

Garet, M. S., Porter, A. C., Desimone, L., Birman, B. F., & Yoon, K. S. (2001). What makes professional development effective?: Results from a national sample of teachers. *American Educational Research Journal, 38*, 915–945.

Goldschmidt, P., & Phelps, G. (2010). Does teacher professional development affect content and pedagogical knowledge: How much and for how long? *Economics of Education Review, 29*, 432–439.

Gregoire, M. (2003). Is it a challenge or a threat?: A dual-process model of teachers' cognition and appraisal processes during conceptual change. *Educational Psychology Review, 15*, 147–179.

Guskey, T. R. (1986). Staff development and the process of teacher change. *Educational Researcher, 15*(5), 5–12.

Guskey, T. R. (2009). Closing the knowledge gap on effective professional development. *Educational Horizons, 87*, 224–233.

Guskey, T., & Yoon, K. (2009). What works in professional development? *Phi Delta Kappan, 90*, 495–500.

Hill, H. (2009). Fixing teacher professional development. *Phi Delta Kappan, 90*, 470–476.

Hochberg, E., & Desimone, L. (2010). Professional development in the accountability context: Building capacity to achieve standards. *Educational Psychologist, 45*, 89–106.

Kazemi, E., & Hubbard, A. (2008). New directions for the design and study of professional development: Attending to the coevolution of teachers' participation across contexts. *Journal of Teacher Education, 59*, 428–441.

Kelcey, B., & Phelps, G. (2013). Considerations for designing group randomized trials of professional development with teacher knowledge outcomes. *Educational Evaluation and Policy Analysis, 35,* 370–390.

Learning Forward. (2012). Standards for professional learning. Retrieved from *http://learningforward.org/standards#.UnAplhYhEdI.*

Lewis, W. E., Walpole, S., & McKenna, M. C. (2014). *Cracking the Common Core: Choosing and using texts in grades 6–12.* New York: Guilford Press.

Marrero, M., Woodruff, K., Schuster, G., & Riccio, J. (2010). Live, online short-courses: A case study of innovative teacher professional development. *International Review of Research in Open and Distance Learning, 11,* 81–95.

McKenna, M. C., & Robinson, R. D. (2012). *Teaching through text: Reading and writing in the content areas* (2nd ed.). Boston: Allyn & Bacon/Vango.

McKenna, M. C., & Walpole, S. (2008). *The literacy coaching challenge: Models and methods for grades K–8.* New York: Guilford Press.

Mouza, C. (2009). Does research-based professional development make a difference?: A longitudinal investigation of teacher learning in technology integration. *Teachers College Record, 111,* 1195–1241.

National Governors Association & Council of Chief State School Officers. (2010). *Common Core State Standards.* Washington, DC: Author.

National Staff Development Council. (2001). NSCD standards for staff development. Retrieved from *www.nsdc.org/standards/index.cfm.*

Neuman, S., & Cunningham, L. (2009). The impact of professional development and coaching on early language and literacy instructional practices. *American Educational Research Journal, 46,* 532–566.

Park Rogers, M. A., Abell, S. K., Marra, R. M., Arbaugh, F., Hutchins, K. L., & Cole, J. S. (2010). Orientations to science teacher professional development: An exploratory study. *Journal of Science Teacher Education, 21,* 309–328.

Reinking, D. (2011). Beyond the laboratory and the lens: New metaphors for literacy research. In P. J. Dunston, L. B. Gambrell, K. Headley, S. K. Fullerton, P. M. Stecker, V. R. Gillis, et al. (Eds.), *Sixtieth yearbook of the Literacy Research Association* (pp. 1–17). Oak Creek, WI: Literary Research Association.

Reinking, D., & Bradley, B. A. (2008). *Formative and design experiments: Approaches to language and literacy research.* New York: Teachers College Press.

Salomon, G., & Perkins, D. N. (1989). Rocky roads to transfer: Rethinking mechanisms of a neglected phenomenon. *Educational Researcher, 24*(2), 113–142.

Shulman, L. S. (1986). Those who understand: Knowledge growth in teaching. *Educational Researcher, 15*(2), 4–14.

Taylor, J. E. (2008). Instructional coaching: The state of the art. In M. M. Mangin & S. R. Stoelinga (Eds.), *Effective teacher leadership: Using research to inform and reform* (pp. 10–35). New York: Teachers College Press.

Timperley, H., & Phillips, G. (2003). Changing and sustaining teachers' expectations through professional development in literacy. *Teaching and Teacher Education, 19,* 627– 641.

Tschannen-Moran, M., & McMaster, P. (2009). Sources of self-efficacy: Four professional development formats and their relationship to self-efficacy and implementation of a new teaching strategy. *Elementary School Journal, 110,* 228–245.

Walpole, S., & McKenna, M. C. (2004). *The literacy coach's handbook: A guide to research-based practice.* New York: Guilford Press.

Walpole, S., & McKenna, M. C. (2009a). Everything you've always wanted to know about literacy coaching but were afraid to ask: A review of policy and research. In K. M. Leander, D. W. Rowe, D. K. Dickinson, M. K. Hundley, R. T. Jiménez, & V. J. Risko (Eds.), *Fifty-eighth yearbook of the National Reading Conference* (pp. 23–33). Oak Creek, WI: National Reading Conference.

Walpole, S., & McKenna, M. C. (2009b). *How to plan differentiated reading instruction: Resources for grades K–3.* New York: Guilford Press.

Walpole, S., & McKenna, M. C. (2013). *The literacy coach's handbook: A guide to research-based practice* (2nd ed.). New York: Guilford Press.

Webster-Wright, A. (2009). Reframing professional development through understanding authentic professional learning. *Review of Educational Research, 79,* 702–739.

Index

Page numbers in *italic* indicate a figure or table